CONSUMER TRANSACTIONS

SELECTED STATUTES AND REGULATIONS

By

MICHAEL M. GREENFIELD
Professor of Law
Washington University

Mineola, New York
THE FOUNDATION PRESS, INC.
1983

ISBN 0-88277-114-0

Greenfield Consumer Trans. UCB
Stat.Supp.

PREFACE

This supplement contains the statutory and regulatory materials referred to in CONSUMER TRANSACTIONS. The federal materials appear first, roughly in the order in which they appear in the casebook. State materials follow, again roughly in the order in which they appear in the casebook.

Omissions are numerous. The table of sections that precedes each lengthy statute indicates which sections of the statute are omitted in their entirety. When only a portion of a section is omitted, an elipsis appears at the point of the omission. Most of the official commentary to the uniform acts is omitted without any indication of the omission.

MICHAEL M. GREENFIELD

St. Louis, Missouri
February, 1983

*

TABLE OF CONTENTS

ALPHABETICAL LISTING

*

CONSUMER TRANSACTIONS

SELECTED STATUTES AND REGULATIONS

*

PART ONE. FEDERAL STATUTES AND REGULATIONS

MOTOR VEHICLE INFORMATION AND COST SAVINGS ACT

TITLE IV—ODOMETER REQUIREMENTS

15 U.S.C. §§ 1981–1991

Table of Sections

---

§ 401. Findings and purpose [15 U.S.C. § 1981]

The Congress hereby finds that purchasers, when buying motor vehicles, rely heavily on the odometer reading as an index of the condition and value of such vehicle; that purchasers are entitled to rely on the odometer reading as an accurate reflection of the mileage actually traveled by the vehicle; that an accurate indication of the mileage traveled by a motor vehicle assists the purchaser in determining its safety and reliability; and that motor vehicles move in the current of interstate and foreign commerce or affect such commerce. It is therefore the purpose of this title to prohibit tampering with odometers on motor vehicles and to establish certain safeguards for the protection of purchasers with respect to the sale of motor vehicles having altered or reset odometers.

§ 402. Definitions [15 U.S.C. § 1982]

As used in this title—

(1) The term "dealer" means any person who has sold 5 or more motor vehicles in the past 12 months to purchasers who in good faith purchase such vehicles for purposes other than resale.

(2) The term "distributor" means any person who has sold 5 or more vehicles in the past 12 months for resale.

(3) The term "odometer" means an instrument for measuring and recording the actual distance a motor vehicle travels while in operation; but shall not include any auxiliary odometer designed to be reset by the operator of the motor vehicle for the purpose of recording mileage on trips.

(4) The term "repair and replacement" means to restore to a sound working condition by replacing the odometer or any part thereof or by correcting what is inoperative.

(5) The term "transfer" means to change ownership by purchase, gift, or any other means.

§ 403. Unlawful devices [15 U.S.C. § 1983]

No person shall advertise for sale, sell, use, or install or cause to be installed, any device which causes an odometer to register any mileage other than the true mileage driven. For purposes of this section, the true mileage driven is that mileage driven by the vehicle as registered by the odometer within the manufacturer's designed tolerance.

§ 404. Unlawful change of mileage [15 U.S.C. § 1984]

No person shall disconnect, reset, or alter or cause to be disconnected, reset, or altered, the odometer of any motor vehicle with intent to change the number of miles indicated thereon.

§ 405. Operation with intent to defraud [15 U.S.C. § 1985]

No person shall, with intent to defraud, operate a motor vehicle on any street or highway knowing that the odometer of such vehicle is disconnected or nonfunctional.

§ 406. Conspiracy [15 U.S.C. § 1986]

No person shall conspire with any other person to violate section 403, 404, 405, 407, or 408 of this title.

§ 407. Lawful service, repair, or replacement [15 U.S.C. § 1987]

(a) Nothing in this title shall prevent the service, repair, or replacement of an odometer, provided the mileage indicated thereon remains the same as before the service, repair, or replacement. Where the odometer is incapable of registering the same mileage as before such service, repair, or replacement, the odometer shall be adjusted to read zero and a notice in writing shall be attached to the left door frame of the vehicle by the owner or his agent specifying the mileage prior to repair or replacement of the odometer and the date on which it was repaired or replaced.

(b)(1) No person shall fail to adjust an odometer or affix a notice regarding such adjustment as required pursuant to subsection (a) of this section.

(2) No person shall, with intent to defraud, remove or alter any notice affixed to a motor vehicle pursuant to subsection (a) of this section.

§ 408. Disclosure requirements [15 U.S.C. § 1988]

(a) Not later than 90 days after October 20, 1972, the Secretary shall prescribe rules requiring any transferor to give the following written disclosure to the transferee in connection with the transfer of ownership of a motor vehicle:

(1) Disclosure of the cumulative mileage registered on the odometer.

(2) Disclosure that the actual mileage is unknown, if the odometer reading is known to the transferor to be different from the number of miles the vehicle has actually traveled.

Such rules shall prescribe the manner in which information shall be disclosed under this section and in which such information shall be retained.

(b) No transferor shall violate any rule prescribed under this section or give a false statement to a transferee in making any disclosure required by such rule.

(c) No transferee who, for purposes of resale, acquires ownership of a motor vehicle shall accept any written disclosure required by any rule prescribed under this section if such disclosure is incomplete.

§ 409. Private civil action [15 U.S.C. § 1989]

(a) Any person who, with intent to defraud, violates any requirement imposed under this title shall be liable in an amount equal to the sum of—

(1) three times the amount of actual damages sustained or $1,500, whichever is the greater; and

(2) in the case of any successful action to enforce the foregoing liability, the costs of the action together with reasonable attorney fees as determined by the court.

(b) An action to enforce any liability created under subsection (a) of this section, may be brought in a United States district court without regard to the amount in controversy, or in any other court of competent jurisdiction, within two years from the date on which the liability arises.

§ 410. Injunctive enforcement [15 U.S.C. § 1990]

(a) The United States district courts shall have jurisdiction, for cause shown and subject to the provisions of rule 65(a) and (b) of the Federal Rules of Civil Procedure, to restrain violations of this title or rules, regulations, or orders issued thereunder. Such actions may be brought by the Attorney General in any United States district court for a district wherein any act, omission, or transaction constituting the violation occurred, or in such court for the district wherein the defendant is found, is an inhabitant, or transacts business. In any action brought under this section, process may be served on a defendant in any other district in which the defendant resides or may be found.

(b) In any action brought under this title, subpoenas for witnesses who are required to attend a United States district court may run into any other district.

§ 411. State enforcement [15 U.S.C. § 1990a]

(a) If any person violates any requirement imposed under this title, the chief law enforcement officer of the State in which such violation occurred may bring any action to—

(1) restrain such violation; or

(2) recover amounts for which such person is liable under section 409 of this title to each person on whose behalf such action is brought.

(b) Any action under subsection (a) of this section may be brought within two years from the date on which the liability arises—

(1) without regard to the amount in controversy, in any appropriate district court of the United States, or

(2) in any court of competent jurisdiction of any State.

§ 412. Civil penalty [15 U.S.C. § 1990b]

(a) Any person who commits any act or causes to be done any act that violates any provision of this title or omits to do any act or causes to be omitted any act that is required by any such provision shall be subject to a civil penalty not to exceed $1,000 for each such violation. A violation of any such provision shall, for purposes of this section, constitute a separate violation with respect to each motor vehicle or device involved, except that the maximum civil penalty shall not exceed $100,000 for any related series of violations.

(b) Any civil penalty under this section shall be assessed by the Secretary and collected in a civil action brought by the Attorney General on behalf of the United States. Before referral of civil penalty claims to the Attorney General, civil penalties may be compromised by the Secretary after affording the person charged with a violation of any section of this subchapter an opportunity to present views and evidence in support thereof to establish that the alleged violation did not occur. In determining the amount of such penalty, the Secretary shall take into account the nature, circumstances, extent, and gravity of the violation committed and, with respect to the person found to have committed such violation, the degree of culpability, any history of prior offenses, ability to pay, effect on ability to continue to do business, and such other matters as justice may require.

§ 413. Criminal penalties [15 U.S.C. § 1990c]

(a) Any person who knowingly and willfully commits any act or causes to be done any act that violates any provision of this title or knowingly and willfully omits to do any act or causes to be omitted any act that is required by any such provision shall be fined not more than $50,000 or imprisoned not more than one year, or both.

(b) Any individual director, officer, or agent of a corporation who knowingly and willfully authorizes, orders, or performs any of the acts or practices constituting in whole or in part a violation of any section of this title shall be subject to penalties under this section without regard to any penalties to which that corporation may be subject under subsection (a) of this section.

§ 414. Inspections and investigations [15 U.S.C. § 1990d]

(a)(1) The Secretary is authorized to conduct any inspection or investigation necessary to enforce this title or any rules, regulations, or orders issued thereunder. Information obtained indicating noncompliance with this title or any rules, regulations, or orders issued thereunder, may be referred to the Attorney General for investigative consideration. In making investigations under this paragraph, the Secretary shall cooperate with appropriate State and local officials to the greatest extent possible consistent with the purposes of this subsection.

. . .

§ 418. Effect on State law [15 U.S.C. § 1991]

This title does not—

(1) annul, alter, or affect the laws of any State with respect to the disconnecting, altering, or tampering with odometers with the intent to defraud, or

(2) exempt any person subject to the provisions of this title from complying with such laws,

except to the extent that those laws are inconsistent with any provision of this title, and then only to the extent of the inconsistency.

NATIONAL HIGHWAY TRAFFIC SAFETY ADMINISTRATION, DEPARTMENT OF TRANSPORTATION

ODOMETER DISCLOSURE REQUIREMENTS

49 C.F.R. Part 580

Table of Sections

---

§ 580.3 Definitions

All terms defined in sections 2 and 402 of the Act are used in their statutory meaning. Other terms used in this part are defined as follows:

"Transferor" means any person who transfers his ownership in a motor vehicle by sale, gift, or any means other than by creation of a security interest.

"Transferee" means any person to whom the ownership in a motor vehicle is transferred by purchase, gift, or any means other than by creation of a security interest.

§ 580.4 Disclosure of odometer information

(a) Before executing any transfer of ownership document, each transferor of a motor vehicle shall furnish to the transferee a written statement signed by the transferor, containing the following information:

(1) The odometer reading at the time of transfer;

(2) The date of transfer;

(3) The transferor's name and current address;

(4) The transferee's name and current address;

(5) The identity of the vehicle, including its make, model, year, and body type, and its vehicle identification number.

(b) In addition to the information provided under paragraph (a) of this section, the statement shall refer to the Motor Vehicle Information and Cost Savings Act and shall state that incorrect information may result in civil liability and civil or criminal penalties.

(c) In addition to the information provided under paragraphs (a) and (b) of this section,

(1) The transferor shall certify that to the best of his knowledge the odometer reading reflects the actual miles or kilometers the vehicle has been driven; or

(2) If the transferor knows that the odometer reading reflects the amount of mileage in excess of the designed mechanical odometer limit of 99,999 miles/kilometers, he shall include a statement to that effect; or

(3) If the transferor knows that the odometer reading differs from the number of miles/kilometers the vehicle has actually traveled and that the difference is greater than that caused by odometer calibration error, he shall include a statement that the odometer reading is not the actual mileage, and should not be relied upon.

(d) In addition to the information provided under paragraphs (a), (b) and (c) of this section, the transferor shall certify that:

(1) The odometer was not altered, set back, or disconnected while in the transferor's possession, and he has no knowledge of anyone else doing so;

(2) The odometer was altered for repair or replacement purposes while in the transferor's possession, and the mileage registered on the repaired or replacement odometer was identical to that before such service; or

(3) The odometer was altered for repair or replacement purposes, the odometer was incapable of registering the same mileage, it was reset to zero, and the mileage on odometer before repair was ______ miles/kilometers.

(e) The transferee shall acknowledge receipt of the disclosure statement by signing it.

(f)(1) If the laws or regulations of the State in which the transfer occurs require the odometer disclosure to be made on the certificate of title or other State documents which evidences ownership, the transferor may make the disclosure required by this section by executing the State certificate of title or such other ownership document. In order to utilize the above documents as substitutes for the Federal odometer disclosure statement, they must contain essentially the same information required by paragraphs (a), (b), (c) and (e) of this section. If the information contained thereon varies in any way from that required for the Federal form, the State must obtain approval from the National Highway Traffic Safety Administration before its certificate of title or other ownership document can be used as a substitute for the Federal form. Such approval may be obtained by submitting a copy of the proposed document to the Office of the Chief Counsel, National Highway Traffic Safety Administration, 400 Seventh Street, SW., Washington, D.C. 20590.

(2) The NHTSA shall respond to the State's request within 30 days of receipt of such request.

(g) If there is no State document as described in paragraph (f) of this section, the transferor shall make the disclosure required by this section by executing the disclosure form specified in § 580.6.

§ 580.6 Disclosure form

ODOMETER MILEAGE STATEMENT

(Federal regulations require you to state the odometer mileage upon transfer of ownership. An inaccurate or untruthful statement may make you liable for damages to your transferee, for attorney fees, and for civil or criminal penalties, pursuant to sections 409, 412, and 413 of the Motor Vehicle Information and Cost Savings Act of 1972 (Pub.L. 92–513, as amended by Pub.L. 94–364).

I, ______ (transferor's name, print), state that the odometer of the vehicle described below now reads ______ miles/kilometers.

Check one box only.

☐ (1) I hereby certify that to the best of my knowledge the odometer reading as stated above reflects the actual mileage of the vehicle described below.

☐ (2) I hereby certify that to the best of my knowledge the odometer reading as stated above reflects the amount of mileage in excess of designed mechanical odometer limit of 99,999 miles/kilometers of the vehicle described below.

☐ (3) I hereby certify that to the best of my knowledge the odometer reading as stated above is NOT the actual mileage of the vehicle described below, and should not be relied upon.

Make Model Body type

Vehicle identification number Year

Check one box only.

☐ (1) I hereby certify that the odometer of said vehicle was not altered, set back, or disconnected while in my possession, and I have no knowledge of anyone else doing so.

☐ (2) I hereby certify that the odometer was altered for repair or replacement purposes while in my possession, and that the mileage registered on the repaired or replacement odometer was identical to that before such service.

☐ (3) I hereby certify that the repaired or replacement odometer was incapable of registering the same mileage, that it was reset to zero, and that the mileage on the original odometer or the odometer before repair was ______ miles.

Transferor's Address (seller) ______________________
(Street)

____
(City) (State) (ZIP Code)

Transferor's Signature (seller) ______________________

Date of Statement ______________________

Transferee's Name and Address (buyer) ______________________

____
(Street)

____
(City) (State) (ZIP Code)

Receipt of copy Acknowledged ______________________

____
(Transferee's signature, buyer)

§ 580.7 Odometer mileage statement retention

Each dealer or distributor of a motor vehicle who is required by this part to execute an odometer disclosure statement shall retain for four years each odometer mileage statement which he receives. He shall also retain for four years a photostat, carbon, or other facsimile copy of each odometer mileage statement which he issues. He shall retain each odometer mileage statement at his primary place of business in an order that is appropriate to his business requirements and that permits systematic retrieval. The statement may be reproduced (e.g., photocopies or put on microfilm) as long as no information or identifying marks such as signatures are lost in the reproduction.

FEDERAL TRADE COMMISSION ACT

15 U.S.C. §§ 41–58

Table of Sections

---

§ 1. Federal Trade Commission established; membership; vacancies; seal [15 U.S.C. § 41]

A commission is created and established, to be known as the Federal Trade Commission (hereinafter referred to as the Commission), which shall be composed of five Commissioners, who shall be appointed by the President, by and with the advice and consent of the

Senate. Not more than three of the Commissioners shall be members of the same political party. . . .

§ 4. Definitions [15 U.S.C. § 44]

The words defined in this section shall have the following meaning when found in this subchapter, to wit:

"Commerce" means commerce among the several States or with foreign nations, or in any Territory of the United States or in the District of Columbia, or between any such Territory and another, or between any such Territory and any State or foreign nation, or between the District of Columbia and any State or Territory or foreign nation.

. . .

§ 5. Unfair methods of competition unlawful; prevention by Commission [15 U.S.C. § 45]

(a) Declaration of unlawfulness; power to prohibit unfair practices

(1) Unfair methods of competition in or affecting commerce, and unfair or deceptive acts or practices in or affecting commerce, are declared unlawful.

(2) The Commission is empowered and directed to prevent persons, partnerships, or corporations, except banks, savings and loan institutions described in section 18(f)(3), common carriers subject to the Acts to regulate commerce, air carriers and foreign air carriers subject to the Federal Aviation Act of 1958, and persons, partnerships, or corporations insofar as they are subject to the Packers and Stockyards Act, 1921, except as provided in section 406(b) of said Act, from using unfair methods of competition in or affecting commerce and unfair or deceptive acts or practices in or affecting commerce.

. . .

(b) Proceeding by Commission; modifying and setting aside orders

Whenever the Commission shall have reason to believe that any such person, partnership, or corporation has been or is using any unfair method of competition or unfair or deceptive act or practice in or affecting commerce, and if it shall appear to the Commission that a proceeding by it in respect thereof would be to the interest of the public, it shall issue and serve upon such person, partnership, or corporation a complaint stating its charges in that respect and containing a notice of a hearing upon a day and at a place therein fixed at least thirty days after the service of said complaint. The person, partnership, or corporation so complained of shall have the right to appear at the place and time so fixed and show cause why an order should not be entered by the Commission requiring such person, partnership, or corporation to cease and desist from the violation of the law so charged in said complaint. Any person, partnership, or corporation may make application, and upon good cause shown may be allowed by the Commission to intervene and appear in said proceeding by counsel or in person. The testimony in any such proceeding shall be reduced to writing and filed in the office of the Commission. If upon such hearing the Commission shall be of the opinion that the method of competition or the act or practice in question is prohibited by this Act, it shall make a report in writing in which it shall state its findings as to the facts and shall issue and cause to be served on such person, partnership, or corporation an order requiring such person, partnership, or corporation to cease and desist from using such method of competition or such act or practice. Until the expiration of the time allowed for filing a petition for review, if no such petition has been duly filed within such time, or, if a petition for review has been filed within such time then until the record in the proceeding has been filed in a court of appeals of the United States, as hereinafter provided, the Commission may at any time, upon such notice and in such manner as it shall deem proper, modify or set aside, in whole or in part, any report or any order made or issued by it under this section. After the expiration of the time allowed for filing a petition for review, if no such petition has been duly filed within such time, the Commission may at any time, after notice and opportunity for hearing, reopen and alter, modify, or set aside, in whole or in part any report or order made or issued by it under this section, whenever in the opinion of the Commission conditions of fact or of law have so changed as to require such action or if the public interest shall so require, except that (1) the said person, partnership, or corporation may, within sixty days after service upon him or it of said report or order entered after such a reopening, obtain a review thereof in the appropriate court of appeals of the United States, in the manner provided in subsection (c) of this section; and (2) in the case of an order, the Commission shall reopen any such order to consider whether such order (including any affirmative relief provision contained in such order) should be altered, modified, or set aside, in whole or in part, if the person, partnership, or corporation involved files a request with the Commission which makes a satisfactory showing that changed conditions of law or fact require such order to be altered, modified, or set aside, in whole or in part. The Commission shall determine whether to alter, modify, or set aside any order of the Commission in response to a request made by a person, partnership, or corporation under paragraph (2) not later than 120 days after the date of the filing of such request.

(c) Review of order; rehearing

Any person, partnership, or corporation required by an order of the Commission to cease and desist from using any method of competition or act or practice may obtain a review of such order in the court of appeals of the United States, within any circuit where the method of competition or the act or practice in question was used or where such person, partnership, or corporation resides or carries on business, by filing in the court, within sixty days from the date of the service of such order, a written petition praying that the order of the Commission be set aside. A copy of such petition shall be forthwith transmitted by the clerk of the court to the Commission, and thereupon the Commission shall file in the court the record in the proceeding, as provided in section 2112 of title 28. Upon such filing of the petition the court shall have jurisdiction of the proceeding and of the question determined therein concurrently with the Commission until the filing of the record and shall have power to make and enter a decree affirming, modifying, or setting aside the order of the Commission, and enforcing the same to the extent that such order is affirmed and to issue such writs as are ancillary to its jurisdiction or are necessary in its judgment to prevent injury to the public or to competitors pendente lite. The findings of the Commission as to the facts, if supported by evidence, shall be conclusive. To the extent that the order of the Commission is affirmed, the court shall thereupon issue its own order commanding obedience to the terms of such order of the Commission. If either party shall apply to the court for leave to adduce additional evidence, and shall show to the satisfaction of the court that such additional evidence is material and that there were reasonable grounds for the failure to adduce such evidence in the proceeding before the Commission, the court may order such additional evidence to be taken before the Commission and to be adduced upon the hearing in such manner and upon such terms and conditions as to the court may seem proper. The Commission may modify its findings as to the facts, or make new findings, by reason of the additional evidence so taken, and it shall file such modified or new findings, which, if supported by evidence, shall be conclusive, and its recommendation, if any, for the modification or setting aside of its original order, with the return of such additional evidence. The judgment and decree of the court shall be final, except that the same shall be subject to review by the Supreme Court upon certiorari, as provided in section 1254 of title 28.

(d) Jurisdiction of court

Upon the filing of the record with it the jurisdiction of the court of appeals of the United States to affirm, enforce, modify, or set aside orders of the Commission shall be exclusive.

(e) Precedence of proceedings; exemption from liability

Such proceedings in the court of appeals shall be given precedence over other cases pending therein, and shall be in every way expedited. . . .

(*l*) Penalty for violation of order; injunctions and other appropriate equitable relief

Any person, partnership, or corporation who violates an order of the Commission after it has become final, and while such order is in effect, shall forfeit and pay to the United States a civil penalty of not more than $10,000 for each violation, which shall accrue to the United States and may be recovered in a civil action brought by the Attorney General of the United States. Each separate violation of such an order shall be a separate offense, except that in a case of a violation through continuing failure to obey or neglect to obey a final order of the Commission, each day of continuance of such failure or neglect shall be deemed a separate offense. In such actions, the United States district courts are empowered to grant mandatory injunctions and such other and further equitable relief as they deem appropriate in the enforcement of such final orders of the Commission.

(m) Civil actions for recovery of penalties for knowing violations of rules and cease and desist orders respecting unfair or deceptive acts or practices; jurisdiction; maximum amount of penalties; continuing violations; de novo determinations; compromise or settlement procedure

(1)(A) The Commission may commence a civil action to recover a civil penalty in a district court of the United States against any person, partnership, or corporation which violates any rule under this Act respecting unfair or deceptive acts or practices (other than an interpretive rule or a rule violation of which the Commission has provided is not an unfair or deceptive act or practice in violation of subsection (a)(1) of this section) with actual knowledge or knowledge fairly implied on the basis of objective circumstances that such act is unfair or deceptive and is prohibited by such rule. In such action, such person, partnership, or corporation shall be liable for a civil penalty of not more than $10,000 for each violation.

(B) If the Commission determines in a proceeding under subsection (b) of this section that any act or practice is unfair or deceptive, and issues a final cease and desist order with respect to such act or practice, then the Commission may commence a civil action to obtain a civil penalty in a district court of the United States against any person, partnership, or corporation which engages in such act or practice—

(1) after such cease and desist order becomes final (whether or not such person, partnership, or corporation was subject to such cease and desist order), and

(2) with actual knowledge that such act or practice is unfair or deceptive and is unlawful under subsection (a)(1) of this section.

In such action, such person, partnership, or corporation shall be liable for a civil penalty of not more than $10,000 for each violation.

(C) In the case of a violation through continuing failure to comply with a rule or with subsection (a)(1) of this section, each day of continuance of such failure shall be treated as a separate violation, for purposes of subparagraphs (A) and (B). In determining the amount of such a civil penalty, the court shall take into account the degree of culpability, any history of prior such conduct, ability to pay, effect on ability to continue to do business, and such other matters as justice may require.

(2) If the cease and desist order establishing that the act or practice is unfair or deceptive was not issued against the defendant in a civil penalty action under paragraph (1)(B) the issues of fact in such action against such defendant shall be tried de novo.

(3) The Commission may compromise or settle any action for a civil penalty if such compromise or settlement is accompanied by a public statement of its reasons and is approved by the court.

§ 6. Additional powers of Commission [15 U.S.C. § 46]

The Commission shall also have power—

(a) Investigation of persons, partnerships, or corporations

To gather and compile information concerning, and to investigate from time to time the organization, business, conduct, practices, and management of any person, partnership, or corporation engaged in or whose business affects commerce, excepting banks, savings and loan institutions described in section 18(f)(3), and common carriers subject to the Act to regulate commerce, and its relation to other persons, partnerships, and corporations.

(b) Reports of persons, partnerships, and corporations

To require, by general or special orders, persons, partnerships, and corporations, engaged in or whose business affects commerce, excepting banks, savings and loan institutions described in section 18(f)(3), and common carriers subject to the Act to regulate commerce, or any class of them, or any of them, respectively, to file with the Commission in such form as the Commission may prescribe annual or special, or both annual and special, reports or answers in writing to specific questions, furnishing to the Commission such information as it may require as to the organization, business, conduct, practices, management, and relation to other corporations, partnerships, and individuals of the respective persons, partnerships, and corporations filing such reports or answers in writing. Such reports and answers shall be made under oath, or otherwise, as the Commission may prescribe, and shall be filed with the Commission within such reasonable period as the Commission may prescribe, unless additional time be granted in any case by the Commission.

. . .

(f) Publication of information; reports

To make public from time to time such portions of the information obtained by it hereunder as are in the public interest; and to make annual and special reports to the Congress and to submit therewith recommendations for additional legislation; and to provide for the publication of its reports and decisions in such form and manner as may be best adapted for public information and use: *Provided,* That the Commission shall not have any authority to make public any trade secret or any commercial or financial information which is obtained from any person and which is privileged or confidential, . . .

(g) Classification of corporations; regulations

From time to time classify corporations and (except as provided in section 18(a)(2)) to make rules and regulations for the purpose of carrying out the provisions of this Act.

. . .

Provided, That the exception of "banks, savings and loan institutions described in section 18(f)(3), and common carriers subject to the Act to regulate commerce" from the Commission's powers defined in clauses (a) and (b) of this section, shall not be construed to limit the Commission's authority to gather and compile information, to investigate, or to require reports or answers from, any person, partnership, or corporation to the extent that such action is necessary to the investigation of any person, partnership, or corporation, group of persons, partnerships, or corporations, or industry which is not engaged or is engaged only incidentally in banking, in business as a savings and loan institution, or in business as a common carrier subject to the Act to regulate commerce.

The Commission shall establish a plan designed to substantially reduce burdens imposed upon small businesses as a result of requirements established by the Commission under clause (b) relating to the filing of quarterly financial reports. Such plan shall (1) be established after consultation with small businesses and persons who use the information contained in such quarterly financial reports; (2) provide for a reduction of the number of small businesses required to file such quarterly financial reports; and (3) make revisions in the forms used for such quarterly financial reports for the purpose of reducing the complexity of such forms. . . .

Nothing in this section (other than the provisions of clause (c) and clause (d)) shall apply to the business of insurance, except that the Commission shall have authority to conduct studies and prepare reports relating to the business of insurance. The Commission may exercise such authority only upon receiving a request which is agreed to by a majority of the members of the Committee on Commerce, Science, and Transportation of the Senate or the Committee on Energy and Commerce of the House of Representatives. The authority to conduct any such study shall expire at the end of the Congress during which the request for such study was made.

§ 8. Information and assistance from departments [15 U.S.C. § 48]

The several departments and bureaus of the Government when directed by the President shall furnish the Commission, upon its request, all records, papers, and information in their possession relating to any corporation subject to any of the provisions of this Act, and shall detail from time to time such officials and employees to the Commission as he may direct.

§ 9. Documentary evidence; depositions; witnesses [15 U.S.C. § 49]

For the purposes of this Act the Commission, or its duly authorized agent or agents, shall at all reasonable times have access to, for the purpose of examination, and the right to copy any documentary evidence of any person, partnership, or corporation being investigated or proceeded against; and the Commission shall have power to require by subpoena the attendance and testimony of witnesses and the production of all such documentary evidence relating to any matter under investigation. Any member of the Commission may sign subpoenas, and members and examiners of the Commission may administer oaths and affirmations, examine witnesses, and receive evidence.

Such attendance of witnesses, and the production of such documentary evidence, may be required from any place in the United States, at any designated place of hearing. And in case of disobedience to a subpoena the Commission may invoke the aid of any court of the United States in requiring the attendance and testimony of witnesses and the production of documentary evidence.

Any of the district courts of the United States within the jurisdiction of which such inquiry is carried on may, in case of contumacy or refusal to obey a subpoena issued to any person, partnership, or corporation issue an order requiring such person, partnership, or corporation to appear before the Commission, or to produce documentary evidence if so ordered, or to give evidence touching the matter in question; and any failure to obey such order of the court may be punished by such court as a contempt thereof.

Upon the application of the Attorney General of the United States, at the request of the Commission, the district courts of the United States shall have jurisdiction to issue writs of mandamus commanding any person, partnership, or corporation to comply with the provisions of this Act or any order of the Commission made in pursuance thereof.

The Commission may order testimony to be taken by deposition in any proceeding or investigation pending under this Act at any stage of such proceeding or investigation. Such depositions may be taken before any person designated by the Commission and having power to administer oaths. Such testimony shall be reduced to writing by the person taking the deposition, or under his direction, and shall then be subscribed by the deponent. Any person may be compelled to appear and depose and to produce documentary evidence in the same manner as witnesses may be compelled to appear and testify and produce documentary evidence before the Commission as hereinbefore provided.

Witnesses summoned before the Commission shall be paid the same fees and mileage that are paid witnesses in the courts of the United States and witnesses whose depositions are taken and the persons taking the same shall severally be entitled to the same fees as are paid for like services in the courts of the United States.

§ 10. Offenses and penalties [15 U.S.C. § 50]

Any person who shall neglect or refuse to attend and testify, or to answer any lawful inquiry or to produce any documentary evidence, if in his power to do so, in obedience to an order of a district court of the United States directing compliance with the subpoena or lawful requirement of the Commission, shall be guilty of an offense and upon conviction thereof by a court of competent jurisdiction shall be punished by a fine of not less than $1,000 nor more than $5,000, or by imprisonment for not more than one year, or by both such fine and imprisonment.

Any person who shall willfully make, or cause to be made, any false entry or statement of fact in any report required to be made under this Act, or who shall willfully make, or cause to be made, any false entry in any account, record, or memorandum kept by any person, partnership, or corporation subject to this Act, or who shall willfully neglect or fail to make, or to cause to be made, full, true, and correct entries in such accounts, records, or memoranda of all facts and transactions appertaining to the business of such person, partnership, or corporation, or who shall willfully remove out of the jurisdiction of the United States, or willfully mutilate, alter, or by any other means falsify any documentary evidence of such person, partnership, or corporation, or who shall willfully refuse to submit to the Commission or to any of its authorized agents, for the purpose of inspection and taking copies, any documentary evidence of such person, partnership, or corporation in his possession or within his control, shall be deemed guilty of an offense against the United States, and shall be subject, upon conviction in any court of the United States of competent jurisdiction, to a fine of not less than $1,000 nor more than

$5,000, or to imprisonment for a term of not more than three years, or to both such fine and imprisonment.

. . .

§ 11. Effect on other statutory provisions [15 U.S.C. § 51]

Nothing contained in this Act shall be construed to prevent or interfere with the enforcement of the provisions of the antitrust Acts or the Acts to regulate commerce, nor shall anything contained in this Act be construed to alter, modify, or repeal the said antitrust Acts or the Acts to regulate commerce or any part or parts thereof.

§ 12. Dissemination of false advertisements [15 U.S.C. § 52]

(a) Unlawfulness

It shall be unlawful for any person, partnership, or corporation to disseminate, or cause to be disseminated, any false advertisement—

(1) By United States mails, or in or having an effect upon commerce, by any means, for the purpose of inducing, or which is likely to induce, directly or indirectly the purchase of food, drugs, devices, or cosmetics; or

(2) By any means, for the purpose of inducing, or which is likely to induce, directly or indirectly, the purchase in or having an effect upon commerce, of food, drugs, devices, or cosmetics.

(b) Unfair or deceptive act or practice

The dissemination or the causing to be disseminated of any false advertisement within the provisions of subsection (a) of this section shall be an unfair or deceptive act or practice in or affecting commerce within the meaning of section 5.

§ 13. False advertisements; injunctions and restraining orders [15 U.S.C. § 53]

(a) Power of Commission; jurisdiction of courts

Whenever the Commission has reason to believe—

(1) that any person, partnership, or corporation is engaged in, or is about to engage in, the dissemination or the causing of the dissemination of any advertisement in violation of section 12, and

(2) that the enjoining thereof pending the issuance of a complaint by the Commission under section 5, and until such complaint is dismissed by the Commission or set aside by the court on review, or the order of the Commission to cease and desist made thereon has become final within the meaning of section 5, would be to the interest of the public,

the Commission by any of its attorneys designated by it for such purpose may bring suit in a district court of the United States or in the

United States court of any Territory, to enjoin the dissemination or the causing of the dissemination of such advertisement. Upon proper showing a temporary injunction or restraining order shall be granted without bond. Any such suit shall be brought in the district in which such person, partnership, or corporation resides or transacts business.

(b) Temporary restraining orders; preliminary injunctions

Whenever the Commission has reason to believe—

(1) that any person, partnership, or corporation is violating, or is about to violate, any provision of law enforced by the Federal Trade Commission, and

(2) that the enjoining thereof pending the issuance of a complaint by the Commission and until such complaint is dismissed by the Commission or set aside by the court on review, or until the order of the Commission made thereon has become final, would be in the interest of the public—

the Commission by any of its attorneys designated by it for such purpose may bring suit in a district court of the United States to enjoin any such act or practice. Upon a proper showing that, weighing the equities and considering the Commission's likelihood of ultimate success, such action would be in the public interest, and after notice to the defendant, a temporary restraining order or a preliminary injunction may be granted without bond: *Provided, however,* That if a complaint is not filed within such period (not exceeding 20 days) as may be specified by the court after issuance of the temporary restraining order or preliminary injunction, the order or injunction shall be dissolved by the court and be of no further force and effect: *Provided further,* That in proper cases the Commission may seek, and after proper proof, the court may issue, a permanent injunction. Any such suit shall be brought in the district in which such person, partnership, or corporation resides or transacts business.

(c) Exception of periodical publications

Whenever it appears to the satisfaction of the court in the case of a newspaper, magazine, periodical, or other publication, published at regular intervals—

(1) that restraining the dissemination of a false advertisement in any particular issue of such publication would delay the delivery of such issue after the regular time therefor, and

(2) that such delay would be due to the method by which the manufacture and distribution of such publication is customarily conducted by the publisher in accordance with sound business practice, and not to any method or device adopted for the evasion of this section or to prevent or delay the issuance of an injunction or restraining order with respect to such false advertisement or any other advertisement,

the court shall exclude such issue from the operation of the restraining order or injunction.

§ 14. False advertisements; penalties [15 U.S.C. § 54]

(a) Imposition of penalties

Any person, partnership, or corporation who violates any provision of section 12(a) shall, if the use of the commodity advertised may be injurious to health because of results from such use under the conditions prescribed in the advertisement thereof, or under such conditions as are customary or usual, or if such violation is with intent to defraud or mislead, be guilty of a misdemeanor, and upon conviction shall be punished by a fine of not more than $5,000 or by imprisonment for not more than six months, or by both such fine and imprisonment; except that if the conviction is for a violation committed after a first conviction of such person, partnership, or corporation, for any violation of such section, punishment shall be by a fine of not more than $10,000 or by imprisonment for not more than one year, or by both such fine and imprisonment: *Provided,* That for the purposes of this section meats and meat food products duly inspected, marked, and labeled in accordance with rules and regulations issued under the Meat Inspection Act shall be conclusively presumed not injurious to health at the time the same leave official "establishments."

(b) Exception of advertising medium or agency

No publisher, radio-broadcast licensee, or agency or medium for the dissemination of advertising, except the manufacturer, packer, distributor, or seller of the commodity to which the false advertisement relates, shall be liable under this section by reason of the dissemination by him of any false advertisement, unless he has refused, on the request of the Commission, to furnish the Commission the name and post-office address of the manufacturer, packer, distributor, seller, or advertising agency, residing in the United States, who caused him to disseminate such advertisement. No advertising agency shall be liable under this section by reason of the causing by it of the dissemination of any false advertisement, unless it has refused, on the request of the Commission, to furnish the Commission the name and post-office address of the manufacturer, packer, distributor, or seller, residing in the United States, who caused it to cause the dissemination of such advertisement.

§ 15. Additional definitions [15 U.S.C. § 55]

For the purposes of sections 12, 13, and 14—

(a) False advertisement

(1) The term "false advertisement" means an advertisement, other than labeling, which is misleading in a material respect; and in determining whether any advertisement is misleading, there shall be

taken into account (among other things) not only representations made or suggested by statement, word, design, device, sound, or any combination thereof, but also the extent to which the advertisement fails to reveal facts material in the light of such representations or material with respect to consequences which may result from the use of the commodity to which the advertisement relates under the conditions prescribed in said advertisement, or under such conditions as are customary or usual. No advertisement of a drug shall be deemed to be false if it is disseminated only to members of the medical profession, contains no false representation of a material fact, and includes, or is accompanied in each instance by truthful disclosure of, the formula showing quantitatively each ingredient of such drug.

(2) In the case of oleomargarine or margarine an advertisement shall be deemed misleading in a material respect if in such advertisement representations are made or suggested by statement, word, grade designation, design, device, symbol, sound, or any combination thereof, that such oleomargarine or margarine is a dairy product, except that nothing contained herein shall prevent a truthful, accurate, and full statement in any such advertisement of all the ingredients contained in such oleomargarine or margarine.

(b) Food

The term "food" means (1) articles used for food or drink for man or other animals, (2) chewing gum, and (3) articles used for components of any such article.

(c) Drug

The term "drug" means (1) articles recognized in the official United States Pharmacopoeia, official Homoeopathic Pharmacopoeia of the United States, or official National Formulary, or any supplement to any of them; and (2) articles intended for use in the diagnosis, cure, mitigation, treatment, or prevention of disease in man or other animals; and (3) articles (other than food) intended to affect the structure or any function of the body of man or other animals; and (4) articles intended for use as a component of any article specified in clause (1), (2), or (3); but does not include devices or their components, parts, or accessories.

(d) Device

The term "device" (except when used in subsection (a) of this section) means an instrument, apparatus, implement, machine, contrivance, implant, in vitro reagent, or other similar or related article, including any component, part, or accessory, which is—

(1) recognized in the official National Formulary, or the United States Pharmacopeia, or any supplement to them,

(2) intended for use in the diagnosis of disease or other conditions, or in the cure, mitigation, treatment, or prevention of disease, in man or other animals, or

(3) intended to affect the structure or any function of the body of man or other animals, and

which does not achieve any of its principal intended purposes through chemical action within or on the body of man or other animals and which is not dependent upon being metabolized for the achievement of any of its principal intended purposes.

(e) Cosmetic

The term "cosmetic" means (1) articles to be rubbed, poured, sprinkled, or sprayed on, introduced into, or otherwise applied to the human body or any part thereof intended for cleansing, beautifying, promoting attractiveness, or altering the appearance, and (2) articles intended for use as a component of any such article; except that such term shall not include soap.

(f) Oleomargarine or margarine

For the purposes of this section and section 407 of the Food, Drug, and Cosmetic Act, the term "oleomargarine" or "margarine" includes—

(1) all substances, mixtures, and compounds known as oleomargarine or margarine;

(2) all substances, mixtures, and compounds which have a consistence similar to that of butter and which contain any edible oils or fats other than milk fat if made in imitation or semblance of butter.

§ 16. Commencement, defense, intervention and supervision of litigation and appeal by Commission or Attorney General; procedure for exercise of authority to litigate or appeal; certification by Commission to Attorney General for criminal proceedings [15 U.S.C. § 56]

(a)(1) Except as otherwise provided in paragraph (2) or (3), if—

(A) before commencing, defending, or intervening in, any civil action involving this Act (including an action to collect a civil penalty) which the Commission, or the Attorney General on behalf of the Commission, is authorized to commence, defend, or intervene in, the Commission gives written notification and undertakes to consult with the Attorney General with respect to such action; and

(B) the Attorney General fails within 45 days after receipt of such notification to commence, defend, or intervene in, such action;

the Commission may commence, defend, or intervene in, and supervise the litigation or, such action and any appeal of such action in its own name by any of its attorneys designated by it for such purpose.

(2) Except as otherwise provided in paragraph (3), in any civil action—

(A) under section 13 (relating to injunctive relief);

(B) under section 19 (relating to consumer redress);

(C) to obtain judicial review of a rule prescribed by the Commission, or a cease and desist order issued under section 5; or

(D) under the second paragraph of section 9 (relating to enforcement of a subpena) and under the fourth paragraph of such section (relating to compliance with section 6);

the Commission shall have exclusive authority to commence or defend, and supervise the litigation of, such action and any appeal of such action in its own name by any of its attorneys designated by it for such purpose, unless the Commission authorizes the Attorney General to do so. The Commission shall inform the Attorney General of the exercise of such authority and such exercise shall not preclude the Attorney General from intervening on behalf of the United States in such action and any appeal of such action as may be otherwise provided by law.

(3)(A) If the Commission makes a written request to the Attorney General, within the 10-day period which begins on the date of the entry of the judgment in any civil action in which the Commission represented itself pursuant to paragraph (1) or (2), to represent itself through any of its attorneys designated by it for such purpose before the Supreme Court in such action, it may do so, if—

(i) the Attorney General concurs with such request; or

(ii) the Attorney General, within the 60-day period which begins on the date of the entry of such judgment—

(a) refuses to appeal or file a petition for writ of certiorari with respect to such civil action, in which case he shall give written notification to the Commission of the reasons for such refusal within such 60-day period; or

(b) the Attorney General fails to take any action with respect to the Commission's request.

(B) In any case where the Attorney General represents the Commission before the Supreme Court in any civil action in which the Commission represented itself pursuant to paragraph (1) or (2), the Attorney General may not agree to any settlement, compromise, or dismissal of such action, or confess error in the Supreme Court with respect to such action, unless the Commission concurs.

(C) For purposes of this paragraph (with respect to representation before the Supreme Court), the term "Attorney General" includes the Solicitor General.

(4) If, prior to the expiration of the 45-day period specified in paragraph (1) of this section or a 60-day period specified in paragraph (3),

any right of the Commission to commence, defend, or intervene in, any such action or appeal may be extinguished due to any procedural requirement of any court with respect to the time in which any pleadings, notice of appeal, or other acts pertaining to such action or appeal may be taken, the Attorney General shall have one-half of the time required to comply with any such procedural requirement of the court (including any extension of such time granted by the court) for the purpose of commencing, defending, or intervening in the civil action pursuant to paragraph (1) or for the purpose of refusing to appeal or file a petition for writ of certiorari and the written notification or failing to take any action pursuant to paragraph 3(A)(ii).

(5) The provisions of this subsection shall apply notwithstanding chapter 31 of title 28, or any other provision of law.

(b) Whenever the Commission has reason to believe that any person, partnership, or corporation is liable for a criminal penalty under this Act, the Commission shall certify the facts to the Attorney General, whose duty it shall be to cause appropriate criminal proceedings to be brought.

§ 17. Separability clause [15 U.S.C. § 57]

If any provision of this Act, or the application thereof to any person, partnership, or corporation, or circumstance, is held invalid, the remainder of this Act, and the application of such provisions to any other person, partnership, corporation, or circumstance, shall not be affected thereby.

§ 18. Unfair or deceptive acts or practices rulemaking proceedings [15 U.S.C. § 57a]

(a) Authority of Commission to prescribe rules and general statements of policy

(1) Except as provided in subsection (i) of this section, the Commission may prescribe—

(A) interpretive rules and general statements of policy with respect to unfair or deceptive acts or practices in or affecting commerce (within the meaning of section 5(a)(1)), and

(B) rules which define with specificity acts or practices which are unfair or deceptive acts or practices in or affecting commerce (within the meaning of section 5(a)(1)), except that the Commission shall not develop or promulgate any trade rule or regulation with regard to the regulation of the development and utilization of the standards and certification activities pursuant to this section. Rules under this subparagraph may include requirements prescribed for the purpose of preventing such acts or practices.

(2) The Commission shall have no authority under this Act, other than its authority under this section, to prescribe any rule with respect to unfair or deceptive acts or practices in or affecting commerce (within the meaning of section 5(a)(1)). The preceding sentence shall not affect any authority of the Commission to prescribe rules (including interpretive rules), and general statements of policy, with respect to unfair methods of competition in or affecting commerce.

(b) Procedures applicable

(1) When prescribing a rule under subsection (a)(1)(B) of this section, the Commission shall proceed in accordance with section 553 of title 5 (without regard to any reference in such section to sections 556 and 557 of such title), and shall also (A) publish a notice of proposed rulemaking stating with particularity the text of the rule, including any alternatives, which the Commission proposes to promulgate, and the reason for the proposed rule; (B) allow interested persons to submit written data, views, and arguments, and make all such submissions publicly available; (C) provide an opportunity for an informal hearing in accordance with subsection (c) of this section; and (D) promulgate, if appropriate, a final rule based on the matter in the rulemaking record (as defined in subsection (e)(1)(B) of this section), together with a statement of basis and purpose.

(2)(A) Prior to the publication of any notice of proposed rulemaking pursuant to paragraph (1)(A), the Commission shall publish an advance notice of proposed rulemaking in the Federal Register. Such advance notice shall—

(i) contain a brief description of the area of inquiry under consideration, the objectives which the Commission seeks to achieve, and possible regulatory alternatives under consideration by the Commission; and

(ii) invite the response of interested parties with respect to such proposed rulemaking, including any suggestions or alternative methods for achieving such objectives.

(B) The Commission shall submit such advance notice of proposed rulemaking to the Committee on Commerce, Science, and Transportation of the Senate and to the Committee on Energy and Commerce of the House of Representatives. The Commission may use such additional mechanisms as the Commission considers useful to obtain suggestions regarding the content of the area of inquiry before the publication of a general notice of proposed rulemaking under paragraph (1)(A).

(C) The Commission shall, 30 days before the publication of a notice of proposed rulemaking pursuant to paragraph (1)(A), submit such notice to the Committee on Commerce, Science, and Transportation of the Senate and to the Committee on Energy and Commerce of the House of Representatives.

(c) Informal hearing procedure

The Commission shall conduct any informal hearings required by subsection (b)(1)(C) of this section in accordance with the following procedure:

(1)(A) The Commission shall provide for the conduct of proceedings under this subsection by hearing officers who shall perform their functions in accordance with the requirements of this subsection.

(B) The officer who presides over the rulemaking proceedings shall be responsible to a chief presiding officer who shall not be responsible to any other officer or employee of the Commission. The officer who presides over the rulemaking proceeding shall make a recommended decision based upon the findings and conclusions of such officer as to all relevant and material evidence, except that such recommended decision may be made by another officer if the officer who presided over the proceeding is no longer available to the Commission.

(C) Except as required for the disposition of ex parte matters as authorized by law, no presiding officer shall consult any person or party with respect to any fact in issue unless such officer gives notice and opportunity for all parties to participate.

(2) Subject to paragraph (3) of this subsection, an interested person is entitled—

(A) to present his position orally or by documentary submission (or both), and

(B) if the Commission determines that there are disputed issues of material fact it is necessary to resolve, to present such rebuttal submissions and to conduct (or have conducted under paragraph (3)(B)) such cross-examination of persons as the Commission determines (i) to be appropriate, and (ii) to be required for a full and true disclosure with respect to such issues.

(3) The Commission may prescribe such rules and make such rulings concerning proceedings in such hearings as may tend to avoid unnecessary costs or delay. Such rules or rulings may include (A) imposition of reasonable time limits on each interested person's oral presentations, and (B) requirements that any cross-examination to which a person may be entitled under paragraph (2) be conducted by the Commission on behalf of that person in such manner as the Commission determines (i) to be appropriate, and (ii) to be required for a full and true disclosure with respect to disputed issues of material fact.

(4)(A) Except as provided in subparagraph (B), if a group of persons each of whom under paragraphs (2) and (3) would be entitled to conduct (or have conducted) cross-examination and who are determined by the Commission to have the same or similar interests in the proceeding cannot agree upon a single representative of such interests for purposes of cross-examination, the Commission may make rules and rulings (i) limiting the representation of such interest, for such purposes, and (ii) governing the manner in which such cross-examination shall be limited.

(B) When any person who is a member of a group with respect to which the Commission has made a determination under subparagraph (A) is unable to agree upon group representation with the other members of the group, then such person shall not be denied under the authority of subparagraph (A) the opportunity to conduct (or have conducted) cross-examination as to issues affecting his particular interests if (i) he satisfies the Commission that he has made a reasonable and good faith effort to reach agreement upon group representation with the other members of the group and (ii) the Commission determines that there are substantial and relevant issues which are not adequately presented by the group representative.

(5) A verbatim transcript shall be taken of any oral presentation, and cross-examination, in an informal hearing to which this subsection applies. Such transcript shall be available to the public.

(d) Statement of basis and purpose accompanying rule; "Commission" defined; judicial review of amendment or repeal of rule; violation of rules

(1) The Commission's statement of basis and purpose to accompany a rule promulgated under subsection (a)(1)(B) of this section shall include (A) a statement as to the prevalence of the acts or practices treated by the rule; (B) a statement as to the manner and context in which such acts or practices are unfair or deceptive; and (C) a statement as to the economic effect of the rule, taking into account the effect on small business and consumers.

(2)(A) The term "Commission" as used in this subsection and subsections (b) and (c) of this section includes any person authorized to act in behalf of the Commission in any part of the rulemaking proceeding.

(B) A substantive amendment to, or repeal of, a rule promulgated under subsection (a)(1)(B) of this section shall be prescribed, and subject to judicial review, in the same manner as a rule prescribed under such subsection. An exemption under subsection (g) of this section shall not be treated as an amendment or repeal of a rule.

(3) When any rule under subsection (a)(1)(B) of this section takes effect a subsequent violation thereof shall constitute an unfair or deceptive act or practice in violation of section 5(a)(1), unless the Commission otherwise expressly provides in such rule.

(e) Judicial review; petition; jurisdiction and venue; rulemaking record; additional submissions and presentations; scope of review and relief; review by Supreme Court; additional remedies

(1)(A) Not later than 60 days after a rule is promulgated under subsection (a)(1)(B) of this section by the Commission, any interested person (including a consumer or consumer organization) may file a petition, in the United States Court of Appeals for the District of Columbia circuit or for the circuit in which such person resides or has his principal place of business, for judicial review of such rule. Copies of the petition shall be forthwith transmitted by the clerk of the court to the Commission or other officer designated by it for that purpose. The provisions of section 2112 of title 28 shall apply to the filing of the rulemaking record of proceedings on which the Commission based its rule and to the transfer of proceedings in the courts of appeals.

(B) For purposes of this section, the term "rulemaking record" means the rule, its statement of basis and purpose, the transcript required by subsection (c)(5) of this section, any written submissions, and any other information which the Commission considers relevant to such rule.

. . .

(5) . . . The contents and adequacy of any statement required by subsection (b)(1)(D) of this section shall not be subject to judicial review in any respect.

(f) Unfair or deceptive acts or practices by banks or savings and loan institutions; promulgation of regulations by Board of Governors of Federal Reserve System and by Federal Home Loan Bank Board; agency enforcement and compliance proceedings; violations; power of other Federal agencies unaffected; reporting requirements

(1) In order to prevent unfair or deceptive acts or practices in or affecting commerce (including acts or practices which are unfair or deceptive to consumers) by banks or savings and loan institutions described in paragraph (3), each agency specified in paragraph (2) or (3) of this subsection shall establish a separate division of consumer affairs which shall receive and take appropriate action upon complaints with respect to such acts or practices by banks or savings and loan institutions described in paragraph (3) subject to its jurisdiction. The Board of Governors of the Federal Reserve System (with respect to banks) and the Federal Home Loan Bank Board (with respect to savings and loan institutions described in paragraph (3)) shall prescribe regulations to carry out the purposes of this section, including regulations defining with specificity such unfair or deceptive acts or practices, and containing requirements prescribed for the purpose of preventing such acts or practices. Whenever the Commission prescribes a rule under subsection (a)(1)(B) of this section, then within 60 days after such rule takes effect each such Board shall promulgate substantially similar regulations prohibiting acts or practices of banks or savings and loan institutions described in paragraph (3), as the case

may be, which are substantially similar to those prohibited by rules of the Commission and which impose substantially similar requirements, unless (A) either such Board finds that such acts or practices of banks or savings and loan institutions described in paragraph (3), as the case may be, are not unfair or deceptive, or (B) the Board of Governors of the Federal Reserve System finds that implementation of similar regulations with respect to banks would seriously conflict with essential monetary and payments systems policies of such Board, and publishes any such finding, and the reasons therefor, in the Federal Register.

(2) Compliance with regulations prescribed under this subsection shall be enforced under section 8 of the Federal Deposit Insurance Act, in the case of—

(A) national banks and banks operating under the code of law for the District of Columbia, by the division of consumer affairs established by the Comptroller of the Currency;

(B) member banks of the Federal Reserve System (other than banks referred to in subparagraph (A)), by the division of consumer affairs established by the Board of Governors of the Federal Reserve System; and

(C) banks insured by the Federal Deposit Insurance Corporation (other than banks referred to in subparagraph (A) or (B)), by the division of consumer affairs established by the Board of Directors of the Federal Deposit Insurance Corporation.

(3) Compliance with regulations prescribed under this subsection shall be enforced under section 5 of the Home Owners' Loan Act of 1933 (12 U.S.C. 1464) with respect to Federal savings and loan associations, section 407 of the National Housing Act (12 U.S.C. 1730) with respect to insured institutions, and sections 6(i) and 17 of the Federal Home Loan Bank Act (12 U.S.C. 1426(i), 1437) with respect to savings and loan institutions which are members of a Federal Home Loan Bank, by a division of consumer affairs to be established by the Federal Home Loan Bank Board pursuant to the Federal Home Loan Bank Act.

(4) For the purpose of the exercise by any agency referred to in paragraph (2) of its powers under any Act referred to in that paragraph, a violation of any regulation prescribed under this subsection shall be deemed to be a violation of a requirement imposed under that Act. In addition to its powers under any provision of law specifically referred to in paragraph (2), each of the agencies referred to in that paragraph may exercise, for the purpose of enforcing compliance with any regulation prescribed under this subsection, any other authority conferred on it by law.

(5) The authority of the Board of Governors of the Federal Reserve System to issue regulations under this subsection does not im-

pair the authority of any other agency designated in this subsection to make rules respecting its own procedures in enforcing compliance with regulations prescribed under this subsection.

(6) Each agency exercising authority under this subsection shall transmit to the Congress each year a detailed report on its activities under this paragraph during the preceding calendar year.

(g) Exemptions and stays from application of rules; procedures

(1) Any person to whom a rule under subsection (a)(1)(B) of this section applies may petition the Commission for an exemption from such rule.

(2) If, on its own motion or on the basis of a petition under paragraph (1), the Commission finds that the application of a rule prescribed under subsection (a)(1)(B) of this section to any person or class of persons is not necessary to prevent the unfair or deceptive act or practice to which the rule relates, the Commission may exempt such person or class from all or part of such rule. Section 553 of title 5 shall apply to action under this paragraph.

(3) Neither the pendency of a proceeding under this subsection respecting an exemption from a rule, nor the pendency of judicial proceedings to review the Commission's action or failure to act under this subsection, shall stay the applicability of such rule under subsection (a)(1)(B) of this section.

(h) Compensation for attorney fees, expert witness fees, etc., incurred by persons in rulemaking proceedings; limitation on amount; establishment of small business outreach program

(1) The Commission may, pursuant to rules prescribed by it, provide compensation for reasonable attorneys fees, expert witness fees, and other costs of participating in a rulemaking proceeding under this section to any person (A) who has, or represents, an interest (i) which would not otherwise be adequately represented in such proceeding, and (ii) representation of which is necessary for a fair determination of the rulemaking proceeding taken as a whole, and (B) who is unable effectively to participate in such proceeding because such person cannot afford to pay costs of making oral presentations, conducting cross-examination, and making rebuttal submissions in such proceeding.

(2) The Commission shall reserve an amount equal to 25 percent of the amount appropriated for the payment of compensation under this subsection for any fiscal year for use in accordance with this paragraph. Such reserved amount shall be available solely for the payment of compensation to persons who either (A) would be regulated by the proposed rule involved; or (B) represent persons who would be so regulated. Any portion of such reserved amount which is not used for the payment of compensation to such persons under this paragraph shall revert to the Treasury of the United States.

(3) The amount of compensation which may be paid to any person under this subsection in connection with the participation by such person in any particular rulemaking proceeding under this section may not exceed $75,000. The aggregate amount of compensation paid under this subsection in any fiscal year to any person for all rulemaking proceedings in which such person participates during such fiscal year may not exceed $50,000.

(4) The aggregate amount of compensation paid to all persons in any fiscal year under this subsection may not exceed $750,000.

(5) The Commission, in connection with the administration of this subsection pursuant to rules prescribed by the Commission under paragraph (1), shall establish a small business outreach program. Such program shall—

(A) solicit public comment from small businesses whose views otherwise would not be adequately represented, in order to ensure a fair determination in rulemaking proceedings under this section; and

(B) encourage the participation of small businesses in the compensation program administered by the Commission under this subsection by disseminating to small businesses information which explains the procedures and requirements applicable to the receipt of compensation under such program.

(i) Restriction on rulemaking authority of Commission respecting children's advertising proceedings pending on May 28, 1980

The Commission shall not have any authority to promulgate any rule in the children's advertising proceeding pending on May 28, 1980, or in any substantially similar proceeding on the basis of a determination by the Commission that such advertising constitutes an unfair act or practice in or affecting commerce.

(j) Meetings with outside parties

(1) For purposes of this subsection, the term "outside party" means any person other than (A) a Commissioner; (B) an officer or employee of the Commission; or (C) any person who has entered into a contract or any other agreement or arrangement with the Commission to provide any goods or services (including consulting services) to the Commission.

(2) Not later than 60 days after May 28, 1980, the Commission shall publish a proposed rule, and not later than 180 days after May 28, 1980, the Commission shall promulgate a final rule, which shall authorize the Commission or any Commissioner to meet with any outside party concerning any rulemaking proceeding of the Commission. Such rule shall provide that—

(A) notice of any such meeting shall be included in any weekly calendar prepared by the Commission; and

(B) a verbatim record or a summary of any such meeting, or of any communication relating to any such meeting, shall be kept, made available to the public, and included in the rulemaking record.

(k) Communications by investigative personnel with staff of Commission concerning matters outside rulemaking record prohibited

Not later than 60 days after May 28, 1980, the Commission shall publish a proposed rule, and not later than 180 days after May 28, 1980, the Commission shall promulgate a final rule, which shall prohibit any officer, employee, or agent of the Commission with any investigative responsibility or other responsibility relating to any rulemaking proceeding within any operating bureau of the Commission, from communicating or causing to be communicated to any Commissioner or to the personal staff of any Commissioner any fact which is relevant to the merits of such proceeding and which is not on the rulemaking record of such proceeding, unless such communication is made available to the public and is included in the rulemaking record. The provisions of this subsection shall not apply to any communication to the extent such communication is required for the disposition of ex parte matters as authorized by law.

§ 19. Civil actions for violations of rules and cease and desist orders respecting unfair or deceptive acts or practices [15 U.S.C. § 57b]

(a) Suits by Commission against persons, partnerships, or corporations; jurisdiction; relief for dishonest or fraudulent acts

(1) If any person, partnership, or corporation violates any rule under this Act respecting unfair or deceptive acts or practices (other than an interpretive rule, or a rule violation of which the Commission has provided is not an unfair or deceptive act or practice in violation of section 5(a)), then the Commission may commence a civil action against such person, partnership, or corporation for relief under subsection (b) of this section in a United States district court or in any court of competent jurisdiction of a State.

(2) If any person, partnership, or corporation engages in any unfair or deceptive act or practice (within the meaning of section 5(a)(1)) with respect to which the Commission has issued a final cease and desist order which is applicable to such person, partnership, or corporation, then the Commission may commence a civil action against such person, partnership, or corporation in a United States district court or in any court of competent jurisdiction of a State. If the Commission satisfies the court that the act or practice to which the cease and desist order relates is one which a reasonable man would

have known under the circumstances was dishonest or fraudulent, the court may grant relief under subsection (b) of this section.

(b) Nature of relief available

The court in an action under subsection (a) of this section shall have jurisdiction to grant such relief as the court finds necessary to redress injury to consumers or other persons, partnerships, and corporations resulting from the rule violation or the unfair or deceptive act or practice, as the case may be. Such relief may include, but shall not be limited to, rescission or reformation of contracts, the refund of money or return of property, the payment of damages, and public notification respecting the rule violation or the unfair or deceptive act or practice, as the case may be; except that nothing in this subsection is intended to authorize the imposition of any exemplary or punitive damages.

(c) Conclusiveness of findings of Commission in cease and desist proceedings; notice of judicial proceedings to injured persons, etc.

(1) If (A) a cease and desist order issued under section 5(b) has become final under section 5g with respect to any person's, partnership's, or corporation's rule violation or unfair or deceptive act or practice, and (B) an action under this section is brought with respect to such person's, partnership's, or corporation's rule violation or act or practice, then the findings of the Commission as to the material facts in the proceeding under section 5(b) with respect to such person's, partnership's, or corporation's rule violation or act or practice, shall be conclusive unless (i) the terms of such cease and desist order expressly provide that the Commission's findings shall not be conclusive, or (ii) the order became final by reason of section 5(g)(1), in which case such finding shall be conclusive if supported by evidence.

(2) The court shall cause notice of an action under this section to be given in a manner which is reasonably calculated, under all of the circumstances, to apprise the persons, partnerships, and corporations allegedly injured by the defendant's rule violation or act or practice of the pendency of such action. Such notice may, in the discretion of the court, be given by publication.

(d) Time for bringing of actions

No action may be brought by the Commission under this section more than 3 years after the rule violation to which an action under subsection (a)(1) of this section relates, or the unfair or deceptive act or practice to which an action under subsection (a)(2) of this section relates; except that if a cease and desist order with respect to any person's, partnership's, or corporation's rule violation or unfair or deceptive act or practice has become final and such order was issued in a proceeding under section 5(b) which was commenced not later than 3 years after the rule violation or act or practice occurred, a civil action may be commenced under this section against such person, partnership, or corporation at any time before the expiration of one year after such order becomes final.

(e) Availability of additional Federal or State remedies; other authority of Commission unaffected

Remedies provided in this section are in addition to, and not in lieu of, any other remedy or right of action provided by State or Federal law. Nothing in this section shall be construed to affect any authority of the Commission under any other provision of law.

§ 20. Civil investigative demands [15 U.S.C. § 57b–1]

(a) Definitions

For purposes of this section:

(1) The terms "civil investigative demand" and "demand" mean any demand issued by the Commission under subsection (c)(1) of this section.

(2) The term "Commission investigation" means any inquiry conducted by a Commission investigator for the purpose of ascertaining whether any person is or has been engaged in any unfair or deceptive acts or practices in or affecting commerce (within the meaning of section 5(a)(1)).

(3) The term "Commission investigator" means any attorney or investigator employed by the Commission who is charged with the duty of enforcing or carrying into effect any provisions relating to unfair or deceptive acts or practices in or affecting commerce (within the meaning of section 5(a)(1)).

(4) The term "custodian" means the custodian or any deputy custodian designated under section 21(b)(2)(A).

(5) The term "documentary material" includes the original or any copy of any book, record, report, memorandum, paper, communication, tabulation, chart, or other document.

(6) The term "person" means any natural person, partnership, corporation, association, or other legal entity, including any person acting under color or authority of State law.

(7) The term "violation" means any act or omission constituting an unfair or deceptive act or practice in or affecting commerce (within the meaning of section 5(a)(1)).

(b) Actions conducted by Commission respecting unfair or deceptive acts or practices in or affecting commerce

For the purpose of investigations performed pursuant to this section with respect to unfair or deceptive acts or practices in or affecting commerce (within the meaning of section 5(a)(1)); all actions of the Commission taken under section 6 and section 9 shall be conducted pursuant to subsection (c) of this section.

(c) Issuance of demand; contents; service; verified return; sworn certificates; answers; taking of oral testimony

(1) Whenever the Commission has reason to believe that any person may be in possession, custody, or control of any documentary material, or may have any information, relevant to unfair or deceptive acts or practices in or affecting commerce (within the meaning of section 5(a)(1)), the Commission may, before the institution of any proceedings under this Act, issue in writing, and cause to be served upon such person, a civil investigative demand requiring such person to produce such documentary material for inspection and copying or reproduction, to file written reports or answers to questions, to give oral testimony concerning documentary material or other information, or to furnish any combination of such material, answers, or testimony.

(2) Each civil investigative demand shall state the nature of the conduct constituting the alleged violation which is under investigation and the provision of law applicable to such violation.

(3) Each civil investigative demand for the production of documentary material shall—

(A) describe each class of documentary material to be produced under the demand with such definiteness and certainty as to permit such material to be fairly identified;

(B) prescribe a return date or dates which will provide a reasonable period of time within which the material so demanded may be assembled and made available for inspection and copying or reproduction; and

(C) identify the custodian to whom such material shall be made available.

(4) Each civil investigative demand for written reports or answers to questions shall—

(A) propound with definiteness and certainty the reports to be produced or the questions to be answered;

(B) prescribe a date or dates at which time written reports or answers to questions shall be submitted; and

(C) identify the custodian to whom such reports or answers shall be submitted.

. . .

(d) Procedures for demand material

Materials received as a result of a civil investigative demand shall be subject to the procedures established in section 21.

(e) Petition for enforcement

Whenever any person fails to comply with any civil investigative demand duly served upon him under this section, or whenever satisfactory copying or reproduction of material requested pursuant to the demand cannot be accomplished and such person refuses to surrender such material, the Commission, through such officers or attorneys as it may designate, may file, in the district court of the United States for any judicial district in which such person resides, is found, or transacts business, and serve upon such person, a petition for an order of such court for the enforcement of this section. All process of any court to which application may be made as provided in this subsection may be served in any judicial district.

. . .

(h) Jurisdiction of court

Whenever any petition is filed in any district court of the United States under this section, such court shall have jurisdiction to hear and determine the matter so presented, and to enter such order or orders as may be required to carry into effect the provisions of this section. Any final order so entered shall be subject to appeal pursuant to section 1291 of title 28. Any disobedience of any final order entered under this section by any court shall be punished as a contempt of such court.

(i) Commission authority to issue subpoenas or make demand for information

Notwithstanding any other provision of law, the Commission shall have no authority to issue a subpoena or make a demand for information, under authority of this Act or any other provision of law, unless such subpoena or demand for information is signed by a Commissioner acting pursuant to a Commission resolution. The Commission shall not delegate the power conferred by this section to sign subpoenas or demands for information to any other person.

(j) Applicability of this section

The provisions of this section shall not—

(1) apply to any proceeding under section 5(b); or

(2) apply to or affect the jurisdiction, duties, or powers of any agency of the Federal Government, other than the Commission, regardless of whether such jurisdiction, duties, or powers are derived in whole or in part, by reference to this Act.

§ 21. Confidentiality [15 U.S.C. § 57b–2]

(a) Definitions

For purposes of this section:

(1) The term "material" means documentary material, written reports or answers to questions, and transcripts of oral testimony.

(2) The term "Federal agency" has the meaning given it in section 552(e) of title 5.

(b) Procedures respecting documents or transcripts of oral testimony received pursuant to compulsory process or investigation

(1) With respect to any document or transcript of oral testimony received by the Commission pursuant to compulsory process in an investigation, a purpose of which is to determine whether any person may have violated any provision of the laws administered by the Commission, the procedures established in paragraph (2) through paragraph (7) shall apply.

(2)(A) The Commission shall designate a duly authorized agent to serve as custodian of documentary material, or written reports or answers to questions, and transcripts of oral testimony, and such additional duly authorized agents as the Commission shall determine from time to time to be necessary to serve as deputies to the custodian.

. . .

(3)(A) The custodian to whom any documentary material, written reports or answers to questions, and transcripts of oral testimony are delivered shall take physical possession of such material, reports or answers, and transcripts, and shall be responsible for the use made of such material, reports or answers, and transcripts, and for the return of material, pursuant to the requirements of this section.

. . .

(C) Except as otherwise provided in this section, while in the possession of the custodian, no documentary material, reports or answers to questions, and transcripts of oral testimony shall be available for examination by any individual other than a duly authorized officer or employee of the Commission without the consent of the person who produced the material or transcripts. Nothing in this section is intended to prevent disclosure to either House of the Congress or to any committee or subcommittee of the Congress, except that the Commission immediately shall notify the owner or provider of any such information of a request for information designated as confidential by the owner or provider.

. . .

(4) Whenever the Commission has instituted a proceeding against a person, partnership, or corporation, the custodian may deliver to any officer or employee of the Commission documentary material, written reports or answers to questions, and transcripts of oral testimony for official use in connection with such proceeding. Upon the completion of the proceeding, the officer or employee shall return to the custodian any such material so delivered which has not been received into the record of the proceeding.

(5) If any documentary material, written reports or answers to questions, and transcripts of oral testimony have been produced in

the course of any investigation by any person pursuant to compulsory process and—

(A) any proceeding arising out of the investigation has been completed; or

(B) no proceeding in which the material may be used has been commenced within a reasonable time after completion of the examination and analysis of all such material and other information assembled in the course of the investigation;

then the custodian shall, upon written request of the person who produced the material, return to the person any such material which has not been received into the record of any such proceeding (other than copies of such material made by the custodian pursuant to paragraph (3)(B)).

(6) The custodian of any documentary material, written reports or answers to questions, and transcripts of oral testimony may deliver to any officers or employees of appropriate Federal law enforcement agencies, in response to a written request, copies of such material for use in connection with an investigation or proceeding under the jurisdiction of any such agency. Such materials shall not be made available to any such agency until the custodian received certification of any officer of such agency that such information will be maintained in confidence and will be used only for official law enforcement purposes. Such documentary material, written reports or answers to questions, and transcripts of oral testimony may be used by any officer or employee of such agency only in such manner and subject to such conditions as apply to the Commission under this section. The custodian may make such materials available to any State law enforcement agency upon the prior certification of any officer of such agency that such information will be maintained in confidence and will be used only for official law enforcement purposes.

. . .

(d) Particular disclosures allowed

(1) The provisions of subsection (c) of this section shall not be construed to prohibit—

(A) the disclosure of information to either House of the Congress or to any committee or subcommittee of the Congress, except that the Commission immediately shall notify the owner or provider of any such information of a request for information designated as confidential by the owner or provider;

(B) the disclosure of the results of any investigation or study carried out or prepared by the Commission, except that no information shall be identified nor shall information be disclosed in such a manner as to disclose a trade secret of any person supplying the trade secret, or to disclose any commercial or financial information which is obtained from any person and which is privileged or confidential;

(C) the disclosure of relevant and material information in Commission adjudicative proceedings or in judicial proceedings to which the Commission is a party; or

(D) the disclosure to a Federal agency of disaggregated information obtained in accordance with section 3512 of title 44, except that the recipient agency shall use such disaggregated information for economic, statistical, or policymaking purposes only, and shall not disclose such information in an individually identifiable form.

(2) Any disclosure of relevant and material information in Commission adjudicative proceedings or in judicial proceedings to which the Commission is a party shall be governed by the rules of the Commission for adjudicative proceedings or by court rules or orders, except that the rules of the Commission shall not be amended in a manner inconsistent with the purposes of this section.

(e) Effect on other statutory provisions limiting disclosure

Nothing in this section shall supersede any statutory provision which expressly prohibits or limits particular disclosures by the Commission, or which authorizes disclosures to any other Federal agency.

(f) Exemption from disclosure

Any material which is received by the Commission in any investigation, a purpose of which is to determine whether any person may have violated any provision of the laws administered by the Commission, and which is provided pursuant to any compulsory process under this subchapter or which is provided voluntarily in place of such compulsory process shall be exempt from disclosure under section 552 of title 5.

§ 22. Rulemaking process [15 U.S.C. § 57b–3]

(a) Definitions

For purposes of this section:

(1) The term "rule" means any rule promulgated by the Commission under section 6 or section 18, except that such term does not include interpretive rules, rules involving Commission management or personnel, general statements of policy, or rules relating to Commission organization, procedure, or practice. Such term does not include any amendment to a rule unless the Commission—

(A) estimates that such amendment will have an annual effect on the national economy of $100,000,000 or more;

(B) estimates that such amendment will cause a substantial change in the cost or price of goods or services which are used extensively by particular industries, which are supplied extensively in particular geographic regions, or which are required in significant quantities by the Federal Government, or by State or local governments; or

(C) otherwise determines that such amendment will have a significant impact upon persons subject to regulation under such amendment and upon consumers.

(2) The term "rulemaking" means any Commission process for formulating or amending a rule.

(b) Notice of proposed rulemaking; regulatory analysis; contents; issuance

(1) In any case in which the Commission publishes notice of a proposed rulemaking, the Commission shall issue a preliminary regulatory analysis relating to the proposed rule involved. Each preliminary regulatory analysis shall contain—

(A) a concise statement of the need for, and the objectives of, the proposed rule;

(B) a description of any reasonable alternatives to the proposed rule which may accomplish the stated objective of the rule in a manner consistent with applicable law; and

(C) for the proposed rule, and for each of the alternatives described in the analysis, a preliminary analysis of the projected benefits and any adverse economic effects and any other effects, and of the effectiveness of the proposed rule and each alternative in meeting the stated objectives of the proposed rule.

(2) In any case in which the Commission promulgates a final rule, the Commission shall issue a final regulatory analysis relating to the final rule. Each final regulatory analysis shall contain—

(A) a concise statement of the need for, and the objectives of, the final rule;

(B) a description of any alternatives to the final rule which were considered by the Commission;

(C) an analysis of the projected benefits and any adverse economic effects and any other effects of the final rule;

(D) an explanation of the reasons for the determination of the Commission that the final rule will attain its objectives in a manner consistent with applicable law and the reasons the particular alternative was chosen; and

(E) a summary of any significant issues raised by the comments submitted during the public comment period in response to the preliminary regulatory analysis, and a summary of the assessment by the Commission of such issues.

(3)(A) In order to avoid duplication or waste, the Commission is authorized to—

(i) consider a series of closely related rules as one rule for purposes of this subsection; and

(ii) whenever appropriate, incorporate any data or analysis contained in a regulatory analysis issued under this subsection in the statement of basis and purpose to accompany any rule promulgated under section 18(a)(1)(B), and incorporate by reference in any preliminary or final regulatory analysis information contained in a notice of proposed rulemaking or a statement of basis and purpose.

(B) The Commission shall include, in each notice of proposed rulemaking and in each publication of a final rule, a statement of the manner in which the public may obtain copies of the preliminary and final regulatory analyses. The Commission may charge a reasonable fee for the copying and mailing of regulatory analyses. The regulatory analyses shall be furnished without charge or at a reduced charge if the Commission determines that waiver or reduction of the fee is in the public interest because furnishing the information primarily benefits the general public.

(4) The Commission is authorized to delay the completion of any of the requirements established in this subsection by publishing in the Federal Register, not later than the date of publication of the final rule involved, a finding that the final rule is being promulgated in response to an emergency which makes timely compliance with the provisions of this subsection impracticable. Such publication shall include a statement of the reasons for such finding.

(5) The requirements of this subsection shall not be construed to alter in any manner the substantive standards applicable to any action by the Commission, or the procedural standards otherwise applicable to such action.

(c) Judicial review

(1) The contents and adequacy of any regulatory analysis prepared or issued by the Commission under this section, including the adequacy of any procedure involved in such preparation or issuance, shall not be subject to any judicial review in any court, except that a court, upon review of a rule pursuant to section 18(e) may set aside such rule if the Commission has failed entirely to prepare a regulatory analysis.

(2) Except as specified in paragraph (1), no Commission action may be invalidated, remanded, or otherwise affected by any court on account of any failure to comply with the requirements of this section.

(3) The provisions of this subsection do not alter the substantive or procedural standards otherwise applicable to judicial review of any action by the Commission.

(d) Regulatory agenda; contents; publication dates in Federal Register

(1) The Commission shall publish at least semiannually a regulatory agenda. Each regulatory agenda shall contain a list of rules which the Commission intends to propose or promulgate during the 12-month period following the publication of the agenda. On the first Monday in October of each year, the Commission shall publish in the Federal Register a schedule showing the dates during the current fiscal year on which the semiannual regulatory agenda of the Commission will be published.

(2) For each rule listed in a regulatory agenda, the Commission shall—

(A) describe the rule;

(B) state the objectives of and the legal basis for the rule; and

(C) specify any dates established or anticipated by the Commission for taking action, including dates for advance notice of proposed rulemaking, notices of proposed rulemaking, and final action by the Commission.

(3) Each regulatory agenda shall state the name, office address, and office telephone number of the Commission officer or employee responsible for responding to any inquiry relating to each rule instead.

(4) The Commission shall not propose or promulgate a rule which was not listed on a regulatory agenda unless the Commission publishes with the rule an explanation of the reasons the rule was omitted from such agenda.

§ 23. Good faith reliance on actions of Board of Governors [15 U.S.C. § 57b–4]

(a) Board of Governors defined

For purposes of this section, the term "Board of Governors" means the Board of Governors of the Federal Reserve System.

(b) Use as defense

Notwithstanding any other provision of law, if—

(1) any person, partnership, or corporation engages in any conduct or practice which allegedly constitutes a violation of any Federal law with respect to which the Board of Governors of the Federal Reserve System has rulemaking authority; and

(2) such person, partnership, or corporation engaged in such conduct or practice in good faith reliance upon, and in conformity

with, any rule, regulation, statement of interpretation, or statement of approval prescribed or issued by the Board of Governors under such Federal law;

then such good faith reliance shall constitute a defense in any administrative or judicial proceeding commenced against such person, partnership, or corporation by the Commission under this Act or in any administrative or judicial proceeding commenced against such person, partnership, or corporation by the Attorney General of the United States, upon request made by the Commission, under any provision of law.

(c) Applicability of subsection (b)

The provisions of subsection (b) of this section shall apply regardless of whether any rule, regulation, statement of interpretation, or statement of approval prescribed or issued by the Board of Governors is amended, rescinded, or held to be invalid by judicial authority or any other authority after a person, partnership, or corporation has engaged in any conduct or practice in good faith reliance upon, and in conformity with, such rule, regulation, statement of interpretation, or statement of approval.

(d) Request for issuance of statement or interpretation concerning conduct or practice

If, in any case in which—

(1) the Board of Governors has rulemaking authority with respect to any Federal law; and

(2) the Commission is authorized to enforce the requirements of such Federal law;

any person, partnership, or corporation submits a request to the Board of Governors for the issuance of any statement of interpretation or statement of approval relating to any conduct or practice of such person, partnership, or corporation which may be subject to the requirements of such Federal law, then the Board of Governors shall dispose of such request as soon as practicable after the receipt of such request.

§ 25. Short title [15 U.S.C. § 58]

This Act may be cited as the "Federal Trade Commission Act."

15 U.S.C. § 57a–1. Congressional review of rules

(a) Promulgation of final rule by Commission; submittal to Congress; effective date

(1) The Federal Trade Commission, after promulgating a final rule, shall submit such final rule to the Congress for review in accordance with this section. Such final rule shall be delivered to each House of the Congress on the same date and to each House of the

Congress while it is in session. Such final rule shall be referred to the Committee on Commerce, Science, and Transportation of the Senate and to the Committee on Energy and Commerce of the House, respectively.

(2) Any such final rule shall become effective in accordance with its terms unless, before the end of the period of 90 calendar days of continuous session after the date such final rule is submitted to the Congress, both Houses of the Congress adopt a concurrent resolution disapproving such final rule.

(b) Congressional authority; disapproval of final rule by concurrent resolution; motion to discharge; appeals; approval of concurrent resolution

(1) The provisions of this subsection are enacted by the Congress—

(A) as an exercise of the rulemaking power of the Senate and the House of Representatives, respectively, and as such they are deemed a part of the rules of each House, respectively, but applicable only with respect to the procedure to be followed in that House in the case of concurrent resolutions which are subject to this section, and such provisions supersede other rules only to the extent that they are inconsistent with such other rules; and

(B) with full recognition of the constitutional right of either House to change the rules (so far as relating to the procedure of that House) at any time, in the same manner and to the same extent as in the case of any other rule of that House.

(2)(A) Any concurrent resolution disapproving a final rule of the Commission shall, upon introduction or receipt from the other House of the Congress, be referred immediately by the presiding officer of such House to the Committee on Commerce, Science, and Transportation of the Senate or to the Committee on Energy and Commerce of the House, as the case may be.

(B) If a committee to which a concurrent resolution is referred does not report such concurrent resolution before the end of the period of 75 calendar days of continuous session of the Congress after the referral of such resolution to the Committee on Commerce, Science, and Transportation of the Senate or to the Committee on Energy and Commerce of the House, as the case may be, under subsection (a)(1) of this section, it shall be in order to move to discharge any such committee from further consideration of such concurrent resolution.

(C)(i) A motion to discharge in the Senate may be made only by a Member favoring the concurrent resolution, shall be privileged (except that it may not be made after the committee has reported a concurrent resolution with respect to the same final rule of the Commission), and debate on such motion shall be limited to not more than 1 hour, to be divided equally between those favoring and those opposing the motion. An amendment to the motion shall not be in order, and it shall not be in order to move to reconsider the vote by which the motion was agreed to or disagreed to. If the motion to discharge is agreed to or disagreed to, the motion may not be renewed, nor may another motion to discharge the committee be made with respect to any other concurrent resolution with respect to the same final rule of the Commission.

(ii) A motion to discharge in the House may be made by presentation in writing to the Clerk. The motion may be called up only if the motion has been signed by one-fifth of the Members of the House. The motion is highly privileged (except that it may not be made after the committee has reported a concurrent resolution of disapproval with respect to the same rule). Debate on such motion shall be limited to not more than 1 hour, the time to be divided equally between those favoring and those opposing the motion. An amendment to the motion is not in order, and it is not in order to move to reconsider the vote by which the motion is agreed to or disagreed to.

(3)(A) When a committee has reported, or has been discharged from further consideration of, a concurrent resolution, it shall be at any time thereafter in order (even though a previous motion to the same effect has been disagreed to) to move to proceed to the consideration of the concurrent resolution. The motion shall be privileged in the Senate and highly privileged in the House of Representatives, and shall not be debatable. An amendment to the motion shall not be in order, and it shall not be in order to move to reconsider the vote by which the motion was agreed to or disagreed to.

(B) Debate on the concurrent resolution shall be limited to not more than 10 hours, which shall be divided equally between those favoring and those opposing such concurrent resolution. A motion further to limit debate shall not be debatable. An amendment to, or motion to recommit, the concurrent resolution shall not be in order, and it shall not be in order to move to reconsider the vote by which such concurrent resolution was agreed to or disagreed to.

(4) Appeals from the decision of the Chair relating to the application of the rules of the Senate or the House of Representatives, as the case may be, to the procedure relating to a concurrent resolution shall be decided without debate.

(5) Notwithstanding any other provision of this subsection, if a House has approved a concurrent resolution with respect to any final rule of the Commission, then it shall not be in order to consider in such House any other concurrent resolution with respect to the same final rule.

(c) Promulgation of final rule in accordance with congressional disapproval; submittal to Congress

(1) If a final rule of the Commission is disapproved by the Congress under subsection (a)(2) of this section, then the Commission may promulgate a final rule which relates to the same acts or practices as the final rule disapproved by the Congress in accordance with this subsection. Shall final rule—

(A) shall be based upon—

(i) the rulemaking record of the final rule disapproved by the Congress; or

(ii) such rulemaking record and the record established in supplemental rulemaking proceedings conducted by the Commission in accordance with section 553 of title 5, in any case in which the Commission determines that it is necessary to supplement the existing rulemaking record; and

(B) may contain such changes as the Commission considers necessary or appropriate.

(2) The Commission, after promulgating a final rule under this subsection, shall submit the final rule to the Congress in accordance with subsection (a)(1) of this section.

(d) Effect of congressional inaction on, or rejection of, a concurrent resolution of disapproval

Congressional inaction on, or rejection of, a concurrent resolution of disapproval under this section shall not be construed as an expression of approval of the final rule involved, and shall not be construed to create any presumption of validity with respect to such final rule.

(e) Preparation of report by Comptroller General respecting congressional review of rules; submittal to Congress

(1) The Comptroller General shall prepare a report which examines the review of Commission rules under this section. Such report shall—

(A) list the final rules submitted to the Congress by the Commission during the period in which this section is in effect;

(B) list the final rules disapproved by the Congress under subsection (a)(2) of this section;

(C) specify the number of instances in which the Commission promulgates a final rule in accordance with subsection (c) of this section; and

(D) include an analysis of any impact which the provisions of this section have had upon the decisionmaking and rulemaking processes of the Commission.

(2) The Comptroller General shall submit the report required in paragraph (1) to the Congress before the end of fiscal year 1982.

(f) Actions in district court of the United States

(1) Any interested party may institute such actions in the appropriate district court of the United States, including actions for declaratory judgment, as may be appropriate to construe the constitutionality of any provision of this section. The district court immediately shall certify all questions of the constitutionality of this section to the United States court of appeals for the circuit involved, which shall hear the matter sitting en banc.

(2) Notwithstanding any other provision of law, any decision on a matter certified under paragraph (1) shall be reviewable by appeal directly to the Supreme Court of the United States. Such appeal shall be brought not later than 20 days after the decision of the court of appeals.

(3) It shall be the duty of the court of appeals and of the Supreme Court of the United States to advance on the docket and to expedite to the greatest possible extent the disposition of any matter certified under paragraph (1).

(g) Congressional adjournments

(1) For purposes of this section—

(A) continuity of session is broken only by an adjournment sine die; and

(B) days on which either House is not in session because of an adjournment of more than 5 days to a day certain are excluded in the computation of the periods specified in subsection (a)(2) of this section and subsection (b) of this section.

(2) If an adjournment sine die of the Congress occurs after the Commission has submitted a final rule under subsection (a)(1) of this section, but such adjournment occurs—

(A) before the end of the period specified in subsection (a)(2) of this section; and

(B) before any action necessary to disapprove the final rule is completed under subsection (a)(2) of this section;

then the Commission shall be required to resubmit the final rule involved at the beginning of the next regular session of the Congress. The period specified in subsection (a)(2) of this section shall begin on the date of such resubmission.

(h) Definitions

For purposes of this section:

(1) The term "Commission" means the Federal Trade Commission.

(2) The term "concurrent resolution" means a concurrent resolution the matter after the resolving clause of which is as follows: "That the Congress disapproves the final rule promulgated by the Federal Trade Commission dealing with the matter of ______, which

final rule was submitted to the Congress on ______.''. (The blank spaces shall be filled appropriately.)

(3) The term ''rule'' means any rule promulgated by the Commission pursuant to the Federal Trade Commission Act (15 U.S.C. 41 et seq.), other than any rule promulgated under section 18(a)(1)(A) of such Act (15 U.S.C. 57a(a)(1)(A)).

FTC RULES

COOLING–OFF PERIOD FOR DOOR–TO–DOOR SALES

16 C.F.R. Part 429

§ 429.1 The Rule

In connection with any door-to-door sale, it constitutes an unfair and deceptive act or practice for any seller to:

(a) Fail to furnish the buyer with a fully completed receipt or copy of any contract pertaining to such sale at the time of its execution, which is in the same language, e.g., Spanish, as that principally used in the oral sales presentation and which shows the date of the transaction and contains the name and address of the seller, and in immediate proximity to the space reserved in the contract for the signature of the buyer or on the front page of the receipt if a contract is not used and in bold face type of a minimum size of 10 points, a statement in substantially the following form:

"You, the buyer, may cancel this transaction at any time prior to midnight of the third business day after the date of this transaction. See the attached notice of cancellation form for an explanation of this right."

(b) Fail to furnish each buyer, at the time he signs the door-to-door sales contract or otherwise agrees to buy consumer goods or services from the seller, a completed form in duplicate, captioned "NOTICE OF CANCELLATION", which shall be attached to the contract or receipt and easily detachable, and which shall contain in ten point bold face type the following information and statements in the same language, e.g., Spanish, as that used in the contract:

NOTICE OF CANCELLATION

[enter date of transaction]

____
(Date)

YOU MAY CANCEL THIS TRANSACTION, WITHOUT ANY PENALTY OR OBLIGATION, WITHIN THREE BUSINESS DAYS FROM THE ABOVE DATE.

IF YOU CANCEL, ANY PROPERTY TRADED IN, ANY PAYMENTS MADE BY YOU UNDER THE CONTRACT OR SALE, AND ANY NEGOTIABLE INSTRUMENT EXECUTED BY YOU WILL BE RETURNED WITHIN 10 BUSINESS DAYS FOLLOW-

ING RECEIPT BY THE SELLER OF YOUR CANCELLATION NOTICE, AND ANY SECURITY INTEREST ARISING OUT OF THE TRANSACTION WILL BE CANCELED.

IF YOU CANCEL, YOU MUST MAKE AVAILABLE TO THE SELLER AT YOUR RESIDENCE, IN SUBSTANTIALLY AS GOOD CONDITION AS WHEN RECEIVED, ANY GOODS DELIVERED TO YOU UNDER THIS CONTRACT OR SALE; OR YOU MAY IF YOU WISH, COMPLY WITH THE INSTRUCTIONS OF THE SELLER REGARDING THE RETURN SHIPMENT OF THE GOODS AT THE SELLER'S EXPENSE AND RISK.

IF YOU DO MAKE THE GOODS AVAILABLE TO THE SELLER AND THE SELLER DOES NOT PICK THEM UP WITHIN 20 DAYS OF THE DATE OF YOUR NOTICE OF CANCELLATION, YOU MAY RETAIN OR DISPOSE OF THE GOODS WITHOUT ANY FURTHER OBLIGATION. IF YOU FAIL TO MAKE THE GOODS AVAILABLE TO THE SELLER, OR IF YOU AGREE TO RETURN THE GOODS TO THE SELLER AND FAIL TO DO SO, THEN YOU REMAIN LIABLE FOR PERFORMANCE OF ALL OBLIGATIONS UNDER THE CONTRACT.

TO CANCEL THIS TRANSACTION, MAIL OR DELIVER A SIGNED AND DATED COPY OF THIS CANCELLATION NOTICE OR ANY OTHER WRITTEN NOTICE, OR SEND A TELEGRAM, TO [Name of seller], AT [address of seller's place of business] NOT LATER THAN MIDNIGHT OF ______ (date).

I HEREBY CANCEL THIS TRANSACTION.

(Date) ______________________

____

(Buyer's signature)

(c) Fail, before furnishing copies of the "Notice of Cancellation" to the buyer, to complete both copies by entering the name of the seller, the address of the seller's place of business, the date of the transaction, and the date, not earlier than the third business day following the date of the transaction, by which the buyer may give notice of cancellation.

(d) Include in any door-to-door contract or receipt any confession of judgment or any waiver of any of the rights to which the buyer is entitled under this section including specifically his right to cancel the sale in accordance with the provisions of this section.

(e) Fail to inform each buyer orally, at the time he signs the contract or purchases the goods or services, of his right to cancel.

(f) Misrepresent in any manner the buyer's right to cancel.

(g) Fail or refuse to honor any valid notice of cancellation by a buyer and within 10 business days after the receipt of such notice, to:

(i) Refund all payments made under the contract or sale; (ii) return any goods or property traded in, in substantially as good condition as when received by the seller; (iii) cancel and return any negotiable instrument executed by the buyer in connection with the contract or sale and take any action necessary or appropriate to terminate promptly any security interest created in the transaction.

(h) Negotiate, transfer, sell, or assign any note or other evidence of indebtedness to a finance company or other third party prior to midnight of the fifth business day following the day the contract was signed or the goods or services were purchased.

(i) Fail, within 10 business days of receipt of the buyer's notice of cancellation, to notify him whether the seller intends to repossess or to abandon any shipped or delivered goods.

Note 1: *Definitions.* For the purposes of this section the following definitions shall apply:

(a) *Door-to-Door Sale*—A sale, lease, or rental of consumer goods or services with a purchase price of $25 or more, whether under single or multiple contracts, in which the seller or his representative personally solicits the sale, including those in response to or following an invitation by the buyer, and the buyer's agreement or offer to purchase is made at a place other than the place of business of the seller. The term "door-to-door sale" does not include a transaction:

(1) Made pursuant to prior negotiations in the course of a visit by the buyer to a retail business establishment having a fixed permanent location where the goods are exhibited or the services are offered for sale on a continuing basis; or

(2) In which the consumer is accorded the right of recision by the provisions of the Consumer Credit Protection Act (15 U.S.C. 1635) or regulations issued pursuant thereto; or

(3) In which the buyer has initiated the contact and the goods or services are needed to meet a bona fide immediate personal emergency of the buyer, and the buyer furnishes the seller with a separate dated and signed personal statement in the buyer's handwriting describing the situation requiring immediate remedy and expressly acknowledging and waiving the right to cancel the sale within 3 business days; or

(4) Conducted and consummated entirely by mail or telephone; and without any other contact between the buyer and the seller or its representative prior to delivery of the goods or performance of the services; or

(5) In which the buyer has initiated the contact and specifically requested the seller to visit his home for the purpose of repairing or performing maintenance upon the buyer's personal property. If in the course of such a visit, the seller sells the buyer the right to receive additional services or goods other than replacement parts neces-

sarily used in performing the maintenance or in making the repairs, the sale of those additional goods or services would not fall within this exclusion; or

(6) Pertaining to the sale or rental of real property, to the sale of insurance or to the sale of securities or commodities by a broker-dealer registered with the Securities and Exchange Commission.

(b) *Consumer Goods or Services*—Goods or services purchased, leased, or rented primarily for personal, family, or household purposes, including courses of instruction or training regardless of the purpose for which they are taken.

(c) *Seller*—Any person, partnership, corporation, or association engaged in the door-to-door sale of consumer goods or services.

(d) *Place of Business*—The main or permanent branch office or local address of a seller.

(e) *Purchase Price*—The total price paid or to be paid for the consumer goods or services, including all interest and service charges.

(f) *Business Day*—Any calendar day except Sunday, or the following business holidays:

New Year's Day, Washington's Birthday, Memorial Day, Independence Day, Labor Day, Columbus Day, Veterans' Day, Thanksgiving Day, and Christmas Day.

Note 2: *Effect on State Laws and Municipal Ordinances.*

(a) The Commission is cognizant of the significant burden imposed upon door-to-door sellers by the various and often inconsistent State laws which provide the buyer with the right to cancel door-to-door sales transactions. However, it does not believe that this constitutes sufficient justification for preempting all of the provisions of such laws or of the ordinances of the political subdivisions of the various States. The Record in the proceedings supports the view that the joint and coordinated efforts of both the Commission and State and local officials are required to insure that a consumer who has purchased from a door-to-door seller something he does not want, does not need, or cannot afford, is accorded a unilateral right to rescind, without penalty, his agreement to purchase the goods or services.

(b) This section will not be construed to annul, or exempt any seller from complying with the laws of any State, or with the ordinances of political subdivisions thereof, regulating door-to-door sales, except to the extent that such laws or ordinances, if they permit door-to-door selling, are directly inconsistent with the provisions of this section. Such laws or ordinances which do not accord the buyer, with respect to the particular transaction, a right to cancel a door-to-door sale which is substantially the same or greater than that provided in this section, or which permit the imposition of any fee or penalty on the buyer for the exercise of such right, or which do not provide for giving the buyer notice of his right to cancel the transaction in substantially the same form and manner provided for in this section, are among those which will be considered directly inconsistent.

*

PRESERVATION OF CONSUMERS' CLAIMS AND DEFENSES

16 C.F.R. Part 433

§ 433.1 Definitions

(a) *Person.* An individual, corporation, or any other business organization.

(b) *Consumer.* A natural person who seeks or acquires goods or services for personal, family, or household use.

(c) *Creditor.* A person who, in the ordinary course of business, lends purchase money or finances the sale of goods or services to consumers on a deferred payment basis; *Provided,* such person is not acting, for the purposes of a particular transaction, in the capacity of a credit card issuer.

(d) *Purchase money loan.* A cash advance which is received by a consumer in return for a "Finance Charge" within the meaning of the Truth in Lending Act and Regulation Z, which is applied, in whole or substantial part, to a purchase of goods or services from a seller who (1) refers consumers to the creditor or (2) is affiliated with the creditor by common control, contract, or business arrangement.

(e) *Financing a sale.* Extending credit to a consumer in connection with a "Credit Sale" within the meaning of the Truth in Lending Act and Regulation Z.

(f) *Contract.* Any oral or written agreement, formal or informal, between a creditor and a seller, which contemplates or provides for cooperative or concerted activity in connection with the sale of goods or services to consumers or the financing thereof.

(g) *Business arrangement.* Any understanding, procedure, course of dealing, or arrangement, formal or informal, between a creditor and a seller, in connection with the sale of goods or services to consumers or the financing thereof.

(h) *Credit card issuer.* A person who extends to cardholders the right to use a credit card in connection with purchases of goods or services.

(i) *Consumer credit contract.* Any instrument which evidences or embodies a debt arising from a "Purchase Money Loan" transaction or a "financed sale" as defined in paragraphs (d) and (e) of this section.

(j) *Seller.* A person who, in the ordinary course of business, sells or leases goods or services to consumers.

§ 433.2 Preservation of consumers' claims and defenses, unfair or deceptive acts or practices

In connection with any sale or lease of goods or services to consumers, in or affecting commerce as "commerce" is defined in the Federal Trade Commission Act, it is an unfair or deceptive act or practice within the meaning of Section 5 of that Act for a seller, directly or indirectly, to:

(a) Take or receive a consumer credit contract which fails to contain the following provision in at least ten point, bold face, type:

NOTICE

ANY HOLDER OF THIS CONSUMER CREDIT CONTRACT IS SUBJECT TO ALL CLAIMS AND DEFENSES WHICH THE DEBTOR COULD ASSERT AGAINST THE SELLER OF GOODS OR SERVICES OBTAINED PURSUANT HERETO OR WITH THE PROCEEDS HEREOF. RECOVERY HEREUNDER BY THE DEBTOR SHALL NOT EXCEED AMOUNTS PAID BY THE DEBTOR HEREUNDER.

or,

(b) Accept, as full or partial payment for such sale or lease, the proceeds of any purchase money loan (as purchase money loan is defined herein), unless any consumer credit contract made in connection with such purchase money loan contains the following provision in at least ten point, bold face, type:

NOTICE

ANY HOLDER OF THIS CONSUMER CREDIT CONTRACT IS SUBJECT TO ALL CLAIMS AND DEFENSES WHICH THE DEBTOR COULD ASSERT AGAINST THE SELLER OF GOODS OR SERVICES OBTAINED WITH THE PROCEEDS HEREOF. RECOVERY HEREUNDER BY THE DEBTOR SHALL NOT EXCEED AMOUNTS PAID BY THE DEBTOR HEREUNDER.

§ 433.3 Exemption of sellers taking or receiving open end consumer credit contracts before November 1, 1977 from requirements of § 433.2(a)

(a) Any seller who has taken or received an open end consumer credit contract before November 1, 1977, shall be exempt from the requirements of 16 CFR Part 433 with respect to such contract provided the contract does not cut off consumers' claims and defenses.

(b) *Definitions.* The following definitions apply to this exemption:

(1) All pertinent definitions contained in 16 CFR 433.1.

(2) Open end consumer credit contract: a consumer credit contract pursuant to which "open end credit" is extended.

(3) "Open end credit": consumer credit extended on an account pursuant to a plan under which a creditor may permit an applicant to make purchases or make loans, from time to time, directly from the creditor or indirectly by use of a credit card, check, or other device, as the plan may provide. The term does not include negotiated advances under an open-end real estate mortgage or a letter of credit.

(4) Contract which does not cut off consumers' claims and defenses: a consumer credit contract which does not constitute or contain a negotiable instrument, or contain any waiver, limitation, term, or condition which has the effect of limiting a consumer's right to assert against any holder of the contract all legally sufficient claims and defenses which the consumer could assert against the seller of goods or services purchased pursuant to the contract.

*

CONSUMER CREDIT PROTECTION ACT

15 U.S.C. §§ 1601–1693r

Table of Sections

TITLE I. TRUTH-IN-LENDING ACT

(15 U.S.C. §§ 1601–1667e)

Table of Sections

CHAPTER 1. GENERAL PROVISIONS

CHAPTER 2. CREDIT TRANSACTIONS

CHAPTER 1. GENERAL PROVISIONS

§ 101. Short title

This title may be cited as the Truth in Lending Act.

§ 102. Findings and declaration of purpose [15 U.S.C. § 1601]

(a) The Congress finds that economic stabilization would be enhanced and the competition among the various financial institutions and other firms engaged in the extension of consumer credit would be strengthened by the informed use of credit. The informed use of credit results from an awareness of the cost thereof by consumers. It is the purpose of this title to assure a meaningful disclosure of credit terms so that the consumer will be able to compare more readily the various credit terms available to him and avoid the uninformed use of credit, and to protect the consumer against inaccurate and unfair credit billing and credit card practices.

(b) The Congress also finds that there has been a recent trend toward leasing automobiles and other durable goods for consumer use as an alternative to instalment credit sales and that these leases have been offered without adequate cost disclosures. It is the purpose of this title to assure a meaningful disclosure of the terms of leases of personal property for personal, family, or household purposes so as to enable the lessee to compare more readily the various lease terms available to him, limit balloon payments in consumer leasing, enable comparison of lease terms with credit terms where appropriate, and to assure meaningful and accurate disclosures of lease terms in advertisements.

§ 103. Definitions and rules of construction [15 U.S.C. § 1602]

(a) The definitions and rules of construction set forth in this section are applicable for the purposes of this title.

(b) The term "*Board*" refers to the Board of Governors of the Federal Reserve System.

(c) The term "*organization*" means a corporation, government or governmental subdivision or agency, trust, estate, partnership, cooperative, or association.

(d) The term "*person*" means a natural person or an organization.

(e) The term "*credit*" means the right granted by a creditor to a debtor to defer payment of debt or to incur debt and defer its payment.

(f) The term "*creditor*" refers only to a person who both (1) regularly extends, whether in connection with loans, sales of property or services, or otherwise, consumer credit which is payable by agreement in more than four installments or for which the payment of a finance charge is or may be required; and (2) is the person to whom the debt arising from the consumer credit transaction is initially payable on the face of the evidence of indebtedness or, if there is no such evidence of indebtedness, by agreement. Notwithstanding the preceding sentence, in the case of an open end credit plan involving a credit card, the card issuer and any person who honors the credit card and offers a discount which is a finance charge are creditors. For the purposes of the requirements imposed under chapter 4 and sections 127(a)(5), 127(a)(6), 127(a)(7), 127(b)(1), 127(b)(2), 127(b)(3), 127(b)(8), and 127(b)(10) of chapter 2 of this title, the term "creditor" shall also include card issuers whether or not the amount due is payable by agreement in more than four installments or the payment of a finance charge is or may be required, and the Board shall, by regulation, apply these requirements to such card issuers, to the extent appropriate, even though the requirements are by their terms applicable only to creditors offering open end credit plans.

(g) The term "*credit sale*" refers to any sale in which the seller is a creditor. The term includes any contract in the form of a bailment or lease if the bailee or lessee contracts to pay as compensation for use a sum substantially equivalent to or in excess of the aggregate value of the property and services involved and it is agreed that the bailee or lessee will become, or for no other or a nominal consideration has the option to become, the owner of the property upon full compliance with his obligations under the contract.

(h) The adjective "*consumer*", used with reference to a credit transaction, characterizes the transaction as one in which the party to whom credit is offered or extended is a natural person, and the money, property, or services which are the subject of the transaction are primarily for personal, family, or household purposes.

(i) The term "*open end credit plan*" means a plan under which the creditor reasonably contemplates repeated transactions, which prescribes the terms of such transactions, and which provides for a finance charge which may be computed from time to time on the outstanding unpaid balance. A credit plan which is an open end credit plan within the meaning of the preceding sentence is an open end credit plan even if credit information is verified from time to time.

(j) The term "*adequate notice*", as used in section 133, means a printed notice to a cardholder which sets forth the pertinent facts clearly and conspicuously so that a person against whom it is to operate could reasonably be expected to have noticed it and understood its meaning. Such notice may be given to a cardholder by printing the notice on any credit card, or on each periodic statement of account, issued to the cardholder, or by any other means reasonably assuring the receipt thereof by the cardholder.

(k) The term "*credit card*" means any card, plate, coupon book or other credit device existing for the purpose of obtaining money, property, labor, or services on credit.

(*l*) The term "*accepted credit card*" means any credit card which the cardholder has requested and received or has signed or has used, or authorized another to use, for the purpose of obtaining money, property, labor, or services on credit.

(m) The term *"cardholder"* means any person to whom a credit card is issued or any person who has agreed with the card issuer to pay obligations arising from the issuance of a credit card to another person.

(n) The term *"card issuer"* means any person who issues a credit card, or the agent of such person with respect to such card.

(*o*) The term *"unauthorized use"*, as used in section 133, means a use of a credit card by a person other than the cardholder who does not have actual, implied, or apparent authority for such use and from which the cardholder receives no benefit.

(p) The term *"discount"* as used in section 167 means a reduction made from the regular price. The term "discount" as used in section 167 shall not mean a surcharge.

(q) The term *"surcharge"* as used in section 103 and section 167 means any means of increasing the regular price to a cardholder which is not imposed upon customers paying by cash, check, or similar means.

(r) The term *"State"* refers to any State, the Commonwealth of Puerto Rico, the District of Columbia, and any territory or possession of the United States.

(s) The term *"agricultural purposes"* includes the production, harvest, exhibition, marketing, transportation, processing, or manufacture of agricultural products by a natural person who cultivates, plants, propagates, or nurtures those agricultural products, including but not limited to the acquisition of farmland, real property with a farm residence, and personal property and services used primarily in farming.

(t) The term *"agricultural products"* includes agricultural, horticultural, viticultural, and dairy products, livestock, wildlife, poultry, bees, forest products, fish and shellfish, and any products thereof, including processed and manufactured products, and any and all products raised or produced on farms and any processed or manufactured products thereof.

(u) The term *"material disclosures"* means the disclosure, as required by this title, of the annual percentage rate, the method of determining the finance charge and the balance upon which a finance charge will be imposed, the amount of the finance charge, the amount to be financed, the total of payments, the number and amount of payments, and the due dates or periods of payments scheduled to repay the indebtedness.

(v) The term *"dwelling"* means a residential structure or mobile home which contains one to four family housing units, or individual units of condominiums or cooperatives.

(w) The term *"residential mortgage transaction"* means a transaction in which a mortgage, deed of trust, purchase money security interest arising under an installment sales contract, or equivalent consensual security interest is created or retained against the consumer's dwelling to finance the acquisition or initial construction of such dwelling.

(x) As used in this section and section 167, the term "*regular price*" means the tag or posted price charged for the property or service if a single price is tagged or posted, or the price charged for the property or service when payment is made by use of an open-end credit plan or a credit card if either (1) no price is tagged or posted, or (2) two prices are tagged or posted, one of which is charged when payment is made by use of an open-end credit plan or a credit card and the other when payment is made by use of cash, check, or similar means. For purposes of this definition, payment by check, draft, or other negotiable instrument which may result in the debiting of an open-end credit plan or a credit cardholder's open-end account shall not be considered payment made by use of the plan or the account.

(y) Any reference to any requirement imposed under this title or any provision thereof includes reference to the regulations of the Board under this title or the provision thereof in question.

(z) The disclosure of an amount or percentage which is greater than the amount or percentage required to be disclosed under this title does not in itself constitute a violation of this title.

§ 104. Exempted transactions [15 U.S.C. § 1603]

This title does not apply to the following:

(1) Credit transactions involving extensions of credit primarily for business, commercial, or agricultural purposes, or to government or governmental agencies or instrumentalities, or to organizations.

(2) Transactions in securities or commodities accounts by a broker-dealer registered with the Securities and Exchange Commission.

(3) Credit transactions, other than those in which a security interest is or will be acquired in real property, or in personal property used or expected to be used as the principal dwelling of the consumer, in which the total amount financed exceeds $25,000.

(4) Transactions under public utility tariffs, if the Board determines that a State regulatory body regulates the charges for the public utility services involved, the charges for delayed payment, and any discount allowed for early payment.

(6) Loans made, insured, or guaranteed pursuant to a program authorized by Title IV of the Higher Education Act of 1965 (20 U.S.C. 1070 et seq.).

§ 105. Regulations [15 U.S.C. § 1604]

(a) The Board shall prescribe regulations to carry out the purposes of this title. These regulations may contain such classifications, differentiations, or other provisions, and may provide for such adjustments and exceptions for any class of transactions, as in the judgment of the Board are necessary or proper to effectuate the purposes of this title, to prevent circumvention or evasion thereof, or to facilitate compliance therewith.

(b) The Board shall publish model disclosure forms and clauses for common transactions to facilitate compliance with the disclosure requirements of this title and to aid the borrower or lessee in understanding the transaction by utilizing readily understandable language to simplify the technical nature of the disclosures. In devising such forms, the Board shall consider the use by creditors or lessors of data processing or similar automated equipment. Nothing in this title may be construed to require a creditor or lessor to use any such model form or clause prescribed by the Board under this section. A creditor or lessor shall be deemed to be in compliance with the disclosure provisions of this title with respect to other than numerical disclosures if the creditor or lessor (1) uses any appropriate model form or clause as published by the Board, or (2) uses any such model form or clause and changes it by (A) deleting any information which is not required by this title, or (B) rearranging the format, if in making such deletion or rearranging the format, the creditor or lessor does not affect the substance, clarity, or meaningful sequence of the disclosure.

(c) Model disclosure forms and clauses shall be adopted by the Board after notice duly given in the Federal Register and an opportunity for public comment in accordance with section 553 of title 5, United States Code.

(d) Any regulation of the Board, or any amendment or interpretation thereof, requiring any disclosure which differs from the disclosures previously required by this chapter, chapter 4, or chapter 5, or by any regulation of the Board promulgated thereunder shall have an effective date of that October 1 which follows by at least six months the date of promulgation, except that the Board may at its discretion take interim action by regulation, amendment, or interpretation to lengthen the period of time permitted for creditors or lessors to adjust their forms to accommodate new requirements or shorten the length of time for creditors or lessors to make such adjustments when it makes a specific finding that such action is necessary to comply with the findings of a court or to prevent unfair or deceptive disclosure practices. Notwithstanding the previous sentence, any creditor or lessor may comply with any such newly promulgated disclosure requirements prior to the effective date of the requirements.

§ 106. Determination of finance charge [15 U.S.C. § 1605]

(a) Except as otherwise provided in this section, the amount of the finance charge in connection with any consumer credit transaction shall be determined as the sum of all charges, payable directly or indirectly by the person to whom the credit is extended, and imposed directly or indirectly by the creditor as an incident to the extension of credit. The finance charge does not include charges of a type payable in a comparable cash transaction. Examples of charges which are included in the finance charge include any of the following types of charges which are applicable.

(1) Interest, time price differential, and any amount payable under a point, discount, or other system of additional charges.

(2) Service or carrying charge.

(3) Loan fee, finder's fee, or similar charge.

(4) Fee for an investigation or credit report.

(5) Premium or other charge for any guarantee or insurance protecting the creditor against the obligor's default or other credit loss.

(b) Charges or premiums for credit life, accident, or health insurance written in connection with any consumer credit transaction shall be included in the finance charge unless

(1) the coverage of the debtor by the insurance is not a factor in the approval by the creditor of the extension of credit, and this fact is clearly disclosed in writing to the person applying for or obtaining the extension of credit; and

(2) in order to obtain the insurance in connection with the extension of credit, the person to whom the credit is extended must give specific affirmative written indication of his desire to do so after written disclosure to him of the cost thereof.

(c) Charges of premiums for insurance, written in connection with any consumer credit transaction, against loss of or damage to property or against liability arising out of the ownership or use of property, shall be included in the finance charge unless a clear and specific statement in writing is furnished by the creditor to the person to whom the credit is extended, setting forth the cost of the insurance if obtained from or through the creditor, and stating that the person to whom the credit is extended may choose the person through which the insurance is to be obtained.

(d) If any of the following items is itemized and disclosed in accordance with the regulations of the Board in connection with any transaction, then the creditor need not include that item in the computation of the finance charge with respect to that transaction:

(1) Fees and charges prescribed by law which actually are or will be paid to public officials for determining the existence of or for

perfecting or releasing or satisfying any security related to the credit transaction.

(2) The premium payable for any insurance in lieu of perfecting any security interest otherwise required by the creditor in connection with the transaction, if the premium does not exceed the fees and charges described in paragraph (1) which would otherwise be payable.

(e) The following items, when charged in connection with any extension of credit secured by an interest in real property, shall not be included in the computation of the finance charge with respect to that transaction:

(1) Fees or premiums for title examination, title insurance, or similar purposes.

(2) Fees for preparation of a deed, settlement statement, or other documents.

(3) Escrows for future payments of taxes and insurance.

(4) Fees for notarizing deeds and other documents.

(5) Appraisal fees.

(6) Credit reports.

§ 107. Determination of annual percentage rate [15 U.S.C. § 1606]

(a) The annual percentage rate applicable to any extension of consumer credit shall be determined, in accordance with the regulations of the Board,

(1) in the case of any extension of credit other than under an open end credit plan, as

(A) that nominal annual percentage rate which will yield a sum equal to the amount of the finance charge when it is applied to the unpaid balances of the amount financed, calculated according to the actuarial method of allocating payments made on a debt between the amount financed and the amount of the finance charge, pursuant to which a payment is applied first to the accumulated finance charge and the balance is applied to the unpaid amount financed; or

(B) the rate determined by any method prescribed by the Board as a method which materially simplifies computation while retaining reasonable accuracy as compared with the rate determined under subparagraph (A).

(2) in the case of any extension of credit under an open end credit plan, as the quotient (expressed as a percentage) of the total finance charge for the period to which it relates divided by the amount upon which the finance charge for that period is based, multiplied by the number of such periods in a year.

(b) Where a creditor imposes the same finance charge for balances within a specified range, the annual percentage rate shall be computed on the median balance within the range, except that if the Board determines that a rate so computed would not be meaningful, or would be materially misleading, the annual percentage rate shall be computed on such other basis as the Board may by regulation require.

(c) The disclosure of an annual percentage rate is accurate for the purpose of this title if the rate disclosed is within a tolerance not greater than one-eighth of 1 per centum more or less than the actual rate or rounded to the nearest one-fourth of 1 per centum. The Board may allow a greater tolerance to simplify compliance where irregular payments are involved.

(d) The Board may authorize the use of rate tables or charts which may provide for the disclosure of annual percentage rates which vary from the rate determined in accordance with subsection (a)(1)(A) by not more than such tolerances as the Board may allow. The Board may not allow a tolerance greater than 8 per centum of that rate except to simplify compliance where irregular payments are involved.

(e) In the case of creditors determining the annual percentage rate in a manner other than as described in subsection (d), the Board may authorize other reasonable tolerances.

§ 108. Administrative enforcement [15 U.S.C. § 1607]

(a) Compliance with the requirements imposed under this title shall be enforced under

(1) section 8 of the Federal Deposit Insurance Act, in the case of

(A) national banks, by the Comptroller of the Currency.

(B) member banks of the Federal Reserve System (other than national banks), by the Board.

(C) banks insured by the Federal Deposit Insurance Corporation (other than members of the Federal Reserve System), by the Board of Directors of the Federal Deposit Insurance Corporation.

(2) section 5(d) of the Home Owners' Loan Act of 1933, section 407 of the National Housing Act, and sections 6(i) and 17 of the Federal Home Loan Bank Act, by the Federal Home Loan Bank Board (acting directly or through the Federal Savings and Loan Insurance Corporation), in the case of any institution subject to any of those provisions.

(3) the Federal Credit Union Act, by the Administrator of the National Credit Union Administration with respect to any Federal credit union.

(4) the Federal Aviation Act of 1958, by the Civil Aeronautics Board with respect to any air carrier or foreign air carrier subject to that Act.

(5) the Packers and Stockyards Act, 1921 (except as provided in section 406 of that Act), by the Secretary of Agriculture with respect to any activities subject to that Act.

(6) the Farm Credit Act of 1971, by the Farm Credit Administration with respect to any Federal land bank, Federal land bank association, Federal intermediate credit bank, or production credit association.

(b) For the purpose of the exercise by any agency referred to in subsection (a) of its powers under any Act referred to in that subsection, a violation of any requirement imposed under this title shall be deemed to be a violation of a requirement imposed under that Act. In addition to its powers under any provision of law specifically referred to in subsection (a), each of the agencies referred to in that subsection may exercise, for the purpose of enforcing compliance with any requirement imposed under this title, any other authority conferred on it by law.

(c) Except to the extent that enforcement of the requirements imposed under this title is specifically committed to some other Government agency under subsection (a), the Federal Trade Commission shall enforce such requirements. For the purpose of the exercise by the Federal Trade Commission of its functions and powers under the Federal Trade Commission Act, a violation of any requirement imposed under this title shall be deemed a violation of a requirement imposed under that Act. All of the functions and powers of the Federal Trade Commission under the Federal Trade Commission Act are available to the Commission to enforce compliance by any person with the requirements imposed under this title, irrespective of whether that person is engaged in commerce or meets any other jurisdictional tests in the Federal Trade Commission Act.

(d) The authority of the Board to issue regulations under this title does not impair the authority of any other agency designated in this section to make rules respecting its own procedures in enforcing compliance with requirements imposed under this title.

(e)(1) In carrying out its enforcement activities under this section, each agency referred to in subsection (a) or (c), in cases where an annual percentage rate or finance charge was inaccurately disclosed, shall notify the creditor of such disclosure error and is authorized in accordance with the provisions of this subsection to require the creditor to make an adjustment to the account of the person to whom credit was extended, to assure that such person will not be required to pay a finance charge in excess of the finance charge actually disclosed or the dollar equivalent of the annual percentage rate actually disclosed, whichever is lower. For the purposes of this subsection, except where such disclosure error resulted from a willful violation which was intended to mislead the person to whom credit was extended, in determining whether a disclosure error has occurred and in calculating any adjustment, (A) each agency shall apply (i) with respect to the annual percentage rate, a tolerance of one-quarter of 1 percent more or less than the actual rate, determined without regard to section 107(c) of this title, and (ii) with respect to the finance charge, a corresponding numerical tolerance as generated by the tolerance provided under this subsection for the annual percentage rate; except that (B) with respect to transactions consummated after two years following the effective date of section 608 of the Truth in Lending Simplification and Reform Act, each agency shall apply (i) for transactions that have a scheduled amortization of ten years or less, with respect to the annual percentage rate, a tolerance not to exceed one-quarter of 1 percent more or less than the actual rate, determined without regard to section 107(c) of this title, but in no event a tolerance of less than the tolerances allowed under section 107(c), (ii) for transactions that have a scheduled amortization of more than ten years, with respect to the annual percentage rate, only such tolerances as are allowed under section 107(c) of this title, and (iii) for all transactions, with respect to the finance charge, a corresponding numerical tolerance as generated by the tolerances provided under this subsection for the annual percentage rate.

(2) Each agency shall require such an adjustment when it determines that such disclosure error resulted from (A) a clear and consistent pattern or practice of violations, (B) gross negligence, or (C) a willful violation which was intended to mislead the person to whom the credit was extended. Notwithstanding the preceding sentence, except where such disclosure error resulted from a willful violation which was intended to mislead the person to whom credit was extended, an agency need not require such an adjustment if it determines that such disclosure error—

(A) resulted from an error involving the disclosure of a fee or charge that would otherwise be excludable in computing the finance charge, including but not limited to violations involving the disclosures described in sections 106(b), (c) and (d) of this title, in which event the agency may require such remedial action as it determines to be equitable, except that for transactions consummated after two years after the effective date of section 608 of the Truth in Lending Simplification and Reform Act, such an adjustment shall be ordered for violations of section 106(b);

(B) involved a disclosed amount which was 10 per centum or less of the amount that should have been disclosed and (i) in cases where the error involved a disclosed finance charge, the annual percentage rate was disclosed correctly, and (ii) in cases where the error involved a disclosed annual percentage rate, the finance charge was disclosed correctly; in which event the agency may require such adjustment as it determines to be equitable;

(C) involved a total failure to disclose either the annual percentage rate or the finance charge, in which event the agency may require such adjustment as it determines to be equitable; or

(D) resulted from any other unique circumstance involving clearly technical and nonsubstantive disclosure violations that do not adversely affect information provided to the consumer and that have not misled or otherwise deceived the consumer.

In the case of other such disclosure errors, each agency may require such an adjustment.

(3) Notwithstanding paragraph (2), no adjustment shall be ordered (A) if it would have a significantly adverse impact upon the safety or soundness of the creditor, but in any such case, the agency may require a partial adjustment in an amount which does not have such an impact except that with respect to any transaction consummated after the effective date of section 608 of the Truth in Lending Simplification and Reform Act, the agency shall require the full adjustment, but permit the creditor to make the required adjustment in partial payments over an extended period of time which the agency considers to be reasonable, (B) if the amount of the adjustment would be less than $1, except that if more than one year has elapsed since the date of the violation, the agency may require that such amount be paid into the Treasury of the United States, or (C) except where such disclosure error resulted from a willful violation which was intended to mislead the person to whom credit was extended, in the case of an open-end credit plan, more than two years after the violation, or in the case of any other extension of credit, as follows:

(i) with respect to creditors that are subject to examination by the agencies referred to in paragraphs (1) through (3) of section 108(a) of this title, except in connection with violations arising from practices identified in the current examination and only in connection with transactions that are consummated after the date of the immediately preceding examination, except that where practices giving rise to violations identified in earlier examinations have not been corrected, adjustments for those violations shall be required in connection with transactions consummated after the date of the examination in which such practices were first identified;

(ii) with respect to creditors that are not subject to examination by such agencies, except in connection with transactions that are consummated after May 10, 1978; and

(iii) in no event after the later of (I) the expiration of the life of the credit extension, or (II) two years after the agreement to extend credit was consummated.

(4)(A) Notwithstanding any other provision of this section, an adjustment under this subsection may be required by an agency referred to in subsection (a) or (c) only by an order issued in accordance with cease and desist procedures provided by the provision of law referred to in such subsections.

(B) In the case of an agency which is not authorized to conduct cease and desist proceedings, such an order may be issued after an agency hearing on the record conducted at least thirty but not more than sixty days after notice of the alleged violation is served on the creditor. Such a hearing shall be deemed to be a hearing which is subject to the provisions of section 8(h) of the Federal Deposit Insurance Act and shall be subject to judicial review as provided therein.

(5) Except as otherwise specifically provided in this subsection and notwithstanding any provision of law referred to in subsection (a) or (c), no agency referred to in subsection (a) or (c) may require a creditor to make dollar adjustments for errors in any requirements under this title, except with regard to the requirements of section 165.

(6) A creditor shall not be subject to an order to make an adjustment, if within sixty days after discovering a disclosure error, whether pursuant to a final written examination report or through the creditor's own procedures, the creditor notifies the person concerned of the error and adjusts the account so as to assure that such person will not be required to pay a finance charge in excess of the finance charge actually disclosed or the dollar equivalent of the annual percentage rate actually disclosed, whichever is lower.

(7) Notwithstanding the second sentence of subsection (e)(1), subsection (e)(3)(C)(i), and subsection (e)(3)(C)(ii), each agency referred to in subsection (a) or (c) shall require an adjustment for an annual percentage rate disclosure error that exceeds a tolerance of one quarter of one percent less than the actual rate, determined without regard to section 107(c) of this title, with respect to any transaction consummated between January 1, 1977, and [October 1, 1982].

§ 109. Views of other agencies [15 U.S.C. § 1608]

In the exercise of its functions under this title, the Board may obtain upon request the views of any other Federal agency which, in the judgment of the Board, exercises regulatory or supervisory functions with respect to any class of creditors subject to this title.

§ 111. Effect on other laws [15 U.S.C. § 1610]

(a)(1) Chapters 1, 2, and 3 do not annul, alter, or affect the laws of any State relating to the disclosure of information in connection with credit transactions, except to the extent that those laws are inconsistent with the provisions of this title, and then only to the extent of the inconsistency. Upon its own motion or upon the request of any creditor, State, or other interested party which is submitted in accordance with procedures prescribed in regulations of the Board, the Board shall determine whether any such inconsistency exists. If the Board determines that a State-required disclosure is inconsistent, creditors located in that State may not make disclosures using the inconsistent term or form, and shall incur no liability under the law of that State for failure to use such term or form, notwithstanding that such determination is subsequently amended, rescinded, or determined by judicial or other authority to be invalid for any reason.

(2) Upon its own motion or upon the request of any creditor, State, or other interested party which is submitted in accordance with procedures prescribed in regulations of the Board, the Board shall determine whether any disclosure required under the law of any State is substantially the same in meaning as a disclosure required under this title. If the Board determines that a State-required disclosure is substantially the same in meaning as a disclosure required by this title, then creditors located in that State may make such disclosure in compliance with such State law in lieu of the disclosure required by this title, except that the annual percentage rate and finance charge shall be disclosed as required by section 122.

(b) This title does not otherwise annul, alter or affect in any manner the meaning, scope or applicability of the laws of any State, including, but not limited to, laws relating to the types, amounts or rates of charges, or any element or elements of charges, permissible under such laws in connection with the extension or use of credit, nor does this title extend the applicability of those laws to any class of persons or transactions to which they would not otherwise apply.

(c) In any action or proceeding in any court involving a consumer credit sale, the disclosure of the annual percentage rate as required under this title in connection with that sale may not be received as evidence that the sale was a loan or any type of transaction other than a credit sale.

(d) Except as specified in sections 125, 130, and 166, this title and the regulations issued thereunder do not affect the validity or enforceability of any contract or obligation under State or Federal law.

§ 112. Criminal liability for willful and knowing violation [15 U.S.C. § 1611]

Whoever willfully and knowingly

(1) gives false or inaccurate information or fails to provide information which he is required to disclose under the provisions of this title or any regulation issued thereunder,

(2) uses any chart or table authorized by the Board under section 107 in such a manner as to consistently understate the annual percentage rate determined under section 107(a)(1)(A), or

(3) otherwise fails to comply with any requirement imposed under this title, shall be fined not more than $5,000 or imprisoned not more than one year, or both.

§ 113. Effect on governmental agencies [15 U.S.C. § 1612]

(a) Any department or agency of the United States which administers a credit program in which it extends, insures, or guarantees consumer credit and in which it provides instruments to a creditor which contain any disclosures required by this title shall, prior to the issuance or continued use of such instruments, consult with the Board to assure that such instruments comply with this title.

(b) No civil or criminal penalty provided under this title for any violation thereof may be imposed upon the United States or any department or agency thereof, or upon any State or political subdivision thereof, or any agency of any State or political subdivision.

(c) A creditor participating in a credit program administered, insured, or guaranteed by any department or agency of the United States shall not be held liable for a civil or criminal penalty under this title in any case in which the violation results from the use of an instrument required by any such department or agency.

(d) A creditor participating in a credit program administered, insured, or guaranteed by any department or agency of the United States shall not be held liable for a civil or criminal penalty under the laws of any State (other than laws determined under section 111 to be inconsistent with this title) for any technical or procedural failure, such as a failure to use a specific form, to make information available at a specific place on an instrument, or to use a specific typeface, as required by State law, which is caused by the use of an instrument required to be used by such department or agency.

§ 114. Reports by Board and Attorney General [15 U.S.C. § 1613]

Each year the Board and the Attorney General shall, respectively, make reports to the Congress concerning the administration of their functions under this title, including such recommendations as the Board and the Attorney General, respectively, deem necessary or appropriate. In addition, each report of the Board shall include its assessment of the extent to which compliance with the requirements imposed under this title is being achieved.

CHAPTER 2. CREDIT TRANSACTIONS

§ 121. General requirement of disclosure [15 U.S.C. § 1631]

(a) Subject to subsection (b), a creditor or lessor shall disclose to the person who is obligated on a consumer lease or a consumer credit transaction the information required under this title. In a transaction involving more than one obligor, a creditor or lessor, except in a transaction under section 125, need not disclose to more than one of such obligors if the obligor given disclosure is a primary obligor.

(b) If a transaction involves one creditor as defined in section 103(f), or one lessor as defined in section 181(3), such creditor or lessor shall make the disclosures. If a transaction involves more than one creditor or lessor, only one creditor or lessor shall be required to make the disclosures. The Board shall by regulation specify which creditor or lessor shall make the disclosures.

(c) The Board may provide by regulation that any portion of the information required to be disclosed by this title may be given in the form of estimates where the provider of such information is not in a position to know exact information.

(d) The Board shall determine whether tolerances for numerical disclosures other than the annual percentage rate are necessary to facilitate compliance with this title, and if it determines that such tolerances are necessary to facilitate compliance, it shall by regulation permit disclosures within such tolerances. The Board shall exercise its authority to permit tolerances for numerical disclosures other than the annual percentage rate so that such tolerances are narrow enough to prevent such tolerances from resulting in misleading disclosures or disclosures that circumvent the purposes of this title.

§ 122. Form of disclosure; additional information [15 U.S.C. § 1632]

(a) Information required by this title shall be disclosed clearly and conspicuously, in accordance with regulations of the Board. The terms "annual percentage rate" and "finance charge" shall be disclosed more conspicuously than other terms, data, or information provided in connection with a transaction, except information relating to the identity of the creditor. Regulations of the Board need not require that disclosures pursuant to this title be made in the order set forth in this title and, except as otherwise provided, may permit the use of terminology different from that employed in this title if it conveys substantially the same meaning.

(b) Any creditor or lessor may supply additional information or explanation with any disclosures required under chapters 4 and 5 and, except as provided in section 128(b)(1), under this chapter.

§ 123. Exemption for State-regulated transactions [15 U.S.C. § 1633]

The Board shall by regulation exempt from the requirements of this chapter any class of credit transactions within any State if it determines that under the law of that State that class of transactions is subject to requirements substantially similar to those imposed under this chapter, and that there is adequate provision for enforcement.

§ 124. Effect of subsequent occurrence [15 U.S.C. § 1634]

If information disclosed in accordance with this chapter is subsequently rendered inaccurate as the result of any act, occurrence, or agreement subsequent to the delivery of the required disclosures, the inaccuracy resulting therefrom does not constitute a violation of this chapter.

§ 125. Right of rescission as to certain transactions [15 U.S.C. § 1635]

(a) Except as otherwise provided in this section, in the case of any consumer credit transaction (including opening or increasing the credit limit for an open end credit plan) in which a security interest, including any such interest arising by operation of law, is or will be retained or acquired in any property which is used as the principal dwelling of the person to whom credit is extended, the obligor shall have the right to rescind the transaction until midnight of the third business day following the consummation of the transaction or the delivery of the information and rescission forms required under this section together with a statement containing the material disclosures required under this title, whichever is later, by notifying the creditor, in accordance with regulations of the Board, of his intention to do so. The creditor shall clearly and conspicuously disclose, in accordance with regulations of the Board, to any obligor in a transaction subject to this section the rights of the obligor under this section. The creditor shall also provide, in accordance with regulations of the Board, appropriate forms for the obligor to exercise his right to rescind any transaction subject to this section.

(b) When an obligor exercises his right to rescind under subsection (a), he is not liable for any finance or other charge, and any security interest given by the obligor, including any such interest arising by operation of law, becomes void upon such a rescission. Within 20 days after receipt of a notice of rescission, the creditor shall return to the obligor any money or property given as earnest money, downpayment, or otherwise, and shall take any action necessary or appropriate to reflect the termination of any security interest created under the transaction. If the creditor has delivered any property to the obligor, the obligor may retain possession of it. Upon the performance of the creditor's obligations under this section, the obligor shall tender the property to the creditor, except that if return of the property in kind would be impracticable or inequitable, the obligor shall tender its reasonable value. Tender shall be made at the location of the property or at the residence of the obligor, at the option of the obligor. If the creditor does not take possession of the property within 20 days after tender by the obligor, ownership of the property vests in the obligor without obligation on his part to pay for it. The procedures prescribed by this subsection shall apply except when otherwise ordered by a court.

(c) Notwithstanding any rule of evidence, written acknowledgment of receipt of any disclosures required under this title by a person to whom information, forms, and a statement is required to be given pursuant to this section does no more than create a rebuttable presumption of delivery thereof.

(d) The Board may, if it finds that such action is necessary in order to permit homeowners to meet bona fide personal financial emergencies, prescribe regulations authorizing the modification or waiver of any rights created under this section to the extent and under the circumstances set forth in those regulations.

(e)(1) This section does not apply to—

(A) a residential mortgage transaction as defined in section 103(w);

(B) a transaction which constitutes a refinancing or consolidation (with no new advances) of the principal balance then due and any accrued and unpaid finance charges of an existing extension of credit by the same creditor secured by an interest in the same property;

(C) a transaction in which an agency of a State is the creditor; or

(D) advances under a preexisting open end credit plan if a security interest has already been retained or acquired and such advances are in accordance with a previously established credit limit for such plan.

(2) The provisions of paragraph (1)(D) shall cease to be effective 3 years after the effective date of the Truth in Lending Simplification and Reform Act.

(f) An obligor's right of rescission shall expire three years after the date of consummation of the transaction or upon the sale of the property, whichever occurs first, notwithstanding the fact that the information and forms required under this section or any other disclosures required under this chapter have not been delivered to the obligor, except that if (1) any agency empowered to enforce the provisions of this title institutes a proceeding to enforce the provisions of this section within three years after the date of consummation of the transaction, (2) such agency finds a violation of section 125, and (3) the obligor's right to rescind is based in whole or in part on any matter involved in such proceeding, then the obligor's right of rescission shall expire three years after the date of consummation of the transaction or upon the earlier sale of the property, or upon the expiration of one year following the conclusion of the proceeding, or any judicial review or period for judicial review thereof, whichever is later.

(g) In any action in which it is determined that a creditor has violated this section, in addition to rescission the court may award relief under section 130 for violations of this title not relating to the right to rescind.

§ 127. Open end consumer credit plans [15 U.S.C. § 1637]

(a) Before opening any account under an open end consumer credit plan, the creditor shall disclose to the person to whom credit is to be extended each of the following items, to the extent applicable:

(1) The conditions under which a finance charge may be imposed, including the time period (if any) within which any credit extended may be repaid without incurring a finance charge, except that the creditor may, at his election and without disclosure, impose no such finance charge if payment is received after the termination of such time period. If no such time period is provided, the creditor shall disclose such fact.

(2) The method of determining the balance upon which a finance charge will be imposed.

(3) The method of determining the amount of the finance charge, including any minimum or fixed amount imposed as a finance charge.

(4) Where one or more periodic rates may be used to compute the finance charge, each such rate, the range of balances to which it is applicable, and the corresponding nominal annual percentage rate determined by multiplying the periodic rate by the number of periods in a year.

(5) Identification of other charges which may be imposed as part of the plan, and their method of computation, in accordance with regulations of the Board.

(6) In cases where the credit is or will be secured, a statement that a security interest has been or will be taken in (A) the property purchased as part of the credit transaction, or (B) property not purchased as part of the credit transaction identified by item or type.

(7) A statement, in a form prescribed by regulations of the Board of the protection provided by sections 161 and 170 to an obligor and the creditor's responsibilities under sections 162 and 170. With respect to one billing cycle per calendar year, at intervals of not less than six months or more than eighteen months, the creditor shall

transmit such statement to each obligor to whom the creditor is required to transmit a statement pursuant to section 127(b) for such billing cycle.

(b) The creditor of any account under an open end consumer credit plan shall transmit to the obligor, for each billing cycle at the end of which there is an outstanding balance in that account or with respect to which a finance charge is imposed, a statement setting forth each of the following items to the extent applicable:

(1) The outstanding balance in the account at the beginning of the statement period.

(2) The amount and date of each extension of credit during the period, and a brief identification, on or accompanying the statement of each extension of credit in a form prescribed by the Board sufficient to enable the obligor either to identify the transaction or to relate it to copies of sales vouchers or similar instruments previously furnished, except that a creditor's failure to disclose such information in accordance with this paragraph shall not be deemed a failure to comply with this chapter or this title if (A) the creditor maintains procedures reasonably adapted to procure and provide such information, and (B) the creditor responds to and treats any inquiry for clarification or documentation as a billing error and an erroneously billed amount under section 161. In lieu of complying with the requirements of the previous sentence, in the case of any transaction in which the creditor and seller are the same person, as defined by the Board, and such person's open end credit plan has fewer than 15,000 accounts, the creditor may elect to provide only the amount and date of each extension of credit during the period and the seller's name and location where the transaction took place if (A) a brief identification of the transaction has been previously furnished, and (B) the creditor responds to and treats any inquiry for clarification or documentation as a billing error and an erroneously billed amount under section 161.

(3) The total amount credited to the account during the period.

(4) The amount of any finance charge added to the account during the period, itemized to show the amounts, if any, due to the application of percentage rates and the amount, if any, imposed as a minimum or fixed charge.

(5) Where one or more periodic rates may be used to compute the finance charge, each such rate, the range of balances to which it is applicable, and, unless the annual percentage rate (determined under section 107(a)(2)) is required to be disclosed pursuant to paragraph (6), the corresponding nominal annual percentage rate determined by multiplying the periodic rate by the number of periods in a year.

(6) Where the total finance charge exceeds 50 cents for a monthly or longer billing cycle, or the pro rata part of 50 cents for a billing

cycle shorter than monthly, the total finance charge expressed as an annual percentage rate (determined under section 107(a)(2)), except that if the finance charge is the sum of two or more products of a rate times a portion of the balance, the creditor may, in lieu of disclosing a single rate for the total charge, disclose each such rate expressed as an annual percentage rate, and the part of the balance to which it is applicable.

(7) The balance on which the finance charge was computed and a statement of how the balance was determined. If the balance is determined without first deducting all credits during the period, that fact and the amount of such payments shall also be disclosed.

(8) The outstanding balance in the account at the end of the period.

(9) The date by which or the period (if any) within which payment must be made to avoid additional finance charges, except that the creditor may, at his election and without disclosure, impose no such additional finance charge if payment is received after such date or the termination of such period.

(10) The address to be used by the creditor for the purpose of receiving billing inquiries from the obligor.

§ 128. Consumer credit not under open end credit plans [15 U.S.C. § 1638]

(a) For each consumer credit transaction other than under an open end credit plan, the creditor shall disclose each of the following items, to the extent applicable:

(1) The identity of the creditor required to make disclosure.

(2)(A) The "amount financed", using that term, which shall be the amount of credit of which the consumer has actual use. This amount shall be computed as follows, but the computations need not be disclosed and shall not be disclosed with the disclosures conspicuously segregated in accordance with subsection (b)(1):

(i) take the principal amount of the loan or the cash price less downpayment and trade-in;

(ii) add any charges which are not part of the finance charge or of the principal amount of the loan and which are financed by the consumer, including the cost of any items excluded from the finance charge pursuant to section 106; and

(iii) subtract any charges which are part of the finance charge but which will be paid by the consumer before or at the time of the consummation of the transaction, or have been withheld from the proceeds of the credit.

(B) In conjunction with the disclosure of the amount financed, a creditor shall provide a statement of the consumer's right to obtain, upon a written request, a written itemization of the amount financed. The statement shall include spaces for a "yes" and "no" indication to be initialed by the consumer to indicate whether the consumer wants a written itemization of the amount financed. Upon receiving an affirmative indication, the creditor shall provide, at the time other disclosures are required to be furnished, a written itemization of the amount financed. For the purposes of this subparagraph, "itemization of the amount financed" means a disclosure of the following items, to the extent applicable:

(i) the amount that is or will be paid directly to the consumer;

(ii) the amount that is or will be credited to the consumer's account to discharge obligations owed to the creditor;

(iii) each amount that is or will be paid to third persons by the creditor on the consumer's behalf, together with an identification of or reference to the third person; and

(iv) the total amount of any charges described in the preceding subparagraph (A)(iii).

(3) The "finance charge", not itemized, using that term.

(4) The finance charge expressed as an "annual percentage rate", using that term. This shall not be required if the amount financed does not exceed $75 and the finance charge does not exceed $5, or if the amount financed exceeds $75 and the finance charge does not exceed $7.50.

(5) The sum of the amount financed and the finance charge, which shall be termed the "total of payments".

(6) The number, amount, and due dates or period of payments scheduled to repay the total of payments.

(7) In a sale of property or services in which the seller is the creditor required to disclose pursuant to section 121(b), the "total sale price", using that term, which shall be the total of the cash price of the property or services, additional charges, and the finance charge.

(8) Descriptive explanations of the terms "amount financed", "finance charge", "annual percentage rate", "total of payments", and "total sale price" as specified by the Board. The descriptive explanation of "total sale price" shall include reference to the amount of the downpayment.

(9) Where the credit is secured, a statement that a security interest has been taken in (A) the property which is purchased as part of the credit transaction, or (B) property not purchased as part of the credit transaction identified by item or type.

(10) Any dollar charge or percentage amount which may be imposed by a creditor solely on account of a late payment, other than a deferral or extension charge.

(11) A statement indicating whether or not the consumer is entitled to a rebate of any finance charge upon refinancing or prepayment in full pursuant to acceleration or otherwise, if the obligation involves a precomputed finance charge. A statement indicating whether or not a penalty will be imposed in those same circumstances if the obligation involves a finance charge computed from time to time by application of a rate to the unpaid principal balance.

(12) A statement that the consumer should refer to the appropriate contract document for any information such document provides about nonpayment, default, the right to accelerate the maturity of the debt, and prepayment rebates and penalties.

(13) In any residential mortgage transaction, a statement indicating whether a subsequent purchaser or assignee of the consumer may assume the debt obligation on its original terms and conditions.

(b)(1) Except as otherwise provided in this chapter, the disclosures required under subsection (a) shall be made before the credit is extended. Except for the disclosures required by subsection (a)(1) of this section, all disclosures required under subsection (a) and any disclosure provided for in subsection (b), (c), or (d) of section 106 shall be conspicuously segregated from all other terms, data, or information provided in connection with a transaction, including any computations or itemization.

(2) In the case of a residential mortgage transaction, as defined in section 103(w), which is also subject to the Real Estate Settlement Procedures Act, good faith estimates of the disclosures required under subsection (a) shall be made in accordance with regulations of the Board under section 121(c) before the credit is extended, or shall be delivered or placed in the mail not later than three business days after the creditor receives the consumer's written application, whichever is earlier. If the disclosure statement furnished within three days of the written application contains an annual percentage rate which is subsequently rendered inaccurate within the meaning of section 107(c), the creditor shall furnish another statement at the time of settlement or consummation.

(c)(1) If a creditor receives a purchase order by mail or telephone without personal solicitation, and the cash price and the total sale price and the terms of financing, including the annual percentage rate, are set forth in the creditor's catalog or other printed material distributed to the public, then the disclosures required under subsection (a) may be made at any time not later than the date the first payment is due.

(2) If a creditor receives a request for a loan by mail or telephone without personal solicitation and the terms of financing, including the annual percentage rate for representative amounts of credit, are set forth in the creditor's printed material distributed to the public, or in the contract of loan or other printed material delivered to the obligor,

then the disclosures required under subsection (a) may be made at any time not later than the date the first payment is due.

(d) If a consumer credit sale is one of a series of consumer credit sales transactions made pursuant to an agreement providing for the addition of the deferred payment price of that sale to an existing outstanding balance, and the person to whom the credit is extended has approved in writing both the annual percentage rate or rates and the method of computing the finance charge or charges, and the creditor retains no security interest in any property as to which he has received payments aggregating the amount of the sales price including any finance charges attributable thereto, then the disclosure required under subsection (a) for the particular sale may be made at any time not later than the date the first payment for that sale is due. For the purposes of this subsection, in the case of items purchased on different dates, the first purchased shall be deemed first paid for, and in the case of items purchased on the same date, the lowest priced shall be deemed first paid for.

§ 130. Civil liability [15 U.S.C. § 1640]

(a) Except as otherwise provided in this section, any creditor who fails to comply with any requirement imposed under this chapter, including any requirement under section 125, or chapter 4 or 5 of this title with respect to any person is liable to such person in an amount equal to the sum of—

(1) any actual damage sustained by such person as a result of the failure;

(2)(A)(i) in the case of an individual action twice the amount of any finance charge in connection with the transaction, or (ii) in the case of an individual action relating to a consumer lease under chapter 5 of this title, 25 per centum of the total amount of monthly payments under the lease, except that the liability under this subparagraph shall not be less than $100 nor greater than $1,000; or

(B) in the case of a class action, such amount as the court may allow, except that as to each member of the class no minimum recovery shall be applicable, and the total recovery under this subparagraph in any class action or series of class actions arising out of the same failure to comply by the same creditor shall not be more than the lesser of $500,000 or 1 per centum of the net worth of the creditor; and

(3) in the case of any successful action to enforce the foregoing liability or in any action in which a person is determined to have a right of rescission under section 125, the costs of the action, together with a reasonable attorney's fee as determined by the court. In determining the amount of award in any class action, the court shall consider, among other relevant factors, the amount of any actual

damages awarded, the frequency and persistence of failures of compliance by the creditor, the resources of the creditor, the number of persons adversely affected, and the extent to which the creditor's failure of compliance was intentional. In connection with the disclosures referred to in section 127, a creditor shall have a liability determined under paragraph (2) only for failing to comply with the requirements of section 125, section 127(a), or of paragraph (4), (5), (6), (7), (8), (9), or (10) of section 127(b) or for failing to comply with disclosure requirements under State law for any term or item which the Board has determined to be substantially the same in meaning under section 111(a)(2) as any of the terms or items referred to in section 127(a) or any of those paragraphs of section 127(b). In connection with the disclosures referred to in section 128, a creditor shall have a liability determined under paragraph (2) only for failing to comply with the requirements of section 125 or of paragraph (2) (insofar as it requires a disclosure of the "amount financed"), (3), (4), (5), (6), or (9) of section 128(a), or for failing to comply with disclosure requirements under State law for any term which the Board has determined to be substantially the same in meaning under section 111(a)(2) as any of the terms referred to in any of those paragraphs of section 128(a). With respect to any failure to make disclosures required under this chapter or chapter 4 or 5 of this title, liability shall be imposed only upon the creditor required to make disclosure, except as provided in section 131.

(b) A creditor or assignee has no liability under this section or section 108 or section 112 for any failure to comply with any requirement imposed under this chapter or chapter 5, if within sixty days after discovering an error, whether pursuant to a final written examination report or notice issued under section 108(e)(1) or through the creditor's or assignee's own procedures, and prior to the institution of an action under this section or the receipt of written notice of the error from the obligor, the creditor or assignee notifies the person concerned of the error and makes whatever adjustments in the appropriate account are necessary to assure that the person will not be required to pay an amount in excess of the charge actually disclosed, or the dollar equivalent of the annual percentage rate actually disclosed, whichever is lower.

(c) A creditor or assignee may not be held liable in any action brought under this section or section 125 for a violation of this title if the creditor or assignee shows by a preponderance of evidence that the violation was not intentional and resulted from a bona fide error notwithstanding the maintenance of procedures reasonably adapted to avoid any such error. Examples of a bona fide error include, but are not limited to, clerical, calculation, computer malfunction and programing, and printing errors, except that an error of legal judgment with respect to a person's obligations under this title is not a bona fide error.

(d) When there are multiple obligors in a consumer credit transaction or consumer lease, there shall be no more than one recovery of damages under subsection (a)(2) for a violation of this title.

(e) Any action under this section may be brought in any United States district court, or in any other court of competent jurisdiction, within one year from the date of the occurrence of the violation. This subsection does not bar a person from asserting a violation of this title in an action to collect the debt which was brought more than one year from the date of the occurrence of the violation as a matter of defense by recoupment or set-off in such action, except as otherwise provided by State law.

(f) No provision of this section, section 108(b), section 108(c), section 108(e), or section 112 imposing any liability shall apply to any act done or omitted in good faith in conformity with any rule, regulation, or interpretation thereof by the Board or in conformity with any interpretation or approval by an official or employee of the Federal Reserve System duly authorized by the Board to issue such interpretations or approvals under such procedures as the Board may prescribe therefor, notwithstanding that after such act or omission has occurred, such rule, regulation, interpretation, or approval is amended, rescinded, or determined by judicial or other authority to be invalid for any reason.

(g) The multiple failure to disclose to any person any information required under this chapter or chapter 4 or 5 of this title to be disclosed in connection with a single account under an open end consumer credit plan, other single consumer credit sale, consumer loan, consumer lease, or other extension of consumer credit, shall entitle the person to a single recovery under this section but continued failure to disclose after a recovery has been granted shall give rise to rights to additional recoveries. This subsection does not bar any remedy permitted by section 125.

(h) A person may not take any action to offset any amount for which a creditor or assignee is potentially liable to such person under subsection (a)(2) against any amount owed by such person, unless the amount of the creditor's or assignee's liability under this title has been determined by judgment of a court of competent jurisdiction in an action of which such person was a party. This subsection does not bar a consumer then in default on the obligation from asserting a violation of this title as an original action, or as a defense or counterclaim to an action to collect amounts owed by the consumer brought by a person liable under this title.

§ 131. Liability of assignees [15 U.S.C. § 1641]

(a) Except as otherwise specifically provided in this title, any civil action for a violation of this title or proceeding under section 108 which may be brought against a creditor may be maintained against any assignee of such creditor only if the violation for which such action or proceeding is brought is apparent on the face of the disclosure statement, except where the assignment was involuntary. For the purpose of this section, a violation apparent on the face of the disclosure statement includes, but is not limited to (1) a disclosure which can be determined to be incomplete or inaccurate from the face of the disclosure statement or other documents assigned, or (2) a disclosure which does not use the terms required to be used by this title.

(b) Except as provided in section 125(c), in any action or proceeding by or against any subsequent assignee of the original creditor without knowledge to the contrary by the assignee when he acquires the obligation, written acknowledgement of receipt by a person to whom a statement is required to be given pursuant to this title shall be conclusive proof of the delivery thereof and, except as provided in subsection (a), of compliance with this chapter. This section does not affect the rights of the obligor in any action against the original creditor.

(c) Any consumer who has the right to rescind a transaction under section 125 may rescind the transaction as against any assignee of the obligation.

§ 132. Issuance of credit cards [15 U.S.C. § 1642]

No credit card shall be issued except in response to a request or application therefor. This prohibition does not apply to the issuance of a credit card in renewal of, or in substitution for, an accepted credit card.

§ 133. Liability of holder of credit card [15 U.S.C. § 1643]

(a)(1) A cardholder shall be liable for the unauthorized use of a credit card only if—

(A) the card is an accepted credit card;

(B) the liability is not in excess of $50;

(C) the card issuer gives adequate notice to the cardholder of the potential liability;

(D) the card issuer has provided the cardholder with a description of a means by which the card issuer may be notified of loss or theft of the card, which description may be provided on the face or reverse side of the statement required by section 127(b) or on a separate notice accompanying such statement;

(E) the unauthorized use occurs before the card issuer has been notified that an unauthorized use of the credit card has occurred or may occur as the result of loss, theft, or otherwise; and

(F) the card issuer has provided a method whereby the user of such card can be identified as the person authorized to use it.

(2) For purposes of this section, a card issuer has been notified when such steps as may be reasonably required in the ordinary course of business to provide the card issuer with the pertinent information have been taken, whether or not any particular officer, employee, or agent of the card issuer does in fact receive such information.

(b) In any action by a card issuer to enforce liability for the use of a credit card, the burden of proof is upon the card issuer to show that the use was authorized or, if the use was unauthorized, then the burden of proof is upon the card issuer to show that the conditions of liability for the unauthorized use of a credit card, as set forth in subsection (a), have been met.

(c) Nothing in this section imposes liability upon a cardholder for the unauthorized use of a credit card in excess of his liability for such use under other applicable law or under any agreement with the card issuer.

(d) Except as provided in this section, a cardholder incurs no liability from the unauthorized use of a credit card.

§ 134. Fraudulent use of credit card [15 U.S.C. § 1644]

(a) Whoever knowingly in a transaction affecting interstate or foreign commerce, uses or attempts or conspires to use any counterfeit, fictitious, altered, forged, lost, stolen, or fraudulently obtained credit card to obtain money, goods, services, or anything else of value which within any one-year period has a value aggregating $1,000 or more; or

(b) Whoever, with unlawful or fraudulent intent, transports or attempts or conspires to transport in interstate or foreign commerce a counterfeit, fictitious, altered, forged, lost, stolen, or fraudulently obtained credit card knowing the same to be counterfeit, fictitious, altered, forged, lost, stolen, or fraudulently obtained; or

(c) Whoever, with unlawful or fraudulent intent, uses any instrumentality of interstate or foreign commerce to sell or transport a counterfeit, fictitious, altered, forged, lost, stolen, or fraudulently obtained credit card knowing the same to be counterfeit, fictitious, altered, forged, lost, stolen, or fraudulently obtained; or

(d) Whoever knowingly receives, conceals, uses, or transports money, goods, services, or anything else of value (except tickets for interstate or foreign transportation) which (1) within any one-year period has a value aggregating $1,000 or more, (2) has moved in or is part of, or which constitutes interstate or foreign commerce, and (3) has been obtained with a counterfeit, fictitious, altered, forged, lost, stolen, or fraudulently obtained credit card; or

(e) Whoever knowingly receives, conceals, uses, sells, or transports in interstate or foreign commerce one or more tickets for interstate or foreign transportation, which (1) within any one-year period have a value aggregating $500 or more, and (2) have been purchased or obtained with one or more counterfeit, fictitious, altered, forged, lost, stolen, or fraudulently obtained credit cards; or

(f) Whoever in a transaction affecting interstate or foreign commerce furnishes money, property, services, or anything else of value, which within any one-year period has a value aggregating $1,000 or more, through the use of any counterfeit, fictitious, altered, forged, lost, stolen, or fraudulently obtained credit card knowing the same to be counterfeit, fictitious, altered, forged, lost, stolen, or fraudulently obtained—

shall be fined not more than $10,000 or imprisoned not more than ten years, or both.

§ 135. Business credit cards [15 U.S.C. § 1645]

The exemption provided by section 104(1) does not apply to the provisions of sections 132, 133, and 134, except that a card issuer and a business or other organization which provides credit cards issued by the same card issuer to ten or more of its employees may by contract agree as to liability of the business or other organization with respect to unauthorized use of such credit cards without regard to the provisions of section 133, but in no case may such business or other organization or card issuer impose liability upon any employee with respect to unauthorized use of such a credit card except in accordance with and subject to the limitations of section 133.

§ 136. Dissemination of annual percentage rates [15 U.S.C. § 1646]

(a) The Board shall collect, publish, and disseminate to the public, on a demonstration basis in a number of standard metropolitan statistical areas to be determined by the Board, the annual percentage rates charged for representative types of nonsale credit by creditors in such areas. For the purpose of this section, the Board is authorized to require creditors in such areas to furnish information necessary for the Board to collect, publish, and disseminate such information.

(b) The Board is authorized to enter into contracts or other arrangements with appropriate persons, organizations, or State agencies to carry out its functions under subsection (a) and to furnish financial assistance in support thereof.

CHAPTER 3. CREDIT ADVERTISING

§ 141. Catalogs and multiple-page advertisements [15 U.S.C. § 1661]

For the purposes of this chapter, a catalog or other multiple-page advertisement shall be considered a single advertisement if it clearly and conspicuously displays a credit terms table on which the information required to be stated under this chapter is clearly set forth.

§ 142. Advertising of downpayments and installments [15 U.S.C. § 1662]

No advertisement to aid, promote, or assist directly or indirectly any extension of consumer credit may state

(1) that a specific periodic consumer credit amount or installment amount can be arranged, unless the creditor usually and customarily arranges credit payments or installments for that period and in that amount.

(2) that a specified downpayment is required in connection with any extension of consumer credit, unless the creditor usually and customarily arranges downpayments in that amount.

§ 143. Advertising of open end credit plans [15 U.S.C. § 1663]

No advertisement to aid, promote, or assist directly or indirectly the extension of consumer credit under an open end credit plan may set forth any of the specific terms of that plan unless it also clearly and conspicuously sets forth all of the following items:

(1) Any minimum or fixed amount which could be imposed.

(2) In any case in which periodic rates may be used to compute the finance charge, the periodic rates expressed as annual percentage rates.

(3) Any other term that the Board may by regulation require to be disclosed.

§ 144. Advertising of credit other than open end plans [15 U.S.C. § 1664]

(a) Except as provided in subsection (b), this section applies to any advertisement to aid, promote, or assist directly or indirectly any consumer credit sale, loan, or other extension of credit subject to the provisions of this title, other than an open end credit plan.

(b) The provisions of this section do not apply to advertisements of residential real estate except to the extent that the Board may by regulation require.

(c) If any advertisement to which this section applies states the rate of a finance charge, the advertisement shall state the rate of that charge expressed as an annual percentage rate.

(d) If any advertisement to which this section applies states the amount of the downpayment, if any, the amount of any installment payment, the dollar amount of any finance charge, or the number of installments or the period of repayment, then the advertisement shall state all of the following items:

(1) The downpayment, if any.

(2) The terms of repayment.

(3) The rate of the finance charge expressed as an annual percentage rate.

§ 145. Nonliability of media [15 U.S.C. § 1665]

There is no liability under this chapter on the part of any owner or personnel, as such, of any medium in which an advertisement appears or through which it is disseminated.

§ 146. Use of annual percentage rate in oral disclosures [15 U.S.C. § 1665a]

In responding orally to any inquiry about the cost of credit, a creditor, regardless of the method used to compute finance charges, shall state rates only in terms of the annual percentage rate, except that in the case of an open end credit plan, the periodic rate also may be stated and, in the case of an other than open end credit plan where a major component of the finance charge consists of interest computed at a simple annual rate, the simple annual rate also may be stated. The Board may, by regulation, modify the requirements of this section or provide an exception from this section for a transaction or class of transactions for which the creditor cannot determine in advance the applicable annual percentage rate.

CHAPTER 4. CREDIT BILLING

§ 161. Correction of billing errors [15 U.S.C. § 1666]

(a) If a creditor, within sixty days after having transmitted to an obligor a statement of the obligor's account in connection with an extension of consumer credit, receives at the address disclosed under section 127(b)(10) a written notice (other than notice on a payment stub or other payment medium supplied by the creditor if the creditor so stipulates with the disclosure required under section 127(a)(7) from the obligor in which the obligor—

(1) sets forth or otherwise enables the creditor to identify the name and account number (if any) of the obligor,

(2) indicates the obligor's belief that the statement contains a billing error and the amount of such billing error, and

(3) sets forth the reasons for the obligor's belief (to the extent applicable) that the statement contains a billing error,

the creditor shall, unless the obligor has, after giving such written notice and before the expiration of the time limits herein specified, agreed that the statement was correct—

(A) not later than thirty days after the receipt of the notice, send a written acknowledgment thereof to the obligor, unless the action required in subparagraph (B) is taken within such thirty-day period, and

(B) not later than two complete billing cycles of the creditor (in no event later than ninety days) after the receipt of the notice and prior to taking any action to collect the amount, or any part thereof, indicated by the obligor under paragraph (2) either—

(i) make appropriate corrections in the account of the obligor, including the crediting of any finance charges on amounts erroneously billed, and transmit to the obligor a notification of such corrections and the creditor's explanation of any change in the amount indicated by the obligor under paragraph (2) and, if any such change is made and the obligor so requests, copies of documentary evidence of the obligor's indebtedness; or

(ii) send a written explanation or clarification to the obligor, after having conducted an investigation, setting forth to the extent applicable the reasons why the creditor believes the account of the obligor was correctly shown in the statement and, upon request of the obligor, provide copies of documentary evidence of the obligor's indebtedness. In the case of a billing error where the obligor alleges that the creditor's billing statement reflects goods not delivered to the obligor or his designee in accordance with the agreement made at the time of the transaction, a creditor may not construe such amount to be correctly shown unless he determines that such goods were actually delivered, mailed, or otherwise sent to the obligor and provides the obligor with a statement of such determination.

After complying with the provisions of this subsection with respect to an alleged billing error, a creditor has no further responsibility under this section if the obligor continues to make substantially the same allegation with respect to such error.

(b) For the purpose of this section, a "billing error" consists of any of the following:

(1) A reflection on a statement of an extension of credit which was not made to the obligor or, if made, was not in the amount reflected on such statement.

(2) A reflection on a statement of an extension of credit for which the obligor requests additional clarification including documentary evidence thereof.

(3) A reflection on a statement of goods or services not accepted by the obligor or his designee or not delivered to the obligor or his designee in accordance with the agreement made at the time of a transaction.

(4) The creditor's failure to reflect properly on a statement a payment made by the obligor or a credit issued to the obligor.

(5) A computation error or similar error of an accounting nature of the creditor on a statement.

(6) Failure to transmit the statement required under section 127(b) of this Act to the last address of the obligor which has been disclosed to the creditor, unless that address was furnished less than twenty days before the end of the billing cycle for which the statement is required.

(7) Any other error described in regulations of the Board.

(c) For the purposes of this section, "action to collect the amount, or any part thereof, indicated by an obligor under paragraph (2)" does not include the sending of statements of account, which may include finance charges on amounts in dispute, to the obligor following written notice from the obligor as specified under subsection (a), if—

(1) the obligor's account is not restricted or closed because of the failure of the obligor to pay the amount indicated under paragraph (2) of subsection (a), and

(2) the creditor indicates the payment of such amount is not required pending the creditor's compliance with this section. Nothing in this section shall be construed to prohibit any action by a creditor to collect any amount which has not been indicated by the obligor to contain a billing error.

(d) Pursuant to regulations of the Board, a creditor operating an open end consumer credit plan may not, prior to the sending of the written explanation or clarification required under paragraph (B)(ii), restrict or close an account with respect to which the obligor has indicated pursuant to subsection (a) that he believes such account to contain a billing error solely because of the obligor's failure to pay the amount indicated to be in error. Nothing in this subsection shall be deemed to prohibit a creditor from applying against the credit limit on the obligor's account the amount indicated to be in error.

(e) Any creditor who fails to comply with the requirements of this section or section 162 forfeits any right to collect from the obligor the amount indicated by the obligor under paragraph (2) of subsection (a) of this section, and any finance charges thereon, except that the amount required to be forfeited under this subsection may not exceed $50.

§ 162. Regulation of credit reports [15 U.S.C. § 1666a]

(a) After receiving a notice from an obligor as provided in section 161(a), a creditor or his agent may not directly or indirectly threaten to report to any person adversely on the obligor's credit rating or credit standing because of the obligor's failure to pay the amount indicated by the obligor under section 161(a)(2), and such amount may not be reported as delinquent to any third party until the creditor has met the requirements of section 161 and has allowed the obligor the same number of days (not less than ten) thereafter to make payment as is provided under the credit agreement with the obligor for the payment of undisputed amounts.

(b) If a creditor receives a further written notice from an obligor that an amount is still in dispute within the time allowed for payment under subsection (a) of this section, a creditor may not report to any third party that the amount of the obligor is delinquent because the obligor has failed to pay an amount which he has indicated under section 161(a)(2), unless the creditor also reports that the amount is in dispute and, at the same time, notifies the obligor of the name and address of each party to whom the creditor is reporting information concerning the delinquency.

(c) A creditor shall report any subsequent resolution of any delinquencies reported pursuant to subsection (b) to the parties to whom such delinquencies were initially reported.

§ 163. Length of billing period [15 U.S.C. § 1666b]

(a) If an open end consumer credit plan provides a time period within which an obligor may repay any portion of the credit extended without incurring an additional finance charge, such additional finance charge may not be imposed with respect to such portion of the credit extended for the billing cycle of which such period is a part unless a statement which includes the amount upon which the finance charge for that period is based was mailed at least fourteen days prior to the date specified in the statement by which payment must be made in order to avoid imposition of that finance charge.

(b) Subsection (a) does not apply in any case where a creditor has been prevented, delayed, or hindered in making timely mailing or delivery of such periodic statement within the time period specified in such subsection because of an act of God, war, natural disaster, strike, or other excusable or justifiable cause, as determined under regulations of the Board.

§ 164. Prompt crediting of payments [15 U.S.C. § 1666c]

Payments received from an obligor under an open end consumer credit plan by the creditor shall be posted promptly to the obligor's account as specified in regulations of the Board. Such regulation shall prevent a finance charge from being imposed on any obligor if the creditor has received the obligor's payment in readily identifiable form in the amount, manner, location, and time indicated by the creditor to avoid the imposition thereof.

§ 165. Treatment of credit balances [15 U.S.C. § 1666d]

Whenever a credit balance in excess of $1 is created in connection with a consumer credit transaction through (1) transmittal of funds to a creditor in excess of the total balance due on an account, (2) rebates of unearned finance charges or insurance premiums, or (3) amounts otherwise owed to or held for the benefit of an obligor, the creditor shall—

(A) credit the amount of the credit balance to the consumer's account;

(B) refund any part of the amount of the remaining credit balance, upon request of the consumer; and

(C) make a good faith effort to refund to the consumer by cash, check, or money order any part of the amount of the credit balance remaining in the account for more than six months, except that no further action is required in any case in which the consumer's current location is not known by the creditor and cannot be traced through the consumer's last known address or telephone number.

§ 166. Prompt notification of returns [15 U.S.C. § 1666e]

With respect to any sales transaction where a credit card has been used to obtain credit, where the seller is a person other than the card issuer, and where the seller accepts or allows a return of the goods or forgiveness of a debit for services which were the subject of such sale, the seller shall promptly transmit to the credit card issuer, a credit statement with respect thereto and the credit card issuer shall credit the account of the obligor for the amount of the transaction.

§ 167. Use of cash discounts [15 U.S.C. § 1666f]

(a)(1) With respect to credit card which may be used for extensions of credit in sales transactions in which the seller is a person other than the card issuer, the card issuer may not, by contract or otherwise, prohibit any such seller from offering a discount to a cardholder to induce the cardholder to pay by cash, check, or similar means rather than use a credit card.

(2) No seller in any sales transaction may impose a surcharge on a cardholder who elects to use a credit card in lieu of payment by cash, check, or similar means.

(b) With respect to any sales transaction, any discount from the regular price offered by the seller for the purpose of inducing payment by cash, checks, or other means not involving the use of an open-end credit plan or a credit card shall not constitute a finance charge as determined under section 106 if such discount is offered to all prospective buyers and its availability is disclosed clearly and conspicuously.

§ 168. Prohibition of tie-in services [15 U.S.C. § 1666g]

Notwithstanding any agreement to the contrary, a card issuer may not require a seller, as a condition to participating in a credit card plan, to open an account with or procure any other service from the card issuer or its subsidiary or agent.

§ 169. Prohibition of offsets [15 U.S.C. § 1666h]

(a) A card issuer may not take any action to offset a cardholder's indebtedness arising in connection with a consumer credit transaction under the relevant credit card plan against funds of the cardholder held on deposit with the card issuer unless—

(1) such action was previously authorized in writing by the cardholder in accordance with a credit plan whereby the cardholder agrees periodically to pay debts incurred in his open end credit account by permitting the card issuer periodically to deduct all or a portion of such debt from the cardholder's deposit account, and

(2) such action with respect to any outstanding disputed amount not be taken by the card issuer upon request of the cardholder.

In the case of any credit card account in existence on the effective date of this section, the previous written authorization referred to in clause (1) shall not be required until the date (after such effective date) when such account is renewed, but in no case later than one year after such effective date. Such written authorization shall be deemed to exist if the card issuer has previously notified the cardholder that the use of his credit card account will subject any funds which the card issuer holds in deposit accounts of such cardholder to offset against any amounts due and payable on his credit card account which have not been paid in accordance with the terms of the agreement between the card issuer and the cardholder.

(b) This section does not alter or affect the right under State law of a card issuer to attach or otherwise levy upon funds of a cardholder held on deposit with the card issuer if that remedy is constitutionally available to creditors generally.

§ 170. Rights of credit card customers [15 U.S.C. § 1666i]

(a) Subject to the limitation contained in subsection (b), a card issuer who has issued a credit card to a cardholder pursuant to an open end consumer credit plan shall be subject to all claims (other than tort claims) and defenses arising out of any transaction in which the credit card is used as a method of payment or extension of credit if (1) the obligor has made a good faith attempt to obtain satisfactory resolution of a disagreement or problem relative to the transaction from the person honoring the credit card; (2) the amount of the initial transaction exceeds $50; and (3) the place where the initial transaction occurred was in the same State as the mailing address previously provided by the cardholder or was within 100 miles from such address, except that the limitations set forth in clauses (2) and (3) with respect to an obligor's right to assert claims and defenses against a card issuer shall not be applicable to any transaction in which the person honoring the credit card (A) is the same person as the card issuer, (B) is controlled by the card issuer, (C) is under direct or indirect common control with the card issuer, (D) is a franchised dealer in the card issuer's products or services, or (E) has obtained the order for such transaction through a mail solicitation made by or participated in by the card issuer in which the cardholder is solicited to enter into such transaction by using the credit card issued by the card issuer.

(b) The amount of claims or defenses asserted by the cardholder may not exceed the amount of credit outstanding with respect to such transaction at the time the cardholder first notifies the card issuer or the person honoring the credit card of such claim or defense. For the purpose of determining the amount of credit outstanding in the preceding sentence, payments and credits to the cardholder's account are deemed to have been applied, in the order indicated, to the payment of: (1) late charges in the order of their entry to the account; (2) finance charges in order of their entry to the account; and (3) debits to the account other than those set forth above, in the order in which each debit entry to the account was made.

§ 171. Relation to State laws [15 U.S.C. § 1666j]

(a) This chapter does not annul, alter, or affect, or exempt any person subject to the provisions of this chapter from complying with the laws of any State with respect to credit billing practices, except to the extent that those laws are inconsistent with any provision of this chapter, and then only to the extent of the inconsistency. The Board is authorized to determine whether such inconsistencies exist. The Board may not determine that any State law is inconsistent with any provision of this chapter if the Board determines that such law gives greater protection to the consumer.

(b) The Board shall by regulation exempt from the requirements of this chapter any class of credit transactions within any State if it determines that under the law of the State that class of transactions is subject to requirements substantially similar to those imposed under this chapter or that such law gives greater protection to the consumer, and that there is adequate provision for enforcement.

(c) Notwithstanding any other provisions of this title, any discount offered under section 167(b) of this title shall not be considered a finance charge or other charge for credit under the usury laws of any State or under the laws of any State relating to disclosure of information in connection with credit transactions, or relating to the types, amounts or rates of charges, or to any element or elements of charges permissible under such laws in connection with the extension or use of credit.

CHAPTER 5. CONSUMER LEASES

§ 181. Definitions [15 U.S.C. § 1667]

For purposes of this chapter—

(1) The term "*consumer lease*" means a contract in the form of a lease or bailment for the use of personal property by a natural person for a period of time exceeding four months, and for a total contractual obligation not exceeding $25,000, primarily for personal, family, or household purposes, whether or not the lessee has the option to purchase or otherwise become the owner of the property at the expiration of the lease, except that such term shall not include any credit sale as defined in section 103(g). Such term does not include a lease for agricultural, business, or commercial purposes, or to a government or governmental agency or instrumentality, or to an organization.

(2) The term "*lessee*" means a natural person who leases or is offered a consumer lease.

(3) The term "*lessor*" means a person who is regularly engaged in leasing, offering to lease, or arranging to lease under a consumer lease.

(4) The term "*personal property*" means any property which is not real property under the laws of the State where situated at the time offered or otherwise made available for lease.

(5) The terms "*security*" and "*security interest*" mean any interest in property which secures payment or performance of an obligation.

§ 182. Consumer lease disclosures [15 U.S.C. § 1667a]

Each lessor shall give a lessee prior to the consummation of the lease a dated written statement on which the lessor and lessee are identified setting out accurately and in a clear and conspicuous manner the following information with respect to that lease, as applicable:

(1) A brief description or identification of the leased property;

(2) The amount of any payment by the lessee required at the inception of the lease;

(3) The amount paid or payable by the lessee for official fees, registration, certificate of title, or license fees or taxes;

(4) The amount of other charges payable by the lessee not included in the periodic payments, a description of the charges and that the lessee shall be liable for the differential, if any, between the anticipated fair market value of the leased property and its appraised actual value at the termination of the lease, if the lessee has such liability;

(5) A statement of the amount or method of determining the amount of any liabilities the lease imposes upon the lessee at the end of the term and whether or not the lessee has the option to purchase the leased property and at what price and time;

(6) A statement identifying all express warranties and guarantees made by the manufacturer or lessor with respect to the leased property, and identifying the party responsible for maintaining or servicing the leased property together with a description of the responsibility;

(7) A brief description of insurance provided or paid for by the lessor or required of the lessee, including the types and amounts of the coverages and costs;

(8) A description of any security interest held or to be retained by the lessor in connection with the lease and a clear identification of the property to which the security interest relates;

(9) The number, amount, and due dates or periods of payments under the lease and the total amount of such periodic payments;

(10) Where the lease provides that the lessee shall be liable for the anticipated fair market value of the property on expiration of the lease, the fair market value of the property at the inception of the lease, the aggregate cost of the lease on expiration, and the differential between them; and

(11) A statement of the conditions under which the lessee or lessor may terminate the lease prior to the end of the term and the amount or method of determining any penalty or other charge for delinquency, default, late payments, or early termination.

The disclosures required under this section may be made in the lease contract to be signed by the lessee. The Board may provide by regulation that any portion of the information required to be disclosed under this section may be given in the form of estimates where the lessor is not in a position to know exact information.

§ 183. Lessee's liability on expiration or termination of lease [15 U.S.C. § 1667b]

(a) Where the lessee's liability on expiration of a consumer lease is based on the estimated residual value of the property such estimated residual value shall be a reasonable approximation of the anticipated actual fair market value of the property on lease expiration. There shall be a rebuttable presumption that the estimated residual value is unreasonable to the extent that the estimated residual value exceeds the actual residual value by more than three times the average payment allocable to a monthly period under the lease. In addition, where the lessee has such liability on expiration of a consumer lease there shall be a rebuttable presumption that the lessor's estimated residual value is not in good faith to the extent that the estimated residual value exceeds the actual residual value by more than three times the average payment allocable to a monthly period under the lease and such lessor shall not collect from the lessee the amount of such excess liability on expiration of a consumer lease unless the lessor brings a successful action with respect to such excess liability. In all actions, the lessor shall pay the lessee's reasonable attorney's fees. The presumptions stated in this section shall not apply to the extent the excess of estimated over actual residual value is due to physical damage to the property beyond reasonable wear and use, or to excessive use, and the lease may set standards for such wear and use if such standards are not unreasonable. Nothing in this subsection shall preclude the right of a willing lessee to make any mutually agreeable final adjustment with respect to such excess residual liability, provided such an agreement is reached after termination of the lease.

(b) Penalties or other charges for delinquency, default, or early termination may be specified in the lease but only at an amount which is reasonable in the light of the anticipated or actual harm caused by the delinquency, default, or early termination, the difficulties of proof of loss, and the inconvenience or nonfeasibility of otherwise obtaining an adequate remedy.

(c) If a lease has a residual value provision at the termination of the lease, the lessee may obtain at his expense, a professional appraisal of the leased property by an independent third party agreed to by both parties. Such appraisal shall be final and binding on the parties.

§ 184. Consumer lease advertising [15 U.S.C. § 1667c]

(a) No advertisement to aid, promote, or assist directly or indirectly any consumer lease shall state the amount of any payment, the number of required payments, or that any or no downpayment or other payment is required at inception of the lease unless the advertisement also states clearly and conspicuously and in accordance with regulations issued by the Board each of the following items of information which is applicable:

(1) That the transaction advertised is a lease.

(2) The amount of any payment required at the inception of the lease or that no such payment is required if that is the case.

(3) The number, amounts, due dates or periods of scheduled payments, and the total of payments under the lease.

(4) That the lessee shall be liable for the differential, if any, between the anticipated fair market value of the leased property and its appraised actual value at the termination of the lease, if the lessee has such liability.

(5) A statement of the amount or method of determining the amount of any liabilities the lease imposes upon the lessee at the end of the term and whether or not the lessee has the option to purchase the leased property and at what price and time.

(b) There is no liability under this section on the part of any owner or personnel, as such, of any medium in which an advertisement appears or through which it is disseminated.

§ 185. Civil liability [15 U.S.C. § 1667d]

(a) Any lessor who fails to comply with any requirement imposed under section 182 or 183 of this chapter with respect to any person is liable to such person as provided in section 130.

(b) Any lessor who fails to comply with any requirement imposed under section 184 of this chapter with respect to any person who suffers actual damage from the violation is liable to such person as provided in section 130. For the purposes of this section, the term "creditor" as used in sections 130 and 131 shall include a lessor as defined in this chapter.

(c) Notwithstanding section 130(e), any action under this section may be brought in any United States district court or in any other court of competent jurisdiction. Such actions alleging a failure to disclose or otherwise comply with the requirements of this chapter shall be brought within one year of the termination of the lease agreement.

§ 186. Relation to State laws [15 U.S.C. § 1667e]

(a) This chapter does not annul, alter, or affect, or exempt any person subject to the provisions of this chapter from complying with, the laws of any State with respect to consumer leases, except to the extent that those laws are inconsistent with any provision of this chapter, and then only to the extent of the inconsistency. The Board is authorized to determine whether such inconsistencies exist. The Board may not determine that any State law is inconsistent with any provision of this chapter if the Board determines that such law gives greater protection and benefit to the consumer.

(b) The Board shall by regulation exempt from the requirements of this chapter any class of lease transactions with any State if it determines that under the law of that State that class of transactions is subject to requirements substantially similar to those imposed under this chapter or that such law gives greater protection and benefit to the consumer, and that there is adequate provision for enforcement.

*

TITLE III. RESTRICTION ON GARNISHMENT

(15 U.S.C. §§ 1671–1677)

Table of Sections

---

§ 301. Findings [15 U.S.C. § 1671]

(a) The Congress finds:

(1) The unrestricted garnishment of compensation due for personal services encourages the making of predatory extensions of credit. Such extensions of credit divert money into excessive credit payments and thereby hinder the production and flow of goods in interstate commerce.

(2) The application of garnishment as a creditors' remedy frequently results in loss of employment by the debtor, and the resulting disruption of employment, production, and consumption constitutes a substantial burden on interstate commerce.

(3) The great disparities among the laws of the several States relating to garnishment have, in effect, destroyed the uniformity of the bankruptcy laws and frustrated the purposes thereof in many areas of the country.

(b) On the basis of the findings stated in subsection (a) of this section, the Congress determines that the provisions of this title are necessary and proper for the purpose of carrying into execution the powers of the Congress to regulate commerce and to establish uniform bankruptcy laws.

§ 302. Definitions [15 U.S.C. § 1672]

For the purposes of this title:

(a) The term "earnings" means compensation paid or payable for personal services, whether denominated as wages, salary, commission, bonus, or otherwise, and includes periodic payments pursuant to a pension or retirement program.

(b) The term "disposable earnings" means that part of the earnings of any individual remaining after the deduction from those earnings of any amounts required by law to be withheld.

(c) The term "garnishment" means any legal or equitable procedure through which the earnings of any individual are required to be withheld for payment of any debt.

§ 303. Restriction on garnishment [15 U.S.C. § 1673]

(a) Except as provided in subsection (b) of this section and in section 305, the maximum part of the aggregate disposable earnings of an individual for any workweek which is subjected to garnishment may not exceed

(1) 25 per centum of his disposable earnings for that week, or

(2) the amount by which his disposable earnings for that week exceed thirty times the Federal minimum hourly wage prescribed by section 6(a)(1) of the Fair Labor Standards Act of 1938 in effect at the time the earnings are payable,

whichever is less. In the case of earnings for any pay period other than a week, the Secretary of Labor shall by regulation prescribe a multiple of the Federal minimum hourly wage equivalent in effect to that set forth in paragraph (2).

(b)(1) The restrictions of subsection (a) of this section do not apply in the case of

(A) any order for the support of any person issued by a court of competent jurisdiction or in accordance with an administrative procedure, which is established by State law, which affords substantial due process, and which is subject to judicial review.

(B) any order of any court of the United States having jurisdiction over cases under chapter 13 of Title 11.

(C) any debt due for any State or Federal tax.

(2) The maximum part of the aggregate disposable earnings of an individual for any workweek which is subject to garnishment to enforce any order for the support of any person shall not exceed—

(A) where such individual is supporting his spouse or dependent child (other than a spouse or child with respect to whose support such order is used), 50 per centum of such individual's disposable earnings for that week; and

(B) where such individual is not supporting such a spouse or dependent child described in clause (A), 60 per centum of such individual's disposable earnings for that week;

except that, with respect to the disposable earnings of any individual for any workweek, the 50 per centum specified in clause (A) shall be deemed to be 55 per centum and the 60 per centum specified in clause

(B) shall be deemed to be 65 per centum, if and to the extent that such earnings are subject to garnishment to enforce a support order with respect to a period which is prior to the twelve-week period which ends with the beginning of such workweek.

(c) No court of the United States or any State, and no State (or officer or agency thereof), may make, execute, or enforce any order or process in violation of this section.

§ 304. Restriction on discharge from employment by reason of garnishment [15 U.S.C. § 1674]

(a) No employer may discharge any employee by reason of the fact that his earnings have been subjected to garnishment for any one indebtedness.

(b) Whoever willfully violates subsection (a) of this section shall be fined not more than $1,000, or imprisoned not more than one year, or both

§ 305. Exemption for State-regulated garnishments [15 U.S.C. § 1675]

The Secretary of Labor may by regulation exempt from the provisions of section 303(a) and (b)(2) of this title garnishments issued under the laws of any State if he determines that the laws of that State provide restrictions on garnishment which are substantially similar to those provided in section 303(a) and (b)(2).

§ 306. Enforcement by Secretary of Labor [15 U.S.C. § 1676]

The Secretary of Labor, acting through the Wage and Hour Division of the Department of Labor, shall enforce the provisions of this title.

§ 307. Effect on State laws [15 U.S.C. § 1677]

This title does not annul, alter, or affect, or exempt any person from complying with, the laws of any State

(1) prohibiting garnishments or providing for more limited garnishments than are allowed under this title, or

(2) prohibiting the discharge of any employee by reason of the fact that his earnings have been subjected to garnishment for more than one indebtedness.

*

TITLE VI. FAIR CREDIT REPORTING ACT

(15 U.S.C. §§ 1681–1681t)

Table of Sections

---

§ 601. Short title

This title may be cited as the Fair Credit Reporting Act.

§ 602. Findings and purpose [15 U.S.C. § 1681]

(a) The Congress makes the following findings:

(1) The banking system is dependent upon fair and accurate credit reporting. Inaccurate credit reports directly impair the efficiency of the banking system, and unfair credit reporting methods undermine the public confidence which is essential to the continued functioning of the banking system.

(2) An elaborate mechanism has been developed for investigating and evaluating the credit worthiness, credit standing, credit capacity, character, and general reputation of consumers.

(3) Consumer reporting agencies have assumed a vital role in assembling and evaluating consumer credit and other information on consumers.

(4) There is a need to insure that consumer reporting agencies exercise their grave responsibilities with fairness, impartiality, and a respect for the consumer's right to privacy.

(b) It is the purpose of this title to require that consumer reporting agencies adopt reasonable procedures for meeting the needs of commerce for consumer credit, personnel, insurance, and other information in a manner which is fair and equitable to the consumer, with regard to the confidentiality, accuracy, relevancy, and proper utilization of such information in accordance with the requirements of this title.

§ 603. Definitions and rules of construction [15 U.S.C. § 1681a]

(a) Definitions and rules of construction set forth in this section are applicable for the purposes of this title.

(b) The term "person" means any individual, partnership, corporation, trust, estate, cooperative, association, government or governmental subdivision or agency, or other entity.

(c) The term "consumer" means an individual.

(d) The term "consumer report" means any written, oral, or other communication of any information by a consumer reporting agency bearing on a consumer's credit worthiness, credit standing, credit capacity, character, general reputation, personal characteristics, or mode of living which is used or expected to be used or collected in whole or in part for the purpose of serving as a factor in establishing the consumer's eligibility for (1) credit or insurance to be used primarily for personal, family, or household purposes, or (2) employment purposes, or (3) other purposes authorized under section 604. The term does not include (A) any report containing information solely as to transactions or experiences between the consumer and the person making the report; (B) any authorization or approval of a specific extension of credit directly or indirectly by the issuer of a credit card or similar device; or (C) any report in which a person who has been requested by a third party to make a specific extension of credit directly or indirectly to a consumer conveys his decision with respect to such request, if the third party advises the consumer of the name and address of the person to whom the request was made and such person makes the disclosures to the consumer required under section 615.

(e) The term "investigative consumer report" means a consumer report or portion thereof in which information on a consumer's character, general reputation, personal characteristics, or mode of living is obtained through personal interviews with neighbors, friends, or associates of the consumer reported on or with others with whom he is acquainted or who may have knowledge concerning any such items of information. However, such information shall not include specific factual information on a consumer's credit record obtained directly from a creditor of the consumer or from a consumer reporting agency when such information was obtained directly from a creditor of the consumer or from the consumer.

(f) The term "consumer reporting agency" means any person which, for monetary fees, dues, or on a cooperative nonprofit basis, regularly engages in whole or in part in the practice of assembling or evaluating consumer credit information or other information on consumers for the purpose of furnishing consumer reports to third parties, and which uses any means or facility of interstate commerce for the purpose of preparing or furnishing consumer reports.

(g) The term "file", when used in connection with information on any consumer, means all of the information on that consumer recorded and retained by a consumer reporting agency regardless of how the information is stored.

(h) The term "employment purposes" when used in connection with a consumer report means a report used for the purpose of evaluating a consumer for employment, promotion, reassignment or retention as an employee.

(i) The term "medical information" means information or records obtained, with the consent of the individual to whom it relates, from licensed physicians or medical practitioners, hospitals, clinics, or other medical or medically related facilities.

§ 604. Permissible purposes of reports [15 U.S.C. § 1681b]

A consumer reporting agency may furnish a consumer report under the following circumstances and no other:

(1) In response to the order of a court having jurisdiction to issue such an order.

(2) In accordance with the written instructions of the consumer to whom it relates.

(3) To a person which it has reason to believe—

(A) intends to use the information in connection with a credit transaction involving the consumer on whom the information is to be furnished and involving the extension of credit to, or review or collection of an account of, the consumer; or

(B) intends to use the information for employment purposes; or

(C) intends to use the information in connection with the underwriting of insurance involving the consumer; or

(D) intends to use the information in connection with a determination of the consumer's eligibility for a license or other benefit granted by a governmental instrumentality required by law to consider an applicant's financial responsibility or status; or

(E) otherwise has a legitimate business need for the information in connection with a business transaction involving the consumer.

§ 605. Obsolete information [15 U.S.C. § 1681c]

(a) Except as authorized under subsection (b) of this section, no consumer reporting agency may make any consumer report containing any of the following items of information:

(1) Cases under Title 11 or under the Bankruptcy Act that, from the date of entry of the order for relief or the date of adjudication, as the case may be, antedate the report by more than 10 years.

(2) Suits and judgments which, from date of entry, antedate the report by more than seven years or until the governing statute of limitations has expired, whichever is the longer period.

(3) Paid tax liens which, from date of payment, antedate the report by more than seven years.

(4) Accounts placed for collection or charged to profit and loss which antedate the report by more than seven years.

(5) Records of arrest, indictment, or conviction of crime which, from date of disposition, release, or parole, antedate the report by more than seven years.

(6) Any other adverse item of information which antedates the report by more than seven years.

(b) The provisions of subsection (a) of this section are not applicable in the case of any consumer credit report to be used in connection with—

(1) a credit transaction involving, or which may reasonably be expected to involve, a principal amount of $50,000 or more;

(2) the underwriting of life insurance involving, or which may reasonably be expected to involve, a face amount of $50,000 or more; or

(3) the employment of any individual at an annual salary which equals, or which may reasonably be expected to equal $20,000, or more.

§ 606. Disclosure of investigative consumer reports [15 U.S.C. § 1681d]

(a) A person may not procure or cause to be prepared an investigative consumer report on any consumer unless—

(1) it is clearly and accurately disclosed to the consumer that an investigative consumer report including information as to his character, general reputation, personal characteristics, and mode of living, whichever are applicable, may be made, and such disclosure (A) is

made in a writing mailed, or otherwise delivered, to the consumer, not later than three days after the date on which the report was first requested, and (B) includes a statement informing the consumer of his right to request the additional disclosures provided for under subsection (b) of this section; or

(2) the report is to be used for employment purposes for which the consumer has not specifically applied.

(b) Any person who procures or causes to be prepared an investigative consumer report on any consumer shall, upon written request made by the consumer within a reasonable period of time after the receipt by him of the disclosure required by subsection (a)(1) of this section, make a complete and accurate disclosure of the nature and scope of the investigation requested. This disclosure shall be made in a writing mailed, or otherwise delivered, to the consumer not later than five days after the date on which the request for such disclosure was received from the consumer or such report was first requested, whichever is the later.

(c) No person may be held liable for any violation of subsection (a) or (b) of this section if he shows by a preponderance of the evidence that at the time of the violation he maintained reasonable procedures to assure compliance with subsection (a) or (b) of this section.

§ 607. Compliance procedures [15 U.S.C. § 1681e]

(a) Every consumer reporting agency shall maintain reasonable procedures designed to avoid violations of section 1681c of this title and to limit the furnishing of consumer reports to the purposes listed under section 1681b of this title. These procedures shall require that prospective users of the information identify themselves, certify the purposes for which the information is sought, and certify that the information will be used for no other purpose. Every consumer reporting agency shall make a reasonable effort to verify the identity of a new prospective user and the uses certified by such prospective user prior to furnishing such user a consumer report. No consumer reporting agency may furnish a consumer report to any person if it has reasonable grounds for believing that the consumer report will not be used for a purpose listed in section 604.

(b) Whenever a consumer reporting agency prepares a consumer report it shall follow reasonable procedures to assure maximum possible accuracy of the information concerning the individual about whom the report relates.

§ 608. Disclosures to governmental agencies [15 U.S.C. § 1681f]

Notwithstanding the provisions of section 604, a consumer reporting agency may furnish identifying information respecting any consumer, limited to his name, address, former addresses, places of employment, or former places of employment, to a governmental agency.

§ 609. Disclosures to consumers [15 U.S.C. § 1681g]

(a) Every consumer reporting agency shall, upon request and proper identification of any consumer, clearly and accurately disclose to the consumer:

(1) The nature and substance of all information (except medical information) in its files on the consumer at the time of the request.

(2) The sources of the information; except that the sources of information acquired solely for use in preparing an investigative consumer report and actually used for no other purpose need not be disclosed: *Provided*, That in the event an action is brought under this subchapter, such sources shall be available to the plaintiff under appropriate discovery procedures in the court in which the action is brought.

(3) The recipients of any consumer report on the consumer which it has furnished—

(A) for employment purposes within the two-year period preceding the request, and

(B) for any other purpose within the six-month period preceding the request.

(b) The requirements of subsection (a) of this section respecting the disclosure of sources of information and the recipients of consumer reports do not apply to information received or consumer reports furnished prior to the effective date of this subchapter except to the extent that the matter involved is contained in the files of the consumer reporting agency on that date.

§ 610. Conditions of disclosure to consumers [15 U.S.C. § 1681h]

(a) A consumer reporting agency shall make the disclosures required under section 609 during normal business hours and on reasonable notice.

(b) The disclosures required under section 609 shall be made to the consumer—

(1) in person if he appears in person and furnishes proper identification; or

(2) by telephone if he has made a written request, with proper identification, for telephone disclosure and the toll charge, if any, for the telephone call is prepaid by or charged directly to the consumer.

(c) Any consumer reporting agency shall provide trained personnel to explain to the consumer any information furnished to him pursuant to section 609.

(d) The consumer shall be permitted to be accompanied by one other person of his choosing, who shall furnish reasonable identification. A consumer reporting agency may require the consumer to furnish a written statement granting permission to the consumer reporting agency to discuss the consumer's file in such person's presence.

(e) Except as provided in sections 616 and 617, no consumer may bring any action or proceeding in the nature of defamation, invasion of privacy, or negligence with respect to the reporting of information against any consumer reporting agency, any user of information, or any person who furnishes information to a consumer reporting agency, based on information disclosed pursuant to section 609, 610, or 615, except as to false information furnished with malice or willful intent to injure such consumer.

§ 611. Procedure in case of disputed accuracy [15 U.S.C. § 1681i]

(a) If the completeness or accuracy of any item of information contained in his file is disputed by a consumer, and such dispute is directly conveyed to the consumer reporting agency by the consumer, the consumer reporting agency shall within a reasonable period of time reinvestigate and record the current status of that information unless it has reasonable grounds to believe that the dispute by the consumer is frivolous or irrelevant. If after such reinvestigation such information is found to be inaccurate or can no longer be verified, the consumer reporting agency shall promptly delete such information. The presence of contradictory information in the consumer's file does not in and of itself constitute reasonable grounds for believing the dispute is frivolous or irrelevant.

(b) If the reinvestigation does not resolve the dispute, the consumer may file a brief statement setting forth the nature of the dispute. The consumer reporting agency may limit such statements to not more than one hundred words if it provides the consumer with assistance in writing a clear summary of the dispute.

(c) Whenever a statement of a dispute is filed, unless there is reasonable grounds to believe that it is frivolous or irrelevant, the consumer reporting agency shall, in any subsequent consumer report containing the information in question, clearly note that it is disputed by the consumer and provide either the consumer's statement or a clear and accurate codification or summary thereof.

(d) Following any deletion of information which is found to be inaccurate or whose accuracy can no longer be verified or any notation as to disputed information, the consumer reporting agency shall, at the request of the consumer, furnish notification that the item has been deleted or the statement codification or summary pursuant to subsection (b) or (c) of this section to any person specifically designated by the consumer who has within two years prior thereto received a consumer report for employment purposes, or within six months prior thereto received a consumer report for any other purpose, which contained the deleted or disputed information. The consumer reporting agency shall clearly and conspicuously disclose to the consumer his rights to make such a request. Such disclosure shall be made at or prior to the time the information is deleted or the consumer's statement regarding the disputed information is received.

§ 612. Charges for certain disclosures [15 U.S.C. § 1681j]

A consumer reporting agency shall make all disclosures pursuant to section 609 and furnish all consumer reports pursuant to section 611d without charge to the consumer if, within thirty days after receipt by such consumer of a notification pursuant to section 615 of this title or notification from a debt collection agency affiliated with such consumer reporting agency stating that the consumer's credit rating may be or has been adversely affected, the consumer makes a request under section 609 or 611(d). Otherwise, the consumer reporting agency may impose a reasonable charge on the consumer for making disclosure to such consumer pursuant to section 609, the charge for which shall be indicated to the consumer prior to making disclosure; and for furnishing notifications, statements, summaries, or codifications to person designated by the consumer pursuant to section 611(d), the charge for which shall be indicated to the consumer prior to furnishing such information and shall not exceed the charge that the consumer reporting agency would impose on each designated recipient for a consumer report except that no charge may be made for notifying such persons of the deletion of information which is found to be inaccurate or which can no longer be verified.

§ 613. Public record information for employment purposes [15 U.S.C. § 1681k]

A consumer reporting agency which furnishes a consumer report for employment purposes and which for that purpose compiles and reports items of information on consumers which are matters of public record and are likely to have an adverse effect upon a consumer's ability to obtain employment shall—

(1) at the time such public record information is reported to the user of such consumer report, notify the consumer of the fact that public record information is being reported by the consumer reporting agency, together with the name and address of the person to whom such information is being reported; or

(2) maintain strict procedures designed to insure that whenever public record information which is likely to have an adverse effect on a consumer's ability to obtain employment is reported it is complete and up to date. For purposes of this paragraph, items of public rec-

ord relating to arrests, indictments, convictions, suits, tax liens, and outstanding judgments shall be considered up to date if the current public record status of the item at the time of the report is reported.

§ 614. Restrictions on investigative consumer reports [15 U.S.C. § 1681*l*]

Whenever a consumer reporting agency prepares an investigative consumer report, no adverse information in the consumer report (other than information which is a matter of public record) may be included in a subsequent consumer report unless such adverse information has been verified in the process of making such subsequent consumer report, or the adverse information was received within the three-month period preceding the date the subsequent report is furnished.

§ 615. Requirements on users of consumer reports [15 U.S.C. § 1681m]

(a) Whenever credit or insurance for personal, family, or household purposes, or employment involving a consumer is denied or the charge for such credit or insurance is increased either wholly or partly because of information contained in a consumer report from a consumer reporting agency, the user of the consumer report shall so advise the consumer against whom such adverse action has been taken and supply the name and address of the consumer reporting agency making the report.

(b) Whenever credit for personal, family, or household purposes involving a consumer is denied or the charge for such credit is increased either wholly or partly because of information obtained from a person other than a consumer reporting agency bearing upon the consumer's credit worthiness, credit standing, credit capacity, character, general reputation, personal characteristics, or mode of living, the user of such information shall, within a reasonable period of time, upon the consumer's written request for the reasons for such adverse action received within sixty days after learning of such adverse action, disclose the nature of the information to the consumer. The user of such information shall clearly and accurately disclose to the consumer his right to make such written request at the time such adverse action is communicated to the consumer.

(c) No person shall be held liable for any violation of this section if he shows by a preponderance of the evidence that at the time of the alleged violation he maintained reasonable procedures to assure compliance with the provisions of subsections (a) and (b) of this section.

§ 616. Civil liability for willful noncompliance [15 U.S.C. § 1681n]

Any consumer reporting agency or user of information which willfully fails to comply with any requirement imposed under this title with respect to any consumer is liable to that consumer in an amount equal to the sum of—

(1) any actual damages sustained by the consumer as a result of the failure;

(2) such amount of punitive damages as the court may allow; and

(3) in the case of any successful action to enforce any liability under this section, the costs of the action together with reasonable attorney's fees as determined by the court.

§ 617. Civil liability for negligent noncompliance [15 U.S.C. § 1681*o*]

Any consumer reporting agency or user of information which is negligent in failing to comply with any requirement imposed under this title with respect to any consumer is liable to that consumer in an amount equal to the sum of—

(1) any actual damages sustained by the consumer as a result of the failure;

(2) in the case of any successful action to enforce any liability under this section, the costs of the action together with reasonable attorney's fees as determined by the court.

§ 618. Jurisdiction of courts; limitation of actions [15 U.S.C. § 1681p]

An action to enforce any liability created under this title may be brought in any appropriate United States district court without regard to the amount in controversy, or in any other court of competent jurisdiction, within two years from the date on which the liability arises, except that where a defendant has materially and willfully misrepresented any information required under this title to be disclosed to an individual and the information so misrepresented is material to the establishment of the defendant's liability to that individual under this title, the action may be brought at any time within two years after discovery by the individual of the misrepresentation.

§ 619. Obtaining information under false pretenses [15 U.S.C. § 1681q]

Any person who knowingly and willfully obtains information on a consumer from a consumer reporting agency under false pretenses shall be fined not more than $5,000 or imprisoned not more than one year, or both.

§ 620. Unauthorized disclosures by officers or employees [15 U.S.C. § 1681r]

Any officer or employee of a consumer reporting agency who knowingly and willfully provides information concerning an individual from the agency's files to a person not authorized to receive that information shall be fined not more than $5,000 or imprisoned not more than one year, or both.

§ 621. Administrative enforcement [15 U.S.C. § 1681s]

(a) Compliance with the requirements imposed under this title shall be enforced under the Federal Trade Commission Act by the Federal Trade Commission with respect to consumer reporting agencies and all other persons subject thereto, except to the extent that enforcement of the requirements imposed under this title is specifically committed to some other government agency under subsection (b) hereof. For the purpose of the exercise by the Federal Trade Commission of its functions and powers under the Federal Trade Commission Act, a violation of any requirement or prohibition imposed under this title shall constitute an unfair or deceptive act or practice in commerce in violation of section 5(a) of the Federal Trade Commission Act and shall be subject to enforcement by the Federal Trade Commission under section 5(b) thereof with respect to any consumer reporting agency or person subject to enforcement by the Federal Trade Commission pursuant to this subsection, irrespective of whether that person is engaged in commerce or meets any other jurisdictional tests in the Federal Trade Commission Act. The Federal Trade Commission shall have such procedural, investigative, and enforcement powers, including the power to issue procedural rules in enforcing compliance with the requirements imposed under this title and to require the filing of reports, the production of documents, and the appearance of witnesses as though the applicable terms and conditions of the Federal Trade Commission Act were part of this title. Any person violating any of the provisions of this title shall be subject to the penalties and entitled to the privileges and immunities provided in the Federal Trade Commission Act as though the applicable terms and provisions thereof were part of this title.

(b) Compliance with the requirements imposed under this title with respect to consumer reporting agencies and persons who use consumer reports from such agencies shall be enforced under—

(1) section 8 of the Federal Deposit Insurance Act, in the case of:

(A) national banks, by the Comptroller of the Currency;

(B) member banks of the Federal Reserve System (other than national banks), by the Federal Reserve Board; and

(C) banks insured by the Federal Deposit Insurance Corporation (other than members of the Federal Reserve System), by the Board of Directors of the Federal Deposit Insurance Corporation.

(2) section 5(d) of the Home Owners Loan Act of 1933, section 407 of the National Housing Act, and sections 6(i) and 17 of the Federal Home Loan Bank Act, by the Federal Home Loan Bank Board (acting directly or through the Federal Savings and Loan Insurance Corporation), in the case of any institution subject to any of those provisions;

(3) the Federal Credit Union Act, by the Administrator of the National Credit Union Administration with respect to any Federal credit union;

(4) the Acts to regulate commerce, by the Interstate Commerce Commission with respect to any common carrier subject to those Acts;

(5) the Federal Aviation Act of 1958, by the Civil Aeronautics Board with respect to any air carrier or foreign air carrier subject to that Act; and

(6) the Packers and Stockyards Act, 1921 (except as provided in section 406 of that Act), by the Secretary of Agriculture with respect to any activities subject to that Act.

(c) For the purpose of the exercise by any agency referred to in subsection (b) of this section of its powers under any Act referred to in that subsection, a violation of any requirement imposed under this title shall be deemed to be a violation of a requirement imposed under that Act. In addition to its powers under any provision of law specifically referred to in subsection (b) of this section, each of the agencies referred to in that subsection may exercise, for the purpose of enforcing compliance with any requirement imposed under this title any other authority conferred on it by law.

§ 622. Relation to State laws [15 U.S.C. § 1681t]

This title does not annul, alter, affect, or exempt any person subject to the provisions of this subchapter from complying with the laws of any State with respect to the collection, distribution, or use of any information on consumers, except to the extent that those laws are inconsistent with any provision of this title and then only to the extent of the inconsistency.

TITLE VII. EQUAL CREDIT OPPORTUNITY ACT

(15 U.S.C. §§ 1691–1691f)

Table of Sections

---

§ 701. Prohibited discrimination; reasons for adverse action [15 U.S.C. § 1691]

(a) It shall be unlawful for any creditor to discriminate against any applicant, with respect to any aspect of a credit transaction—

(1) on the basis of race, color, religion, national origin, sex or marital status, or age (provided the applicant has the capacity to contract);

(2) because all or part of the applicant's income derives from any public assistance program; or

(3) because the applicant has in good faith exercised any right under this chapter.

(b) It shall not constitute discrimination for purposes of this title for a creditor—

(1) to make an inquiry of marital status if such inquiry is for the purpose of ascertaining the creditor's rights and remedies applicable to the particular extension of credit and not to discriminate in a determination of credit-worthiness;

(2) to make an inquiry of the applicant's age or of whether the applicant's income derives from any public assistance program if such inquiry is for the purpose of determining the amount and probable continuance of income levels, credit history, or other pertinent element of credit-worthiness as provided in regulations of the Board;

(3) to use any empirically derived credit system which considers age if such system is demonstrably and statistically sound in accordance with regulations of the Board, except that in the operation of

such system the age of an elderly applicant may not be assigned a negative factor or value; or

(4) to make an inquiry or to consider the age of an elderly applicant when the age of such applicant is to be used by the creditor in the extension of credit in favor of such applicant.

(c) It is not a violation of this section for a creditor to refuse to extend credit offered pursuant to—

(1) any credit assistance program expressly authorized by law for an economically disadvantaged class of persons;

(2) any credit assistance program administered by a nonprofit organization for its members or an economically disadvantaged class of persons; or

(3) any special purpose credit program offered by a profit-making organization to meet special social needs which meets standards prescribed in regulations by the Board;

if such refusal is required by or made pursuant to such program.

(d)(1) Within thirty days (or such longer reasonable time as specified in regulations of the Board for any class of credit transaction) after receipt of a completed application for credit, a creditor shall notify the applicant of its action on the application.

(2) Each applicant against whom adverse action is taken shall be entitled to a statement of reasons for such action from the creditor. A creditor satisfies this obligation by—

(A) providing statements of reasons in writing as a matter of course to applicants against whom adverse action is taken; or

(B) giving written notification of adverse action which discloses (i) the applicant's right to a statement of reasons within thirty days after receipt by the creditor of a request made within sixty days after such notification, and (ii) the identity of the person or office from which such statement may be obtained. Such statement may be given orally if the written notification advises the applicant of his right to have the statement of reasons confirmed in writing on written request.

(3) A statement of reasons meets the requirements of this section only if it contains the specific reasons for the adverse action taken.

(4) Where a creditor has been requested by a third party to make a specific extension of credit directly or indirectly to an applicant, the notification and statement of reasons required by this subsection may be made directly by such creditor, or indirectly through the third party, provided in either case that the identity of the creditor is disclosed.

(5) The requirements of paragraph (2), (3), or (4) may be satisfied by verbal statements or notifications in the case of any creditor who did not act on more than one hundred and fifty applications during

the calender year preceding the calender year in which the adverse action is taken, as determined under regulations of the Board.

(6) For purposes of this subsection, the term "adverse action" means a denial or revocation of credit, a change in the terms of an existing credit arrangement, or a refusal to grant credit in substantially the amount or on substantially the terms requested. Such term does not include a refusal to extend additional credit under an existing credit arrangement where the applicant is delinquent or otherwise in default, or where such additional credit would exceed a previously established credit limit.

§ 702. Definitions [15 U.S.C. § 1691a]

(a) The definitions and rules of construction set forth in this section are applicable for the purposes of this title.

(b) The term "applicant" means any person who applies to a creditor directly for an extension, renewal, or continuation of credit, or applies to a creditor indirectly by use of an existing credit plan for an amount exceeding a previously established credit limit.

(c) The term "Board" refers to the Board of Governors of the Federal Reserve System.

(d) The term "credit" means the right granted by a creditor to a debtor to defer payment of debt or to incur debts and defer its payment or to purchase property or services and defer payment therefor.

(e) The term "creditor" means any person who regularly extends, renews, or continues credit; any person who regularly arranges for the extension, renewal, or continuation of credit; or any assignee of an original creditor who participates in the decision to extend, renew, or continue credit.

(f) The term "person" means a natural person, a corporation, government or governmental subdivision or agency, trust, estate, partnership, cooperative, or association.

(g) Any reference to any requirement imposed under this title or any provision thereof includes reference to the regulations of the Board under this title or the provision thereof in question.

§ 703. Regulations [15 U.S.C. § 1691b]

(a) The Board shall prescribe regulations to carry out the purposes of this title. These regulations may contain but are not limited to such classifications, differentiation, or other provision, and may provide for such adjustments and exceptions for any class of transactions, as in the judgment of the Board are necessary or proper to effectuate the purposes of this title, to prevent circumvention or evasion thereof, or to facilitate or substantiate compliance therewith. In particular, such regulations may exempt from one or more of the provisions of this subchapter any class of transactions not primarily for personal, family, or household purposes, if the Board makes an express finding that the application of such provision or provisions would not contribute substantially to carrying out the purposes of this title. Such regulations shall be prescribed as soon as possible after the date of enactment of this Act, but in no event later than the effective date of this Act.

(b) The Board shall establish a Consumer Advisory Council to advise and consult with it in the exercise of its functions under the Consumer Credit Protection Act and to advise and consult with it concerning other consumer related matters it may place before the Council. In appointing the members of the Council, the Board shall seek to achieve a fair representation of the interests of creditors and consumers. The Council shall meet from time to time at the call of the Board. Members of the Council who are not regular full-time employees of the United States shall, while attending meetings of such Council, be entitled to receive compensation at a rate fixed by the Board, but not exceeding $100 per day, including travel time. Such members may be allowed travel expenses, including transportation and subsistence, while away from their homes or regular place of business.

§ 704. Administrative enforcement [15 U.S.C. § 1691c]

(a) Compliance with the requirements imposed under this title shall be enforced under:

(1) Section 8 of the Federal Deposit Insurance Act, in the case of—

(A) national banks, by the Comptroller of the Currency,

(B) member banks of the Federal Reserve System (other than national banks), by the Board,

(C) banks insured by the Federal Deposit Insurance Corporation (other than members of the Federal Reserve System), by the Board of Directors of the Federal Deposit Insurance Corporation.

(2) Section 5(d) of the Home Owners' Loan Act of 1933, section 407 of National Housing Act, and sections 6(i) and 17 of the Federal Home Loan Bank Act, by the Federal Home Loan Bank Board (acting directly or through the Federal Savings and Loan Insurance Corporation), in the case of any institution subject to any of those provisions.

(3) The Federal Credit Union Act, by the Administrator of the National Credit Union Administration with respect to any Federal Credit Union.

(4) The Acts to regulate commerce, by the Interstate Commerce Commission with respect to any common carrier subject to those Acts.

(5) The Federal Aviation Act of 1958, by the Civil Aeronautics Board with respect to any air carrier or foreign air carrier subject to that Act.

(6) The Packers and Stockyards Act, 1921 (except as provided in section 406 of that Act), by the Secretary of Agriculture with respect to any activities subject to that Act.

(7) The Farm Credit Act of 1971, by the Farm Credit Administration with respect to any Federal land bank, Federal land bank association, Federal intermediate credit bank, and production credit association;

(8) The Securities Exchange Act of 1934, by the Securities and Exchange Commission with respect to brokers and dealers; and

(9) The Small Business Investment Act of 1958, by the Small Business Administration, with respect to small business investment companies.

(b) For the purpose of the exercise by any agency referred to in subsection (a) of this section of its powers under any Act referred to in that subsection, a violation of any requirement imposed under this title shall be deemed to be a violation of a requirement imposed under that Act. In addition to its powers under any provision of law specifically referred to in subsection (a) of this section, each of the agencies referred to in that subsection may exercise for the purpose of enforcing compliance with any requirement imposed under this title, any other authority conferred on it by law. The exercise of the authorities of any of the agencies referred to in subsection (a) of this section for the purpose of enforcing compliance with any requirement imposed under this title shall in no way preclude the exercise of such authorities for the purpose of enforcing compliance with any other provision of law not relating to the prohibition of discrimination on the basis of sex or marital status with respect to any aspect of a credit transaction.

(c) Except to the extent that enforcement of the requirements imposed under this title is specifically committed to some other Government agency under subsection (a) of this section, the Federal Trade Commission shall enforce such requirements. For the purpose of the exercise by the Federal Trade Commission of its functions and powers under the Federal Trade Commission Act, a violation of any requirement imposed under this title shall be deemed a violation of a requirement imposed under that Act. All of the functions and powers of the Federal Trade Commission under the Federal Trade Commission Act are available to the Commission to enforce compliance by any person with the requirements imposed under this title, irrespective of whether that person is engaged in commerce or meets any other jurisdictional tests in the Federal Trade Commission Act, including the power to enforce any Federal Reserve Board regulation promulgated under this title in the same manner as if the violation had been a violation of a Federal Trade Commission trade regulation rule.

(d) The authority of the Board to issue regulations under this title does not impair the authority of any other agency designated in this section to make rules respecting its own procedures in enforcing compliance with requirements imposed under this title.

§ 705. Relation to State laws [15 U.S.C. § 1691d]

(a) A request for the signature of both parties to a marriage for the purpose of creating a valid lien, passing clear title, waiving inchoate rights to property, or assigning earnings, shall not constitute discrimination under this title: *Provided, however,* That this provision shall not be construed to permit a creditor to take sex or marital status into account in connection with the evaluation of creditworthiness of any applicant.

(b) Consideration or application of State property laws directly or indirectly affecting creditworthiness shall not constitute discrimination for purposes of this title.

(c) Any provision of State law which prohibits the separate extension of consumer credit to each party to a marriage shall not apply in any case where each party to a marriage voluntarily applies for separate credit from the same creditor: *Provided,* That in any case where such a State law is so preempted, each party to the marriage shall be solely responsible for the debt so contracted.

(d) When each party to a marriage separately and voluntarily applies for and obtains separate credit accounts with the same creditor, those accounts shall not be aggregated or otherwise combined for purposes of determining permissible finance charges or permissible loan ceilings under the laws of any State or of the United States.

(e) Where the same act or omission constitutes a violation of this title and of applicable State law, a person aggrieved by such conduct may bring a legal action to recover monetary damages either under this title or under such State law, but not both. This election of remedies shall not apply to court actions in which the relief sought does not include monetary damages or to administrative actions.

(f) This title does not annul, alter, or affect, or exempt any person subject to the provisions of this title from complying with, the laws of any State with respect to credit discrimination, except to the extent that those laws are inconsistent with any provision of this title, and then only to the extent of the inconsistency. The Board is authorized to determine whether such inconsistencies exist. The Board may not determine that any State law is inconsistent with any provision of this title if the Board determines that such law gives greater protection to the applicant.

(g) The Board shall by regulation exempt from the requirements of sections 701 and 702 any class of credit transactions within any State if it determines that under the law of that State that class of transactions is subject to requirements substantially similar to those imposed under this title or that such law gives greater protection to the applicant, and that there is adequate provision for enforcement. Failure to comply with any requirement of such State law in any transaction so exempted shall constitute a violation of this title for the purposes of section 706.

§ 706. Civil liability [15 U.S.C. § 1691e]

(a) Any creditor who fails to comply with any requirement imposed under this title shall be liable to the aggrieved applicant for any actual damages sustained by such applicant acting either in an individual capacity or as a member of a class.

(b) Any creditor, other than a government or governmental subdivision or agency, who fails to comply with any requirement imposed under this title shall be liable to the aggrieved applicant for punitive damages in an amount not greater than $10,000, in addition to any actual damages provided in subsection (a) of this section, except that in the case of a class action the total recovery under this subsection shall not exceed the lesser of $500,000 or 1 per centum of the net worth of the creditor. In determining the amount of such damages in any action, the court shall consider, among other relevant factors, the amount of any actual damages awarded, the frequency and persistance of failures of compliance by the creditor, the resources of the creditor, the number of persons adversely affected, and the extent to which the creditor's failure of compliance was intentional.

(c) Upon application by an aggrieved applicant, the appropriate United States district court or any other court of competent jurisdiction may grant such equitable and declaratory relief as is necessary to enforce the requirements imposed under this title.

(d) In the case of any successful action under subsection (a), (b), or (c) of this section, the costs of the action, together with a reasonable attorney's fee as determined by the court, shall be added to any damages awarded by the court under such subsection.

(e) No provision of this title imposing liability shall apply to any act done or omitted in good faith in conformity with any official rule, regulation, or interpretation thereof by the Board or in conformity with any interpretation or approval by an official or employee of the Federal Reserve System duly authorized by the Board to issue such interpretations or approvals under such procedures as the Board may prescribe therefor, notwithstanding that after such act or omission has occurred, such rule, regulation, interpretation, or approval is amended, rescinded, or determined by judicial or other authority to be invalid for any reason.

(f) Any action under this section may be brought in the appropriate United States district court without regard to the amount in controversy, or in any other court of competent jurisdiction. No such action shall be brought later than two years from the date of the occurrence of the violation, except that—

(1) whenever any agency having responsibility for administrative enforcement under section 704 commences an enforcement proceeding within two years from the date of the occurrence of the violation,

(2) whenever the Attorney General commences a civil action under this section within two years from the date of the occurrence of the violation,

then any applicant who has been a victim of the discrimination which is the subject of such proceeding or civil action may bring an action under this section not later than one year after the commencement of that proceeding or action.

(g) The agencies having responsibility for administrative enforcement under section 704, if unable to obtain compliance with section 701, are authorized to refer the matter to the Attorney General with a recommendation that an appropriate civil action be instituted.

(h) When a matter is referred to the Attorney General pursuant to subsection (g) of this section, or whenever he has reason to believe that one or more creditors are engaged in a pattern or practice in violation of this title, the Attorney General may bring a civil action in any appropriate United States district court for such relief as may be appropriate, including injunctive relief.

(i) No person aggrieved by a violation of this title and by a violation of section 805 of the Civil Rights Act of 1968 shall recover under this title and section 812 of the Civil Rights Act of 1968 if such violation is based on the same transaction.

(j) Nothing in this title shall be construed to prohibit the discovery of a creditor's credit granting standards under appropriate discovery procedures in the court or agency in which an action or proceeding is brought.

§ 707. Annual reports to Congress [15 U.S.C. § 1691f]

Each year, the Board and the Attorney General shall, respectively, make reports to the Congress concerning the administration of their functions under this title, including such recommendations as the Board and the Attorney General, respectively deem necessary or appropriate. In addition, each report of the Board shall include its assessment of the extent to which compliance with the requirements of this title is being achieved, and a summary of the enforcement actions taken by each of the agencies assigned administrative enforcement responsibilities under section 704.

§ 709. Short title

This title may be cited as the "Equal Credit Opportunity Act."

*

TITLE VIII. FAIR DEBT COLLECTION PRACTICES ACT

(15 U.S.C. §§ 1692–1692m)

Table of Sections

---

§ 801. Short title

This title may be cited as the "Fair Debt Collection Practices Act."

§ 802. Findings and purpose [15 U.S.C. § 1692]

(a) There is abundant evidence of the use of abusive, deceptive, and unfair debt collection practices by many debt collectors. Abusive debt collection practices contribute to the number of personal bankruptcies, to marital instability, to the loss of jobs, and to invasions of individual privacy.

(b) Existing laws and procedures for redressing these injuries are inadequate to protect consumers.

(c) Means other than misrepresentation or other abusive debt collection practices are available for the effective collection of debts.

(d) Abusive debt collection practices are carried on to a substantial extent in interstate commerce and through means and instrumentalities of such commerce. Even where abusive debt collection practices are purely intrastate in character, they nevertheless directly affect interstate commerce.

(e) It is the purpose of this title to eliminate abusive debt collection practices by debt collectors, to insure that those debt collectors who refrain from using abusive debt collection practices are not competitively disadvantaged, and to promote consistent State action to protect consumers against debt collection abuses.

§ 803. Definitions [15 U.S.C. § 1692a]

As used in this title—

(1) The term "Commission" means the Federal Trade Commission.

(2) The term "communication" means the conveying of information regarding a debt directly or indirectly to any person through any medium.

(3) The term "consumer" means any natural person obligated or allegedly obligated to pay any debt.

(4) The term "creditor" means any person who offers or extends credit creating a debt or to whom a debt is owed, but such term does not include any person to the extent that he receives an assignment or transfer of a debt in default solely for the purpose of facilitating collection of such debt for another.

(5) The term "debt" means any obligation or alleged obligation of a consumer to pay money arising out of a transaction in which the money, property, insurance, or services which are the subject of the transaction are primarily for personal, family, or household purposes, whether or not such obligation has been reduced to judgment.

(6) The term "debt collector" means any person who uses any instrumentality of interstate commerce or the mails in any business the principal purpose of which is the collection of any debts, or who regularly collects or attempts to collect, directly or indirectly, debts owed or due or asserted to be owed or due another. Notwithstanding the exclusion provided by clause (G) of the last sentence of this paragraph, the term includes any creditor who, in the process of collecting his own debts, uses any name other than his own which would indicate that a third person is collecting or attempting to collect such debts. For the purpose of section 808(6), such term also includes any person who uses any instrumentality of interstate commerce or the mails in any business the principal purpose of which is the enforcement of security interests. The term does not include—

(A) any officer or employee of a creditor while, in the name of the creditor, collecting debts for such creditor;

(B) any person while acting as a debt collector for another person, both of whom are related by common ownership or affiliated by corporate control, if the person acting as a debt collector does so only for persons to whom it is so related or affiliated and if the principal business of such person is not the collection of debts;

(C) any officer or employee of the United States or any State to the extent that collecting or attempting to collect any debt is in the performance of his official duties;

(D) any person while serving or attempting to serve legal process on any other person in connection with the judicial enforcement of any debt;

(E) any nonprofit organization which, at the request of consumers, performs bona fide consumer credit counseling and assists consumers in the liquidation of their debts by receiving payments from such consumers and distributing such amounts to creditor;

(F) any attorney-at-law collecting a debt as an attorney on behalf of and in the name of a client; and

(G) any person collecting or attempting to collect any debt owed or due or asserted to be owed or due another to the extent such activity (i) is incidental to a bona fide fiduciary obligation or a bona fide escrow arrangement; (ii) concerns a debt which was originated by such person; (iii) concerns a debt which was not in default at the time it was obtained by such person; or (iv) concerns a debt obtained by such person as a secured party in a commercial credit transaction involving the creditor.

(7) The term "location information" means a consumer's place of abode and his telephone number at such place, or his place of employment.

(8) The term "State" means any State, territory, or possession of the United States, the District of Columbia, the Commonwealth of Puerto Rico, or any political subdivision of any of the foregoing.

§ 804. Acquisition of location information [15 U.S.C. § 1692b]

Any debt collector communicating with any person other than the consumer for the purpose of acquiring location information about the consumer shall—

(1) identify himself, state that he is confirming or correcting location information concerning the consumer, and, only if expressly requested, identify his employer;

(2) not state that such consumer owes any debt;

(3) not communicate with any such person more than once unless requested to do so by such person or unless the debt collector reasonably believes that the earlier response of such person is erroneous or incomplete and that such person now has correct or complete location information;

(4) not communicate by post card;

(5) not use any language or symbol on any envelope or in the contents of any communication effected by the mails or telegram that indicates that the debt collector is in the debt collection business or that the communication relates to the collection of a debt; and

(6) after the debt collector knows the consumer is represented by an attorney with regard to the subject debt and has knowledge of, or can readily ascertain, such attorney's name and address, not communicate with any person other than that attorney, unless the attorney fails to respond within a reasonable period of time to communication from the debt collector.

§ 805. Communication in connection with debt collection [15 U.S.C. § 1692c]

(a) Communication with the consumer generally—Without the prior consent of the consumer given directly to the debt collector or the express permission of a court of competent jurisdiction, a debt collector may not communicate with a consumer in connection with the collection of any debt—

(1) at any unusual time or place or a time or place known or which should be known to be inconvenient to the consumer. In the absence of knowledge of circumstances to the contrary, a debt collector shall assume that the convenient time for communicating with a consumer is after 8 o'clock antimeridian and before 9 o'clock postmeridian, local time at the consumer's location;

(2) if the debt collector knows the consumer is represented by an attorney with respect to such debt and has knowledge of, or can readily ascertain, such attorney's name and address, unless the attorney fails to respond within a reasonable period of time to a communication from the debt collector or unless the attorney consents to direct communication with the consumer; or

(3) at the consumer's place of employment if the debt collector knows or has reason to know that the consumer's employer prohibits the consumer from receiving such communication.

(b) Communication with third parties—Except as provided in section 804, without the prior consent of the consumer given directly to the debt collector, or the express permission of a court of competent jurisdiction, or as reasonably necessary to effectuate a postjudgment judicial remedy, a debt collector may not communicate, in connection with the collection of any debt, with any person other than the consumer, his attorney, a consumer reporting agency if otherwise permitted by law, the creditor, the attorney of the creditor, or the attorney of the debt collector.

(c) Ceasing communication—If a consumer notifies a debt collector in writing that the consumer refuses to pay a debt or that the consumer wishes the debt collector to cease further communication with the consumer, the debt collector shall not communicate further with the consumer with respect to such debt, except—

(1) to advise the consumer that the debt collector's further efforts are being terminated;

(2) to notify the consumer that the debt collector or creditor may invoke specified remedies which are ordinarily invoked by such debt collector or creditor; or

(3) where applicable, to notify the consumer that the debt collector or creditor intends to invoke a specified remedy.

If such notice from the consumer is made by mail, notification shall be complete upon receipt.

(d) For the purpose of this section, the term "consumer" includes the consumer's spouse, parent (if the consumer is a minor), guardian, executor, or administrator.

§ 806. Harassment or abuse [15 U.S.C. § 1692d]

A debt collector may not engage in any conduct the natural consequence of which is to harass, oppress, or abuse any person in connection with the collection of a debt. Without limiting the general application of the foregoing, the following conduct is a violation of this section:

(1) The use or threat of use of violence or other criminal means to harm the physical person, reputation, or property of any person.

(2) The use of obscene or profane language or language the natural consequence of which is to abuse the hearer or reader.

(3) The publication of a list of consumers who allegedly refuse to pay debts, except to a consumer reporting agency or to persons meeting the requirements of section 603(f) or 604(3) of this Act.

(4) The advertisement for sale of any debt to coerce payment of the debt.

(5) Causing a telephone to ring or engaging any person in telephone conversation repeatedly or continuously with intent to annoy, abuse, or harass any person at the called number.

(6) Except as provided in section 804, the placement of telephone calls without meaningful disclosure of the caller's identity.

§ 807. False or misleading representations [15 U.S.C. § 1692e]

A debt collector may not use any false, deceptive, or misleading representation or means in connection with the collection of any debt.

Without limiting the general application of the foregoing, the following conduct is a violation of this section:

(1) The false representation or implication that the debt collector is vouched for, bonded by, or affiliated with the United States or any State, including the use of any badge, uniform, or facsimile thereof.

(2) The false representation of—

(A) the character, amount, or legal status of any debt; or

(B) any services rendered or compensation which may be lawfully received by any debt collector for the collection of a debt.

(3) The false representation or implication that any individual is an attorney or that any communication is from an attorney.

(4) The representation or implication that nonpayment of any debt will result in the arrest or imprisonment of any person or the seizure, garnishment, attachment, or sale of any property or wages of any person unless such action is lawful and the debt collector or creditor intends to take such action.

(5) The threat to take any action that cannot legally be taken or that is not intended to be taken.

(6) The false representation or implication that a sale, referral, or other transfer of any interest in a debt shall cause the consumer to—

(A) lose any claim or defense to payment of the debt; or

(B) become subject to any practice prohibited by this subchapter.

(7) The false representation or implication that the consumer committed any crime or other conduct in order to disgrace the consumer.

(8) Communicating or threatening to communicate to any person credit information which is known or which should be known to be false, including the failure to communicate that a disputed debt is disputed.

(9) The use or distribution of any written communication which simulates or is falsely represented to be a document authorized, issued, or approved by any court, official, or agency of the United States or any State, or which creates a false impression as to its source, authorization or approval.

(10) The use of any false representation or deceptive means to collect or attempt to collect any debt or to obtain information concerning a consumer.

(11) Except as otherwise provided for communications to acquire location information under section 1692b of this title, the failure to disclose clearly in all communications made to collect a debt or to obtain information about a consumer, that the debt collector is attempting to collect a debt and that any information obtained will be used for that purpose.

(12) The false representation or implication that accounts have been turned over to innocent purchasers for value.

(13) The false representation or implication that documents are legal process.

(14) The use of any business, company, or organization name other than the true name of the debt collector's business, company, or organization.

(15) The false representation or implication that documents are not legal process forms or do not require action by the consumer.

(16) The false representation or implication that a debt collector operates or is employed by a consumer reporting agency as defined by section 603(f) of this Act.

§ 808. Unfair practices [15 U.S.C. § 1692f]

A debt collector may not use unfair or unconscionable means to collect or attempt to collect any debt. Without limiting the general application of the foregoing, the following conduct is a violation of this section:

(1) The collection of any amount (including any interest, fee, charge, or expense incidental to the principal obligation) unless such amount is expressly authorized by the agreement creating the debt or permitted by law.

(2) The acceptance by a debt collector from any person of a check or other payment instrument postdated by more than five days unless such person is notified in writing of the debt collector's intent to deposit such check or instrument not more than ten nor less than three business days prior to such deposit.

(3) The solicitation by a debt collector of any postdated check or other postdated payment instrument for the purpose of threatening or instituting criminal prosecution.

(4) Depositing or threatening to deposit any postdated check or other postdated payment instrument prior to the date on such check or instrument.

(5) Causing charges to be made to any person for communications by concealment of the true purpose of the communication. Such charges include, but are not limited to, collect telephone calls and telegram fees.

(6) Taking or threatening to take any nonjudicial action to effect dispossession or disablement of property if—

(A) there is no present right to possession of the property claimed as collateral through an enforceable security interest;

(B) there is no present intention to take possession of the property; or

(C) the property is exempt by law from such dispossession or disablement.

(7) Communicating with a consumer regarding a debt by post card.

(8) Using any language or symbol, other than the debt collector's address, on any envelope when communicating with a consumer by use of the mails or by telegram, except that a debt collector may use his business name if such name does not indicate that he is in the debt collection business.

§ 809. Validation of debts [15 U.S.C. § 1692g]

(a) Within five days after the initial communication with a consumer in connection with the collection of any debt, a debt collector shall, unless the following information is contained in the initial communication or the consumer has paid the debt, send the consumer a written notice containing—

(1) the amount of the debt;

(2) the name of the creditor to whom the debt is owed;

(3) a statement that unless the consumer, within thirty days after receipt of the notice, disputes the validity of the debt, or any portion thereof, the debt will be assumed to be valid by the debt collector;

(4) a statement that if the consumer notifies the debt collector in writing within the thirty-day period that the debt, or any portion thereof, is disputed, the debt collector will obtain verification of the debt or a copy of a judgment against the consumer and a copy of such verification or judgment will be mailed to the consumer by the debt collector; and

(5) a statement that, upon the consumer's written request within the thirty-day period, the debt collector will provide the consumer with the name and address of the original creditor, if different from the current creditor.

(b) If the consumer notifies the debt collector in writing within the thirty-day period described in subsection (a) of this section that the debt, or any portion thereof, is disputed, or that the consumer requests the name and address of the original creditor, the debt collector shall cease collection of the debt, or any disputed portion thereof, until the debt collector obtains verification of the debt or a copy of a judgment, or the name and address of the original creditor, and a copy of such verification or judgment, or name and address of the original creditor, is mailed to the consumer by the debt collector.

(c) The failure of a consumer to dispute the validity of a debt under this section may not be construed by any court as an admission of liability by the consumer.

§ 810. Multiple debts [15 U.S.C. § 1692h]

If any consumer owes multiple debts and makes any single payment to any debt collector with respect to such debts, such debt collector may not apply such payment to any debt which is disputed by the consumer and, where applicable, shall apply such payment in accordance with the consumer's directions.

§ 811. Legal actions by debt collectors [15 U.S.C. § 1692i]

(a) Any debt collector who brings any legal action on a debt against any consumer shall—

(1) in the case of an action to enforce an interest in real property securing the consumer's obligation, bring such action only in a judicial district or similar legal entity in which such real property is located; or

(2) in the case of an action not described in paragraph (1), bring such action only in the judicial district or similar legal entity—

(A) in which such consumer signed the contract sued upon; or

(B) in which such consumer resides at the commencement of the action.

(b) Nothing in this subchapter shall be construed to authorize the bringing of legal actions by debt collectors.

§ 812. Furnishing certain deceptive forms [15 U.S.C. § 1692j]

(a) It is unlawful to design, compile, and furnish any form knowing that such form would be used to create the false belief in a consumer that a person other than the creditor of such consumer is participating in the collection of or in an attempt to collect a debt such consumer allegedly owes such creditor, when in fact such person is not so participating.

(b) Any person who violates this section shall be liable to the same extent and in the same manner as a debt collector is liable under section 813 for failure to comply with a provision of this title.

§ 813. Civil liability [15 U.S.C. § 1692k]

(a) Except as otherwise provided by this section, any debt collector who fails to comply with any provision of this title with respect to any person is liable to such person in an amount equal to the sum of—

(1) any actual damage sustained by such person as a result of such failure;

(2)(A) in the case of any action by an individual, such additional damages as the court may allow, but not exceeding $1,000; or

(B) in the case of a class action, (i) such amount for each named plaintiff as could be recovered under subparagraph (A), and (ii) such amount as the court may allow for all other class members, without regard to a minimum individual recovery, not to exceed the lesser of $500,000 or 1 per centum of the net worth of the debt collector; and

(3) in the case of any successful action to enforce the foregoing liability, the costs of the action, together with a reasonable attorney's fee as determined by the court. On a finding by the court that an action under this section was brought in bad faith and for the purpose of harassment, the court may award to the defendant attorney's fees reasonable in relation to the work expended and costs.

(b) In determining the amount of liability in any action under subsection (a) of this section, the court shall consider, among other relevant factors—

(1) in any individual action under subsection (a)(2)(A) of this section, the frequency and persistence of noncompliance by the debt collector, the nature of such noncompliance, and the extent to which such noncompliance was intentional; or

(2) in any class action under subsection (a)(2)(B) of this section, the frequency and persistence of noncompliance by the debt collector, the nature of such noncompliance, the resources of the debt collector, the number of persons adversely affected, and the extent to which the debt collector's noncompliance was intentional.

(c) A debt collector may not be held liable in any action brought under this title if the debt collector shows by a preponderance of evidence that the violation was not intentional and resulted from a bona fide error notwithstanding the maintenance of procedures reasonably adapted to avoid any such error.

(d) An action to enforce any liability created by this title may be brought in any appropriate United States district court without regard to the amount in controversy, or in any other court of competent jurisdiction, within one year from the date on which the violation occurs.

(e) No provision of this section imposing any liability shall apply to any act done or omitted in good faith in conformity with any advisory opinion of the Commission, notwithstanding that after such act or omission has occurred, such opinion is amended, rescinded, or determined by judicial or other authority to be invalid for any reason.

§ 814. Administrative enforcement [15 U.S.C. § 1692*l*]

(a) Compliance with this title shall be enforced by the Commission, except to the extent that enforcement of the requirements imposed under this title is specifically committed to another agency under subsection (b) of this section. For purpose of the exercise by the Commission of its functions and powers under the Federal Trade

Commission Act, a violation of this title shall be deemed an unfair or deceptive act or practice in violation of that Act. All of the functions and powers of the Commission under the Federal Trade Commission Act are available to the Commission to enforce compliance by any person with this title, irrespective of whether that person is engaged in commerce or meets any other jurisdictional tests in the Federal Trade Commission Act, including the power to enforce the provisions of this title in the same manner as if the violation had been a violation of a Federal Trade Commission trade regulation rule.

(b) Compliance with any requirements imposed under this title shall be enforced under—

(1) section 8 of Federal Deposit Insurance Act, in the case of—

(A) national banks, by the Comptroller of the Currency;

(B) member banks of the Federal Reserve System (other than national banks), by the Federal Reserve Board; and

(C) banks the deposits or accounts of which are insured by the Federal Deposit Insurance Corporation (other than members of the Federal Reserve System), by the Board of Directors of the Federal Deposit Insurance Corporation;

(2) section 5(d) of the Home Owners Loan Act of 1933, section 407 of the National Housing Act, and sections 6(i) and 17 of the Federal Home Loan Bank Act, by the Federal Home Loan Bank Board (acting directly or through the Federal Savings and Loan Insurance Corporation), in the case of any institution subject to any of those provisions;

(3) the Federal Credit Union Act, by the Administrator of the National Credit Union Administration with respect to any Federal credit union;

(4) the Acts to regulate commerce, by the Interstate Commerce Commission with respect to any common carrier subject to those Acts;

(5) the Federal Aviation Act of 1958, by the Civil Aeronautics Board with respect to any air carrier or any foreign air carrier subject to that Act; and

(6) the Packers and Stockyards Act, 1921 (except as provided in section 406 of that Act), by the Secretary of Agriculture with respect to any activities subject to that Act.

(c) For the purpose of the exercise by any agency referred to in subsection (b) of this section of its powers under any Act referred to in that subsection, a violation of any requirement imposed under this title shall be deemed to be a violation of a requirement imposed under that Act. In addition to its powers under any provision of law specifically referred to in subsection (b) of this section, each of the agencies referred to in that subsection may exercise, for the purpose of enforcing compliance with any requirement imposed under this title any other authority conferred on it by law, except as provided in subsection (d) of this section.

(d) Neither the Commission nor any other agency referred to in subsection (b) of this section may promulgate trade regulation rules or other regulations with respect to the collection of debts by debt collectors as defined in this title.

§ 815. Reports to Congress by the Commission [15 U.S.C. § 1692m]

(a) Not later than one year after the effective date of this subchapter and at one-year intervals thereafter, the Commission shall make reports to the Congress concerning the administration of its functions under this subchapter, including such recommendations as the Commission deems necessary or appropriate. In addition, each report of the Commission shall include its assessment of the extent to which compliance with this title is being achieved and a summary of the enforcement actions taken by the Commission under section 814.

(b) In the exercise of its functions under this title, the Commission may obtain upon request the views of any other Federal agency which exercises enforcement functions under section 814.

§ 816. Relation to State laws [15 U.S.C. § 1692n]

This title does not annul, alter, or affect, or exempt any person subject to the provisions of this title from complying with the laws of any State with respect to debt collection practices, except to the extent that those laws are inconsistent with any provision of this title, and then only to the extent of the inconsistency. For purposes of this section, a State law is not inconsistent with this title if the protection such law affords any consumer is greater than the protection provided by this title.

§ 817. Exemption for State regulation [15 U.S.C. § 1692*o*]

The Commission shall by regulation exempt from the requirements of this title any class of debt collection practices within any State if the Commission determines that under the law of that State that class of debt collection practices is subject to requirements substantially similar to those imposed by this title, and that there is adequate provision for enforcement.

TITLE IX. ELECTRONIC FUND TRANSFER ACT

(15 U.S.C. §§ 1693–1693r)

Table of Sections

---

§ 901. Short title

This Act may be cited as the "Electronic Fund Transfer Act."

§ 902. Findings and purpose [15 U.S.C. § 1693]

(a) The Congress finds that the use of electronic systems to transfer funds provides the potential for substantial benefits to consumers. However, due to the unique characteristics of such systems, the application of existing consumer protection legislation is unclear, leaving the rights and liabilities of consumers, financial institutions, and intermediaries in electronic fund transfers undefined.

(b) It is the purpose of this title to provide a basic framework establishing the rights, liabilities, and responsibilities of participants in electronic fund transfer systems. The primary objective of this title, however, is the provision of individual consumer rights.

§ 903. Definitions [15 U.S.C. § 1693a]

As used in this title—

(1) the term "accepted card or other means of access" means a card, code, or other means of access to a consumer's account for the purpose of initiating electronic fund transfers when the person to whom such card or other means of access was issued has requested and received or has signed or has used, or authorized another to use, such card or other means of access for the purpose of transferring money between accounts or obtaining money, property, labor, or services;

(2) the term "account" means a demand deposit, savings deposit, or other asset account (other than an occasional or incidental credit balance in an open end credit plan as defined in section 103(i) of this Act), as described in regulations of the Board, established primarily for personal, family, or household purposes, but such term does not include an account held by a financial institution pursuant to a bona fide trust agreement;

(3) the term "Board" means the Board of Governors of the Federal Reserve System;

(4) the term "business day" means any day on which the offices of the consumer's financial institution involved in an electronic fund transfer are open to the public for carrying on substantially all of its business functions;

(5) the term "consumer" means a natural person;

(6) the term "electronic fund transfer" means any transfer of funds, other than a transaction originated by check, draft, or similar paper instrument, which is initiated through an electronic terminal, telephonic instrument, or computer or magnetic tape so as to order, instruct, or authorize a financial institution to debit or credit an account. Such term includes, but is not limited to, point-of-sale transfers, automated teller machine transactions, direct deposits or withdrawals of funds, and transfers initiated by telephone. Such term does not include—

(A) any check guarantee or authorization service which does not directly result in a debit or credit to a consumer's account:

(B) any transfer of funds, other than those processed by automated clearinghouse, made by a financial institution on behalf of a consumer by means of a service that transfers funds held at either Federal Reserve banks or other depository institutions and which is not designed primarily to transfer funds on behalf of a consumer;

(C) any transaction the primary purpose of which is the purchase or sale of securities or commodities through a broker-dealer registered with or regulated by the Securities and Exchange Commission;

(D) any automatic transfer from a savings account to a demand deposit account pursuant to an agreement between a consumer and a financial institution for the purpose of covering an overdraft or maintaining an agreed upon minimum balance in the consumer's demand deposit account; or

(E) any transfer of funds which is initiated by a telephone conversation between a consumer and an officer or employee of a financial institution which is not pursuant to a prearranged plan and under which periodic or recurring transfers are not contemplated;

as determined under regulations of the Board;

(7) the term "electronic terminal" means an electronic device, other than a telephone operated by a consumer, through which a consumer may initiate an electronic fund transfer. Such term includes, but is not limited to, point-of-sale terminals, automated teller machines, and cash dispensing machines;

(8) the term "financial institution" means a State or National bank, a State or Federal savings and loan association, a mutual savings bank, a State or Federal credit union, or any other person who, directly or indirectly, holds an account belonging to a consumer;

(9) the term "preauthorized electronic fund transfer" means an electronic fund transfer authorized in advance to recur at substantially regular intervals;

(10) the term "State" means any State, territory, or possession of the United States, the District of Columbia, the Commonwealth of Puerto Rico, or any political subdivision of any of the foregoing; and

(11) the term "unauthorized electronic fund transfer" means an electronic fund transfer from a consumer's account initiated by a person other than the consumer without actual authority to initiate such transfer and from which the consumer receives no benefit, but the term does not include any electronic fund transfer (A) initiated by a person other than the consumer who was furnished with the card, code, or other means of access to such consumer's account by such consumer, unless the consumer has notified the financial institution involved that transfers by such other person are no longer authorized, (B) initiated with fraudulent intent by the consumer or any person acting in concert with the consumer, or (C) which constitutes an error committed by a financial institution.

§ 904. Regulations [15 U.S.C. § 1693b]

(a) The Board shall prescribe regulations to carry out the purposes of this title. In prescribing such regulations, the Board shall:

(1) consult with the other agencies referred to in section 917 and take into account, and allow for, the continuing evolution of electronic banking services and the technology utilized in such services,

(2) prepare an analysis of economic impact which considers the costs and benefits to financial institutions, consumers, and other users of electronic fund transfers, including the extent to which additional documentation, reports, records, or other paper work would be required, and the effects upon competition in the provision of electronic banking services among large and small financial institutions and the availability of such services to different classes of consumers, particularly low income consumers,

(3) to the extent practicable, the Board shall demonstrate that the consumer protections of the proposed regulations outweigh the compliance costs imposed upon consumers and financial institutions, and

(4) any proposed regulations and accompanying analyses shall be sent promptly to Congress by the Board.

(b) The Board shall issue model clauses for optional use by financial institutions to facilitate compliance with the disclosure requirements of section 905 and to aid consumers in understanding the rights and responsibilities of participants in electronic fund transfers by utilizing readily understandable language. Such model clauses shall be adopted after notice duly given in the Federal Register and opportunity for public comment in accordance with section 553 of Title 5. With respect to the disclosures required by section 905(a)(3) and (4), the Board shall take account of variations in the services and charges under different electronic fund transfer systems and, as appropriate, shall issue alternative model clauses for disclosure of these differing account terms.

(c) Regulations prescribed hereunder may contain such classifications, differentiations, or other provisions, and may provide for such adjustments and exceptions for any class of electronic fund transfers, as in the judgment of the Board are necessary or proper to effectuate the purposes of this title, to prevent circumvention or evasion thereof, or to facilitate compliance therewith. The Board shall by regulation modify the requirements imposed by this title on small financial institutions if the Board determines that such modifications are necessary to alleviate any undue compliance burden on small financial institutions and such modifications are consistent with the purpose and objective of this title.

(d) In the event that electronic fund transfer services are made available to consumers by a person other than a financial institution holding a consumer's account, the Board shall by regulation assure that the disclosures, protections, responsibilities, and remedies created by this title are made applicable to such persons and services.

§ 905. Terms and conditions of transfers [15 U.S.C. § 1693c]

(a) The terms and conditions of electronic fund transfers involving a consumer's account shall be disclosed at the time the consumer contracts for an electronic fund transfer service, in accordance with regulations of the Board. Such disclosures shall be in readily understandable language and shall include, to the extent applicable—

(1) the consumer's liability for unauthorized electronic fund transfers and, at the financial institution's option, notice of the advisability of prompt reporting of any loss, theft, or unauthorized use of a card, code, or other means of access;

(2) the telephone number and address of the person or office to be notified in the event the consumer believes that an unauthorized electronic fund transfer has been or may be effected;

(3) the type and nature of electronic fund transfers which the consumer may initiate, including any limitations on the frequency or dollar amount of such transfers, except that the details of such limitations need not be disclosed if their confidentiality is necessary to maintain the security of an electronic fund transfer system, as determined by the Board;

(4) any charges for electronic fund transfers or for the right to make such transfers;

(5) the consumer's right to stop payment of a preauthorized electronic fund transfer and the procedure to initiate such a stop payment order;

(6) the consumer's right to receive documentation of electronic fund transfers under section 906;

(7) a summary, in a form prescribed by regulations of the Board, of the error resolution provisions of section 908 and the consumer's rights thereunder. The financial institution shall thereafter transmit such summary at least once per calendar year;

(8) the financial institution's liability to the consumer under section 910; and

(9) under what circumstances the financial institution will in the ordinary course of business disclose information concerning the consumer's account to third persons.

(b) A financial institution shall notify a consumer in writing at least twenty-one days prior to the effective date of any change in any term or condition of the consumer's account required to be disclosed under subsection (a) of this section if such change would result in greater cost or liability for such consumer or decreased access to the consumer's account. A financial institution may, however, implement a change in the terms or conditions of an account without prior notice when such change is immediately necessary to maintain or restore the security of an electronic fund transfer system or a consumer's account. Subject to subsection (a)(3) of this section, the Board shall require subsequent notification if such a change is made permanent.

(c) For any account of a consumer made accessible to electronic fund transfers prior to the effective date of this title, the information required to be disclosed to the consumer under subsection (a) of this section shall be disclosed not later than the earlier of—

(1) the first periodic statement required by section 906(c) after the effective date of this title; or

(2) thirty days after the effective date of this title.

§ 906. Documentation of transfers; periodic statements [15 U.S.C. § 1693d]

(a) For each electronic fund transfer initiated by a consumer from an electronic terminal, the financial institution holding such consumer's account shall, directly or indirectly, at the time the transfer is initiated, make available to the consumer written documentation of such transfer. The documentation shall clearly set forth to the extent applicable—

(1) the amount involved and date the transfer is initiated;

(2) the type of transfer;

(3) the identity of the consumer's account with the financial institution from which or to which funds are transferred;

(4) the identity of any third party to whom or from whom funds are transferred; and

(5) the location or identification of the electronic terminal involved.

(b) For a consumer's account which is scheduled to be credited by a preauthorized electronic fund transfer from the same payor at least once in each successive sixty-day period, except where the payor provides positive notice of the transfer to the consumer, the financial institution shall elect to provide promptly either positive notice to the consumer when the credit is made as scheduled, or negative notice to the consumer when the credit is not made as scheduled, in accordance with regulations of the Board. The means of notice elected shall be disclosed to the consumer in accordance with section 905.

(c) A financial institution shall provide each consumer with a periodic statement for each account of such consumer that may be accessed by means of an electronic fund transfer. Except as provided in subsections (d) and (e) of this section, such statement shall be provided at least monthly for each monthly or shorter cycle in which an electronic fund transfer affecting the account has occurred, or every three months, whichever is more frequent. The statement, which may include information regarding transactions other than electronic fund transfers, shall clearly set forth—

(1) with regard to each electronic fund transfer during the period, the information described in subsection (a) of this section, which may be provided on an accompanying document;

(2) the amount of any fee or charge assessed by the financial institution during the period for electronic fund transfers or for account maintenance;

(3) the balances in the consumer's account at the beginning of the period and at the close of the period; and

(4) the address and telephone number to be used by the financial institution for the purpose of receiving any statement inquiry or notice of account error from the consumer. Such address and telephone number shall be preceded by the caption "Direct Inquiries To:" or other similar language indicating that the address and number are to be used for such inquiries or notices.

(d) In the case of a consumer's passbook account which may not be accessed by electronic fund transfers other than preauthorized electronic fund transfers crediting the account, a financial institution may, in lieu of complying with the requirements of subsection (c) of this section, upon presentation of the passbook provide the consumer in writing with the amount and date of each such transfer involving the account since the passbook was last presented.

(e) In the case of a consumer's account, other than a passbook account, which may not be accessed by electronic fund transfers other than preauthorized electronic fund transfers crediting the account, the financial institution may provide a periodic statement on a quarterly basis which otherwise complies with the requirements of subsection (c) of this section.

(f) In any action involving a consumer, any documentation required by this section to be given to the consumer which indicates that an electronic fund transfer was made to another person shall be admissible as evidence of such transfer and shall constitute prima facie proof that such transfer was made.

§ 907. Preauthorized transfers [15 U.S.C. § 1693e]

(a) A preauthorized electronic fund transfer from a consumer's account may be authorized by the consumer only in writing, and a copy of such authorization shall be provided to the consumer when made. A consumer may stop payment of a preauthorized electronic fund transfer by notifying the financial institution orally or in writing at any time up to three business days preceding the scheduled date of such transfer. The financial institution may require written confirmation to be provided to it within fourteen days of an oral notification if, when the oral notification is made, the consumer is advised of such requirement and the address to which such confirmation should be sent.

(b) In the case of preauthorized transfers from a consumer's account to the same person which may vary in amount, the financial institution or designated payee shall, prior to each transfer, provide reasonable advance notice to the consumer, in accordance with regulations of the Board, of the amount to be transferred and the scheduled date of the transfer.

§ 908. Error resolution [15 U.S.C. § 1693f]

(a) If a financial institution, within sixty days after having transmitted to a consumer documentation pursuant to section 906(a), (c), or (d) or notification pursuant to section 906(b), receives oral or written notice in which the consumer—

(1) sets forth or otherwise enables the financial institution to identify the name and account number of the consumer;

(2) indicates the consumer's belief that the documentation, or, in the case of notification pursuant to section 906(b), the consumer's account, contains an error and the amount of such error; and

(3) sets forth the reasons for the consumer's belief (where applicable) that an error has occurred,

the financial institution shall investigate the alleged error, determine whether an error has occurred, and report or mail the results of such investigation and determination to the consumer within ten business days. The financial institution may require written confirmation to be provided to it within ten business days of an oral notification of error if, when the oral notification is made, the consumer is advised of such requirement and the address to which such confirmation should be sent. A financial institution which requires written confirmation in accordance with the previous sentence need not provisionally recredit a consumer's account in accordance with subsection (c) of this section, nor shall the financial institution be liable under subsection (e) of this section if the written confirmation is not received within the ten-day period referred to in the previous sentence.

(b) If the financial institution determines that an error did occur, it shall promptly, but in no event more than one business day after such determination, correct the error, subject to section 909, including the crediting of interest where applicable.

(c) If a financial institution receives notice of an error in the manner and within the time period specified in subsection (a) of this section, it may, in lieu of the requirements of subsections (a) and (b) of this section, within ten business days after receiving such notice provisionally recredit the consumer's account for the amount alleged to be in error, subject to section 909, including interest where applicable, pending the conclusion of its investigation and its determination of whether an error has occurred. Such investigation shall be concluded not later than forty-five days after receipt of notice of the error. During the pendency of the investigation, the consumer shall have full use of the funds provisionally recredited.

(d) If the financial institution determines after its investigation pursuant to subsection (a) or (c) of this section that an error did not occur, it shall deliver or mail to the consumer an explanation of its findings within 3 business days after the conclusion of its investigation, and upon request of the consumer promptly deliver or mail to the consumer reproductions of all documents which the financial institution relied on to conclude that such error did not occur. The financial institution shall include notice of the right to request reproductions with the explanation of its findings.

(e) If in any action under section 915, the court finds that—

(1) the financial institution did not provisionally recredit a consumer's account within the ten-day period specified in subsection (c) of this section, and the financial institution (A) did not make a good faith investigation of the alleged error, or (B) did not have a reasonable basis for believing that the consumer's account was not in error; or

(2) the financial institution knowingly and willfully concluded that the consumer's account was not in error when such conclusion could not reasonably have been drawn from the evidence available to the financial institution at the time of its investigation,

then the consumer shall be entitled to treble damages determined under section 915(a)(1).

(f) For the purpose of this section, an error consists of—

(1) an unauthorized electronic fund transfer;

(2) an incorrect electronic fund transfer from or to the consumer's account;

(3) the omission from a periodic statement of an electronic fund transfer affecting the consumer's account which should have been included;

(4) a computational error by the financial institution;

(5) the consumer's receipt of an incorrect amount of money from an electronic terminal;

(6) a consumer's request for additional information or clarification concerning an electronic fund transfer or any documentation required by this title; or

(7) any other error described in regulations of the Board.

§ 909. Consumer liability for unauthorized transfers [15 U.S.C. § 1693g]

(a) A consumer shall be liable for any unauthorized electronic fund transfer involving the account of such consumer only if the card or other means of access utilized for such transfer was an accepted card or other means of access and if the issuer of such card, code, or other means of access has provided a means whereby the user of such card, code, or other means of access can be identified as the person authorized to use it, such as by signature, photograph, or fingerprint or by electronic or mechanical confirmation. In no event, however, shall a consumer's liability for an unauthorized transfer exceed the lesser of—

(1) $50; or

(2) the amount of money or value of property or services obtained in such unauthorized electronic fund transfer prior to the time the financial institution is notified of, or otherwise becomes aware of, circumstances which lead to the reasonable belief that an unauthorized electronic fund transfer involving the consumer's account has been or may be effected. Notice under this paragraph is sufficient when such steps have been taken as may be reasonably required in the ordinary course of business to provide the financial institution with the pertinent information, whether or not any particular officer, employee, or agent of the financial institution does in fact receive such information.

Notwithstanding the foregoing, reimbursement need not be made to the consumer for losses the financial institution establishes would not have occurred but for the failure of the consumer to report within sixty days of transmittal of the statement (or in extenuating circumstances such as extended travel or hospitalization, within a reasonable time under the circumstances) any unauthorized electronic fund transfer or account error which appears on the periodic statement provided to the consumer under section 906. In addition, reimbursement need not be made to the consumer for losses which the financial institution establishes would not have occurred but for the failure of the consumer to report any loss or theft of a card or other means of access within two business days after the consumer learns of the loss or theft (or in extenuating circumstances such as extended travel or hospitalization, within a longer period which is reasonable under the circumstances), but the consumer's liability under this subsection in any such case may not exceed a total of $500, or the amount of unauthorized electronic fund transfers which occur following the close of two business days (or such longer period) after the consumer learns of the loss or theft but prior to notice to the financial institution under this subsection, whichever is less.

(b) In any action which involves a consumer's liability for an unauthorized electronic fund transfer, the burden of proof is upon the financial institution to show that the electronic fund transfer was authorized or, if the electronic fund transfer was unauthorized, then the burden of proof is upon the financial institution to establish that the conditions of liability set forth in subsection (a) of this section have been met, and, if the transfer was initiated after the effective date of section 905, that the disclosures required to be made to the consumer under section 905(a)(1) and (2) were in fact made in accordance with such section.

(c) In the event of a transaction which involves both an unauthorized electronic fund transfer and an extension of credit as defined in section 103(e) of this Act pursuant to an agreement between the consumer and the financial institution to extend such credit to the consumer in the event the consumer's account is overdrawn, the limitation on the consumer's liability for such transaction shall be determined solely in accordance with this section.

(d) Nothing in this section imposes liability upon a consumer for an unauthorized electronic fund transfer in excess of his liability for such a transfer under other applicable law or under any agreement with the consumer's financial institution.

(e) Except as provided in this section, a consumer incurs no liability from an unauthorized electronic fund transfer.

§ 910. Liability of financial institutions [15 U.S.C. § 1693h]

(a) Subject to subsections (b) and (c) of this section, a financial institution shall be liable to a consumer for all damages proximately caused by—

(1) the financial institution's failure to make an electronic fund transfer, in accordance with the terms and conditions of an account, in the correct amount or in a timely manner when properly instructed to do so by the consumer, except where—

(A) the consumer's account has insufficient funds;

(B) the funds are subject to legal process or other encumbrance restricting such transfer;

(C) such transfer would exceed an established credit limit;

(D) an electronic terminal has insufficient cash to complete the transaction; or

(E) as otherwise provided in regulations of the Board;

(2) the financial institution's failure to make an electronic fund transfer due to insufficient funds when the financial institution failed to credit, in accordance with the terms and conditions of an account, a deposit of funds to the consumer's account which would have provided sufficient funds to make the transfer, and

(3) the financial institution's failure to stop payment of a preauthorized transfer from a consumer's account when instructed to do so in accordance with the terms and conditions of the account.

(b) A financial institution shall not be liable under subsection (a) (1) or (2) of this section if the financial institution shows by a preponderance of the evidence that its action or failure to act resulted from—

(1) an act of God or other circumstance beyond its control, that it exercised reasonable care to prevent such an occurrence, and that it exercised such diligence as the circumstances required; or

(2) a technical malfunction which was known to the consumer at the time he attempted to initiate an electronic fund transfer or, in the case of a preauthorized transfer, at the time such transfer should have occurred.

(c) In the case of a failure described in subsection (a) of this section which was not intentional and which resulted from a bona fide error, notwithstanding the maintenance of procedures reasonably adapted to avoid any such error, the financial institution shall be liable for actual damages proved.

§ 911. Issuance of cards or other means of access [15 U.S.C. § 1693i]

(a) No person may issue to a consumer any card, code, or other means of access to such consumer's account for the purpose of initiating an electronic fund transfer other than—

(1) in response to a request or application therefor; or

(2) as a renewal of, or in substitution for, an accepted card, code, or other means of access, whether issued by the initial issuer or a successor.

(b) Notwithstanding the provisions of subsection (a) of this section, a person may distribute to a consumer on an unsolicited basis a card, code, or other means of access for use in initiating an electronic fund transfer from such consumer's account, if—

(1) such card, code, or other means of access is not validated;

(2) such distribution is accompanied by a complete disclosure, in accordance with section 905, of the consumer's rights and liabilities which will apply if such card, code, or other means of access is validated;

(3) such distribution is accompanied by a clear explanation, in accordance with regulations of the Board, that such card, code, or other means of access is not validated and how the consumer may dispose of such code, card, or other means of access if validation is not desired; and

(4) such card, code, or other means of access is validated only in response to a request or application from the consumer, upon verification of the consumer's identity.

(c) For the purpose of subsection (b) of this section, a card, code, or other means of access is validated when it may be used to initiate an electronic fund transfer.

§ 912. Suspension of obligations [15 U.S.C. § 1693j]

If a system malfunction prevents the effectuation of an electronic fund transfer initiated by a consumer to another person, and such other person has agreed to accept payment by such means, the consumer's obligation to the other person shall be suspended until the malfunction is corrected and the electronic fund transfer may be completed, unless such other person has subsequently, by written request, demanded payment by means other than an electronic fund transfer.

§ 913. Compulsory use of electronic fund transfers [15 U.S.C. § 1693k]

No person may—

(1) condition the extension of credit to a consumer on such consumer's repayment by means of preauthorized electronic fund transfers; or

(2) require a consumer to establish an account for receipt of electronic fund transfers with a particular financial institution as a condition of employment or receipt of a government benefit.

§ 914. Waiver of rights [15 U.S.C. § 1693*l*]

No writing or other agreement between a consumer and any other person may contain any provision which constitutes a waiver of any right conferred or cause of action created by this title. Nothing in this section prohibits, however, any writing or other agreement which grants to a consumer a more extensive right or remedy or greater protection than contained in this title or a waiver given in settlement of a dispute or action.

§ 915. Civil liability [15 U.S.C. § 1693m]

(a) Except as otherwise provided by this section and section 910, any person who fails to comply with any provision of this title with respect to any consumer, except for an error resolved in accordance with section 908, if liable to such consumer in an amount equal to the sum of—

(1) any actual damage sustained by such consumer as a result of such failure;

(2)(A) in the case of an individual action, an amount not less than $100 nor greater than $1,000; or

(B) in the case of a class action, such amount as the court may allow, except that (i) as to each member of the class no minimum recovery shall be applicable, and (ii) the total recovery under this subparagraph in any class action or series of class actions arising out of the same failure to comply by the same person shall not be more than the lesser of $500,000 or 1 per centum of the net worth of the defendant; and

(3) in the case of any successful action to enforce the foregoing liability, the costs of the action, together with a reasonable attorney's fee as determined by the court.

(b) In determining the amount of liability in any action under subsection (a) of this section, the court shall consider, among other relevant factors—

(1) in any individual action under subsection (a)(2)(A) of this section, the frequency and persistence of noncompliance, the nature of such noncompliance, and the extent to which the noncompliance was intentional; or

(2) in any class action under subsection (a)(2)(B) of this section, the frequency and persistence of noncompliance, the nature of such noncompliance, the resources of the defendant, the number of persons adversely affected, and the extent to which the noncompliance was intentional.

(c) Except as provided in section 910, a person may not be held liable in any action brought under this section for a violation of this title if the person shows by a preponderance of evidence that the violation was not intentional and resulted from a bona fide error notwithstanding the maintenance of procedures reasonably adapted to avoid any such error.

(d) No provision of this section or section 916 imposing any liability shall apply to—

(1) any act done or omitted in good faith in conformity with any rule, regulation, or interpretation thereof by the Board or in conformity with any interpretation or approval by an official or employee of the Federal Reserve System duly authorized by the Board to issue such interpretations or approvals under such procedures as the Board may prescribe therefor; or

(2) any failure to make disclosure in proper form if a financial institution utilized an appropriate model clause issued by the Board,

notwithstanding that after such act, omission, or failure has occurred, such rule, regulation, approval, or model clause is amended, rescinded, or determined by judicial or other authority to be invalid for any reason.

(e) A person has no liability under this section for any failure to comply with any requirement under this title if, prior to the institution of an action under this section, the person notifies the consumer concerned of the failure, complies with the requirements of this title, and makes an appropriate adjustment to the consumer's account and pays actual damages or, where applicable, damages in accordance with section 910.

(f) On a finding by the court that an unsuccessful action under this section was brought in bad faith or for purposes of harassment, the court shall award to the defendant attorney's fees reasonable in relation to the work expended and costs.

(g) Without regard to the amount in controversy, any action under this section may be brought in any United States district court, or in any other court of competent jurisdiction, within one year from the date of the occurrence of the violation.

§ 916. Criminal liability [15 U.S.C. § 1693n]

(a) Whoever knowingly and willfully—

(1) gives false or inaccurate information or fails to provide information which he is required to disclose by this title or any regulation issued thereunder; or

(2) otherwise fails to comply with any provision of this title;

shall be fined not more than $5,000 or imprisoned not more than one year, or both.

(b) Whoever—

(1) knowingly, in a transaction affecting interstate or foreign commerce, uses or attempts or conspires to use any counterfeit, fictitious, altered, forged, lost, stolen, or fraudulently obtained debit instrument to obtain money, goods, services, or anything else of value which within any one-year period has a value aggregating $1,000 or more; or

(2) with unlawful or fraudulent intent, transports or attempts or conspires to transport in interstate or foreign commerce a counterfeit, fictitious, altered, forged, lost, stolen, or fraudulently obtained debit instrument knowing the same to be counterfeit, fictitious, altered, forged, lost, stolen, or fraudulently obtained; or

(3) with unlawful or fraudulent intent, uses any instrumentality of interstate or foreign commerce to sell or transport a counterfeit, fictitious, altered, forged, lost, stolen, or fraudulently obtained debit instrument knowing the same to be counterfeit, fictitious, altered, forged, lost, stolen, or fraudulently obtained; or

(4) knowingly receives, conceals, uses, or transports money, goods, services, or anything else of value (except tickets for interstate or foreign transportation) which (A) within any one-year pe-

riod has a value aggregating $1,000 or more, (B) has moved in or is part of, or which constitutes interstate or foreign commerce, and (C) has been obtained with a counterfeit, fictitious, altered, forged, lost, stolen, or fraudulently obtained debit instrument; or

(5) knowingly receives, conceals, uses, sells, or transports in interstate or foreign commerce one or more tickets for interstate or foreign transportation, which (A) within any one-year period have a value aggregating $500 or more, and (B) have been purchased or obtained with one or more counterfeit, fictitious, altered, forged, lost, stolen, or fraudulently obtained debit instrument; or

(6) in a transaction affecting interstate or foreign commerce, furnishes money, property, services, or anything else of value, which within any one-year period has a value aggregating $1,000 or more, through the use of any counterfeit, fictitious, altered, forged, lost, stolen, or fraudulently obtained debit instrument knowing the same to be counterfeit, fictitious, altered, forged, lost, stolen, or fraudulently obtained—

shall be fined not more than $10,000 or imprisoned not more than ten years, or both.

(c) As used in this section, the term "debit instrument" means a card, code, or other device, other than a check, draft, or similar paper instrument, by the use of which a person may initiate an electronic fund transfer.

§ 917. Administrative enforcement [15 U.S.C. § 1693*o*]

(a) Compliance with the requirements imposed under this title shall be enforced under—

(1) section 8 of the Federal Deposit Insurance Act, in the case of—

(A) national banks, by the Comptroller of the Currency;

(B) member banks of the Federal Reserve System (other than national banks), by the Board;

(C) banks insured by the Federal Deposit Insurance Corporation (other than members of the Federal Reserve System), by the Board of Directors of the Federal Deposit Insurance Corporation;

(2) section 5(d) of the Home Owners' Loan Act of 1933, section 407 of the National Housing Act, and sections 6(i) and 17 of the Federal Home Loan Bank Act, by the Federal Home Loan Bank Board (acting directly or through the Federal Savings and Loan Insurance Corporation), in the case of any institution subject to any of those provisions;

(3) the Federal Credit Union Act, by the Administrator of the National Credit Union Administration with respect to any Federal credit union;

(4) the Federal Aviation Act of 1958, by the Civil Aeronautics Board, with respect to any air carrier or foreign air carrier subject to that Act; and

(5) the Securities Exchange Act of 1934, by the Securities and Exchange Commission, with respect to any broker or dealer subject to that Act.

(b) For the purpose of the exercise by any agency referred to in subsection (a) of this section of its powers under any Act referred to in that subsection, a violation of any requirement imposed under this title shall be deemed to be a violation of a requirement imposed under that Act. In addition to its powers under any provision of law specifically referred to in subsection (a) of this section, each of the agencies referred to in that subsection may exercise, for the purpose of enforcing compliance with any requirement imposed under this title, any other authority conferred on it by law.

(c) Except to the extent that enforcement of the requirements imposed under this title is specifically committed to some other Government agency under subsection (a) of this section, the Federal Trade Commission shall enforce such requirements. For the purpose of the exercise by the Federal Trade Commission of its functions and powers under the Federal Trade Commission Act, a violation of any requirement imposed under this title shall be deemed a violation of a requirement imposed under that Act. All of the functions and powers of the Federal Trade Commission under the Federal Trade Commission Act are available to the Commission to enforce compliance by any person subject to the jurisdiction of the Commission with the requirements imposed under this title, irrespective of whether that person is engaged in commerce or meets any other jurisdictional tests in the Federal Trade Commission Act.

§ 918. Reports to Congress [15 U.S.C. § 1693p]

(a) Not later than twelve months after the effective date of this subchapter and at one-year intervals thereafter, the Board and the Attorney General shall, respectively, make reports to the Congress concerning the administration of their functions under this title, including such recommendations as the Board and the Attorney General, respectively, deem necessary or appropriate. In addition, each report of the Board shall include its assessment of the extent to which compliance with this title is being achieved, and a summary of the enforcement actions taken under section 917. In such report, the Board shall particularly address the effects of this title on the costs and benefits to financial institutions and consumers, on competition, on the introduction of new technology, on the operations of financial institutions, and on the adequacy of consumer protection. The report of the Attorney General shall also contain an analysis of the impact of this title on the operation, workload, and efficiency of the Federal courts.

(b) In the exercise of its functions under this title, the Board may obtain upon request the views of any other Federal agency which, in the judgment of the Board, exercises regulatory or supervisory functions with respect to any class of persons subject to this title.

§ 919. Relation to State laws [15 U.S.C. § 1693q]

This title does not annul, alter, or affect the laws of any State relating to electronic fund transfers, except to the extent that those laws are inconsistent with the provisions of this title, and then only to the extent of the inconsistency. A State law is not inconsistent with this title if the protection such law affords any consumer is greater than the protection afforded by this title. The Board shall, upon its own motion or upon the request of any financial institution, State, or other interested party, submitted in accordance with procedures prescribed in regulations of the Board, determine whether a State requirement is inconsistent or affords greater protection. If the Board determines that a State requirement is inconsistent, financial institutions shall incur no liability under the law of that State for a good faith failure to comply with that law, notwithstanding that such determination is subsequently amended, rescinded, or determined by judicial or other authority to be invalid for any reason. This title does not extend the applicability of any such law to any class of persons or transactions to which it would not otherwise apply.

§ 920. Exemption for State regulation [15 U.S.C. § 1693r]

The Board shall by regulation exempt from the requirements of this title any class of electronic fund transfers within any State if the Board determines that under the law of that State that class of electronic fund transfers is subject to requirements substantially similar to those imposed by this title, and that there is adequate provision for enforcement.

FEDERAL RESERVE BOARD, REGULATION Z, TRUTH-IN-LENDING

12 C.F.R. Part 226

Table of Sections

Subpart A. General

Subpart B. Open-End Credit

Subpart C. Closed-End Credit

Subpart D. Miscellaneous

SUBPART A. GENERAL

§ 226.1 Authority, purpose, coverage, organization, enforcement and liability

(a) *Authority.* This regulation, known as Regulation Z, is issued by the Board of Governors of the Federal Reserve System to implement the federal Truth in Lending and Fair Credit Billing Acts, which are contained in title I of the Consumer Credit Protection Act, as amended (15 USC 1601 et seq.).

(b) *Purpose.* The purpose of this regulation is to promote the informed use of consumer credit by requiring disclosures about its terms and cost. The regulation also gives consumers the right to cancel certain credit transactions that involve a lien on a consumer's principal dwelling, regulates certain credit card practices, and provides a means for fair and timely resolution of credit billing disputes. The regulation does not govern charges for consumer credit.

(c) *Coverage.* (1) In general, this regulation applies to each individual or business that offers or extends credit when four conditions are met: (i) the credit is offered or extended to consumers; (ii) the offering or extention of credit is done regularly;[1] (iii) the credit is subject to a finance charge or is payable by a written agreement in more than four installments; and (iv) the credit is primarily for personal, family, or household purposes.

(2) If a credit card is involved, however, certain provisions apply even if the credit is not subject to a finance charge, or is not payable by a written agreement in more than four installments, or if the credit card is to be used for business purposes.

. . .

1. The meaning of "regularly" is explained in the definition of "creditor" in section 226.2(a).

§ 226.2 Definitions and rules of construction

(a) *Definitions.* For purposes of this regulation, the following definitions apply:

(1) "*Act*" means the Truth in Lending Act (15 USC 1601 et seq.).

(2) "*Advertisement*" means a commercial message in any medium that promotes, directly or indirectly, a credit transaction.

(3) "*Arranger of credit*" means a person who regularly arranges for the extension of consumer credit [2] by another person if:

(i) A finance charge may be imposed for that credit, or the credit is payable by written agreement in more than four installments (not including a downpayment); and

(ii) The person extending the credit is not a creditor. The term does not include a person (such as a real estate broker) when arranging seller financing of a dwelling or real property.

(4) "*Billing cycle*" or "*cycle*" means the interval between the days or dates of regular periodic statements. These intervals shall be equal and no longer than a quarter of a year. An interval will be considered equal if the number of days in the cycle does not vary more than four days from the regular day or date of the periodic statement.

(5) "*Board*" means the Board of Governors of the Federal Reserve System.

(6) "*Business day*" means a day on which a creditor's offices are open to the public for carrying on substantially all of its business functions. However, for purposes of rescission under sections 226.15 and 226.23, the term means all calendar days except Sundays and the legal public holidays specified in 5 USC 6103(a), such as New Year's Day, Washington's Birthday, Memorial Day, Independence Day, Labor Day, Columbus Day, Veterans Day, Thanksgiving Day, and Christmas Day.

(7) "*Card issuer*" means a person that issues a credit card or that person's agent with respect to the card.

(8) "*Cardholder*" means a natural person to whom a credit card is issued for consumer credit purposes, or a natural person who has agreed with the card issuer to pay consumer credit obligations arising from the issuance of a credit card to another natural person. For purposes of section 226.12(a) and (b), the term includes any person to whom a credit card is issued for any purpose, including business, commercial, or agricultural use, or a person who has agreed with the the

2. A person regularly arranges for the extension of consumer credit only if it arranged credit more than 25 times (or more than 5 times for transactions secured by a dwelling) in the preceding calendar year. If a person did not meet these numerical standards in the preceding calendar year, the numerical standards shall be applied to the current calendar year.

card issuer to pay obligations arising from the issuance of such a credit card to another person.

(9) *"Cash price"* means the price at which a creditor, in the ordinary course of business, offers to sell for cash the property or service that is the subject of the transaction. At the creditor's option, the term may include the price of accessories, services related to the sale, service contracts and taxes and fees for license, title, and registration. The term does not include any finance charge.

(10) *"Closed-end credit"* means consumer credit other than "open-end credit" as defined in this section.

(11) *"Consumer"* means a cardholder or a natural person to whom consumer credit is offered or extended. However, for purposes of rescission under sections 226.15 and 226.23, the term also includes a natural person in whose principal dwelling a security interest is or will be retained or acquired, if that person's ownership interest in the dwelling is or will be subject to the security interest.

(12) *"Consumer credit"* means credit offered or extended to a consumer primarily for personal, family, or household purposes.

(13) *"Consummation"* means the time that a consumer becomes contractually obligated on a credit transaction.

(14) *"Credit"* means the right to defer payment of debt or to incur debt and defer its payment.

(15) *"Credit card"* means any card, plate, coupon book, or other single credit device that may be used from time to time to obtain credit.

(16) *"Credit sale"* means a sale in which the seller is a creditor. The term includes a bailment or lease (unless terminable without penalty at any time by the consumer) under which the consumer—

(i) Agrees to pay as compensation for use a sum substantially equivalent to, or in excess of, the total value of the property and services involved; and

(ii) Will become (or has the option to become), for no additional consideration or for nominal consideration, the owner of the property upon compliance with the agreement.

(17) *"Creditor"* means:

(i) A person (A) who regularly extends consumer credit [3] that is subject to a finance charge or is payable by written agreement in more than four installments (not including a downpayment), and (B) to whom the obligation is initially payable, either on the

3. A person regularly extends consumer credit only if it extended credit more than 25 times (or more than 5 times for transactions secured by a dwelling) in the preceding calendar year. If a person did not meet these numerical standards in the preceding calendar year, the numerical standards shall be applied to the current calendar year.

face of the note or contract, or by agreement when there is no note or contract.

(ii) An arranger of credit.

(iii) For purposes of sections 226.4(c)(8) (Discounts), 226.9(d) (Finance charge imposed at time of transaction), and 226.12(e) (Prompt notification of returns and crediting of refunds), a person that honors a credit card.

(iv) For purposes of subpart B, any card issuer that extends either open-end credit or credit that is not subject to a finance charge and is not payable by written agreement in more than four installments.

(v) For purposes of subpart B (except for the finance charge disclosures contained in sections 226.6(a) and 226.7(d) through (g) and the right of rescission set forth in section 226.15) and subpart C, any card issuer that extends closed-end credit that is subject to a finance charge or is payable by written agreement in more than four installments.

(18) "*Downpayment*" means an amount, including the value of any property used as a trade-in paid to a seller to reduce the cash price of goods or services purchased in a credit sale transaction. A deferred portion of a downpayment may be treated as part of the downpayment if it is payable not later than the due date of the second otherwise regularly scheduled payment and is not subject to a finance charge.

(19) "*Dwelling*" means a residential structure that contains one to four units, whether or not that structure is attached to real property. The term includes an individual condominium unit, cooperative unit, mobile home, and trailer, it if is used as a residence.

(20) "*Open-end credit*" means consumer credit extended by a creditor under a plan in which—

(i) The creditor reasonably contemplates repeated transactions;

(ii) The creditor may impose a finance charge from time to time on an outstanding unpaid balance; and

(iii) The amount of credit that may be extended to the consumer during the term of the plan (up to any limit set by the creditor) is generally made available to the extent that any outstanding balance is repaid.

(21) "*Periodic rate*" means a rate of finance charge that is or may be imposed by a creditor on a balance for a day, week, month, or other subdivision of a year.

(22) "*Person*" means a natural person or an organization, including a corporation, partnership, proprietorship, association, cooperative, estate, trust, or government unit.

(23) "*Prepaid finance charge*" means any finance charge paid separately in cash or by check before or at consummation of a transaction, or withheld from the proceeds of the credit at any time.

(24) "*Residential mortgage transaction*" means a transaction in which a mortgage, deed of trust, purchase money security interest arising under an installment sales contract, or equivalent consensual security interest is created or retained in the consumer's principal dwelling to finance the acquisition or initial construction of that dwelling.

(25) "*Security interest*" means an interest in property that secures performance of a consumer credit obligation and that is recognized by state or federal law. It does not include incidental interests such as interests in proceeds, accessions, additions, fixtures, insurance proceeds (whether or not the creditor is a loss payee or beneficiary), premium rebates, or interests in after-acquired property. For purposes of disclosure under sections 226.6 and 226.18, the term does not include an interest that arises solely by operation of law. However, for purposes of the right of rescission under sections 226.15 and 226.23, the term does include interests that arise solely by operation of law.

(26) "*State*" means any state, the District of Columbia, the Commonwealth of Puerto Rico, and any territory or possession of the United States.

(b) *Rules of construction.* For purposes of this regulation, the following rules of construction apply:

(1) Where appropriate, the singular form of a word includes the plural form and plural includes singular.

(2) Where the words "obligation" and "transaction" are used in this regulation, they refer to a consumer credit obligation or transaction, depending upon the context. Where the word "credit" is used in this regulation, it means "consumer credit" unless the context clearly indicates otherwise.

(3) Unless defined in this regulation, the words used have the meanings given to them by state law or contract.

(4) Footnotes have the same legal effect as the text of the regulation.

§ 226.3 Exempt transactions

This regulation does not apply to the following;

(a) *Business, commercial, agricultural, or organizational credit.*[4] (1) An extension of credit primarily for a business, commercial or agricultural purpose.

4. Extensions of credit that are exempt under paragraph (a)(1) and (2) remain subject to section 226.12(a) and (b) governing the issuance of credit cards and the liability for their unauthorized use.

(2) An extension of credit to other than a natural person, including credit to government agencies or instrumentalities.

(b) *Credit over $25,000 not secured by real property or a dwelling.* An extension of credit not secured by real property, or by personal property used or expected to be used as the principal dwelling of the consumer, in which the amount financed exceeds $25,000 or in which there is an express written commitment to extend credit in excess of $25,000.

(c) *Public utility credit.* An extension of credit that involves public utility services provided through pipe, wire, other connected facilities, or radio or similar transmission (including extensions of such facilities), if the charges for service, delayed payment, or any discounts for prompt payment are filed with or regulated by any government unit. The financing of durable goods or home improvements by a public utility is not exempt.

(d) *Securities or commodities accounts.* Transactions in securities or commodities accounts in which credit is extended by a broker-dealer registered with the Securities and Exchange Commission or the Commodity Futures Trading Commission.

(e) *Home fuel budget plans.* An installment agreement for the purchase of home fuels in which no finance charge is imposed.

§ 226.4 Finance charge

(a) *Definition.* The finance charge is the cost of consumer credit as a dollar amount. It includes any charge payable directly or indirectly by the consumer and imposed directly or indirectly by the creditor as an incident to or a condition of the extension of credit. It does not include any charge of a type payable in a comparable cash transaction.

(b) *Examples of finance charges.* The finance charge includes the following types of charges, except for charges specifically excluded by paragraphs (c) through (e) of this section:

(1) Interest, time price differential, and any amount payable under an add-on or discount system of additional charges.

(2) Service, transaction, activity, and carrying charges, including any charge imposed on a checking or other transaction account to the extent that the charge exceeds the charge for a similar account without a credit feature.

(3) Points, loan fees, assumption fees, finder's fees, and similar charges.

(4) Appraisal, investigation, and credit report fees.

(5) Premiums or other charges for any guarantee or insurance protecting the creditor against the consumer's default or other credit loss.

(6) Charges imposed on a creditor by another person for purchasing or accepting a consumer's obligation, if the consumer is required to pay the charges in cash, as an addition to the obligation, or as a deduction from the proceeds of the obligation.

(7) Premiums or other charges for credit life, accident, health, or loss-of-income insurance, written in connection with a credit transaction.

(8) Premiums or other charges for insurance against loss of or damage to property, or against liability arising out of the ownership or use of property, written in connection with a credit transaction.

(9) Discounts for the purpose of inducing payment by a means other than the use of credit.

(c) *Charges excluded from the finance charge.* The following charges are not finance charges:

(1) Application fees charged to all applicants for credit, whether or not credit is actually extended.

(2) Charges for actual unanticipated late payment, for exceeding a credit limit, or for delinquency, default, or a similar occurrence.

(3) Charges imposed by a financial institution for paying items that overdraw an account, unless the payment of such items and the imposition of the charge were previously agreed upon in writing.

(4) Fees charged for participation in a credit plan, whether assessed on an annual or other periodic basis.

(5) Seller's points.

(6) Interest forfeited as a result of an interest reduction required by law on a time deposit used as security for an extension of credit.

(7) The following fees in a transaction secured by real property or in a residential mortgage transaction, if the fees are bona fide and reasonable in amount:

(i) Fees for title examination, abstract of title, title insurance, property survey, and similar purposes.

(ii) Fees for preparing deeds, mortgages, and reconveyance, settlement, and similar documents.

(iii) Notary, appraisal, and credit report fees.

(iv) Amounts required to be paid into escrow or trustee accounts if the amounts would not otherwise be included in the finance charge.

(8) Discounts offered to induce payment for a purchase by cash, check, or other means, as provided in section 167(b) of the act.

(d) *Insurance.* (1) Premiums for credit life, accident, health, or loss-of-income insurance may be excluded from the finance charge if the following conditions are met:

(i) The insurance coverage is not required by the creditor, and this fact is disclosed.

(ii) The premium for the initial term of insurance coverage is disclosed. If the term of insurance is less than the term of the transaction, the term of insurance also shall be disclosed. The premium may be disclosed on a unit-cost basis only in open-end credit transactions, closed-end credit transactions by mail or telephone under section 226.17(g), and certain closed-end credit transactions involving an insurance plan that limits the total amount of indebtedness subject to coverage.

(iii) The consumer signs or initials an affirmative written request for the insurance after receiving the disclosures specified in this paragraph. Any consumer in the transaction may sign or initial the request.

(2) Premiums for insurance against loss of or damage to property, or against liability arising out of the ownership or use of property,[5] may be excluded from the finance charge if the following conditions are met:

(i) The insurance coverage may be obtained from a person of the consumer's choice,[6] and this fact is disclosed.

(ii) If the coverage is obtained from or through the creditor, the premium for the initial term of insurance coverage shall be disclosed. If the term of insurance is less than the term of the transaction, the term of insurance shall also be disclosed. The premium may be disclosed on a unit-cost basis only in open-end credit transactions, closed-end credit transactions by mail or telephone under section 226.17(g), and certain closed-end credit transactions involving an insurance plan that limits the total amount of indebtedness subject to coverage.

(e) *Certain security interest charges.* If itemized and disclosed, the following charges may be excluded from the finance charge:

(1) Taxes and fees prescribed by law that actually are or will be paid to public officials for determining the existence of or for perfecting, releasing, or satisfying a security interest.

(2) The premium for insurance in lieu of perfecting a security interest to the extent that the premium does not exceed the fees described in paragraph (e)(1) of this section that otherwise would be payable.

5. This includes single interest insurance if the insurer waives all right of subrogation against the consumer.

6. A creditor may reserve the right to refuse to accept, for reasonable cause, an insurer offered by the consumer.

(f) *Prohibited offsets.* Interest, dividends, or other income received or to be received by the consumer on deposits or investments shall not be deducted in computing the finance charge.

SUBPART B. OPEN-END CREDIT

§ 226.5 General disclosure requirements

(a) *Form of disclosures.* (1) The creditor shall make the disclosures required by this subpart clearly and conspicuously in writing,[7] in a form that the consumer may keep.[8]

(2) The terms "finance charge" and "annual percentage rate," when required to be disclosed with a corresponding amount or percentage rate, shall be more conspicuous than any other required disclosure.[9]

(b) *Time of disclosures.* (1) *Initial disclosures.* The creditor shall furnish the initial disclosure statement required by section 226.6 before the first transaction is made under the plan.

(2) *Periodic statements.* (i) The creditor shall mail or deliver a periodic statement as required by section 226.7 for each billing cycle at the end of which an account has a debit or credit balance of more than $1 or on which a finance charge has been imposed. A periodic statement need not be sent for an account if the creditor deems it uncollectible, or if delinquency collection proceedings have been instituted, or if furnishing the statement would violate federal law.

(ii) The creditor shall mail or deliver the periodic statement at least 14 days prior to any date or the end of any time period required to be disclosed under section 226.7(j) in order for the consumer to avoid an additional finance or other charge.[10] A creditor that fails to meet this requirement shall not collect any finance or other charge imposed as a result of such failure.

(c) *Basis of disclosures and use of estimates.* Disclosures shall reflect the terms of the legal obligation between the parties. If any information necessary for accurate disclosure is unknown to the creditor, it shall make the disclosure based on the best information reasonably available and shall state clearly that the disclosure is an estimate.

7. The disclosure required by section 226.9(d) when a finance charge is imposed at the time of a transaction need not be written.

8. The alternative summary billing rights statement provided for in section 226.9(a)(2), and the disclosures made under section 226.10(b) about payment requirements need not be in a form that the consumer can keep.

9. The terms need not be more conspicuous when used under section 226.7(d) on periodic statements and under section 226.16 in advertisements.

10. This timing requirement does not apply if the creditor is unable to meet the requirement because of an act of God, war, civil disorder, natural disaster, or strike.

(d) *Multiple creditors; multiple consumers.* If the credit plan involves more than one creditor, only one set of disclosures shall be given, and the creditors shall agree among themselves which creditor must comply with the requirements that this regulation imposes on any or all of them. If there is more than one consumer, the disclosures may be made to any consumer who is primarily liable on the account. If the right of rescission under section 226.15 is applicable, however, the disclosures required by sections 226.6 and 226.15(b) shall be made to each consumer having the right to rescind.

(e) *Effect of subsequent events.* If a disclosure becomes inaccurate because of an event that occurs after the creditor mails or delivers the disclosures, the resulting inaccuracy is not a violation of this regulation, although new disclosures may be required under section 226.9(c).

§ 226.6 Initial disclosure statement

The creditor shall disclose to the consumer, in terminology consistent with that to be used on the periodic statement, each of the following items, to the extent applicable:

(a) *Finance charge.* The circumstances under which a finance charge will be imposed and an explanation of how it will be determined, as follows:

(1) A statement of when finance charges begin to accrue, including an explanation of whether or not any time period exists within which any credit extended may be repaid without incurring a finance charge. If such a time period is provided, a creditor may, at its option and without disclosure, impose no finance charge when payment is received after the time period's expiration.

(2) A disclosure of each periodic rate that may be used to compute the finance charge, the range of balances to which it is applicable,[11] and the corresponding annual percentage rate.[12] When different periodic rates apply to different types of transactions, the types of transactions to which the periodic rates apply shall also be disclosed.

(3) An explanation of the method used to determine the balance on which the finance charge may be computed.

(4) An explanation of how the amount of any finance charge will be determined,[13] including a description of how any finance charge other than the periodic rate will be determined.

11. A creditor is not required to adjust the range of balances disclosure to reflect the balance below which only a minimum charge applies.

12. If a creditor is offering a variable rate plan, the creditor shall also disclose: (1) the circumstances under which the rate(s) may increase; (2) any limitations on the increase; and (3) the effect(s) of an increase.

13. If no finance charge is imposed when the outstanding balance is less than a certain amount, no disclosure is required of that fact or of the balance be-

(b) *Other charges.* The amount of any charge other than a finance charge that may be imposed as part of the plan, or an explanation of how the charge will be determined.

(c) *Security interests.* The fact that the creditor has or will acquire a security interest in the property purchased under the plan, or in other property identified by item or type.

(d) *Statement of billing rights.* A statement that outlines the consumer's rights and the creditor's responsibilities under sections 226.12(c) and 226.13 and that is substantially similar to the statement found in appendix G.

§ 226.7 Periodic statement

The creditor shall furnish the consumer with a periodic statement that discloses the following items, to the extent applicable:

(a) *Previous balance.* The account balance outstanding at the beginning of the billing cycle.

(b) *Identification of transactions.* An identification of each credit transaction in accordance with section 226.8.

(c) *Credits.* Any credit to the account during the billing cycle, including the amount and the date of crediting. The date need not be provided if a delay in crediting does not result in any finance or other charge.

(d) *Periodic rates.* Each periodic rate that may be used to compute the finance charge, the range of balances to which it is applicable,[14] and the corresponding annual percentage rate.[15] If different periodic rates apply to different types of transactions, the types of transactions to which the periodic rates apply shall also be disclosed.

(e) *Balance on which finance charge computed.* The amount of the balance to which a periodic rate was applied and an explanation of how that balance was determined. When a balance is determined without first deducting all credits and payments made during the billing cycle, that fact and the amount of the credits and payments shall be disclosed.

(f) *Amount of finance charge.* The amount of any finance charge debited or added to the account during the billing cycle, using the term "finance charge." The components of the finance charge shall be individually itemized and identified to show the amount(s) due to the application of any periodic rates and the amount(s) of any other type of finance charge. If there is more than one periodic rate, the amount of the finance charge attributable to each rate need not be separately itemized and identified.

low which no finance charge will be imposed.

14. See footnotes 11 and 13.

15. If a variable rate plan is involved, the creditor shall disclose the fact that the periodic rate(s) may vary.

(g) *Annual percentage rate.* When a finance charge is imposed during the billing cycle, the annual percentage rate(s) determined under section 226.14, using the term "annual percentage rate."

(h) *Other charges.* The amounts, itemized and identified by type, of any charges other than finance charges debited to the account during the billing cycle.

(i) *Closing date of billing cycle; new balance.* The closing date of the billing cycle and the account balance outstanding on that date.

(j) *Free-ride period.* The date by which or the time period within which the new balance or any portion of the new balance must be paid to avoid additional finance charges. If such a time period is provided, a creditor may, at its option and without disclosure, impose no finance charge when payment is received after the time period's expiration.

(k) *Address for notice of billing errors.* The address to be used for notice of billing errors. Alternatively, the address may be provided on the billing rights statement permitted by section 226.9(a)(2).

§ 226.8 Identification of transactions

The creditor shall identify credit transactions on or with the first periodic statement that reflects the transaction by furnishing the following information, as applicable.[16]

(a) *Sale credit.* For each credit transaction involving the sale of property or services, the following rules shall apply:

(1) *Copy of credit document provided.* When an actual copy of the receipt or other credit document is provided with the first periodic statement reflecting the transaction, the transaction is sufficiently identified if the amount of the transaction and either the date of the transaction or the date of debiting the transaction to the consumer's account are disclosed on the copy or on the periodic statement.

(2) *Copy of credit document not provided—creditor and seller same or related person(s).* When the creditor and the seller are the same person or related persons, and an actual copy of the receipt or other credit document is not provided with the periodic statement, the

16. Failure to disclose the information required by this section shall not be deemed a failure to comply with the regulation if: (1) the creditor maintains procedures reasonably adapted to obtain and provide the information; and (2) the creditor treats an inquiry for clarification or documentation as a notice of a billing error, including correcting the account in accordance with section 226.13(e). This applies to transactions that take place outside a state, as defined in section 226.2(a), whether or not the creditor maintains procedures reasonably adapted to obtain the required information.

creditor shall disclose the amount and date of the transaction, and a brief identification [17] of the property or services purchased.[18]

(3) *Copy of credit document not provided—creditor and seller not same or related person(s).* When the creditor and seller are not the same person or related persons, and an actual copy of the receipt or other credit document is not provided with the periodic statement, the creditor shall disclose the amount and date of the transaction; the seller's name; and the city, and state or foreign country where the transaction took place.[19]

(b) *Nonsale credit.* A nonsale credit transaction is sufficiently identified if the first periodic statement reflecting the transaction discloses a brief identification of the transaction; [20] the amount of the transaction; and at least one of the following dates: the date of the transaction, the date or debiting the transaction to the consumer's account, or, if the consumer signed the credit document, the date appearing on the document. If an actual copy of the receipt or other credit document is provided and that copy shows the amount and at least one of the specified dates, the brief identification may be omitted.

§ 226.9 Subsequent disclosure requirements

(a) *Furnishing statement of billing rights.*

(1) *Annual statement.* The creditor shall mail or deliver the billing rights statement required by section 226.6(d) at least once per calendar year, at intervals of not less than 6 months nor more than 18 months, either to all consumers or to each consumer entitled to receive a periodic statement under section 226.5(b)(2) for any one billing cycle.

(2) *Alternative summary statement.* As an alternative to paragraph (a)(1) of this section, the creditor may mail or deliver, on or

17. As an alternative to the brief identification, the creditor may disclose a number or symbol that also appears on the receipt or other credit document given to the consumer, if the number or symbol reasonably identifies that transaction with that creditor, and if the creditor treats an inquiry for clarification or documentation as a notice of a billing error, including correcting the account in accordance with section 226.13(e).

18. An identification of property or services may be replaced by the seller's name and location of the transaction when: (1) the creditor and the seller are the same person; (2) the creditor's open-end plan has fewer than 15,000 accounts; (3) the creditor provides the consumer with point-of-sale documentation for that transaction; and (4) the creditor treats an inquiry for clarification or documentation as a notice of a billing error, including correcting the account in accordance with section 226.13(e).

19. The creditor may omit the address or provide any suitable designation that helps the consumer to identify the transaction when the transaction (1) took place at a location that is not fixed; (2) took place in the consumer's home; or (3) was a mail or telephone order.

20. See footnote 17.

with each periodic statement, a statement substantially similar to that in appendix G.

(b) *Disclosures for supplemental credit devices and additional features.* (1) If a creditor within 30 days after mailing or delivering the initial disclosures under section 226.6(a), adds a credit feature to the consumer's account or mails or delivers to the consumer a credit device for which the finance charge terms are the same as those previously disclosed, no additional disclosures are necessary. After 30 days, if the creditor adds a credit feature or furnishes a credit device (other than as a renewal, resupply, or the original issuance of a credit card) on the same finance charge terms, the creditor shall disclose, before the consumer uses the feature or device for the first time, that it is for use in obtaining credit under the terms previously disclosed.

(2) Whenever a credit feature is added or a credit device is mailed or delivered, and the finance charge terms for the feature or device differ from disclosures previously given, the disclosures required by section 226.6(a) that are applicable to the added feature or device shall be given before the consumer uses the feature or device for the first time.

(c) *Change in terms.* (1) *Written notice required.* Whenever any term required to be disclosed under section 226.6 is changed or the required minimum periodic payment is increased, the creditor shall mail or deliver written notice of the change to each consumer who may be affected. The notice shall be mailed or delivered at least 15 days prior to the effective date of the change. The 15-day timing requirement does not apply if the change has been agreed to by the consumer, or if a periodic rate or other finance charge is increased because of the consumer's delinquency or default; the notice shall be given, however, before the effective date of the change.

(2) *Notice not required.* No notice under this section is required when the change involves late-payment charges, charges for documentary evidence, or over-the-limit charges; a reduction of any component of a finance or other charge; suspension of future credit privileges or termination of an account or plan; or when the change results from an agreement involving a court proceeding, or from the consumer's default or delinquency (other than an increase in the periodic rate or other finance charge).

(d) *Finance charge imposed at time of transaction.* (1) Any person, other than the card issuer, who imposes a finance charge at the time of honoring a consumer's credit card, shall disclose the amount of that finance charge prior to its imposition.

(2) The card issuer, if other than the person honoring the consumer's credit card, shall have no responsibility for the disclosure required by paragraph (d)(1) of this section, and shall not consider any such charge for purposes of sections 226.6 and 226.7.

§ 226.10 Prompt crediting of payments

(a) *General rule.* A creditor shall credit a payment to the consumer's account as of the date of receipt, except when a delay in crediting does not result in a finance or other charge or except as provided in paragraph (b) of this section.

(b) *Specific requirements for payments.* If a creditor specifies, on or with the periodic statement, requirements for the consumer to follow in making payments, but accepts a payment that does not conform to the requirements, the creditor shall credit the payment within five days of receipt.

(c) *Adjustment of account.* If a creditor fails to credit a payment, as required by paragraphs (a) or (b) of this section, in time to avoid the imposition of finance or other charges, the creditor shall adjust the consumer's account so that the charges imposed are credited to the consumer's account during the next billing cycle.

§ 226.11 Treatment of credit balances

When a credit balance in excess of $1 is created on a credit account (through transmittal of funds to a creditor in excess of the total balance due on an account, through rebates of unearned finance charges or insurance premiums, or through amounts otherwise owed to or held for the benefit of a consumer), the creditor shall—

(a) Credit the amount of the credit balance to the consumer's account;

(b) Refund any part of the remaining credit balance within seven business days from receipt of a written request from the consumer; and

(c) Make a good faith effort to refund to the consumer by cash, check, or money order, or credit to a deposit account of the consumer, any part of the credit balance remaining in the account for more than six months. No further action is required if the consumer's current location is not known to the creditor and cannot be traced through the consumer's last known address or telephone number.

§ 226.12 Special credit card provisions

(a) *Issuance of credit cards.* Regardless of the purpose for which a credit card is to be used, including business, commercial, or agricultural use, no credit card shall be issued to any person except—

(1) In response to an oral or written request or application for the card; or

(2) As a renewal of, or substitute for, an accepted credit card.[21]

21. For purposes of this section, "accepted credit card" means any credit card that a cardholder has requested or applied for and received, or has signed,

(b) *Liability of cardholder for unauthorized use.* (1) *Limitation on amount.* The liability of a cardholder for unauthorized use [22] of a credit card shall not exceed the lesser of $50 or the amount of money, property, labor, or services obtained by the unauthorized use before notification to the card issuer under paragraph (b)(3) of this section.

(2) *Conditions of liability.* A cardholder shall be liable for unauthorized use of a credit card only if—

(i) The credit card is an accepted credit card;

(ii) The card issuer has provided adequate notice [23] of the cardholder's maximum potential liability and of means by which the card issuer may be notified of loss or theft of the card. The notice shall state that the cardholder's liability shall not exceed $50 (or any lesser amount) and that the cardholder may give oral or written notification, and shall describe a means of notification (for example, a telephone number, an address, or both); and

(iii) The card issuer has provided a means to identify the cardholder on the account or the authorized user of the card.

(3) *Notification to card issuer.* Notification to a card issuer is given when steps have been taken as may be reasonably required in the ordinary course of business to provide the card issuer with the pertinent information about the loss, theft, or possible unauthorized use of a credit card, regardless of whether any particular officer, employee, or agent of the card issuer does, in fact, receive the information. Notification may be given, at the option of the person giving it, in person, by telephone, or in writing. Notification in writing is considered given at the time of receipt or, whether or not received, at the expiration of the time ordinarily required for transmission, whichever is earlier.

(4) *Effect of other applicable law or agreement.* If state law or an agreement between a cardholder and the card issuer imposes lesser liability than that provided in this paragraph, the lesser liability shall govern.

(5) *Business use of credit cards.* If 10 or more credit cards are issued by one card issuer for use by the employees of an organization, this section does not prohibit the card issuer and the organiza-

used, or authorized another person to use to obtain credit. Any credit card issued as a renewal or substitute in accordance with this paragraph becomes an accepted credit card when received by the cardholder.

22. "Unauthorized use" means the use of a credit card by a person, other than the cardholder, who does not have actual, implied, or apparent authority for such use, and from which the cardholder receives no benefit.

23. "Adequate notice" means a printed notice to a cardholder that sets forth clearly the pertinent facts so that the cardholder may reasonably be expected to have noticed it and understood its meaning. The notice may be given by any means reasonably assuring receipt by the cardholder.

tion from agreeing to liability for unauthorized use without regard to this section. However, liability for unauthorized use may be imposed on an employee of the organization, by either the card issuer or the organization, only in accordance with this section.

(c) *Right of cardholder to assert claims or defenses against card issuer.*[24] (1) *General rule.* When a person who honors a credit card fails to resolve satisfactorily a dispute as to property or services purchased with the credit card in a consumer credit transaction, the cardholder may assert against the card issuer all claims (other than tort claims) and defenses arising out of the transaction and relating to the failure to resolve the dispute. The cardholder may withhold payment up to the amount of credit outstanding for the property or services that gave rise to the dispute and any finance or other charges imposed on that amount.[25]

(2) *Adverse credit reports prohibited.* If, in accordance with paragraph (c)(1) of this section, the cardholder withholds payment of the amount of credit outstanding for the disputed transaction, the card issuer shall not report that amount as delinquent until the dispute is settled or judgment is rendered.

(3) *Limitations.* The rights stated in paragraphs (c)(1) and (2) of this section apply only if—

(i) The cardholder has made a good faith attempt to resolve the dispute with the person honoring the credit card; and

(ii) The amount of credit extended to obtain the property or services that result in the assertion of the claim or defense by the cardholder exceeds $50, and the disputed transaction occurred in the same state as the cardholder's current designated address or, if not within the same state, within 100 miles from that address.[26]

24. This paragraph does not apply to the use of a check guarantee card or a debit card in connection with an overdraft credit plan, or to a check guarantee card used in connection with cash advance checks.

25. The amount of the claim or defense that the cardholder may assert shall not exceed the amount of credit outstanding for the disputed transaction at the time the cardholder first notifies the card issuer or the person honoring the credit card of the existence of the claim or defense. To determine the amount of credit outstanding for purposes of this section, payments and other credits shall be applied to: (1) late charges in the order of entry to the account; then to (2) finance charges in the order of entry to the account; and then to (3) any other debits in the order of entry to the account. If more than one item is included in a single extension of credit, credits are to be distributed pro rata according to prices and applicable taxes.

26. The limitations stated in paragraph (c)(3)(ii) of this section shall not apply when the person honoring the credit card: (1) is the same person as the card issuer; (2) is controlled by the card issuer directly or indirectly; (3) is under the direct or indirect control of a third person that also directly or indirectly controls the card issuer; (4) controls the card issuer directly or indirectly; (5) is a franchised dealer in the card issuer's products or services; or (6) has obtained the order for the disputed transaction through a mail solicitation made or participated in by the card issuer.

(d) *Offsets by card issuer prohibited.* (1) A card issuer may not take any action, either before or after termination of credit card privileges, to offset a cardholder's indebtedness arising from a consumer credit transaction under the relevant credit card plan against funds of the cardholder held on deposit with the card issuer.

(2) This paragraph does not alter or affect the right of a card issuer acting under state or federal law to do any of the following with regard to funds of a cardholder held on deposit with the card issuer if the same procedure is constitutionally available to creditors generally: obtain or enforce a consensual security interest in the funds; attach or otherwise levy upon the funds; or obtain or enforce a court order relating to the funds.

(3) This paragraph does not prohibit a plan, if authorized in writing by the cardholder, under which the card issuer may periodically deduct all or part of the cardholder's credit card debt from a deposit account held with the card issuer (subject to the limitations in section 226.13(d)(1)).

(e) *Prompt notification of returns and crediting of refunds.* (1) When a creditor other than the card issuer accepts the return of property or forgives a debt for services that is to be reflected as a credit to the consumer's credit card account, that creditor shall, within seven business days from accepting the return or forgiving the debt, transmit a credit statement to the card issuer through the card issuer's normal channels for credit statements.

(2) The card issuer shall, within three business days from receipt of a credit statement, credit the consumer's account with the amount of the refund.

(3) If a creditor other than a card issuer routinely gives cash refunds to consumers paying in cash, the creditor shall also give credit or cash refunds to consumers using credit cards, unless it discloses at the time the transaction is consummated that credit or cash refunds for returns are not given. This section does not require refunds for returns nor does it prohibit refunds in kind.

(f) *Discounts: tie-in arrangements.* No card issuer may, by contract or otherwise—

(1) Prohibit any person who honors a credit card from offering a discount to a consumer to induce the consumer to pay by cash, check, or similar means rather than by use of a credit card or its underlying account for the purchase of property or services; or

(2) Require any person who honors the card issuer's credit card to open or maintain any account or obtain any other service not essential to the operation of the credit card plan from the card issuer or any other person, as a condition of participation in a credit card plan. If maintenance of an account for clearing purposes is determined to be essential to the operation of the credit card plan, it may be re-

quired only if no service charges or minimum balance requirements are imposed.

(g) *Relation to Electronic Fund Transfer Act and Regulation E.* For guidance on whether Regulation Z or Regulation E applies in instances involving both credit and electronic fund transfer aspects, refer to Regulation E, 12 CFR 205.5(c) regarding issuance and 205.6(d) regarding liability for unauthorized use. On matters other than issuance and liability, this section applies to the credit aspects of combined credit/electronic fund transfer transactions, as applicable.

§ 226.13 Billing-error resolution [27]

(a) *Definition of billing error.* For purposes of this section, the term "billing error" means:

(1) A reflection on or with a periodic statement of an extension of credit that is not made to the consumer or to a person who has actual, implied, or apparent authority to use the consumer's credit card or open-end credit plan.

(2) A reflection on or with a periodic statement of an extension of credit that is not identified in accordance with the requirements of sections 226.7(b) and 226.8.

(3) A reflection on or with a periodic statement of an extension of credit for property or services not accepted by the consumer or the consumer's designee, or not delivered to the consumer or the consumer's designee as agreed.

(4) A reflection on a periodic statement of the creditor's failure to credit properly a payment or other credit issued to the consumer's account.

(5) A reflection on a periodic statement of a computational or similar error of an accounting nature that is made by the creditor.

(6) A reflection on a periodic statement of an extension of credit for which the consumer requests additional clarification, including documentary evidence.

(7) The creditor's failure to mail or deliver a periodic statement to the consumer's last known address if that address was received by the creditor, in writing, at least 20 days before the end of the billing cycle for which the statement was required.

27. A creditor shall not accelerate any part of the consumer's indebtedness or restrict or close a consumer's account solely because the consumer has exercised in good faith rights provided by this section. A creditor may be subject to the forfeiture penalty under section 161(e) of the act for failure to comply with any of the requirements of this section.

(b) *Billing-error notice.*[28] A billing-error notice is a written notice [29] from a consumer that—

(1) Is received by a creditor at the address disclosed under section 226.7(k) no later than 60 days after the creditor transmitted the first periodic statement that reflects the alleged billing error;

(2) Enables the creditor to identify the consumer's name and account number; and

(3) To the extent possible, indicates the consumer's belief and the reasons for the belief that a billing error exists, and the type, date, and amount of the error.

(c) *Time for resolution; general procedures.*

(1) The creditor shall mail or deliver written acknowledgment to the consumer within 30 days of receiving a billing-error notice, unless the creditor has complied with the appropriate resolution procedures of paragraphs (e) and (f) of this section, as applicable, within the 30-day period; and

(2) The creditor shall comply with the appropriate resolution procedures of paragraphs (e) and (f) of this section, as applicable, within two complete billing cycles (but in no event later than 90 days) after receiving a billing-error notice.

(d) *Rules pending resolution.* Until a billing error is resolved under paragraphs (e) or (f) of this section, the following rules apply:

(1) *Consumer's right to withhold disputed amount; collection action prohibited.* The consumer need not pay (and the creditor may not try to collect) any portion of any required payment that the consumer believes is related to the disputed amount (including related finance or other charges).[30] If the cardholder maintains a deposit account with the card issuer and has agreed to pay the credit card indebtedness by periodic deductions from the cardholder's deposit account, the card issuer shall not deduct any part of the disputed amount or related finance or other charges if a billing error notice is received any time up to three business days before the scheduled payment date.

28. The creditor need not comply with the requirements of paragraphs (c) through (g) of this section if the consumer concludes that no billing error occurred and voluntarily withdraws the billing-error notice.

29. The creditor may require that the written notice not be made on the payment medium or other material accompanying the periodic statement if the creditor so stipulates in the billing rights statement required by sections 226.6(d) and 226.9(a).

30. A creditor is not prohibited from taking action to collect any undisputed portion of the item or bill; from deducting any disputed amount and related finance or other charges from the consumer's credit limit on the account; or from reflecting a disputed amount and related finance or other charges on a periodic statement, provided that the creditor indicates on or with the periodic statement that payment of any disputed amount and related finance or other charges is not required pending the creditor's compliance with this section.

(2) *Adverse credit reports prohibited.* The creditor or its agent shall not (directly or indirectly) make or threaten to make an adverse report to any person about the consumer's credit standing, or report that an amount or account is delinquent, because the consumer failed to pay the disputed amount or related finance or other charges.

(e) *Procedures if billing error occurred as asserted.* If a creditor determines that a billing error occurred as asserted, it shall within the time limits in paragraph (c)(2) of this section—

(1) Correct the billing error and credit the consumer's account with any disputed amount and related finance or other charges, as applicable; and

(2) Mail or deliver a correction notice to the consumer.

(f) *Procedures if different billing error or no billing error occurred.* If, after conducting a reasonable investigation,[31] a creditor determines that no billing error occurred or that a different billing error occurred from that asserted, the creditor shall within the time limits in paragraph (c)(2) of this section—

(1) Mail or deliver to the consumer an explanation that sets forth the reasons for the creditor's belief that the billing error alleged by the consumer is incorrect in whole or in part;

(2) Furnish copies of documentary evidence of the consumer's indebtedness, if the consumer so requests; and

(3) If a different billing error occurred, correct the billing error and credit the consumer's account with any disputed amount and related finance or other charges, as applicable.

(g) *Creditor's rights and duties after resolution.* If a creditor, after complying with all of the requirements of this section, determines that a consumer owes all or part of the disputed amount and related finance or other charges, the creditor—

(1) Shall promptly notify the consumer in writing of the time when payment is due and the portion of the disputed amount and related finance or other charges that the consumer still owes;

(2) Shall allow any time period disclosed under sections 226.6(a)(1) and 226.7(j), during which the consumer can pay the amount due under paragraph (g)(1) of this section without incurring additional finance or other charges;

(3) May report an account or amount as delinquent because the amount due under paragraph (g)(1) of this section remains unpaid af-

31. If a consumer submits a billing error notice alleging either the nondelivery of property or services under paragraph (a)(3) of this section or that information appearing on a periodic statement is incorrect because a person honoring the consumer's credit card has made an incorrect report to the card issuer, the creditor shall not deny the assertion unless it conducts a reasonable investigation and determines that the property or services were actually delivered, mailed, or sent as agreed or that the information was correct.

ter the creditor has allowed any time period disclosed under sections 226.6(a)(1) and 226.7(j) or 10 days (whichever is longer) during which the consumer can pay the amount; but

(4) May not report that an amount or account is delinquent because the amount due under paragraph (g)(1) of the section remains unpaid, if the creditor receives (within the time allowed for payment in paragraph (g)(3) of this section) further written notice from the consumer that any portion of the billing error is still in dispute, unless the creditor also—

(i) Promptly reports that the amount or account is in dispute;

(ii) Mails or delivers to the consumer (at the same time the report is made) a written notice of the name and address of each person to whom the creditor makes a report; and

(iii) Promptly reports any subsequent resolution of the reported delinquency to all persons to whom the creditor has made a report.

(h) *Reassertion of billing error.* A creditor that has fully complied with the requirements of this section has no further responsibilities under this section (other than as provided in paragraph (g)(4) of this section) if a consumer reasserts substantially the same billing error.

(i) *Relation to Electronic Fund Transfer Act and Regulation E.* If an extension of credit is incident to an electronic fund transfer, under an agreement between a consumer and a financial institution to extend credit when the consumer's account is overdrawn or to maintain a specified minimum balance in the consumer's account, the creditor shall comply with the requirements of Regulation E, 12 CFR 205.11, governing error resolution rather than those of paragraphs (a), (b), (c), (e), (f), and (h) of this section.

§ 226.14 Determination of annual percentage rate

(a) *General rule.* The annual percentage rate is a measure of the cost of credit, expressed as a yearly rate. An annual percentage rate shall be considered accurate if it is not more than 1/8 of 1 percentage point above or below the annual percentage rate determined in accordance with this section.

(b) *Annual percentage rate for initial disclosures and for advertising purposes.* Where one or more periodic rates may be used to compute the finance charge, the annual percentage rate(s) to be disclosed for purposes of sections 226.6(a)(2) and 226.16(b)(2) shall be computed by multiplying each periodic rate by the number of periods in a year.

(c) *Annual percentage rate for periodic statements.* The annual percentage rate(s) to be disclosed for purposes of section 226.7(d) shall be computed by multiplying each periodic rate by the number of periods in a year and, for purposes of section 226.7(g), shall be determined as follows:

(1) If the finance charge is determined solely by applying one or more periodic rates, at the creditor's option, either—

(i) By multiplying each periodic rate by the number of periods in a year; or

(ii) By dividing the total finance charge for the billing cycle by the sum of the balances to which the periodic rates were applied and multiplying the quotient (expressed as a percentage) by the number of billing cycles in a year.

(2) If the finance charge imposed during the billing cycle is or includes a minimum, fixed, or other charge not due to the application of a periodic rate, other than a charge with respect to any specific transaction during the billing cycle, by dividing the total finance charge for the billing cycle by the amount of the balance(s) to which it is applicable [32] and multiplying the quotient (expressed as a percentage) by the number of billing cycles in a year.[33]

(3) If the finance charge imposed during the billing cycle is or includes a charge relating to a specific transaction during the billing cycle (even if the total finance charge also includes any other minimum, fixed, or other charge not due to the application of a periodic rate), by dividing the total finance charge imposed during the billing cycle by the total of all balances and other amounts on which a finance charge was imposed during the billing cycle without duplication, and multiplying the quotient (expressed as a percentage) by the number of billing cycles in a year,[34] except that the annual percentage rate shall not be less than the largest rate determined by multiplying each periodic rate imposed during the billing cycle by the number of periods in a year.[35]

(4) If the finance charge imposed during the billing cycle is or includes a minimum, fixed, or other charge not due to the application of a periodic rate and the total finance charge imposed during the billing cycle does not exceed 50 cents for a monthly or longer billing cycle, or the pro rata part of 50 cents for a billing cycle shorter than monthly, at the creditor's option, by multiplying each applicable periodic rate by the number of periods in a year, notwithstanding the provisions of paragraphs (c)(2) and (3) of this section.

32. If there is no balance to which the finance charge is applicable, an annual percentage rate cannot be determined under this section.

33. Where the finance charge imposed during the billing cycle is or includes a loan fee, points, or similar charge that relates to the opening of the account, the amount of such charge shall not be included in the calculation of the annual percentage rate.

34. See appendix F regarding determination of the denominator of the fraction under this paragraph.

35. See footnote 33.

(d) *Calculations where daily periodic rate applied.* If the provisions of paragraphs (c)(1)(ii) or (2) of this section apply and all or a portion of the finance charge is determined by the application of one or more daily periodic rates, the annual percentage rate may be determined either—

(1) By dividing the total finance charge by the average of the daily balances and multiplying the quotient by the number of billing cycles in a year; or

(2) By dividing the total finance charge by the sum of the daily balances and multiplying the quotient by 365.

§ 226.15 Right of rescission

(a) *Consumer's right to rescind.* (1)(i) Except as provided in paragraph (a)(1)(ii) of this section, in a credit plan in which a security interest is or will be retained or acquired in a consumer's principal dwelling, each consumer whose ownership interest is or will be subject to the security interest shall have the right to rescind: each credit extension made under the plan; the plan when the plan is opened; a security interest when added or increased to secure an existing plan; and the increase when a credit limit on the plan is increased.

(ii) As provided in section 125(e) of the act, the consumer does not have the right to rescind each credit extension made under the plan if such extension is made in accordance with a previously established credit limit for the plan.

(2) To exercise the right to rescind, the consumer shall notify the creditor of the rescission by mail, telegram, or other means of written communication. Notice is considered given when mailed, or when filed for telegraphic transmission, or, if sent by other means, when delivered to the creditor's designated place of business.

(3) The consumer may exercise the right to rescind until midnight of the third business day following the occurrence described in paragraph (a)(1) of this section that gave rise to the right of rescission, delivery of the notice required by pargraph (b) of this section, or delivery of all material disclosures,[36] whichever occurs last. If the required notice and material disclosures are not delivered, the right to rescind shall expire three years after the occurrence giving rise to the right of rescission, or upon transfer of all of the consumer's interest in the property, or upon sale of the property, whichever occurs first.

36. The term "material disclosures" means the information that must be provided to satisfy the requirements in section 226.6 with regard to the method of determining the finance charge and the balance upon which a finance charge will be imposed, the annual percentage rate, and the amount or method of determining the amount of any membership or participation fee that may be imposed as part of the plan.

In the case of certain administrative proceedings, the rescission period shall be extended in accordance with section 125(f) of the act.

(4) When more than one consumer has the right to rescind, the exercise of the right by one consumer shall be effective as to all consumers.

(b) *Notice of right to rescind.* In any transaction or occurrence subject to rescission, a creditor shall deliver two copies of the notice of the right to rescind to each consumer entitled to rescind. The notice shall identify the transaction or occurrence and clearly and conspicuously disclose the following:

(1) The retention or acquisition of a security interest in the consumer's principal dwelling.

(2) The consumer's right to rescind, as described in paragraph (a)(1) of this section.

(3) How to exercise the right to rescind, with a form for that purpose, designating the address of the creditor's place of business.

(4) The effects of rescission, as described in paragraph (d) of this section.

(5) The date the rescission period expires.

(c) *Delay of creditor's performance.* Unless a consumer waives the right to rescind under paragraph (e) of this section, no money shall be disbursed other than in escrow, no services shall be performed, and no materials delivered until after the rescission period has expired and the creditor is reasonably satisfied that the consumer has not rescinded. A creditor does not violate this section if a third party with no knowledge of the event activating the rescission right does not delay in providing materials or services, as long as the debt incurred for those materials or services is not secured by the property subject to rescission.

(d) *Effects of rescission.* (1) When a consumer rescinds a transaction, the security interest giving rise to the right of rescission becomes void, and the consumer shall not be liable for any amount, including any finance charge.

(2) Within 20 calendar days after receipt of a notice of rescission, the creditor shall return any money or property that has been given to anyone in connection with the transaction and shall take any action necessary to reflect the termination of the security interest.

(3) If the creditor has delivered any money or property, the consumer may retain possession until the creditor has met its obligation under paragraph (d)(2) of this section. When the creditor has complied with that paragraph, the consumer shall tender the money or property to the creditor or, where the latter would be impracticable or inequitable, tender its reasonable value. At the consumer's option, tender of property may be made at the location of the property or at

the consumer's residence. Tender of money must be made at the creditor's designated place of business. If the creditor does not take possession of the money or property within 20 calendar days after the consumer's tender, the consumer may keep it without further obligation.

(4) The procedures outlined in paragraphs (d)(2) and (3) of this section may be modified by court order.

(e) *Consumer's waiver of right to rescind.* The consumer may modify or waive the right to rescind if the consumer determines that the extension of credit is needed to meet a bona fide personal financial emergency. To modify or waive the right, the consumer shall give the creditor a dated written statement that describes the emergency, that specifically modifies or waives the right to rescind, and that bears the signatures of the consumers entitled to rescind. Printed forms for this purpose are prohibited.

(f) *Exempt transactions.* The right to rescind does not apply to the following:

(1) A residential mortgage transaction.

(2) A credit plan in which a state agency is a creditor.

§ 226.16 Advertising

(a) *Actually available terms.* If an advertisement for credit states specific credit terms, it shall state only those terms that actually are or will be arranged or offered by the creditor.

(b) *Advertisement of terms that require additional disclosures.* If any of the terms required to be disclosed under section 226.6 is set forth in an advertisement, the advertisement shall also clearly and conspicuously set forth the following:

(1) Any minimum, fixed, transaction, activity or similar charge that could be imposed.

(2) Any periodic rate that may be applied expressed as an annual percentage rate as determined under section 226.14(b). If the plan provides for a variable periodic rate, that fact shall be disclosed.

(3) Any membership or participation fee that could be imposed.

(c) *Catalogs and multiple-page advertisements.* (1) If a catalog or other multiple-page advertisement gives information in a table or schedule in sufficient detail to permit determination of the disclosures required by paragraph (b) of this section, it shall be considered a single advertisement if—

(i) The table or schedule is clearly and conspicuously set forth; and

(ii) Any statement of terms set forth in section 226.6 appearing anywhere else in the catalog or advertisement clearly refers to that page on which the table or schedule begins.

(2) A catalog or multiple-page advertisement complies with this paragraph if the table or schedule of terms includes all appropriate disclosures for a representative scale of amounts up to the level of the more commonly sold higher-priced property or services offered.

SUBPART C. CLOSED–END CREDIT

§ 226.17 General disclosure requirements

(a) *Form of disclosures.* (1) The creditor shall make the disclosures required by this subpart clearly and conspicuously in writing, in a form that the consumer may keep. The disclosures shall be grouped together, shall be segregated from everything else, and shall not contain any information not directly related [37] to the disclosures required under section 226.18.[38] The itemization of the amount financed under section 226.18(c)(1) must be separate from the other disclosures under that section.

(2) The terms "finance charge" and "annual percentage rate," when required to be disclosed under section 226.18(d) and (e) together with a corresponding amount or percentage rate, shall be more conspicuous than any other disclosure, except the creditor's identity under section 226.18(a).

(b) *Time of disclosures.* The creditor shall make disclosures before consummation of the transaction. In certain residential mortgage transactions, special timing requirements are set forth in section 226.19. In certain transactions involving mail or telephone orders or a series of sales, the timing of the disclosures may be delayed in accordance with paragraphs (g) and (h) of this section.

(c) *Basis of disclosures and use of estimates.*

(1) The disclosures shall reflect the terms of the legal obligation between the parties.

(2) If any information necessary for an accurate disclosure is unknown to the creditor, it shall make the disclosure based on the best information reasonably available and shall state that the disclosure is an estimate.

37. The disclosures may include an acknowledgment of receipt, the date of the transaction, and the consumer's name, address, and account number.

38. The following disclosures may be made together or separately from other required disclosures: the creditor's identity under section 226.18(a), the variable rate example under section 226.18(f)(4), insurance under section 226.18(n), and certain security interest charges under section 226.18(*o*).

(3) The creditor may disregard the effects of the following in making calculations and disclosures:

(i) That payments must be collected in whole cents.

(ii) That dates of scheduled payments and advances may be changed because the scheduled date is not a business day.

(iii) That months have different numbers of days.

(iv) The occurrence of leap year.

(4) In making calculations and disclosures, the creditor may disregard any irregularity in the first period that falls within the limits described below and any payment schedule irregularity that results from the irregular first period—

(i) For transactions in which the term is less than 1 year, a first period not more than 6 days shorter or 13 days longer than a regular period;

(ii) For transactions in which the term is at least 1 year and less than 10 years, a first period not more than 11 days shorter or 21 days longer than a regular period; and

(iii) For transactions in which the term is at least 10 years, a first period shorter than or not more than 32 days longer than a regular period.

(5) If an obligation is payable on demand, the creditor shall make the disclosures based on an assumed maturity of one year. If an alternate maturity date is stated in the legal obligation between the parties, the disclosures shall be based on that date.

(6)(i) A series of advances under an agreement to extend credit up to a certain amount may be considered as one transaction.

(ii) When a multiple-advance loan to finance the construction of a dwelling may be permanently financed by the same creditor, the construction phase and the permanent phase may be treated as either one transaction or more than one transaction.

(d) *Multiple creditors; multiple consumers.* If a transaction involves more than one creditor, only one set of disclosures shall be given and the creditors shall agree among themselves which creditor must comply with the requirements that this regulation imposes on any or all of them. If there is more than one consumer, the disclosures may be made to any consumer who is primarily liable on the obligation. If the transaction is rescindable under section 226.23, however, the disclosures shall be made to each consumer who has the right to rescind.

(e) *Effect of subsequent events.* If a disclosure becomes inaccurate because of an event that occurs after the creditor delivers the required disclosures, the inaccuracy is not a violation of this regulation, although new disclosures may be required under paragraph (f) of this section, section 226.19, or section 226.20.

(f) *Early disclosures.* If disclosures are given before the date of consummation of a transaction and a subsequent event makes them inaccurate, the creditor shall disclose the changed terms before consummation, if the annual percentage rate in the consummated transaction varies from the annual percentage rate disclosed under section 226.18(e) by more than 1/8 of 1 percentage point in a regular transaction, or more than 1/4 of 1 percentage point in an irregular transaction, as defined in section 226.22(a).

(g) *Mail or telephone orders—delay in disclosures.* If a creditor receives a purchase order or a request for an extension of credit by mail, telephone, or any other written or electronic communication without face-to-face or direct telephone solicitation, the creditor may delay the disclosures until the due date of the first payment, if the following information for representative amounts or ranges of credit is made available in written form to the consumer or to the public before the actual purchase order or request:

(1) The cash price or the principal loan amount.

(2) The total sale price.

(3) The finance charge.

(4) The annual percentage rate, and if the rate may increase after consummation, the following disclosures:

(i) The circumstances under which the rate may increase.

(ii) Any limitations on the increase.

(iii) The effect of an increase.

(5) The terms of repayment.

(h) *Series of sales—delay in disclosures.* If a credit sale is one of a series made under an agreement providing that subsequent sales may be added to an outstanding balance, the creditor may delay the required disclosures until the due date of the first payment for the current sale, if the following two conditions are met:

(1) The consumer has approved in writing the annual percentage rate or rates, the range of balances to which they apply, and the method of treating any unearned finance charge on an existing balance.

(2) The creditor retains no security interest in any property after the creditor has received payments equal to the cash price and any finance charge attributable to the sale of that property. For purposes of this provision, in the case of items purchased on different dates, the first purchased is deemed the first item paid for; in the case of items purchased on the same date, the lowest priced is deemed the first item paid for.

(i) *Interim student credit extensions.* For each transaction involving an interim credit extension under a student credit program, the creditor need not make the following disclosures: the finance charge under section 226.18(d), the payment schedule under section 226.18(g), the total of payments under section 226.18(h), or the total sale price under section 226.18(j).

§ 226.18 Content of disclosures

For each transaction, the creditor shall disclose the following information as applicable:

(a) *Creditor.* The identity of the creditor making the disclosures.

(b) *Amount financed.* The "amount financed," using that term, and a brief description such as "the amount of credit provided to you or on your behalf." The amount financed is calculated by—

(1) Determining the principal loan amount or the cash price (subtracting any downpayment);

(2) Adding any other amounts that are financed by the creditor and are not part of the finance charge; and

(3) Subtracting any prepaid finance charge.

(c) *Itemization of amount financed.* (1) A separate written itemization of the amount financed, including: [39]

(i) The amount of any proceeds distributed directly to the consumer.

(ii) The amount credited to the consumer's account with the creditor.

(iii) Any amounts paid to other persons by the creditor on the consumer's behalf. The creditor shall identify those persons.[40]

(iv) The prepaid finance charge.

(2) The creditor need not comply with paragraph (c)(1) of this section if the creditor provides a statement that the consumer has the right to receive a written itemization of the amount financed, together with a space for the consumer to indicate whether it is desired, and the consumer does not request it.

(d) *Finance charge.* The "finance charge," using that term, and a brief description such as "the dollar amount the credit will cost you." [41]

39. Good faith estimates of settlement costs provided for transactions subject to the Real Estate Settlement Procedures Act (12 USC 2601 et seq.) may be substituted for the disclosures required by paragraph (c) of this section.

40. The following payees may be described using generic or other general terms and need not be further identified: public officials or government agencies, credit reporting agencies, appraisers, and insurance companies.

41. The finance charge shall be considered accurate if it is not more than $5 above or below the exact finance charge in a transaction involving an amount financed of $1,000 or less, or not more than $10 above or below the exact finance charge in a transaction involving an amount financed of more than $1,000.

(e) *Annual percentage rate.* The "annual percentage rate," using that term, and a brief description such as "the cost of your credit as a yearly rate." [42]

(f) *Variable rate.* If the annual percentage rate may increase after consummation, the following disclosures: [43]

(1) The circumstances under which the rate may increase.

(2) Any limitations on the increase.

(3) The effect of an increase.

(4) An example of the payment terms that would result from an increase.

(g) *Payment schedule.* The number, amounts, and timing of payments scheduled to repay the obligation.

(1) In a demand obligation with no alternate maturity date, the creditor may comply with this paragraph by disclosing the due dates or payment periods of any scheduled interest payments for the first year.

(2) In a transaction in which a series of payments varies because a finance charge is applied to the unpaid principal balance, the creditor may comply with this paragraph by disclosing the following information:

(i) The dollar amounts of the largest and smallest payments in the series.

(ii) A reference to the variations in the other payments in the series.

(h) *Total of payments.* The "total of payments," using that term, and a descriptive explanation such as "the amount you will have paid when you have made all scheduled payments." [44]

(i) *Demand feature.* If the obligation has a demand feature, that fact shall be disclosed. When the disclosures are based on an assumed maturity of one year as provided in section 226.17(c)(5), that fact shall also be disclosed.

(j) *Total sale price.* In a credit sale, the "total sale price," using that term, and a descriptive explanation (including the amount of any downpayment) such as "the total price of your purchase on credit, including your downpayment of $______." The total sale price is the

42. For any transaction involving a finance charge of $5 or less on an amount financed of $75 or less, or a finance charge of $7.50 or less on an amount financed of more than $75, the creditor need not disclose the annual percentage rate.

43. Information provided in accordance with variable rate regulations of other federal agencies may be substituted for the disclosures required by paragraph (f) of this section.

44. In any transaction involving a single payment, the creditor need not disclose the total of payments.

sum of the cash price, the items described in paragraph (b)(2), and the finance charge disclosed under paragraph (d) of this section.

(k) *Prepayment.* (1) When an obligation includes a finance charge computed from time to time by application of a rate to the unpaid principal balance, a statement indicating whether or not a penalty may be imposed if the obligation is prepaid in full.

(2) When an obligation includes a finance charge other than the finance charge described in paragraph (k)(1) of this section, a statement indicating whether or not the consumer is entitled to a rebate of any finance charge if the obligation is prepaid in full.

(*l*) *Late payment.* Any dollar or percentage charge that may be imposed before maturity due to a late payment, other than a deferral or extension charge.

(m) *Security interest.* The fact that the creditor has or will acquire a security interest in the property purchased as part of the transaction, or in other property identified by item or type.

(n) *Insurance.* The items required by section 226.4(d) in order to exclude certain insurance premiums from the finance charge.

(*o*) *Certain security interest charges.* The disclosures required by section 226.4(e) in order to exclude from the finance charge certain fees prescribed by law or certain premiums for insurance in lieu of perfecting a security interest.

(p) *Contract reference.* A statement that the consumer should refer to the appropriate contract document for information about nonpayment, default, the right to accelerate the maturity of the obligation, and prepayment rebates and penalties. At the creditor's option, the statement may also include a reference to the contract for further information about security interests and, in a residential mortgage transaction, about the creditor's policy regarding assumption of the obligation.

(q) *Assumption policy.* In a residential mortgage transaction, a statement whether or not a subsequent purchaser of the dwelling from the consumer may be permitted to assume the remaining obligation on its original terms.

(r) *Required deposit.* If the creditor requires the consumer to maintain a deposit as a condition of the specific transaction, a statement that the annual percentage rate does not reflect the effect of the required deposit.[45]

45. A required deposit need not include, for example: (1) an escrow account for items such as taxes, insurance or repairs; (2) a deposit that earns not less than 5 percent per year; or (3) payments under a Morris Plan.

§ 226.19 Certain residential mortgage transactions

(a) *Time of disclosure.* In a residential mortgage transaction subject to the Real Estate Settlement Procedures Act (12 USC 2601 et seq.) the creditor shall make good faith estimates of the disclosures required by section 226.18 before consummation, or shall deliver or place them in the mail not later than three business days after the creditor receives the consumer's written application, whichever is earlier.

(b) *Redisclosure required.* If the annual percentage rate in the consummated transaction varies from the annual percentage rate disclosed under section 226.18(e) by more than 1/8 of 1 percentage point in a regular transaction or more than 1/4 of 1 percentage point in an irregular transaction, as defined in section 226.22, the creditor shall disclose the changed terms no later than consummation or settlement.

§ 226.20 Subsequent disclosure requirements

(a) *Refinancings.* A refinancing occurs when an existing obligation that was subject to this subpart is satisfied and replaced by a new obligation undertaken by the same consumer. A refinancing is a new transaction requiring new disclosures to the consumer. The new finance charge shall include any unearned portion of the old finance charge that is not credited to the existing obligation. The following shall not be treated as a refinancing:

(1) A renewal of a single payment obligation with no change in the original terms.

(2) A reduction in the annual percentage rate with a corresponding change in the payment schedule.

(3) An agreement involving a court proceeding.

(4) A change in the payment schedule or a change in collateral requirements as a result of the consumer's default or delinquency, unless the rate is increased, or the new amount financed exceeds the unpaid balance plus earned finance charge and premiums for continuation of insurance of the types described in section 226.4(d).

(5) The renewal of optional insurance purchased by the consumer and added to an existing transaction, if disclosures relating to the initial purchase were provided as required by this subpart.

(b) *Assumptions.* An assumption occurs when a creditor expressly agrees in writing with a subsequent consumer to accept that consumer as a primary obligor on an existing residential mortgage transaction. Before the assumption occurs, the creditor shall make new disclosures to the subsequent consumer, based on the remaining obligation. If the finance charge originally imposed on the existing obligation was an add-on or discount finance charge, the creditor need only disclose:

(1) The unpaid balance of the obligation assumed.

(2) The total charges imposed by the creditor in connection with the assumption.

(3) The information required to be disclosed under section 226.18(k), (*l*), (m), and (n).

(4) The annual percentage rate originally imposed on the obligation.

(5) The payment schedule under section 226.18(g) and the total of payments under section 226.18(h), based on the remaining obligation.

§ 226.21 Treatment of credit balances

When a credit balance in excess of $1 is created in connection with a transaction (through transmittal of funds to a creditor in excess of the total balance due on an account, through rebates of unearned finance charges or insurance premiums, or through amounts otherwise owed to or held for the benefit of a consumer), the creditor shall—

(a) Credit the amount of the credit balance to the consumer's account;

(b) Refund any part of the remaining credit balance, upon the written request of the consumer; and

(c) Make a good faith effort to refund to the consumer by cash, check, or money order, or credit to a deposit account of the consumer, any part of the credit balance remaining in the account for more than 6 months, except that no further action is required if the consumer's current location is not known to the creditor and cannot be traced through the consumer's last known address or telephone number.

§ 226.22 Determination of annual percentage rate

(a) *Accuracy of annual percentage rate.* (1) The annual percentage rate is a measure of the cost of credit, expressed as a yearly rate, that relates the amount and timing of value received by the consumer to the amount and timing of payments made. The annual percentage rate shall be determined in accordance with either the actuarial method or the United States Rule method. Explanations, equations and instructions for determining the annual percentage rate in accordance with the actuarial method are set forth in appendix J to this regulation.

(2) As a general rule, the annual percentage rate shall be considered accurate if it is not more than 1/8 of 1 percentage point above or below the annual percentage rate determined in accordance with paragraph (a)(1) of this section.

(3) In an irregular transaction, the annual percentage rate shall be considered accurate if it is not more than 1/4 of 1 percentage point above or below the annual percentage rate determined in accordance with paragraph (a)(1) of this section.[46]

(b) *Computation tools.* (1) The Regulation Z Annual Percentage Rate Tables produced by the Board may be used to determine the annual percentage rate, and any rate determined from those tables in accordance with the accompanying instructions complies with the requirements of this section. Volume I of the tables applies to single-advance transactions involving up to 480 monthly payments or 104 weekly payments. It may be used for regular transactions and for transactions with any of the following irregularities: an irregular first period, an irregular first payment, and an irregular final payment. Volume II of the tables applies to transactions involving multiple advances and any type of payment or period irregularity.

(2) Creditors may use any other computation tool in determining the annual percentage rate if the rate so determined equals the rate determined in accordance with appendix J, within the degree of accuracy set forth in paragraph (a) of this section.

(c) *Single add-on rate transactions.* If a single add-on rate is applied to all transactions with maturities up to 60 months and if all payments are equal in amount and period, a single annual percentage rate may be disclosed for all those transactions, so long as it is the highest annual percentage rate for any such transaction.

(d) *Certain transactions involving ranges of balances.* For purposes of disclosing the annual percentage rate referred to in section 226.17(g)(4) (Mail or Telephone Orders—Delay in Disclosures) and (h) (Series of Sales—Delay in Disclosures), if the same finance charge is imposed on all balances within a specified range of balances, the annual percentage rate computed for the median balance may be disclosed for all the balances. However, if the annual percentage rate computed for the median balance understates the annual percentage rate computed for the lowest balance by more than 8 percent of the latter rate, the annual percentage rate shall be computed on whatever lower balance will produce an annual percentage rate that does not result in an understatement of more than 8 percent of the rate determined on the lowest balance.

§ 226.23 Right of rescission

(a) *Consumer's right to rescind.* (1) In a credit transaction in which a security interest is or will be retained or acquired in a con-

46. For purposes of paragraph (a)(3) of this section, an irregular transaction is one that includes one or more of the following features: multiple advances, irregular payment periods, or irregular payment amounts (other than an irregular first period or an irregular first or final payment).

sumer's principal dwelling, each consumer whose ownership interest is or will be subject to the security interest shall have the right to rescind the transaction, except for transactions described in paragraph (f) of this section.[47]

(2) To exercise the right to rescind, the consumer shall notify the creditor of the rescission by mail, telegram or other means of written communication. Notice is considered given when mailed, when filed for telegraphic transmission or, if sent by other means, when delivered to the creditor's designated place of business.

(3) The consumer may exercise the right to rescind until midnight of the third business day following consummation, delivery of the notice required by paragraph (b) of this section, or delivery of all material disclosures,[48] whichever occurs last. If the required notice or material disclosures are not delivered, the right to rescind shall expire three years after consummation, upon transfer of all of the consumer's interest in the property, or upon sale of the property, whichever occurs first. In the case of certain administrative proceedings, the rescission period shall be extended in accordance with section 125(f) of the act.

(4) When more than one consumer in a transaction has the right to rescind, the exercise of the right by one consumer shall be effective as to all consumers.

(b) *Notice of right to rescind.* In a transaction subject to rescission, a creditor shall deliver two copies of the notice of the right to rescind to each consumer entitled to rescind. The notice shall be on a separate document that identifies the transaction and shall clearly and conspicuously disclose the following:

(1) The retention or acquisition of a security interest in the consumer's principal dwelling.

(2) The consumer's right to rescind the transaction.

(3) How to exercise the right to rescind, with a form for that purpose, designating the address of the creditor's place of business.

(4) The effects of rescission, as described in paragraph (d) of this section.

(5) The date the rescission period expires.

47. For purposes of this section, the addition to an existing obligation of a security interest in a consumer's principal dwelling is a transaction. The right of rescission applies only to the addition of the security interest and not the existing obligation. The creditor shall deliver the notice required by paragraph (b) of this section but need not deliver new material disclosures. Delivery of the required notice shall begin the rescission period.

48. The term "material disclosures" means the required disclosures of the annual percentge rate, the finance charge, the amount financed, the total of payments, and the payment schedule.

(c) *Delay of creditor's performance.* Unless a consumer waives the right of rescission under paragraph (e) of this section, no money shall be disbursed other than in escrow, no services shall be performed and no materials delivered until the rescission period has expired and the creditor is reasonably satisfied that the consumer has not rescinded.

(d) *Effects of rescission.* (1) When a consumer rescinds a transaction, the security interest giving rise to the right of rescission becomes void and the consumer shall not be liable for any amount, including any finance charge.

(2) Within 20 calendar days after receipt of a notice of rescission, the creditor shall return any money or property that has been given to anyone in connection with the transaction and shall take any action necessary to reflect the termination of the security interest.

(3) If the creditor has delivered any money or property, the consumer may retain possession until the creditor has met its obligation under paragraph (d)(2) of this section. When the creditor has complied with that paragraph, the consumer shall tender the money or property to the creditor, or, where the latter would be impracticable or inequitable, tender its reasonable value. At the consumer's option, tender of property may be made at the location of the property or at the consumer's residence. Tender of money must be made at the creditor's designated place of business. If the creditor does not take possession of the money or property within 20 calendar days after the consumer's tender, the consumer may keep it without further obligation.

(4) The procedures outlined in paragraphs (d)(2) and (3) of this section may be modified by court order.

(e) *Consumer's waiver of right to rescind.* The consumer may modify or waive the right to rescind if the consumer determines that the extension of credit is needed to meet a bona fide personal financial emergency. To modify or waive the right, the consumer shall give the creditor a dated written statement that describes the emergency, specifically modifies or waives the right to rescind, and bears the signature of all of the consumers entitled to rescind. Printed forms for this purpose are prohibited.

(f) *Exempt transactions.* The right to rescind does not apply to the following:

(1) A residential mortgage transaction.

(2) A refinancing or consolidation by the same creditor of an extension of credit already secured by the consumer's principal dwelling. If the new amount financed exceeds the unpaid principal balance plus any earned unpaid finance charge on the existing debt, this exemption applies only to the existing debt and its security interest.

(3) A transaction in which a state agency is a creditor.

(4) An advance, other than an initial advance, in a series of advances or in a series of single-payment obligations that is treated as a single transaction under section 226.17(c)(6), if the notice required by paragraph (b) of this section and all material disclosures have been given to the consumer.

(5) A renewal of optional insurance premiums that is not considered a refinancing under section 226.20(a)(5).

§ 226.24 Advertising

(a) *Actually available terms.* If an advertisement for credit states specific credit terms, it shall state only those terms that actually are or will be arranged or offered by the creditor.

(b) *Advertisement of rate of finance charge.* If an advertisement states a rate of finance charge, it shall state the rate as an "annual percentage rate," using that term. If the annual percentage rate may be increased after consummation, the advertisement shall state that fact. The advertisement shall not state any other rate, except that a simple annual rate or periodic rate that is applied to an unpaid balance may be stated in conjunction with, but not more conspicuously than, the annual percentage rate.

(c) *Advertisement of terms that require additional disclosures.* (1) If any of the following terms is set forth in an advertisement, the advertisement shall meet the requirements of paragraph (c)(2) of this section:

(i) The amount or percentage of any downpayment.

(ii) The number of payments or period of repayment.

(iii) The amount of any payment.

(iv) The amount of any finance charge.

(2) An advertisement stating any of the terms in paragraph (c)(1) of this section shall state the following terms,[49] as applicable:

(i) The amount or percentage of the downpayment.

(ii) The terms of repayment.

(iii) The "annual percentage rate," using that term, and, if the rate may be increased after consummation, that fact.

(d) *Catalogs and multiple-page advertisements.* (1) If a catalog or other multiple-page advertisement gives information in a table or schedule in sufficient detail to permit determination of the disclosures

49. An example of one or more typical extensions of credit with a statement of all the terms applicable to each may be used.

required by paragraph (c)(2) of this section, it shall be considered a single advertisement if—

(i) The table or schedule is clearly set forth; and

(ii) Any statement of the credit terms in paragraph (c)(1) of this section appearing anywhere else in the catalog or advertisement clearly refers to the page on which the table or schedule begins.

(2) A catalog or multiple-page advertisement complies with paragraph (c)(2) of this section if the table or schedule of terms includes all appropriate disclosures for a representative scale of amounts up to the level of the more commonly sold higher-priced property or services offered.

SUBPART D. MISCELLANEOUS

§ 226.25 Record retention

(a) *General rule.* A creditor shall retain evidence of compliance with this regulation (other than advertising requirements under sections 226.16 and 226.24) for two years after the date disclosures are required to be made or action is required to be taken. The administrative agencies responsible for enforcing the regulation may require creditors under their jurisdictions to retain records for a longer period if necessary to carry out their enforcement responsibilities under section 108 of the act.

(b) *Inspection of records.* A creditor shall permit the agency responsible for enforcing this regulation with respect to that creditor to inspect its relevant records for compliance.

§ 226.26 Use of annual percentage rate in oral disclosures

(a) *Open-end credit.* In an oral response to a consumer's inquiry about the cost of open-end credit, only the annual percentage rate or rates shall be stated, except that the periodic rate or rates also may be stated. If the annual percentage rate cannot be determined in advance because there are finance charges other than a periodic rate, the corresponding annual percentage rate shall be stated, and other cost information may be given.

(b) *Closed-end credit.* In an oral response to a consumer's inquiry about the cost of closed-end credit, only the annual percentage rate shall be stated, except that a simple annual rate or periodic rate also may be stated if it is applied to an unpaid balance. If the annual percentage rate cannot be determined in advance, the annual percentage rate for a sample transaction shall be stated, and other cost information for the consumer's specific transaction may be given.

§ 226.27 Spanish language disclosures

All disclosures required by this regulation shall be made in the English language, except in the Commonwealth of Puerto Rico, where creditors may, at their option, make disclosures in the Spanish language. If Spanish disclosures are made, English disclosures shall be provided on the consumer's request, either in substitution for or in addition to the Spanish disclosures. This requirement for providing English disclosures on request shall not apply to advertisements subject to sections 226.16 and 226.24 of this regulation.

§ 226.28 Effect on state laws

(a) *Inconsistent disclosure requirements.* (1) State law requirements that are inconsistent with the requirements contained in chapter 1 (General Provisions), chapter 2 (Credit Transactions), or chapter 3 (Credit Advertising) of the act and the implementing provisions of this regulation are preempted to the extent of the inconsistency. A state law is inconsistent if it requires a creditor to make disclosures or take actions that contradict the requirements of the federal law. A state law is contradictory if it requires the use of the same term to represent a different amount or a different meaning than the federal law, or if it requires the use of a term different from that required in the federal law to describe the same item. A creditor, state, or other interested party may request the Board to determine whether a state law requirement is inconsistent. After the Board determines that a state law is inconsistent, a creditor may not make disclosures using the inconsistent term or form.

(2)(i) State law requirements are inconsistent with the requirements contained in sections 161 (Correction of Billing Errors) or 162 (Regulation of Credit Reports) of the act and the implementing provisions of this regulation and are preempted if they provide rights, responsibilities, or procedures for consumers or creditors that are different from those required by the federal law. However, a state law that allows a consumer to inquire about an open-end credit account and imposes on the creditor an obligation to respond to such inquiry after the time allowed in the federal law for the consumer to submit written notice of a billing error shall not be preempted in any situation where the time period for making written notice under this regulation has expired. If a creditor gives written notice of a consumer's rights under such state law, the notice shall state that reliance on the longer time period available under state law may result in the loss of important rights that could be preserved by acting more promptly under federal law; it shall also explain that the state law provisions apply only after expiration of the time period for submitting a proper written notice of a billing error under the federal law. If the state disclosures are made on the same side of a page as the required federal disclosures, the state disclosures shall appear under a demarcation line below the federal disclosures, and the federal disclosures shall be identified by a heading indicating that they are made in compliance with federal law.

(ii) State law requirements are inconsistent with the requirements contained in chapter 4 (Credit Billing) of the act (other than sections 161 or 162) and the implementing provisions of this regulation and are preempted if the creditor cannot comply with state law without violating federal law.

(iii) A state may request the Board to determine whether its law is inconsistent with chapter 4 of the act and its implementing provisions.

(b) *Equivalent disclosure requirements.* If the Board determines that a disclosure required by state law (other than a requirement relating to the finance charge or annual percentage rate) is substantially the same in meaning as a disclosure required under the act or this regulation, creditors in that state may make the state disclosure in lieu of the federal disclosure. A creditor, state, or other interested party may request the Board to determine whether a state disclosure is substantially the same in meaning as a federal disclosure.

(c) *Request for determination.* The procedures under which a request for a determination may be made under this section are set forth in appendix A.

§ 226.29 State exemptions

(a) *General rule.* Any state may apply to the Board to exempt a class of transactions within the state from the requirements of chapter 2 (Credit Transactions) or chapter 4 (Credit Billing) of the act and the corresponding provisions of this regulation. The Board shall grant an exemption if it determines that—

(1) The state law is substantially similar to the federal law or, in the case of chapter 4, affords the consumer greater protection than the federal law; and

(2) There is adequate provision for enforcement.

(b) *Civil liability.* (1) No exemptions granted under this section shall extend to the civil liability provisions of sections 130 and 131 of the act.

(2) If an exemption has been granted, the disclosures required by the applicable state law (except any additional requirements not imposed by federal law) shall constitute the disclosures required by this act.

(c) *Applications.* The procedures under which a state may apply for an exemption under this section are set forth in appendix B.

APPENDIX F. Annual Percentage Rate Computations for Certain Open-End Credit Plans

In determining the denominator of the fraction under section 226.14(c)(3), no amount will be used more than once when adding the sum of the balances [1] subject to periodic rates to the sum of the amounts subject to specific transaction charges. In every case, the full amount of transactions subject to specific transaction charges shall be included in the denominator. Other balances or parts of balances shall be included according to the manner of determining the balance subject to a periodic rate, as illustrated in the following examples of accounts on monthly billing cycles:

1. Previous balance—none.

A specific transaction of $100 occurs on the first day of the billing cycle. The average daily balance is $100. A specific transaction charge of 3 percent is applicable to the specific transaction. The periodic rate is 1½ percent applicable to the average daily balance. The numerator is the amount of the finance charge, which is $4.50. The denominator is the amount of the transaction (which is $100), plus the amount by which the balance subject to the periodic rate exceeds the amount of the specific transactions (such excess in this case is 0), totaling $100.

The annual percentage rate is the quotient (which is 4½ percent) multiplied by 12 (the number of months in a year), i.e., 54 percent.

2. Previous balance—$100.

A specific transaction of $100 occurs at the midpoint of the billing cycle. The average daily balance is $150. A specific transaction charge of 3 percent is applicable to the specific transaction. The periodic rate is 1½ percent applicable to the average daily balance. The numerator is the amount of the finance charge which is $5.25. The denominator is the amount of the transaction (which is $100), plus the amount by which the balance subject to the periodic rate exceeds the amount of the specific transaction (such excess in this case is $50), totaling $150. As explained in example 1, the annual percentage rate is $3\frac{1}{2}\% \times 12 = 42\%$.

3. If, in example 2, the periodic rate applies only to the previous balance, the numerator is $4.50 and the denominator is $200 (the amount of the transaction, $100, plus the balance subject only to the periodic rate, the $100 previous balance). As explained in example 1, the annual percentage rate is $2\frac{1}{4}\% \times 12 = 27\%$.

4. If, in example 2, the periodic rate applies only to an adjusted balance (previous balance less payments and credits) and the consumer made a payment of $50 at the midpoint of the billing cycle, the nu-

1. Where a portion of the finance charge is determined by application of one or more daily periodic rates, the phrase "sum of the balances" shall also mean the "average of daily balances."

merator is $3.75 and the denominator is $150 (the amount of the transaction, $100, plus the balance subject to the periodic rate, the $50 adjusted balance). As explained in example 1, the annual percentage rate is $2^1/_2\% \times 12 = 30\%$.

5. Previous balance—$100.

A specific transaction (check) of $100 occurs at the midpoint of the billing cycle. The average daily balance is $150. The specific transaction charge is $.25 per check. The periodic rate is $1^1/_2$ percent applied to the average daily balance. The numerator is the amount of the finance charge, which is $2.50 and includes the $.25 check charge and the $2.25 resulting from the application of the periodic rate. The denominator is the full amount of the specific transaction (which is $100) plus the amount by which the average daily balance exceeds the amount of the specific transaction (which in this case is $50), totaling $150. As explained in example 1, the annual percentage rate would be $1^2/_3\% \times 12 = 20\%$.

6. Previous balance—none.

A specific transaction of $100 occurs at the midpoint of the billing cycle. The average daily balance is $50. The specific transaction charge is 3 percent of the transaction amount or $3.00. The periodic rate is $1^1/_2$ percent per month applied to the average daily balance. The numerator is the amount of the finance charge, which is $3.75, including the $3.00 transaction charge and $.75 resulting from application of the periodic rate. The denominator is the full amount of the specific transaction ($100) plus the amount by which the balance subject to the periodic rate exceeds the amount of the transaction ($0). Where the specific transaction amount exceeds the balance subject to the periodic rate, the resulting number is considered to be zero rather than a negative number ($50 − $100 = −$50). The denominator, in this case, is $100. As explained in example 1, the annual percentage rate is $3^3/_4\% \times 12 = 45\%$.

APPENDIX G. Open-End Model Forms and Clauses

G–1. Balance Computation Methods Model Clauses (§§ 226.6 and 226.7)

G–2. Liability for Unauthorized Use Model Clause (§ 226.12)

G–3. Long-Form Billing-Error Rights Model Form (§§ 226.6 and 226.9)

G–4. Alternative Billing-Error Rights Model Form (§ 226.9)

G–5. Rescission Model Form (When Opening an Account) (§ 226.15)

G–6. Rescission Model Form (For Each Transaction) (§ 226.15)

G–7. Rescission Model Form (When Increasing the Credit Limit) (§ 226.15) [Omitted]

G–8. Rescission Model Form (When Adding a Security Interest) (§ 226.15) [Omitted]

G–9. Rescission Model Form (When Increasing the Security) (§ 226.15) [Omitted]

G–1. Balance Computation Methods Model Clauses

(a) *Adjusted balance method*

We figure [a portion of] the finance charge on your account by applying the periodic rate to the "adjusted balance" of your account. We get the "adjusted balance" by taking the balance you owed at the end of the previous billing cycle and subtracting [any unpaid finance charges and] any payments and credits received during the present billing cycle.

(b) *Previous balance method*

We figure [a portion of] the finance charge on your account by applying the periodic rate to the amount you owe at the beginning of each billing cycle [minus any unpaid finance charges]. We do not subtract any payments or credits received during the billing cycle. [The amount of payments and credits to your account this billing cycle was $________.]

(c) *Average daily balance method (excluding current transactions)*

We figure [a portion of] the finance charge on your account by applying the periodic rate to the "average daily balance" of your account (excluding current transactions). To get the "average daily balance" we take the beginning balance of your account each day and subtract any payments or credits [and any unpaid finance charges]. We do not add in any new [purchases/advances/loans]. This gives us the daily balance. Then, we add all the daily balances for the billing cycle together and divide the total by the number of days in the billing cycle. This gives us the "average daily balance."

(d) *Average daily balance method (including current transactions)*

We figure [a portion of] the finance charge on your account by applying the periodic rate to the "average daily balance" of your account (including current transactions). To get the "average daily balance" we take the beginning balance of your account each day, add any new [purchases/advances/loans], and subtract any payments or credits, [and unpaid finance charges]. This gives us the daily balance. Then, we add up all the daily balances for the billing cycle and divide the total by the number of days in the billing cycle. This gives us the "average daily balance."

G–2. Liability for Unauthorized Use Model Clause

You may be liable for the unauthorized use of your credit card [or other term that describes the credit card]. You will not be liable for unauthorized use that occurs after you notify [name of card issuer or its designee] at [address], orally or in writing, of the loss, theft, or possible unauthorized use. In any case, your liability will not exceed [insert $50 or any lesser amount under agreement with the cardholder].

G–3. Long-Form Billing-Error Rights Model Form

YOUR BILLING RIGHTS KEEP THIS NOTICE FOR FUTURE USE

This notice contains important information about your rights and our responsibilities under the Fair Credit Billing Act.

Notify Us In Case of Errors or Questions About Your Bill

If you think your bill is wrong, or if you need more information about a transaction on your bill, write us [on a separate sheet] at [address] [the address listed on your bill]. Write to us as soon as possible. We must hear from you no later than 60 days after we sent you the first bill on which the error or problem appeared. You can telephone us, but doing so will not preserve your rights.

In your letter, give us the following information:

- Your name and account number.
- The dollar amount of the suspected error.
- Describe the error and explain, if you can, why you believe there is an error. If you need more information, describe the item you are not sure about.

If you have authorized us to pay your credit card bill automatically from your savings or checking account, you can stop the payment on any amount you think is wrong. To stop the payment your letter must reach us three business days before the automatic payment is scheduled to occur.

Your Rights and Our Responsibilities After We Receive Your Written Notice

We must acknowledge your letter within 30 days, unless we have corrected the error by then. Within 90 days, we must either correct the error or explain why we believe the bill was correct.

After we receive your letter, we cannot try to collect any amount you question, or report you as delinquent. We can continue to bill you for the amount you question, including finance charges, and we can apply any unpaid amount against your credit limit. You do not have to pay any questioned amount while we are investigating, but you are still obligated to pay the parts of your bill that are not in question.

If we find that we made a mistake on your bill, you will not have to pay any finance charges related to any questioned amount. If we didn't make a mistake, you may have to pay finance charges, and you will have to make up any missed payments on the questioned amount. In either case, we will send you a statement of the amount you owe and the date that it is due.

If you fail to pay the amount that we think you owe, we may report you as delinquent. However, if our explanation does not satisfy you and you write to us within ten days telling us that you still refuse to pay, we must tell anyone we report you to that you have a question about your bill. And, we must tell you the name of anyone we reported you to. We must tell anyone we report you to that the matter has been settled between us when it finally is.

If we don't follow these rules, we can't collect the first $50 of the questioned amount, even if your bill was correct.

Special Rule for Credit Card Purchases

If you have a problem with the quality of property or services that you purchased with a credit card, and you have tried in good faith to correct the problem with the merchant, you may have the right not to pay the remaining amount due on the property or services. There are two limitations on this right:

(a) You must have made the purchase in your home state or, if not within your home state within 100 miles of your current mailing address; and

(b) The purchase price must have been more than $50.

These limitations do not apply if we own or operate the merchant, or if we mailed you the advertisement for the property or services.

G–4. Alternative Billing-Error Rights Model Form

BILLING RIGHTS SUMMARY

In Case of Errors or Questions About Your Bill

If you think your bill is wrong, or if you need more information about a transaction on your bill, write us [on a separate sheet] at [address] [the address shown on your bill] as soon as possible. We must hear from you no later than 60 days after we sent you the first bill on which the error or problem appeared. You can telephone us, but doing so will not preserve your rights.

In your letter, give us the following information:

- Your name and account number.
- The dollar amount of the suspected error.

- Describe the error and explain, if you can, why you believe there is an error. If you need more information, describe the item you are unsure about.

You do not have to pay any amount in question while we are investigating, but you are still obligated to pay the parts of your bill that are not in question. While we investigate your question, we cannot report you as delinquent or take any action to collect the amount you question.

Special Rule for Credit Card Purchases

If you have a problem with the quality of goods or services that you purchased with a credit card, and you have tried in good faith to correct the problem with the merchant, you may not have to pay the remaining amount due on the goods or services. You have this protection only when the purchase price was more than $50 and the purchase was made in your home state or within 100 miles of your mailing address. (If we own or operate the merchant, or if we mailed you the advertisement for the property or services, all purchases are covered regardless of amount or location of purchase.)

G–5. Rescission Model Form (When Opening An Account)

NOTICE OF RIGHT TO CANCEL

1. Your Right to Cancel

We have agreed to establish an open-end credit account for you, and you have agreed to give us a [mortgage/lien/security interest] [on/in] your home as security for the account. You have a legal right under federal law to cancel the account, without cost, within three business days after the latest of the following events:

(1) the opening date of your account which is ________; or

(2) the date you received your Truth-in-Lending disclosures; or

(3) the date you received this notice of your right to cancel the account.

If you cancel the account, the [mortgage/lien/security interest] [on/in] your home is also cancelled. Within 20 days of receiving your notice, we must take the necessary steps to reflect the fact that the [mortgage/lien/security interest] [on/in] your home has been cancelled. We must return to you any money or property you have given to us or to anyone else in connection with the account.

You may keep any money or property we have given you until we have done the things mentioned above, but you must then offer to return the money or property. If it is impractical or unfair for you to return the property, you must offer its reasonable value. You may offer to return the property at your home or at the location of the property. Money must be returned to the address shown below. If we do not take possession of the money or property within 20 calendar days of your offer, you may keep it without further obligation.

2. How to Cancel.

If you decide to cancel the account, you may do so by notifying us, in writing, at

(*creditor's name and business address*).

You may use any written statement that is signed and dated by you and states your intention to cancel, or you may use this notice by dating and signing below. Keep one copy of this notice no matter how you notify us because it contains important information about your rights.

If you cancel by mail or telegram, you must send the notice no later than midnight of

(*date*)

(or midnight of the third business day following the latest of the three events listed above). If you send or deliver your written notice to cancel some other way, it must be delivered to the above address no later than that time.

I WISH TO CANCEL.

______________________________ ____________

Consumer's Signature Date

G–6. Rescission Model Form (For Each Transaction)

NOTICE OF RIGHT TO CANCEL

1. Your Right to Cancel

We have extended credit to you under your open-end credit account. This extension of credit will increase the amount you owe on your account. We already have a [mortgage/lien/security interest] [on/in] your home as security for your account. You have a legal right under federal law to cancel the extension of credit, without cost, within three business days after the latest of the following events:

(1) the date of the additional extension of credit which is ______; or

(2) the date you received your Truth-in-Lending disclosures; or

(3) the date you received this notice of your right to cancel the additional extension of credit.

If you cancel the additional extension of credit, your cancellation will only apply to the additional amount and to any increase in the [mortgage/lien/security interest] that resulted because of the additional amount. It will not affect the amount you presently owe, and it will not affect the [mortgage/lien/security interest] we already have [on/in] your home. Within 20 calendar days after we receive your notice of cancellation, we must take the necessary steps to reflect the fact that any increase in the [mortgage/lien/security interest] [on/in] your home has been cancelled. We must also return to you any money or property you have given to us or to anyone else in connection with this extension of credit.

You may keep any money or property we have given you until we have done the things mentioned above, but you must then offer to return the money or property. If it is impractical or unfair for you to return the property, you must offer its reasonable value. You may offer to return the property at your home or at the location of the property. Money must be returned to the address shown below. If we do not take possession of the money or property within 20 calendar days of your offer, you may keep it without further obligation.

2. How to Cancel

If you decide to cancel the additional extension of credit, you may do so by notifying us, in writing, at

(*creditor's name and business address*).

You may use any written statement that is signed and dated by you and states your intention to cancel, or you may use this notice by dating and signing below. Keep one copy of this notice no matter how you notify us because it contains important information about your rights.

If you cancel by mail or telegram, you must send the notice no later than midnight of

(*date*)

(or midnight of the third business day following the latest of the three events listed above). "If you send or deliver your written notice to cancel some other way, it must be delivered to the above address no later than that time."

I WISH TO CANCEL

Consumer's Signature   Date

APPENDIX H. Closed-End Model Forms and Clauses

H–1. Credit Sale Model Form (§ 226.18)
H–2. Loan Model Form (§ 226.18)
H–3. Amount Financed Itemization Model Form (§ 226.18(c))
H–4. Variable-Rate Model Clauses (§ 226.18(f))
H–5. Demand Feature Model Clauses (§ 226.18(i))
H–6. Assumption Policy Model Clause (§ 226.18(q))
H–7. Required Deposit Model Clause (§ 226.18(r))
H–8. Rescission Model Form (General) (§ 226.23)
H–9. Rescission Model Form (Refinancing) (§ 226.23) [Omitted]
H–10. Credit Sale Sample [Omitted]
H–11. Installment Loan Sample [Omitted]
H–12. Refinancing Sample [Omitted]
H–13. Mortgage with Demand Feature Sample [Omitted]
H–14. Variable-Rate Mortgage Sample [Omitted]
H–15. Graduated-Payment Mortgage Sample [Omitted]

H–1. Credit Sale Model Form

ANNUAL PERCENTAGE RATE The cost of your credit as a yearly rate. %	**FINANCE CHARGE** The dollar amount the credit will cost you. $	Amount Financed The amount of credit provided to you or on your behalf. $	Total of Payments The amount you will have paid after you have made all payments as scheduled. $	Total Sale Price The total cost of your purchase on credit, including your downpayment of $ ________. $

You have the right to receive at this time an itemization of the Amount Financed.
☐ I want an itemization. ☐ I do not want an itemization.

Your payment schedule will be:

Number of Payments	Amount of Payments	When Payments Are Due

Insurance
Credit life insurance and credit disability insurance are not required to obtain credit, and will not be provided unless you sign and agree to pay the additional cost.

Type	Premium	Signature	
Credit Life		I want credit life insurance.	Signature
Credit Disability		I want credit disability insurance.	Signature
Credit Life and Disability		I want credit life and disability insurance.	Signature

You may obtain property insurance from anyone you want that is acceptable to (creditor). If you get the insurance from (creditor), you will pay $ ________.

Security: You are giving a security interest in:
☐ the goods or property being purchased.
☐ (brief description of other property).

Filing fees $ ________ **Non-filing insurance** $ ________

Late Charge: If a payment is late, you will be charged $ ________ / ________ % of the payment.

Prepayment: If you pay off early, you
☐ may ☐ will not have to pay a penalty.
☐ may ☐ will not be entitled to a refund of part of the finance charge.

See your contract documents for any additional information about nonpayment, default, any required repayment in full before the scheduled date, and prepayment refunds and penalties.

e means an estimate

H–2. Loan Model Form

ANNUAL PERCENTAGE RATE The cost of your credit as a yearly rate.	**FINANCE CHARGE** The dollar amount the credit will cost you.	**Amount Financed** The amount of credit provided to you or on your behalf.	**Total of Payments** The amount you will have paid after you have made all payments as scheduled.
%	$	$	$

You have the right to receive at this time an itemization of the Amount Financed.
☐ I want an itemization. ☐ I do not want an itemization.

Your payment schedule will be:

Number of Payments	Amount of Payments	When Payments Are Due

Insurance
Credit life insurance and credit disability insurance are not required to obtain credit, and will not be provided unless you sign and agree to pay the additional cost.

Type	Premium	Signature
Credit Life		I want credit life insurance. ______ Signature
Credit Disability		I want credit disability insurance. ______ Signature
Credit Life and Disability		I want credit life and disability insurance. ______ Signature

You may obtain property insurance from anyone you want that is acceptable to (creditor). If you get the insurance from (creditor), you will pay $__________.

Security: You are giving a security interest in:
☐ the goods or property being purchased.
☐ (brief description of other property).

Filing fees $________ **Non-filing insurance** $________

Late Charge: If a payment is late, you will be charged $________/________% of the payment.

Prepayment: If you pay off early, you
☐ may ☐ will not have to pay a penalty.
☐ may ☐ will not be entitled to a refund of part of the finance charge.

See your contract documents for any additional information about nonpayment, default, any required repayment in full before the scheduled date, and prepayment refunds and penalties.

e means an estimate

H–3. Amount Financed Itemization Model Form

Itemization of the Amount Financed of $______________

$______ Amount given to you directly

$______ Amount paid on your account

Amount paid to others on your behalf

$______ to [public officials] [credit bureau] [appraiser] [insurance company]

$______ to (*name of another creditor*)

$______ to (*other*)

$______ Prepaid finance charge

H-4. Variable-Rate Model Clauses

The annual percentage rate may increase during the term of this transaction if:

[the prime interest rate of (*creditor*) increases.]

[the balance in your deposit account falls below $______.]

[you terminate your employment with (*employer*).]

[The interest rate will not increase above ______%.]

[The maximum interest rate increase at one time will be ______%.]

[The rate will not increase more than once every (*time period*).]

Any increase will take the form of:

[higher payment amounts.]

[more payments of the same amount.]

[a larger amount due at maturity.]

Example based on the specific transaction

[If the interest rate increases by ______% in (*time period*),

[your regular payments will increase to $______.]

[you will have to make ______ additional payments.]

[your final payment will increase to $______.]]

Example based on a typical transaction

[If your loan were for $______ at ______% for (*term*) and the rate increased to ______% in (*time period*),

[your regular payments would increase by $______.]

[you would have to make ______ additional payments.]

[your final payment would increase by $______.]]

H-5. Demand Feature Model Clauses

This obligation [is payable on demand.] [has a demand feature.]

[All disclosures are based on an assumed maturity of one year.]

H-6. Assumption Policy Model Clause

Assumption: Someone buying your house [may, subject to conditions, be allowed to] [cannot] assume the remainder of the mortgage on the original terms.

H–7. Required Deposit Model Clause

The annual percentage rate does not take into account your required deposit.

H–8. Rescission Model Form (General)

NOTICE OF RIGHT TO CANCEL

Your Right to Cancel

You are entering into a transaction that will result in a [mortgage/lien/security interest] [on/in] your home. You have a legal right under federal law to cancel this transaction, without cost, within three business days from whichever of the following events occurs last:

(1) the date of the transaction, which is ______; or

(2) the date you received your Truth in Lending disclosures; or

(3) the date you received this notice of your right to cancel.

If you cancel the transaction, the [mortgage/lien/security interest] is also cancelled. Within 20 calendar days after we receive your notice, we must take the steps necessary to reflect the fact that the [mortgage/lien/security interest] [on/in] your home has been cancelled, and we must return to you any money or property you have given to us or to anyone else in connection with this transaction.

You may keep any money or property we have given you until we have done the things mentioned above, but you must then offer to return the money or property. If it is impractical or unfair for you to return the property, you must offer its reasonable value. You may offer to return the property at your home or at the location of the property. Money must be returned to the address below. If we do not take possession of the money or property within 20 calendar days of your offer, you may keep it without further obligation.

How to Cancel

If you decide to cancel this transaction, you may do so by notifying us in writing, at

(*creditor's name and business address*).

You may use any written statement that is signed and dated by you and states your intention to cancel, or you may use this notice by dating and signing below. Keep one copy of this notice because it contains important information about your rights.

If you cancel by mail or telegram, you must send the notice no later than midnight of

(*date*)

(or midnight of the third business day following the latest of the three events listed above). If you send or deliver your written notice to cancel some other way, it must be delivered to the above address no later than that time.

I WISH TO CANCEL

______________________________ __________

Consumer's Signature Date

APPENDIX J. Annual Percentage Rate Computations for Closed-End Credit Transactions

(a) *Introduction.* (1) Section 226.22(a) of Regulation Z provides that the annual percentage rate for other than open-end credit transactions shall be determined in accordance with either the actuarial method or the United States Rule method. This appendix contains an explanation of the actuarial method as well as equations, instructions and examples of how this method applies to single-advance and multiple-advance transactions.

(2) Under the actuarial method, at the end of each unit period (or fractional unit period) the unpaid balance of the amount financed is increased by the finance charge earned during that period and is decreased by the total payment (if any) made at the end of that period. The determination of unit periods and fractional unit periods shall be consistent with the definitions and rules in paragraphs (b)(3), (4) and (5) of this section and the general equation in paragraph (b)(8) of this section.

(3) In contrast, under the United States Rule method, at the end of each payment period, the unpaid balance of the amount financed is increased by the finance charge earned during that payment period and is decreased by the payment made at the end of that payment period. If the payment is less than the finance charge earned, the adjustment of the unpaid balance of the amount financed is postponed until the end of the next payment period. If at that time the sum of the two payments is still less than the total earned finance charge for the two payment periods, the adjustment of the unpaid balance of the amount financed is postponed still another payment period, and so forth.

(b) *Instructions and equations for the actuarial method.* (1) *General rule.* The annual percentage rate shall be the nominal annual percentage rate determined by multiplying the unit-period rate by the number of unit periods in a year.

(2) *Term of the transaction.* The term of the transaction begins on the date of its consummation, except that if the finance charge or

any portion of it is earned beginning on a later date, the term begins on the later date. The term ends on the date the last payment is due, except that if an advance is scheduled after that date, the term ends on the later date. For computation purposes, the length of the term shall be equal to the time interval between any point in time on the beginning date to the same point in time on the ending date.

(3) *Definitions of time intervals.* (i) A period is the interval of time between advances or between payments and includes the interval of time between the date the finance charge begins to be earned and the date of the first advance thereafter or the date of the first payment thereafter, as applicable.

(ii) A common period is any period that occurs more than once in a transaction.

(iii) A standard interval of time is a day, week, semimonth, month, or a multiple of a week or a month up to, but not exceeding, one year.

(iv) All months shall be considered equal. Full months shall be measured from any point in time on a given date of a given month to the same point in time on the same date of another month. If a series of payments (or advances) is scheduled for the last day of each month, months shall be measured from the last day of the given month to the last day of another month. If payments (or advances) are scheduled for the 29th or 30th of each month, the last day of February shall be used when applicable.

(4) *Unit period.* (i) In all transactions other than a single-advance, single-payment transaction, the unit period shall be that common period, not to exceed one year, that occurs most frequently in the transaction, except that—

(A) If two or more common periods occur with equal frequency, the smaller of such common periods shall be the unit period; or

(B) If there is no common period in the transaction, the unit period shall be that period which is the average of all periods rounded to the nearest whole standard interval of time. If the average is equally near two standard intervals of time, the lower shall be the unit period.

(ii) In a single-advance, single-payment transaction, the unit period shall be the term of the transaction, but shall not exceed one year.

(5) *Number of unit periods between two given dates.* (i) The number of days between two dates shall be the number of 24-hour intervals between any point in time on the first date to the same point in time on the second date.

(ii) If the unit period is a month, the number of full unit periods between two dates shall be the number of months measured back from the later date. The remaining fraction of a unit period shall be the number of days measured forward from the earlier date to the beginning of the first full unit period, divided by 30. If the unit period is a month, there are 12 unit periods per year.

(iii) If the unit period is a semimonth or a multiple of a month not exceeding 11 months, the number of days between two dates shall be 30 times the number of full months measured back from the later date, plus the number of remaining days. The number of full unit periods and the remaining fraction of a unit period shall be determined by dividing such number of days by 15 in the case of a semimonthly unit period or by the appropriate multiple of 30 in the case of a multimonthly unit period. If the unit period is a semimonth, the number of unit periods per year shall be 24. If the number of unit periods is a multiple of a month, the number of unit periods per year shall be 12 divided by the number of months per unit period.

(iv) If the unit period is a day, a week, or a multiple of a week, the number of full unit periods and the remaining fractions of a unit period shall be determined by dividing the number of days between the two given dates by the number of days per unit period. If the unit period is a day, the number of unit periods per year shall be 365. If the unit period is a week or a multiple of a week, the number of unit periods per year shall be 52 divided by the number of weeks per unit period.

(v) If the unit period is a year, the number of full unit periods between two dates shall be the number of full years (each equal to 12 months) measured back from the later date. The remaining fraction of a unit period shall be—

(A) The remaining number of months divided by 12 if the remaining interval is equal to a whole number of months, or

(B) The remaining number of days divided by 365 if the remaining interval is *not* equal to a whole number of months.

(vi) In a single-advance, single-payment transaction in which the term is less than a year and is equal to a whole number of months, the number of unit periods in the term shall be one, and the number of unit periods per year shall be 12 divided by the number of months in the term or 365 divided by the number of days in the term.

(vii) In a single-advance, single-payment transaction in which the term is less than a year and is *not* equal to a whole number of months, the number of unit periods in the term shall be one, and the number of unit periods per year shall be 365 divided by the number of days in the term.

(6) *Percentage rate for a fraction of a unit period.* The percentage rate of finance charge for a fraction (less than one) of a unit period shall be equal to such fraction multiplied by the percentage rate of finance charge per unit period.

(7) *Symbols.* The symbols used to express the terms of a transaction in the equation set forth in paragraph (b)(8) of this section are defined as follows:

A_k = The amount of the kth advance.

q_k = The number of full unit periods from the beginning of the term of the transaction to the kth advance.

e_k = The fraction of a unit period in the time interval from the beginning of the term of the transaction to the kth advance.

m = The number of advances.

P_j = The amount of the jth payment.

t_j = The number of full unit periods from the beginning of the term of the transaction to the jth payment.

f_j = The fraction of a unit period in the time interval from the beginning of the term of the transaction to the jth payment.

n = The number of payments.

i = The percentage rate of finance charge per unit period, expressed as a decimal equivalent.

Symbols used in the examples shown in this appendix are defined as follows:

$\ddot{a}_{\overline{x}|}$ = The present value of 1 per unit period for x unit periods, first payment due immediately.

$$= 1 + \frac{1}{(1+i)} + \frac{1}{(1+i)^2} + \dots\dots + \frac{1}{(1+i)^{x-1}}$$

w = The number of unit periods per year.

I = wi × 100 = The nominal annual percentage rate.

(8) *General equation.* The following equation sets forth the relationship among the terms of a transaction:

$$\frac{A_1}{(1+e_1i)(1+i)^{q_1}} + \frac{A_2}{(1+e_2i)(1+i)^{q_2}} +$$

$$\ldots + \frac{A_m}{(1+e_mi)(1+i)^{q_m}} =$$

$$\frac{P_1}{(1+f_1i)(1+i)^{t_1}} + \frac{P_2}{(1+f_2i)(1+i)^{t_2}} +$$

$$\ldots + \frac{P_n}{(1+f_ni)(1+i)^{t_n}}$$

(9) *Solution of general equation by iteration process.* (i) The general equation in paragraph (b)(8) of this section, when applied to a simple transaction in which a loan of $1000 is repaid by 36 monthly payments of $33.61 each, takes the special form:

$$A = \frac{33.61\,\ddot{a}_{\overline{36}|}}{(1+i)}$$

Step 1:

Let I_1 = estimated annual percentage rate =	12.50%
Evaluate expression for A, letting $i = I_1/(100w)$ =	.010416667
Result (referred to as A') =	1004.674391

Step 2:

Let $I_2 = I_1 + .1$ =	12.60%
Evaluate expression for A, letting $i = I_2/(100w)$ =	.010500000
Result (referred to as A") =	1003.235366

Step 3:

Interpolate for I (annual percentage rate):

$$I = I_1 + .1\left[\frac{(A - A')}{(A'' - A')}\right] = 12.50 +$$

$$.1\left[\frac{(1000.000000 - 1004.674391)}{(1003.235366 - 1004.674391)}\right]$$

$$= 12.82483042\%$$

Step 4:

First iteration, let I_1
= 12.82483042% and
repeat Steps 1, 2, and 3
obtaining a new I = 12.82557859%

Second iteration, let I_1
= 12.82557859% and
repeat Steps 1, 2, and 3
obtaining a new I = 12.82557529%

In this case, no further iterations are required to obtain the annual percentage rate correct to two decimal places, 12.83%.

(ii) When the iteration approach is used, it is expected that calculators or computers will be programmed to carry all available decimals throughout the calculation and that enough iterations will be performed to make virtually certain that the annual percentage rate obtained, when rounded to two decimals, is correct. Annual percentage rates in the examples below were obtained by using a 10-digit programmable calculator and the iteration procedure described above.

(c) *Examples for the actuarial method.* (1) *Single-advance transaction, with or without an odd first period, and otherwise regular.* The general equation in paragraph (b)(8) of this section can be put in the following special form for this type of transaction:

$$A = \frac{1}{(1+fi)(1+i)^t}\left(P\, \ddot{a}_{\overline{n}|}\right)$$

Example (i): Monthly payments (regular first period):
Amount advanced (A) = \$5000. Payment (P) = \$230.
Number of payments (n) = 24.
Unit period = 1 month. Unit periods per year (w) = 12.
Advance, 1–10–78. First payment, 2–10–78.
From 1–10–78 through 2–10–78 = 1 unit period. (t = 1; f = 0)
Annual percentage rate
(I) = wi = .0969 = 9.69%

Example (ii): Monthly payments (long first period):
Amount advanced (A) = \$6000. Payment (P) = \$200.
Number of payments (n) = 36.
Unit period = 1 month. Unit periods per year (w) = 12.
Advance, 2–10–78. First payment, 4–1–78.
From 3–1–78 through 4–1–78 = 1 unit period. (t = 1)
From 2–10–78 through 3–1–78 = 19 days. (f = 19/30)

Annual percentage rate

(I) = wi = .1182 = 11.82%

. . .

(2) *Single-advance transaction, with an odd first payment, with or without an odd first period, and otherwise regular.* The general equation in paragraph (b)(8) of this section can be put in the following special form for this type of transaction:

$$A = \frac{1}{(1+fi)(1+i)^t}\left[P_1 + \frac{P\ddot{a}_{\overline{n-1}|}}{(1+i)}\right]$$

Example (i): Monthly payments (regular first period and irregular first payment):

Amount advanced (A) = \$5000. First payment (P_1) = \$250.

Regular payment (P) = \$230. Number of payments (n) = 24.

Unit period = 1 month. Unit periods per year (w) = 12.

Advance, 1–10–78. First payment, 2–10–78.

From 1–10–78 through 2–10–78 = 1 unit period. (t = 1; f = 0)

Annual percentage rate

(I) = wi = .1008 = 10.08%

. . .

(3) *Single-advance transaction, with an odd final payment, with or without an odd first period, and otherwise regular.* The general equation in paragraph (b)(8) of this section can be put in the following special form for this type of transaction:

$$A = \frac{1}{(1+fi)(1+i)^t}\left[P\,\ddot{a}_{\overline{n-1}|} + \frac{P_n}{(1+i)^{n-1}}\right]$$

Example (i): Monthly payments (regular first period and irregular final payment):

Amount advanced (A) = \$5000. Regular payment (P) = \$230.

Final payment (P_n) = \$280. Number of payments (n) = 24.

Unit period = 1 month. Unit periods per year (w) = 12.

Advance, 1–10–78. First payment, 2–10–78.

From 1–10–78 through 2–10–78 = 1 unit period. (t = 1; f = 0)

Annual percentage rate

(I) = wi = .1050 = 10.50%

. . .

(5) *Single-advance, single-payment transaction.* The general equation in paragraph (b)(8) of this section can be put in the special

forms below for single advance, single payment transactions. Forms 1 through 3 are for the direct determination of the annual percentage rate under special conditions. Form 4 requires the use of the iteration procedure of paragraph (b)(9) of this section and can be used for all single-advance, single-payment transactions regardless of term.

Form 1—Term less than one year:

$$I = 100w\left(\frac{P}{A} - 1\right)$$

Form 2—Term more than one year but less than two years:

$$I = \frac{50}{f}\left\{\left[(1+f)^2 + 4f\left(\frac{P}{A} - 1\right)\right]^{1/2} - (1+f)\right\}$$

Form 3—Term equal to exactly a year or exact multiple of a year:

$$I = 100\left[\left(\frac{P}{A}\right)^{1/t} - 1\right]$$

Form 4—Special form for iteration procedure (no restriction on term):

$$A = \frac{P}{(1+fi)(1+i)^t}$$

Example (i): Single-advance, single-payment (term of less than one year, measured in days):

Amount advanced (A) = \$1000. Payment (P) = \$1080.

Unit period = 255 days. Unit periods per year (w) = 365/255.

Advance, 1–3–78. Payment, 9–15–78.

From 1–3–78 through 9–15–78 = 255 days. (t = 1; f = 0)

Annual percentage rate

(I) = wi = .1145 = 11.45%. (Use form 1 or 4.)

Example (ii): Single-advance, single-payment (term of less than one year, measured in exact calendar months):

Amount advanced (A) = \$1000. Payment (P) = \$1044.

Unit period = 6 months. Unit periods per year (w) = 2.

Advance, 7–15–78. Payment, 1–15–79.

From 7–15–78 through 1–15–79 = 6 mos. (t = 1; f = 0)

Annual percentage rate

(I) = wi = .0880 = 8.80%. (Use form 1 or 4.)

Example (iii): Single-advance, single-payment (term of more than one year but less than two years, fraction measured in exact months):

Amount advanced (A) = \$1000. Payment (P) = \$1135.19.

Unit period = 1 year. Unit periods per year (w) = 1.

Advance, 7–17–78. Payment, 1–17–80.

From 1–17–79 through 1–17–80 = 1 unit period. (t = 1)

From 7–17–78 through 1–17–79 = 6 mos. (f = 6/12)

Annual percentage rate

(I) = wi = .0876 = 8.76%. (Use form 2 or 4.)

Example (iv): Single-advance, single-payment (term of exactly two years):

Amount advanced (A) = \$1000. Payment (P) = \$1240.

Unit period = 1 year. Unit periods per year (w) = 1.

Advance, 1–3–78. Payment, 1–3–80.

From 1–3–78 through 1–3–79 = 1 unit period. (t = 2; f = 0)

Annual percentage rate

(I) = wi = .1136 = 11.36%. (Use form 3 or 4.)

. . .

FEDERAL RESERVE BOARD, REGULATION M, CONSUMER LEASING

12 C.F.R. Part 213

Table of Sections

---

§ 213.1 General provisions

(a) *Authority.* This regulation, known as Regulation M, is issued by the Board of Governors of the Federal Reserve System to implement the consumer leasing portions of the Truth in Lending Act, which is title I of the Consumer Credit Protection Act, as amended (15 USC 1601 et seq.).

(b) *Purpose.* The purpose of this regulation is to assure that lessees of personal property are given meaningful disclosures of lease terms, to delimit the ultimate liability of lessees in leasing personal property and to require meaningful and accurate disclosures of lease terms in advertising.

. . .

§ 213.2 Definitions and rules of construction

(a) *Definitions.* For the purposes of this regulation, unless the context indicates otherwise, the following definitions apply:

(1) "*Act*" means the Truth in Lending Act (15 USC 1601 et seq.).

(2) "*Advertisement*" means any commercial message in any newspaper, magazine, leaflet, flyer or catalog, on radio, television or public address system, in direct mail literature or other printed mate-

rial on any interior or exterior sign or display, in any window display, in any point-of-transaction literature or price tag which is delivered or made available to a lessee or prospective lessee in any manner whatsoever.

(3) "*Agricultural purpose*" means a purpose related to the production, harvest, exhibition, marketing, transportation, processing, or manufacture of agricultural products by a natural person who cultivates, plants, propagates, or nurtures those agricultural products, including but not limited to the acquisition of personal property and services used primarily in farming. "Agricultural products" includes agricultural, horticultural, viticultural, and dairy products, livestock, wildlife, poultry, bees, forest products, fish and shellfish, and any products thereof, including processed and manufactured products, and any and all products raised or produced on farms and any processed or manufactured products thereof.

(4) "*Arrange for lease of personal property*" means to provide or offer to provide a lease which is or will be extended by another person under a business or other relationship pursuant to which the person arranging such lease:

(i) Receives or will receive a fee, compensation, or other consideration for such service; or

(ii) Has knowledge of the lease terms and participates in the preparation of the contract documents required in connection with the lease.

(5) "*Board*" refers to the Board of Governors of the Federal Reserve System.

(6) "*Consumer lease*" means a contract in the form of a bailment or lease for the use of personal property by a natural person primarily for personal, family or household purposes, for a period of time exceeding four months, for a total contractual obligation not exceeding $25,000, whether or not the lessee has the option to purchase or otherwise become the owner of the property at the expiration of the lease. It does not include a lease which meets the definition of a credit sale in Regulation Z, 12 CFR part 226.2(a), nor does it include a lease for agricultural, business or commercial purposes or one made to an organization.

(7) "*Lessee*" means a natural person who leases under, or who is offered a consumer lease.

(8) "*Lessor*" means a person who, in the ordinary course of business regularly leases, offers to lease, or arranges for the leasing of personal property under a consumer lease.

(9) "*Organization*" means a corporation, trust, estate, partnership, cooperative, association, government, or governmental subdivision, agency, or instrumentality.

(10) "*Period*" means a day, week, month, or other subdivision of a year.

(11) "*Person*" means a natural person or an organization.

(12) "*Personal property*" means any property which is not real property under the law of the state where it is located at the time it is offered or made available for lease.

(13) "*Real property*" means property which is real property under the law of the state in which it is located.

(14) "*Realized value*" means (i) the price received by the lessor for the leased property at disposition, (ii) the highest offer for disposition, or (iii) the fair market value at the end of the lease term.

(15) "*Security interest*" and "*security*" mean any interest in property which secures payment or performance of an obligation. The terms include, but are not limited to, security interests under the Uniform Commercial Code, real property mortgages, deeds of trust, and other consensual or confessed liens whether or not recorded, mechanic's, materialman's, artisan's, and other similar liens, vendor's liens in both real and personal property, any lien on property arising by operation of law, and any interest in a lease when used to secure payment or performance of an obligation.

(16) "*State*" means any state, the District of Columbia, the Commonwealth of Puerto Rico, and any territory or possession of the United States.

(17) "*Total lease obligation*" equals the total of (i) the scheduled periodic payments under the lease, (ii) any nonrefundable cash payment required of the lessee or agreed upon by the lessor and lessee or any trade-in allowance made at consummation, and (iii) the estimated value of the leased property at the end of the lease term.

(18) "*Value at consummation*" equals the cost to the lessor of the leased property including, if applicable, any increase or markup by the lessor prior to consummation.

(b) *Rules of construction.* For purposes of this regulation, the following rules of construction apply:

(1) Unless the context indicates otherwise, "lease" shall be construed to mean "consumer lease."

(2) A transaction shall be considered consummated at the time a contractual relationship is created between the lessor and lessee, irrespective of the time of the performance of either party.

(3) Captions and catchlines are intended solely as aids to convenient reference, and no inference as to the intent of any provision may be drawn from them.

§ 213.3 Exempted transactions

This regulation does not apply to lease transactions of personal property which are incident to the lease of real property and which provide that (a) the lessee has no liability for the value of the property at the end of the lease term except for abnormal wear and tear, and (b) the lessee has no option to purchase the leased property.

§ 213.4 Disclosures

(a) *General requirements.* (1) Any lessor shall, in accordance with this regulation and to the extent applicable, make the disclosures required by paragraph (g) of this section with respect to any consumer lease. Such disclosures shall be made clearly, conspicuously, in meaningful sequence, and in accordance with the further requirements of this section. All numerical amounts and percentages shall be stated in figures and shall be printed in not less than the equivalent of 10-point type, .075 inch computer type, or elite size typewritten numerals, or shall be legibly handwritten.

(2) Disclosures shall be made prior to the consummation of the lease on a dated written statement which identifies the lessor and the lessee, and a copy of the statement shall be given to the lessee at that time. All of the disclosures shall be made together on either (i) the contract or other instrument evidencing the lease on the same page and above the place for the lessee's signature; or (ii) a separate statement which identifies the lease transaction.

(3) In any lease of multiple items, the description required by paragraph (g)(1) of this section may be provided on a separate statement or statements which are incorporated by reference in the disclosure statement required by paragraph (a) of this section.

(4) All disclosures required to be given by this regulation shall be made in the English language except in the Commonwealth of Puerto Rico, where disclosures may be made in the Spanish language with English language disclosures provided upon the customer's request, either in substitution for the Spanish disclosures or as additional information in accordance with paragraph (b) of this section.

(b) *Additional information.* At the lessor's option, additional information or explanations may be supplied with any disclosure required by this regulation, but none shall be stated, utilized, or placed so as to mislead or confuse the lessee or contradict, obscure, or detract attention from the information required to be disclosed. Any lessor who elects to make disclosures specified in any provision of state law which, under section 213.7 of this regulation, is inconsistent with the requirements of the act and this regulation may—

(1) Make such inconsistent disclosures on a separate paper apart from the disclosures made pursuant to this regulation; or

(2) Make such inconsistent disclosures on the same statement on which disclosures required by this regulation are made, provided:

(i) All disclosures required by this regulation appear separately and above any other disclosures,

(ii) Disclosures required by this regulation are identified by a clear and conspicuous heading indicating that they are made in compliance with federal law, and

(iii) All inconsistent disclosures appear separately and below a conspicuous demarcation line, and are identified by a clear and conspicuous heading indicating that the statements made thereafter are inconsistent with the disclosure requirements of the federal Consumer Leasing Act.

(c) *Multiple lessors; multiple lessees.* When a transaction involves more than one lessor, only one lessor need make the disclosures required by this regulation, and the one that discloses shall be the one chosen by the lessors. When a lease involves more than one lessee, the disclosures may be made to any lessee who is primarily liable on the lease.

(d) *Unknown-information estimate.* If, at the time disclosures must be made, an amount or other item of information required to be disclosed, or needed to determine a required disclosure, is unknown or not available to the lessor and the lessor has made a reasonable effort to ascertain it, the lessor may use an estimated amount or an approximation of the information, provided the estimate or approximation is clearly identified as such, is reasonable, is based on the best information available to the lessor, and is not used for the purpose of circumventing or evading the disclosure requirements of this regulation. Notwithstanding the requirement of this paragraph that the estimate be based on the best information available, a lessor is not precluded in a purchase option lease from understating the estimated value of the leased property at the end of the term in computing the total lease obligation as required in paragraph (g)(15)(i) of this section.

(e) *Effect of subsequent occurrence.* If information required to be disclosed in accordance with this regulation is subsequently rendered inaccurate as a result of any act, occurrence, or agreement subsequent to the delivery of the required disclosures, the inaccuracy resulting therefrom does not constitute a violation of this regulation.[1]

1. Such acts, occurrences, or agreements include the failure of the lessee to perform his obligations under the contract and such actions by the lessor as may be proper to protect his interests in such circumstances. Such failure may result in the liability of the lessee to pay delinquency charges, collection costs, or expenses of the lessor for perfection or acquisition of any security interest or amounts advanced by the lessor on behalf of the lessee in connection with insurance, repairs to, or preservation of leased property.

(f) *Leap year.* Any variance in any term required under this regulation to be disclosed, or stated in any advertisement, which occurs by reason of the addition of February 29 in each leap year, may be disregarded, and such term may be disclosed or stated without regard to such variance.

(g) *Specific disclosure requirements.* In any lease subject to this section, the following items, as applicable, shall be disclosed:

(1) A brief description of the leased property, sufficient to identify the property to the lessee and lessor.

(2) The total amount of any payment, such as a refundable security deposit paid by cash, check or similar means, advance payment, capitalized cost reduction or any trade-in allowance, appropriately identified, to be paid by the lessee at consummation of the lease.

(3) The number, amount, and due dates or periods of payments scheduled under the lease and the total amount of such periodic payments.

(4) The total amount paid or payable by the lessee during the lease term for official fees, registration, certificate of title, license fees, or taxes.

(5) The total amount of all other charges, individually itemized, payable by the lessee to the lessor, which are not included in the periodic payments. This total includes the amount of any liabilities the lease imposes upon the lessee at the end of the term, but excludes the potential difference between the estimated and realized values, required to be disclosed under paragraph (g)(13) of this section.

(6) A brief identification of insurance in connection with the lease including (i) if provided or paid for by the lessor, the types and amounts of coverages and cost to the lessee, or (ii) if not provided or paid for by the lessor, the types and amounts of coverages required of the lessee.

(7) A statement identifying any express warranties or guarantees available to the lessee made by the lessor or manufacturer with respect to the leased property.

(8) An identification of the party responsible for maintaining or servicing the leased property together with a brief description of the responsibility, and a statement of reasonable standards for wear and use, if the lessor sets such standards.

(9) A description of any security interest, other than a security deposit disclosed under paragraph (g)(2) of this section, held or to be retained by the lessor in connection with the lease and a clear identification of the property to which the security interest relates.

(10) The amount or method of determining the amount of any penalty or other charge for delinquency, default, or late payments.

(11) A statement of whether or not the lessee has the option to purchase the leased property and, if at the end of the lease term, at what price, and, if prior to the end of the lease term, at what time, and the price or method of determining the price.

(12) A statement of the conditions under which the lessee or lessor may terminate the lease prior to the end of the lease term and the amount or method of determining the amount of any penalty or other charge for early termination.

(13) A statement that the lessee shall be liable for the difference between the estimated value of the property and its realized value at early termination or the end of the lease term, if such liability exists.

(14) Where the lessee's liability at early termination or at the end of the lease term is based on the estimated value of the leased property, a statement that the lessee may obtain at the end of the lease term or at early termination, at the lessee's expense, a professional appraisal of the value which could be realized at sale of the leased property by an independent third party agreed to by the lessee and the lessor, which appraisal shall be final and binding on the parties.

(15) Where the lessee's liability at the end of the lease term is based upon the estimated value of the leased property:

(i) The value of the property at consummation of the lease, the itemized total lease obligation at the end of the lease term, and the difference between them.

(ii) That there is a rebuttable presumption that the estimated value of the leased property at the end of the lease term is unreasonable and not in good faith to the extent that it exceeds the realized value by more than three times the average payment allocable to a monthly period, and that the lessor cannot collect the amount of such excess liability unless the lessor brings a successful action in court in which the lessor pays the lessee's attorney's fees, and that this provision regarding the presumption and attorney's fees does not apply to the extent the excess of estimated value over realized value is due to unreasonable wear or use, or excessive use.

(iii) A statement that the requirements of paragraph (g)(15)(ii) of this section do not preclude the right of a willing lessee to make any mutually agreeable final adjustment regarding such excess liability.

(h) *Renegotiations or extensions.* If any existing lease is renegotiated or extended, such renegotiation or extension shall be considered a new lease subject to the disclosure requirements of this regulation, except that the requirements of this paragraph shall not apply to (1) a lease of multiple items where a new item(s) is provided or a previously leased item(s) is returned, and the average payment allocable to a monthly period is not changed by more than 25 percent, or (2) a lease which is extended for not more than six months on a month-to-month basis or otherwise.

§ 213.5 Advertising

(a) *General rule.* No advertisement to aid, promote, or assist directly or indirectly any consumer lease may state that a specific lease of any property at specific amounts or terms is available unless the lessor usually and customarily leases or will lease such property at those amounts or terms.

(b) *Catalogs and multipage advertisements.* If a catalog or other multiple-page advertisement sets forth or gives information in sufficient detail to permit determination of the disclosures required by this section in a table or schedule of lease terms, such catalog or multiple-page advertisement shall be considered a single advertisement provided—

(1) The table or schedule and the disclosures made therein are set forth clearly and conspicuously, and

(2) Any statement of lease terms appearing in any place other than in that table or schedule of lease terms clearly and conspicuously refers to the page or pages on which that table or schedule appears, unless that statement discloses all of the lease terms required to be stated under this section.

(c) *Terms that require additional information.* No advertisement to aid, promote, or assist directly or indirectly any consumer lease shall state the amount of any payment, the number of required payments, or that any or no downpayment or other payment is required at consummation of the lease unless the advertisement also states clearly and conspicuously each of the following items of information as applicable:

(1) That the transaction advertised is a lease.

(2) The total amount of any payment such as a security deposit or capitalized cost reduction required at the consummation of the lease, or that no such payments are required.

(3) The number, amounts, due dates or periods of scheduled payments, and the total of such payments under the lease.

(4) A statement of whether or not the lessee has the option to purchase the leased property and at what price and time. The method of determining the price may be substituted for disclosure of the price.

(5) A statement of the amount or method of determining the amount of any liabilities the lease imposes upon the lessee at the end of the term and a statement that the lessee shall be liable for the difference, if any, between the estimated value of the leased property and its realized value at the end of the lease term, if the lessee has such liability.

(d) *Multiple-item leases; merchandise tags.* If a merchandise tag for an item normally included in a multiple-item lease sets forth information which would require additional disclosures under paragraph (c) of this section, such merchandise tag need not contain such additional disclosures, provided it clearly and conspicuously refers to a sign or display which is prominently posted in the lessor's showroom. Such sign or display shall contain a table or schedule of those items of information to be disclosed under paragraph (c) of this section.

§ 213.6 Preservation and inspection of evidence of compliance

(a) Evidence of compliance with the requirements imposed under this regulation, other than advertising requirements under section 213.5, shall be preserved by the lessor for a period of not less than two years after the date such disclosure is required to be made.

(b) Each lessor shall, when directed by the appropriate administrative enforcement authority designated in section 108 of the act, permit that authority or its duly authorized representative to inspect its relevant records and evidence of compliance with this regulation.

§ 213.7 Inconsistent state requirements

(a) *Preemption.* A state law which is similar in nature, purpose, scope, intent, effect, or requisites to a section of chapter 5 of the act is not inconsistent with the act or this regulation within the meaning of section 186(a) of the act if the lessor can comply with the state law without violating this regulation. If a lessor cannot comply with a state law without violating a provision of this regulation which implements a section of chapter 5 of the act, such state law is inconsistent with the requirements of the act and this regulation within the meaning of section 186(a) of the act and is preempted.

(b) *Procedures.* A state, through its governor, attorney general, or other appropriate official having primary enforcement or interpretative responsibilities for its consumer leasing law, may apply to the Board for a determination that the state law offers greater protection and benefit to lessees than a comparable provision(s) of chapter 5 of the act and its implementing provision(s) in this regulation, or is otherwise not inconsistent with chapter 5 of the act and this regulation, or for a determination with respect to any issues not clearly covered by paragraph (a) of this section as to the consistency or inconsistency of a state law with chapter 5 of the act or its implementing provisions in this regulation.

§ 213.8 Exemption of certain state-regulated transactions

(a) *Exemption for state-regulated transactions.* In accordance with the provisions of appendix A to Regulation M, any state may make application to the Board for exemption of any class of transactions within the state from the requirements of chapter 5 of the act and the corresponding provisions of this regulation, provided that—

(1) The Board determines that under the law of that state, that class of transactions is subject to requirements substantially similar to those imposed under chapter 5 of the act and the corresponding provisions of this regulation; or the lessee is afforded greater protection and benefit than is afforded under chapter 5 of the act, and

(2) There is adequate provision for enforcement.

(b) *Procedures and criteria.* The procedures and criteria under which a state may apply for the determination provided for in paragraph (a) of this section are set forth in appendix A to Regulation M.

(c) *Civil liability.* In order to assure that the concurrent jurisdiction of federal and state courts created in sections 130(e) and 185(c) of the act shall continue to have substantive provisions to which such jurisdiction shall apply, and generally to aid in implementing the act with respect to any class of transactions exempted pursuant to paragraph (a) of this section and appendix A, the Board pursuant to sections 105 and 186(b) of the act hereby prescribes that—

(1) No such exemptions shall be deemed to extend to the civil liability provisions of sections 130, 131, and 185 of the act; and

(2) After an exemption has been granted, the disclosure requirements of the applicable state law shall constitute the disclosure requirements of the act, except to the extent that such state law imposes disclosure requirements not imposed by the act. Information required under such state law with the exception of those provisions which impose disclosure requirements not imposed by the act shall, accordingly, constitute a "requirement imposed" under chapter 5 of the act for the purpose of section 130(a).

APPENDIX A. Procedures and Criteria for State Exemptions from the Consumer Leasing Act

. . .

(c) *Criteria for determination.* The Board will consider the following criteria along with any other relevant information in making a determination whether the laws of a state impose requirements substantially similar to or provide greater protection and benefit to lessees than under chapter 5, and whether there is adequate provision for enforcement of such laws:

(1) In order for provisions of state law to be substantially similar to or provide greater protection and benefit to lessees than the provision of chapter 5, the provisions of state law shall require that

(i) Definitions and rules of construction import the same meaning and have the same application as those prescribed under section 213.2 of this regulation;

(ii) Lessors make all of the applicable disclosures required by this regulation and within the same (or more stringent) time periods as are prescribed by this regulation;

(iii) Lessors abide by obligations substantially similar to those prescribed by chapter 5, under conditions substantially similar to (or more stringent than) those prescribed in chapter 5;

(iv) Lessors abide by the same (or more stringent) prohibitions as are provided in chapter 5;

(v) Lessees need comply with no obligations or responsibilities which are more costly or burdensome as a condition of exercising any of the rights or gaining the benefits and protections in the state law which correspond to those afforded by chapter 5, than those obligations or responsibilities imposed upon lessees in chapter 5; and

(vi) Substantially similar or more favorable rights and protections are provided to lessees under conditions substantially similar to or more favorable (to lessees) than those afforded by chapter 5.

(2) In determining whether the provisions for enforcement of the state law referred to in paragraph (b)(1) of this appendix are adequate, consideration will be given to the extent to which, under the laws of the state, provision is made for

(i) Administrative enforcement, including necessary facilities, personnel and funding;

(ii) Criminal liability for willful and knowing violation with penalties substantially similar to those prescribed under section 112 of the act, except that more severe criminal penalties may be prescribed;

(iii) Civil liability for failure to comply with the provisions of the state law substantially similar to that provided under sections 130, 131 and 185(b) of the act, except that more severe civil liability penalties may be prescribed;

(iv) In leases where the lessee's liability at the end of the lease term is based on the estimated value of the leased property, a limitation on the lessee's liability at the end of the lease term substantially similar to that provided in section 183(a) of the act, and a provision requiring that penalties be reasonably substantially similar to that provided in section 183(b) of the act, except that stricter standards on end-term liability and penalty provisions may be prescribed; and

(v) A statute of limitations with respect to civil liability of substantially similar duration to that provided under section 185(c) of the act, except that a longer duration may be provided.

. . .

APPENDIX B. Procedures and Criteria for Board Determination Regarding Preemption

. . .

(c) *Criteria for determination.* The Board will consider the following criteria along with any other relevant information, in addition to the criteria set forth in section 213.7 of this regulation, in making a determination of whether or not state law is inconsistent with a provision of chapter 5. In order for provisions of state law to be determined to be consistent with a provision of chapter 5, the provisions of state law shall, to the extent relevant to the determination, require that—

(1) Definitions and rules of construction import the same meaning and have the same application as those prescribed by this regulation;

(2) Lessors make all of the applicable disclosures required by the corresponding provision of chapter 5 and this regulation, and within the same (or more stringent) time periods as those prescribed by this regulation;

(3) Lessors abide by obligations substantially similar to those prescribed by a provision of chapter 5 under conditions substantially similar (or more stringent) to those in chapter 5;

(4) Lessors abide by the same (or more stringent) prohibitions as are provided by chapter 5;

(5) Lessees need comply with no obligations or responsibilities which are more costly or burdensome as a condition of exercising any of the rights or gaining the benefits and protections provided in the state law, which correspond to those afforded by chapter 5, than those obligations or responsibilities imposed on lessees in chapter 5; and

(6) Lessees are to have rights and protections substantially similar to or more favorable than those provided by the corresponding provisions of chapter 5 under conditions and within time periods which are substantially similar to or more favorable (to lessees) than those prescribed by chapter 5.[5]

. . .

5. A state may make a showing that in certain limited readily identifiable circumstances a law which may otherwise be inconsistent with a provision of chapter 5 is not inconsistent under the criteria set forth in paragraph (c) of this appendix. The Board may determine such state law to be consistent only under those circumstances but will make no such determination if doing so would mislead or confuse lessees.

APPENDIX C. Model Forms

C-1. Model Open-End or Finance Vehicle Lease Disclosures

Date ________________

These disclosures are provided pursuant to the Federal Consumer Leasing Act.

1. LESSOR(S) ________________ LESSEE(S) ________________

2. Description of leased property

Year	Make	Model	Body Style	Vehicle ID #

3. (a) Initial Charges, consisting of
☐ Capitalized Cost Reduction ☐ Trade-in Allowance ☐ ________ $________

(b) Other Charges Payable at Inception, consisting of
☐ Advance Monthly Payment of ________
☐ Refundable Security Deposit ☐ Delivery Charge $________
☐ Registration Fees ☐ ________

Total Payment Due at Inception: $________

4. (a) Basic Monthly Payment: $________

(b) Other Charges Payable Monthly:
☐ Maintenance ☐ Registration Fees $________
☐ Insurance ☐ ________

Total Monthly Payment: $________

5. Term of this lease: ________
The first monthly payment of $________ is due on ________; ________ subsequent payments of $________ on the ____ of each month thereafter.

6. Total of Basic Monthly Payments: $________

7. Total of Other Charges Payable to Lessor:
☐ Disposition $________ ☐ Maintenance $________
☐ ________ $________ $________

8. Fees and Taxes
Total amount you will pay during the term for official fees, registration, certificate of title, license fees and taxes. $________

9. Insurance
The following types and amounts of insurance will be acquired in connection with this lease: ________

☐ We (lessor) will provide the insurance coverage quoted above for a total premium cost of $________.
☐ You (lessee) agree to provide insurance coverage in the amounts and types indicated above. $________

10. Estimated ________ value of the vehicle at the end of the lease term:
(Your liability for this sum may be limited. See Item 14.) $________

11. Total Lease Obligation: $________
(Items 3(a), 6 and 10.)

12. Initial Value of Vehicle: $________

13. Difference:
(Item 11 less Item 12.) $________

14. End of Term Liability

(a) The estimated value of the vehicle stated in Item 10 is based on a reasonable, good faith estimate of the value of the vehicle at the end of the lease term. If the actual value of the vehicle at that time is *greater* than the estimated value, you will have no further liability under this lease, except for other charges already incurred [and are entitled to a credit or refund of any surplus].

If the actual value of the vehicle is *less* than the estimated value, you will be liable for any difference up to $________ (3 times Item 4(a)). For any difference in excess of that amount, you will be liable only if

1. Excessive use or damage [as described in Item 15] [representing more than normal wear and tear] resulted in an unusually low value at the end of the term.
2. You voluntarily agree with us after the end of the lease term to make a higher payment.
3. The matter is not otherwise resolved and we win a lawsuit against you seeking a higher payment.

Should we bring a lawsuit against you, we must prove that our original estimate of the value of the leased property at the

[C6647]

end of the lease term was reasonable and was made in good faith. For example, we might prove that the actual value was less than the original estimated value, although the original estimate was reasonable, because of an unanticipated decline in value for that type of vehicle.

Unless we prove that the excess amount owed was the result of excessive use or unreasonable wear and tear, we will pay your reasonable attorney's fees.

(b) If you disagree with the value we assign to the vehicle, you may obtain, at your own expense, from an independent third party agreeable to both of us, a professional appraisal of the ________ value of the leased vehicle which could be realized at sale. The appraised value shall then be used as the actual value.

15. Standards for Wear and Use

The following standards are applicable for determining unreasonable or excessive wear and use of the leased vehicle: ________

16. Maintenance

[You are responsible for the following maintenance and servicing of the leased vehicle: ________.]

[We are responsible for the following maintenance and servicing of the leased vehicle: ________.]

17. Warranties

The leased vehicle is subject to the following express warranties: ________.

18. Early Termination and Default

(a) You may terminate this lease before the end of the lease term under the following conditions: ________.

The charge for such early termination is ________.

(b) We may terminate this lease before the end of the lease term under the following conditions: ________.

Upon such termination we shall be entitled to the following charge(s) for ________.

(c) To the extent these charges take into account the value of the vehicle at the end of the lease term, you have the same right to a professional appraisal as that stated in Item 14(b).

19. Security Interest

We reserve a security interest of the following type in the property listed below to secure performance of your obligations under this lease: ________.

20. Late Payments

The charge for late payments is ________.

21. Option to Purchase

[You have an option to purchase the leased vehicle at the following times: ________.

If at the end of the term, the price will be $________.

If prior to the end of the term, the price will be $________.]

[You have no option to purchase the leased vehicle.]

[C6648]

Instructions for Completion of Model Open-End or Finance Vehicle Lease Disclosures

General Instructions

Completion of this form may be facilitated by reference to the following instructions. Any question to the permissibility or accuracy of a specific disclosure may be answered by reference to Regulation M, 12 CFR Part 213.

Information which is required to be disclosed may be estimated if the information is unknown or unavailable, provided that the information is clearly identified as an estimate, and the estimate is based on the best information available and is reasonable.

Any inapplicable disclosures should be deleted. This form is based on a monthly periodic payment. Any lessor whose lease contemplates a different payment period should change the form where it refers to "monthly" amounts to read "weekly" or other time period, as appropriate.

All numerical amounts must be stated in figures and shall be printed in not less than the equivalent of ten point type or elite typewritten numerals or legibly handwritten. Paragraph numbers need not be printed in ten point type or its equivalent.

Specific Instructions

Item 1. The disclosures must be made on a written dated statement. All lessors and lessees must be identified by name. If, for example, one person arranges the lease and another person enters into the lease, both must be identified as lessors. An address may augment the identification but need not be supplied as part of the disclosure form.

Item 2. This disclosure provides a brief description of the leased property. Lessors may include a more detailed description including, for example, special accessories. There is no requirement that a vehicle identification number for the vehicle be disclosed.

Item 3. This disclosure shows the total amount of any initial payment the customer must make when the lease is entered into. The components of the initial payment *must* be identified and *may*, at the lessor's option, be itemized with respect to dollar amount.

This item is divided into two distinct parts. The items identified in 3(a) are those which are included in the calculation of the "Total Lease Obligation." Those which appear in 3(b) are not included in the "Total Lease Obligation." For convenient reference and to provide the customer with the total amount due at the inception of the lease, subtotals for 3(a) and 3(b) are provided as well as a combined total of 3(a) and 3(b) (shown as "Total Payment Due at Inception").

The term "Capitalized Cost Reduction" is used to indicate payment in the nature of a downpayment which reduces the value of the leased vehicle to be amortized over the term of the lease.

The "Advance Monthly Payment" is the total of all amounts collected at the inception of the lease which are to be attributed to a monthly payment(s). For example, if the first month's rental payment is collected at the inception, the form might read "Advance Monthly Payment of the first month's rent" or a similar phrase. If the last month's payment, or any other payment in the nature of rental for a portion of the term, is collected at the inception, appropriate language should be provided to describe the components of the "Advance Monthly Payment."

Checklists are provided for both 3(a) and 3(b) to aid in identifying their components. Blank spaces and check boxes are provided to identify any other elements which are to be included in these items.

Item 4. This item discloses the payment the lessee must make each payment period. This item is divided into two parts. The terms in 4(a) are those portions of each payment which are included in the computation of the "Total Lease Obligation." This item includes sales/use taxes paid on the periodic (monthly) payment. The terms in 4(b) are not included in the "Total Lease Obligation." For convenient reference and to provide the customer with the total amount of each payment, subtotals are provided for 4(a) and 4(b) as well as the combined total of 4(a) and 4(b) (shown as the "Total Monthly Payment"). The components of 4(a) and 4(b) may be itemized as to dollar amount.

Item 5. This item discloses the term of the lease, the date of the first periodic payment and the dates or periods of all subsequent periodic payments. The blank spaces should be filled in with the appropriate terms. For example, after the phrase "Term of this lease:" the lessor may place the words "24 months" or "April 2, 1977, through April 2, 1979," as appropriate. In the blank spaces provided after the phrase "The first monthly payment of:" should be the appropriate amount and date. The first monthly payment may be part or all of the "Advance Monthly Payment" disclosed under 3(b). The phrase "subsequent payments of" should be preceded by the appropriate number of payments and followed with the appropriate terms, such as "$100.00 on the 2d of each month thereafter."

Item 6. This item discloses the total of the basic monthly payments payable over the term of the lease. This figure is computed by multiplying the basic monthly payment from Item 4(a) by the number of subsequent payments in Item 5 and adding to the product the basic portion of the first monthly payment. This figure will be used in computing the "Total Lease Obligation."

Item 7. This item discloses the total of other charges payable to the lessor. This excludes charges for official fees, taxes, insurance and charges disclosed as totals under other items. The individual components must be identified and itemized as to amount. A blank check box is provided in order to add to the list, as necessary.

Item 8. This item discloses the total amount to be paid by the lessee during the lease term for taxes and other official fees.

Item 9. This item requires disclosure of the types and amounts of insurance coverage, with their total premium cost, if the insurance is provided by the lessor. In the alternative, only the types and amounts of coverage required of the lessee must be disclosed if the lessee provides the insurance coverage. The disclosure is to be completed by identifying the types and amounts of insurance coverage following the colon at the end of the first sentence. If the lessor is to provide the coverage the top check box should be filled in and the total premium cost indicated in the blank space provided. Otherwise the bottom check box should be filled in.

Item 10. This item provides for disclosure of the estimated value of the leased vehicle at the end of the term, an element of the "Total Lease Obligation." A blank space is provided in which to indicate whether the value shown is, for example, "retail" or "wholesale" value.

Items 11, 12 and 13. These items provide for disclosure of the difference between the "Total Lease Obligation" and the vehicle's value at the inception of the lease. The definition of "Total Lease Obligation" is the sum of any initial charges (Item 3(a)), the total of basic monthly payments (Item 6) and the estimated value of the property at the end of the term (Item 10). The "Total Lease Obligation" does not include items such as refundable security deposits and insurance premiums.

Item 14. This item provides disclosures with respect to the lessee's liability at the end of the lease term. The bracketed phrase in the second sentence is appropriate only where the lessee will be given any surplus resulting from the disposition. The lessor may, in Item 14(a)1, reference the standards set forth in Item 15, if the lessor set such standards. If the lessor does not set standards for wear and use, the second bracketed phrase should be used. Item 14(b) discloses the lessee's right to an independent appraisal. The blank space in Item 14(b) is provided to indicate whether the value of the appraisal should be, for example, "wholesale" or "retail." This item should be consistent with the type of value used in Item 10.

Item 15. This item discloses reasonable standards for wear and use established by the lessor. The lessor is permitted but not required to set such standards. Therefore, the disclosure may be omitted by lessors who do not set standards for wear and use.

Item 16. This item provides for disclosure of the maintenance and servicing responsibilities of the parties. These responsibilities may be allocated either to the lessor or to the lessee, or may be divided between them.

Item 17. This item discloses all express warranties on the leased property made by the manufacturer or lessor and available to the lessee. A brief identification of the warranty must be supplied. A reference to the standard manufacturer's warranty, for example, would suffice.

Item 18. This item discloses the conditions under which the lessee may terminate the lease prior to the end of the lease term. It also discloses the amount or method of determining the amount of the charge which the lessee must pay for early termination. This item should disclose the conditions under which the lessor may terminate the lease prior to the end of the term, such as default. This item should also be used to disclose the amount or method of determining the amount of any default charges. The charges or method of determining the charges for early termination by the lessor other than for lessee's default should be separately specified in this item.

Item 19. This disclosure of the security taken must include, in the space provided, a brief identification of the types of security interests and an identification of the property covered by each.

Item 20. This disclosure indicates the amount or method of determining the amount of any charges for late payment.

Item 21. This item provides alternative disclosures covering the several options a lessor may offer to a lessee to purchase the leased property. A lessor should use the disclosures applicable to the lease plan used. For example, if no option to purchase is offered, only the last sentence of the item should be used. If the lessor offers an option to purchase, the times at which it may be exercised must be supplied. The price must be disclosed for an option exercised at the end of the term and the price or method of computing the price for an option exercised during the lease term must be supplied.

C–2. Model Closed-End or Net Vehicle Lease Disclosures

Date ______

These disclosures are provided pursuant to the Federal Consumer Leasing Act.

1. LESSOR(S) ______ LESSEE(S) ______

2. Description of leased property

Year	Make	Model	Body Style	Vehicle ID #

3. Total Payment Due at Inception:
☐ Capitalized Cost Reduction ☐ Delivery Charge
☐ Trade-in Allowance ☐ Registration Fees
☐ Advance Monthly Payment of ______
☐ Refundable Security Deposit ☐ ______ $______

4. Term of this lease:
The first monthly payment of $______ is due on ______; ______ subsequent payments of $______ on the ______ of each month thereafter.

5. Total Monthly Payment: $______

6. Total of Monthly Payments: $______

7. Total of Other Charges Payable to Lessor:
☐ Disposition $______ ☐ Maintenance $______
☐ ______ $______ $______

8. Fees and Taxes
Total amount you will pay during the term for official fees, registration, certificate of title, license fees and taxes. $______

9. Insurance
The following types and amounts of insurance will be acquired in connection with this lease:
______
☐ We (lessor) will provide the insurance coverage quoted above for a total premium cost of $______
☐ You (lessee) agree to provide insurance coverage in the amounts and types indicated above. $______

10. Standards for Wear and Use
The following standards are applicable for determining unreasonable or excessive wear and use of the leased vehicle: ______

11. Maintenance
[You are responsible for the following maintenance and servicing of the leased vehicle: ______]
[We are responsible for the following maintenance and servicing of the leased vehicle: ______]

[C6649]

12. Warranties
The leased vehicle is subject to the following express warranties: ______________________________

13. Early Termination and Default
(a) You may terminate this lease before the end of the lease term under the following conditions: ______________________________

The charge for such early termination is: ______________________________

(b) We may terminate this lease before the end of the lease term under the following conditions: ______________________________

Upon such termination we shall be entitled to the following charge(s) for ______________________________

(c) To the extent that these charges take into account the value of the vehicle at the end of the lease term, if you disagree with the value we assign to the vehicle, you may obtain at your own expense, from an independent third party agreeable to both of us, a professional appraisal of the ______________ value of the leased vehicle which could be realized at sale. The appraised value shall then be used as the actual value.

14. Security Interest
We reserve a security interest of the following type in the property listed below to secure performance of your obligations under this lease: ______________________________

15. Late Payments
The charge for late payments is ______________________________

16. Lessee's Option to Purchase
[You have an option to purchase the leased vehicle at the following times: ______________________________

If at the end of the term, the price will be $______________.
If prior to the end of the term, the price will be $______________________________]

[You have no option to purchase the leased vehicle.]

[C6650]

Instructions for Completion of Model Closed-End or Net Vehicle Lease Disclosures

General Instructions

Completion of this form may be facilitated by reference to the following instructions. Any question as to the permissibility or accuracy of a specific disclosure may be answered by reference to Regulation M, 12 CFR Part 213.

Information which is required to be disclosed may be estimated if the information is unknown or unavailable, provided that the information is clearly identified as an estimate and the estimate is based on the best information available and is reasonable.

Any inapplicable disclosures should be deleted. This form is based on a monthly periodic payment. Any lessor whose lease contemplates a different payment period should change the form where it refers to "monthly" amounts to read "weekly" or other time period, as appropriate. All numerical amounts must be stated in figures and shall be printed in not less than the equivalent of ten point type or elite typewritten numerals or legibly handwritten. Paragraph numbers need not be printed in ten point type or its equivalent.

Specific Instructions

Item 1. The disclosures must be made on a written dated statement. All lessors and lessees must be identified by name. If, for example, one person arranges the lease and another person enters into the lease, both must be identified as lessors. An address may augment the identification but need not be supplied as part of the disclosure form.

Item 2. This disclosure provides a brief description of the leased property. Lessors may include a more detailed description including, for example, special accessories. There is no requirement that a vehicle identification number for the vehicle be disclosed.

Item 3. This disclosure shows the total amount of any initial payment the customer must make when the lease is entered into. The components of the initial payment *must* be identified and *may*, at the lessor's option, be itemized with respect to dollar amount.

The term "Capitalized Cost Reduction" is used to indicate a payment in the nature of a downpayment which reduces the value of the leased vehicle to be amortized over the term of the lease.

The "Advance Monthly Payment" is the total of all amounts collected at the inception of the lease which are to be attributed to a monthly payment(s). For example, if the first month's rental payment is collected at the inception, the form might read "Advance Monthly Payment of the first month's rent" or a similar phrase. If the last month's payment, or any other payment in the nature of rental for a portion of the term, is collected at the inception, appropriate language should be provided to describe the components of the "Advance Monthly Payment."

Checklists are provided to aid in identifying the components. Blank spaces and check boxes are provided to identify any other elements which are to be included in this item.

Item 4. This item discloses the term of the lease, the date of the first periodic payment and the dates or periods of all subsequent periodic payments. The blank spaces should be filled in with the appropriate terms. For example, after the phrase "Term of this lease:" the lessor may place the words "24 months" or "April 2, 1977, through April 2, 1979," as appropriate. In the blank spaces provided after the phrase "The first monthly payment of:" should be the appropriate amount and date. The first monthly payment may be part or all of the "Advance Monthly Payment" disclosed under Item 3. The phrase "subsequent payments of" should be preceded by the appropriate number of payments and followed with the appropriate terms, such as "$100.00 on the 2d of each month thereafter."

Item 5. This item discloses the payment the lessee must make each payment period. The component parts of the "Total Monthly Payment" may but need not be identified and itemized as to amount.

Item 6. This item discloses the total of the monthly payments payable over the term of the lease. This figure is computed by multiplying the monthly payment from Item 5 by the number of subsequent payments in Item 4 and adding the first monthly payment to the product.

Item 7. This item discloses the total of other charges payable to the lessor. This excludes charges for official fees, taxes, insurance and charges disclosed as totals under other items. The individual components must be identified and itemized as to amount. A blank check box is provided in order to add to the list, as necessary.

Item 8. This item discloses the total amount to be paid by the lessee during the lease term for taxes and other official fees.

Item 9. This item requires disclosure of the types and amounts of insurance coverage, with their total premium cost, if the insurance is provided by the lessor. In the alternative, only the types and amounts of coverage required of the lessee must be disclosed if the lessee provides the insurance coverage. The disclosure is to be completed by identifying the types and amounts of insurance coverage following the colon at the end of the first sentence. If the lessor is to provide the coverage the top check box should be filled in and the total premium cost indicated in the blank space provided. Otherwise the bottom check box should be filled in.

Item 10. This item discloses reasonable standards for wear and use established by the lessor. The lessor is permitted but not required to set such standards. Therefore, the disclosure may be omitted by lessors who do not set standards for wear and use.

Item 11. This item provides for disclosure of the maintenance and servicing responsibilities of the parties. These responsibilities may be allocated either to the lessor or to the lessee, or may be divided between them.

Item 12. This item discloses all express warranties on the leased property made by the manufacturer or lessor and available to the lessee. A brief identification of the warranty must be supplied. A reference to the standard manufacturer's warranty, for example, would suffice.

Item 13. This item discloses the conditions under which the lessee may terminate the lease prior to the end of the lease term. It also discloses the amount or method of determining the amount of the charge which the lessee must pay for early termination. This item should disclose the conditions under which the lessor may terminate the lease prior to the end of the term, such as default. This item should also be used to disclose the amount or method of determining the amount of any default charges. The charges or method of determining the charges for early termination by the lessor other than for lessee's default should be separately specified in this item. The blank space in 13(c) is provided to indicate whether the appraisal should be, for example, "retail" or "wholesale."

Item 14. This disclosure of the security taken must include, in the space provided, a brief identification of the types of security interests and an identification of the property covered by each.

Item 15. This disclosure indicates the amount or method of determining the amount of any charges for late payment.

Item 16. This item provides alternative disclosures covering the several options a lessor may offer to a lessee to purchase the leased property. A lessor should use the disclosures applicable to the lease plan used. For example, if no option to purchase is offered, only the last sentence of the item should be used. If the lessor offers an option to purchase, the times at which it may be exercised must be supplied. The price must be disclosed for an option exercised at the end of the term and the price or method of computing the price for an option exercised during the lease term must be supplied.

*

FEDERAL RESERVE BOARD, REGULATION B, EQUAL CREDIT OPPORTUNITY

12 C.F.R. Part 202

Table of Sections

§ 202.1 Authority, scope, enforcement, penalties and liabilities, interpretations

(a) *Authority and scope.* This part comprises the regulations issued by the Board of Governors of the Federal Reserve System pursuant to Title VII (Equal Credit Opportunity Act) of the Consumer Credit Protection Act, as amended (15 U.S.C. 1601 et seq.). Except as otherwise provided herein, this part applies to all persons who are creditors, as defined in § 202.2(1).

. . .

(d) *Issuance of staff interpretations.* (1) Unofficial staff interpretations will be issued at the staff's discretion where the protection of section 706(e) of the Act is neither requested nor required, or where a rapid response is necessary.

(2)(i) Official staff interpretations will be issued at the discretion of designated officials. No such interpretation will be issued approving creditors' forms or statements. . . .

(4) Pursuant to section 706(e) of the Act, the Board has designated the Director and other officials of the Division of Consumer Affairs as officials "duly authorized" to issue, at their discretion, official staff interpretations of this part.

§ 202.2 Definitions and rules of construction

For the purposes of this part, unless the context indicates otherwise, the following definitions and rules of construction shall apply:[2]

(a) *Account* means an extension of credit. When employed in relation to an account, the word *use* refers only to open end credit.

(b) *Act* means the Equal Credit Opportunity Act (Title VII of the Consumer Credit Protection Act).

(c) *Adverse action.* (1) For the purposes of notification of action taken, statement of reasons for denial, and record retention, the term means:

(i) A refusal to grant credit in substantially the amount or on substantially the terms requested by an applicant unless the creditor offers to grant credit other than in substantially the amount or on substantially the terms requested by the applicant and the applicant uses or expressly accepts the credit offered; or

(ii) A termination of an account or an unfavorable change in the terms of an account that does not affect all or a substantial portion of a classification of a creditor's accounts; or

2. Note that some of the definitions in this part are not identical to those in 12 CFR Part 226 (Regulation Z).

(iii) A refusal to increase the amount of credit available to an applicant when the applicant requests an increase in accordance with procedures established by the creditor for the type of credit involved.

(2) The term does not include:

(i) A change in the terms of an account expressly agreed to by an applicant; or

(ii) Any action or forbearance relating to an account taken in connection with inactivity, default, or delinquency as to that account; or

(iii) A refusal or failure to authorize an account transaction at a point of sale or loan, except when the refusal is a termination or an unfavorable change in the terms of an account that does not affect all or a substantial portion of a classification of the creditor's accounts or when the refusal is a denial of an application to increase the amount of credit available under the account; or

(iv) A refusal to extend credit because applicable law prohibits the creditor from extending the credit requested; or

(v) A refusal to extend credit because the creditor does not offer the type of credit or credit plan requested.

(3) An action that falls within the definition of both paragraphs (c)(1) and (c)(2) of this section shall be governed by the provisions of paragraph (c)(2) of this section.

(d) *Age* refers only to natural persons and means the number of fully elapsed years from the date of an applicant's birth.

(e) *Applicant* means any person who requests or who has received an extension of credit from a creditor, and includes any person who is or may be contractually liable regarding an extension of credit other than a guarantor, surety, endorser, or similar party.

(f) *Application* means an oral or written request for an extension of credit that is made in accordance with procedures established by a creditor for the type of credit requested. The term does not include the use of an account or line of credit to obtain an amount of credit that does not exceed a previously established credit limit. A *completed application for credit* means an application in connection with which a creditor has received all the information that the creditor regularly obtains and considers in evaluating applications for the amount and type of credit requested (including, but not limited to, credit reports, any additional information requested from the applicant, and any approvals or reports by governmental agencies or other persons that are necessary to guarantee, insure, or provide security for the credit or collateral); provided however, that the creditor has exercised reasonable diligence in obtaining such information. Where an application is incomplete respecting matters that the applicant can complete, a creditor shall make a reasonable effort to notify the applicant of the incompleteness and shall allow the applicant a reasonable opportunity to complete the application.

(g) *Board* means the Board of Governors of the Federal Reserve System.

(h) *Consumer credit* means credit extended to a natural person in which the money, property, or service that is the subject of the transaction is primarily for personal, family, or household purposes.

(i) *Contractually liable* means expressly obligated to repay all debts arising on an account by reason of an agreement to that effect.

(j) *Credit* means the right granted by a creditor to an applicant to defer payment of a debt, incur debt and defer its payment, or purchase property or services and defer payment therefor.

(k) *Credit card* means any card, plate, coupon book, or other single credit device existing for the purpose of being used from time to time upon presentation to obtain money, property, or services on credit.

(*l*) *Creditor* means a person who, in the ordinary course of business, regularly participates in the decision of whether or not to extend credit. The term includes a creditor's assignee, transferee, or subrogee who so participates. For purposes of §§ 202.4 and 202.5(a), the term also includes a person who, in the ordinary course of business, regularly refers applicants or prospective applicants to creditors, or selects or offers to select creditors to whom requests for credit may be made. A person is not a creditor regarding any violation of the Act or this part committed by another creditor unless the person knew or had reasonable notice of the act, policy, or practice that constituted the violation before its involvement with the credit transaction. The term does not include a person whose only participation in a credit transaction involves honoring a credit card.

(m) *Credit transaction* means every aspect of an applicant's dealings with a creditor regarding an application for, or an existing extension of, credit including, but not limited to, information requirements; investigation procedures; standards of creditworthiness; terms of credit; furnishing of credit information; revocation, alteration, or termination of credit; and collection procedures.

(n) *Discriminate against an applicant* means to treat an applicant less favorably than other applicants.

(*o*) *Elderly* means an age of 62 or older.

(p) *Empirically derived credit system.* (1) The term means a credit scoring system that evaluates an applicant's creditworthiness primarily by allocating points (or by using a comparable basis for assigning weights) to key attributes describing the applicant and other aspects of the transaction. In such a system, the points (or weights) assigned to each attribute, and hence the entire score:

(i) Are derived from an empirical comparison of sample groups or the population of creditworthy and non-creditworthy applicants of a creditor who applied for credit within a reasonable preceding period of time; and

(ii) Determine, alone or in conjunction with an evaluation of additional information about the applicant, whether an applicant is deemed creditworthy.

(2) *A demonstrably and statistically sound, empirically derived credit system* is a system:

(i) In which the data used to develop the system, if not the complete population consisting of all applicants, are obtained from the applicant file by using appropriate sampling principles;

(ii) Which is developed for the purpose of predicting the creditworthiness of applicants with respect to the legitimate business interests of the creditor utilizing the system, including, but not limited to, minimizing bad debt losses and operating expenses in accordance with the creditor's business judgment;

(iii) Which, upon validation using appropriate statistical principles, separates creditworthy and non-creditworthy applicants at a statistically significant rate; and

(iv) Which is periodically revalidated as to its predictive ability by the use of appropriate statistical principles and is adjusted as necessary to maintain its predictive ability.

(3) A creditor may use a demonstrably and statistically sound, empirically derived credit system obtained from another person or may obtain credit experience from which such a system may be developed. Any such system must satisfy the tests set forth in paragraphs (p)(1) and (2) of this section; provided that, if a creditor is unable during the development process to validate the system based on its own credit experience in accordance with paragraph (p)(2)(iii) of this section, then the system must be validated when sufficient credit experience becomes available. A system that fails this validity test shall henceforth be deemed not to be a demonstrably and statistically sound, empirically derived credit system for that creditor.

(q) *Extend credit and extension of credit* mean the granting of credit in any form and include, but are not limited to, credit granted in addition to any existing credit or credit limit; credit granted pursuant to an open end credit plan; the refinancing or other renewal of credit, including the issuance of a new credit card in place of an expiring credit card or in substitution for an existing credit card; the consolidation of two or more obligations; or the continuance of existing credit without any special effort to collect at or after maturity.

(r) *Good faith* means honesty in fact in the conduct or transaction.

(s) *Inadvertent error* means a mechanical, electronic, or clerical error that a creditor demonstrates was not intentional and occurred notwithstanding the maintenance of procedures reasonably adapted to avoid any such error.

(t) *Judgmental system of evaluating applicants* means any system for evaluating the creditworthiness of an applicant other than a demonstrably and statistically sound, empirically derived credit system.

(u) *Marital status* means the state of being unmarried, married, or separated, as defined by applicable State law. For the purposes of this part, the term "unmarried" includes persons who are single, divorced, or widowed.

(v) *Negative factor or value,* in relation to the age of elderly applicants, means utilizing a factor, value, or weight that is less favorable regarding elderly applicants than the creditor's experience warrants or is less favorable than the factor, value, or weight assigned to the class of applicants that are not classified as elderly applicants and are most favored by a creditor on the basis of age.

(w) *Open end credit* means credit extended pursuant to a plan under which a creditor may permit an applicant to make purchases or obtain loan from time to time directly from the creditor or indirectly by use of a credit card, check, or other device as the plan may provide. The term does not include negotiated advances under an open end real estate mortgage or a letter of credit.

(x) *Person* means a natural person, corporation, government or governmental subdivision or agency, trust, estate, partnership, cooperative, or association.

(y) *Pertinent element of creditworthiness,* in relation to a judgmental system of evaluating applicants, means any information about applicants that a creditor obtains and considers and that has a demonstrable relationship to a determination of creditworthiness.

(z) *Prohibited basis* means race, color, religion, national origin, sex, marital status, or age (provided that the applicant has the capacity to enter into a binding contract); the fact that all or part of the applicant's income derives from any public assistance program, or the fact that the applicant has in good faith exercised any right under the Consumer Credit Protection Act [3] or any State law upon which an exemption has been granted by the Board.

3. The first clause of the definition is not limited to characteristics of the applicant. Therefore, "prohibited basis" as used in this part refers not only to the race, color, religion, national origin, sex, marital status, or age of an applicant (or of partners or officers of an applicant), but refers also to the characteristics of individuals with whom an applicant deals. This means, for example, that, under the

(aa) *Public assistance program* means any Federal, State, or local governmental assistance program that provides a continuing, periodic income supplement, whether premised on entitlement or need. The term includes, but is not limited to, Aid to Families with Dependent Children, food stamps, rent and mortgage supplement or assistance programs, Social Security and Supplemental Security Income, and unemployment compensation.

(bb) *State* means any State, the District of Columbia, the Commonwealth of Puerto Rico, or any territory or possession of the United States.

(cc) Captions and catchlines are intended solely as aids to convenient reference, and no inference as to the substance of any provision of this part may be drawn from them.

(dd) Footnotes shall have the same legal effect as the text of the regulation, whether they are explanatory or illustrative in nature.

§ 202.3 Special treatment for certain classes of transactions

(a) *Classes of transactions afforded special treatment.* Pursuant to section 703(a) of the Act, the following classes of transactions are afforded specialized treatment:

(1) Extensions of credit relating to transactions under public utility tariffs involving services provided through pipe, wire, or other connected facilities if the charges for such public utility services, the charges for delayed payment, and any discount allowed for early payment are filed with, or reviewed or regulated by, an agency of the Federal Government, a State, or a political subdivision thereof;

(2) Extensions of credit subject to regulation under section 7 of the Securities Exchange Act of 1934 or extensions of credit by a broker or dealer subject to regulation as a broker or dealer under the Securities Exchange Act of 1934;

general rule stated in § 202.4, a creditor may not discriminate against a non-Jewish applicant because of that person's business dealings with Jews, or discriminate against an applicant because of the characteristics of persons to whom the extension of credit relates (e.g., the prospective tenants in an apartment complex to be constructed with the proceeds of the credit requested), or because of the characteristics of other individuals residing in the neighborhood where the property offered as collateral is located. A creditor may take into account, however, any applicable law, regulation, or executive order restricting dealings with citizens or governments of other countries or imposing limitations regarding credit extended for their use.

The second clause is limited to an applicant's receipt of public assistance income and to an applicant's good faith exercise of rights under the Consumer Credit Protection Act or applicable State law.

(3) Extensions of incidental consumer credit, other than of the types described in paragraph (a)(1) and (2) of this section:

(i) That are not made pursuant to the terms of a credit card account;

(ii) On which no finance charge as defined in § 226.4 of this Title (Regulation Z, 12 CFR 226.4) is or may be imposed; and

(iii) That are not payable by agreement in more than four installments;

(4) Extensions of credit primarily for business or commercial purposes, including extensions of credit primarily for agricultural purposes, but excluding extensions of credit of the types described in paragraphs (a)(1) and (2) of this section; and

(5) Extensions of credit made to governments or governmental subdivisions, agencies, or instrumentalities.

(b) *Public utilities credit.* The following provisions of this part shall not apply to extensions of credit of the type described in paragraph (a)(1) of this section:

(1) Section 202.5(d)(1) concerning information about marital status;

(2) Section 202.10 relating to furnishing of credit information; and

(3) Section 202.12(b) relating to record retention.

(c) *Securities credit.* The following provisions of this part shall not apply to extensions of credit of the type described in paragraph (a)(2) of this section:

(1) Section 202.5(c) concerning information about a spouse or former spouse;

(2) Section 202.5(d)(1) concerning information about marital status;

(3) Section 202.5(d)(3) concerning information about the sex of an applicant;

(4) Section 202.7(b) relating to designation of name, but only to the extent necessary to prevent violation of rules regarding an account in which a broker or dealer has an interest, or rules necessitating the aggregation of accounts of spouses for the purpose of determining controlling interests, beneficial interests, beneficial ownership, or purchase limitations and restrictions;

(5) Section 202.7(c) relating to action concerning open end accounts, but only to the extent the action taken is on the basis of a change of name or marital status;

(6) Section 202.7(d) relating to signatures of a spouse or other person;

(7) Section 202.10 relating to furnishing of credit information; and

(8) Section 202.12(b) relating to record retention.

(d) *Incidental credit.* The following provisions of this part shall not apply to extensions of credit of the type described in paragraph (a)(3) of this section:

(1) Section 202.5(c) concerning information about a spouse or former spouse;

(2) Section 202.5(d)(1) concerning information about marital status;

(3) Section 202.5(d)(2) concerning information about income derived from alimony, child support, or separate maintenance payments;

(4) Section 202.5(d)(3) concerning information about the sex of an applicant to the extent necessary for medical records or similar purposes;

(5) Section 202.7(d) relating to signatures of a spouse or other person;

(6) Section 202.9 relating to notifications;

(7) Section 202.10 relating to furnishing of credit information; and

(8) Section 202.12(b) relating to record retention.

(e) *Business credit.* The following provisions of this part shall not apply to extensions of credit of the type described in paragraph (a)(4) of this section:

(1) Section 202.5(d)(1) concerning information about marital status;

(2) Section 202.9 relating to notifications, unless an applicant, within 30 days after oral or written notification that adverse action has been taken, requests in writing the reasons for such action;

(3) Section 202.10 relating to furnishing of credit information; and

(4) Section 202.12(b) relating to record retention, unless an applicant, within 90 days after adverse action has been taken, requests in writing that the records relating to the application be retained.

(f) *Governmental credit.* Except for § 202.1 relating to authority, scope, enforcement, penalties and liabilities, and interpretation, § 202.2 relating to definitions and rules of construction, this section, § 202.4 relating to the general rule prohibiting discrimination, § 202.6(a) relating to the use of information, § 202.11 relating to State laws, and § 202.12(a) relating to the retention of prohibited information, the provisions of this part shall not apply to extensions of credit of the type described in paragraph (a)(5) of this section.

§ 202.4 General rules prohibiting discrimination

A creditor shall not discriminate against an applicant on a prohibited basis regarding any aspect of a credit transaction.

§ 202.5 Rules concerning applications

(a) *Discouraging applications.* A creditor shall not make any oral or written statement, in advertising or otherwise, to applicants or prospective applicants that would discourage on a prohibited basis a reasonable person from making or pursuing an application.

(b) *General rules concerning requests for information.* (1) Except as otherwise provided in this section, a creditor may request any information in connection with an application.[4]

(2) Notwithstanding any other provision of this section, a creditor shall request an applicant's race/national origin, sex, and marital status as required in § 202.13 (information for monitoring purposes). In addition, a creditor may obtain such information as may be required by a regulation, order, or agreement issued by, or entered into with, a court or an enforcement agency (including the Attorney General or a similar State official) to monitor or enforce compliance with the Act, this part, or other Federal or State statute or regulation.

(3) The provisions of this section limiting permissible information requests are subject to the provisions of § 202.7(e) regarding insurance and § 202.8(c) and (d) regarding special purpose credit programs.

(c) *Information about a spouse or former spouse.* (1) Except as permitted in this subsection, a creditor may not request any information concerning the spouse or former spouse of an applicant.

(2) A creditor may request any information concerning an applicant's spouse (or former spouse under paragraph (c)(2)(v) of this section) that may be requested about the applicant if:

(i) The spouse will be permitted to use the account; or

(ii) The spouse will be contractually liable upon the account; or

(iii) The applicant is relying on the spouse's income as a basis for repayment of the credit requested; or

(iv) The applicant resides in a community property State or property upon which the applicant is relying as a basis for repayment of the credit requested is located in such a State; or

(v) The applicant is relying on alimony, child support, or separate maintenance payments from a spouse or former spouse as a basis for repayment of the credit requested.

(3) A creditor may request an applicant to list any account upon which the applicant is liable and to provide the name and address in

4. This subsection is not intended to limit or abrogate any Federal or State law regarding privacy, privileged information, credit reporting limitations, or similar restrictions on obtainable information. Furthermore, permission to request information should not be confused with how it may be utilized, which is governed by § 202.6 (rules concerning evaluations of applications).

which such account is carried. A creditor may also ask the names in which an applicant has previously received credit.

(d) *Information a creditor may not request.* (1) If an applicant applies for an individual, unsecured account, a creditor shall not request the applicant's marital status, unless the applicant resides in a community property State or property upon which the applicant is relying as a basis for repayment of the credit requested is located in such a State.[5] Where an application is for other than individual, unsecured credit, a creditor may request an applicant's marital status. Only the terms "married," "unmarried," and "separated" shall be used, and a creditor may explain that the category "unmarried" includes single, divorced, and widowed persons.

(2) A creditor shall not inquire whether any income stated in an application is derived from alimony, child support, or separate maintenance payments, unless the creditor appropriately discloses to the applicant that such income need not be revealed if the applicant does not desire the creditor to consider such income in determining the applicant's creditworthiness. Since a general inquiry about income, without further specification, may lead an applicant to list alimony, child support, or separate maintenance payments, a creditor shall provide an appropriate notice to an applicant before inquiring about the source of an applicant's income, unless the terms of the inquiry (such as an inquiry about salary, wages, investment income, or similarly specified income) tend to preclude the unintentional disclosure of alimony, child support, or separate maintenance payments.

(3) A creditor shall not request the sex of an applicant. An applicant may be requested to designate a title on an application form (such as Ms., Miss, Mr., or Mrs.) if the form appropriately discloses that the designation of such a title is optional. An application form shall otherwise use only terms that are neutral as to sex.

(4) A creditor shall not request information about birth control practices, intentions concerning the bearing or rearing of children, or capability to bear children. This does not preclude a creditor from inquiring about the number and ages of an applicant's dependents or about dependent-related financial obligations or expenditures, provided such information is requested without regard to sex, marital status, or any other prohibited basis.

5. This provision does not preclude requesting relevant information that may indirectly disclose marital status, such as asking about liability to pay alimony, child support, or separate maintenance; the source of income to be used as a basis for the repayment of the credit requested, which may disclose that it is a spouse's income; whether any obligation disclosed by the applicant has a co-obligor, which may disclose that the co-obligor is a spouse or former spouse; or the ownership of assets, which may disclose the interest of a spouse, when such assets are relied upon in extending the credit. Such inquiries are allowed by the general rule of subparagraph (b)(1) of this section.

(5) A creditor shall not request the race, color, religion, or national origin of an applicant or any other person in connection with a credit transaction. A creditor may inquire, however, as to an applicant's permanent residence and immigration status.

(e) *Application forms.* A creditor need not use written applications. If a creditor chooses to use written forms, it may design its own, use forms prepared by another person, or use the appropriate model application forms contained in Appendix B. If a creditor chooses to use an Appendix B form, it may change the form:

(1) By asking for additional information not prohibited by this section;

(2) By deleting any information request; or

(3) By rearranging the format without modifying the substance of the inquiries; provided that in each of these three instances the appropriate notices regarding the optional nature of courtesy titles, the option to disclose alimony, child support, or separate maintenance, and the limitation concerning marital status inquiries are included in the appropriate places if the items to which they relate appear on the creditor's form. If a creditor uses an appropriate Appendix B model form or to the extent that it modifies such a form in accordance with the provisions of clauses (2) or (3) of the preceding sentence or the instructions to Appendix B, that creditor shall be deemed to be acting in compliance with the provisions of paragraphs (c) and (d) of this section.

§ 202.6 Rules concerning evaluation of applications

(a) *General rule concerning use of information.* Except as otherwise provided in the Act and this part, a creditor may consider in evaluating an application any information that the creditor obtains, so long as the information is not used to discriminate against an applicant on a prohibited basis.[7]

(b) *Specific rules concerning use of information.* (1) Except as provided in the Act and this part, a creditor shall not take a prohibited basis into account in any system of evaluating the creditworthiness of applicants.[8]

7. The legislative history of the Act indicates that the Congress intended an "effects test" concept, as outlined in the employment field by the Supreme Court in the cases of Griggs v. Duke Power Co., 401 U.S. 424 (1971), and Albemarle Paper Co. v. Moody, 422 U.S. 405 (1975), to be applicable to a creditor's determination of creditworthiness. See Senate Report to accompany H.R. 6516, No. 94–589, pp. 4–5; House Report to accompany H.R. 6516, N. 94–210, p. 5.

8. This provision does not prevent a creditor from considering the marital status of an applicant or the source of an applicant's income for the purpose of ascertaining the creditor's rights and remedies applicable to the particular extension of credit and not to discriminate in a determination of creditworthiness. Fur-

(2)(i) Except as permitted in this section, a creditor shall not take into account an applicant's age (*Provided,* That the applicant has the capacity to enter into a binding contract) or whether an applicant's income derives from any public assistance program.

(ii) In a demonstrably and statistically sound, empirically derived credit system, a creditor may use an applicant's age as a predictive variable, provided that the age of an elderly applicant is not assigned a negative factor or value.

(iii) In a judgmental system of evaluating creditworthiness, a creditor may consider an applicant's age or whether an applicant's income derives from any public assistance program only for the purpose of determining a pertinent element of creditworthiness.[9]

(iv) In any system of evaluating creditworthiness, a creditor may consider the age of an elderly applicant when such age is to be used to favor the elderly applicant in extending credit.

(3) A creditor shall not use, in evaluating the creditworthiness of an applicant, assumptions or aggregate statistics relating to the likelihood that any group of persons will bear or rear children or, for that reason, will receive diminished or interrupted income in the future.

(4) A creditor shall not take into account the existence of a telephone listing in the name of an applicant for consumer credit. A creditor may take into account the existence of a telephone in the residence of such an applicant.

(5) A creditor shall not discount or exclude from consideration the income of an applicant or the spouse of the applicant because of a prohibited basis or because the income is derived from part-time employment or from an annuity, pension, or other retirement benefit; but a creditor may consider the amount and probable continuance of

thermore, a prohibited basis may be considered in accordance with § 202.8 (special purpose credit programs).

9. Concerning income derived from a public assistance program, a creditor may consider, for example, the length of time an applicant has been receiving such income; whether an applicant intends to continue to reside in the jurisdiction in relation to residency requirements for benefits; and the status of an applicant's dependents to ascertain whether benefits that the applicant is presently receiving will continue.

Concerning age, a creditor may consider, for example, the occupation and length of time to retirement of an applicant to ascertain whether the applicant's income (including retirement income, as applicable) will support the extension of credit until its maturity; or the adequacy of any security offered if the duration of the credit extension will exceed the life expectancy of the applicant. An elderly applicant might not qualify for a five-percent down, 30-year mortgage loan because the duration of the loan exceeds the applicant's life expectancy and the cost of realizing on the collateral might exceed the applicant's equity. The same applicant might qualify with a larger downpayment and a shorter loan maturity. A creditor could also consider an applicant's age, for example to assess the significance of the applicant's length of employment or residence (a young applicant may have just entered the job market; an elderly applicant may recently have retired and moved from a long-time residence).

any income in evaluating an applicant's creditworthiness. Where an applicant relies on alimony, child support, or separate maintenance payments in applying for credit, a creditor shall consider such payments as income to the extent that they are likely to be consistently made. Factors that a creditor may consider in determining the likelihood of consistent payments include, but are not limited to, whether the payments are received pursuant to a written agreement or court decree; the length of time that the payments have been received; the regularity of receipt; the availability of procedures to compel payment; and the creditworthiness of the payor, including the credit history of the payor where available to the creditor under the Fair Credit Reporting Act or other applicable laws.

(6) To the extent that a creditor considers credit history in evaluating the creditworthiness of similarly qualified applicants for a similar type and amount of credit, in evaluating an applicant's creditworthiness, a creditor shall consider (unless the failure to consider results from an inadvertent error):

(i) The credit history, when available, of accounts designated as accounts that the applicant and a spouse are permitted to use or for which both are contractually liable;

(ii) On the applicant's request, any information that the applicant may present tending to indicate that the credit history being considered by the creditor does not accurately reflect the applicant's creditworthiness; and

(iii) On the applicant's request, the credit history, when available, of any account reported in the name of the applicant's spouse or former spouse that the applicant can demonstrate accurately reflects the applicant creditworthiness.

(7) A creditor may consider whether an applicant is a permanent resident of the United States, the applicant's immigration status, and such additional information as may be necessary to ascertain its rights and remedies regarding repayment.

(c) *State property laws.* A creditor's consideration or application of State property laws directly or indirectly affecting creditworthiness shall not constitute unlawful discrimination for the purposes of the Act or this part.

§ 202.7 Rules concerning extensions of credit

(a) *Individual accounts.* A creditor shall not refuse to grant an individual account to a creditworthy applicant on the basis of sex, marital status, or any other prohibited basis.

(b) *Designation of name.* A creditor shall not prohibit an applicant from opening or maintaining an account in a birth-given first name and a surname that is the applicant's birth-given surname, the spouse's surname, or a combined surname.

(c) *Action concerning existing open end accounts.* (1) In the absence of evidence of inability or unwillingness to repay, a creditor shall not take any of the following actions regarding an applicant who is contractually liable on an existing open end account on the basis of the applicant's reaching a certain age or retiring, or on the basis of a change in the applicant's name or marital status:

(i) Require a reapplication; or

(ii) Change the terms of the account; or

(iii) Terminate the account.

(2) A creditor may require a reapplication regarding an open end account on the basis of a change in an applicant's marital status where the credit granted was based on income earned by the applicant's spouse if the applicant's income alone at the time of the original application would not support the amount of credit currently extended.

(d) *Signature of spouse or other person.* (1) Except as provided in this subsection, a creditor shall not require the signature of an applicant's spouse or other person, other than a joint applicant, on any credit instrument if the applicant qualifies under the creditor's standards of creditworthiness for the amount and terms of the credit requested.

(2) If an applicant requests unsecured credit and relies in part upon property to establish creditworthiness, a creditor may consider State law; the form of ownership of the property; its susceptibility to attachment, execution, severance, and partition; and other factors that may affect the value to the creditor of the applicant's interest in the property. If necessary to satisfy the creditor's standards of creditworthiness, the creditor may require the signature of the applicant's spouse or other person on any instrument necessary, or reasonably believed by the creditor to be necessary, under applicable State law to make the property relied upon available to satisfy the debt in the event of default.

(3) If a married applicant requests unsecured credit and resides in a community property State or if the property upon which the applicant is relying is located in such a State, a creditor may require the signature of the spouse on any instrument necessary, or reasonably believed by the creditor to be necessary, under applicable State law to make the community property available to satisfy the debt in the event of default if:

(i) Applicable State law denied the applicant power to manage or control sufficient community property to qualify for the amount of credit requested under the creditor's standards of creditworthiness; and

(ii) The applicant does not have sufficient separate property to qualify for the amount of credit requested without regard to community property.

(4) If an applicant requests secured credit, a creditor may require the signature of the applicant's spouse or other person on any instrument necessary, or reasonably believed by the creditor to be necessary, under applicable State law to make the property being offered as security available to satisfy the debt in the event of default, for example, any instrument to create a valid lien, pass clear title, waive inchoate rights, or assign earnings.

(5) If, under a creditor's standards of creditworthiness, the personal liability of an additional party is necessary to support the extension of the credit requested,[10] a creditor may request that the applicant obtain a co-signer, guarantor, or the like. The applicant's spouse may serve as an additional party, but a creditor shall not require that the spouse be the additional party. For the purposes of paragraph (d) of this section, a creditor shall not impose requirements upon an additional party that the creditor may not impose upon an applicant.

(e) *Insurance.* Differentiation in the availability, rates, and terms on which credit-related casualty insurance or credit life, health, accident, or disability insurance is offered or provided to an applicant shall not constitute a violation of the Act or this part; but a creditor shall not refuse to extend credit and shall not terminate an account because credit life, health, accident, or disability insurance is not available on the basis of the applicant's age. Notwithstanding any other provision of this part, information about the age, sex, or marital status of an applicant may be requested in an application for insurance.

§ 202.8 Special purpose credit programs

(a) *Standards for programs.* Subject to the provisions of paragraph (b) of this section, the Act and this part are not violated if a creditor refuses to extend credit to the applicant solely because the applicant does not qualify under the special requirements that define eligibility for the following types of special purpose credit programs:

(1) Any credit assistance program expressly authorized by Federal or State law for the benefit of an economically disadvantaged class of persons; or

(2) Any credit assistance program offered by a not-for-profit organization, as defined under section 501(c) of the Internal Revenue Code

10. If an applicant requests individual credit relying on the separate income of another person, a creditor may require the signature of the other person to make the income available to pay the debt.

of 1954, as amended, for the benefit of its members or for the benefit of an economically disadvantaged class of persons; or

(3) Any special purpose credit program offered by a for-profit organization or in which such an organization participates to meet special social needs, provided that:

(i) The program is established and administered pursuant to a written plan that (A) identifies the class or classes of persons that the program is designed to benefit and (B) sets forth the procedures and standards for extending credit pursuant to the program; and

(ii) The program is established and administered to extend credit to a class of persons who, pursuant to the customary standards of creditworthiness used by the organization extending the credit, either probably would not receive such credit or probably would receive it on less favorable terms than are ordinarily available to other applicants applying to the organization for a similar type and amount of credit.

(b) *Applicability of other rules.* (1) All of the provisions of this part shall apply to each of the special purpose credit programs described in paragraph (a) of this section to the extent that those provisions are not inconsistent with the provisions of this section.

(2) A program described in paragraphs (a)(2) or (a)(3) of this section shall qualify as a special purpose credit program under paragraph (a) of this section only if it was established and is administered so as not to discriminate against an applicant on the basis of race, color, religion, national origin, sex, marital status, age (*Provided,* That the applicant has the capacity to enter into a binding contract), income derived from a public assistance program, or good faith exercise of any right under the Consumer Credit Protection Act or any State law upon which an exemption has been granted therefrom by the Board; except that all program participants may be required to share one or more of those characteristics so long as the program was not established and is not administered with the purpose of evading the requirements of the Act or this part.

(c) *Special rule concerning requests and use of information.* If all participants in a special purpose credit program described in paragraph (a) of this section are or will be required to possess one or more common characteristics relating to race, color, religion, national origin, sex, marital status, age, or receipt of income from a public assistance program and if the special purpose credit program otherwise satisfies the requirements of paragraph (a) of this section, then, notwithstanding the prohibitions of §§ 202.5 and 202.6, the creditor may request of an applicant and may consider, in determining eligibility for such program, information regarding the common characteristics required for eligibility. In such circumstances, the solicitation and consideration of that information shall not constitute unlawful discrimination for the purposes of the Act or this part.

(d) *Special rule in the case of financial need.* If financial need is or will be one of the criteria for the extension of credit under a special purpose credit program described in paragraph (a) of this section, then, notwithstanding the prohibitions of §§ 202.5 and 202.6, the creditor may request and consider, in determining eligibility for such program, information regarding an applicant's marital status, income from alimony, child support, or separate maintenance, and the spouse's financial resources. In addition, notwithstanding the prohibitions of § 202.7(d), a creditor may obtain the signature of an applicant's spouse or other person on an application or credit instrument relating to a special purpose program if required by Federal or State law. In such circumstances, the solicitation and consideration of that information and the obtaining of a required signature shall not constitute unlawful discrimination for the purposes of the Act or this part.

§ 202.9 Notifications

(a) *Notification of action taken, ECOA notice, and statement of specific reasons*—(1) *Notification of action taken.* A creditor shall notify an applicant of action taken within:

(i) 30 days after receiving a completed application concerning the creditor's approval of, or adverse action regarding, the application (notification of approval may be expressed by implication, where, for example, the applicant receives a credit card, money, property, or services in accordance with the application);

(ii) 30 days after taking adverse action on an uncompleted application;

(iii) 30 days after taking adverse action regarding an existing account; and

(iv) 90 days after the creditor has notified the applicant of an offer to grant credit other than in substantially the amount or on substantially the terms requested by the applicant if the applicant during those 90 days has not expressly accepted or used the credit offered.

(2) *Content of notification.* Any notification given to an applicant against whom adverse action taken shall be in writing and shall contain: a statement of the action taken; a statement of the provisions of section 701(a) of the Act; the name and address of the Federal agency that administers compliance concerning the creditor giving the notification; and

(i) A statement of specific reasons for the action taken; or

(ii) A disclosure of the applicant's right to a statement of reasons within 30 days after receipt by the creditor of a request made within 60 days of such notification, the disclosure to include the name, address, and telephone number of the person or office from which the statement of reasons can be obtained. If the creditor chooses to provide the statement of reasons orally, the notification shall also include a disclosure of the applicant's right to have any oral statement of reasons confirmed in writing within 30 days after a written request for confirmation is received by the creditor.

(3) *Multiple applicants.* If there is more than one applicant, the notification need only be given to one of them, but must be given to the primary applicant where one is readily apparent.

(4) *Multiple creditors.* If a transaction involves more than one creditor and the applicant expressly accepts or uses the credit offered, this section does not require notification of adverse action by any creditor. If a transaction involves more than one creditor and either no credit is offered or the applicant does not expressly accept or use any credit offered, then each creditor taking adverse action must comply with this section. The required notification may be provided indirectly through a third party, which may be one of the creditors, provided that the identity of each creditor taking adverse action is disclosed. Whenever the notification is to be provided through a third party, a creditor shall not be liable for any act or omission of the third party that constitutes a violation of this section if the creditor accurately and in a timely manner provided the third party with the information necessary for the notification and was maintaining procedures reasonably adapted to avoid any such violation.

(b) *Form of ECOA notice and statement of specific reasons*—(1) *ECOA notice.* A creditor satisfies the requirements of paragraph (a)(2) of this section regarding a statement of the provisions of section 701(a) of the Act and the name and address of the appropriate Federal enforcement agency if it provides the following notice, or one that is substantially similar:

> The Federal Equal Credit Opportunity Act prohibits creditors from discriminating against credit applicants on the basis of race, color, religion, national origin, sex, marital status, age (provided that the applicant has the capacity to enter into a binding contract); because all or part of the applicant's income derives from any public assistance program; or because the applicant has in good faith exercised any right under the Consumer Credit Protection Act. The Federal agency that administers compliance with this law concerning this creditor is (name and address as specified by the appropriate agency listed in Appendix A).

The sample notice printed above may be modified immediately following the required references to the Federal Act and enforcement agency to include references to any similar State statute or regulation and to a State enforcement agency.

(2) *Statement of specific reasons.* A statement of reasons for adverse action shall be sufficient if it is specific and indicates the principal reason(s) for the adverse action. A creditor may formulate its own statement of reasons in checklist or letter form or may use all or a portion of the sample form printed below, which, if properly completed, satisfies the requirements of paragraph (a)(2)(i) of this section. Statements that the adverse action was based on the creditor's internal standards or policies or that the applicant failed to achieve the qualifying score on the creditor's credit scoring system are insufficient.

STATEMENT OF CREDIT DENIAL,
TERMINATION, OR CHANGE

Date ____________

Applicant's Name: ______________________________________

Applicant's Address: ____________________________________

____

Description of Account, Transaction, or Requested Credit:

____

____

Description of Adverse Action Taken:

____

____

PRINCIPAL REASON(S) FOR ADVERSE ACTION
CONCERNING CREDIT

- ☐ Credit application incomplete
- ☐ Insufficient credit references
- ☐ Unable to verify credit references
- ☐ Temporary or irregular employment
- ☐ Unable to verify employment
- ☐ Length of employment
- ☐ Insufficient income
- ☐ Excessive obligations
- ☐ Unable to verify income
- ☐ Inadequate collateral
- ☐ We do not grant credit to any applicant on the terms and conditions you request.
- ☐ Too short a period of residence
- ☐ Temporary residence
- ☐ Unable to verify residence

☐ No credit file
☐ Insufficient credit file
☐ Delinquent credit obligations
☐ Garnishment, attachment, foreclosure, repossession, or suit
☐ Bankruptcy
☐ Other specify: ______________________________

DISCLOSURE OF USE OF INFORMATION OBTAINED FROM AN OUTSIDE SOURCE

☐ Disclosure inapplicable
☐ Information obtained in a report from a consumer reporting agency

Name: ______________________________
____

Street Address: ______________________________
____

Phone: ______________________________

☐ Information obtained from an outside source other than a consumer reporting agency. Under the Fair Credit Reporting Act, you have the right to make a written request, within 60 days of receipt of this notice, for disclosure of the nature of the adverse information.

Creditor's name: ______________________________

Creditor's address: ______________________________
____

Creditor's telephone number: ______________________________

[Add ECOA Notice]

(3) *Other information.* The notification required by paragraph (a)(1) of this section may include other information so long as it does not detract from the required content. This notification also may be combined with any disclosures required under other titles of the Consumer Credit Protection Act or any other law, provided that all requirements for clarity and placement are satisfied; and it may appear on either or both sides of the paper if there is a clear reference on the front to any information on the back.

(c) *Oral notifications.* The applicable requirements of this section are satisfied by oral notifications (including statements of specific reasons) in the case of any creditor that did not receive more than 150 applications during the calendar year immediately preceding the calendar year in which the notification of adverse action is to be given to a particular applicant.

(d) *Withdrawn applications.* Where an applicant submits an application and the parties contemplate that the applicant will inquire about its status, if the creditor approves the application and the applicant has not inquired within 30 days after applying, then the creditor may treat the application as withdrawn and need not comply with paragraph (a)(1) of this section.

(e) *Failure of compliance.* A failure to comply with this section shall not constitute a violation when caused by an inadvertent error; provided that, on discovering the error, the creditor corrects it as soon as possible and commences compliance with the requirements of this section.

(f) *Notification.* A creditor notifies an applicant when a writing addressed to the applicant is delivered or mailed to the applicant's last known address or, in the case of an oral notification, when the creditor communicates with the applicants.

§ 202.10 Furnishing of credit information

(a) *Accounts established on or after June 1, 1977.* (1) For every account established on or after June 1, 1977, a creditor that furnishes credit information shall:

(i) Determine whether an account offered by the creditor is one that an applicant's spouse is permitted to use or upon which the spouses are contractually liable other than as guarantors, sureties, endorsers, or similar parties; and

(ii) Designate any such account to reflect the fact of participation of both spouses,[11]

(2) Except as provided in paragraph (a)(3) of this section, if a creditor furnishes credit information concerning an account designated under this section (or designated prior to the effective date of this part) to a consumer reporting agency, it shall furnish the information in a manner that will enable the agency to provide access to the information in the name of each spouse.

(3) If a creditor furnishes credit information concerning an account designated under this section (or designated prior to the effective date of this part) in response to an inquiry regarding a particular applicant, it shall furnish the information in the name of the spouse about whom such information is requested.[12]

11. A creditor need not distinguish between participation as a user or as a contractually liable party.

12. If a creditor learns that new parties have undertaken payment on an account, then the subsequent history of the account shall be furnished in the names of the new parties and need not continue to be furnished in the names of the former parties.

(b) *Accounts established prior to June 1, 1977.* For every account established prior to and in existence on June 1, 1977, a creditor that furnishes credit information shall either:

(1) Not later than June 1, 1977

(i) Determine whether the account is one that an applicant's spouse, if any, is permitted to use or upon which the spouses are contractually liable other than as guarantors, sureties, endorsers, or similar parties;

(ii) Designate any such account to reflect the fact of participation of both spouses: [13] and

(iii) Comply with the reporting requirements of paragraphs (a) (2) and (a)(3) of this section; or

(2) Mail or deliver to all applicants, or all married applicants, in whose name an account is carried on the creditor's records one copy of the notice set forth below.[14] The notice may be mailed with a billing statement or other mailing. All such notices shall be mailed or delivered by October 1, 1977. As to open end accounts, this requirement may be satisfied by mailing one notice at any time prior to October 2, 1977, regarding each account for which a billing statement is sent between June 1 and October 1, 1977. The notice may be supplemented as necessary to permit identification of the account by the creditor or by a consumer reporting agency. A creditor need only send notices relating to those accounts on which it lacks the information necessary to make the proper designation regarding participation or contractual liability.

NOTICE

CREDIT HISTORY FOR MARRIED PERSONS

The Federal Equal Credit Opportunity Act prohibits credit discrimination on the basis of race, color, religion, national origin, sex, marital status, age (provided that a person has the capacity to enter into a binding contract); because all or part of a person's income derives from any public assistance program; or because a person in good faith has exercised any right under the Federal Consumer Credit Protection Act. Regulations under the Act give married persons the right to have credit information included in credit reports in the name of both the wife and the husband if both use or are responsible for the account. This right was created, in part, to insure that credit histories will be available to women who become divorced or widowed.

13. See footnote 11.

14. A creditor may delete the references to the "use" of an account when providing notices regarding closed end accounts.

If your account with us is one that both husband and wife signed for or is an account that is being used by one of you who did not sign, then you are entitled to have us report credit information relating to the account in both your names. If you choose to have credit information concerning your account with us reported in both your names, please complete and sign the statement below and return it to us.

Federal regulations provide that signing your name below will not change your or your spouse's legal liability on the account. Your signature will only request that credit information be reported in both your names.

If you do not complete and return the form below, we will continue to report your credit history in the same way that we do now.

When you furnish credit information on this account, please report all information concerning the account in both our names.

____
Account number

____
Print or type name

____
Print or type name

____
Signature of either spouse

(c) *Requests to change manner in which information is reported.* Within 90 days after receipt of a properly completed request to change the manner in which information is reported to consumer reporting agencies and others regarding an account described in paragraph (b) of this section a creditor shall designate the account to reflect the fact of participation of both spouses. When furnishing information concerning any such account, the creditor shall comply with the reporting requirements of subparagraphs (a)(2) and (a)(3) of this section. The signature of an applicant or the applicant's spouse on a request to change the manner in which information concerning an account is furnished shall not alter the legal liability of either spouse upon the account or require the creditor to change the name in which the account is carried.

(d) *Inadvertent errors.* A failure to comply with this section shall not constitute a violation when caused by an inadvertent error; *Provided,* That, on discovering the error the creditor corrects it as soon as possible and commences compliance with the requirements of this section.

§ 202.11 Relation to State law

(a) *Inconsistent State laws.* Except as otherwise provided in this section, this part alters, affects, or preempts only those State laws that are inconsistent with this part and then only to the extent of the inconsistency. A State law is not inconsistent with this part if it is more protective of an applicant.

(b) *Preempted provisions of State law.* (1) State law is deemed to be inconsistent with the requirements of the Act and this part and less protective of an applicant within the meaning of section 705(f) of the Act to the extent that such law:

(i) Requires or permits a practice or act prohibited by the Act or this part;

(ii) Prohibits the individual extension of consumer credit to both parties to a marriage if each spouse individually and voluntarily applies for such credit;

(iii) Prohibits inquiries or collection of data required to comply with the Act or this part;

(iv) Prohibits asking age or considering age in a demonstrably and statistically sound, empirically derived credit system, to determine a pertinent element of creditworthiness, or to favor an elderly applicant; or

(v) Prohibits inquiries necessary to establish or administer a special purpose credit program as defined by § 202.8.

(2) A determination as to whether a State law is inconsistent with the requirements of the Act and this part will be made only in response to a request for a formal Board interpretation. All requests for such interpretations, in addition to meeting the requirements of § 202.1(d), shall comply with the applicable provisions of subsections (b)(1) and (2) of Supplement I to this part. A determination shall be based on the factors enumerated in this subsection and, as applicable, subsection (c) of Supplement I. Notice of the interpretation shall be provided as specified in subsection (e)(1) of Supplement I, but the interpretation shall be effective in accordance with § 202.1. The interpretation shall be subject to revocation or modification at any time, as provided in subsection (g)(4) of Supplement I.

(c) *Finance charges and loan ceilings.* If married applicants voluntarily apply for and obtain individual accounts with the same creditor, the accounts shall not be aggregated or otherwise combined for purposes of determining permissible finance charges or permissible loan ceilings under any Federal or State law. Permissible loan ceiling laws shall be construed to permit each spouse to become individually liable up to the amount of the loan ceilings, less the amount for which the applicant is jointly liable.[16]

(d) *State and Federal laws not affected.* This section does not alter or annul any provision of State property laws, laws relating to the disposition of decedents' estates, or Federal or State banking regulations directed only towards insuring the solvency of financial institutions.

(e) *Exemption for State regulated transactions.* (1) In accordance with the provisions of Supplement I to this part, any State may apply to the Board for an exemption from the requirements of sections 701 and 702 of the Act and the corresponding provisions of this part for any class of credit transactions within the State. The Board will grant such an exemption if:

(i) The Board determines that, under the law of that State, that class of credit transactions is subject to requirements substantially similar to those imposed under sections 701 and 702 of the Act and the corresponding provisions of this part, or that applicants are afforded greater protection than is afforded under Sections 701 and 702 of the Act and the corresponding provisions of this part; and

(ii) There is adequate provision for State enforcement.

(2) In order to assure that the concurrent jurisdiction of Federal and State courts created in section 706(f) of the Act will continue to have substantive provisions to which such jurisdiction shall apply; to allow Federal enforcement agencies to retain their authority regarding any class of credit transactions exempted pursuant to paragraph (e)(1) of this section and Supplement I; and, generally, to aid in implementing the Act:

(i) No such exemption shall be deemed to extend to the civil liability provisions of section 706 or the administrative enforcement provisions of section 704 of the Act; and

(ii) After an exemption has been granted, the requirements of the applicable State law shall constitute the requirements of the Act and this part, except to the extent such State law imposes requirements not imposed by the Act or this part.

(3) Exemptions granted by the Board to particular classes of credit transactions within specified States will be set forth in Supplement II to this part.

16. For example, in a State with a permissible loan ceiling of $1,000, if a married couple were jointly liable for unpaid debt in the amount of $250, each spouse could subsequently become individually liable for $750.

§ 202.12 Record retention

(a) *Retention of prohibited information.* Retention in a creditor's files of any information, the use of which in evaluating applications is prohibited by the Act or this part, shall not constitute a violation of the Act or this part where such information was obtained:

(1) From any source prior to March 23, 1977;[17] or

(2) At any time from consumer reporting agencies; or

(3) At any time from any applicant or others without the specific request of the creditor; or

(4) At any time as required to monitor compliance with the Act and this part or other Federal or State statutes or regulations.

(b) *Preservation of records.* (1) for 25 months after the date that a creditor notifies an applicant of action taken on an application, the creditor shall retain as to that application in original form or a copy thereof.[18]

(i) Any application form that it receives, any information required to be obtained concerning characteristics of an applicant to monitor compliance with the Act and this part or other similar law, and any other written or recorded information used in evaluating the application and not return to the applicant at the applicant's request;

(ii) A copy of the following documents if furnished to the applicant in written form (or, if furnished orally, any notation or memorandum with respect thereto made by the creditor):

(A) The notification of action taken; and

(B) The statement of specific reasons for adverse action; and

(iii) Any written statement submitted by the applicant alleging a violation of the Act or this part.

(2) For 25 months after the date that a creditor notifies an applicant of adverse action regarding an account, other than in connection with an application, the creditor shall retain as to that account, in original form or a copy thereof:

(i) Any written or recorded information concerning such adverse action; and

(ii) Any written statement submitted by the applicant alleging a violation of the Act or this part.

17. Pursuant to the October 28, 1975 version of Regulation B, the applicable date for sex and marital status information is June 30, 1976.

18. "A copy thereof" includes carbon copies, photocopies, microfilm or microfiche copies or copies produced by any accurate information retrieval system. A creditor who uses a computerized or mechanized system need not keep a written copy of a document if it can regenerate the precise text of the document upon request.

(3) In addition to the requirements of paragraphs (b)(1) and (2), of this section, any creditor that has actual notice that it is under investigation or is subject to an enforcement proceeding for an alleged violation of the Act or this part by an enforcement agency charged with monitoring that creditor's compliance with the Act and this part, or that has been served with notice of an action filed pursuant to section 706 of the Act and § 202.1(b) or (c) of this part, shall retain the information required in paragraphs (b)(1) and (2) of this section until final disposition of the matter, unless an earlier time is allowed by order of the agency or court.

(4) In any transaction involving more than one creditor, any creditor not required to comply with § 202.9 (notifications) shall retain for the time period specified in paragraph (b) of this section all written or recorded information in its possession concerning the applicant, including a notation of action taken in connection with any adverse action.

(c) *Failure of compliance.* A failure to comply with this section shall not constitute a violation when caused by an inadvertent error.

§ 202.13 Information for monitoring purposes

(a) *Scope and information requested.* (1) For the purpose of monitoring compliance with the provisions of the Act and this part, any creditor that receives an application for consumer credit relating to the purchase of residential real property, where the extension of credit is to be secured by a lien on such property, shall request as part of any written application for such credit the following information regarding the applicant and joint applicant (if any):

(i) Race/national origin, using the categories American Indian or Alaskan Native; Asian or Pacific Islander; Black; White; Hispanic; Other (Specify);

(ii) Sex;

(iii) Marital status, using the categories married, unmarried, and separated; and

(iv) Age.

(2) "Residential real property" means improved real property used or intended to be used for residential purposes, including single family homes, dwellings for from two to four families, and individual units of condominiums and cooperatives.

(b) *Method of obtaining information.* Questions regarding race/national origin, sex, marital status, and age may be listed at the creditor's option, either on the application form or on a separate form that refers to the application.

(c) *Disclosure to applicant and joint applicant.* The applicant and joint applicant (if any) shall be informed that the information regarding race/national origin, sex, marital status, and age is being requested by the Federal government for the purpose of monitoring compliance with Federal anti-discrimination statutes and that those statutes prohibit creditors from discriminating against applicants on those bases. The applicant and joint applicant shall be asked, but not required, to supply the requested information. If the applicant or joint applicant chooses not to provide the information or any part of it, that fact shall be noted on the form on which the information is obtained.

(d) *Substitute monitoring program.* Any monitoring program required by an agency charged with administrative enforcement under section 704 of the Act may be substituted for the requirements contained in paragraphs (a), (b) and (c) of this section.

*

FEDERAL RESERVE BOARD, REGULATION E, ELECTRONIC FUND TRANSFERS

12 C.F.R. Part 205

Table of Sections

---

§ 205.1 Authority, purpose, and scope

(a) *Authority.* This regulation, issued by the Board of Governors of the Federal Reserve System, implements Title IX (Electronic Fund Transfer Act) of the Consumer Credit Protection Act, as amended (15 U.S.C. 1601 et seq.).

(b) *Purpose and Scope.* In November 1978, the Congress enacted the Electronic Fund Transfer Act. The Congress found that the use of electronic systems to transfer funds provides the potential for substantial benefits to consumers, but that the unique characteristics of these systems make the application of existing consumer protection laws unclear, leaving the rights and liabilities of users of electronic fund transfer systems undefined. The Act establishes the basic rights, liabilities, and responsibilities of consumers who use electronic money transfer services and of financial institutions that offer these services. This regulation is intended to carry out the purposes of the Act, including, primarily, the protection of individual consumers engaging in electronic transfers. Except as otherwise provided, this regulation applies to all persons who are financial institutions as defined in § 205.2(i).

§ 205.2 Definitions and rules of construction

For the purposes of this regulation, the following definitions apply, unless the context indicates otherwise:

(a)(1) "Access device" means a card, code, or other means of access to a consumer's account, or any combination thereof, that may be used by the consumer for the purpose of initiating electronic fund transfers.

(2) An access device becomes an "accepted access device" when the consumer to whom the access device was issued:

(i) Requests and receives, or signs, or uses, or authorizes another to use, the access device for the purpose of transferring money between accounts or obtaining money, property, labor or services;

(ii) Requests validation of an access device issued on an unsolicited basis; or

(iii) Receives an access device issued in renewal of, or in substitution for, an accepted access device, whether such access device is issued by the initial financial institution or a successor.

(b) "Account" means a demand deposit (checking), savings, or other consumer asset account (other than an occasional or incidental credit balance in a credit plan) held either directly or indirectly by a financial institution and established primarily for personal, family, or household purposes.

(c) "Act" means the Electronic Fund Transfer Act (Title IX of the Consumer Credit Protection Act, 15 U.S.C. 1601 et seq.).

(d) "Business day" means any day on which the offices of the consumer's financial institution are open to the public for carrying on substantially all business functions.

(e) "Consumer" means a natural person.

(f) "Credit" means the right granted by a financial institution to a consumer to defer payment of debt, incur debt and defer its payment, or purchase property or services and defer payment therefor.

(g) "Electronic fund transfer" means any transfer of funds, other than a transaction originated by check, draft, or similar paper instrument, that is initiated through an electronic terminal, telephone, or computer or magnetic tape for the purpose of ordering, instructing, or authorizing a financial institution to debit or credit an account. The term includes, but is not limited to, point-of-sale transfers, automated teller machine transfers, direct deposits or withdrawals of funds, and transfers initiated by telephone. The term does not include payments made by check, draft, or similar paper instrument at an electronic terminal.

(h) "Electronic terminal" means an electronic device, other than a telephone operated by a consumer, through which a consumer may initiate an electronic fund transfer. The term includes, but is not limited to, point-of-sale terminals, automated teller machines, and cash dispensing machines.

(i) "Financial institution" means a State or National bank, a State or Federal savings and loan association, a State or Federal mutual savings bank, a State or Federal credit union, or any other person who, directly or indirectly, holds an account belonging to a consumer. The term also includes any person who issues an access device and agrees with a consumer to provide electronic fund transfer services.

(j) "Preauthorized electronic fund transfer" means an electronic fund transfer authorized in advance to recur at substantially regular intervals.

(k) "State" means any State, territory or possession of the United States, the District of Columbia, the Commonwealth of Puerto Rico, or any political subdivision of any of the above.

(*l*) "Unauthorized electronic fund transfer" means an electronic fund transfer from a consumer's account initiated by a person other than the consumer without actual authority to initiate the transfer and from which the consumer receives no benefit. The term does not include any electronic fund transfer (1) initiated by a person who was furnished with the access device to the consumer's account by the consumer, unless the consumer has notified the financial institution involved that transfers by that person are no longer authorized, (2) initiated with fraudulent intent by the consumer or any person acting in concert with the consumer, or (3) that is initiated by the financial institution or its employee.

(m) Footnotes have the same legal effect as the text of the regulation.

§ 205.3 Exemptions

This Act and this regulation do not apply to the following:

(a) *Check guarantee or authorization services.* Any service that guarantees payment or authorizes acceptance of a check, draft, or similar paper instrument and that does not directly result in a debit or credit to a consumer's account.

(b) *Wire transfers.* Any wire transfer of funds for a consumer through the Federal Reserve Communications System or other similar network that is used primarily for transfers between financial institutions or between businesses.

(c) *Certain securities or commodities transfers.* Any transfer the primary purpose of which is the purchase or sale of securities or commodities regulated by the Securities and Exchange Commission or the Commodity Futures Trading Commission.

(d) *Certain automatic transfers.* Any transfer under an agreement between a consumer and a financial institution which provides that the institution will initiate individual transfers without a specific request from the consumer.

(1) Between a consumer's accounts within the financial institution, such as a transfer from a checking account to a savings account;

(2) Into a consumer's account by the financial institution, such as the crediting of interest to a savings account;[1a]

(3) From a consumer's account to an account of the financial institution, such as a loan payment; [1a] or

(4) From a consumer's account to an account of another consumer, within the financial institution, who is a member of the transferor's family.

(e) *Certain telephone-initiated transfers.* Any transfer of funds that (1) is initiated by a telephone conversation between a consumer and an officer or employee of a financial institution and (2) is not under a telephone bill-payment or other prearranged plan or agreement in which periodic or recurring transfers are contemplated.

(f) *Trust accounts.* Any trust account held by a financial institution under a bona fide trust agreement.

(g) *Preauthorized transfers to small financial institutions.* (1) Any preauthorized transfer to or from an account if the assets of the account-holding financial institution are $25 million or less on December 31.[1a]

(2) If the account-holding financial institution's assets subsequently exceed $25 million, the institution's exemption for this class of transfers shall terminate one year from the end of the calendar year in which the assets exceed $25 million.

§ 205.4 Special requirements

(a) *Services offered by two or more financial institutions.* Two or more financial institutions that jointly provide electronic fund transfer services may contract among themselves to comply with the requirements that this regulation imposes on any or all of them.

1a. The financial institution remains subject to section 913 of the act regarding compulsory use of electronic fund transfers. A financial institution may, however, require the automatic repayment of credit that is extended under an overdraft credit plan or that is extended to maintain a specified minimum balance in the consumer's account. Financial institutions also remain subject to sections 915 and 916 regarding civil and criminal liability.

When making disclosures under §§ 205.7 and 205.8, a financial institution that provides electronic fund transfer services under an agreement with other financial institutions need make only those disclosures which are within its knowledge and the purview of its relationship with the consumer for whom it holds an account.

(b) *Multiple accounts and account holders.* (1) If a consumer holds two or more accounts at a financial institution, the institution may combine the disclosures required by the regulation into one statement (for example, the financial institution may mail or deliver a single periodic statement or annual error resolution notice to a consumer for multiple accounts held by that consumer at that institution).

(2) If two or more consumers hold a joint account from or to which electronic fund transfers can be made, the financial institution need provide only one set of the disclosures required by the regulation for each account.

(c) *Additional information; disclosures required by other laws.* At the financial institution's option, additional information or disclosures required by other laws (for example, Truth in Lending disclosures) may be combined with the disclosures required by this regulation.

§ 205.5 Issuance of access devices

(a) *General rule.* A financial institution may issue an access device to a consumer only:

(1) In response to an oral or written request or application for the device; [1b] or

(2) As a renewal of, or in substitution for, an accepted access device, whether issued by the initial financial institution or a successor.

(3) As a renewal of, or in substitution for, an access device issued before February 8, 1979 (other than an accepted access device, which can be renewed or substituted under paragraph (a)(2) of this section), provided that the disclosures set forth in §§ 205.7(a)(1), (2), and (3) accompany the renewal or substitute device; except that for a renewal or substitution that occurs before July 1, 1979, the disclosures may be sent within a reasonable time after the renewal or substitute device is issued.

(b) *Exception.* Notwithstanding the provisions of paragraph (a)(1) of this section, a financial institution may distribute an access device to a consumer on an unsolicited basis if:

(1) The access device is not validated;

1b. In the case of a joint account, a financial institution may issue an access device to each account holder for whom the requesting holder specifically requests an access device.

(2) The distribution is accompanied by a complete disclosure, in accordance with § 205.7(a), of the consumer's rights and liabilities that will apply if the access device is validated;

(3) The distribution is accompanied by a clear explanation that the access device is not validated and how the consumer may dispose of the access device if validation is not desired; and

(4) The access device is validated only in response to the consumer's oral or written request or application for validation and after verification of the consumer's identity by any reasonable means, such as by photograph, fingerprint, personal visit, or signature comparison. An access device is considered validated when a financial institution has performed all procedures necessary to enable a consumer to use it to initiate an electronic fund transfer.

(c) *Relation to Truth in Lending.* (1) The Act and this regulation govern

(i) Issuance of access devices;

(ii) Addition to an accepted credit card, as defined in 12 CFR 226.2(a) (Regulation Z), of the capability to intitiate electronic fund transfers; and

(iii) Issuance of access devices that permit credit extensions only under a preexisting agreement between a consumer and a financial institution to extend the credit when the consumer's account is overdrawn or to maintain a specified minimum balance in the consumer's account.

(2) The Truth in Lending Act (15 U.S.C. 1601 et seq.) and 12 CFR Part 226 (Regulation Z), which prohibit the unsolicited issuance of credit cards, govern

(i) Issuance of credit cards as defined in 12 CFR 226.2(r);

(ii) Addition of a credit feature to an accepted access device; and

(iii) Issuance of credit cards that are also access devices, except as provided in paragraph (c)(1)(iii) of this section.

§ 205.6 Liability of consumer for unauthorized transfers

(a) *General rule.* A consumer is liable, within the limitations described in paragraph (b) of this section, for unauthorized electronic fund transfers involving the consumer's account only if:

(1) The access device used for the unauthorized transfers is an accepted access device;

(2) The financial institution has provided a means (such as by signature, photograph, fingerprint, or electronic or mechanical confirmation) to identify the consumer to whom the access device was issued; and

(3) The financial institution has provided the following information, in writing, to the consumer:

(i) A summary of the consumer's liability under this section, or under other applicable law or agreement, for unauthorized electronic fund transfers and, at the financial institution's option, notice of the advisability of promptly reporting loss or theft of the access device or unauthorized transfers.

(ii) The telephone number and address of the person or office to be notified in the event the consumer believes that an unauthorized electronic fund transfer has been or may be made.

(iii) The financial institution's business days, as determined under § 205.2(d), unless applicable State law or an agreement between the consumer and the financial institution sets a liability limit not greater than $50.

(b) *Limitations on amount of liability.* The amount of a consumer's liability for an unauthorized electronic fund transfer or a series of related unauthorized transfers shall not exceed $50 or the amount of unauthorized transfers that occur before notice to the financial institution under paragraph (c) of this section, whichever is less, unless one or both of the following exceptions apply:

(1) If the consumer fails to notify the financial institution within 2 business days after learning of the loss or theft of the access device, the consumer's liability shall not exceed the lesser of $500 or the sum of

(i) $50 or the amount of unauthorized electronic fund transfers that occur before the close of the 2 business days, whichever is less, and

(ii) the amount of unauthorized electronic fund transfers that the financial institution establishes would not have occurred but for the failure of the consumer to notify the institution within 2 business days after the consumer learns of the loss or theft of the access device, and that occur after the close of 2 business days and before notice to the financial institution.

(2) If the consumer fails to report within 60 days of transmittal of the periodic statement any unauthorized electronic fund transfer that appears on the statement, the consumer's liability shall not exceed the sum of

(i) The lesser of $50 or the amount of unauthorized electronic fund transfers that appear on the periodic statement or that occur during the 60-day period, and

(ii) The amount of unauthorized electronic fund transfers that occur after the close of the 60 days and before notice to the financial institution and that the financial institution establishes would not have occurred but for the failure of the consumer to notify the financial institution within that time.

(3) Paragraphs (b)(1) and (2) of this section may both apply in some circumstances. Paragraph (b)(1) shall determine the consumer's liability for any unauthorized transfers that appear on the periodic statement and occur before the close of the 60-day period, and paragraph (b)(2)(ii) shall determine liability for transfers that occur after the close of the 60-day period.

(4) If a delay in notifying the financial institution was due to extenuating circumstances, such as extended travel or hospitalization, the time periods specified above shall be extended to a reasonable time.

(5) If applicable State law or an agreement between the consumer and financial institution imposes lesser liability than that provided in paragraph (b) of this section, the consumer's liability shall not exceed that imposed under that law or agreement.

(c) *Notice to financial institution.* For purposes of this section, notice to a financial institution is given when a consumer takes such steps as are reasonably necessary to provide the financial institution with the pertinent information, whether or not any particular officer, employee, or agent of the financial institution does in fact receive the information. Notice in writing is considered given at the time the consumer deposits the notice in the mail or delivers the notice for transmission by any other usual means to the financial institution. Notice in writing is considered given at the time of receipt or, whether or not received, at the expiration of the time ordinarily required for transmission, whichever is earlier. Notice is also considered given when the financial institution becomes aware of circumstances that lead to the reasonable belief that an unauthorized electronic fund transfer involving the consumer's account has been or may be made.

(d) *Relation to Truth in Lending.* (1) A consumer's liability for an unauthorized electronic fund transfer shall be determined solely in accordance with this section if the electronic fund transfer

(i) Was initiated by use of an access device that is also a credit card as defined in 12 CFR 226.2(r), or

(ii) Involves an extension of credit under an agreement between a consumer and a financial institution to extend the credit when the consumer's account is overdrawn or to maintain a specified minimum balance in the consumer's account.

(2) A consumer's liability for unauthorized use of a credit card that is also an access device but that does not involve an electronic fund transfer shall be determined solely in accordance with the Truth in Lending Act and 12 CFR Part 226 (Regulation Z).

§ 205.7 Initial disclosure of terms and conditions

(a) *Content of disclosures.* At the time a consumer contracts for an electronic fund transfer service or before the first electronic fund transfer is made involving a consumer's account, a financial institution shall disclose to the consumer, in a readily understandable written statement that the consumer may retain, the following terms and conditions of the electronic fund transfer service, as applicable:

(1) A summary of the consumer's liability under § 205.6, or other applicable law or agreement, for unauthorized electronic fund transfers and, at the financial institution's option, the advisability of promptly reporting loss or theft of the access device or unauthorized transfers.

(2) The telephone number and address of the person or office to be notified when the consumer believes that an unauthorized electronic fund transfer has been or may be made.

(3) The financial institution's business days, as determined under § 205.2(d).

(4) The type of electronic fund transfers that the consumer may make and any limitations on the frequency and dollar amount of transfers. The details of the limitations need not be disclosed if their confidentiality is essential to maintain the security of the electronic fund transfer system.

(5) Any charges for electronic fund transfers or for the right to make transfers.

(6) A summary of the consumer's right to receive documentation of electronic fund transfers, as provided in §§ 205.9, 205.10(a), and 205.10(d).

(7) A summary of the consumer's right to stop payment of a preauthorized electronic fund transfer and the procedure for initiating a stop-payment order, as provided in § 205.10(c).

(8) A summary of the financial institution's liability to the consumer for its failure to make or to stop certain transfers under § 910 of the Act.

(9) The circumstances under which the financial institution in the ordinary course of business will disclose information to third parties concerning the consumer's account.

(10) A notice that is substantially similar to the following notice concerning error resolution procedures and the consumer's rights under them:

IN CASE OF ERRORS OR QUESTIONS ABOUT YOUR ELECTRONIC TRANSFERS

Telephone us at [insert phone number]

or

Write us at [insert address]

as soon as you can, if you think your statement or receipt is wrong or if you need more information about a transfer listed on the statement or receipt. We must hear from you no later than 60 days after we sent you the FIRST statement on which the problem or error appeared.

(1) Tell us your name and account number (if any).

(2) Describe the error or the transfer you are unsure about, and explain as clearly as you can why you believe it is an error or why you need more information.

(3) Tell us the dollar amount of the suspected error.

If you tell us orally, we may require that you send us your complaint or question in writing within 10 business days.

We will tell you the results of our investigation within 10 business days after we hear from you and will correct any error promptly. If we need more time, however, we may take up to 45 days to investigate your complaint or question. If we decide to do this, we will recredit your account within 10 business days for the amount you think is in error, so that you will have the use of the money during the time it takes us to complete our investigation. If we ask you to put your complaint or question in writing and we do not receive it within 10 business days, we may not recredit your account.

If we decide that there was no error, we will send you a written explanation within 3 business days after we finish our investigation. You may ask for copies of the documents that we used in our investigation.

(b) *Timing of disclosures for accounts in existence on May 10, 1980.* A financial institution shall mail or deliver to the consumer the information required by paragraph (a) of this section on or before June 9, 1980, or with the first periodic statement required by § 205.9(b) after May 10, 1980, whichever is earlier, for any account that is open on May 10, and

(1) From or to which electronic fund transfers were made prior to May 10, 1980;

(2) With respect to which a contract for such transfers was entered into between a consumer and a financial institution; or

(3) For which an access device was issued to a consumer.

§ 205.8 Change in terms; error resolution notice

(a) *Change in terms.* A financial institution shall mail or deliver a written notice to the consumer at least 21 days before the effective date of any change in a term or condition required to be disclosed under § 205.7(a) if the change would result in increased fees or charges, increased liability for the consumer, fewer types of available electronic fund transfers, or stricter limitations on the frequency or dollar amounts of transfers. Prior notice need not be given where an immediate change in terms or conditions is necessary to maintain or restore the security of an electronic fund transfer system or account. However, if a change required to be disclosed under this paragraph is to be made permanent, the financial institution shall provide written notice of the change to the consumer on or with the next regularly scheduled periodic statement or within 30 days, unless disclosure would jeopardize the security of the system or account. However, if such a change is to be made permanent, the financial institution shall provide written notice of the change to the consumer on or with the next regularly scheduled periodic statement or within 30 days, unless disclosure would jeopardize the security of the system or account.

(b) *Error resolution notice.* For each account from or to which electronic fund transfers can be made, a financial institution shall mail or deliver to the consumer, at least once each calendar year, the notice set forth in § 205.7(a)(10). Alternatively, a financial institution may mail or deliver a notice that is substantially similar to the following notice on or with each periodic statement required by § 205.9(b):

IN CASE OF ERRORS OR QUESTIONS ABOUT YOUR ELECTRONIC TRANSFERS

Telephone us at [insert telephone number]

or

Write us at [insert address]

as soon as you can, if you think your statement or receipt is wrong or if you need more information about a transfer on the statement or receipt. We must hear from you no later than 60 days after we sent you the FIRST statement on which the error or problem appeared.

(1) Tell us your name and account number (if any).

(2) Describe the error or the transfer you are unsure about, and explain as clearly as you can why you believe there is an error or why you need more information.

(3) Tell us the dollar amount of the suspected error.

We will investigate your complaint and will correct any error promptly. If we take more than 10 business days to do this, we will recredit your account for the amount you think is in error, so that you will have use of the money during the time it takes us to complete our investigation.

§ 205.9 Documentation of transfers

(a) *Receipts at electronic terminals.* At the time an electronic fund transfer is initiated at an electronic terminal by a consumer, the financial institution shall make available [2] to the consumer a written receipt of the transfer(s) that clearly sets forth the following information, as applicable:

(1) The amount of the transfer. A charge for the transfer may be included in this amount if the terminal is owned or operated by a person other than the financial institution holding the consumer's account, provided the amount of the charge is disclosed on the receipt and on a sign posted on or at the terminal.

(2) The calendar date the consumer initiated the transfer.

(3) The type of transfer and the type of the consumer's account(s) [3] to or from which funds are transferred, such as "withdrawal from checking," "transfer from savings to checking," or "payment from savings." These descriptions may be used for transfers to or from accounts that are similar in function to checking accounts (such as share draft or negotiable order of withdrawal accounts) or to savings accounts (such as share accounts). Codes may be used only if they are explained elsewhere on the receipt.

(4) A number or code that uniquely identifies the consumer initiating the transfer, the consumer's account(s), or the access device used to initiate the transfer.

(5) The location (in a form prescribed by paragraph (b)(1)(iv) of this section) of the terminal at which the transfer was initiated or an identification (such as a code or terminal number).

(6) The name of any third party to or from whom funds are transferred; a code may be used only if it is explained elsewhere on the receipt. This requirement does not apply if the name is provided by the consumer in a form that the electronic terminal cannot duplicate on the receipt.

2. A financial institution may arrange for a third party, such as a merchant to make the receipt available.

3. If more than one account of the same type may be accessed by a single access device, the accounts must be uniquely identified unless the terminal is incapable of such identification and was purchased or ordered by the financial institution prior to February 6, 1980. In a point-of-sale transfer, the type of account need not be identified if the access device used may access only one account at point of sale. The type of account need not be identified if the access device may access only one account at that terminal.

(b) *Periodic statements.* For any account to or from which electronic fund transfers can be made, the financial institution shall mail or deliver a statement for each monthly or shorter cycle in which an electronic fund transfer has occurred, but at least a quarterly statement if no transfer has occurred. The statement shall include the following, as applicable:

(1) For each electronic fund transfer occurring during the cycle,[4]

(i) The amount of the transfer. If a transfer charge was added at the time of initiation by the owner or operator of an electronic terminal in accordance with paragraph (a)(1) of this section, that charge may be included in the amount of the transfer.

(ii) The date the transfer was credited or debited to the consumer's account.

(iii) The type of transfer and the type of the consumer's account(s) to or from which funds were transferred.

(iv) For each transfer initiated by the consumer at an electronic terminal [4a], the location that appeared on the receipt or, if an identification (such as a code or terminal number) was used, that identification and one of the following descriptions of the terminal's location:

(A) The address, including number and street (the number may be omitted if the street alone uniquely identifies the terminal location) or intersection, city, and state or foreign country; [5]

(B) A generally accepted name for a specific location (such as a branch of the financial institution, a shopping center, or an airport), city, and state or foreign country; [6] or

(C) The name of the entity at whose place of business the terminal is located or which owns or operates the terminal (such as the financial institution [7] or the seller of goods or services), city, and state or foreign country.[8]

4. The information required by paragraph (b)(1) of this section may be provided on accompanying documents. Codes explained on the statement or on accompanying documents are acceptable.

4a. A financial institution need not identify the terminal location for deposits of cash, checks, drafts, or similar paper instruments at electronic terminals.

5. The city and state may be omitted if all the terminals owned or operated by the financial institution providing the statement (or by the system in which it participates) are located in the same city. The state may be omitted if all the terminals owned or operated by the financial institution providing the statement (or by the system in which it participates) are located in that state. The state may also be omitted for transfers occurring at terminals within 50 miles of the financial institution's main office.

6. See footnote 5.

7. If the financial institution providing the statement owns or operates terminals at more than one location, it shall describe the location of its electronic terminals by use of paragraphs (b)(1)(iv)(A) or (B) of this section.

8. See footnote 5.

(v) The name of any third party to or from whom funds were transferred.[9]

(2) The number(s) of the consumer's account(s) for which the statement is issued.

(3) The total amount of any fees or charges, other than a finance charge under 12 CFR 226.7(b)(1)(iv), assessed against the account during the statement period for electronic fund transfers or the right to make such transfers, or for account maintenance.

(4) The balances in the consumer's account(s) at the beginning and at the close of the statement period.

(5) The address and telephone number to be used for inquiry or notice of errors, preceded by "Direct Inquiries To:" or similar language. Alternatively, the address and telephone number may be provided on the notice of error resolution procedures set forth in § 205.8(b).

(6) If the financial institution uses the notice procedure set forth in § 205.10(a)(1)(iii), the telephone number the consumer may call to ascertain whether a preauthorized transfer to the consumer's account has occurred.

(c) *Documentation for certain passbook accounts.* In the case of a consumer's passbook account which may not be accessed by any electronic fund transfers other than preauthorized transfers to the account,[9a] the financial institution may, in lieu of complying with paragraph (b) of this section, upon presentation of the consumer's passbook, provide the consumer with documentation by entering in the passbook or on a separate document the amount and date of each electronic fund transfer made since the passbook was last presented.

(d) *Periodic statements for certain non-passbook accounts.* If a consumer's account other than a passbook account may not be accessed by any electronic fund transfers other than preauthorized transfers to the account,[9a] the financial institution need provide the periodic statement required by paragraph (b) of this section only quarterly.

(e) *Use of abbreviations.* A financial institution may use commonly accepted or readily understandable abbreviations in complying with the documentation requirements of this section.

(f) *Receipt requirements for certain cash-dispensing terminals.* The failure of a financial institution to comply with the requirement

9. A financial institution need not identify third parties whose names appear on checks, drafts, or similar paper instruments deposited to the consumer's account at an electronic terminal.

9a. Accounts that also are accessible by the intra-institutional transfers described in paragraph (h) of this section may continue to be documented in accordance with paragraph (c) or (d) of this section.

of paragraph (a) of this section that a receipt be made available to the consumer at the time an electronic fund transfer is initiated at an electronic terminal shall not constitute a violation of the Act or this regulation, provided:

(1) The transfer occurs at an electronic terminal that:

(i) Does not permit transfers other than cash withdrawals by the consumer,

(ii) Cannot make a receipt available to the consumer at the time the transfer is initiated,

(iii) Cannot be modified to provide a receipt at that time, and

(iv) Was purchased or ordered by the financial institution prior to February 6, 1980; and

(2) The financial institution mails or delivers a written receipt to the consumer that complies with the other requirements of paragraph (a) of this section on the next business day following the transfer.

(g) *Delayed effective date for certain periodic statement requirements.* The failure of a financial institution to describe an electronic fund transfer in accordance with the requirements of paragraphs (b)(1)(iv) and (v) of this section shall not constitute a violation of the Act or this regulation unless the transfer occurs on or after August 10, 1980, if, when a transfer involves a payment to another person, the financial institution, upon the consumer's request, and without charge, promptly provides the consumer with proof that such a payment was made.

(h) *Periodic statements for certain intra-institutional transfers.* A financial institution need not provide the periodic statement required by paragraph (b) of this section for an account accessed only by electronic fund transfers initiated by the consumer to or from another account of the consumer for which the financial institution documents transfers in compliance with paragraph (b) of this section.

(i) *Documentation for foreign-initiated transfers.* Failure to provide the terminal receipt and periodic statement required by paragraphs (a) and (b) of this section for a particular electronic fund transfer shall not be deemed a failure to comply with this regulation, if:

(1) the transfer is not initiated in a state as defined in § 205.2(k); and

(2) in accordance with § 205.11, the financial institution treats an inquiry for clarification or documentation as a notice of error and corrects the error.

§ 205.10 Preauthorized transfers

(a) *Preauthorized transfers to a consumer's account.* (1) Where a consumer's account is scheduled to be credited by a preauthorized electronic fund transfer from the same payor at least once every 60 days, except where the payor provides positive notice to the consumer that the transfer has been initiated, the financial institution shall provide notice by one of the following means:

(i) The institution shall transmit oral or written notice to the consumer, within 2 business days after the transfer, that the transfer occurred;

(ii) The institution shall transmit oral or written notice to the consumer, within 2 business days after the date on which the transfer was scheduled to occur, that the transfer did not occur; or

(iii) The institution shall provide a readily available telephone line that the consumer may call to ascertain whether or not the transfer occurred, and shall disclose the telephone number on the initial disclosures required by § 205.7 and on each periodic statement.

(2) A financial institution that receives a preauthorized transfer of the type described in paragraph (a)(1) of this section shall credit the amount of the transfer as of the day the funds for the transfer are received.

(b) *Preauthorized transfers from a consumer's account; written authorization.* Preauthorized electronic fund transfers from a consumer's account may be authorized by the consumer only in writing, and a copy of the authorization shall be provided to the consumer by the party that obtains the authorization from the consumer.

(c) *Consumer's right to stop payment.* A consumer may stop payment of a preauthorized electronic fund transfer from the consumer's account by notifying the financial institution orally or in writing at any time up to 3 business days before the scheduled date of the transfer. The financial institution may require written confirmation of the stop-payment order to be made within 14 days of an oral notification if, when the oral notification is made, the requirement is disclosed to the consumer together with the address to which confirmation should be sent. If written confirmation has been required by the financial institution, the oral stop-payment order shall cease to be binding 14 days after it has been made.

(d) *Notice of transfers varying in amount.* Where a preauthorized electronic fund transfer from the consumer's account varies in amount from the previous transfer relating to the same authorization, or the preauthorized amount, the financial institution or the designated payee shall mail or deliver, at least 10 days before the scheduled transfer date, a written notice of the amount and scheduled date of the transfer. If the financial institution or designated payee informs the consumer of the right to receive notice of all varying transfers, the consumer may elect to receive notice only when a transfer does not fall within a specified range of amounts or, alternatively, only when a transfer differs from the most recent transfer by more than an agreed-upon amount.

§ 205.11 Procedures for resolving errors

(a) *Definition of error.* For purposes of this section, the term "error" means:

(1) A unauthorized electronic fund transfer;

(2) An incorrect electronic fund transfer to or from the consumer's account;

(3) The omission from a periodic statement of an electronic fund transfer to or from the consumer's account that should have been included;

(4) A computational or bookkeeping error made by the financial institution relating to an electronic fund transfer;

(5) The consumer's receipt of an incorrect amount of money from an electronic terminal;

(6) An electronic fund transfer not identified in accordance with the requirements of §§ 205.9 or 205.10(a); or

(7) A consumer's request for any documentation required by §§ 205.9 or 205.10(a), or for additional information or clarification concerning an electronic fund transfer. This includes any request for documentation, information, or clarification in order to assert an error within the meaning of paragraphs (a)(1) through (6) of this section. It does not include a routine inquiry about the balance in the consumer's account or a request for duplicate copies of documentation or other information that is made only for tax or other recordkeeping purposes.

(b) *Notice of error from consumer.* (1) A notice of an error is an oral or written notice from the consumer that

(i) Is received by the financial institution [10] no later than 60 days after the institution

(A) Transmitted a periodic statement or provided documentation under § 205.9(c) on which the alleged error is first reflected; or

(B) Transmitted additional information, clarification, or documentation described in paragraph (a)(7) of this section that was initially requested in accordance with paragraph (b)(1)(i)(A) of this section;

10. A financial institution may require the consumer to give notice only at the telephone number or address disclosed by the institution, provided the institution maintains reasonable procedures to refer the consumer to the specified telephone number or address if the consumer attempts to give notice to the institution in a different manner.

(ii) Enables the financial institution to identify the consumer's name and account number; and

(iii) Except for errors described in paragraph (a)(7) of this section, indicates the consumer's belief, and the reasons for that belief, that an error exists in the consumer's account or is reflected on documentation required by §§ 205.9 or 205.10(a), and indicates to the extent possible the type, the date, and the amount of the error.

(2) A financial institution may require a written confirmation to be received within 10 business days of an oral notice if, when the oral notice is given, the consumer is advised of the requirement and of the address to which confirmation must be sent.

(c) *Investigation of errors.* (1) After receiving a notice of an error, the financial institution shall promptly investigate the alleged error, determine whether an error occurred, and transmit the results of its investigation and determination to the consumer within 10 business days.

(2) As an alternative to the 10-business-day requirement of paragraph (c)(1) of this section, the financial institution shall investigate the alleged error and determine whether an error occurred, promptly but in no event later than 45 calendar days after receiving a notice of an error, and shall transmit the results of its investigation and determination to the consumer, provided

(i) The financial institution provisionally recredits the consumer's account in the amount of the alleged error (including interest where applicable) within 10 business days after receiving the notice of error. If the financial institution has a reasonable basis for believing that an unauthorized electronic fund transfer may have occurred and that it has satisfied the requirements of § 205.6(a), it may withhold a maximum of $50 from the amount recredited;

(ii) The financial institution, promptly but no later than 2 business days after the provisional recrediting, orally reports or mails or delivers notice to the consumer of the amount and date of the recrediting and of the fact that the consumer will have full use of the funds pending the determination of whether an error occurred;

(iii) The financial institution gives the consumer full use of the funds provisionally recredited during the investigation; and

(iv) If the financial institution determines that no error occurred and debits the account, the institution gives notice of the debiting and continues to honor certain items as required by paragraph (f)(2) of this section.

(3) A financial institution that requires but does not receive timely written confirmation of oral notice of an error shall comply with all

requirements of this section except that it need not provisionally recredit the consumer's account.

(4) If a notice of an error involves an electronic fund transfer that was not initiated in a state as defined in § 205.2(k), the applicable time periods for action in subsections (c), (e), and (f) shall be 20 business days in place of 10 business days, and 90 calendar days in place of 45 calendar days.

(d) *Extent of required investigation.* (1) A financial institution complies with its duty to investigate, correct, and report its determination regarding an error described in paragraph (a)(7) of this section by transmitting the requested information, clarification, or documentation within the time limits set forth in paragraph (c) of this section. If the institution has provisionally recredited the consumer's account in accordance with paragraph (c)(2) of this section, it may debit the amount upon transmitting the requested information, clarification, or documentation.

(2) Except in the case of services covered by § 205.14, a financial institution's review of its own records regarding an alleged error will satisfy its investigation responsibilities under paragraph (c) of this section if the alleged error concerns a transfer to or from a third party and there is no agreement between the financial institution and the third party [11] regarding the type of electronic fund transfer alleged in the error.

(3) A financial institution may make, without investigation, a final correction to a consumer's account in the amount or manner alleged by the consumer to be in error, but must comply with all other applicable requirements of this section.

(e) *Procedures after financial institution determines that error occurred.* If the financial institution determines that an error occurred, it shall

(1) Promptly, but no later than 1 business day after its determination, correct the error (subject to the liability provisions of §§ 205.6(a) and (b)), including, where applicable, the crediting of interest and the refunding of any fees or charges imposed, and

(2) Promptly, but in any event within the 10-business-day or 45-day time limits, orally report or mail or deliver to the consumer notice

11. Institutions do not have an agreement for purposes of paragraph (d)(2) of this section solely because they participate in transactions under the federal recurring payments program, or that are cleared through an automated or other clearing house or similar arrangement for the clearing and settlement of fund transfers generally, or because they agree to be bound by the rules of such arrangements. An agreement that a third party will honor an access device is an agreement for purposes of this paragraph.

of the correction and, if applicable, notice that a provisional credit has been made final.[12]

(f) *Procedures after financial institution determines that no error occurred.* If the financial institution determines that no error occurred or that an error occurred in a different manner or amount from that described by the consumer,

(1) The financial institution shall mail or deliver to the consumer a written explanation of its findings within 3 business days after concluding its investigation, but in no event later than 10 business days after receiving notice of the error if the institution is proceeding under paragraph (c)(1) of this section. The explanation shall include notice of the consumer's right to request the documents upon which the institution relied in making its determination.

(2) Upon debiting a provisionally recredited amount, the financial institution

(i) Shall orally report or mail or deliver notice to the consumer of the date and amount of the debiting and the fact that the financial institution will honor checks, drafts, or similar paper instruments payable to third parties and preauthorized transfers from the consumer's account (using the provisionally recredited funds) for 5 business days after transmittal of the notice.

(ii) Shall honor checks, drafts, or similar paper instruments payable to third parties and preauthorized transfers from the consumer's account (without charge to the consumer as a result of an overdraft) for 5 business days after transmittal of the notice. The institution need only honor items that it would have paid if the provisionally recredited funds had not been debited.

(3) Upon the consumer's request, the financial institution shall promptly mail or deliver to the consumer copies of the documents on which it relied in making its determination.

(g) *Withdrawal of notice of error.* The financial institution has no further error resolution responsibilities as to a consumer's assertion of an error if the consumer concludes that no error did in fact occur and voluntarily withdraws the notice.

(h) *Reassertion of error.* A financial institution that has fully complied with the requirements of this section with respect to an error has no further responsibilities under this section if the consumer subsequently reasserts the same error, regardless of the manner in which it is reasserted. This paragraph does not preclude the assertion of an error defined in paragraphs (a)(1) through (6) of this section following the assertion of an error described in paragraph (a)(7) of this section regarding the same electronic fund transfer.

12. This notice requirement may be satisfied by a notice on a periodic statement that is mailed or delivered within the 10-business-day or 45-day time limits and that clearly identifies the correction to the consumer's account.

(i) *Relation to Truth in Lending.* Where an electronic fund transfer also involves an extension of credit under an agreement between a consumer and a financial institution to extend credit when the consumer's account is overdrawn or to maintain a specified minimum balance in the consumer's account, the financial institution shall comply with the requirements of this section rather than those of 12 CFR 226.2(j), 226.2(cc), and 226.14(a) governing error resolution.

§ 205.12 Relation to state law

(a) *Preemption of inconsistent state laws.* The Board shall determine, upon the request of any state, financial institution, or other interested party, whether the Act and this regulation preempt state laws relating to electronic fund transfers. Only those state laws that are inconsistent with the Act and this regulation shall be preempted and then only to the extent of the inconsistency. A state law is not inconsistent with the Act and this regulation if it is more protective of a consumer.

(b) *Standards for preemption.* The following are examples of the standards the Board will apply in determining whether a state law, or a provision of that law, is inconsistent with the Act and this regulation. Inconsistency may exist when state law:

(1) Requires or permits a practice or act prohibited by the Act or this regulation;

(2) Provides for consumer liability for unauthorized electronic fund transfers which exceeds that imposed by the Act and this regulation;

(3) Provides for longer time periods than the Act and this regulation for investigation and correction of errors alleged by a consumer, or fails to provide for the recrediting of the consumer's account during the institution's investigation of errors as set forth in § 205.11(c); or

(4) Provides for initial disclosures, periodic statements, or receipts that are different in content from that required by the Act and this regulation except to the extent that the disclosures relate to rights granted to consumers by the state law and not by the Act or this regulation.

(c) *Procedures for preemption.* Any request for a determination shall include the following:

(1) A copy of the full text of the state law in question, including any regulatory implementation or judicial interpretation of that law;

(2) A comparison of the provisions of state law with the corresponding provisions in the Act and this regulation, together with a discussion of reasons why specific provisions of state law are either

consistent or inconsistent with corresponding sections of the Act and this regulation; and

(3) A comparison of the civil and criminal liability for violation of state law with the provisions of sections 915 and 916(a) of the Act.

(d) *Exemption for state-regulated transfers.* (1) Any state may apply to the Board for an exemption from the requirements of the Act and the corresponding provisions of this regulation for any class of electronic fund transfers within the state. The Board will grant such an exemption if the Board determines that:

(i) Under the law of the state that class of electronic fund transfers is subject to requirements substantially similar to those imposed by the Act and the corresponding provisions of this regulation, and

(ii) There is adequate provision for state enforcement.

(2) To assure that the federal and state courts will continue to have concurrent jurisdiction, and to aid in implementing the Act:

(i) No exemption shall extend to the civil liability provisions of section 915 of the Act; and

(ii) After an exemption has been granted, for the purposes of section 915 of the Act, the requirements of the applicable state law shall constitute the requirements of the Act and this regulation, except to the extent the state law imposes requirements not imposed by the Act or this regulation.

§ 205.13 Administrative enforcement

. . .

(b) *Issuance of staff interpretations.* (1) Unofficial staff interpretations are issued at the staff's discretion where the protection of section 915(d) of the Act is neither requested nor required, or where a rapid response is necessary.

(2)(i) Official staff interpretations are issued at the discretion of designated officials. No interpretations will be issued approving financial institutions' forms or statements. . . .

(4) Pursuant to section 915(d) of the Act, the Board has designated the Director and other officials of the Division of Consumer and Community Affairs as officials "duly authorized" to issue, at their discretion, official staff interpretations of this regulation.

(c) *Record retention.* (1) Evidence of compliance with the requirements imposed by the Act and this regulation shall be preserved by any person subject to the Act and this regulation for a period of not less than 2 years. Records may be stored by use of microfiche, microfilm, magnetic tape, or other methods capable of accurately retaining and reproducing information.

(2) Any person subject to the Act and this regulation that has actual notice that it is being investigated or is subject to an enforcement proceeding by an agency charged with monitoring that person's compliance with the Act and this regulation, or that has been served with notice of an action filed under section 910, 915, or 916(a) of the Act, shall retain the information required in paragraph (c)(1) of this section that pertains to the action or proceeding until final disposition of the matter, unless an earlier time is allowed by order of the agency or court.

§ 205.14 Services offered by financial institutions not holding consumer's account

(a) *Compliance by service-providing institution.* Except as provided in this section, where a financial institution issues an access device to a consumer to be used for initiating electronic fund transfers to or from the consumer's account held by another financial institution, and the service-providing institution does not have an agreement with the account-holding institution regarding the service, the service-providing institution shall comply with all requirements of the Act and this regulation that relate to the service or the electronic fund transfers made by the consumer under the service. For this purpose, the following special rules shall apply:

(1) Section 205.6 shall require the service-providing institution to reimburse the consumer for unauthorized electronic fund transfers in excess of the limits set by that section.

(2) Sections 205.7, 205.8, and 205.9 shall require the service-providing institution to provide those disclosures and documentation that are within its knowledge and the purview of its relationship with the consumer.

(3) Section 205.11(b)(1)(i) shall require the service-providing institution to extend by a reasonable time the time periods within which notice of an error must be received if a delay in notifying the service-providing institution was due to the fact that the consumer initially notified or attempted to notify the account-holding institution.

(4) Sections 205.11(c)(2)(i) and (e)(1) shall require the service-providing institution to transfer funds, in the appropriate amount and within the applicable time period, to the consumer's account at the account-holding institution.

(5) Section 205.11(c)(2)(ii) shall require the service-providing institution to disclose the date on which it initiates a transfer to effect the provisional recredit.

(6) Section 205.11(f)(2) shall require the service-providing institution to notify the account-holding institution of the date until which the account-holding institution must honor any debit to the account as required by § 205.11(f)(2). If an overdraft results, the service-provid-

ing institution shall promptly reimburse the account-holding institution in the amount of the overdraft.

(b) *Compliance by account-holding institution.* An account-holding institution described in paragraph (a) of this section need not comply with the requirements of the Act and this regulation with respect to electronic fund transfers to or from the consumer's account made by the service-providing institution, except that the account-holding institution shall comply with § 205.11 by

(1) Promptly providing, upon the request of the service-providing institution information or copies of documents required for the purpose of investigating alleged errors or furnishing copies of documents to the consumer; and

(2) Honoring debits to the account in accordance with § 205.11(f)(2).

(c) *Definition of agreement.* For purposes of this section, an agreement between the service-providing and the account-holding institutions regarding the electronic fund transfer service refers to a specific agreement(s) among institutions (or among institutions and another person that participates in the operation of the service) which sets forth the rights and obligations of the institutions with respect to a service involving the issuance of an access device to the consumer. Institutions do not have such an agreement solely because they participate in transactions that are cleared through an automated or other clearing house or similar arrangement for the clearing and settlement of fund transfers generally, or because they agree to be bound by the rules of such an arrangement.

APPENDIX A. Model Disclosure Clauses

This appendix contains model disclosure clauses for optional use by financial institutions to facilitate compliance with the disclosure requirements of sections 205.5(a)(3), (b)(2), and (b)(3), 205.6(a)(3), and 205.7. Section 915(d)(2) of the Act provides that use of these clauses in conjunction with other requirements of the regulation will protect financial institutions from liability under sections 915 and 916 of the Act to the extent that the clauses accurately reflect the institutions' electronic fund transfer services.

Financial institutions need not use any of the clauses, but may use clauses of their own design in conjunction with the model clauses. The inapplicable words or portions of phrases in parentheses should be deleted. The underscored catchlines are not part of the clauses and should not be used as such. Financial institutions may make alterations, substitutions, or additions in the clauses in order to reflect the services offered, such as technical changes (e.g., substitution of a trade name for the word "card," deletion of inapplicable services, or substitution of lesser liability limits in section A(2)). Sections A(3) and A(9) include references to a telephone number and address. Where two or more of these clauses are used in a disclosure, the telephone number and address need not be repeated if referenced.

SECTION A(1)—DISCLOSURE THAT ACCESS DEVICE IS NOT VALIDATED AND HOW TO DISPOSE OF DEVICE IF VALIDATION IS NOT DESIRED (§ 205.5(b)(3))

(a) *Accounts using cards.* You cannot use the enclosed card to transfer money into or out of your account until we have validated it. If you do not want to use the card, please (destroy it at once by cutting it in half).

FINANCIAL INSTITUTION MAY ADD VALIDATION INSTRUCTIONS HERE

(b) *Accounts using codes.* You cannot use the enclosed code to transfer money into or out of your account until we have validated it. If you do not want to use the code, please (destroy this notice at once).

FINANCIAL INSTITUTION MAY ADD VALIDATION INSTRUCTIONS HERE

SECTION A(2)—DISCLOSURE OF CONSUMER'S LIABILITY FOR UNAUTHORIZED TRANSFERS AND OPTIONAL DISCLOSURE OF ADVISABILITY OF PROMPT REPORTING (§ 205.7(a)(1))

(a) *Liability disclosure.* (Tell us AT ONCE if you believe your (card) (code) has been lost or stolen. Telephoning is the best way of keeping your possible losses down. You could lose all the money in your account (plus your maximum overdraft line of credit). If you tell us within 2 business days, you can lose no more the $50 if someone used your (card) (code) without your permission.) (If you believe your (card) (code) has been lost or stolen, and you tell us within 2 business days after you learn of the loss or theft, you can lose no more than $50 if someone used your (card) (code) without your permission.)

If you do NOT tell us within 2 business days after you learn of the loss or theft of your (card) (code), and we can prove we could have stopped someone from using your (card) (code) without your permission if you had told us, you could lose as much as $500.

Also, if your statement shows transfers that you did not make, tell us at once. If you do not tell us within 60 days after the statement was mailed to you, you may not get back any money you lost after the 60 days if we can prove that we could have stopped someone from taking the money if you had told us in time.

If a good reason (such as a long trip or a hospital stay) kept you from telling us, we will extend the time periods.

SECTION A(3)—DISCLOSURE OF TELEPHONE NUMBER AND ADDRESS TO BE NOTIFIED IN EVENT OF UNAUTHORIZED TRANSFER (§ 205.7(a)(2))

(a) *Address and telephone number.* If you believe your (card) (code) has been lost or stolen or that someone has transferred or may transfer money from your account without your permission, call:

____
[Telephone number]

____

or write:

____
[Name of person or office to be notified]

____
[Address]

SECTION A(4)—DISCLOSURE OF WHAT CONSTITUTES BUSINESS DAY OF INSTITUTION (§ 205.7(a)(3))

(a) *Business day disclosure.* Our business days are (Monday through Friday) (Monday through Saturday) (any day including Saturdays and Sundays). Holidays are (not) included.

SECTION A(5)—DISCLOSURE OF TYPES OF AVAILABLE TRANSFERS AND LIMITS ON TRANSFERS (§ 205.7(a)(4))

(a) *Account access.* You may use your (card) (code) to (1) withdraw cash from your (checking) (or) (savings) account.

(2) Make deposits to your (checking) (or) (savings) account.

(3) Transfer funds between your checking and savings accounts whenever you request.

(4) Pay for purchases at places that have agreed to accept the (card) (code).

(5) Pay bills directly (by telephone) from your (checking) (or) (savings) account in the amounts and on the days you request.

Some of these services may not be available at all terminals.

(b) *Limitations on frequency of transfers.*

(1) You may make only [insert number, e.g., 3] cash withdrawals from our terminals each [insert time period, e.g., week].

(2) You can use your telephone bill-payment service to pay [insert number] bills each ([insert time period]) (telephone call).

(3) You can use our point-of-sale transfer service for [insert number] transactions each [insert time period].

(4) For security reasons, there are (other) limits on the number of transfers you can make using our (terminals) (telephone bill-payment service) (point-of-sale transfer service).

(c) *Limitations on dollar amounts of transfers.*

(1) You may withdraw up to [insert dollar amount] from our terminals each ([insert time period]) (time you use the (card) (code)).

(2) You may buy up to [insert dollar amount] worth of goods or services each ([insert time period]) (time you use the (card) (code)) in our point-of-sale transfer service.

SECTION A(6)—DISCLOSURE OF CHARGES FOR TRANSFERS OF RIGHT TO MAKE TRANSFERS (§ 205.7(a)(5))

(a) *Per transfer charge.* We will charge you [insert dollar amount] for each transfer you make using our (automated teller machines) (telephone bill-payment service) (point-of-sale transfer service).

(b) *Fixed charge.* We will charge you [insert dollar amount] each [insert time period] for our (automated teller machine service) (telephone bill-payment service) (point-of-sale transfer service).

(c) *Average or minimum balance charge.* We will only charge you for using our (automated teller machines) (telephone bill-payment service) (point-of-sale transfer service) if the (average) (minimum) balance in your (checking account) (savings account) (accounts) falls below [insert dollar amount]. If it does, we will charge you [insert dollar amount] each (transfer) ([insert time period]).

SECTION A(7)—DISCLOSURE OF ACCOUNT INFORMATION TO THIRD PARTIES (§ 205.7(a)(9))

(a) *Account information disclosure.* We will disclose information to third parties about your account or the transfers you make: (1) Where it is necessary for completing transfers, or

(2) In order to verify the existence and condition of your account for a third party, such as a credit bureau or merchant, or

(3) In order to comply with government agency or court orders, or

(4) If you give us your written permission.

SECTION A(8)—DISCLOSURE OF RIGHT TO RECEIVE DOCUMENTATION OF TRANSFERS (§ 205.7(a)(6))

(a) *Terminal transfers.* You can get a receipt at the time you make any transfer to or from your account using one of our (automated teller machines) (or) (point-of-sale terminals).

(b) *Preauthorized credits.* If you have arranged to have direct deposits made to your account at least once every 60 days from the same person or company.

(we will let you know if the deposit is (not) made.)

(the person or company making the deposit will tell you every time they send us the money.)

(you can call us at (insert telephone number) to find out whether or not the deposit has been made.)

(c) *Periodic statements.* You will get a (monthly) (quarterly) account statement (unless there are no transfers in a particular month. In any case you will get the statement at least quarterly).

(d) *Passbook account where the only possible electronic fund transfers are preauthorized credits.* If you bring your passbook to us, we will record any electronic deposits that were made to your account since the last time you brought in your passbook.

SECTION A(9)—DISCLOSURE OF RIGHT TO STOP PAYMENT OF PREAUTHORIZED TRANSFERS, PROCEDURE FOR DOING SO, RIGHT TO RECEIVE NOTICE OF VARYING AMOUNTS, AND FINANCIAL INSTITUTION'S LIABILITY FOR FAILURE TO STOP PAYMENT (§ 205.7(a)(6), (7), and (8))

(a) *Right to stop payment and procedure for doing so.* If you have told us in advance to make regular payments out of your account, you can stop any of these payments. Here's how:

Call us at (insert telephone number), or write us at (insert address), in time for us to receive your request 3 business days or more before the payment is scheduled to be made. If you call, we may also require you to put your request in writing and get it to us within 14 days after you call. (We will charge you (insert amount) for each stop-payment order you give.)

(b) *Notice of varying amounts.* If these regular payments may vary in amount, (we) (the person you are going to pay) will tell you, 10 days before each payment, when it will be made and how much it will be. (You may choose instead to get this notice only when the payment would differ by more than a certain amount from the previous payment, or when the amount would fall outside certain limits that you set.)

(c) *Liability for failure to stop payment of preauthorized transfer.* If you order us to stop one of these payments 3 business days or more before the transfer is scheduled, and we do not do so, we will be liable for your losses or damages.

SECTION A(10)—DISCLOSURE OF FINANCIAL INSTITUTION'S LIABILITY FOR FAILURE TO MAKE TRANSFERS (§ 205.7(a)(8))

(a) *Liability for failure to make transfers.* If we do not complete a transfer to or from your account on time or in the correct amount according to our agreement with you, we will be liable for your losses or damages. However, there are some exceptions. We will not be liable, for instance:

- If, through no fault of ours, you do not have enough money in your account to make the transfer.
- If the transfer would go over the credit limit on your overdraft line.
- If the automated teller machine where you are making the transfer does not have enough cash.
- If the (terminal) (system) was not working properly and you knew about the breakdown when you started the transfer.

- If circumstances beyond our control (such as fire or flood) prevent the transfer, despite reasonable precautions that we have taken.
- There may be other exceptions stated in our agreement with you.

*

CONSUMER PRODUCT SAFETY ACT

15 U.S.C. §§ 2051–2083

Table of Sections

Sec.

§ 1. Short title

This Act may be cited as the "Consumer Product Safety Act."

§ 2. Findings and purposes [15 U.S.C. § 2051]

(a) The Congress finds that—

(1) an unacceptable number of consumer products which present unreasonable risks of injury are distributed in commerce;

(2) complexities of consumer products and the diverse nature and abilities of consumers using them frequently result in an inability of users to anticipate risks and to safeguard themselves adequately;

(3) the public should be protected against unreasonable risks of injury associated with consumer products;

(4) control by State and local governments of unreasonable risks of injury associated with consumer products is inadequate and may be burdensome to manufacturers;

(5) existing Federal authority to protect consumers from exposure to consumer products presenting unreasonable risks of injury is inadequate; and

(6) regulation of consumer products the distribution or use of which affects interstate or foreign commerce is necessary to carry out this chapter.

(b) The purposes of this Act are—

(1) to protect the public against unreasonable risks of injury associated with consumer products;

(2) to assist consumers in evaluating the comparative safety of consumer products;

(3) to develop uniform safety standards for consumer products and to minimize conflicting State and local regulations; and

(4) to promote research and investigation into the causes and prevention of product-related deaths, illnesses, and injuries.

§ 3. Definitions [15 U.S.C. § 2052]

(a) For purposes of this Act:

(1) The term "consumer product" means any article, or component part thereof, produced or distributed (i) for sale to a consumer for use in or around a permanent or temporary household or residence, a school, in recreation, or otherwise, or (ii) for the personal use, consumption or enjoyment of a consumer in or around a permanent or

temporary household or residence, a school, in recreation, or otherwise; but such term does not include—

(A) any article which is not customarily produced or distributed for sale to, or use or consumption by, or enjoyment of, a consumer,

(B) tobacco and tobacco products,

(C) motor vehicles or motor vehicle equipment . . .

(D) pesticides . . .

(E) . . .

(F) aircraft, aircraft engines, propellers, or appliances . . .

(G) boats which could be subjected to safety regulation under the Federal Boat Safety Act of 1971; vessels, and appurtenances to vessels (other than such boats), which could be subjected to safety regulation under title 52 of the Revised Statutes or other marine safety statutes administered by the department in which the Coast Guard is operating; and equipment . . . to the extent that a risk of injury associated with the use of such equipment on boats or vessels could be eliminated or reduced by actions taken under any statute referred to in this subparagraph,

(H) drugs, devices, or cosmetics . . . or

(I) food. . . .

Such term includes any mechanical device which carries or conveys passengers along, around, or over a fixed or restricted route or course or within a defined area for the purpose of giving its passengers amusement, which is customarily controlled or directed by an individual who is employed for that purpose and who is not a consumer with respect to such device, and which is not permanently fixed to a site. Such term does not include such a device which is permanently fixed to a site. . . .

(2) The term "consumer product safety rule" means a consumer products safety standard described in section 7(a), or a rule under this Act declaring a consumer product a banned hazardous product.

(3) The term "risk of injury" means a risk of death, personal injury, or serious or frequent illness.

(4) The term "manufacturer" means any person who manufactures or imports a consumer product.

(5) The term "distributor" means a person to whom a consumer product is delivered or sold for purposes of distribution in commerce, except that such term does not include a manufacturer or retailer of such product.

(6) The term "retailer" means a person to whom a consumer product is delivered or sold for purposes of sale or distribution by such person to a consumer.

(7)(A) The term "private labeler" means an owner of a brand or trademark on the label of a consumer product which bears a private label.

(B) A consumer product bears a private label if (i) the product (or its container) is labeled with the brand or trademark of a person other than a manufacturer of the product, (ii) the person with whose brand or trademark the product (or container) is labeled has authorized or caused the product to be so labeled, and (iii) the brand or trademark of a manufacturer of such product does not appear on such label.

(8) The term "manufactured" means to manufacture, produce, or assemble.

(9) The term "Commission" means the Consumer Product Safety Commission, established by section 4.

(10) The term "State" means a State, the District of Columbia, the Commonwealth of Puerto Rico, the Virgin Islands, Guam, Wake Island, Midway Island, Kingman Reef, Johnston Island, the Canal Zone, American Samoa, or the Trust Territory of the Pacific Islands.

(11) The terms "to distribute in commerce" and "distribution in commerce" mean to sell in commerce, to introduce or deliver for introduction into commerce, or to hold for sale or distribution after introduction into commerce.

(12) The term "commerce" means trade, traffic, commerce, or transportation—

(A) between a place in a State and any place outside thereof, or

(B) which affects trade, traffic, commerce, or transportation described in subparagraph (A).

(13) The terms "import" and "importation" include reimporting a consumer product manufactured or processed, in whole or in part, in the United States.

(14) The term "United States", when used in the geographic sense, means all of the States (as defined in paragraph (10)).

(b) A common carrier, contract carrier, or freight forwarder shall not, for purposes of this Act, be deemed to be a manufacturer, distributor, or retailer of a consumer product solely by reason of receiving or transporting a consumer product in the ordinary course of its business as such a carrier or forwarder.

§ 4. Consumer Product Safety Commission [15 U.S.C. § 2053]

(a) An independent regulatory commission is hereby established, to be known as the Consumer Product Safety Commission, consisting of five Commissioners who shall be appointed by the President, by and with the advice and consent of the Senate. The Chairman shall be appointed by the President, by and with the advice and consent of the Senate, from among the members of the Commission. An individual may be appointed as a member of the Commission and as Chairman at the same time. Any member of the Commission may be removed by the President for neglect of duty or malfeasance in office but for no other cause.

. . .

§ 5. Product safety information and research [15 U.S.C. § 2054]

(a) The Commission shall—

(1) maintain an Injury Information Clearinghouse to collect, investigate, analyze, and disseminate injury data, and information, relating to the causes and prevention of death, injury, and illness associated with consumer products;

(2) conduct such continuing studies and investigations of deaths, injuries, diseases, other health impairments, and economic losses resulting from accidents involving consumer products as it deems necessary;

(3) following publication of an advance notice of proposed rulemaking or a notice of proposed rulemaking for a product safety rule under any rulemaking authority administered by the Commission, assist public and private organizations or groups of manufacturers, administratively and technically, in the development of safety standards addressing the risk of injury identified in such notice; and

(4) to the extent practicable and appropriate (taking into account the resources and priorities of the Commission), assist public and private organizations or groups of manufacturers, administratively and technically, in the development of product safety standards and test methods.

(b) The Commission may—

(1) conduct research, studies, and investigations on the safety of consumer products and on improving the safety of such products;

(2) test consumer products and develop product safety test methods and testing devices; and

(3) offer training in product safety investigation and test methods.

. . .

§ 7. Consumer product safety standards [15 U.S.C. § 2056]

(a) The Commission may promulgate consumer product safety standards in accordance with the provisions of section 9. A consumer product safety standard shall consist of one or more of any of the following types of requirements:

(1) Requirements expressed in terms of performance requirements.

(2) Requirements that a consumer product be marked with or accompanied by clear and adequate warnings or instructions, or requirements respecting the form of warnings or instructions.

Any requirement of such a standard shall be reasonably necessary to prevent or reduce an unreasonble risk of injury associated with such product.

(b) The Commission shall rely upon voluntary consumer product safety standards rather than promulgate a consumer product safety standard prescribing requirements described in subsection (a) of this section whenever compliance with such voluntary standards would eliminate or adequately reduce the risk of injury addressed and it is likely that there will be substantial compliance with such voluntary standards.

(c) If any person participates with the Commission in the development of a consumer product safety standard, the Commission may agree to contribute to the person's cost with respect to such participation, in any case in which the Commission determines that such contribution is likely to result in a more satisfactory standard than would be developed without such contribution, and that the person is financially responsible. Regulations of the Commission shall set forth the items of cost in which it may participate, and shall exclude any contribution to the acquisition of land or buildings. Payments under agreements entered into under this subsection may be made without regard to section 529 of Title 31.

§ 8. Banned hazardous products [15 U.S.C. § 2057]

Whenever the Commission finds that—

(1) a consumer product is being, or will be, distributed in commerce and such consumer product presents an unreasonable risk of injury; and

(2) no feasible consumer product safety standard under this Act would adequately protect the public from the unreasonable risk of injury associated with such product,

the Commission may, in accordance with section 9, promulgate a rule declaring such product a banned hazardous product.

§ 9. Administrative procedure applicable to promulgation of consumer product safety rules [15 U.S.C. § 2058]

(a) A proceeding for the development of a consumer product safety rule shall be commenced by the publication in the Federal Register of an advance notice of proposed rulemaking which shall—

(1) identify the product and the nature of the risk of injury associated with the product;

(2) include a summary of each of the regulatory alternatives under consideration by the Commission (including voluntary consumer product safety standards);

(3) include information with respect to any existing standard known to the Commission which may be relevant to the proceedings, together with a summary of the reasons why the Commission believes preliminarily that such standard does not eliminate or adequately reduce the risk of injury identified in paragraph (1);

(4) invite interested persons to submit to the Commission, within such period as the Commission shall specify in the notice (which period shall not be less than 30 days or more than 60 days after the date of publication of the notice), comments with respect to the risk of injury identified by the Commission, the regulatory alternatives being considered, and other possible alternatives for addressing the risk;

(5) invite any person (other than the Commission) to submit to the Commission, within such period as the Commission shall specify in the notice (which period shall not be less than 30 days after the date of publication of the notice), an existing standard or a portion of a standard as a proposed consumer product safety standard; and

(6) invite any person (other than the Commission) to submit to the Commission, within such period as the Commission shall specify in the notice (which period shall not be less than 30 days after the date of publication of the notice), a statement of intention to modify or develop a voluntary consumer product safety standard to address the risk of injury identified in paragraph (1) together with a description of a plan to modify or develop the standard.

The Commission shall transmit such notice within 10 calendar days to the Committee on Commerce, Science, and Transportation of the Senate and the Committee on Energy and Commerce of the House of Representatives.

(b)(1) If the Commission determines that any standard submitted to it in response to an invitation in a notice published under subsection (a)(5) of this section if promulgated (in whole, in part, or in combination with any other standard submitted to the Commission or any part of such a standard) as a consumer product safety standard, would eliminate or adequately reduce the risk of injury identified in the notice under subsection (a)(1), of this section, the Commission may publish such standard, in whole, in part, or in such combination and with nonmaterial modifications, as a proposed consumer product safety rule.

(2) If the Commission determines that—

(A) compliance with any standard submitted to it in response to an invitation in a notice published under subsection (a)(6) of this section is likely to result in the elimination or adequate reduction of the risk of injury identified in the notice, and

(B) it is likely that there will be substantial compliance with such standard,

the Commission shall terminate any proceeding to promulgate a consumer product safety rule respecting such risk of injury and shall publish in the Federal Register a notice which includes the determination of the Commission and which notifies the public that the Commission will rely on the voluntary standard to eliminate or reduce the risk of injury.

(c) No consumer product safety rule may be proposed by the Commission unless, not less than 60 days after publication of the notice required in subsection (a) of this section, the Commission publishes in the Federal Register the text of the proposed rule, including any alternatives, which the Commission proposes to promulgate, together with a preliminary regulatory analysis containing—

(1) a preliminary description of the potential benefits and potential costs of the proposed rule, including any benefits or costs that cannot be quantified in monetary terms, and an identification of those likely to receive the benefits and bear the costs;

(2) a discussion of the reasons any standard or portion of a standard submitted to the Commission under subsection (a)(5) of this section was not published by the Commission as the proposed rule or part of the proposed rule;

(3) a discussion of the reasons for the Commission's preliminary determination that efforts proposed under subsection (a)(6) of this section and assisted by the Commission as required by section 5(a)(3) would not, within a reasonable period of time, be likely to result in the development of a voluntary consumer product safety standard that would eliminate or adequately reduce the risk of injury addressed by the proposed rule; and

(4) a description of any reasonable alternatives to the proposed rule, together with a summary description of their potential costs and benefits, and a brief explanation of why such alternatives should not be published as a proposed rule.

The Commission shall transmit such notice within 10 calendar days to the Committee on Commerce, Science, and Transportation of the Senate and the Committee on Energy and Commerce of the House of Representatives.

(d)(1) Within 60 days after the publication under subsection (c) of this section of a proposed consumer product safety rule respecting a risk of injury associated with a consumer product, the Commission shall—

(A) promulgate a consumer product safety rule respecting the risk of injury associated with such product, if it makes the findings required under subsection (f) of this section, or

(B) withdraw the applicable notice of proposed rulemaking if it determines that such rule is not (i) reasonably necessary to eliminate or reduce an unreasonable risk of injury associated with the product, or (ii) in the public interest;

except that the Commission may extend such 60-day period for good cause shown (if it publishes its reasons therefor in the Federal Register).

(2) Consumer product safety rules shall be promulgated in accordance with section 553 of title 5 except that the Commission shall give interested persons an opportunity for the oral presentation of data, views, or arguments, in addition to an opportunity to make written submissions. A transcript shall be kept of any oral presentation.

(e) A consumer product safety rule shall express in the rule itself the risk of injury which the standard is designed to eliminate or reduce. In promulgating such a rule the Commission shall consider relevant available product data including the results of research, development, testing, and investigation activities conducted generally and pursuant to this Act. In the promulgation of such a rule the Commission shall also consider and take into account the special needs of elderly and handicapped persons to determine the extent to which such persons may be adversely affected by such rule.

(f)(1) Prior to promulgating a consumer product safety rule, the Commission shall consider, and shall make appropriate findings for inclusion in such rule with respect to—

(A) the degree and nature of the risk of injury the rule is designed to eliminate or reduce;

(B) the approximate number of consumer products, or types or classes thereof, subject to such rule;

(C) the need of the public for the consumer products subject to such rule, and the probable effect of such rule upon the utility, cost, or availability of such products to meet such need; and

(D) any means of achieving the objective of the order while minimizing adverse effects on competition or disruption or dislocation of manufacturing and other commercial practices consistent with the public health and safety.

(2) The Commission shall not promulgate a consumer product safety rule unless it has prepared, on the basis of the findings of the Commission under paragraph (1) and on other information before the Commission, a final regulatory analysis of the rule containing the following information:

(A) A description of the potential benefits and potential costs of the rule, including costs and benefits that cannot be quantified in monetary terms, and the identification of those likely to receive the benefits and bear the costs.

(B) A description of any alternatives to the final rule which were considered by the Commission, together with a summary description of their potential benefits and costs and a brief explanation of the reasons why these alternatives were not chosen.

(C) A summary of any significant issues raised by the comments submitted during the public comment period in response to the preliminary regulatory analysis, and a summary of the assessment by the Commission of such issues.

The Commission shall publish its final regulatory analysis with the rule.

(3) The Commission shall not promulgate a consumer product safety rule unless it finds (and includes such finding in the rule)—

(A) that the rule (including its effective date) is reasonably necessary to eliminate or reduce an unreasonable risk of injury associated with such product;

(B) that the promulgation of the rule is in the public interest;

(C) in the case of a rule declaring the product a banned hazardous product, that no feasible consumer product safety standard under this chapter would adequately protect the public from the unreasonable risk of injury associated with such product;

(D) in the case of a rule which relates to a risk of injury with respect to which persons who would be subject to such rule have adopted and implemented a voluntary consumer product safety standard, that—

(i) compliance with such voluntary consumer product safety standard is not likely to result in the elimination or adequate reduction of such risk of injury; or

(ii) it is unlikely that there will be substantial compliance with such voluntary consumer product safety standard;

(E) that the benefits expected from the rule bear a reasonable relationship to its costs; and

(F) that the rule imposes the least burdensome requirement which prevents or adequately reduces the risk of injury for which the rule is being promulgated.

(4)(A) Any preliminary or final regulatory analysis prepared under subsection (c) or (f)(2) of this section shall not be subject to independent judicial review, except that when an action for judicial review of a rule is instituted, the contents of any such regulatory analysis shall constitute part of the whole rulemaking record of agency action in connection with such review.

(B) The provisions of subparagraph (A) shall not be construed to alter the substantive or procedural standards otherwise applicable to judicial review of any action by the Commission.

(g)(1) Each consumer product safety rule shall specify the date such rule is to take effect not exceeding 180 days from the date promulgated, unless the Commission finds, for good cause shown, that a later effective date is in the public interest and publishes its reasons for such finding. The effective date of a consumer product safety standard under this chapter shall be set at a date at least 30 days after the date of promulgation unless the Commission for good cause shown determines that an earlier effective date is in the public interest. In no case may the effective date be set at a date which is earlier than the date of promulgation. A consumer product safety standard shall be applicable only to consumer products manufactured after the effective date.

(2) The Commission may by rule prohibit a manufacturer of a consumer product from stockpiling any product to which a consumer product safety rule applies, so as to prevent such manufacturer from circumventing the purpose of such consumer product safety rule. For purposes of this paragraph, the term "stockpiling" means manufacturing or importing a product between the date of promulgation of such consumer product safety rule and its effective date at a rate which is significantly greater (as determined under the rule under this paragraph) than the rate at which such product was produced or imported during a base period (prescribed in the rule under this paragraph) ending before the date of promulgation of the consumer product safety rule.

(h) The Commission may by rule amend or revoke any consumer product safety rule. Such amendment or revocation shall specify the date on which it is to take effect which shall not exceed 180 days from the date the amendment or revocation is published unless the Commission finds for good cause shown that a later effective date is in the public interest and publishes its reasons for such finding. Where an amendment involves a material change in a consumer product safety rule, sections 7 and 8 of this Act, and subsections (a) through (g) of this section shall apply. In order to revoke a consumer product safety rule, the Commission shall publish a proposal to revoke such rule in the Federal Register, and allow oral and written presentations in accordance with subsection (d)(2) of this section. It may revoke such rule only if it determines that the rule is not reasonably necessary to eliminate or reduce an unreasonable risk of injury associated with the product. Section 11 shall apply to any amendment of a consumer product safety rule which involves a material change and to any revocation of a consumer product safety rule, in the same manner and to the same extent as such section applies to the Commission's action in promulgating such a rule.

§ 11. Judicial review of consumer product safety rules [15 U.S.C. § 2060]

(a) Not later than 60 days after a consumer product safety rule is promulgated by the Commission, any person adversely affected by such rule, or any consumer or consumer organization, may file a petition with the United States court of appeals for the District of Columbia or for the circuit in which such person, consumer, or organization resides or has his principal place of business for judicial review of such rule. . . .

§ 12. Imminent hazards [15 U.S.C. § 2061]

(a) The Commission may file in a United States district court an action (1) against an imminently hazardous consumer product for seizure of such product under subsection (b)(2) of this section, or (2) against any person who is a manufacturer, distributor, or retailer of such product, or (3) against both. Such an action may be filed notwithstanding the existence of a consumer product safety rule applicable to such product, or the pendency of any administrative or judicial proceedings under any other provision of this Act. As used in this section, and hereinafter in this Act, the term "imminently hazardous consumer product" means a consumer product which presents imminent and unreasonable risk of death, serious illness, or severe personal injury.

(b)(1) The district court in which such action is filed shall have jurisdiction to declare such product an imminently hazardous consumer product, and (in the case of an action under subsection (a)(2) of this section) to grant (as ancillary to such declaration or in lieu thereof) such temporary or permanent relief as may be necessary to protect the public from such risk. Such relief may include a mandatory order requiring the notification of such risk to purchasers of such product known to the defendant, public notice, the recall, the repair or the replacement of, or refund for, such product.

(2) In the case of an action under subsection (a)(1) of this section, the consumer product may be proceeded against by process of libel for the seizure and condemnation of such product in any United States district court within the jurisdiction of which such consumer product is found. Proceedings and cases instituted under the author-

ity of the preceding sentence shall conform as nearly as possible to proceedings in rem in admiralty.

(c) Where appropriate, concurrently with the filing of such action or as soon thereafter as may be practicable, the Commission shall initiate a proceeding to promulgate a consumer product safety rule applicable to the consumer product with respect to which such action is filed.

. . .

§ 14. Product certification and labeling [15 U.S.C. § 2063]

(a)(1) Every manufacturer of a product which is subject to a consumer product safety standard under this Act and which is distributed in commerce (and the private labeler of such product if it bears a private label) shall issue a certificate which shall certify that such product conforms to all applicable consumer product safety standards, and shall specify any standard which is applicable. Such certificate shall accompany the product or shall otherwise be furnished to any distributor or retailer to whom the product is delivered. Any certificate under this subsection shall be based on a test of each product or upon a reasonable testing program; shall state the name of the manufacturer or private labeler issuing the certificate; and shall include the date and place of manufacture.

(2) In the case of a consumer product for which there is more than one manufacturer or more than one private labeler, the Commission may by rule designate one or more of such manufacturers or one or more of such private labelers (as the case may be) as the persons who shall issue the certificate required by paragraph (1) of this subsection, and may exempt all other manufacturers of such product or all other private labelers of the product (as the case may be) from the requirement under paragraph (1) to issue a certificate with respect to such product.

(b) The Commission may by rule prescribe reasonable testing programs for consumer products which are subject to consumer product safety standards under this chapter and for which a certificate is required under subsection (a) of this section. Any test or testing program on the basis of which a certificate is issued under subsection (a) of this section may, at the option of the person required to certify the product, be conducted by an independent third party qualified to perform such tests or testing programs.

(c) The Commission may by rule require the use and prescribe the form and content of labels which contain the following information (or that portion of it specified in the rule)—

(1) The date and place of manufacture of any consumer product.

(2) A suitable identification of the manufacturer of the consumer product, unless the product bears a private label in which case it shall identify the private labeler and shall also contain a code mark which will permit the seller of such product to identify the manufacturer thereof to the purchaser upon his request.

(3) In the case of a consumer product subject to a consumer product safety rule, a certification that the product meets all applicable consumer product safety standards and a specification of the standards which are applicable.

Such labels, where practicable, may be required by the Commission to be permanently marked on or affixed to any such consumer product. The Commission may, in appropriate cases, permit information required under paragraphs (1) and (2) of this subsection to be coded.

§ 15. Notification and repair, replacement, or refund [15 U.S.C. § 2064]

(a) For purposes of this section, the term "substantial product hazard" means—

(1) a failure to comply with an applicable consumer product safety rule which creates a substantial risk of injury to the public, or

(2) a product defect which (because of the pattern of defect, the number of defective products distributed in commerce, the severity of the risk, or otherwise) creates a substantial risk of injury to the public.

(b) Every manufacturer of a consumer product distributed in commerce, and every distributor and retailer of such product, who obtains information which reasonably supports the conclusion that such product—

(1) fails to comply with an applicable consumer product safety rule; or

(2) contains a defect which could create a substantial product hazard described in subsection (a)(2) of this section,

shall immediately inform the Commission of such failure to comply or of such defect, unless such manufacturer, distributor, or retailer has actual knowledge that the Commission has been adequately informed of such defect or failure to comply.

(c) If the Commission determines (after affording interested persons, including consumers and consumer organizations, an opportunity for a hearing in accordance with subsection (f) of this section) that a product distributed in commerce presents a substantial product hazard and that notification is required in order to adequately protect the public from such substantial product hazard, the Commission may order the manufacturer or any distributor or retailer of the product to take any one or more of the following actions:

(1) To give public notice of the defect or failure to comply.

(2) To mail notice to each person who is a manufacturer, distributor, or retailer of such product.

(3) To mail notice to every person to whom the person required to give notice knows such product was delivered or sold.

Any such order shall specify the form and content of any notice required to be given under such order.

(d) If the Commission determines (after affording interested parties, including consumers and consumer organizations, an opportunity for a hearing in accordance with subsection (f) of this section) that a product distributed in commerce presents a substantial product hazard and that action under this subsection is in the public interest, it may order the manufacturer or any distributor or retailer of such product to take whichever of the following actions the person to whom the order is directed elects:

(1) To bring such product into conformity with the requirements of the applicable consumer product safety rule or to repair the defect in such product.

(2) To replace such product with a like or equivalent product which complies with the applicable consumer product safety rule or which does not contain the defect.

(3) To refund the purchase price of such product (less a reasonable allowance for use, if such product has been in the possession of a consumer for one year or more (A) at the time of public notice under subsection (c) of this section, or (B) at the time the consumer receives actual notice of the defect or noncompliance, whichever first occurs).

An order under this subsection may also require the person to whom it applies to submit a plan, satisfactory to the Commission, for taking action under whichever of the preceding paragraphs of this subsection under which such person has elected to act. The Commission shall specify in the order the persons to whom refunds must be made if the person to whom the order is directed elects to take the action described in paragraph (3). If an order under this subsection is directed to more than one person, the Commission shall specify which person has the election under this subsection. An order under this subsection may prohibit the person to whom it applies from manufacturing for sale, offering for sale, distributing in commerce, or importing into the customs territory of the United States (as defined in general headnote 2 to the Tariff Schedules of the United States), or from doing any combination of such actions, the product with respect to which the order was issued.

(e)(1) No charge shall be made to any person (other than a manufacturer, distributor, or retailer) who avails himself of any remedy provided under an order issued under subsection (d) of this section, and the person subject to the order shall reimburse each person (other than a manufacturer, distributor, or retailer) who is entitled to such a remedy for any reasonable and foreseeable expenses incurred by such person in availing himself of such remedy.

(2) An order issued under subsection (c) or (d) of this section with respect to a product may require any person who is a manufacturer, distributor, or retailer of the product to reimburse any other person who is a manufacturer, distributor, or retailer of such product for such other person's expenses in connection with carrying out the order, if the Commission determines such reimbursement to be in the public interest.

(f) An order under subsection (c) or (d) of this section may be issued only after an opportunity for a hearing in accordance with section 554 of Title 5, except that, if the Commission determines that any person who wishes to participate in such hearing is a part of a class of participants who share an identity of interest, the Commission may limit such person's participation in such hearing to participation through a single representative designated by such class (or by the Commission if such class fails to designate such a representative).

(g)(1) If the Commission has initiated a proceeding under this section for the issuance of an order under subsection (d) of this section with respect to a product which the Commission has reason to believe presents a substantial product hazard, the Commission (without regard to section 27(b)(7)) or the Attorney General may, in accordance with section 12(d)(1), apply to a district court of the United States for the issuance of a preliminary injunction to restrain the distribution in commerce of such product pending the completion of such proceeding. If such a preliminary injunction has been issued, the Commission (or the Attorney General if the preliminary injunction was issued upon an application of the Attorney General) may apply to the issuing court for extentions of such preliminary injunction.

(2) Any preliminary injunction, and any extention of a preliminary injunction, issued under this subsection with respect to a product shall be in effect for such period as the issuing court prescribes not to exceed a period which extends beyond the thirtieth day from the date of the issuance of the preliminary injunction (or, in the case of a preliminary injunction which has been extended, the date of its extension) or the date of the completion or termination of the proceeding under this section respecting such product, whichever date occurs first.

(3) The amount in controversy requirement of section 1331 of Title 28 does not apply with respect to the jurisdiction of a district court

of the United States to issue or extend a preliminary injunction under this subsection.

§ 17. Imported products [15 U.S.C. § 2066]

(a) Any consumer product offered for importation into the customs territory of the United States (as defined in general headnote 2 to the Tariff Schedules of the United States) shall be refused admission into such customs territory if such product—

(1) fails to comply with an applicable consumer product safety rule;

(2) is not accompanied by a certificate required by section 14 or is not labeled in accordance with regulations under section 14(c);

(3) is or has been determined to be an imminently hazardous consumer product in a proceeding brought under section 12;

(4) has a product defect which constitutes a substantial product hazard (within the meaning of section 15(a)(2); or

(5) is a product which was manufactured by a person who the Commission has informed the Secretary of the Treasury is in violation of subsection (g) of this section.

. . .

§ 19. Prohibited acts [15 U.S.C. § 2068]

(a) It shall be unlawful for any person to—

(1) manufacture for sale, offer for sale, distribute in commerce, or import into the United States any consumer product which is not in conformity with an applicable consumer product safety standard under this Act;

(2) manufacture for sale, offer for sale, distribute in commerce, or import into the United States any consumer product which has been declared a banned hazardous product by a rule under this Act;

(3) fail or refuse to permit access to or copying of records, or fail or refuse to establish or maintain records, or fail or refuse to make reports or provide information, or fail or refuse to permit entry or inspection, as required under this Act or rule thereunder;

(4) fail to furnish information required by section 15(b);

(5) fail to comply with an order issued under section 15(c) or (d) (relating to notification, to repair, replacement, and refund, and to prohibited acts);

(6) fail to furnish a certificate required by section 14 or issue a false certificate if such person in the exercise of due care has reason to know that such certificate is false or misleading in any material respect; or to fail to comply with any rule under section 14(c) (relating to labeling);

(7) fail to comply with any rule under section 9(d)(2) (relating to stockpiling); or

(8) fail to comply with any rule under section 13 (relating to prior notice and description of new consumer products);

(9) fail to comply with any rule under section 27(e) (relating to provision of performance and technical data);

(10) fail to comply with any rule or requirement under section 35 (relating to labeling and testing of cellulose insulation); and

(11) fail to file a statement with the Commission pursuant to section 18(b).

(b) Paragraphs (1) and (2) of subsection (a) of this section shall not apply to any person (1) who holds a certificate issued in accordance with section 14(a) to the effect that such consumer product conforms to all applicable consumer product safety rules, unless such person knows that such consumer product does not conform, or (2) who relies in good faith on the representation of the manufacturer or a distributor of such product that the product is not subject to an applicable product safety rule.

§ 20. Civil penalties [15 U.S.C. § 2069]

(a)(1) Any person who knowingly violates section 19 shall be subject to a civil penalty not to exceed $2,000 for each such violation. Subject to paragraph (2), a violation of section 19(a)(1), (2), (4), (5), (6), (7), (8), (9), or (10) shall constitute a separate offense with respect to each consumer product involved, except that the maximum civil penalty shall not exceed $500,000 for any related series of violations. A violation of section 19(a)(3) shall constitute a separate violation with respect to each failure or refusal to allow or perform an act required thereby; and, if such violation is a continuing one, each day of such violation shall constitute a separate offense, except that the maximum civil penalty shall not exceed $500,000 for any related series of violations.

(2) The second sentence of paragraph (1) of this subsection shall not apply to violations of paragraph (1) or (2) of section 19(a)—

(A) if the person who violated such paragraphs is not the manufacturer or private labeler or a distributor of the products involved, and

(B) if such person did not have either (i) actual knowledge that his distribution or sale of the product violated such paragraphs or (ii) notice from the Commission that such distribution or sale would be a violation of such paragraphs.

(b) In determining the amount of any penalty to be sought upon commencing an action seeking to assess a penalty for a violation of section 19(a), the Commission shall consider the nature of the product defect, the severity of the risk of injury, the occurrence or absence of injury, the number of defective products distributed, and the appropriateness of such penalty in relation to the size of the business of the person charged.

(c) Any civil penalty under this section may be compromised by the Commission. In determining the amount of such penalty or whether it should be remitted or mitigated and in what amount, the Commission shall consider the appropriateness of such penalty to the size of the business of the person charged, the nature of the product defect, the severity of the risk of injury, the occurrence or absence of injury, and the number of defective products distributed. The amount of such penalty when finally determined, or the amount agreed on compromise, may be deducted from any sums owing by the United States to the person charged.

(d) As used in the first sentence of subsection (a)(1) of this section, the term "knowingly" means (1) the having of actual knowledge, or (2) the presumed having of knowledge deemed to be possessed by a reasonable man who acts in the circumstances, including knowledge obtainable upon the exercise of due care to ascertain the truth of representations.

§ 21. Criminal penalties [15 U.S.C. § 2070]

(a) Any person who knowingly and willfully violates section 19 after having received notice of noncompliance from the Commission shall be fined not more than $50,000 or be imprisoned not more than one year, or both.

(b) Any individual director, officer, or agent of a corporation who knowingly and willfully authorizes, orders, or performs any of the acts or practices constituting in whole or in part a violation of section 19 and who has knowledge of notice of noncompliance received by the corporation from the Commission, shall be subject to penalties under this section without regard to any penalties to which that corporation may be subject under subsection (a) of this section.

§ 22. Injunctive enforcement and seizure [15 U.S.C. § 2071]

(a) The United States district courts shall have jurisdiction to take the following action:

(1) Restrain any violation of section 19.

(2) Restrain any person from manufacturing for sale, offering for sale, distributing in commerce, or importing into the United States a product in violation of an order in effect under section 15(d).

(3) Restrain any person from distributing in commerce a product which does not comply with a consumer product safety rule.

Such actions may be brought by the Commission (without regard to section 27(b)(7)(A)) or by the Attorney General in any United States district court for a district wherein any act, omission, or transaction constituting the violation occurred, or in such court for the district wherein the defendant is found or transacts business. In any action under this section process may be served on a defendant in any other district in which the defendant resides or may be found.

(b) Any consumer product—

(1) which fails to conform with an applicable consumer product safety rule, or

(2) the manufacture for sale, offering for sale, distribution in commerce, or the importation into the United States of which has been prohibited by an order in effect under section 15(d),

when introduced into or while in commerce or while held for sale after shipment in commerce shall be liable to be proceeded against on libel of information and condemned in any district court of the United States within the jurisdiction of which such consumer product is found. Proceedings in cases instituted under the authority of this subsection shall conform as nearly as possible to proceedings in rem in admiralty. Whenever such proceedings involving substantially similar consumer products are pending in courts of two or more judicial districts they shall be consolidated for trial by order of any such court upon application reasonably made by any party in interest upon notice to all other parties in interest.

§ 23. Suits for damages by persons injured [15 U.S.C. § 2072]

(a) Any person who shall sustain injury by reason of any knowing (including willful) violation of a consumer product safety rule, or any other rule or order issued by the Commission may sue any person who knowingly (including willfully) violated any such rule or order in any district court of the United States in the district in which the defendant resides or is found or has an agent, shall recover damages sustained, and may, if the court determines it to be in the interest of justice, recover the costs of suit, including reasonable attorneys' fees (determined in accordance with section 11(f)) and reasonable expert witnesses' fees: *Provided,* That the matter in controversy exceeds the sum or value of $10,000, exclusive of interest and costs, unless such action is brought against the United States, any agency thereof, or any officer or employee thereof in his official capacity.

(b) Except when express provision is made in a statute of the United States, in any case in which the plaintiff is finally adjudged to be entitled to recover less than the sum or value of $10,000, computed without regard to any setoff or counterclaim to which the defendant may be adjudged to be entitled, and exclusive of interests and costs, the district court may deny costs to the plaintiff and, in addition, may impose costs on the plaintiff.

(c) The remedies provided for in this section shall be in addition to and not in lieu of any other remedies provided by common law or under Federal or State law.

§ 24. Private enforcement of product safety rules and of section 15 orders [15 U.S.C. § 2073]

Any interested person (including any individual or nonprofit, business, or other entity) may bring an action in any United States district court for the district in which the defendant is found or transacts business to enforce a consumer product safety rule or an order under section 15, and to obtain appropriate injunctive relief. Not less than thirty days prior to the commencement of such action, such interested person shall give notice by registered mail to the Commission, to the Attorney General, and to the person against whom such action is directed. Such notice shall state the nature of the alleged violation of any such standard or order, the relief to be requested, and the court in which the action will be brought. No separate suit shall be brought under this section if at the time the suit is brought the same alleged violation is the subject of a pending civil or criminal action by the United States under this chapter. In any action under this section the court may in the interest of justice award the costs of suit, including reasonable attorneys' fees (determined in accordance with section 11(f)) and reasonable expert witnesses' fees.

§ 25. Effect on private remedies [15 U.S.C. § 2074]

(a) Compliance with consumer product safety rules or other rules or orders under this Act shall not relieve any person from liability at common law or under State statutory law to any other person.

(b) The failure of the Commission to take any action or commence a proceeding with respect to the safety of a consumer product shall not be admissible in evidence in litigation at common law or under State statutory law relating to such consumer product.

(c) Subject to sections 6(a)(2) and 6(b) but notwithstanding section 6(a)(1), (1) any accident or investigation report made under this Act by an officer or employee of the Commission shall be made available to the public in a manner which will not identify any injured person or any person treating him, without the consent of the person so identified, and (2) all reports on research projects, demonstration projects, and other related activities shall be public information.

§ 27. Additional functions of Commission [15 U.S.C. § 2076]

. . .

(j) The Commission shall prepare and submit to the President and the Congress at the beginning of each regular session of Congress a comprehensive report on the administration of this Act for the preceding fiscal year. Such report shall include—

(1) a thorough appraisal, including statistical analyses, estimates, and long-term projections, of the incidence of injury and effects to the population resulting from consumer products, with a breakdown, insofar as practicable, among the various sources of such injury;

(2) a list of consumer product safety rules prescribed or in effect during such year;

(3) an evaluation of the degree of observance of consumer product safety rules, including a list of enforcement actions, court decisions, and compromises of alleged violations, by location and company name;

(4) a summary of outstanding problems confronting the administration of this Act in order of priority;

(5) an analysis and evaluation of public and private consumer product safety research activities;

(6) a list, with a brief statement of the issues, of completed or pending judicial actions under this Act;

(7) the extent to which technical information was disseminated to the scientific and commercial communities and consumer information was made available to the public;

(8) the extent of cooperation between Commission officials and representatives of industry and other interested parties in the implementation of this Act, including a log or summary of meetings held between Commission officials and representatives of industry and other interested parties;

(9) an appraisal of significant actions of State and local governments relating to the responsibilities of the Commission;

(10) with respect to voluntary consumer product safety standards for which the Commission has participated in the development through monitoring or offering of assistance and with respect to voluntary consumer product safety standards relating to risks of injury that are the subject of regulatory action by the Commission, a description of—

(A) the number of such standards adopted;

(B) the nature and number of the products which are the subject of such standards;

(C) the effectiveness of such standards in reducing potential harm from consumer products;

(D) the degree to which staff members of the Commission participate in the development of such standards;

(E) the amount of resources of the Commission devoted to encouraging development of such standards; and

(F) such other information as the Commission determines appropriate or necessary to inform the Congress on the current status of the voluntary consumer product safety standard program; and

(11) such recommendations for additional legislation as the Commission deems necessary to carry out the purposes of this Act.

. . .

§ 36. Congressional veto of consumer product safety rules [15 U.S.C. § 2083]

(a) The Commission shall transmit to the Secretary of the Senate and the Clerk of the House of Representatives a copy of any consumer product safety rule promulgated by the Commission under section 9.

(b) Any rule specified in subsection (a) of this section shall not take effect if—

(1) within the 90 calendar days of continuous session of the Congress which occur after the date of the promulgation of such rule, both Houses of the Congress adopt a concurrent resolution, the matter after the resolving clause of which is as follows (with the blank spaces appropriately filled): "That the Congress disapproves the consumer product safety rule which was promulgated by the Consumer Product Safety Commission with respect to   and which was transmitted to the Congress on   and disapproves the rule for the following reasons: ."; or

(2) within the 60 calendar days of continuous session of the Congress which occur after the date of the promulgation of such rule, one House of the Congress adopts such concurrent resolution and transmits such resolution to the other House and such resolution is not disapproved by such other House within the 30 calendar days of continuous session of the Congress which occur after the date of such transmittal.

(c) Congressional inaction on, or rejection of, a concurrent resolution of disapproval under this section shall not be construed as an expression of approval of the rule involved, and shall not be construed to create any presumption of validity with respect to such rule.

(d) For purposes of this section—

(1) continuity of session is broken only by an adjournment of the Congress sine die; and

(2) the days on which either House is not in session because of an adjournment of more than 3 days to a day certain are excluded in the computation of the periods of continuous session of the Congress specified in subsection (b) of this section.

MAGNUSON–MOSS WARRANTY ACT

15 U.S.C. §§ 2301–2312

Table of Sections

---

§ 101. Definitions [15 U.S.C. § 2301]

For the purposes of this title:

(1) The term "consumer product" means any tangible personal property which is distributed in commerce and which is normally used for personal, family, or household purposes (including any such property intended to be attached to or installed in any real property without regard to whether it is so attached or installed).

(2) The term "Commission" means the Federal Trade Commission.

(3) The term "consumer" means a buyer (other than for purposes of resale) of any consumer product, any person to whom such product is transferred during the duration of an implied or written warranty (or service contract) applicable to the product, and any other person who is entitled by the terms of such warranty (or service contract) or under applicable State law to enforce against the warrantor (or service contractor) the obligations of the warranty (or service contract).

(4) The term "supplier" means any person engaged in the business of making a consumer product directly or indirectly available to consumers.

(5) The term "warrantor" means any supplier or other person who gives or offers to give a written warranty or who is or may be obligated under an implied warranty.

(6) The term "written warranty" means—

(A) any written affirmation of fact or written promise made in connection with the sale of a consumer product by a supplier to a buyer which relates to the nature of the material or workmanship and affirms or promises that such material or workmanship is defect free or will meet a specified level of performance over a specified period of time, or

(B) any undertaking in writing in connection with the sale by a supplier of a consumer product to refund, repair, replace, or take other remedial action with respect to such product in the event that such product fails to meet the specifications set forth in the undertaking,

which written affirmation, promise, or undertaking becomes part of the basis of the bargain between a supplier and a buyer for purposes other than resale of such product.

(7) The term "implied warranty" means an implied warranty arising under State law (as modified by sections 108 and 104(a)) in connection with the sale by a supplier of a consumer product.

(8) The term "service contract" means a contract in writing to perform, over a fixed period of time or for a specified duration, services relating to the maintenance or repair (or both) of a consumer product.

(9) The term "reasonable and necessary maintenance" consists of those operations (A) which the consumer reasonably can be expected to perform or have performed and (B) which are necessary to keep any consumer product performing its intended function and operating at a reasonable level of performance.

(10) The term "remedy" means whichever of the following actions the warrantor elects:

(A) repair,

(B) replacement, or

(C) refund;

except that the warrantor may not elect refund unless (i) the warrantor is unable to provide replacement and repair is not commercially practicable or cannot be timely made, or (ii) the consumer is willing to accept such refund.

(11) The term "replacement" means furnishing a new consumer product which is identical or reasonably equivalent to the warranted consumer product.

(12) The term "refund" means refunding the actual purchase price (less reasonable depreciation based on actual use where permitted by rules of the Commission).

(13) The term "distributed in commerce" means sold in commerce, introduced or delivered for introduction into commerce, or held for sale or distribution after introduction into commerce.

(14) The term "commerce" means trade, traffic, commerce, or transportation—

(A) between a place in a State and any place outside thereof, or

(B) which affects trade, traffic, commerce, or transportation described in subparagraph (A).

(15) The term "State" means a State, the District of Columbia, the Commonwealth of Puerto Rico, the Virgin Islands, Guam, the Canal Zone, or American Samoa. The term "State law" includes a law of the United States applicable only to the District of Columbia or only to a territory or possession of the United States; and the term "Federal law" excludes any State law.

§ 102. Warranty provisions [15 U.S.C. § 2302]

(a) In order to improve the adequacy of information available to consumers, prevent deception, and improve competition in the marketing of consumer products, any warrantor warranting a consumer product to a consumer by means of a written warranty shall, to the extent required by rules of the Commission, fully and conspicuously disclose in simple and readily understood language the terms and conditions of such warranty. Such rules may require inclusion in the written warranty of any of the following items among others:

(1) The clear identification of the names and addresses of the warrantors.

(2) The identity of the party or parties to whom the warranty is extended.

(3) The products or parts covered.

(4) A statement of what the warrantor will do in the event of a defect, malfunction, or failure to conform with such written warranty—at whose expense—and for what period of time.

(5) A statement of what the consumer must do and expenses he must bear.

(6) Exceptions and exclusions from the terms of the warranty.

(7) The step-by-step procedure which the consumer should take in order to obtain performance of any obligation under the warranty, including the identification of any person or class of persons authorized to perform the obligations set forth in the warranty.

(8) Information respecting the availability of any informal dispute settlement procedure offered by the warrantor and a recital, where the warranty so provides, that the purchaser may be required to re-

sort to such procedure before pursuing any legal remedies in the courts.

(9) A brief, general description of the legal remedies available to the consumer.

(10) The time at which the warrantor will perform any obligations under the warranty.

(11) The period of time within which, after notice of a defect, malfunction, or failure to conform with the warranty, the warrantor will perform any obligations under the warranty.

(12) The characteristics or properties of the products, or parts thereof, that are not covered by the warranty.

(13) The elements of the warranty in words or phrases which would not mislead a reasonable, average consumer as to the nature or scope of the warranty.

(b)(1)(A) The Commission shall prescribe rules requiring that the terms of any written warranty on a consumer product be made available to the consumer (or prospective consumer) prior to the sale of the product to him.

(B) The Commission may prescribe rules for determining the manner and form in which information with respect to any written warranty of a consumer product shall be clearly and conspicuously presented or displayed so as not to mislead the reasonable, average consumer, when such information in contained in advertising, labeling, point-of-sale material, or other representations in writing.

(2) Nothing in this [Act] (other than paragraph (3) of this subsection) shall be deemed to authorize the Commission to prescribe the duration of written warranties given or to require that a consumer product or any of its components be warranted.

(3) The Commission may prescribe rules for extending the period of time a written warranty or service contract is in effect to correspond with any period of time in excess of a reasonable period (not less than 10 days) during which the consumer is deprived of the use of such consumer product by reason of failure of the product to conform with the written warranty or by reason of the failure of the warrantor (or service contractor) to carry out such warranty (or service contract) within the period specified in the warranty (or service contract).

(c) No warrantor of a consumer product may condition his written or implied warranty of such product on the consumer's using, in connection with such product, any article or service (other than article or service provided without charge under the terms of the warranty) which is identified by brand, trade, or corporate name; except that the prohibition of this subsection may be waived by the Commission if—

(1) the warrantor satisfies the Commission that the warranted product will function properly only if the article or service so identified is used in connection with the warranted product, and

(2) the Commission finds that such a waiver is in the public interest.

The Commission shall identify in the Federal Register, and permit public comment on, all applications for waiver of the prohibition of this subsection, and shall publish in the Federal Register its disposition of any such application, including the reasons therefor.

(d) The Commission may by rule devise detailed substantive warranty provisions which warrantors may incorporate by reference in their warranties.

(e) The provisions of this section apply only to warranties which pertain to consumer products actually costing the consumer more than $5.

§ 103. Designation of warranties [15 U.S.C. § 2303]

(a) Any warrantor warranting a consumer product by means of a written warranty shall clearly and conspicuously designate such warranty in the following manner, unless exempted from doing so by the Commission pursuant to subsection (c) of this section:

(1) If the written warranty meets the Federal minimum standards for warranty set forth in section 104 of this Act, then it shall be conspicuously designated a "full (statement of duration) warranty".

(2) If the written warranty does not meet the Federal minimum standards for warranty set forth in section 104 of this Act, then it shall be conspicuously designated a "limited warranty".

(b) Sections 102, 103 and 104 shall not apply to statements or representations which are similar to expressions of general policy concerning customer satisfaction and which are not subject to any specific limitations.

(c) In addition to exercising the authority pertaining to disclosure granted in section 102 of this Act, the Commission may by rule determine when a written warranty does not have to be designated either "full (statement of duration)" or "limited" in accordance with this section.

(d) The provisions of subsections (a) and (c) of this section apply only to warranties which pertain to consumer products actually costing the consumer more than $10 and which are not designated "full (statement of duration) warranties".

§ 104. Federal minimum standards for warranty [15 U.S.C. § 2304]

(a) In order for a warrantor warranting a consumer product by means of a written warranty to meet the Federal minimum standards for warranty—

(1) such warrantor must as a minimum remedy such consumer product within a reasonable time and without charge, in the case of a defect, malfunction, or failure to conform with such written warranty;

(2) notwithstanding section 108(b), such warrantor may not impose any limitation on the duration of any implied warranty on the product;

(3) such warrantor may not exclude or limit consequential damages for breach of any written or implied warranty on such product, unless such exclusion or limitation conspicuously appears on the face of the warranty; and

(4) if the product (or a component part thereof) contains a defect or malfunction after a reasonable number of attempts by the warrantor to remedy defects or malfunctions in such product, such warrantor must permit the consumer or elect either a refund for, or replacement without charge of, such product or part (as the case may be). The Commission may by rule specify for purposes of this paragraph, what constitutes a reasonable number of attempts to remedy particular kinds of defects or malfunctions under different circumstances. If the warrantor replaces a component part of a consumer product, such replacement shall include installing the part in the product without charge.

(b)(1) In fulfilling the duties under subsection (a) of this section respecting a written warranty, the warrantor shall not impose any duty other than notification upon any consumer as a condition of securing remedy of any consumer product which malfunctions, is defective, or does not conform to the written warranty unless the warrantor has demonstrated in a rulemaking proceeding, or can demonstrate in an administrative or judicial enforcement proceeding (including private enforcement), or in an informal dispute settlement proceeding, that such a duty is reasonable.

(2) Notwithstanding paragraph (1), a warrantor may require, as a condition to replacement of, or refund for, any consumer product under subsection (a) of this section, that such consumer product shall be made available to the warrantor free and clear of liens, and other encumbrances, except as otherwise provided by rule or order of the Commission in cases in which such a requirement would not be practicable.

(3) The Commission may, by rule define in detail the duties set forth in subsection (a) of this section and the applicability of such

duties to warrantors of different categories of consumer products with "full (statement of duration)" warranties.

(4) The duties under subsection (a) of this section extend from the warrantor to each person who is a consumer with respect to the consumer product.

(c) The performance of the duties under subsection (a) of this section shall not be required of the warrantor if he can show that the defect, malfunction, or failure of any warranted consumer product to conform with a written warranty, was caused by damage (not resulting from defect or malfunction) while in the possession of the consumer, or unreasonable use (including failure to provide reasonable and necessary maintenance).

(d) For purposes of this section and of section 102(c), the term "without charge" means that the warrantor may not assess the consumer for any costs the warrantor or his representatives incur in connection with the required remedy of a warranted consumer product. An obligation under subsection (a)(1)(A) of this section to remedy without charge does not necessarily require the warrantor to compensate the consumer for incidental expenses; however, if any incidental expenses are incurred because the remedy is not made within a reasonable time or because the warrantor imposed an unreasonable duty upon the consumer as a condition of securing remedy, then the consumer shall be entitled to recover reasonable incidental expenses which are so incurred in any action against the warrantor.

(e) If a supplier designates a warranty applicable to a consumer product as a "full (statement of duration)" warranty, then the warranty on such product shall, for purposes of any action under section 110(d) or under any State law, be deemed to incorporate at least the minimum requirements of this section and rules prescribed under this section.

§ 105. Full and limited warranting of a consumer product [15 U.S.C. § 2305]

Nothing in this [Act] shall prohibit the selling of a consumer product which has both full and limited warranties if such warranties are clearly and conspicuously differentiated.

§ 106. Service contracts [15 U.S.C. § 2306]

(a) The Commission may prescribe by rule the manner and form in which the terms and conditions of service contracts shall be fully, clearly, and conspicuously disclosed.

(b) Nothing in this [Act] shall be construed to prevent a supplier or warrantor from entering into a service contract with the consumer in addition to or in lieu of a written warranty if such contract fully, clearly, and conspicuously discloses its terms and conditions in simple and readily understood language.

§ 107. Designation of representatives [15 U.S.C. § 2307]

Nothing in this [Act] shall be construed to prevent any warrantor from designating representatives to perform duties under the written or implied warranty: *Provided,* That such warrantor shall make reasonable arrangements for compensation of such designated representatives, but no such designation shall relieve the warrantor of his direct responsibilites to the consumer or make the representative a cowarrantor.

§ 108. Limitation on disclaimer of implied warranties [15 U.S.C. § 2308]

(a) No supplier may disclaim or modify (except as provided in subsection (b) of this section) any implied warranty to a consumer with respect to such consumer product if (1) such supplier makes any written warranty to the consumer with respect to such consumer product, or (2) at the time of sale, or within 90 days thereafter, such supplier enters into a service contract with the consumer which applies to such consumer product.

(b) For purposes of this [Act] (other than section 104(a)(2)), implied warranties may be limited in duration to the duration of a written warranty of reasonable duration, if such limitation is conscionable and is set forth in clear and unmistakable language and prominently displayed on the face of the warranty.

(c) A disclaimer, modification, or limitation made in violation of this section shall be ineffective for purposes of this [Act] and State law.

§ 109. Commission rules [15 U.S.C. § 2309]

(a) Any rule prescribed under this [Act] shall be prescribed in accordance with section 553 of Title 5; except that the Commission shall give interested persons an opportunity for oral presentations of data, views, and arguments, in addition to written submissions. A transcript shall be kept of any oral presentation. Any such rule shall be subject to judicial review under section 18(e) of the Federal Trade Commission Act in the same manner as rules prescribed under section 18(a)(1)(B) of such Act, except that section 18(e)(3)(B) of such Act shall not apply.

(b) The Commission shall initiate within one year after January 4, 1975, a rulemaking proceeding dealing with warranties and warranty practices in connection with the sale of used motor vehicles; and, to the extent necessary to supplement the protections offered the consumer by this [Act] shall prescribe rules dealing with such warranties and practices. In prescribing rules under this subsection, the Commission may exercise any authority it may have under this [Act], or other law, and in addition it may require disclosure that a used motor vehicle is sold without any warranty and specify the form and content of such disclosure.

§ 110. Remedies [15 U.S.C. § 2310]

(a)(1) Congress hereby declares it to be its policy to encourage warrantors to establish procedures whereby consumer disputes are fairly and expeditiously settled through informal dispute settlement mechanisms.

(2) The Commission shall prescribe rules setting forth minimum requirements for any informal dispute settlement procedure which is incorporated into the terms of a written warranty to which any provision of this [Act] applies. Such rules shall provide for participation in such procedure by independent or governmental entities.

(3) One or more warrantors may establish an informal dispute settlement procedure which meets the requirements of the Commission's rules under paragraph (2). If—

(A) a warrantor establishes such a procedure,

(B) such procedure, and its implementation, meets the requirements of such rules, and

(C) he incorporates in a written warranty a requirement that the consumer resort to such procedure before pursuing any legal remedy under this section respecting such warranty,

then (i) the consumer may not commence a civil action (other than a class action) under subsection (d) of this section unless he initially resorts to such procedure; and (ii) a class of consumers may not proceed in a class action under subsection (d) of this section except to the extent the court determines necessary to establish the representative capacity of the named plaintiffs, unless the named plaintiffs (upon notifying the defendant that they are named plaintiffs in a class action with respect to a warranty obligation) initially resort to such procedure. In the case of such a class action which is brought in a district court of the United States, the representative capacity of the named plaintiffs shall be established in the application of rule 23 of the Federal Rules of Civil Procedure. In any civil action arising out of a warranty obligation and relating to a matter considered in such a procedure, any decision in such procedure shall be admissible in evidence.

(4) The Commission on its own initiative may, or upon written complaint filed by any interested person shall, review the bona fide operation of any dispute settlement procedure resort to which is stated in a written warranty to be a prerequisite to pursuing a legal remedy under this section. If the Commission finds that such procedure

or its implementation fails to comply with the requirements of the rules under paragraph (2), the Commission may take appropriate remedial action under any authority it may have under this chapter or any other provision of law.

(5) Until rules under paragraph (2) take effect, this subsection shall not affect the validity of any informal dispute settlement procedure respecting consumer warranties, but in any action under subsection (d) of this section, the court may invalidate any such procedure if it finds that such procedure is unfair.

(b) It shall be a violation of section 5(a)(1) of the Federal Trade Commission Act for any person to fail to comply with any requirement imposed on such person by this [Act] (or a rule thereunder) or to violate any prohibition contained in this [Act] (or a rule thereunder).

(c)(1) The district courts of the United States shall have jurisdiction of any action brought by the Attorney General (in his capacity as such), or by the Commission by any of its attorneys designated by it for such purpose, to restrain (A) any warrantor from making a deceptive warranty with respect to a consumer product, or (B) any person from failing to comply with any requirement imposed on such person by or pursuant to this [Act] or from violating any prohibition contained in this [Act]. Upon proper showing that, weighing the equities and considering the Commission's or Attorney General's likelihood of ultimate success, such action would be in the public interest and after notice to the defendant, a temporary restraining order or preliminary injunction may be granted without bond. In the case of an action brought by the Commission, if a complaint under section 5 of the Federal Trade Commission Act is not filed within such period (not exceeding 10 days) as may be specified by the court after the issuance of the temporary restraining order or preliminary injunction, the order or injunction shall be dissolved by the court and be of no further force and effect. Any suit shall be brought in the district in which such person resides or transacts business. Whenever it appears to the court that the ends of justice require that other persons should be parties in the action, the court may cause them to be summoned whether or not they reside in the district in which the court is held, and to that end process may be served in any district.

(2) For the purposes of this subsection, the term "deceptive warranty" means (A) a written warranty which (i) contains an affirmation, promise, description, or representation which is either false or fraudulent, or which, in light of all of the circumstances, would mislead a reasonable individual exercising due care; or (ii) fails to contain information which is necessary in light of all of the circumstances, to make the warranty not misleading to a reasonable individual exercising due care; or (B) a written warranty created by the use of such terms as "guaranty" or "warranty", if the terms and

conditions of such warranty so limit its scope and application as to deceive a reasonable individual.

(d)(1) Subject to subsections (a)(3) and (e) of this section, a consumer who is damaged by the failure of a supplier, warrantor, or service contractor to comply with any obligation under this [Act], or under a written warranty, implied warranty, or service contract, may bring suit for damages and other legal and equitable relief—

(A) in any court of competent jurisdiction in any State or the District of Columbia; or

(B) in an appropriate district court of the United States, subject to paragraph (3) of this subsection.

(2) If a consumer finally prevails in any action brought under paragraph (1) of this subsection, he may be allowed by the court to recover as part of the judgment a sum equal to the aggregate amount of cost and expenses (including attorneys' fees based on actual time expended) determined by the court to have been reasonably incurred by the plaintiff for or in connection with the commencement and prosecution of such action, unless the court in its discretion shall determine that such an award of attorneys' fees would be inappropriate.

(3) No claim shall be cognizable in a suit brought under paragraph (1)(B) of this subsection—

(A) if the amount in controversy of any individual claim is less than the sum or value of $25;

(B) if the amount in controversy is less than the sum or value of $50,000 (exclusive of interest and costs) computed on the basis of all claims to be determined in this suit; or

(C) if the action is brought as a class action, and the number of named plaintiffs is less than one hundred.

(e) No action (other than a class action or an action respecting a warranty to which subsection (a)(3) of this section applies) may be brought under subsection (d) of this section for failure to comply with any obligation under any written or implied warranty or service contract, and a class of consumers may not proceed in a class action under such subsection with respect to such a failure except to the extent the court determines necessary to establish the representative capacity of the named plaintiffs, unless the person obligated under the warranty or service contract is afforded a reasonable opportunity to cure such failure to comply. In the case of such a class action (other than a class action respecting a warranty to which subsection (a)(3) of this section applies) brought under subsection (d) of this section for breach of any written or implied warranty or service contract, such reasonable opportunity will be afforded by the named plaintiffs and they shall at that time notify the defendant that they are acting on behalf of the class. In the case of such a class action which is brought in a district court of the United States, the representative capacity of the named plaintiffs shall be established in the application of rule 23 of the Federal Rules of Civil Procedure.

(f) For purposes of this section, only the warrantor actually making a written affirmation of fact, promise, or undertaking shall be deemed to have created a written warranty, and any rights arising thereunder may be enforced under this section only against such warrantor and no other person.

§ 111. Effect on other laws [15 U.S.C. § 2311]

(a)(1) Nothing contained in this [Act] shall be construed to repeal, invalidate, or supersede the Federal Trade Commission Act or any statute defined therein as an Antitrust Act.

(2) Nothing in this [Act] shall be construed to repeal, invalidate, or supersede the Federal Seed Act and nothing in this [Act] shall apply to seed for planting.

(b)(1) Nothing in this [Act] shall invalidate or restrict any right or remedy of any consumer under State law or any other Federal law.

(2) Nothing in this [Act] (other than sections 108 and 104(a)(2) and (4)) shall (A) affect the liability of, or impose liability on, any person for personal jury, or (B) supersede any provision of State law regarding consequential damages for injury to the person or other injury.

(c)(1) Except as provided in subsection (b) of this section and in paragraph (2) of this subsection, a State requirement—

> (A) which relates to labeling or disclosure with respect to written warranties or performance thereunder;
>
> (B) which is within the scope of an applicable requirement of sections 102, 103, and 104 (and rules implementing such sections), and
>
> (C) which is not identical to a requirement of section 102, 103, or 104 (or a rule thereunder),

shall not be applicable to written warranties complying with such sections (or rules thereunder).

(2) If, upon application of an appropriate State agency, the Commission determines (pursuant to rules issued in accordance with section 109) that any requirement of such State covering any transaction to which this [Act] applies (A) affords protection to consumers greater than the requirements of this [Act] and (B) does not unduly burden interstate commerce, then such State requirement shall be applicable (notwithstanding the provisions of paragraph (1) of this subsection) to the extent specified in such determination for so long as the State administers and enforces effectively any such greater requirement.

(d) This chapter (other than section 102(c)) shall be inapplicable to any written warranty the making or content of which is otherwise governed by Federal law. If only a portion of a written warranty is so governed by Federal law, the remaining portion shall be subject to this [Act].

§ 112. Effective dates [15 U.S.C. 2312]

(a) Except as provided in subsection (b) of this section, this [Act] shall take effect 6 months after January 4, 1975, but shall not apply to consumer products manufactured prior to such date.

. . .

FEDERAL TRADE COMMISSION RULES, REGULATIONS, STATEMENTS AND INTERPRETATIONS UNDER THE MAGNUSON–MOSS WARRANTY ACT

16 C.F.R. Parts 700–703

PART 700. INTERPRETATIONS OF MAGNUSON–MOSS WARRANTY ACT

Table of Sections

---

§ 700.1 Products covered

(a) The Act applies to written warranties on tangible personal property which is normally used for personal, family, or household purposes. This definition includes property which is intended to be attached to or installed in any real property without regard to whether it is so attached or installed. This means that a product is a "consumer product" if the use of that type of product is not uncommon. The percentage of sales or the use to which a product is put by any individual buyer is not determinative. For example, products such as automobiles and typewriters which are used for both personal and commercial purposes come within the definition of consumer product. Where it is unclear whether a particular product is covered under the definition of consumer product, any ambiguity will be resolved in favor of coverage.

(b) Agricultural products such as farm machinery, structures and implements used in the business or occupation of farming are not covered by the Act where their personal, family, or household use is uncommon. However, those agricultural products normally used for personal or household gardening (for example, to produce goods for personal consumption, and not for resale) are consumer products under the Act.

(c) The definition of "Consumer product" limits the applicability of the Act to personal property, "including any such property intended to be attached to or installed in any real property without regard to whether it is so attached or installed." This provision brings under the Act separate items of equipment attached to real property, such as air conditioners, furnaces, and water heaters.

(d) The coverage of separate items of equipment attached to real property includes, but is not limited to, appliances and other thermal, mechanical, and electrical equipment. (It does not extend to the wiring, plumbing, ducts, and other items which are integral component parts of the structure.) State law would classify many such products as fixtures to, and therefore a part of, realty. The statutory definition is designed to being such products under the Act regardless of whether they may be considered fixtures under state law.

(e) The coverage of building materials which are not separate items of equipment is based on the nature of the purchase transaction. An analysis of the transaction will determine whether the goods are real or personal property. The numerous products which go into the construction of a consumer dwelling are all consumer products when sold "over the counter," as by hardware and building supply retailers. This is also true where a consumer contracts for the purchase of such materials in connection with the improvement, repair, or modification of a home (for example, paneling, dropped ceilings, siding, roofing, storm windows, remodeling). However, where such products are at the time of sale integrated into the structure of a dwelling they are not consumer products as they cannot be practically distinguished from realty. Thus, for example, the beams, wallboard, wiring, plumbing, windows, roofing, and other structural components of a dwelling are not consumer products when they are sold as part of real estate covered by a written warranty.

(f) In the case where a consumer contracts with a builder to construct a home, a substantial addition to a home, or other realty (such as a garage or an in-ground swimming pool) the building materials to be used are not consumer products. Although the materials are separately identifiable at the time the contract is made, it is the intention of the parties to contract for the construction of realty which will integrate the component materials. Of course, as noted above, any separate items of equipment to be attached to such realty are consumer products under the Act.

(g) Certain provisions of the Act apply only to products actually costing the consumer more than a specified amount. Section 103 applies to consumer products actually costing the consumer more than $10, excluding tax. The $10 minimum will be interpreted to include multiple-packaged items which may individually sell for less than $10, but which have been packaged in a manner that does not permit breaking the package to purchase an item or items at a price less than $10. Thus, a written warranty on a dozen items packaged and priced for sale at $12 must be designated, even though identical items may be offered in smaller quantities at under $10. This interpretation applies in the same manner to the minimum dollar limits in section 102 and rules promulgated under that section.

(h) Warranties on replacement parts and components used to repair consumer products are covered; warranties on services are not covered. Therefore, warranties which apply solely to a repairer's workmanship in performing repairs are not subject to the Act. Where a written agreement warrants both the parts provided to effect a repair and the workmanship in making that repair, the warranty must comply with the Act and the rules thereunder.

(i) The Act covers written warranties on consumer products "distributed in commerce" as that term is defined in section 101(3). Thus, by its terms the Act arguably applies to products exported to foreign jurisdictions. However, the public interest would not be served by the use of Commission resources to enforce the Act with respect to such products. Moreover, the legislative intent to apply the requirements of the Act to such products is not sufficiently clear to justify such an extraordinary result. The Commission does not contemplate the enforcement of the Act with respect to consumer products exported to foreign jurisdictions. Products exported for sale at military post exchanges remain subject to the same enforcement standards as products sold within the United States, its territories and possessions.

§ 700.2 Date of manufacture

Section 112 of the Act provides that the Act shall apply only to those consumer products manufactured after July 4, 1975. When a consumer purchases repair of a consumer product the date of manufacture of any replacement parts used is the measuring date for determining coverage under the Act. The date of manufacture of the consumer product being repaired is in this instance not relevant. Where a consumer purchases or obtains on an exchange basis a rebuilt consumer product, the date that the rebuilding process is completed determines the Act's applicability.

§ 700.3 Written warranty

(a) The Act imposes specific duties and liabilities on suppliers who offer written warranties on consumer products. Certain representations, such as energy efficiency ratings for electrical appliances, care labeling of wearing apparel, and other product information disclosures may be express warranties under the Uniform Commercial Code. However, these disclosures alone are not written warranties under this Act. Section 101(6) provides that a written affirmation of fact or a written promise of a specified level of performance must relate to a specified period of time in order to be considered a "written warranty."[1] A product information disclosure without a specified time period to which the disclosure relates is therefore not a written warranty. In addition, section 111(d) exempts from the Act (except section 102(c)) any written warranty the making or content of which is required by federal law. The Commission encourages the disclosure of product information which is not deceptive and which may benefit consumers, and will not construe the Act to impede information disclosure in product advertising or labeling.

(b) Certain terms, or conditions, of sale of a consumer product may not be "written warranties" as that term is defined in section 101(6), and should not be offered or described in a manner that may deceive consumers as to their enforceability under the Act. For example, a seller of consumer products may give consumers an unconditional right to revoke acceptance of goods within a certain number of days after delivery without regard to defects or failure to meet a specified level of performance. Or a seller may permit consumers to return products for any reason for credit toward purchase of another item. Such terms of sale taken alone are not written warranties under the Act. Therefore, suppliers should avoid any characterization of such terms of sale as warranties. The use of such terms as "free trial period" and "trade-in credit policy" in this regard would be appropriate. Furthermore, such terms of sale should be stated separately from any written warranty. Of course, the offering and performance of such terms of sale remain subject to section 5 of the Federal Trade Commission Act, 15 U.S.C. 45.

(c) The Magnuson-Moss Warranty Act generally applies to written warranties covering consumer products. Many consumer products are covered by warranties which are neither intended for, nor enforceable by, consumers. A common example is a warranty given by a component supplier to a manufacturer of consumer products. (The manufacturer may, in turn, warrant these components to consumers.) The component supplier's warranty is generally given solely to the product manufacturer, and is neither intended to be conveyed to the consumer nor brought to the consumer's attention in connection with the sale. Such warranties are not subject to the Act, since a written warranty under section 101(6) of the Act must become "part of the

1. A "written warranty" is also created by a written affirmation of fact or a written promise that the product is defect free, or by a written undertaking of remedial action within the meaning of section 101(6)(B).

basis of the bargain between a supplier and a buyer for purposes other than resale." However, the Act applies to a component supplier's warranty in writing which is given to the consumer. An example is a supplier's written warranty to the consumer covering a refrigerator that is sold installed in a boat or recreational vehicle. The supplier of the refrigerator relies on the boat or vehicle assembler to convey the written agreement to the consumer. In this case, the supplier's written warranty is to a consumer, and is covered by the Act.

§ 700.4 Parties "Actually making" a written warranty

Section 110(f) of the Act provides that only the supplier "actually making" a written warranty is liable for purposes of FTC and private enforcement of the Act. A supplier who does no more than distribute or sell a consumer product covered by a written warranty offered by another person or business and which identifies that person or business as the warrantor is not liable for failure of the written warranty to comply with the Act or rules thereunder. However, other actions and written and oral representations of such a supplier in connection with the offer or sale of a warranted product may obligate that supplier under the Act. If under state law the supplier is deemed to have "adopted" the written affirmation of fact, promise, or undertaking, the supplier is also obligated under the Act. Suppliers are advised to consult state law to determine those actions and representations which may make them co-warrantors, and therefore obligated under the warranty of the other person or business.

§ 700.5 Expressions of general policy

(a) Under section 103(b), statements or representations of general policy concerning customer satisfaction which are not subject to any specific limitation need not be designated as full or limited warranties, and are exempt from the requirements of sections 102, 103, and 104 of the Act and rules thereunder. However, such statements remain subject to the enforcement provisions of section 110 of the Act, and to section 5 of the Federal Trade Commission Act, 15 U.S.C. 45.

(b) The section 103(b) exemption applies only to general policies, not to those which are limited to specific consumer products manufactured or sold by the supplier offering such a policy. In addition, to qualify for an exemption under section 103(b) such policies may not be subject to any specific limitations. For example, policies which have an express limitation of duration or a limitation of the amount to be refunded are not exempted. This does not preclude the imposition of reasonable limitations based on the circumstances in each instance a consumer seeks to invoke such an agreement. For instance, a warrantor may refuse to honor such an expression of policy where a consumer has used a product for 10 years without previously expressing any dissatisfaction with the product. Such a refusal would not be a specific limitation under this provision.

§ 700.6 Designation of warranties

(a) Section 103 of the Act provides that written warranties on consumer products manufactured after July 4, 1975, and actually costing the consumer more than $10, excluding tax, must be designated either "Full (statement of duration) Warranty" or "Limited Warranty". Warrantors may include a statement of duration in a limited warranty designation. The designation or designations should appear clearly and conspicuously as a caption, or prominent title, clearly separated from the text of the warranty. The full (statement of duration) warranty and limited warranty are the exclusive designations permitted under the Act, unless a specific exception is created by rule.

(b) Section 104(b)(4) states that "the duties under subsection (a) (of section 104) extend from the warrantor to each person who is a consumer with respect to the consumer product." Section 101(3) defines a consumer as "a buyer (other than for purposes of resale) of any consumer product, any person to whom such product is transferred during the duration of an implied or written warranty (or service contract) applicable to the product. . . ." Therefore, a full warranty may not expressly restrict the warranty rights of a transferee during its stated duration. However, where the duration of a full warranty is defined solely in terms of first purchaser ownership there can be no violation of section 104(b)(4), since the duration of the warranty expires, by definition, at the time of transfer. No rights of a subsequent transferee are cut off as there is no transfer of ownership "during the duration of (any) warranty." Thus, these provisions do not preclude the offering of a full warranty with its duration determined exclusively by the period during which the first purchaser owns the product, or uses it in conjunction with another product. For example, an automotive battery or muffler warranty may be designated as "full warranty for as long as you own your car." Because this type of warranty leads the consumer to believe that proof of purchase is not needed so long as he or she owns the product a duty to furnish documentary proof may not be reasonably imposed on the consumer under this type of warranty. The burden is on the warrantor to prove that a particular claimant under this type of warranty is not the original purchaser or owner of the product. Warrantors or their designated agents may, however, ask consumers to state or affirm that they are the first purchaser of the product.

§ 700.7 Use of warranty registration cards

(a) Under section 104(b)(1) of the Act a warrantor offering a full warranty may not impose on consumers any duty other than notification of a defect as a condition of securing remedy of the defect or malfunction, unless such additional duty can be demonstrated by the warrantor to be reasonable. Warrantors have in the past stipulated the return of a "warranty registration" or similar card. By "warranty registration card" the Commission means a card which must be returned by the consumer shortly after purchase of the product and which is stipulated or implied in the warranty to be a condition precedent to warranty coverage and performance.

(b) A requirement that the consumer return a warranty registration card or a similar notice as a condition of performance under a full warranty is an unreasonable duty. Thus, a provision such as, "This warranty is void unless the warranty registration card is returned to the warrantor" is not permissible in a full warranty, nor is it permissible to imply such a condition in a full warranty.

(c) This does not prohibit the use of such registration cards where a warrantor suggests use of the card as one possible means of proof of the date the product was purchased. For example, it is permissible to provide in a full warranty that a consumer may fill out and return a card to place on file proof of the date the product was purchased. Any such suggestion to the consumer must include notice that failure to return the card will not affect rights under the warranty, so long as the consumer can show in a reasonable manner the date the product was purchased. Nor does this interpretation prohibit a seller from obtaining from purchasers at the time of sale information requested by the warrantor.

§ 700.8 Warrantor's decision as final

A warrantor shall not indicate in any written warranty or service contract either directly or indirectly that the decision of the warrantor, service contractor, or any designated third party is final or binding in any dispute concerning the warranty or service contract. Nor shall a warrantor or service contractor state that it alone shall determine what is a defect under the agreement. Such statements are deceptive since section 110(d) of the Act gives state and federal courts jurisdiction over suits for breach of warranty and service contract.

§ 700.9 Duty to install under a full warranty

Under section 104(a)(1) of the Act, the remedy under a full warranty must be provided to the consumer without charge, If the warranted product has utility only when installed, a full warranty must provide such installation without charge regardless of whether or not the consumer originally paid for installation by the warrantor or his agent. However, this does not preclude the warrantor from imposing on the consumer a duty to remove, return, or reinstall where such duty can be demonstrated by the warrantor to meet the standard of reasonableness under section 104(b)(1).

§ 700.10 Section 102(c)

(a) Section 102(c) prohibits tying arrangements that condition coverage under a written warranty on the consumer's use of an article or service identified by brand, trade, or corporate name unless that article or service is provided without charge to the consumer.

(b) Under a limited warranty that provides only for replacement of defective parts and no portion of labor charges, section 102(c) prohibits a condition that the consumer use only service (labor) identified by the warrantor to install the replacement parts. A warrantor or his designated representative may not provide parts under the warranty in a manner which impedes or precludes the choice by the consumer of the person or business to perform necessary labor to install such parts.

(c) No warrantor may condition the continued validity of a warranty on the use of only authorized repair service and/or authorized replacement parts for non-warranty service and maintenance. For example, provisions such as, "this warranty is void if service is performed by anyone other than an authorized 'ABC' dealer and all replacement parts must be genuine 'ABC' parts, and the like, are prohibited where the service or parts are not covered by the warranty. These provisions violate the Act in two ways. First, they violate the section 102(c) ban against tying arrangements. Second, such provisions are deceptive under section 110 of the Act, because a warrantor cannot, as a matter of law, avoid liability under a written warranty where a defect is unrelated to the use by a consumer of "unauthorized" articles or service. This does not preclude a warrantor from expressly excluding liability for defects or damage caused by such "unauthorized" articles or service; nor does it preclude the warrantor from denying liability where the warrantor can demonstrate that the defect or damage was so caused.

§ 700.11 Written warranty, service contract, and insurance distinguished for purposes of compliance under the Act

(a) The Act recognizes two types of agreements which may provide similar coverage of consumer products, the written warranty, and the service contract. In addition, other agreements may meet the statutory definitions of either "written warranty" or "service contract," but are sold and regulated under state law as contracts of insurance. One example is the automobile breakdown insurance policies sold in many jurisdictions and regulated by the state as a form of casualty insurance. The McCarran-Ferguson Act, 15 U.S.C. 1011 et seq., precludes jurisdiction under federal law over "the business of insurance" to the extent an agreement is regulated by state law as insurance. Thus, such agreements are subject to the Magnuson-Moss Warranty Act only to the extent they are not regulated in a particular state as the business of insurance.

(b) "Written warranty" and "service contract" are defined in sections 101(6) and 101(8) of the Act, respectively. A written warranty must be "part of the basis of the bargain." This means that it must be conveyed at the time of sale of the consumer product and the consumer must not give any consideration beyond the purchase price of the consumer product in order to benefit from the agreement. It is not a requirement of the Act that an agreement obligate a supplier of the consumer product to a written warranty, but merely that it be part of the basis of the bargain between a supplier and a consumer. This contemplates written warranties by third-party non-suppliers.

(c) A service contract under the Act must meet the definitions of section 101(8). An agreement which would meet the definition of written warranty in section 101(6)(A) or (B) but for its failure to satisfy the basis of the bargain test is a service contract. For example, an agreement which calls for some consideration in addition to the purchase price of the consumer product, or which is entered into at some date after the purchase of the consumer product to which it applies, is a service contract. An agreement which relates only to the performance of maintenance and/or inspection services and which is not an undertaking, promise, or affirmation with respect to a specified level of performance, or that the product is free of defects in materials or workmanship, is a service contract. An agreement to perform periodic cleaning and inspection of a product over a specified period of time, even when offered at the time of sale and without charge to the consumer, is an example of such a service contract.

PART 701. DISCLOSURE OF WRITTEN CONSUMER PRODUCT WARRANTY TERMS AND CONDITIONS

Table of Sections

---

§ 701.1 Definitions

(a) "The Act" means the Magnuson-Moss Warranty Federal Trade Commission Improvement Act, 15 U.S.C. 2301, et seq.

(b) "Consumer product" means any tangible personal property which is distributed in commerce and which is normally used for personal, family, or household purposes (including any such property intended to be attached to or installed in any real property without regard to whether it is so attached or installed). Products which are purchased solely for commercial or industrial use are excluded solely for purposes of this Part.

(c) "Written warranty" means:

(1) Any written affirmation of fact or written promise made in connection with the sale of a consumer product by a supplier to a buyer which relates to the nature of the material or workmanship and affirms or promises that such material or workmanship is defect free or will meet a specified level of performance over a specified period of time, or

(2) Any undertaking in writing in connection with the sale by a supplier of a consumer product to refund, repair, replace, or take other remedial action with respect to such product in the event that such product fails to meet the specifications set forth in the undertaking, which written affirmation, promise or undertaking becomes part of the basis of the bargain between a supplier and a buyer for purposes other than resale of such product.

(d) "Implied warranty" means an implied warranty arising under State law (as modified by secs. 104(a) and 108 of the Act) in connection with the sale by a supplier of a consumer product.

(e) "Remedy" means whichever of the following actions the warrantor elects:

(1) Repair,

(2) Replacement, or

(3) Refund; except that the warrantor may not elect refund unless: (i) The warrantor is unable to provide replacement and repair is not commercially practicable or cannot be timely made, or

(ii) The consumer is willing to accept such refund.

(f) "Supplier" means any person engaged in the business of making a consumer product directly or indirectly available to consumers.

(g) "Warrantor" means any supplier or other person who gives or offers to give a written warranty.

(h) "Consumer" means a buyer (other than for purposes of resale or use in the ordinary course of the buyer's business) of any consumer product, any person to whom such product is transferred during the duration of an implied or written warranty applicable to the product, and any other such person who is entitled by the terms of such warranty or under applicable State law to enforce against the warrantor the obligations of the warranty.

(i) "On the face of the warranty" means:

(1) Where the warranty is a single sheet with printing on both sides of the sheet or where the warranty is comprised of more than one sheet, the page on which the warranty text begins;

(2) Where the warranty is included as part of a larger document, such as a use and care manual, the page in such document on which the warranty text begins.

§ 701.2 Scope

The regulations in this part establish requirements for warrantors for disclosing the terms and conditions of written warranties on consumer products actually costing the consumer more than $15.00.

§ 701.3 Written warranty terms

(a) Any warrantor warranting to a consumer by means of a written warranty a consumer product actually costing the consumer more than $15.00 shall clearly and conspicuously disclose in a single document in simple and readily understood language, the following items of information:

(1) The identity of the party or parties to whom the written warranty is extended, if the enforceability of the written warranty is limited to the original consumer purchaser or is otherwise limited to persons other than every consumer owner during the term of the warranty;

(2) A clear description and identification of products, or parts, or characteristics, or components or properties covered by and where necessary for clarification, excluded from the warranty;

(3) A statement of what the warrantor will do in the event of a defect, malfunction or failure to conform with the written warranty, including the items or services the warrantor will pay for or provide, and, where necessary for clarification, those which the warrantor will not pay for or provide;

(4) The point in time or event on which the warranty term commences, if different from the purchase date, and the time period or other measurement of warranty duration;

(5) A step-by-step explanation of the procedure which the consumer should follow in order to obtain performance of any warranty obligation, including the persons or class of persons authorized to perform warranty obligations. This includes the name(s) of the warrantor(s), together with: The mailing address(es) of the warrantor(s), and/or the name or title and the address of any employee or department of the warrantor responsible for the performance of warranty obligations, and/or a telephone number which consumers may use without charge to obtain information on warranty performance;

(6) Information respecting the availability of any informal dispute settlement mechanism elected by the warrantor in compliance with Part 703 of this subchapter;

(7) Any limitations on the duration of implied warranties, disclosed on the face of the warranty as provided in Section 108 of the Act, accompanied by the following statement:

> Some states do not allow limitations on how long an implied warranty lasts, so the above limitation may not apply to you.

(8) Any exclusions of or limitations on relief such as incidental or consequential damages, accompanied by the following statement, which may be combined with the statement required in paragraph (a)(7) of this section:

> Some states do not allow the exclusion or limitation of incidental or consequential damages, so the above limitation or exclusion may not apply to you.

(9) A statement in the following language:

> This warranty gives you specific legal rights, and you may also have other rights which vary from state to state.

(b) Paragraphs (a)(1) through (9) of this section shall not be applicable with respect to statements of general policy on emblems, seals or insignias issued by third parties promising replacement or refund if a consumer product is defective, which statements contain no representation or assurance of the quality or performance characteristics of the product; provided that (1) the disclosures required by paragraphs (a)(1) through (9) of this section are published by such third parties in each issue of a publication with a general circulation, and (2) such disclosures are provided free of charge to any consumer upon written request.

§ 701.4 Owner registration cards

When a warrantor employs any card such as an owner's registration card, a warranty registration card, or the like, and the return of such card is a condition precedent to warranty coverage and performance, the warrantor shall disclose this fact in the warranty. If the return of such card reasonably appears to be a condition precedent to warranty coverage and performance, but is not such a condition, that fact shall be disclosed in the warranty.

PART 702. PRE–SALE AVAILABILITY OF WRITTEN WARRANTY TERMS

Table of Sections

§ 702.1 Definitions

(a) "The Act" means the Magnuson-Moss Warranty Federal Trade Commission Improvement Act, 15 U.S.C. 2301, et seq.

(b) "Consumer product" means any tangible personal property which is distributed in commerce and which is normally used for personal, family, or household purposes (including any such property intended to be attached to or installed in any real property without regard to whether it is so attached or installed). Products which are purchased solely for commercial or industrial use are excluded solely for purposes of this part.

(c) "Written warranty" means:

(1) Any written affirmation of fact or written promise made in connection with the sale of a consumer product by a supplier to a buyer which relates to the nature of the material or workmanship and affirms or promises that such material or workmanship is defect free or will meet a specified level of performance over a specified period of time, or

(2) Any undertaking in writing in connection with the sale by a supplier of a consumer product to refund, repair, replace, or take other remedial action with respect to such product in the event that such product fails to meet the specifications set forth in the undertaking, which written affirmation, promise or undertaking becomes part of the basis of the bargain between a supplier and a buyer for purposes other than resale of such product.

(d) "Warrantor" means any supplier or other person who gives or offers to give a written warranty.

(e) "Seller" means any person who sells or offers for sale for purposes other than resale or use in the ordinary course of the buyer's business any consumer product.

(f) "Supplier" means any person engaged in the business of making a consumer product directly or indirectly available to consumers.

(g) "Binder" means a locking binder, notebook, or similar system which will provide the consumer with convenient access to copies of product warranties.

§ 702.2 Scope

The regulations in this part establish requirements for sellers and warrantors for making the terms of any written warranty on a consumer product available to the consumer prior to sale.

§ 702.3 Pre-sale availability of written warranty terms

The following requirements apply to consumer products actually costing the consumer more than $15.00:

(a) *Duties of the seller.* Except as provided in paragraphs (c) through (d) of this section, the seller of a consumer product with a written warranty shall:

(1) Make available for the prospective buyer's review, prior to sale, the text of such written warranty by the use of one or more of the following means:

(i) Clearly and conspicuously displaying the text of the written warranty in close conjunction to each warranted product; and/or

(ii) Maintaining a binder or series of binders which contain(s) copies of the warranties for the products sold in each department in which any consumer product with a written warranty is offered for sale. Such binder(s) shall be maintained in each such department, or in a location which provides the prospective buyer with ready access to such binder(s), and shall be prominently entitled "Warranties" or other similar title which clearly identifies the binder(s). Such binder(s) shall be indexed according to product or warrantor and shall be maintained up to date when new warranted products or models or new warranties for existing products are introduced into the store or department by substituting superseding warranties and by adding new warranties as appropriate. The seller shall either:

(A) Display such binder(s) in a manner reasonably calculated to elicit the prospective buyer's attention; or

(B) Make the binders available to prospective buyers on request, and place signs reasonably calculated to elicit the prospective buyer's attention in prominent locations in the store or department advising such prospective buyers of the availability of the binders, including instructions for obtaining access; and/or

(iii) Displaying the package of any consumer product on which the text of the written warranty is disclosed, in a manner such that the warranty is clearly visible to prospective buyers at the point of sale; and/or

(iv) Placing in close proximity to the warranted consumer product a notice which discloses the text of the written warranty, in a manner which clearly identifies to prospective buyers the product to which the notice applies;

(2) Not remove or obscure any warranty disclosure materials provided by a warrantor, except:

(i) Where such removal is necessary for store window displays, fashion shows, or picture taking; or

(ii) Where the seller otherwise, through means provided for in paragraph (a)(1) of this section, makes the terms of the warranty information available to the consumer.

(b) *Duties of the warrantor.* (1) A warrantor who gives a written warranty warranting to a consumer a consumer product actually costing the consumer more than $15.00 shall:

(i) Provide sellers with warranty materials necessary for such sellers to comply with the requirements set forth in paragraph (a) of this section, by the use of one or more by the following means:

(A) Providing a copy of the written warranty with every warranted consumer product; and/or

(B) Providing a tag, sign, sticker, label, decal or other attachment to the product, which contains the full text of the written warranty; and/or

(C) Printing on or otherwise attaching the text of the written warranty to the package, carton, or other container if that package, carton or other container is normally used for display purposes. If the warrantor elects this option a copy of the written warranty must also accompany the warranted product; and/or

(D) Providing a notice, sign, or poster disclosing the text of a consumer product warranty. If the warrantor elects this option, a copy of the written warranty must also accompany each warranted product.

(ii) Provide catalog, mail order, and door-to-door sellers with copies of written warranties necessary for such sellers to comply with the requirements set forth in paragraphs (c) and (d) of this section.

(2) Paragraph (a)(1) of this section shall not be applicable with respect to statements of general policy on emblems, seals or insignias issued by third parties promising replacement or refund if a consumer product is defective, which statements contain no representation or assurance of the quality or performance characteristics of the product; provided that (i) the disclosures required by § 701.3(a)(1) through (9) of this part are published by such third parties in each issue of a publication with a general circulation, and (ii) such disclosures are provided free of charge to any consumer upon written request.

(c) *Catalog and Mail Order Sales.* (1) For purposes of this paragraph:

(i) "Catalog or mail order sales", means any offer for sale, or any solicitation for an order for a consumer product with a written warranty, which includes instructions for ordering the product which do not require a personal visit to the seller's establishment.

(ii) "Close conjunction" means on the page containing the description of the warranted product, or on the page facing that page.

(2) Any seller who offers for sale to consumers consumer products with written warranties by means of a catalog or mail order solicitation shall:

(i) Clearly and conspicuously disclose in such catalog or solicitation in close conjunction to the description of warranted product, or in an information section of the catalog or solicitation clearly referenced, including a page number, in close conjunction to the description of the warranted product, *either:*

(A) The full text of the written warranty; or

(B) That the written warranty can be obtained free upon specific written request, and the address where such warranty can be obtained. If this option is elected, such seller shall promptly provide a copy of any written warranty requested by the consumer.

(d) *Door-to-door sales.* (1) For purposes of this paragraph:

(i) "Door-to-door sale" means a sale of consumer products in which the seller or his representative personally solicits the sale, including those in response to or following an invitation by a buyer, and the buyer's agreement to offer to purchase is made at a place other than the place of business of the seller.

(ii) "Prospective buyer" means an individual solicited by a door-to-door seller to buy a consumer product who indicates sufficient interest in that consumer product or maintains sufficient contact with the seller for the seller reasonably to conclude that the person solicited is considering purchasing the product.

(2) Any seller who offers for sale to consumers consumer products with written warranties by means of door-to-door sales shall, prior to the consummation of the sale, disclose the fact that the sales representative has copies of the warranties for the warranted products being offered for sale, which may be inspected by the prospective buyer at any time during the sales presentation. Such disclosure shall be made orally and shall be included in any written materials shown to prospective buyers.

PART 703. INFORMAL DISPUTE SETTLEMENT PROCEDURES

Table of Sections

---

§ 703.1 Definitions

(a) "The Act" means the Magnuson-Moss Warranty—Federal Trade Commission Improvement Act, 15 U.S.C. 2301, *et seq.*

(b) "Consumer product" means any tangible personal property which is distributed in commerce and which is normally used for personal, family, or household purposes (including any such property intended to be attached to or installed in any real property without regard to whether it is so attached or installed).

(c) "Written warranty" means:

(1) Any written affirmation of fact or written promise made in connection with the sale of a consumer product by a supplier to a buyer which relates to the nature of the material or workmanship and affirms or promises that such material or workmanship is defect free or will meet a specified level of performance over a specified period of time, or

(2) Any undertaking in writing in connection with the sale by a supplier of a consumer product to refund, repair, replace, or take other remedial action with respect to such product in the event that such product fails to meet the specifications set forth in the undertaking, which written affirmation, promise or undertaking becomes part of the basis of the bargain between a supplier and a buyer for purposes other than resale of such product.

(d) "Warrantor" means any person who gives or offers to give a written warranty which incorporates an informal dispute settlement mechanism.

(e) "Mechanism" means an informal dispute settlement procedure which is incorporated into the terms of a written warranty to which any provision of Title I of the Act applies, as provided in Section 110 of the Act.

(f) "Members" means the person or persons within a Mechanism actually deciding disputes.

(g) "Consumer" means a buyer (other than for purposes of resale) of any consumer product, any person to whom such product is transferred during the duration of a written warranty applicable to the product, and any other person who is entitled by the terms of such warranty or under applicable state law to enforce against the warrantor the obligations of the warranty.

(h) "On the face of the warranty" means:

(1) If the warranty is a single sheet with printing on both sides of the sheet, or if the warranty is comprised of more than one sheet, the page on which the warranty text begins;

(2) If the warranty is included as part of a longer document, such as a use and care manual, the page in such document on which the warranty text begins.

§ 703.2 Duties of warrantor

(a) The warrantor shall not incorporate into the terms of a written warranty a Mechanism that fails to comply with the requirements contained in §§ 703.3–703.8 of this part. This paragraph shall not prohibit a warrantor from incorporating into the terms of a written warranty the step-by-step procedure which the consumer should take in order to obtain performance of any obligation under the warranty as described in section 102(a)(7) of the Act and required by Part 701 of this subchapter.

(b) The warrantor shall disclose clearly and conspicuously at least the following information on the face of the written warranty:

(1) A statement of the availability of the informal dispute settlement mechanism;

(2) The name and address of the Mechanism, or the name and a telephone number of the Mechanism which consumers may use without charge;

(3) A statement of any requirement that the consumer resort to the Mechanism before exercising rights or seeking remedies created by Title I of the Act; together with the disclosure that if a consumer chooses to seek redress by pursuing rights and remedies not created by Title I of the Act, resort to the Mechanism would not be required by any provision of the Act; and

(4) A statement, if applicable, indicating where further information on the Mechanism can be found in materials accompanying the product, as provided in § 703.2(c) of this section.

(c) The warrantor shall include in the written warranty or in a separate section of materials accompanying the product, the following information:

(1) Either (i) a form addressed to the Mechanism containing spaces requesting the information which the Mechanism may require for prompt resolution of warranty disputes; or (ii) a telephone number of the Mechanism which consumers may use without charge;

(2) The name and address of the Mechanism;

(3) A brief description of Mechanism procedures;

(4) The time limits adhered to by the Mechanism; and

(5) The types of information which the Mechanism may require for prompt resolution of warranty disputes.

(d) The warrantor shall take steps reasonably calculated to make consumers aware of the Mechanism's existence at the time consumers experience warranty disputes. Nothing contained in paragraphs (b), (c), or (d) of this section shall limit the warrantor's option to encourage consumers to seek redress directly from the warrantor as long as the warrantor does not expressly require consumers to seek redress directly from the warrantor. The warrantor shall proceed fairly and expeditiously to attempt to resolve all disputes submitted directly to the warrantor.

(e) Whenever a dispute is submitted directly to the warrantor, the warrantor shall, within a reasonable time, decide whether, and to what extent, it will satisfy the consumer, and inform the consumer of its decision. In its notification to the consumer of its decision, the warrantor shall include the information required in § 703.2(b) and (c) of this section.

(f) The warrantor shall: (1) Respond fully and promptly to reasonble requests by the Mechanism for information relating to disputes;

(2) Upon notification of any decision of the Mechanism that would require action on the part of the warrantor, immediately notify the Mechanism whether, and to what extent, warrantor will abide by the decision; and

(3) Perform any obligations it has agreed to.

(g) The warrantor shall act in good faith in determining whether, and to what extent, it will abide by a Mechanism decision.

(h) The warrantor shall comply with any reasonable requirements imposed by the Mechanism to fairly and expeditiously resolve warranty disputes.

MINIMUM REQUIREMENTS OF THE MECHANISM

§ 703.3 Mechanism organization

(a) The Mechanism shall be funded and competently staffed at a level sufficient to ensure fair and expeditious resolution of all disputes, and shall not charge consumers any fee for use of the Mechanism.

(b) The warrantor and the sponsor of the Mechanism (if other than the warrantor) shall take all steps necessary to ensure that the Mechanism, and its members and staff, are sufficiently insulated from the warrantor and the sponsor, so that the decisions of the members and the performance of the staff are not influenced by either the warrantor or the sponsor. Necessary steps shall include, at a minimum, committing funds in advance, basing personnel decisions solely on merit, and not assigning conflicting warrantor or sponsor duties to Mechanism staff persons.

(c) The Mechanism shall impose any other reasonable requirements necessary to ensure that the members and staff act fairly and expeditiously in each dispute.

§ 703.4 Qualification of members

(a) No member deciding a dispute shall be: (1) A party to the dispute, or an employee or agent of a party other than for purposes of deciding disputes; or

(2) A person who is or may become a party in any legal action, including but not limited to class actions, relating to the product or complaint in dispute, or an employee or agent of such person other than for purposes of deciding disputes. For purposes of this paragraph (a) a person shall not be considered a "party" solely because he or she acquires or owns an interest in a party solely for investment, and the acquisition or ownership of an interest which is offered to the general public shall be prima facie evidence of its acquisition or ownership solely for investment.

(b) When one or two members are deciding a dispute, all shall be persons having no direct involvement in the manufacture, distribution, sale or service of any product. When three or more members are deciding a dispute, at least two-thirds shall be persons having no direct involvement in the manufacture, distribution, sale or service of any product. "Direct involvement" shall not include acquiring or owning an interest solely for investment, and the acquisition or ownership of an interest which is offered to the general public shall be prima facie evidence of its acquisition or ownership solely for investment. Nothing contained in this section shall prevent the members from consulting with any persons knowledgeable in the technical, commercial or other areas relating to the product which is the subject of the dispute.

(c) Members shall be persons interested in the fair and expeditious settlement of consumer disputes.

§ 703.5 Operation of the Mechanism

(a) The Mechanism shall establish written operating procedures which shall include at least those items specified in paragraphs (b) through (j) of this section. Copies of the written procedures shall be made available to any person upon request.

(b) Upon notification of a dispute, the Mechanism shall immediately inform both the warrantor and the consumer of receipt of the dispute.

(c) The Mechanism shall investigate, gather and organize all information necessary for a fair and expeditious decision in each dispute. When any evidence gathered by or submitted to the Mechanism raises issues relating to the number of repair attempts, the length of repair periods, the possibility of unreasonable use of the product, or any other issues relevant in light of Title I of the Act (or rules thereunder), including issues relating to consequential damages, or any other remedy under the Act (or rules thereunder), the Mechanism shall investigate these issues. When information which will or may be used in the decision, submitted by one party, or a consultant under § 703.4(b) of this part, or any other source tends to contradict facts submitted by the other party, the Mechanism shall clearly, accurately, and completely disclose to both parties the contradictory information (and its source) and shall provide both parties an opportunity to explain or rebut the information and to submit additional materials. The Mechanism shall not require any information not reasonably necessary to decide the dispute.

(d) If the dispute has not been settled, the Mechanism shall, as expeditiously as possible but at least within 40 days of notification of the dispute, except as provided in paragraph (e) of this section:

(1) Render a fair decision based on the information gathered as described in paragraph (c) of this section, and on any information submitted at an oral presentation which conforms to the requirements of paragraph (f) of this section (A decision shall include any remedies appropriate under the circumstances, including repair, replacement, refund, reimbursement for expenses, compensation for damages, and any other remedies available under the written warranty or the Act (or rules thereunder); and a decision shall state a specified reasonably time for performance);

(2) Disclose to the warrantor its decision and the reasons therefor;

(3) If the decision would require action on the part of the warrantor, determine whether, and to what extent, warrantor will abide by its decision; and

(4) Disclose to the consumer its decision, the reasons therefor, warrantor's intended actions (if the decision would require action on the part of the warrantor), and the information described in paragraph (g) of this section. For purposes of this paragraph (d) a dispute shall be deemed settled when the Mechanism has ascertained from the consumer that:

(i) The dispute has been settled to the consumer's satisfaction; and (ii) the settlement contains a specified reasonable time for performance.

(e) The Mechanism may delay the performance of its duties under paragraph (d) of this section beyond the 40 day time limit;

(1) Where the period of delay is due solely to failure of a consumer to provide promptly his or her name and address, brand name and model number of the product involved, and a statement as to the nature of the defect or other complaint; or

(2) For a 7 day period in those cases where the consumer has made no attempt to seek redress directly from the warrantor.

(f) The Mechanism may allow an oral presentation by a party to a dispute (or a party's representative) only if: (1) Both warrantor and consumer expressly agree to the presentation;

(2) Prior to agreement the Mechanism fully discloses to the consumer the following information:

(i) That the presentation by either party will take place only if both parties so agree, but that if they agree, and one party fails to appear at the agreed upon time and place, the presentation by the other party may still be allowed;

(ii) That the members will decide the dispute whether or not an oral presentation is made;

(iii) The proposed date, time and place for the presentation; and

(iv) A brief description of what will occur at the presentation including, if applicable, parties' rights to bring witnesses and/or counsel; and

(3) Each party has the right to be present during the other party's oral presentation. Nothing contained in this paragraph (b) of this section shall preclude the Mechanism from allowing an oral presentation by one party, if the other party fails to appear at the agreed upon time and place, as long as all of the requirements of this paragraph have been satisfied.

(g) The Mechanism shall inform the consumer, at the time of disclosure required in paragraph (d) of this section that:

(1) If he or she is dissatisfied with its decision or warrantor's intended actions, or eventual performance, legal remedies, including use of small claims court, may be pursued;

(2) The Mechanism's decision is admissible in evidence as provided in section 110(a)(3) of the Act; and

(3) The consumer may obtain, at reasonable cost, copies of all Mechanism records relating to the consumer's dispute.

(h) If the warrantor has agreed to perform any obligations, either as part of a settlement agreed to after notification to the Mechanism of the dispute or as a result of a decision under paragraph (d) of this section, the Mechanism shall ascertain from the consumer within 10 working days of the date for performance whether performance has occurred.

(i) A requirement that a consumer resort to the Mechanism prior to commencement of an action under section 110(d) of the Act shall be satisfied 40 days after notification to the Mechanism of the dispute or when the Mechanism completes all of its duties under paragraph (d) of this section, whichever occurs sooner. Except that, if the Mechanism delays performance of its paragraph (d) of this section duties as allowed by paragraph (e) of this section, the requirement that the consumer initially resort to the Mechanism shall not be satisfied until the period of delay allowed by paragraph (e) of this section has ended.

(j) Decisions of the Mechanism shall not be legally binding on any person. However, the warrantor shall act in good faith, as provided in § 703.2(g) of this part. In any civil action arising out of a warranty obligation and relating to a matter considered by the Mechanism, any decision of the Mechanism shall be admissible in evidence, as provided in section 110(a)(3) of the Act.

§ 703.6 Recordkeeping

(a) The Mechanism shall maintain records on each dispute referred to it which shall include:

(1) Name, address and telephone number of the consumer;

(2) Name, address, telephone number and contact person of the warrantor;

(3) Brand name and model number of the product involved;

(4) The date of receipt of the dispute and the date of disclosure to the consumer of the decision;

(5) All letters or other written documents submitted by either party;

(6) All other evidence collected by the Mechanism relating to the dispute, including summaries of relevant and material portions of telephone calls and meetings between the Mechanism and any other person (including consultants described in § 703.4(b) of this part);

(7) A summary of any relevant and material information presented by either party at an oral presentation;

(8) The decision of the members including information as to date, time and place of meeting, and the identity of members voting; or information on any other resolution;

(9) A copy of the disclosure to the parties of the decision;

(10) A statement of the warrantor's intended action(s);

(11) Copies of follow-up letters (or summaries of relevant and material portions of follow-up telephone calls) to the consumer, and responses thereto; and

(12) Any other documents and communications (or summaries of relevant and material portions of oral communications) relating to the dispute.

(b) The Mechanism shall maintain an index of each warrantor's disputes grouped under brand name and subgrouped under product model.

(c) The Mechanism shall maintain an index for each warrantor as will show:

(1) All disputes in which the warrantor has promised some performance (either by settlement or in response to a Mechanism decision) and has failed to comply; and

(2) All disputes in which the warrantor has refused to abide by a Mechanism decision.

(d) The Mechanism shall maintain an index as will show all disputes delayed beyond 40 days.

(e) The Mechanism shall compile semi-annually and maintain statistics which show the number and percent of disputes in each of the following categories:

(1) Resolved by staff of the Mechanism and warrantor has complied;

(2) Resolved by staff of the Mechanism, time for compliance has occurred, and warrantor has not complied;

(3) Resolved by staff of the Mechanism and time for compliance has not yet occurred;

(4) Decided by members and warrantor has complied;

(5) Decided by members, time for compliance has occurred, and warrantor has not complied;

(6) Decided by members and time for compliance has not yet occurred;

(7) Decided by members adverse to the consumer;

(8) No jurisdiction;

(9) Decision delayed beyond 40 days under § 703.5(e)(1) of this part;

(10) Decision delayed beyond 40 days under § 703.5(e)(2) of this part;

(11) Decision delayed beyond 40 days for any other reason; and

(12) Pending decision.

(f) The Mechanism shall retain all records specified in paragraphs (a) through (e) of this section for at least 4 years after final disposition of the dispute.

§ 703.7 Audits

(a) The Mechanism shall have an audit conducted at least annually, to determine whether the Mechanism and its implementation are in compliance with this part. All records of the Mechanism required to be kept under § 703.6 of this part shall be available for audit.

(b) Each audit provided for in paragraph (a) of this section shall include at a minimum the following:

(1) Evaluation of warrantors' efforts to make consumers aware of the Mechanism's existence as required in § 703.2(d) of this part;

(2) Review of the indexes maintained pursuant to § 703.6(b), (c), and (d) of this part; and

(3) Analysis of a random sample of disputes handled by the Mechanism to determine the following:

(i) Adequacy of the Mechanism's complaint and other forms, investigation, mediation and follow-up efforts, and other aspects of complaint handling; and

(ii) Accuracy of the Mechanism's statistical compilations under § 703.6(e) of this part. (For purposes of this subparagraph "analysis" shall include oral or written contact with the consumers involved in each of the disputes in the random sample.)

(c) A report of each audit under this section shall be submitted to the Federal Trade Commission, and shall be made available to any person at reasonable cost. The Mechanism may direct its auditor to delete names of parties to disputes, and identity of products involved, from the audit report.

(d) Auditors shall be selected by the Mechanism. No auditor may be involved with the Mechanism as a warrantor, sponsor or member, or employee or agent thereof, other than for purposes of the audit.

§ 703.8 Openness of records and proceedings

(a) The statistical summaries specified in § 703.6(e) of this part shall be available to any person for inspection and copying.

(b) Except as provided under paragraphs (a) and (e) of this section, and paragraph (c) of § 703.7 of this part, all records of the Mechanism may be kept confidential, or made available only on such terms and conditions, or in such form, as the Mechanism shall permit.

(c) The policy of the Mechanism with respect to records made available at the Mechanism's option shall be set out in the procedures under § 703.5(a) of this part; the policy shall be applied uniformly to all requests for access to or copies of such records.

(d) Meetings of the members to hear and decide disputes shall be open to observers on reasonable and nondiscriminatory terms. The identity of the parties and products involved in disputes need not be disclosed at meetings.

(e) Upon request the Mechanism shall provide to either party to a dispute:

(1) Access to all records relating to the dispute; and

(2) Copies of any records relating to the dispute, at reasonble cost.

(f) The Mechanism shall make available to any person upon request, information relating to the qualifications of Mechanism staff and members.

PART TWO. STATE STATUTES

DECEPTIVE PRACTICES ACTS (LITTLE–FTC ACTS)

New Jersey (N.J.Stat.Ann. § 56:8–2)
Massachusetts (Mass.Gen.Laws Ann. ch. 93A, § 2)
Oregon (Ore.Rev.Stat. § 646.608)
Uniform Consumer Sales Practices Act

NEW JERSEY

N.J.Stat.Ann. § 56:8–2

§ 56:8–2. Fraud, etc., in connection with sale or advertisement of merchandise or real estate as unlawful practice

The act, use or employment by any person of any unconscionable commercial practice, deception, fraud, false pretense, false promise, misrepresentation, or the knowing concealment, suppression, or omission of any material fact with intent that others rely upon such concealment, suppression or omission, in connection with the sale or advertisement of any merchandise or real estate, or with the subsequent performance of such person as aforesaid, whether or not any person has in fact been misled, deceived or damaged thereby, is declared to be an unlawful practice; provided, however, that nothing herein contained shall apply to the owner or publisher of newspapers, magazines, publications or printed matter wherein such advertisement appears, or to the owner or operator of a radio or television station which disseminates such advertisement when the owner, publisher, or operator has no knowledge of the intent, design or purpose of the advertiser.

MASSACHUSETTS

Mass.Gen.Laws Ann. ch. 93A, § 2

§ 2. Unfair Methods of Competition, etc., Declared Unlawful; Legislative Intent; Duties of Attorney General; etc.

(a) Unfair methods of competition and unfair or deceptive acts or practices in the conduct of any trade or commerce are hereby declared unlawful.

(b) It is the intent of the legislature that in construing paragraph (a) of this section in actions brought under sections four, nine and eleven, the courts will be guided by the interpretations given by the

Federal Trade Commission and the Federal Courts to section 5(a)(1) of the Federal Trade Commission Act (15 U.S.C. 45(a)(1)), as from time to time amended.

(c) The attorney general may make rules and regulations interpreting the provisions of subsection 2(a) of this chapter. Such rules and regulations shall not be inconsistent with the rules, regulations and decisions of the Federal Trade Commission and the Federal Courts interpreting the provisions of 15 U.S.C. 45(a)(1) (The Federal Trade Commission Act), as from time to time amended.

OREGON

Ore.Rev.Stat. § 646.608

§ 646.608 Unlawful business, trade practices; proof; Attorney General's rules

(1) A person engages in an unlawful practice when in the course of the person's business, vocation or occupation the person:

(a) Passes off real estate, goods or services as those of another;

(b) Causes likelihood of confusion or of misunderstanding as to the source, sponsorship, approval, or certification of real estate, goods or services;

(c) Causes likelihood of confusion or of misunderstanding as to affiliation, connection, or association with, or certification by, another;

(d) Uses deceptive representations or designations of geographic origin in connection with real estate, goods or services;

(e) Represents that real estate, goods or services have sponsorship, approval, characteristics, ingredients, uses, benefits, quantities or qualities that they do not have or that a person has a sponsorship, approval, status, qualification, affiliation, or connection that he does not have;

(f) Represents that real estate or goods are original or new if they are deteriorated, altered, reconditioned, reclaimed, used or secondhand;

(g) Represents that real estate, goods or services are of a particular standard, quality, or grade, or that real estate or goods are of a particular style or model, if they are of another;

(h) Disparages the real estate, goods, services, property or business of a customer or another by false or misleading representations of fact;

(i) Advertises real estate, goods or services with intent not to provide them as advertised, or with intent not to supply reasonably expectable public demand, unless the advertisement discloses a limitation of quantity;

(j) Makes false or misleading representations of fact concerning the reasons for, existence of, or amounts of price reductions;

(k) Makes false or misleading representations concerning credit availability or the nature of the transaction or obligation incurred;

(*l*) Makes false or misleading representations relating to commissions or other compensation to be paid in exchange for permitting real estate, goods or services to be used for model or demonstration purposes or in exchange for submitting names of potential customers;

(m) Performs service on or dismantles any goods or real estate when not authorized by the owner or apparent owner thereof;

(n) Solicits potential customers by telephone or door to door as a seller unless the person provides the information required under ORS 646.611;

(*o*) In a sale, rental or other disposition of real estate, goods or services, gives or offers to give a rebate or discount or otherwise pays or offers to pay value to the customer in consideration of the customer giving to the person the names of prospective purchasers, lessees, or borrowers, or otherwise aiding the person in making a sale, lease, or loan to another person, if earning the rebate, discount or other value is contingent upon occurrence of an event subsequent to the time the customer enters into the transaction;

(p) Makes any false or misleading statement about a prize, contest or promotion used to publicize a product, business or service;

(q) Promises to deliver real estate, goods or services within a certain period of time with intent not to deliver them as promised;

(r) Organizes or induces or attempts to induce membership in a pyramid club;

(s) Makes false or misleading representations of fact concerning the offering price of, or the person's cost for real estate, goods or services;

(t) Concurrent with tender or delivery of any real estate, goods or services fails to disclose any known material defect or material nonconformity; or

(u) Engages in any other unfair or deceptive conduct in trade or commerce.

(2) A representation under subsection (1) of this section . . . may be any manifestation of any assertion by words or conduct, including, but not limited to, a failure to disclose a fact.

(3) In order to prevail in an action or suit . . . a prosecuting attorney need not prove competition between the parties or actual confusion or misunderstanding.

(4) No action or suit shall be brought under paragraph (u) of subsection (1) of this section unless the Attorney General has first established a rule . . . declaring the conduct to be unfair or deceptive in trade or commerce.

UNIFORM CONSUMER SALES PRACTICES ACT

Table of Sections

---

§ 1. [Purposes, Rules of Construction]

This Act shall be construed liberally to promote the following policies:

(1) to simplify, clarify, and modernize the law governing consumer sales practices;

(2) to protect consumers from suppliers who commit deceptive and unconscionable sales practices;

(3) to encourage the development of fair consumer sales practices;

(4) to make state regulation of consumer sales practices not inconsistent with the policies of the Federal Trade Commission Act relating to consumer protection; and

(5) to make uniform the law, including the administrative rules, with respect to the subject of this Act among those states which enact it.

§ 2. [Definitions]

As used in this Act:

(1) "consumer transaction" means a sale, lease, assignment, award by chance, or other disposition of an item of goods, a service, or an intangible [except securities] to an individual for purposes that are primarily personal, family, or household, or that relate to a business opportunity that requires both his expenditure of money or property and his personal services on a continuing basis and in which he has not been previously engaged, or a solicitation by a supplier with respect to any of these dispositions;

(2) "Enforcing Authority" means [appropriate official or officials];

(3) "final judgment" means a judgment, including any supporting opinion, that determines the rights of the parties and concerning which appellate remedies have been exhausted or the time for appeal has expired;

(4) "person" means an individual, corporation, government, governmental subdivision or agency, business trust, estate, trust, partnership, association, cooperative, or any other legal entity;

(5) "supplier" means a seller, lessor, assignor, or other person who regularly solicits, engages in, or enforces consumer transactions, whether or not he deals directly with the consumer.

§ 3. [Deceptive Consumer Sales Practices]

(a) A deceptive act or practice by a supplier in connection with a consumer transaction violates this Act whether it occurs before, during, or after the transaction.

(b) Without limiting the scope of subsection (a), the act or practice of a supplier in indicating any of the following is deceptive:

(1) that the subject of a consumer transaction has sponsorship, approval, performance characteristics, accessories, uses, or benefits it does not have;

(2) that the subject of a consumer transaction is of a particular standard, quality, grade, style, or model, if it is not;

(3) that the subject of a consumer transaction is new, or unused, if it is not, or that the subject of a consumer transaction has been used to an extent that is materially different from the fact;

(4) that the subject of a consumer transaction is available to the consumer for a reason that does not exist;

(5) that the subject of a consumer transaction has been supplied in accordance with a previous representation, if it has not;

(6) that the subject of a consumer transaction will be supplied in greater quantity than the supplier intends;

(7) that replacement or repair is needed, if it is not;

(8) that a specific price advantage exists, if it does not;

(9) that the supplier has a sponsorship, approval, or affiliation he does not have;

(10) that a consumer transaction involves or does not involve a warranty, a disclaimer of warranties, particular warranty terms, or other rights, remedies, or obligations if the indication is false; or

(11) that the consumer will receive a rebate, discount, or other benefit as an inducement for entering into a consumer transaction in return for giving the supplier the names of prospective consumers or otherwise helping the supplier to enter into other consumer transactions, if receipt of the benefit is contingent on an event occurring after the consumer enters into the transaction.

§ 4. [Unconscionable Consumer Sales Practices]

(a) An unconscionable act or practice by a supplier in connection with a consumer transaction violates this Act whether it occurs before, during, or after the transaction.

(b) The unconscionability of an act or practice is a question of law for the court. If it is claimed or appears to the court that an act or practice may be unconscionable, the parties shall be given a reasonable opportunity to present evidence as to its setting, purpose and effect to aid the court in making its determination.

(c) In determining whether an act or practice is unconscionable, the court shall consider circumstances such as the following of which the supplier knew or had reason to know:

(1) that he took advantage of the inability of the consumer reasonably to protect his interests because of his physical infirmity, ignorance, illiteracy, inability to understand the language of an agreement, or similar factors;

(2) that when the consumer transaction was entered into the price grossly exceeded the price at which similar property or services were readily obtainable in similar transaction by like consumers;

(3) that when the consumer transaction was entered into the consumer was unable to receive a substantial benefit from the subject of the transaction;

(4) that when the consumer transaction was entered into there was no reasonable probability of payment of the obligation in full by the consumer;

(5) that the transaction he induced the consumer to enter into was excessively one-sided in favor of the supplier; or

(6) that he made a misleading statement of opinion on which the consumer was likely to rely to his detriment.

Commissioner's Comment

[Subsecs. (a) and (b)]. These subsections forbid unconscionable advertising techniques, unconscionable contract terms, and unconscionable debt collection practices. As under Uniform Commercial Code § 2–302 (1962 Official Text with Comments), unconscionability is a question of law for the court. Unconscionability typically involves conduct by which a supplier seeks to induce or to require a consumer to assume risks which materially exceed the benefits to him of a related consumer transaction.

[Subsecs. (c)]. "Knowledge or reason to know" often will be established by a supplier's course of conduct. Although probative, this scienter is not invariably required in order to establish unconscionability under § 4(a).

[Subsec. (c)(1)]. This subsection includes such conduct as selling an English-language encyclopedia set for personal use to a Spanish-American bachelor laborer who does not read English, or using legal verbiage in a manner which can not be readily comprehended by a low-income consumer who both reads and speaks English.

[Subsec. (c)(2)]. This subsection includes such conduct as a home solicitation sale of a set of cookware to a housewife for $375 in an area where a set of comparable quality is readily available to such a housewife for $125 or less.

[Subsec. (c)(3)]. This subsection includes such conduct as the sale of two expensive vacuum cleaners to two poor families whom the salesman knows, or has reason to know, share the same apartment and the same rug.

[Subsec. (c)(4)]. This subsection includes such conduct as the sale of goods, services, or intangibles to a low-income consumer whom the salesman knows, or has reason to know, does not have sufficient income to make the stipulated payments.

[Subsec. (c)(5)]. This subsection includes such conduct as requiring a consumer to sign a one-sided adhesion contract which contains a penalty clause, an acceleration clause, a confession-of-judgment clause, a disclaimer of all warranties, and a clause permitting the supplier, but not the consumer, to cancel the contract at will. As indicated by this illustration, this subsection applies to contract terms which result in an excessively one-sided consumer transaction even though some or all of the contract terms are lawful in and of themselves. The exemption from the Act by subsection 14(a)(1) of acts or practices required or specifically permitted by or under federal or state law should accordingly be reconciled with this subsection by exempting only required or specifically permitted aggregations of contract terms and required or specifically permitted contract terms.

[Subsec. (c)(6)]. This subsection applies to misleading subjective expressions of opinion on which a supplier should reasonably expect a consumer to rely to his detriment. For example, a violation of this subsection would occur if a prospective purchaser asked a supplier what the useful life of a paint job was and the supplier, with reason to know that repainting would be necessary within two years, responded, "in my opinion the paint will wear like iron." Overt factual misstatements expressed in the form of opinion are dealt with by § 3's proscription of deceptive consumer sales practices. For example, a violation of § 3 would occur if a prospective purchaser asked a supplier what the useful life of a two-year paint job was and the supplier responded, "in my opinion repainting will not be necessary for five years."

§ 4A. [Jurisdiction and Service of Process]

[(a) The [______] court of this state [may exercise] [has] jurisdiction over any supplier as to any act or practice in this State governed by this Act or as to any claim arising from a consumer transaction subject to this Act.]

[(b) In addition to any other method provided by [rule or] statute, personal jurisdiction over a supplier may be acquired in a civil action or proceeding instituted in the [______] court by the service of process in the following manner. If a supplier engages in any act or practice in this State governed by this Act, or engages in a consumer transaction subject to this Act, he may designate an agent upon whom service of process may be made in this State. The agent must be a resident of or a corporation authorized to do business in this State. The designation must be in writing and filed with the [Secretary of State]. If no designation is made and filed, or if process cannot be served in this State upon the designated agent, whether or not the supplier is a resident of this State or is authorized to do business in this State, process may be served upon the [Secretary of State], but service upon him is not effective unless the plaintiff promptly mails a copy of the process and pleadings by registered or certified mail to the defendant at his last reasonably ascertainable address. An affidavit of compliance with this section must be filed with the clerk of the court on or before the return day of the process, if any, or within any future time the court allows.]

Commissioners' Comment

[Subsec. (a)]. This optional subsection grants the courts of an enacting state jurisdiction with respect to violations of the Act. It may be omitted in states where an express statutory grant of judicial jurisdiction is unnecessary.

[Subsec. (b)]. This optional subsection provides a method for obtaining personal jurisdiction over out-of-state suppliers who have violated the Act. It may be omitted in states with comparable "long-arm" statutes.

§ 5. [Duties of the Enforcing Authority]

(A) The Enforcing Authority shall:

(1) enforce this Act throughout the State;

(2) cooperate with state and local officials, officials of other states, and officials of the Federal government in the administration of comparable statutes;

(3) inform consumers and suppliers on a continuing basis of the provisions of this Act and of acts or practices that violate this Act, including mailing information concerning final judgments to persons who request it, for which he may charge a reasonable fee to cover the expense;

(4) receive and act on complaints;

(5) maintain a public file of (i) final judgments rendered under this Act that have been either reported officially or made available for public dissemination under Section 5(a)(3), (ii) final consent judgments, and (iii), to the extent the Enforcing Authority considers appropriate, assurances of voluntary compliance; and

(6) report [annually on or before January 1] to the [Governor and Legislature] on the operations of his office and on the acts or practices occurring in this State that violate this Act.

(b) The Enforcing Authority's report shall include a statement of the investigatory and enforcement procedures and policies of his office, of the number of investigations and enforcement proceedings instituted and of their disposition, and of the other activities of his office and of other persons to carry out the purposes of this Act.

(c) In carrying out his duties, the Enforcing Authority may not publicly disclose the identity of a person investigated unless his identity has become a matter of public record in an enforcement proceeding or he has consented to public disclosure.

§ 6. [General Powers of the Enforcing Authority]

(a) The Enforcing Authority may conduct research, hold public hearings, make inquiries, and publish studies relating to consumer sales acts or practices.

(b) The Enforcing Authority shall adopt substantive rules that prohibit with specificity acts or practices that violate Section 3 and appropriate procedural rules.

§ 7. [Rule-making Requirements]

Alternative A

[The [State Administrative Procedure Act] applies to administrative action taken by the Enforcing Authority under this Act.]

Alternative B

[(a) In addition to complying with other rule-making requirements imposed by this Act, the Enforcing Authority shall:

(1) adopt as a rule a description of the organization of his office, stating the general course and method of operation of his office and methods whereby the public may obtain information or make submissions or requests;

(2) adopt rules of practice setting forth the nature and requirements of all formal and informal procedures available, including a description of the forms and instructions used by the Enforcing Authority or his office; and

(3) make available for public inspection all rules, written statements of policy, and interpretations formulated, adopted, or used by the Enforcing Authority in discharging his functions.

(b) A rule of the Enforcing Authority is invalid, and may not be invoked by the Enforcing Authority for any purpose, until it has been made available for public inspection under subsection (a). This provision does not apply to a person who has knowledge of a rule before engaging in an act or practice that violates this Act.]

Commissioners' Comment

Alternative A may be enacted in states that have administrative procedure acts. If a state does not have an administrative procedure act, Alternative B should be selected. The provisions in Alternative B and the accompanying optional §§ 7A–7E are derived from Uniform Consumer Credit Code §§ 6.403–408 (1969 Official Text with Comments).

§ 8. [Investigatory Powers of the Enforcing Authority]

(a) If, by his own inquiries or as a result of complaints, the Enforcing Authority has reason to believe that a person has engaged in, is engaging in, or is about to engage in an act or practice that violates this Act, he may administer oaths and affirmations, subpoena witnesses or matter, and collect evidence.

(b) If matter that the Enforcing Authority subpoenas is located outside this State, the person subpoenaed may either make it available to the Enforcing Authority at a convenient location within the State or pay the reasonable and necessary expenses for the Enforcing Authority or his representative to examine the matter at the place where it is located. The Enforcing Authority may designate representatives, including officials of the state in which the matter is located, to inspect the matter on his behalf, and he may respond to similar requests from officials of other states.

(c) Upon failure of a person without lawful excuse to obey a subpoena and upon reasonable notice to all persons affected, the Enforcing Authority may apply to the [______] court for an order compelling compliance.

(d) [After consultation with the Attorney General,] the Enforcing Authority may request that an individual who refuses to comply with a subpoena on the ground that testimony or matter may incriminate him be ordered by the court to provide the testimony or matter. Except in a prosecution for [perjury] [false swearing], an individual who complies with a court order to provide testimony or matter after asserting a privilege against self-incrimination to which he is entitled by law, may not be subjected to a criminal proceeding or to a civil penalty with respect to the transaction concerning which he is required to testify or produce relevant matter. This subsection does not apply to damages recoverable under Section 11(b) or to civil sanctions imposed under Section 9(a)(2).

§ 9. [Remedies of the Enforcing Authority]

(a) The Enforcing Authority may bring an action:

(1) to obtain a declaratory judgment that an act or practice violates this Act; or

(2) to enjoin, in accordance with the principles of equity, a supplier who has violated, is violating, or is otherwise likely to violate this Act;

(3) to recover actual damages, or obtain relief under subsection (b)(2), on behalf of consumers who complained to the Enforcing Authority before he instituted enforcement proceedings under this Act.

(b)(1) The Enforcing Authority may bring a class action on behalf of consumers for the actual damages caused by an act or practice specified as violating this Act in a rule adopted by the Enforcing Authority under Section 6(b) before the consumer transactions on which the action is based, or declared to violate Section 3 or 4 by final judgment of [insert the appropriate court or courts of general jurisdiction and appellate courts] of this State that was either reported officially or made available for public dissemination under Section 5(a)(3) by the Enforcing Authority [10] days before the consumer transactions on which the action is based, or, with respect to a supplier who agreed to it, was prohibited specifically by the terms of a consent judgment that became final before the consumer transactions on which the action is based.

(2) On motion of the Enforcing Authority and without bond in an action under this subsection, the court may make appropriate orders, including appointment of a master or receiver or sequestration of assets, to reimburse consumers found to have been damaged, or to carry out a transaction in accordance with consumers' reasonable expectations, or to strike or limit the application of unconscionable clauses of contracts to avoid an unconscionable result, or to grant other ap-

propriate relief. The court may assess the expenses of a master or receiver against a supplier.

(3) If a supplier shows by a preponderance of the evidence that a violation of this Act resulted from a bona fide error notwithstanding the maintenance of procedures reasonably adapted to avoid the error, recovery under Section 9(b) is limited to the amount, if any, by which the supplier was unjustly enriched by the violation.

(4) If an act or practice that violates this Act unjustly enriches a supplier and damages can be computed with reasonable certainty, damages recoverable on behalf of consumers who cannot be located with due diligence [shall escheat to the State] [shall be allocated under the Uniform Disposition of Unclaimed Property Act].

(5) No action may be brought by the Enforcing Authority under this subsection more than 2 years after the occurrence of a violation of this Act, or more than one year after the last payment in a consumer transaction involved in a violation of this Act, whichever is later.

(c) The Enforcing Authority may terminate an investigation or an action other than a class action upon acceptance of a supplier's written assurance of voluntary compliance with this Act. Acceptance of an assurance may be conditioned on a commitment to reimburse consumers or take other appropriate corrective action. An assurance is not evidence of a prior violation of this Act. However, unless an assurance has been rescinded by agreement of the parties or voided by a court for good cause, subsequent failure to comply with the terms of an assurance is prima facie evidence of a violation of this Act.

§ 10. [Coordination With Other Supervision]

(a) If the Enforcing Authority receives a complaint or other information relating to noncompliance with this Act by a supplier who is subject to other supervision in this State, the Enforcing Authority shall inform the official or agency having that supervision. The Enforcing Authority may request information about such suppliers from the official or agency.

(b) The Enforcing Authority and any other official or agency in this State having supervisory authority over a supplier shall consult and assist each other in maintaining compliance with this Act. Within the scope of their authority, they may jointly or separately make investigations, prosecute suits, and take other official action they consider appropriate.

§ 11. [Private Remedies]

(a) Whether he seeks or is entitled to damages or has an adequate remedy at law, a consumer may bring an action to:

(1) obtain a declaratory judgment that an act or practice violates this Act; or

(2) enjoin, in accordance with the principles of equity, a supplier who has violated, is violating, or is otherwise likely to violate this Act.

(b) Except in a class action, a consumer who suffers loss as a result of a violation of this Act may recover actual damages or [$100], whichever is greater.

(c) Whether a consumer seeks or is entitled to recover damages or has an adequate remedy at law, he may bring a class action for declaratory judgment, an injunction, and appropriate ancillary relief, except damages, against an act or practice that violates this Act.

(d)(1) A consumer who suffers loss as a result of a violation of this Act may bring a class action for the actual damages caused by an act or practice (i) specified as violating this Act in a rule adopted by the Enforcing Authority under Section 6(b) before the consumer transactions on which the action is based, or (ii) declared to violate Section 3 or 4 by a final judgment of [insert the appropriate court or courts of general jurisdiction and appellate courts] of this State that was either reported officially or made available for public dissemination under Section 5(a)(3) by the Enforcing Authority [10] days before the consumer transaction on which the action is based, or (iii) with respect to a supplier who agreed to it, was prohibited specifically by the terms of a consent judgment which became final before the consumer transactions on which the action is based.

(2) If a supplier shows by a preponderance of the evidence that a violation of this Act resulted from a bona fide error notwithstanding the maintenance of procedures reasonably adapted to avoid the error, recovery under this section is limited to the amount, if any, by which the supplier was unjustly enriched by the violation.

(3) If an act or practice that violates this Act unjustly enriches a supplier and the damages can be computed with reasonable certainty, damages recoverable on behalf of consumers who cannot be located with due diligence [shall escheat to the State] [shall be allocated under the Uniform Disposition of Unclaimed Property Act].

(e) Except for services performed by the Enforcing Authority, the court may award to the prevailing party a reasonable attorney's fee limited to the work reasonably performed if:

(1) the consumer complaining of the act or practice that violates this Act has brought or maintained an action he knew to be ground-

less; or a supplier has committed an act or practice that violates this Act; and

(2) an action under this section has been terminated by a judgment or required by the court to be settled under Section 13(a).

(f) Except for consent judgments entered before testimony is taken, a final judgment in favor of the Enforcing Authority under Section 9 is admissible as prima facie evidence of the facts on which it is based in later proceedings under this section against the same person or a person in privity with him.

(g) When a judgment under this section becomes final, the prevailing party shall mail a copy to the Enforcing Authority for inclusion in the public file maintained under Section 5(a)(5).

(h) An action under this section must be brought within 2 years after occurrence of a violation of this Act, within one year after the last payment in a consumer transaction involved in a violation of this Act, or within one year after the termination of proceedings by the Enforcing Authority with respect to a violation of this Act, whichever is later. However, when a supplier sues a consumer, he may assert as a counterclaim any claim under this Act arising out of the transaction on which suit is brought.

§ 12. [Class Actions]

(a) An action may be maintained as a class action under this Act only if:

(1) the class is so numerous that joinder of all members is impracticable;

(2) there are questions of law or fact common to the class;

(3) the claims or defenses of the representative parties are typical of the claims or defenses of the class;

(4) the representative parties will fairly and adequately protect the interests of the class; and

(5) either:

(A) the prosecution of separate actions by or against individual members of the class would create a risk of:

(i) inconsistent or varying adjudications with respect to individual members of the class which would establish incompatible standards of conduct for the party opposing the class; or

(ii) adjudications with respect to individual members of the class which would as a practical matter be dispositive of the interests of the other members not parties to the adjudications or substantially impair or impede their ability to protect their interests; or

(B) the party opposing the class has acted or refused to act on grounds generally applicable to the class, thereby making appropriate final injunctive relief or corresponding declaratory relief with respect to the class as a whole; or

(C) the court finds that the questions of law or fact common to the members of the class predominate over any questions affecting only individual members, and that a class action is superior to other available methods for the fair and efficient adjudication of the controversy.

(b) The matters pertinent to the findings under subsection (a)(5)(C) include:

(1) the interest of members of the class in individually controlling the prosecution or defense of separate actions;

(2) the extent and nature of any litigation concerning the controversy already commenced by or against members of the class;

(3) the desirability or undesirability of concentrating the litigation of the claims in the particular forum; and

(4) the difficulties likely to be encountered in the management of a class action.

(c) As soon as practicable after the commencement of an action brought as a class action, the court shall determine by order whether it is to be so maintained. An order under this subsection may be conditional, and may be amended before the decision on the merits.

(d) In a class action maintained under subsection (a)(5)(C) the court may direct to the members of the class the best notice practicable under the circumstances, including individual notice to all members who can be identified through reasonable effort. The notice shall advise each member that:

(1) the court will exclude him from the class, if he so requests by a specified date;

(2) the judgment, whether favorable or not, will include all members who do not request exclusion; and

(3) any member who does not request exclusion may, if he desires, enter an appearance through his counsel.

(e) When appropriate, an action may be brought or maintained as a class action with respect to particular issues, or a class may be divided into subclasses and each subclass treated as a class.

(f) In the conduct of a class action the court may make appropriate orders:

(1) determining the course of proceedings or prescribing measures to prevent undue repetition or complication in the presentation of evidence or argument;

(2) requiring, for the protection of the members of the class or otherwise for the fair conduct of the action, that notice be given in the manner the court directs to some or all of the members or to the Enforcing Authority of any step in the action, or of the proposed extent of the judgment, or of the opportunity of members to signify whether they consider the representation fair and adequate, to intervene and present claims or defenses, or otherwise to come into the action;

(3) imposing conditions on the representative parties or on intervenors;

(4) requiring that the pleadings be amended to eliminate allegations as to representation of absent persons, and that the action proceed accordingly; or

(5) dealing with similar procedural matters.

(g) A class action shall not be dismissed or compromised without approval of the court. Notice of the proposed dismissal or compromise shall be given to all members of the class in such manner as the court directs.

(h) The judgment in an action maintained as a class action under subsection (a)(5)(A) or (B), whether or not favorable to the class, shall describe those whom the court finds to be members of the class. The judgment in a class action maintained under subsection (a)(5)(C), whether or not favorable to the class, shall specify or describe those to whom the notice provided in subsection (d) was directed, and who have not requested exclusion, and whom the court finds to be members of the class.

Commissioners' Comment

In order to facilitate its administration, this section is modeled closely on Federal Rule of Civil Procedure 23. The principal substantive deviation from the federal approach appears in § 12(d). Unlike its federal counterpart, § 12(d) allows a court discretion with respect to providing class members notice of an opportunity to exclude themselves from class actions based on the existence of common questions of law or fact. On the other hand, like the federal rule, § 12 permits actions against a class of defendants as well as actions on behalf of a plaintiff-class.

§ 13. [Special Provisions Relating to Class Actions]

(a)(1) A defendant in a class action may file a written offer of settlement. If it is not accepted within a reasonable time by a plaintiff class representative, the defendant may file an affidavit reciting the rejection. The court may determine that the offer has enough merit to present to the members of the class. If is so determines, it shall order a hearing to determine whether the offer should be approved. It shall give the best notice of the hearing that is practicable under the circumstances, including notice to each member who can be identified through reasonable effort. The notice shall specify the terms of the offer and a reasonable period within which members of the class who request it are entitled to be excluded from the class. The statute of limitations for those who are excluded pursuant to this subsection is tolled for the period the class action has been pending, plus an additional year.

(2) If a member who has previously lost an opportunity to be excluded from the class is excluded at his request in response to notice of the offer of settlement during the period specified under paragraph (1), he may not thereafter participate in a class action respecting the same consumer transaction, unless the court later disapproves the offer of settlement or approves a settlement materially different from that proposed in the original offer of settlement. After the expiration of the period specified under paragraph (1), a member of the class is not entitled to be excluded from it.

(3) If the court later approves the offer of settlement, including changes, if any, required by the court in the interest of a just settlement of the action, it shall enter a judgment, which is binding on all persons who are then members of the class. If the court disapproves the offer or approves a settlement materially different from that proposed in the original offer, notice shall be given to a person who was excluded from the action at his request in response to notice of the offer under paragraph (1) that he is entitled to rejoin the class, and, in the case of approval, participate in the settlement.

(b) On the commencement of a class action under Section 11, the class representative shall mail by certified mail with return receipt requested or personally serve a copy of the complaint on the Enforcing Authority. Within 30 days after the receipt of a copy of the complaint, but not thereafter, the Enforcing Authority may intervene in the class action.

Commissioners' Comment

This section permits a court in its discretion to require settlement of actions that have been brought on behalf of a plaintiff-class. In order to do so, the court must notify individual class members of an opportunity to exclude themselves from the settlement proceedings. As long as they have not had a prior opportunity to exclude themselves from a class action under § 12, persons who exclude themselves from a class action under § 13(a) thereafter can maintain either class or individual actions with respect to the same consumer transaction. However, with the two exceptions noted in § 13(a)(2) and (3), persons who have had a prior opportunity to exclude themselves under § 12 and later exclude themselves under § 13(a) thereafter can maintain only individual actions with respect to the same consumer transaction. If the court determines that a supplier has avoided a finding that he violated this

Act by resort to § 13, the court may award a reasonable attorney's fee to the representative of the consumer class, § 11(e).

. . .

§ 14. [Application]

(a) This Act does not apply to:

(1) an act or practice required or specifically permitted by or under Federal law, or by or under State law;

(2) a publisher, broadcaster, printer, or other person engaged in the dissemination of information or the reproduction of printed or pictorial matter insofar as the information or matter has been disseminated or reproduced on behalf of others without actual knowledge that it violated this Act;

(3) a claim for personal injury or death or a claim for damage to property other than the property that is the subject of the consumer transaction; or

(4) the credit terms of a transaction otherwise subject to this Act.

(b) A person alleged to have violated this Act has the burden of showing the applicability of this Section.

Commissioners' Comment

. . .

[Subsec. (a)(3)]. This subsection has primary application to product liability claims. To the extent that joinder is appropriate, it does not bar the joinder of a product liability claim with a related claim for violation of this Act, § 15.

[Subsec. (a)(4)]. This subsection exempts only the credit terms of a consumer transaction. For example, advertising and contractual provisions with respect to the finance charge in a consumer transaction would be exempt, but advertising and contractual provisions with respect to the nature or quality of the subject of a consumer transaction would not be exempt.

. . .

§ 15. [Effect on Other Remedies]

The remedies of this Act are in addition to remedies otherwise available for the same conduct under state or local law, except that a class action relating to a transaction governed by this Act may be brought only as prescribed by this Act.

*

RETAIL INSTALLMENT SALES ACT

N.J.Stat.Ann. §§ 17:16C–1 to 16C–61

Table of Sections

---

§ 17:16C–1. Definitions

In this act, unless the context otherwise requires, the following words and terms shall have the following meanings:

(a) "Goods" means all chattels personal which are primarily for personal, family or household purposes, including merchandise certificates and coupons to be exchanged for goods or services, having a cash price of $10,000.00 or less, but not including money or other choses in action. Goods shall not include chattels personal sold for commercial or business use.

(b) "Retail installment contract" means any contract, other than a retail charge account or an instrument reflecting a sale pursuant thereto, entered into in this State between a retail seller and a retail buyer evidencing an agreement to pay the retail purchase price of goods or services, which are primarily for personal, family or household purposes, or any part thereof, in two or more installments over a period of time. This term includes a security agreement, chattel mortgage, conditional sales contract, or other similar instrument and any contract for the bailment or leasing of goods by which the bailee or lessee agrees to pay as compensation a sum substantially equivalent to or in excess of the value of the goods, and by which it is agreed that the bailee or lessee is bound to become, or has the option of becoming, the owner of such goods upon full compliance with the terms of such retail installment contract.

(c) "Retail seller" means a person who sells or agrees to sell goods or services under a retail installment contract or a retail charge account to a retail buyer, and shall include a motor vehicle installment seller.

(d) "Retail buyer" means a person who buys or agrees to buy goods or services from a retail seller, not for the purpose of resale, pursuant to a retail installment contract or a retail charge account.

(e) "Person" means an individual, partnership, firm, corporation, banking institution, association or any other group of individuals however organized.

(f) "Sales finance company" means and includes any person engaging in this State in the business of acquiring or arranging for the acquisition of retail installment contracts or obligations incurred pursuant to retail charge accounts by purchase, discount, pledge or otherwise from a retail seller which is not wholly owned by or does not wholly own such person, and any person engaging, directly or indirectly, in the business of soliciting the purchase of retail installment contracts or obligations incurred pursuant to retail charge accounts from a retail seller which is not wholly owned by or does not wholly own such person, or in the business of aiding the retail seller in selling, assigning or arranging for the sale or assignment of retail installment contracts or obligations incurred pursuant to retail charge accounts, and any person other than a retail seller who enters into a retail charge account with a retail buyer.

(g) "Motor vehicle" includes all vehicles used for transportation upon a highway propelled otherwise than by muscular power, excepting such vehicles as run only upon rails or tracks.

(h) "Motor vehicle installment seller" means a dealer in motor vehicles, who is required to be licensed under chapter 10 of Title 39 of the Revised Statutes and who sells or offers to sell a motor vehicle to a retail buyer under a retail installment contract.

(i) "Cash price" means the minimum price for which the goods or services subject to a retail installment contract or a retail charge account or other goods or services of like kind and quality may be purchased for cash from the seller by the buyer, as stated in the retail installment contract, the retail charge account or an instrument reflecting a sale pursuant thereto.

(j) "Down payment" means all payments made in cash or in goods or partly in cash and partly in goods, received by the retail seller prior to or substantially contemporaneous with either the execution of the retail installment contract or the delivery of the goods, whichever occurs later.

(k) "Official fees" means the filing or other fees required by law to be paid to a public officer to perfect an interest or lien, on the goods, retained or taken by a retail seller under a retail installment contract and motor vehicle license and transfer fees paid to the State.

(*l*) "Time price differential" means the amount or amounts, however denominated or computed, in addition to the cash price or prices, to be paid by the retail buyer for the privilege of purchasing goods or services pursuant to a retail installment contract or a retail charge account. The term does not include the amount, if a separate charge is made therefor, for insurance and official fees.

(m) "Holder" means any person, including a retail seller, who is entitled to the rights of a retail seller under a retail installment contract or retail charge account.

(n) "Banking institution" means any bank, national banking association, savings bank, or Federally chartered savings bank authorized to do business in this State, and for the purposes of this act only, an association as defined in section 5 of the "Savings and Loan Act (1963)" P.L.1963, c. 144 (c. 17:12B–5).

(*o*) "Commissioner" means the Commissioner of Banking of New Jersey and includes his deputies or any salaried employee of the Department of Banking named or appointed by the said commissioner to perform any function in the administration or enforcement of this act.

(p) "Payment-period" means the period of time scheduled by a retail installment contract to elapse between the days upon which installment payments are scheduled to be made on such contract; except that, when installment payments are scheduled to be omitted, pursuant to section 26, "payment-period" means the period of time scheduled by the contract to elapse between the days upon which installment payments are scheduled to be made during that portion of the contract period in which no installment payment is scheduled to be omitted.

(q) "Contract period" means the period beginning on the date of a retail installment contract and ending on the date scheduled by the contract for the payment of the final installment.

(r) "Retail charge account" means any account, other than a retail installment contract or a home repair contract which is subject to the "Home Repair Financing Act" (P.L.1960, c. 41; C. 17:16C–62 et seq.), established by an agreement which prescribes the terms under which a retail buyer may from time to time purchase or lease goods or services which are primarily for personal, family or household purposes, and under which the unpaid balance thereunder, whenever incurred, is payable in one or more installments and under which a time price differential may be added in each billing period as provided herein. Retail charge account also includes all accounts arising out of the utilization by the holder of a credit card, letter of credit or other credit identification issued by a sales finance company, giving the holder the privilege of using the credit card, letter of credit or other credit identification to become a retail buyer in transactions out of which debt arises: (1) by the sales finance company's payment or agreement to pay the retail buyer's obligations; or (2) by the sales finance company's purchase from the retail seller of the obligations of the user of the credit card, letter of credit or other credit identification as a retail buyer.

(s) "Services" means and includes work, labor and services, professional and otherwise which are primarily for personal, family or household purposes but does not include services which are subject to the "Home Repair Financing Act," and insurance premiums financing which is subject to the "Insurance Premium Finance Company Act" (P.L.1968, c. 221; C. 17:16D–1 et seq.).

(t) "Billing period" means the time interval between regular periodic billing statement dates. In the case of monthly billing periods, such intervals shall be considered equal intervals of time if the billing date of a billing period does not vary more than 4 days from the billing date of the immediately preceding billing period. In the case of billing periods which are not monthly, the permissible variation in billing dates shall be that proportion of 4 days (adjusted to the nearest whole number) which the number of days in the billing period bears to 30.

(u) "Professional services" means services rendered or performed by a person authorized by law to practice a recognized profession whose practice is regulated by law and the performance of which services requires knowledge of an advanced type in a field of learning acquired by a prolonged formal course of specialized instruction and study as distinguished from general academic instruction or apprenticeship and training.

§ 17:16C–2. Necessity of license

No person shall hereafter engage in or continue to engage in the business of a sales finance company or in the business of a motor vehicle installment seller in this State without first obtaining a license from the commissioner as provided for in this act; provided, however, that no sales finance company shall be required to obtain a license to engage in the business of a motor vehicle installment seller for the purpose of disposing of any goods to which it has obtained title as a result of legal or contract right under any retail installment contract; and provided, further, that any banking institution authorized to do business in this State shall be authorized to transact business as a sales finance company, subject to all of the provisions of this act, except that it shall not be required to obtain a license or pay a license fee hereunder.

§ 17:16C–4. Issuance or refusal of license

Within 60 days after the filing of the application and the payment of the fees hereinafter set forth the commissioner shall either:

(a) Issue and deliver to the applicant a license to engage in the business of a sales finance company or a motor vehicle installment seller in accordance with the provisions of this act at the location specified in the said application; or

(b) Refuse to issue the license for any reason for which he may suspend, revoke or refuse to renew any license under section 10 of this act.

§ 17:16C–10. Suspension, revocation or refusal to renew license; notice; grounds

The commissioner may suspend, revoke or refuse to renew any license issued hereunder, upon 10 days' notice in writing, forwarded by registered or certified mail to the principal place of business of such licensee, stating the contemplated action and in general the grounds therefor, and after reasonable opportunity to be heard, if he shall find that the licensee or any owner, director, officer, member, partner, employee or agent of such licensee has:

(a) Made any material misstatement in the application;

(b) Knowingly or without the exercise of due care failed to comply with or violated any provisions of this or any other act relating to retail installment contracts or retail charge accounts;

(c) Defrauded any retail buyer or willfully failed to perform any written agreement with any retail buyer;

(d) Willfully misrepresented or failed to disclose any of the material particulars or the nature thereof required to be stated or furnished to the retail buyer under this act or any other laws of this State relating to retail installment contracts or retail charge accounts;

(e) Knowingly taken any instrument evidencing a retail installment contract which was signed in blank; or

(f) Otherwise demonstrated unworthiness, bad faith or dishonesty.

No license issued under this act to a motor vehicle installment seller shall be valid unless such seller is the holder of a valid and subsisting license issued pursuant to chapter 10 of Title 39 of the Revised Statutes.

§ 17:16C–11. Suspension, revocation or refusal to renew particular license or all licenses issued to licensee

The commissioner may suspend, revoke or refuse to renew the particular license with respect to which grounds for revocation, suspension or refusal to renew may occur or exist, or, if he finds that such grounds for suspension or revocation are of general application to all offices, or more than 1 office, operated by the licensee, he may revoke, suspend or refuse to renew all of the licenses issued to the licensee or such number of licenses as such grounds apply to, as the case may be.

§ 17:16C–15. Investigations by commissioner

The commissioner, if he has reasonable cause to believe that any licensee, or any other person, has violated any of the provisions of this act or of any other law relating to retail installment sales or contracts, shall have the power to make such investigations as he shall deem necessary, and may examine the books, accounts, records and files of such licensee or any other such person believed to have violated this act or any other law relating to retail installment sales or contracts.

§ 17:16C–16. Subpoenas; oaths and affirmations, power to administer

The commissioner shall have power to issue subpoenas to compel the attendance of witnesses and the production of documents, papers, books, records and other evidence before him in any matter over which he has jurisdiction, control or supervision pertaining to this act. The commissioner shall have the power to administer oaths and affirmations to any person whose testimony is required.

§ 17:16C–18. Maintenance of books, accounts and records

Every retail seller, sales finance company and holder shall maintain at its place or places of business in this State such books, accounts and records relating to all transactions within this act as will enable the commissioner to enforce full compliance with the provisions of this act.

§ 17:16C–20. Information to be shown in books, accounts and records

The commissioner is hereby authorized to prescribe the minimum information to be shown in such books, accounts and records of the licensee so that such records will enable the commissioner to determine compliance with the provisions of this act.

§ 17:16C–21. Retail installment contract; writing required; agreements between retail buyer and seller; signatures

Every retail installment contract shall be in writing and shall contain all of the agreements between the retail buyer and retail seller relating to the installment sale of the goods purchased and shall be signed both by the retail buyer and the retail seller.

§ 17:16C–22. Contents of retail installment contract; blank spaces

Every retail installment contract shall state the names and addresses of all parties thereto, the date when signed by the retail buyer, and shall contain a description of the goods sold which shall be sufficient for identification. No retail installment contract shall be signed by any party thereto when such contract contains blank spaces to be filled in after such contract has been signed; however, this provision shall not apply to serial numbers or other identifying marks which are not available for the description of the goods at the time of the execution of the contract.

§ 17:16C–23. Copy of contract to be furnished to buyer

A copy of the retail installment contract shall be furnished by the retail seller to the retail buyer at the time the retail buyer signs the contract except that such copy need not contain the signature of the retail seller. Such copy shall be furnished the retail buyer without charge.

§ 17:16C–24. Notice to buyer in retail installment contract

Every retail installment contract shall contain the following notice printed prominently, in the form herein indicated, in 10-point bold type or larger, directly above the notice required by section 25:

"NOTICE TO RETAIL BUYER

Do not sign this contract in blank.

You are entitled to a copy of the contract at the time you sign.

Keep it to protect your legal rights."

§ 17:16C–25. Acknowledgment by buyer of receipt of copy of contract

Any acknowledgment by the retail buyer of receipt of a copy of the contract shall be printed or written in a size equal to at least 10-point bold type and, if contained in the contract, shall appear directly above the space provided in the contract form for the signature of the retail buyer.

§ 17:16C–26. Payment of time balance in substantially equal amounts on dates separated by substantially equal payment-periods; exceptions

Every retail installment contract shall provide for the payment of the time balance in substantially equal amounts on dates separated by substantially equal payment-periods; except that the retail seller may defer the initial installment for a period of 60 days or for a period of 180 days on seasonal goods sold out of season; and, provided, further, that when appropriate for the purpose of facilitating payment, in accordance with a retail buyer's intermittent income, a contract may provide for payment on a schedule which reduces or omits payments over a period or periods not in excess of 93 days in any 12-month period or a contract may provide an installment schedule which reduces or omits payments over any period or periods of time during which period or periods the retail buyer's income is reduced or suspended. When a retail installment contract provides for unequal or irregular installments, the time price differential shall not exceed the effective rate provided in section 41, having due regard for the schedule of installments. When in any retail installment contract the purchase of goods is combined with the purchase of food, the time balance on which is stated as one amount, that part of the time balance on the sale of goods shall be subject to the provisions of this section, but that part of the time balance on the purchase of food may be payable in a shorter time and added to the equal payment installment on goods.

§ 17:16C–27. Separate items to be set forth in retail installment contract

Every retail installment contract shall set forth the following separate items:

(a) The cash price of the goods which are the subject matter of the retail installment contract;

(b) The down payment made by the retail buyer, indicating whether made in cash or in goods or partly in cash and partly in goods. The amount of the payment in cash and in goods shall be shown separately. A description of the goods, if any, sufficient for identification, shall be shown;

(c) The unpaid cash balance which shall be the difference between the cash price (subsection (a)) and the down payment (subsection (b));

(d) The amount, if any, if a separate charge is made therefor, included for insurance and other benefits, specifying the coverages and benefits;

(e) The amount of official fees;

(f) The principal balance, which is the sum of subsections (c), (d) and (e);

(g) The amount of the time price differential;

(h) The time balance, which is the sum of subsections (f) and (g), owed by the retail buyer to the retail seller, the number of installments required, the amount of each installment expressed in dollars and the due date or period thereof;

(i) The time sales price, which is the sum of subsections (b) and (h).

§ 17:16C–28. Inclusion in retail installment contract of additional goods purchased after original agreement; additional statements

Whenever a retail installment contract by its terms permits the inclusion of additional goods purchased after the original agreement, and such goods are so purchased and the amount due on the new purchase is combined with an unpaid balance on any prior purchase so as to permit the retail seller to retain title to or reserve a lien upon all goods under the combined agreement, the retail seller shall, at the time of the additional purchase, deliver to the retail buyer and attach to the original agreement:

(a) A statement containing all the information with respect to the additional purchase required to be included in a retail installment contract; and

(b) A statement showing the amount due on the agreement immediately previous to the new purchase, the amount due after the new purchase, the payments agreed to be made thereafter, and the number of additional months required to complete the payments.

§ 17:16C–29. Allocation of payment on continuing agreement after addition of additional purchases; prepayment; redemption of separate purchases

Whenever a payment is made on such a continuing agreement after additional purchases have been added, the payment shall be considered as allocated among each of the separate purchases included, in full to the purchase made earliest in time, and the retail seller before repossessing or attempting to repossess any goods under any such agreement shall actually allocate in such manner all such payments made to him by the retail buyer. When the amount owing on any separate purchase has been fully paid, the goods so paid for shall become the absolute property of the retail buyer and shall not be subject to repossession for any subsequent default on the agreement. The retail buyer under any such agreement may at any time prepay the amount due on any of the separate purchases and in case of repossession may redeem any of such separate purchases by payment of the amount due on such purchase alone.

§ 17:16C–30. Insurance at retail buyer's expense; dual protection

Where title to or a lien upon goods sold by the retail seller is retained or taken by the retail seller the retail buyer may be required to insure the goods at the retail buyer's expense for the protection of the retail seller or subsequent holder which insurance may be purchased by the holder. Such insurance shall be written for the dual protection of the retail buyer and the retail seller or subsequent holder to the extent of his interest in the goods and shall be limited to insurance against substantial risk of damage, destruction, or theft of such goods and shall be upon terms and conditions, which are reasonable and appropriate, considering the type and conditions of such goods. When the retail buyer fails or is unable to acquire insurance or the retail seller or subsequent holder is unable to purchase insurance covering the dual protection of the retail buyer and retail seller or subsequent holder, the retail seller or holder may purchase a single interest insurance policy on the goods and may collect the premium therefor from the retail buyer.

§ 17:16C–31. Selection of insurer acceptable to retail seller; inclusion of premium in contract; cancellation of insurance by holder after repossession and sale

The retail buyer shall have the privilege of supplying insurance on the goods through an agent or broker of his own selection and selecting an insurance company acceptable to the retail seller; provided, however, the inclusion of the premium for such insurance in the retail installment contract, when the retail buyer selects the company, agent or broker, shall be optional with the retail seller. The amount, if any, included for such insurance shall not exceed the premiums chargeable in accordance with the applicable rates filed with the commissioner for such insurance. The retail seller or holder, if the premium for dual insurance on the goods is included in a retail installment contract, shall within 25 days after the execution of the retail installment contract send or cause to be sent to the retail buyer a policy or policies or certificate of insurance, written by an insurance company authorized to do business in this State, clearly setting forth the amount of the premium, the kind or kinds of insurance and the scope of the coverage and all the terms, exceptions, limitations, restrictions and conditions of the contract or contracts of insurance. The holder of a retail installment contract shall, if the goods described therein have been repossessed and sold, cancel any insurance on the goods and any other insurance or other benefits then in force and shall credit the amount of the return premium thereon to the unpaid balance outstanding on the retail installment contract.

§ 17:16C–32. Notice that policy required in sale of motor vehicle includes no liability or property damage coverage

Whenever, in the sale of a motor vehicle, the retail buyer is required, under the provisions of this act, to provide a policy of insurance and such policy of insurance does not contain the liability insurance required by section 1 of P.L.1972, c. 197 (C. 39:6B–1), the retail installment contract shall contain, immediately following the statement therein concerning insurance, the following notice printed prominently, in the form herein indicated or in such other form as may be approved by the commissioner, in 10-point type or larger:

> "THIS DOES NOT INCLUDE INSURANCE ON YOUR LIABILITY FOR BODILY INJURY OR PROPERTY DAMAGE. WITHOUT SUCH INSURANCE, YOU MAY NOT OPERATE THIS VEHICLE ON PUBLIC HIGHWAYS."

§ 17:16C–33. Additional insurance; cancellation rights

In addition to insurance on the goods, by agreement with the retail buyer, the retail seller may purchase such other insurance and other benefits as the retail buyer shall contract for; provided, however, that the retail buyer may cancel such additional insurance and other benefits, other than credit life and credit accident and health insurance, at any time prior to the expiration of such insurance contracts or benefits.

§ 17:16C–34. Cancellation of insurance policies; crediting next maturing installment of contract with refund

If any policy or policies or certificates of insurance or other benefits are canceled, or the premiums thereon adjusted, the unearned insurance premium refund or refund on other benefits received by the retail seller or subsequent holder of the retail installment contract shall be credited to the next maturing installments of the retail installment contract, except to the extent applied toward payment for similar insurance protecting the interest of the buyer and the retail seller or holder of the contract or any of them; provided that in the case of credit life or credit accident and health insurance, the refund to the buyer shall be made in accordance with chapter 169 of the laws of 1958 [§ 17:38A–1 et seq.], and provided further that if the amount of such refund is less than the minimum prescribed by the commissioner, no refund need be made.

§ 17:16C–34.1 Retail charge account; terms; regulations; effective date of accounts

(a) A retail charge account may be entered into between a retail buyer and a retail seller or a person wholly owned by or which wholly owns a retail seller or between a retail buyer and a sales finance company on its own behalf or on behalf of one or more retail sellers from whom the sales finance company may purchase or acquire the obligations of the retail buyer incurred pursuant to a retail charge account.

(b) A retail charge account shall be subject to such provisions not inconsistent with this act or otherwise prohibited by law which may be agreed upon, but shall be subject to the requirements for open end credit accounts as prescribed by regulations of the Board of Governors of the Federal Reserve System issued pursuant to Title I of the Consumer Credit Protection Act, referred to in this act as the "Truth in Lending Act and Regulations."

(c) A retail charge account shall become effective when an agreement is signed by the retail buyer or when the retail buyer or someone authorized by the retail buyer makes a purchase pursuant to the terms of the account.

§ 17:16C–35. Prohibited contract provisions; acceleration clause

No retail installment contract or retail charge account or separate instruments executed in connection therewith shall contain any acceleration clause under which any part or all of the balance, not yet matured, may be declared immediately due and payable because the retail seller or holder deems himself to be insecure and any such provision shall be void and unenforceable.

§ 17:16C–36. Waiver of right of action by retail buyer against seller, holder, etc.

No retail installment contract or retail charge account or separate instruments executed in connection therewith shall contain any provisions whereby the retail buyer waives any right of action or defense against the retail seller, sales finance company, holder or other person acting on his or her behalf for any illegal act committed in the collection of the payments under the contract or account or in the repossession of the goods, the subject of the retail installment contract or retail charge account and any such provision shall be void and unenforceable.

§ 17:16C–37. Power of attorney to confess judgment; other powers of attorney

No retail installment contract or retail charge account or separate instruments executed in connection therewith shall contain any power of attorney to confess judgment or any other power of attorney and any such provision shall be void and unenforceable.

§ 17:16C–38. Relief of retail seller from liability under contract

No retail installment contract or retail charge account or separate instruments executed in connection therewith shall contain any provision relieving the retail seller from liability for any legal remedies which the retail buyer may have against the retail seller under the contract or account and any such provision shall be void and unenforceable.

§ 17:16C–38.1 Remedy of buyer against seller; provision relieving holder or other assignee from liability; prohibition

No retail installment contract shall contain any provision relieving the holder, or other assignee, from liability for any civil remedy sounding in contract which the retail buyer may have against the retail seller under the retail installment contract or under any separate instrument executed in connection therewith.

§ 17:16C–38.2 Imprint of words "consumer note" on face of note; note not a negotiable instrument or security interest; subjection of subsequent holder to claims and defenses of buyer

No retail installment contract shall require or entail the execution of any note unless such note shall have printed the words "CONSUMER NOTE" in 10-point bold type or larger on the face thereof. Such a note with the words "CONSUMER NOTE" printed thereon shall be subject to the terms and conditions of the retail installment contract and shall not be a negotiable instrument within the meaning of chapter 3 (Commercial Paper) N.J.S. 12A:3–101 et seq., or a security interest within the meaning of chapter 9 (Secured Transactions) N.J.S. 12A:9–101 et seq. of the Uniform Commercial Code. Any subsequent holder of a consumer note shall be subject to all claims and defenses of the retail buyer against the retail seller arising out of the transaction but no such claim or defense may be asserted against such holder in excess of the time sales price under the retail installment contract for any sale, except that, in the case of the sale of a new motor vehicle, as defined in R.S. 39:10–2, no claim or defense may be asserted against such holder in excess of the time balance under the retail installment contract. No claim or defense which the retail buyer may have against the retail seller arising otherwise than out of the retail installment contract or any separate instrument executed in connection therewith shall be asserted against any subsequent holder.

§ 17:16C–38.3 Violations; penalty

Any person who procures the execution of a note in violation of this act shall be liable to a penalty of not more than $500.00 for each offense.

§ 17:16C–38.4 Execution of note in violation of act; disallowance of finance, collection, etc., charges

In the event that a note is executed in connection with a retail installment contract in violation of this act, no finance, delinquency, collection, repossession or refinancing charges may be recovered in any action or proceeding based on the contract or the consumer note.

§ 17:16C–39. Assignment of salary, wages, commissions or other compensation for services

No retail seller, sales finance company or holder shall at any time take in a retail installment contract, a retail charge account or in a separate instrument, any assignment of or order for the payment of any salary, wages, commissions, or other compensation for services, or any part thereof, earned or to be earned and any such provision shall be void and unenforceable.

§ 17:16C–39.1 Real property mortgage as additional security; prohibition

No retail installment contract, retail charge account or separate instrument executed in connection therewith shall contain any provision whereby the retail seller, sales finance company or holder takes a real property mortgage as additional security in connection with a retail sale. Any such provision shall be void and unenforceable.

§ 17:16C–40. Loan of money or advance of credit to retail buyer; rate of interest

No retail seller, sales finance company or holder shall make any loan of money or advance of credit to a retail buyer on or in connection with any retail installment contract or retail charge account and charge, contract for or receive thereon a greater rate of interest than he would otherwise be permitted by law to charge except in accordance with the provisions of this act; provided, however, that nothing contained in this section shall prohibit a banking institution from making any loan which it otherwise is permitted by law to make.

§ 17:16C–40.1 Loan secured by purchase money security interest to finance purchase of motor vehicle

A sales finance company licensed under the provisions of [this Act] or any act replacing or succeeding thereto which regulates "retail installment sales," may loan to any one person any sum of money up to a maximum of $10,000.00 secured by a purchase money security interest to finance the purchase of a passenger motor vehicle not intended to be used for the transportation of passengers for hire or upon a contract basis. The principal amount of such loan may be repaid in not more than 48 substantially equal monthly installments. Notwithstanding the provisions of R.S. 31:1–1 or any other law to the contrary, the sales finance company may charge interest at a rate or rates agreed to by the sales finance company and the borrower. Such interest shall be computed on the full amount of such loan for the period from the making of the loan to the date of maturity of the final installment, and shall be added to the principal amount of the loan. For the purpose of this act, a purchase money security interest is hereby defined to be a security interest taken by a sales finance company, pursuant to the provisions of chapter 9 of Title 12A of the New Jersey Statutes, in connection with and as security for an advance of money on behalf of a retail buyer of a motor vehicle of the motor vehicle dealer in payment of the unpaid balance of the cash price.

Effective on the first day of the twelfth month following the effective date of this act, when the unpaid balance owing upon a precomputed loan is repaid in full or the maturity of the unpaid balance of such loan is accelerated before the date scheduled for the payment of the final installment, the association shall allow a credit on account of the precomputed interest, calculated according to the actuarial refund method, as if all payments were made as scheduled, or if deferred, as deferred; provided, however, that if the loan is prepaid within 12 months after the first payment is due, an association may charge a prepayment penalty of not more than (a) $20.00 on any loan up to and including $2,000.00; (b) an amount equal to 1% of the loan on any loan greater than $2,000.00 and up to and including $5,000.00; and (c) $100.00 on any loan exceeding $5,000.00.

§ 17:16C–40.2 Violation of provisions; revocation or suspension of license

A violation of any provision of this act shall be cause for the revocation or suspension of the license of the sales finance company by the commissioner upon notice and opportunity to be heard in accordance with the provisions of P.L.1958, chapter 68 [§ 17:1–8.5 et seq.].

§ 17:16C–41. Time price differential; rates; computation

A retail seller and a motor vehicle installment seller, under the provisions of this act, shall have authority to charge, contract for, receive or collect a time price differential as defined in this act, on any retail installment contract evidencing the sale of goods or services in an amount or amounts as agreed to by the retail seller or motor vehicle installment seller and the buyer on motor vehicles and on all other goods or services.

The retail installment contract may provide for an increase, or may provide for a decrease, or both, in the time price differential applicable to the contract. No increase during the entire loan term shall result in an interest rate of more than 6% per annum over the rate applicable initially, nor shall the rate be raised more than 3% per annum during any 12-month period. The lender shall not be obligated to decrease the interest rate more than 6% over the term of the loan, nor more than 3% per annum during any 12-month period. If a rate increase is applied to the loan, the lender shall also be obligated to adopt and implement uniform standards for decreasing the rate. If the contract provides for the possibility of an increase or decrease, or both, in the rate, that fact shall be clearly described in plain language, in at least 8-point bold face type on the face of the contract. No rate increase shall take effect during the first 3 years of the term of the contract, or thereafter, (a) unless at least 90 days prior to the effective date of the first such increase, or 30 days prior to the effective date of any subsequent increase, a written notice has been mailed or delivered to the retail buyer that clearly and conspicuously describes such increase, and (b) unless at least 365 days have elapsed without any increase. No increase during the entire contract term shall result in an interest rate of more than 6% per annum over the rate applicable initially, nor shall the rate be raised more than 3% per annum during any 12-month period.

If the retail installment contract does provide that the time price differential may be increased then, notwithstanding the provisions of section 43 of P.L.1960, c. 40 (C. 17:16C–43), when the unpaid balance owing upon a contract is paid in full or the maturity of the unpaid balance of such contract is accelerated before the date scheduled for the payment of the final installment, the holder of the contract shall allow a credit on account of the precomputed time price differential calculated according to the actuarial refund method, as if all payments were made as scheduled, or if deferred, as deferred; provided, however, that if the contract is prepaid within 12 months after the first payment is due, a holder may charge a prepayment penalty of not more than (a) $20.00 on any contract up to and including $2,000.00; (b) an amount equal to 1% of the loan on any contract greater than $2,000.00 and up to and including $5,000.00; and (c) $100.00 on any contract exceeding $5,000.00. Effective on the first day of the twelfth month following the effective date of this act, if the retail installment contract does provide for a time price differential, then, notwithstanding the provisions of section 43 of P.L.1960, c. 40 (C. 17:16C–43), when the unpaid balance owing upon a contract is paid in full or the maturity of the unpaid balance of such contract is accelerated before the date scheduled for the payment of the final installment, the holder of the contract shall allow a credit on account of the precomputed time price differential calculated according to the actuarial refund method, as if all payments were made as scheduled, or if deferred, as deferred; provided, however, that if the contract is prepaid within 12 months after the first payment is due, a holder may charge a prepayment penalty of not more than (a) $20.00 on any contract up to and including $2,000.00; (b) an amount equal to 1% of the loan on any contract greater than $2,000.00 and up to and including $5,000.00; and (c) $100.00 on any contract exceeding $5,000.00.

The time price differential shall be computed on the amount of the principal balance as determined in section 27(f), from the date of the contract to the due date of the final installment, notwithstanding the fact that the contract is to be repaid in installments.

If the time price differential so computed is less than $12.00, and if the due date of the last installment of the contract is more than 8 months after the date of the contract, a charge of not more than $12.00 may be made in lieu of the time price differential. If the time price differential so computed is less than $10.00, and if the due date of the last installment of the contract is 8 months or less after the date of contract, a charge of not more than $10.00 may be made in lieu of the time price differential.

§ 17:16C-42. Delinquency or collection charge for default in payment; attorney's fees

(a) The holder of any retail installment contract may collect a delinquency or collection charge for default in the payment of any such contract or any installment thereof, if provided for in the contract when such default shall have continued for a period of 10 days, such charge not to exceed 5% of each installment in default or the sum of $5.00, whichever is the lesser. Such charge may be collected by the holder of the retail installment contract or charged to the buyer's retail installment contract account. If charged to the buyer's retail installment contract account, such charge shall be made within 35 days from the date of such default and then a written notification that such charge has been made shall be mailed to the retail buyer within 5 days from the date when such charge was made.

(b) The retail installment contract or retail charge account may provide for the payment of attorney's fees not exceeding 20% of the first $500.00 and 10% on any excess of the amount due and payable under such contract or account when referred to an attorney, not a salaried employee of the holder of the contract or account, for collection.

§ 17:16C-43. Prepayment; credit on account

When the balance owing on a retail installment contract is repaid in full at any time before the end of the contract period, the holder of the contract shall allow a credit on account of the time price differential, the amount of which shall be determined by the application of the formula $C = AN \div D$, in which "C" represents the amount of the credit to be given; "A" represents the amount of the time price differential, less an acquisition cost of $15.00; "D" represents an amount determined as follows: there shall be ascribed to each payment-period included in the contract period, beginning with the first payment-period scheduled by the contract, the cardinal number descriptive of the number of payment-periods scheduled by the contract to elapse from the beginning of each such payment-period to the end of the contract period, and the sum of all such cardinal numbers shall constitute the quantity "D"; and "N" represents the difference between the quantity "D" and the sum of all the cardinal numbers ascribed to the payment-periods which have elapsed, in whole or in part, from the date of the contract to the date upon which such repayment is made. This section shall not apply when the amount of the credit is less than $1.00.

§ 17:16C–44. Extension of scheduled due date; reduction of amount of installments; additional charge; options

The holder of a retail installment contract may extend the scheduled due date of any retail installment contract and defer the scheduled due date of any or all installment payments, or reduce the amount of any or all installments and may, as a consideration therefor, make a total additional charge not to exceed the amount ascertained under either of the following methods of computation at the respective rates indicated by the following options:

Option 1. The additional charge shall be computed on the amount of the scheduled installment on installments extended, deferred or reduced for the period or periods for which each installment or part thereof is extended, deferred or reduced at the following rates on contracts originally in the respective classifications set forth in section 41 of this act:

Class I. 1% per month;

Class II. 1½% per month;

Class III. 2% per month;

Class IV. 2% per month.

Option 2. The holder of a retail installment contract by written agreement may renew the entire unpaid balance on any retail installment contract and may make a charge therefor at the rates charged in the original contract from the date of renewal to the maturity of the final installment. The amount of the balance to be renewed shall be obtained by adding to the existing unpaid balance on the original contract, the cost of any insurance or other benefits for the period of the extension and any accrued default charges and refunding the unearned portion of the time price differential charged according to the formula provided in section 43 of this act; provided, however, that in computing the unearned time price differential charge no allowance shall be taken for the amount of the acquisition cost permitted therein.

§ 17:16C–44.1 Retail charge account; time price differential; rate; computation

(a) Notwithstanding any other law to the contrary, a retail seller, sales finance company, banking institution or other holder may charge, receive and collect a time price differential in each billing period on obligations incurred pursuant to any retail charge account, which shall be determined as specified in the terms of the account, subject to the limitations provided herein. Such time price differential for each monthly billing period shall not exceed the amount resulting from applying the periodic rates provided herein to the greater of the following amounts (including unpaid time price differentials):

(i) The average daily balance of the account for such billing period, or

(ii) The balance of the account at the beginning or end of such billing period.

The periodic rate or rates shall not exceed an amount agreed to by the retail seller, sales finance company, banking institution, or other holder and the retail buyer.

The terms of the retail charge account may provide that the time price differential may be increased or may be decreased or both from time to time provided, however, that no increase shall be effective unless: (1) at least 90 days prior to the effective date of the first such increase, or 30 days prior to the effective date of any subsequent increase, a written notice has been mailed or delivered to the retail buyer that clearly and conspicuously describes such change and the indebtedness to which it applies and states that the incurrence by the retail buyer or another person authorized by him of any further indebtedness under the plan to which the agreement relates on or after the effective date of the increase specified in the notice shall constitute acceptance of the increase and (b) either the retail buyer agrees in writing to the increase or the retail buyer or another person authorized by him incurs such further indebtedness on or after the effective date of the increase stated in the notice. The provisions of this paragraph permitting an increase in the time price differential shall not apply in the case of an agreement which expressly prohibits changing of the time price differential or which provides limitations on changing of the time price differential which are more restrictive than the requirements of this paragraph. If the terms of the retail charge account provide for the possibility of an increase or decrease, or both, in the time price differential, that fact shall be clearly described in plain language, in at least 8-point bold face type on the face of the written notice.

Notwithstanding the foregoing limitation, if the terms of the account so provide, the time price differential may be computed on the median amount within a specified range. Such time price differential for each monthly billing period shall not exceed the amount resulting from applying the respective periodic rates specified above to the median amount within the specified range in which the greater of the amounts specified in (i) and (ii) is included; provided, subject to the classifications and differentiations as may reasonably be established by the retail seller, sales finance company, banking institution or other holder, the same time price differential is charged on all balances within the specified range and provided further that the time price differential determined by applying the respective periodic rates specified above to the median amount within the range does not exceed by more than 8% the amount of the time price differential determined by applying the respective periodic rates specified above to the lowest amount in the range.

(b) If the billing period is not monthly, the maximum periodic rate shall be that rate which bears the same relation to the respective periodic rates per month specified above as the number of days in the billing period bears to 30.

(c) Notwithstanding the limitation provided in (a) above, for any monthly billing period in which a time price differential may be charged pursuant to the terms of the account a minimum time price differential of not more than $0.50 may be charged; if the billing period is not monthly, a minimum time price differential may be charged in such amount which bears the same relation to $0.50 as the number of days in the billing period bears to 30.

§ 17:16C–45. Limitation on sale, transfer or assignment of obligation or evidence of indebtedness by retail seller

No retail seller under a retail installment contract, executed in this State, shall sell, transfer or assign the obligation represented by such contract or any evidence of indebtedness thereunder to any person who is not authorized as a sales finance company pursuant to the provisions of this act, except that such obligation or evidence of indebtedness may be sold, transferred or assigned to a State or national bank outside of this State if the retail installment contract is retained by the retail seller or sales finance company and collection of payments thereon is made to the retail seller or sales finance company.

§ 17:16C–46. Sale, transfer or assignment without notice to retail buyer; payment or tender to last known holder

If a retail installment contract is lawfully sold, transferred or assigned, pursuant to the provisions of this act, and a written notice of such sale, transfer or assignment setting forth the name and address of the new holder and of the person authorized to receive future payments on such contract is not given to the retail buyer, any payment or tender of payment made to and any service of notice on the last known holder by the retail buyer shall be binding upon any subsequent holder.

§ 17:16C–47. Assignment of aggregation of retail installment contracts as collateral security for bona fide commercial loan

The provisions of section 45 shall not apply to any assignment of an aggregation of retail installment contracts, which is executed by a retail seller or sales finance company as collateral security only for a bona fide commercial loan, and under which, in the absence of default or other bona fide breach of the contract, ownership of the assigned retail installment contracts remains vested in the retail seller or sales finance company, and collection of payments on such assigned contracts is made by the retail seller or sales finance company; and provided such assignment of contracts is not made for the purpose of evading or circumventing the provisions of this act.

§ 17:16C–47.1 Purchases of retail installment contract or retail charge account by sales finance company; terms, conditions and price

A sales finance company may purchase a retail installment contract or obligations incurred pursuant to a retail charge account from a retail seller or sales finance company on such terms and conditions and for such price as may be mutually agreed upon.

§ 17:16C–48. Furnishing statement of retail buyer's account

Upon written request from the retail buyer, the retail seller or holder of the retail installment contract shall give or forward to the retail buyer within 10 days from receipt of the written request a written statement of the retail buyer's account, showing the dates and amounts of all payments made or credited to the account and the total amount, if any, unpaid under such contract. No more than 2 such statements shall be required from a holder in any 12-month period.

§ 17:16C–49. Receipt for payment; contents

Whenever payment is made on account of any retail installment contract in cash, the person receiving such payment shall, at the time of receiving such payment, furnish to the retail buyer, or the person making such payment on behalf of the retail buyer, a complete written receipt therefor, showing the date, identification of the account and the amount paid.

§ 17:16C–50. Additional charges prohibited; exceptions

No retail seller, sales finance company, or holder shall charge, contract for, collect or receive from any retail buyer, directly or indirectly, any further or other amount for costs, charges, insurance premiums, examination, appraisal service, brokerage, commission, expense, interest, discount, fees, fines, penalties or other things of value in connection with retail installment contracts or retail charge accounts other than the charges permitted by this act, except court costs, attorney fees and the expenses of retaking and storing repossessed goods which are authorized by law.

§ 17:16C–51. Collection of charges if sale not made prohibited; status of deposit on contemplated purchase of goods

No retail seller shall collect or retain any amount whatsoever in connection with the contemplated sale of goods under a retail installment sales contract, if such sale is not made; provided, however, that nothing contained herein shall affect the legal status of a deposit paid by a prospective retail buyer to a retail seller as a binder on the contemplated purchase of goods.

§ 17:16C–52. Duties of holder upon payment in full

With respect to Class I, Class II, and Class III goods as defined in section 41, upon payment in full by the retail buyer of the time balance and other amounts lawfully due under a retail installment contract, the holder shall:

(a) Return to the retail buyer the original instruments evidencing indebtedness or constituting security under a retail installment contract, which were signed by the retail buyer or his sureties or guarantors in conjunction with such contract, excepting such instruments as are filed or recorded with a public official and retained in the files of such official;

(b) Release all security interest in the goods or in any collateral security to the obligation of the retail buyer under such contract;

(c) Deliver to the retail buyer such good and sufficient assignments and certificates of title as may be necessary to vest the retail buyer with complete evidence of title.

With respect to Class IV goods as defined in section 41, the holder, upon payment in full by the retail buyer of the time balance and other amounts lawfully due under a retail installment contract, shall furnish the retail buyer with such instrument as the commissioner may by regulation provide.

§ 17:16C–54. Unauthorized costs and charges

Whenever, in any retail installment contract or retail charge account under this act, the retail seller, sales finance company or holder has knowingly charged, contracted for or received from the retail buyer any costs or charges not authorized by this act, all costs and charges in connection with such contract or account, other than for insurance authorized by this act, shall be void and unenforceable, and any such costs or charges other than for insurance authorized by this act shall be applied to the unpaid balance or, if the account has been fully paid, remitted to the retail buyer, and the retail buyer shall be entitled to recover all such costs or charges.

§ 17:16C–56. Violations of act; penalty; enforcement by summary proceedings

(a) Any person conducting business under this act and any director, officer, partner, member, employee, agent, or representative thereof who shall knowingly violate any provision of this act or shall directly or indirectly counsel, aid or abet such violation shall be liable to a penalty of not more than $500.00 for each offense.

(b) The penalties provided for by this act shall be sued for and recovered by and in the name of the commissioner and shall be collected and enforced by summary proceedings pursuant to the Penalty Enforcement Law (N.J.S. 2A:58–1 et seq.).

*

SMALL LOAN ACT

Code of Ala. tit. 5, ch. 18

Tables of Sections

---

§ 5–18–1. Short title

This chapter shall be known and may be cited as the Alabama Small Loan Act.

§ 5–18–2. Legislative findings of fact and declaration of intent

(a) The legislature finds as facts and determines that:

(1) There exists among citizens of this state a widespread demand for small loans. The scope and intensity of this demand have been increased progressively by many social and economic forces;

(2) The expense of making and collecting small loans, which are usually made on comparatively unsubstantial security to wage earners, salaried employees and other persons of relatively low incomes, is necessarily high in relation to the amounts lent;

(3) Such loans cannot be made profitably under the limitations imposed by existing laws relating to interest and usury. These limitations have tended to exclude lawful enterprises from the small loan field. Since the demand for small loans cannot be legislated out of existence, many small borrowers have been left to the mercy of those willing to bear the opprobrium and risk the penalties of usury for a large profit;

(4) Interest charges are often disguised by the use of subterfuges to evade the usury law. These subterfuges are so complicated and technical that the usual borrower of small sums is defenseless even if he is aware of the usurious nature of the transaction and of his legal rights;

(5) As a result, borrowers of small sums are being exploited to the injury of the borrower, his dependents and the general public. Charges are generally exorbitant in relation to those necessary to the conduct of a legitimate small loan business, trickery and fraud are common and oppressive collection practices are prevalent; and

(6) These evils characterize and distinguish loans of $749.00 or less. Legislation to control this class of loans is necessary to protect the public welfare.

(b) It is the intent of the legislature in enacting this law to bring under public supervision those engaged in the business of making such loans, to eliminate practices that facilitate abuse of borrowers, to establish a system of regulation for the purpose of insuring honest and efficient small loan service and of stimulating competitive reductions in charges, to allow lenders who meet the conditions of this chapter a rate of charge sufficiently high to permit a business profit and to provide the administrative machinery necessary for effective enforcement.

§ 5–18–3. Definitions

The following terms, when used in this chapter, shall have the following meanings, unless the context clearly requires a different meaning. The meaning ascribed to the singular form shall apply also to the plural.

(1) Person. Such term shall include individuals, copartnerships, associations, trusts, corporations and any other legal entities.

(2) License. A license, issued under the authority of this chapter, to make loans in accordance with the provisions of this chapter at a single place of business.

(3) Licensee. A person to whom one or more licenses have been issued.

(4) Supervisor. The supervisor of the bureau of loans of the state banking department.

(5) Bureau. The bureau of loans of the state banking department.

(6) Cash advance. The amount of cash or its equivalent that the borrower actually receives or is paid at his direction or on his behalf.

§ 5-18-4. License—Required; exemptions; penalties for violation of section

(a) *License required.*—No person shall engage in the business of lending in amounts of $749.00 or less and contract for, exact or receive, directly or indirectly, on or in connection with any such loan, any charges whether for interest, insurance, compensation, consideration or expense, which in the aggregate are greater than the interest that the lender would be permitted by law to charge for a loan of money if he were not a licensee under this chapter, except as provided in and authorized by this chapter and without first having obtained a license from the supervisor. For the purpose of this section, a loan shall be deemed to be in the amount of $749.00 or less if the net amount or value advanced to or on behalf of the borrower, after deducting all payments for interest, expenses and charges of any nature taken substantially contemporaneously with the making of the loan, does not exceed $749.00.

(b) *Exemptions.*—This chapter shall not apply to any person doing business under the authority of, and as permitted by, any law of this state or of the United States relating to banks, trust companies, savings or building and loan associations, credit unions as defined by law nor to any lawful, bona fide pawnbroking business, nor shall this chapter apply to any person making loans to their tenants engaged in agriculture, nor to loans by agricultural suppliers to persons whose principal business is farming, nor shall it apply to agricultural credit corporations or associations organized under an act of the congress of the United States, nor shall it apply to the business of financing the purchase of motor vehicles, refrigerators or other personal property, nor shall it apply to loans insured or guaranteed by the United States or any of its agencies.

(c) *Evasions.*—The provisions of subsection (a) of this section shall apply to any person who seeks to evade its application by any device, subterfuge or pretense whatsoever including, but not thereby limiting the generality of the foregoing: the loan, forbearance, use or sale of credit (as guarantor, surety, endorser, comaker or otherwise), money, insurance, goods or things in action; the use of collateral or related sales or purchases of goods or services or agreements to sell or purchase, whether real or pretended; and, receiving or charging compensation for goods or services, whether or not sold, delivered or provided and the real or pretended negotiation, arrangement or procurement of a loan through any use of activity of a third person, whether real or fictitious.

(d) *Penalties.*—Whoever violates or participates in the violation of any provision of this section shall be guilty of a misdemeanor and, upon conviction thereof, shall be punishable by a fine of not more than $500.00 nor less than $100.00, or by imprisonment for not more than six months, or by both such fine and imprisonment in the discretion of the court. Any contract of loan in the making or collection of which any act shall have been done which violates this section shall be void, and the lender shall have no right to collect, receive or retain any principal, interest or charges whatsoever.

§ 5-18-5. Same—Application; fees

Application for a license shall be in writing, under oath and in the form prescribed by the supervisor. The application shall give the approximate location where the business is to be conducted and shall contain such further relevant information as the supervisor may require, including the names and addresses of the partners, officers, directors or trustees and of such of the principal owners or members as will provide the basis for the investigations and findings contemplated by section 5-18-6. At the time of making such application, the applicant shall pay to the supervisor the sum of $100.00 as a fee for investigating the application. All licensees under this chapter shall pay an annual license fee of $200.00, which shall be due on October 1 of each year and shall be for a one-year period ending September 30 following and shall be delinquent on November 1 of each year, and there shall be a penalty of 10 percent added to such license fee upon delinquency and collected by the bureau. If any applicant licensed under this chapter for the first time shall commence business after April 1 in any year, the amount of the license fee shall be one half of the amount of a full year's license fee. The amount of the license fee and penalties if any shall be paid to the supervisor of the bureau of loans, who shall remit the same to the treasurer of the state of Alabama as provided by law. The license provided for in this chapter shall be in addition to all other licenses now or hereafter provided for by law and shall be in addition to the tax provided for by chapter 16 of Title 40; and the amount of the license fee levied by this section shall not be credited upon or deducted from, in whole or in part, the tax levied by said chapter 16 as to the current state tax year or as to any prior or subsequent state tax year. No refunds for the current or any prior or subsequent state tax year or any portion of the tax levied by said chapter 16 shall be made on the ground that the license fee levied by this section was not credited upon or deducted from the tax levied by said chapter 16, and no civil action shall lie to enforce any claim for such refund.

§ 5-18-6. Same—Investigation of application; issuance or denial of license

(a) *Investigation of application.*—Upon the filing of such application and the payment of such fees, the supervisor shall investigate the facts concerning the application and the requirements provided for in subsection (b) of this section. The supervisor shall grant or deny such application for a license within 90 days from the filing thereof with the required information and fees unless the period is extended by written agreement between the applicant and the supervisor.

(b) *Issuance of license.*—If the supervisor shall find that the liquid assets, financial responsibility, experience, character and the general fitness of the applicant are such as to warrant the belief that the business will be operated lawfully, honestly, fairly and efficiently, within the purposes of this chapter, and that allowing such applicant to engage in the business would promote the convenience and advantage of the community in which the business of the applicant is to be conducted, he shall thereupon enter an order granting such application and file his findings with the bureau and forthwith issue and deliver a license to the applicant.

(c) *Denial of license.*—If the supervisor shall not so find, he shall notify the applicant in writing who may request a hearing on the application. The request for a hearing must be within 30 days of the rejection, with the hearing to be held within 30 days of the date of the request. After such hearing or if no hearing is demanded, the supervisor may deny such application by written order accompanied by his findings of fact and shall deliver a copy of such order and findings to the applicant. The investigation fee shall be retained by the supervisor while the license fee shall be returned to the applicant.

§ 5-18-7. Same—Contents; posting; continuing effect

(a) *Contents of license; posting.*—Each license shall state the address at which the business is to be conducted and shall state fully the name of the licensee and, if the licensee is a copartnership or association, the names of the members thereof and, if a corporation, the date and place of its incorporation. Each license shall be kept conspicuously posted in the licensed place of business and shall not be transferable or assignable.

(b) *Continuing effect of license.*—Each license shall remain in full force and effect until surrendered, revoked or suspended as provided in this chapter.

§ 5–18–8. Same—Place of business of licensee

(a) *Separate license for each place of business.*—Not more than one place of business shall be maintained under the same license, but the supervisor may issue additional licenses to the same licensee upon his compliance with all the provisions of this chapter governing the issuance of the first or original license.

(b) *Removal.*—No change in the place of business of a licensee to a location outside of the original municipality shall be permitted under the same license. When a licensee wishes to change his place of business within the same municipality, he shall give written notice thereof to the supervisor who shall investigate the facts and, if he shall find the proposed location is reasonably accessible to borrowers under existing loan contracts, shall enter an order permitting the change and shall amend the license accordingly. If the supervisor shall not so find, he shall enter an order denying the licensee such permission in the manner specified in and subject to the provisions of subsection (c) of section 5–18–6.

(c) *Residence of borrower.*—Nothing in this chapter shall be construed to restrict the loans of any licensee to residents of the community in which the licensed place of business is situated.

§ 5–18–9. Same—Revocation, suspension, etc.; investigation of complaints

(a) *Revocation of license.*—The supervisor shall, upon 10 days' written notice to the licensee stating the contemplated action and in general the grounds therefor and upon reasonable opportunity to be heard, revoke any license issued under this chapter if he finds that:

(1) The licensee has failed to pay the annual license fee;

(2) The licensee, either knowingly or without the exercise of due care to prevent the same, has violated any provisions of this chapter or any regulation or order lawfully made pursuant to and within the authority of this chapter;

(3) Any fact or condition exists which, if it had existed or had been known to exist at the time of the original application for such license, clearly would have justified the supervisor in refusing originally to issue such license; except, that the license shall not be revoked because of convenience and advantage; or

(4) The licensee is guilty of using unreasonable collection tactics.

(b) *Suspension of license.*—If the supervisor finds that probable cause for revocation of any license exists and that enforcement of the chapter requires immediate suspension of such license pending investigation, he may, upon three days' written notice and a hearing, enter an order suspending such license for a period not exceeding 30 days.

(c) *Records and notice.*—Whenever the supervisor shall revoke or suspend a license issued pursuant to this chapter, he shall enter an order to that effect and forthwith notify the licensee of the revocation or suspension. Within five days after the entry of such an order he shall file with the bureau his findings and a summary of the evidence supporting them, and he shall forthwith deliver a copy thereof to the licensee.

(d) *Surrender of license.*—Any licensee may surrender any license by delivering it to the supervisor with written notice of its surrender, but such surrender shall not affect his civil or criminal liability for acts committed prior thereto.

(e) *Preexisting contracts.*—No revocation, suspension or surrender of any license shall impair or affect the obligation of any preexisting contract between the licensee and any borrower.

(f) *Reinstatement of license.*—The supervisor may reinstate suspended licenses or issue new licenses to a person whose license or licenses have been revoked if no fact or condition then exists which clearly would have justified the supervisor in refusing originally to issue such license under this chapter.

(g) *Complaints of violation investigated.*—The supervisor shall, upon sworn complaint of any borrower, investigate or cause to be investigated any alleged violation of this chapter.

§ 5–18–10. Examinations of licensees; investigations; enforcement powers of supervisor

(a) *Annual examinations of licensees.*—At least once each year and at such other time as may be deemed necessary by the supervisor of the bureau of loans, an examination shall be made of the place of business of each licensee and of the loans, transactions, books, papers and records of such licensee so far as they pertain to the business licensed under this chapter. As cost of examination, the licensee shall pay to the bureau of loans the actual cost of each examination, the amount of which shall be reasonably prescribed under rules and regulations promulgated by the superintendent of banks; provided, however, the cost for each day of examination by each examiner shall not exceed eight times the average hourly rate for auditing purposes as charged by three recognized certified public accountancy firms in the city of Montgomery, Alabama. In addition thereto, the licensee shall pay as per diem the amount authorized by law for state employees traveling inside the state in the service of the state. All such fees shall be paid into the special fund set up by the state treasury pursuant to section 5–2A–20, and used in the supervision and examination of licensees.

(b) *Investigations.*—For the purpose of discovering violations of this chapter or of securing information lawfully required hereunder, the supervisor or his duly authorized representatives may at any time investigate the business and examine the books, accounts, papers and records used therein of (1) any licensee, (2) any other person engaged in the business described in subsection (a) of section 5–18–4 or participating in such business as principal, agent, broker or otherwise and (3) any person who the supervisor has reasonable cause to believe is violating or is about to violate any provisions of this chapter, whether or not such person shall claim to be within the authority or beyond the scope of this chapter. For purposes of this section, any person who shall advertise for, solicit or hold himself out as willing to make loan transactions in the amount or of the value of $749.00 or less shall be presumed to be engaged in the business described in subsection (a) of section 5–18–4.

(c) *Access to records; witnesses.*—For the purposes of this section, the supervisor or his duly authorized representatives shall have and be given free access to the offices and places of business, files, safes and vaults of all such persons and shall have authority to require the attendance of any person and to examine him under oath relative to such loans or such business or to the subject matter of any examination, investigation or hearing.

(d) *Cease and desist orders; injunctions; receivers.*—Whenever the supervisor has reasonable cause to believe that any person is violating or is threatening to or intends to violate any provision of this chapter, he may in addition to all actions provided for in this chapter and in addition to all other remedies that he may have at law and without prejudice thereto enter an order requiring such person to desist or to refrain from such violation, and an action may be brought on the relation of the attorney general or the supervisor to enjoin such person from engaging in or continuing such violation or from doing any act or acts in furtherance thereof. In any such action, an order or judgment may be entered awarding such preliminary or final injunction as may be deemed proper. In addition to all other means provided by law for the enforcement of a restraining order or injunction, the court in which such action is brought shall have power and jurisdiction to impound and to appoint a receiver for the property and business of the defendant, including books, papers, documents and records pertaining thereto or so much thereof as the court may deem reasonably necessary to prevent violations of this chapter through or by means of the use of said property and business. Such receiver, when appointed and qualified, shall have such powers and duties as to custody, collection, administration, winding up and liquidation of such property and business as shall from time to time be conferred upon him by the court.

§ 5–18–11. Books, accounts and records of licensees; annual report

(a) *Books and records.*—Each licensee shall keep and use in his business such books, accounts and records as will enable the supervisor to determine whether such licensee is complying with the provisions of this chapter and with the orders and regulations lawfully made by the supervisor hereunder. Each licensee shall preserve such books, accounts and records for at least two years after making the final entry on any loan recorded therein.

(b) *Annual report.*

(1) Each licensee shall annually, on or before May 1, file a report with the supervisor as to each licensed place of business under this chapter, covering the preceding calendar year. This report shall include the following information, all reported in accordance with sound and generally accepted accounting practice:

a. Balance sheets at the beginning and end of the period;

b. A statement of income and expenses for the period;

c. A reconciliation of surplus or net earnings with the balance sheets;

d. A schedule of assets used and useful in the business;

e. An analysis of charges, sizes of loans and types of security on loans and an analysis of delinquent accounts;

f. An analysis of suits, repossessions and sales of chattels; and

g. The type of business organization and, if the licensee is a corporation, the principal officers and the resident agent, the partners if the licensee is a partnership or the owner if a sole proprietorship.

(2) If the licensee conducts other businesses or is affiliated with other licensees under this chapter, or if any other situation exists under which allocations are necessary, the licensee shall make such allocation according to appropriate and reasonable methods.

(3) If the licensee is affiliated with other licensees under this chapter, a composite report may be filed on behalf of all affiliated licensees within the state of Alabama, but such composite report shall not be required by the supervisor.

(4) Such report shall be made under oath and shall be in the form prescribed by the supervisor who shall make and publish annually an analysis and recapitulation of such reports.

§ 5-18-12. Promulgation of rules, regulations and orders by supervisor; furnishing of certified copies of licenses, regulations or orders

(a) *Rules, regulations and orders.*—The supervisor shall have authority to make reasonable rules, regulations and orders for the administration and enforcement of this chapter, in addition hereto and not inconsistent herewith. Such regulation or order shall be referenced to the section or sections of the chapter which set forth the legislative standard which it interprets or to which it applies. Every regulation shall be promulgated by an order, and any ruling, demand, requirement or similar administrative act may be promulgated by an order. Every order shall be in writing, shall state its effective date and the date of its promulgation and shall be entered in an indexed permanent book which shall be a public record. A copy of every order promulgating a regulation and of every other order containing a requirement of general application shall be mailed to each licensee at least 10 days before the effective date thereof. The failure of a licensee to receive a copy of the regulations shall not exempt him from the duty of compliance with the valid regulations lawfully issued.

(b) *Certified copies of official documents.*—On application of any person and payment of the costs thereof, the supervisor shall furnish, under his seal and signed by him or his deputy a certified copy of any license, regulation or order. In any court or proceeding, such copy shall be prima facie evidence of the fact of the issuance of such license, regulation or order.

§ 5-18-13. Advertising, etc., of rates, terms or conditions for loans; schedule of rates of charge to be displayed

(a) *Advertising, etc.*—No licensee or other person subject to this chapter shall advertise, display, distribute or broadcast or cause to permit to be advertised, displayed, distributed or broadcast in any manner whatsoever any false, misleading or deceptive statement or representation with regard to the rates, terms or conditions for loans in the amount or of the value of $749.00 or less. The supervisor may require that charges or rates of charge, if stated by a licensee, be stated fully and clearly in such manner as he may deem necessary to prevent misunderstanding thereof by prospective borrowers. The supervisor may permit or require licensees to refer in their advertising to the fact that their business is under state supervision, subject to conditions imposed by him to prevent an erroneous impression as to the scope or degree of protections provided by this chapter.

(b) *Schedule of charges.*—Each licensee shall prominently display in each licensed place of business a full and accurate schedule of the rates of charge upon all classes of loans currently to be made by him.

§ 5-18-14. Conduct of other business in office of licensee; loan business confined to licensed offices; acceptance of liens on real estate as security for loans

(a) *Other business in same office.*—No licensee shall conduct the business of making loans under this chapter within any office, suite, room or place of business in which any other business is solicited or engaged in or in association or conjunction with any other business until three days' written notice of an intention so to do has been given the supervisor. Upon receipt of written notification, the supervisor may investigate the facts and, if he finds that the character of the licensee and the nature of the other business warrant belief that such conduct of business would conceal violation or evasion of this chapter or of regulations lawfully made hereunder, he shall enter an order directing the licensee to discontinue said other business. The order shall be entered in the manner specified in and subject to the provisions of subsection (c) of section 5-18-6.

(b) *Business confined to licensed office.*—No licensee shall conduct the business of making loans provided for by this chapter under any name or at any place of business within this state other than that stated in the license. Nothing in this section shall prevent the making of loans by mail nor prohibit accommodations to individual borrowers when necessitated by sickness or other emergency situations.

(c) *Liens on real estate.*—No licensee shall take a lien upon real estate as security for any loan made under this chapter, except such lien as is created by law through the entry or recording of a judgment.

§ 5-18-15. Interest rates, charges and fees

(a) *Maximum rates of interest and charge.*—Every licensee under this chapter may contract for and receive as interest on any loan of money not exceeding $749.00 an amount at a rate not exceeding three percent a month on that part of the unpaid principal balance not in excess of $200.00, two percent a month on that part of the unpaid principal balance in excess of $200.00 but not exceeding $749.00.

(b) *Charges on loans of seventy-five dollars or less.*—On a cash advance of $75.00 or less a licensee may charge, in lieu of the charges specified in subsection (a) of this section, not in excess of $1.00 for each $5.00 of cash advanced to the borrower, up to the amount of $75.00, and a period of at least 15 days must be allowed for the repayment of each $5.00 of the cash advanced. Such charges cannot be assessed by any subterfuge or device on any loan over $75.00 or on any balance of $75.00 or less when the original cash advanced was greater than $75.00.

(c) *Method of computing charges.*

(1) Interest or charges on loans made under this chapter shall not be paid, deducted, discounted or received in advance or compounded, but the rate of charge authorized by this section may be precomputed as provided in subdivision (2) of this subsection.

For the purpose of this section one month shall be that period of time from any date in a month to a corresponding date in the next month and, if there is not such corresponding date, then to the next day of the next month, and a day shall be considered one thirtieth of a month when computation is made for a fraction of a month.

(2) When the loan contract requires repayment in substantially equal and consecutive monthly installments of principal and charges or interest combined, the charges or interest may be precomputed at the agreed monthly or periodic rate not in excess of that provided for in subsection (a) or (b) of this section on scheduled unpaid principal balances according to the terms of the contract and added to the principal of the loan. Every payment may be applied to the combined total of principal and precomputed charge until the contract is fully paid. The acceptance or payment of charges on loans made under the provisions of this subsection shall not be deemed to constitute payment, deduction or receipt thereof in advance nor compounding under subdivision (1) above.

(d) *Refunds.*

(1) When any loan contract is paid in full by cash, a new loan, renewal or otherwise one month or more before the final installment date, the licensee shall refund or credit the borrower with that portion of the total charges which shall be due the borrower as determined by schedules prepared under the rule of seventy-eighths or sum of the digits principle as follows: The amount of the refund or credit shall be as great a proportion of the total charges originally contracted for as the sum of the periodic time balances of the contract scheduled to follow the date of prepayment bears to the sum of all the periodic time balances of the contract, both sums to be determined according to the payment schedule originally contracted for.

(2) If the loan contract is not prepaid in full but becomes partially prepaid in an amount equal to three or more installments, the licensee shall reduce the balance due by the amount that would be required to be refunded for prepayment in full on the date of such partial prepayment and compute charges as payments are made thereafter in the manner prescribed in subdivision (1) of subsection (c) of this section, or the licensee may with the consent of the borrower reschedule the remaining installments and precompute charges as prescribed in subdivision (2) of subsection (c) of this section.

(e) *Default or extension charges.*—If the contract so provides, the additional charge for any installment past due 15 or more days, whether by reason of default or extension agreement, may be three percent of the installment past due, and said amount may be charged once and no more. It is the intent of this subsection that if the payment date of all wholly unpaid installments is deferred or extended one or more full months and the contract so provides, the licensee may charge and collect a deferment or default charge only on the installment which is delinquent at the date the contract is extended or deferred.

(f) *Rules and regulations.*—In addition to the general authority granted to him by subsection (a) of section 5–18–12, the supervisor shall have power and authority to make such rules and regulations as he may deem necessary or advisable to insure that rebates, default charges and deferment charges are so computed, paid to or collected from borrowers that the total charges collected by licensees under subdivision (2) of subsection (c) of this section are substantially equivalent to charges authorized to be collected by licensees under subsection (a) or (b) of this section.

(g) *Recording fees.*—The licensee may collect from the borrower the actual fees paid a public official or agency of the state for filing, recording or releasing any instrument securing the loan.

(h) *Further charges; splitting of contracts; certain contracts void.*—No further or other charges shall be directly or indirectly contracted for or received by any licensee, including insurance premiums of any kind, except those specifically authorized by this chapter. No licensee shall divide into separate parts any contract made for the purpose of or with the effect of obtaining charges in excess of those authorized by this section. All balances due to a licensee from any person as a borrower, or as an endorser, guarantor or surety for any borrower or otherwise, or due from any husband or wife, jointly or severally, shall be considered a part of any loan being made by a licensee to such person for the purpose of computing charges. If any amount in excess of the charges permitted by this section is charged, contracted for or received, except as the result of an accidental and bona fide error of computation, the contract of loan shall be void and the licensee shall have no right to collect or receive any cash advanced, charges or recompense whatsoever, the licensee and the several members, officers, directors, agents and employees thereof who shall have participated in such violation shall be guilty of a misdemeanor and, upon conviction thereof, shall be punishable by a fine of not more than $500.00 and not less than $100.00 or by imprisonment of not more than six months, or by both such fine and imprisonment in the discretion of the court. Any borrower may recover the full amount of principal and charges paid by him on any contract made in violation of this section, together with a reasonable attorney fee, by an action at law brought within 12 months from the date of the last payment of principal or charges on such contract.

(i) *Installment payments; contract period.*—No licensee shall enter into any contract of loan under this chapter in which the borrower agrees to make any scheduled repayment of the cash advance more than 25 calendar months from the date of making such contract of loan. Every loan contract shall require payment of the cash advance and charges in installments which shall be payable at approximately equal periodic intervals; except, that payment dates may be omitted to accommodate borrowers with seasonal incomes. No installment contracted for shall be substantially larger than any preceding installment.

(j) *Interest after due date of final installment.*—Interest as provided in this section shall not accrue or be recovered or charged on any loan made under this chapter for any longer than six months after the due date of the final installment of principal or interest. After the expiration of said six-month period, interest may be charged at a rate not to exceed eight percent per annum.

(k) *Inducing borrower to become obligated under more than one contract.*—No licensee shall induce or permit any person or any husband and wife, jointly or severally, to become obligated directly or contingently or both under more than one contract of loan at the same time for the purpose of obtaining a higher rate of charge than would otherwise be permitted by this section. It shall be unlawful for any licensee to evade or attempt to evade this section by inducing a customer to borrow from another loan company in which he has a pecuniary interest or with whom he has an arrangement for exchange of customers.

§ 5-18-16. Duties of licensees as to making and payment of loans

(a) *Copy of contract or statement; receipts; payment in advance; release of obligation and security.*—Every licensee shall:

(1) At the time a loan is made deliver to the borrower or, if there are two or more borrowers, to one of them a copy of the loan contract or a written statement in the English language showing in clear and distinct terms:

a. The name and address of the lender and one of the primary obligors on the loan;

b. The date of the loan contract;

c. Schedule of installments or description thereof;

d. The cash advance;

e. The face amount of the note evidencing the loan;

f. The amount collected or paid for insurance, if any;

g. The amount collected or paid for filing or other fees allowed by this chapter; and

h. The collateral or security for the loan.

(2) Give to the person making any cash payment on account of any loan a receipt at the time such payment is made which receipt need only show the total amount of such cash payment. No receipt shall be required in the case of payments made by the borrower's check or money order, and the use of a coupon book system shall be deemed in compliance with this section.

(3) Permit the payment to be made in advance in any amount on any contract of loan at any time during a licensee's regular business hours.

(4) Upon repayment of the loan in full, mark plainly every obligation and security signed by any obligor with the word "Paid" or "Cancelled," and release any mortgage, restore any pledge and cancel and return any note and any assignment given to the licensee.

(b) *Confessions of judgment; incomplete instruments.*—No licensee shall:

(1) Take any confession of judgment or any power of attorney running to himself or to any third person to confess judgment or to appear for the borrower in a judicial proceeding; nor

(2) Take any note or promise to pay that does not disclose the total amount to be repaid, a schedule of payments or a description thereof and the agreed rate or aggregate amount of charge, nor any instrument in which blanks are left to be filled in after execution.

(c) *Installments.*—Every loan contract shall provide for repayment of principal and charges at approximately equal periodic intervals of time, which shall be so arranged that no installment is substantially greater in amount than any preceding installment.

(d) *Contract in violation of section void.*—Any contract of loan in the making or collection of which any provision of this section shall have been violated, either knowingly or without the exercise of due care to prevent the same, shall be void, and the licensee shall have no right to collect, receive or retain any principal, charges or recompense whatsoever.

§ 5–18–17. Insurance in connection with credit transaction

(a) With respect to any insurance written in connection with any credit transaction under this chapter, the creditor shall be subject to the same restrictions, prohibitions, powers and allowances as any creditor bank, retail establishment, sales finance company, licensee or any other creditor under section 5–19–20; and shall be subject to the same rates and regulations promulgated pursuant to that section. In no case shall the insurance with respect to any credit transaction exceed the amount and term of the credit.

(b) Insurance sold by a licensee or its agents shall be regulated by the supervisor of the bureau of loans. All such insurance shall be written by a company authorized to conduct business in the state of Alabama.

§ 5–18–18. Charges, rates, etc., as to loans of more than $749.00

If a licensee makes a loan in excess of $749.00, the charges authorized by this chapter shall not apply to any part of the loan. The rates on the entire amount of the loan shall be governed by section 8–8–1 or 8–8–2. The foregoing prohibition shall also apply to any licensee who permits any person as borrower or as endorser, guarantor or surety for any borrower or otherwise or any husband and wife, jointly or severally, to owe directly or contingently or both to the licensee at any time a sum of more than $749.00 for principal. The supervisor may suspend or revoke the license of any licensee who violates this section in the manner prescribed by section 5–18–9, and the penalties provided for in section 5–18–24 shall apply to any person, firm or corporation violating this section.

§ 5–18–19. Collection of loans made outside state

Any loans made outside this state in accordance with the law applicable to such loan in the state in which the loan was made may be collected in this state.

§ 5–18–20. Review of orders, etc., of supervisor

In addition to any other remedy he may have, any licensee and any person considering himself aggrieved by any act or order of the supervisor under this chapter may, within 30 days from the entry of the order complained of, or within 60 days of the act complained of if there is no order, petition the circuit court of Montgomery county for review of such act or order; provided, that such petition shall be docketed, heard and tried in the same manner as other extraordinary writs issued by the court and a copy of the petition and order setting the same for hearing shall be served on the supervisor, giving him such notice of the time and place of the hearing as may be directed by the court.

§ 5–18–21. Applicability of chapter to actions on debts or evidences of indebtedness

In any civil action filed on any debt or evidence of any indebtedness governed hereby in any court, the judge thereof shall not render any judgment by default, nil dicit or otherwise until he has heard the testimony of the licensee or of a representative of such licensee, and the judge must on his own motion interrogate such licensee or such other witness to determine whether there has been any violation of the provisions of this chapter and whether any charges have been contracted for, made or received in excess of the amount allowed under this chapter. If it shall be made to appear that the provisions of this chapter have been violated or that charges in excess of those allowed have been contracted for, made or received, then the action shall be dismissed at the cost of the plaintiff. In any such action the plaintiff must allege that he is a licensee under this chapter; and, if such plaintiff is subject to this chapter and fails to allege in his complaint that he is a licensee hereunder or if it is shown to the court that he is subject to this chapter and is not a licensee, then the court ex mero motu shall dismiss the action at the cost of the plaintiff. No garnishment shall issue in such civil action or in connection therewith until after judgment has been entered.

§ 5–18–22. Modification, amendment or repeal of chapter

This chapter or any part thereof may be modified, amended or repealed so as to effect a cancellation or alteration of any license or right of a licensee hereunder; provided, that such cancellation or alteration shall not impair or affect the obligation of any preexisting lawful contract between any licensee and any borrower.

§ 5–18–23. Maintenance of listing of licensees doing business in state; public access to reports, etc.

(a) The supervisor shall cause to be kept on file in the bureau of loans, open to public inspection during business hours, an alphabetical listing of all licensees doing business in Alabama, and such list shall reveal the true ownership of the licensee companies. If the company is a corporation, the list shall indicate the name of the corporation, the address of the home office and the names and addresses of its officers and directors.

(b) Except as provided in subsection (a) of this section, all applications, reports and other papers and documents submitted by licensees to the supervisor or to the bureau shall be open to public inspection only upon approval of the supervisor, but the supervisor shall not deny any person access to such records when the disclosure thereof to such person is in the public interest.

§ 5–18–24. Penalties for violation of provisions of chapter

Any person, firm, corporation or association who shall willfully violate any of the provisions of this chapter for which a specific penalty is not specifically provided shall be guilty of a misdemeanor and, upon conviction thereof, shall be punished by a fine of not more than $500.00 nor less than $100.00 or by imprisonment for not more than six months, or by both such fine and imprisonment in the discretion of the court.

*

CREDIT INSURANCE ACT

MODEL BILL TO PROVIDE FOR THE REGULATION OF CREDIT LIFE INSURANCE AND CREDIT ACCIDENT AND HEALTH INSURANCE

Promulgated by the National Association of Insurance Commissioners (1977)

Table of Sections

---

§ 1. Purpose

The purpose of this Act is to promote the public welfare by regulating credit life insurance and credit accident and health insurance. Nothing in this Act is intended to prohibit or discourage reasonable competition. The provisions of this Act shall be liberally construed.

§ 2. Scope and Definitions

A. Citation and Scope

(1) This Act may be cited as "The Model Act for the Regulation of Credit Life Insurance and Credit Accident and Health Insurance."

(2) All life insurance and all accident and health insurance in connection with loans or other credit transactions shall be subject to the

provisions of this Act, except such insurance in connection with a loan or other credit transaction of more than ten years duration; nor shall insurance be subject to the provisions of this Act where the issuance of such insurance is an isolated transaction on the part of the insurer not related to an agreement or a plan for insuring debtors of the creditor.

B. Definitions

For the purpose of this Act:

(1) "Credit life insurance" means insurance on the life of a debtor pursuant to or in connection with a specific loan or other credit transaction;

(2) "Credit accident and health insurance" means insurance on a debtor to provide indemnity for payments becoming due on a specific loan or other credit transaction while the debtor is disabled as defined in the policy;

(3) "Creditor" means the lender of money or vendor or lessor of goods, services, or property, rights or privileges, for which payment is arranged through a credit transaction, or any successor to the right, title or interest of any such lender, vendor, or lessor, and an affiliate, associate or subsidiary of any of them or any director, officer or employee of any of them or any other person in any way associated with any of them;

(4) "Debtor" means a borrower of money or a purchaser or lessee of goods, services, property, rights or privileges for which payment is arranged through a credit transaction;

(5) "Indebtedness" means the total amount payable by a debtor to a creditor in connection with a loan or other credit transaction;

(6) "Commissioner" means (Insurance Supervisory Authority of the State).

§ 3. Forms of Credit Life Insurance and Credit Accident and Health Insurance

Credit life insurance and credit accident and health insurance shall be issued only in the following forms:

A. Individual policies of life insurance issued to debtors on the term plan;

B. Individual policies of accident and health insurance issued to debtors on a term plan or disability benefit provisions in individual policies of credit life insurance;

C. Group policies of life insurance issued to creditors providing insurance upon the lives of debtors on the term plan;

D. Group policies of accident and health insurance issued to creditors on a term plan insuring debtors or disability benefit provisions in group credit life insurance policies to provide such coverage.

§ 4. Amount of Credit Life Insurance and Credit Accident and Health Insurance

A. Credit Life Insurance

(1) The initial amount of credit life insurance shall not exceed the total amount repayable under the contract of indebtedness and, where an indebtedness is repayable in substantially equal installments, the amount of insurance shall at no time exceed the scheduled or actual amount of unpaid indebtedness, whichever is greater.

Note: If desired the following provisions may be added as subsection (2) and (3).

(2) Notwithstanding the provisions of the above paragraph, insurance on agricultural credit transaction commitments, not exceeding one year in duration may be written up to the amount of the loan commitment, on a non-decreasing or level term plan.

(3) Notwithstanding the provisions of paragraph A(1) of this or any other subsection, insurance on educational credit transaction commitments may be written for the amount of the portion of such commitment that has not been advanced by the creditor.

B. Credit Accident and Health Insurance

The total amount of periodic indemnity payable by credit accident and health insurance in the event of disability, as defined in the policy, shall not exceed the aggregate of the periodic scheduled unpaid installments of the indebtedness; and the amount of each periodic indemnity payment shall not exceed the original indebtedness divided by the number of periodic installments.

§ 5. Term of Credit Life Insurance and Credit Accident and Health Insurance

The term of any credit life insurance or credit accident and health insurance shall, subject to acceptance by the insurer, commence on the date when the debtor becomes obligated to the creditor, except that, where a group policy provides coverage with respect to existing obligations, the insurance on a debtor with respect to such indebtedness shall commence on the effective date of the policy. Where evidence of insurability is required and such evidence is furnished more than thirty (30) days after the date when the debtor becomes obligated to the creditor, the term of the insurance may commence on the date on which the insurance company determines the evidence to be satisfactory, and in such event there shall be an appropriate refund or adjustment of any charge to the debtor for insurance. The term of such insurance shall not extend more than fifteen days beyond the scheduled maturity date of the indebtedness except when extended without additional cost to the debtor. If the indebtedness is discharged due to renewal or refinancing prior to the scheduled maturity date, the insurance in force shall be terminated before any new insurance may be issued in connection with the renewed or refinanced indebtedness. In all cases of termination prior to scheduled maturity, a refund shall be paid or credited as provided in Section 8.

§ 6. Provisions of Policies and Certificates of Insurance: Disclosure to Debtors

A. All credit life insurance and credit accident and health insurance shall be evidenced by an individual policy, or in the case of group insurance by a certificate of insurance, which individual policy or group certificate of insurance shall be delivered to the debtor.

B. Each individual policy or group certificate of credit life insurance, and/or credit accident and health insurance shall, in addition to other requirements of law, set forth the name and home office address of the insurer, the name or names of the debtor or in the case of a certificate under a group policy, the identity by name or otherwise of the debtor, the premium or amount of payment, if any, by the debtor separately for credit life insurance and credit accident and health insurance, a description of the coverage including the amount and term thereof, and any exceptions, limitations and restrictions, and shall state that the benefits shall be paid to the creditor to reduce or extinguish the unpaid indebtedness and, wherever the amount of insurance may exceed the unpaid indebtedness, that any such excess shall be payable to a beneficiary, other than the creditor, named by the debtor or to his estate.

C. Said individual policy or group certificate of insurance shall be delivered to the insured debtor at the time the indebtedness is incurred except as hereinafter provided.

D. If said individual policy or group certificate of insurance is not delivered to the debtor at the time the indebtedness is incurred, a copy of the application for such policy or a notice of proposed insurance, signed by the debtor and setting forth the name and home office address of the insurer, the name or names of the debtor, the premium or amount of payment by the debtor, if any, separately for credit life insurance and credit accident and health insurance, the amount, term and a brief description of the coverage provided, shall be delivered to the debtor at the time such indebtedness is incurred. The copy of the application for, or notice of proposed insurance, shall also refer exclusively to insurance coverage, and shall be separate and apart from the loan, sale or other credit statement of account, instrument or agreement, unless the information required by this subsection is prominently set forth therein. Upon acceptance of the insurance by the insurer and within thirty (30) days of the date upon which the indebtedness is incurred, the insurer shall cause the individual policy or group certificates of insurance to be delivered to the debtor. Said application or notice of proposed insurance shall state that upon acceptance by the insurer, the insurance shall become effective as provided in Section 5.

E. If the named insurer does not accept the risk, then and in such event the debtor shall receive a policy or certificate of insurance setting forth the name and home office address of the substituted insurer and the amount of the premium to be charged, and if the amount of premium is less than that set forth in the notice of proposed insurance an appropriate refund shall be made.

§ 7. Filing, Approval and Withdrawal of Forms

A. All policies, certificates of insurance, notices of proposed insurance, applications for insurance, endorsements and riders delivered or issued for delivery in this State and the schedules of premium rates pertaining thereto shall be filed with the Commissioner.

B. The Commissioner shall within thirty (30) days after the filing of any such policies, certificates of insurance, notices of proposed insurance, applications for insurance, endorsements and riders, disapprove any such form if the benefits provided therein are not reasonable in relation to the premium charge, or if it contains provisions which are unjust, unfair, inequitable, misleading, deceptive or encourage misrepresentation of the coverage, or are contrary to any provision of the Insurance Code or of any rule or regulation promulgated thereunder.

C. If the Commissioner notifies the insurer that the form is disapproved, it is unlawful thereafter for such insurer to issue or use such form. In such notice, the Commissioner shall specify the reason for his disapproval and state that a hearing will be granted within twenty (20) days after request in writing by the insurer. No such policy, certificate of insurance, notice of proposed insurance, nor any application, endorsement or rider, shall be issued or used until the expiration of thirty (30) days after it has been so filed, unless the Commissioner shall give his prior written approval thereto.

D. The Commissioner may, at any time after a hearing held not less than twenty (20) days after written notice to the insurer, withdraw his approval of any such form on any ground set forth in subsection B above. The written notice of such hearing shall state the reason for the proposed withdrawal.

E. It is not lawful for the insurer to issue such forms or use them after the effective date of such withdrawal.

F. If a group policy of credit life insurance or credit accident and health insurance

(i) has been delivered in this State before the effective date of this Act, or

(ii) has been or is delivered in another State before or after the effective date of this Act,

the insurer shall be required to file only the group certificate and notice of proposed insurance delivered or issued for delivery in this State as specified in subsections B and D of Section 6 of this Act and such forms shall be approved by the Commissioner if they conform with the requirements specified in said subsections and if the schedules of premium rates applicable to the insurance evidenced by such certificate or notice are not in excess of the insurer's schedules of premium rates filed with the Commissioner; provided, however, the premium rate in effect on existing group policies may be continued until the first policy anniversary date following the date this Act becomes operative as provided in Section 12.

G. Any order or final determination of the Commissioner under the provisions of this section shall be subject to judicial review.

§ 8. Premiums and Refunds

A. Any insurer may revise its schedules of premium rates from time to time, and shall file such revised schedules with the Commissioner. No insurer shall issue any credit life insurance policy or credit accident and health insurance policy for which the premium rate exceeds that determined by the schedules of such insurer as then on file with the Commissioner.

B. Each individual policy, or group certificate shall provide that in the event of termination of the insurance prior to the scheduled maturity date of the indebtedness, any refund of an amount paid by the debtor for insurance shall be paid or credited promptly to the person entitled thereto; provided, however, that the Commissioner shall prescribe a minimum refund and no refund which would be less than such minimum need be made. The formula to be used in computing such refund shall be filed with and approved by the Commissioner.

C. If a creditor requires a debtor to make any payment for credit life insurance or credit accident and health insurance and an individual policy or group certificate of insurance is not issued, the creditor shall immediately give written notice to such debtor and shall promptly make an appropriate credit to the account.

D. The amount charged to a debtor for any credit life or credit health and accident insurance shall not exceed the premiums charged by the insurer, as computed at the time the charge to the debtor is determined.

Note: Where a state prohibits payments for insurance by the debtor in connection with credit transactions, the following paragraph may be included.

E. Nothing in this Act shall be construed to authorize any payments for insurance now prohibited under any statute, or rule thereunder, governing credit transactions.

§ 9. Issuance of Policies

All policies of credit life insurance and credit accident and health insurance shall be delivered or issued for delivery in this state only by an insurer authorized to do an insurance business therein, and shall be issued only through holders of licenses or authorizations issued by the Commissioner.

§ 10. Claims

A. All claims shall be promptly reported to the insurer or its designated claim representative, and the insurer shall maintain adequate claim files. All claims shall be settled as soon as possible and in accordance with the terms of the insurance contract.

B. All claims shall be paid either by draft drawn upon the insurer or by check of the insurer to the order of the claimant to whom payment of the claim is due pursuant to the policy provisions, or upon direction of such claimant to one specified.

C. No plan or arrangement shall be used whereby any person, firm or corporation other than the insurer or its designated claim representative shall be authorized to settle or adjust claims. The creditor shall not be designated as claim representative for the insurer in adjusting claims; provided, that a group policyholder may, by arrangement with the group insurer, draw drafts or checks in payment of claims due to the group policyholder subject to audit and review by the insurer.

§ 11. Existing Insurance—Choice of Insurer

When credit life insurance or credit accident and health insurance is required as additional security for any indebtedness, the debtor shall, upon request to the creditor, have the option of furnishing the required amount of insurance through existing policies of insurance owned or controlled by him or of procuring and furnishing the required coverage through any insurer authorized to transact an insurance business within this state.

§ 12. Enforcement

The Commissioner may, after notice and hearing, issue such rules and regulations as he deems appropriate for the supervision of this

Act. Whenever the Commissioner finds that there has been a violation of this Act or any rules or regulations issued pursuant thereto, and after written notice thereof and hearing given to the insurer or other person authorized or licensed by the Commissioner, he shall set forth the details of his findings together with an order for compliance by a specified date. Such order shall be binding on the insurer and other person authorized or licensed by the Commissioner on the date specified unless sooner withdrawn by the Commissioner or a stay thereof has been ordered by a court of competent jurisdiction. The provisions of Sections 5, 6, 7 and 8 of this Act shall not be operative until ninety (90) days after the effective date of this Act, and the Commissioner in his discretion may extend by not more than an additional ninety (90) days the initial period within which the provisions of said sections shall not be operative.

§ 13. Judicial Review

Any party to the proceeding affected by an order of the Commissioner shall be entitled to judicial review by following the procedure set forth in (insert applicable section).

§ 14. Penalties

In addition to any other penalty provided by law, any person, firm or corporation which violates an order of the Commissioner after it has become final, and while such order is in effect, shall, upon proof thereof to the satisfaction of the court, forfeit and pay to the State of (insert state) a sum not to exceed $250.00 which may be recovered in a civil action, except that if such violation is found to be willful, the amount of such penalty shall be a sum not to exceed $1,000.00. The Commissioner, in his discretion, may revoke or suspend the license or certificate of authority of the person, firm or corporation guilty of such violation. Such order for suspension or revocation shall be upon notice and hearing, and shall be subject to judicial review as provided in Section 13 of this Act.

§ 15. Separability Provision

If any provision of this Act, or the application of such provision to any person or circumstances, shall be held invalid, the remainder of the Act, and the application of such provision to any person or circumstances other than those as to which it is held invalid, shall not be affected thereby.

UNIFORM COMMERCIAL CODE

Table of Sections

ARTICLE 1. GENERAL PROVISIONS

PART 1. SHORT TITLE, CONSTRUCTION, APPLICATION AND SUBJECT MATTER OF THE ACT

PART 2. GENERAL DEFINITIONS AND PRINCIPLES OF INTERPRETATION

ARTICLE 2. SALES

PART 1. SHORT TITLE, GENERAL CONSTRUCTION AND SUBJECT MATTER

PART 2. FORM, FORMATION AND READJUSTMENT OF CONTRACT

PART 3. GENERAL OBLIGATION AND CONSTRUCTION OF CONTRACT

PART 4. TITLE, CREDITORS AND GOOD FAITH PURCHASERS [Omitted]

PART 5. PERFORMANCE

PART 6. BREACH, REPUDIATION AND EXCUSE

PART 7. REMEDIES

ARTICLE 3. COMMERCIAL PAPER

PART 1. SHORT TITLE, FORM AND INTERPRETATION

PART 5. PRESENTMENT, NOTICE OF DISHONOR AND PROTEST [Omitted]

PART 6. DISCHARGE [Omitted]

PART 7. ADVICE OF INTERNATIONAL SIGHT DRAFT [Omitted]

PART 8. MISCELLANEOUS [Omitted]

ARTICLE 4. BANK DEPOSITS AND COLLECTIONS [Omitted]

ARTICLE 5. LETTERS OF CREDIT [Omitted]

ARTICLE 6. BULK TRANSFERS [Omitted]

ARTICLE 7. WAREHOUSE RECEIPTS, BILLS OF LADING AND OTHER DOCUMENTS OF TITLE

PART 1. GENERAL [Omitted]

PART 2. WAREHOUSE RECEIPTS: SPECIAL PROVISIONS

PART 3. BILLS OF LADING: SPECIAL PROVISIONS [Omitted]

PART 4. WAREHOUSE RECEIPTS AND BILLS OF LADING: GENERAL OBLIGATIONS [Omitted]

PART 5. WAREHOUSE RECEIPTS AND BILLS OF LADING: NEGOTIATION AND TRANSFER [Omitted]

ARTICLE 8. INVESTMENT SECURITIES [Omitted]

ARTICLE 9. SECURED TRANSACTIONS; SALES OF ACCOUNTS AND CHATTEL PAPER

PART 1. SHORT TITLE, APPLICABILITY AND DEFINITIONS

PART 2. VALIDITY OF SECURITY AGREEMENT AND RIGHTS OF PARTIES THERETO

PART 3. RIGHTS OF THIRD PARTIES; PERFECTED AND UNPERFECTED SECURITY INTERESTS; RULES OF PRIORITY [Omitted]

PART 4. FILING [Omitted]

ARTICLE 1. GENERAL PROVISIONS

PART 1. SHORT TITLE, CONSTRUCTION, APPLICATION AND SUBJECT MATTER OF THE ACT

§ 1–101. Short Title

This Act shall be known and may be cited as Uniform Commercial Code.

§ 1–102. Purposes; Rules of Construction; Variation by Agreement

(1) This Act shall be liberally construed and applied to promote its underlying purposes and policies.

(2) Underlying purposes and policies of this Act are

(a) to simplify, clarify and modernize the law governing commercial transactions;

(b) to permit the continued expansion of commercial practices through custom, usage and agreement of the parties;

(c) to make uniform the law among the various jurisdictions.

(3) The effect of provisions of this Act may be varied by agreement, except as otherwise provided in this Act and except that the obligations of good faith, diligence, reasonableness and care prescribed by this Act may not be disclaimed by agreement but the parties may by agreement determine the standards by which the performance of such obligations is to be measured if such standards are not manifestly unreasonable.

(4) The presence in certain provisions of this Act of the words "unless otherwise agreed" or words of similar import does not imply that the effect of other provisions may not be varied by agreement under subsection (3).

(5) In this Act unless the context otherwise requires

(a) words in the singular number include the plural, and in the plural include the singular;

(b) words of the masculine gender include the feminine and the neuter, and when the sense so indicates words of the neuter gender may refer to any gender.

§ 1-103. Supplementary General Principles of Law Applicable

Unless displaced by the particular provisions of this Act, the principles of law and equity, including the law merchant and the law relative to capacity to contract, principal and agent, estoppel, fraud, misrepresentation, duress, coercion, mistake, bankruptcy, or other validating or invalidating cause shall supplement its provisions.

§ 1-104. Construction Against Implicit Repeal

This Act being a general act intended as a unified coverage of its subject matter, no part of it shall be deemed to be impliedly repealed by subsequent legislation if such construction can reasonably be avoided.

§ 1-105. Territorial Application of the Act; Parties' Power to Choose Applicable Law

(1) Except as provided hereafter in this section, when a transaction bears a reasonable relation to this state and also to another state or nation the parties may agree that the law either of this state or of such other state or nation shall govern their rights and duties. Failing such agreement this Act applies to transactions bearing an appropriate relation to this state.

. . .

§ 1–106. Remedies to Be Liberally Administered

(1) The remedies provided by this Act shall be liberally administered to the end that the aggrieved party may be put in as good a position as if the other party had fully performed but neither consequential or special nor penal damages may be had except as specifically provided in this Act or by other rule of law.

(2) Any right or obligation declared by this Act is enforceable by action unless the provision declaring it specifies a different and limited effect.

PART 2. GENERAL DEFINITIONS AND PRINCIPLES OF INTERPRETATION

§ 1–201. General Definitions

Subject to additional definitions contained in the subsequent Articles of this Act which are applicable to specific Articles or Parts thereof, and unless the context otherwise requires, in this Act:

(1) "Action" in the sense of a judicial proceeding includes recoupment, counterclaim, set-off, suit in equity and any other proceedings in which rights are determined.

(2) "Aggrieved party" means a party entitled to resort to a remedy.

(3) "Agreement" means the bargain of the parties in fact as found in their language or by implication from other circumstances including course of dealing or usage of trade or course of performance as provided in this Act (Sections 1–205 and 2–208). Whether an agreement has legal consequences is determined by the provisions of this Act, if applicable; otherwise by the law of contracts (Section 1–103). (Compare "Contract".)

(4) "Bank" means any person engaged in the business of banking.

(5) "Bearer" means the person in possession of an instrument, document of title, or certified security payable to bearer or indorsed in blank.

(6) "Bill of lading" means a document evidencing the receipt of goods for shipment issued by a person engaged in the business of transporting or forwarding goods, and includes an airbill. "Airbill" means a document serving for air transportation as a bill of lading does for marine or rail transportation, and includes an air consignment note or air waybill.

(7) "Branch" includes a separately incorporated foreign branch of a bank.

(8) "Burden of establishing" a fact means the burden of persuading the triers of fact that the existence of the fact is more probable than its non-existence.

(9) "Buyer in ordinary course of business" means a person who in good faith and without knowledge that the sale to him is in violation of the ownership rights or security interest of a third party in the goods buys in ordinary course from a person in the business of selling goods of that kind but does not include a pawnbroker. All persons who sell minerals or the like (including oil and gas) at wellhead or minehead shall be deemed to be persons in the business of selling goods of that kind. "Buying" may be for cash or by exchange of other property or on secured or unsecured credit and includes receiving goods or documents of title under a pre-existing contract for sale but does not include a transfer in bulk or as security for or in total or partial satisfaction of a money debt.

(10) "Conspicuous": A term or clause is conspicuous when it is so written that a reasonable person against whom it is to operate ought to have noticed it. A printed heading in capitals (as: NON-NEGOTIABLE BILL OF LADING) is conspicuous. Language in the body of a form is "conspicuous" if it is in larger or other contrasting type or color. But in a telegram any stated term is "conspicuous". Whether a term or clause is "conspicuous" or not is for decision by the court.

(11) "Contract" means the total legal obligation which results from the parties' agreement as affected by this Act and any other applicable rules of law. (Compare "Agreement".)

(12) "Creditor" includes a general creditor, a secured creditor, a lien creditor and any representative of creditors, including an assignee for the benefit of creditors, a trustee in bankruptcy, a receiver in equity and an executor or administrator of an insolvent debtor's or assignor's estate.

(13) "Defendant" includes a person in the position of defendant in a cross-action or counterclaim.

(14) "Delivery" with respect to instruments, documents of title, chattel paper, or certificated securities means voluntary transfer of possession.

(15) "Document of title" includes bill of lading, dock warrant, dock receipt, warehouse receipt or order for the delivery of goods, and also any other document which in the regular course of business or financing is treated as adequately evidencing that the person in possession of it is entitled to receive, hold and dispose of the document and the goods it covers. To be a document of title a document must purport to be issued by or addressed to a bailee and purport to cover goods in the bailee's possession which are either identified or are fungible portions of an identified mass.

(16) "Fault" means wrongful act, omission or breach.

(17) "Fungible" with respect to goods or securities means goods or securities of which any unit is, by nature or usage of trade, the equivalent of any other like unit. Goods which are not fungible shall

be deemed fungible for the purposes of this Act to the extent that under a particular agreement or document unlike units are treated as equivalents.

(18) "Genuine" means free of forgery or counterfeiting.

(19) "Good faith" means honesty in fact in the conduct or transaction concerned.

(20) "Holder" means a person who is in possession of a document of title or an instrument or a certificated investment security drawn, issued, or indorsed to him or his order or to bearer or in blank.

(21) To "honor" is to pay or to accept and pay, or where a credit so engages to purchase or discount a draft complying with the terms of the credit.

(22) "Insolvency proceedings" includes any assignment for the benefit of creditors or other proceedings intended to liquidate or rehabilitate the estate of the person involved.

(23) A person is "insolvent" who either has ceased to pay his debts in the ordinary course of business or cannot pay his debts as they become due or is insolvent within the meaning of the federal bankruptcy law.

(24) "Money" means a medium of exchange authorized or adopted by a domestic or foreign government as a part of its currency.

(25) A person has "notice" of a fact when

(a) he has actual knowledge of it; or

(b) he has received a notice or notification of it; or

(c) from all the facts and circumstances known to him at the time in question he has reason to know that it exists.

A person "knows" or has "knowledge" of a fact when he has actual knowledge of it. "Discover" or "learn" or a word or phrase of similar import refers to knowledge rather than to reason to know. The time and circumstances under which a notice or notification may cease to be effective are not determined by this Act.

(26) A person "notifies" or "gives" a notice or notification to another by taking such steps as may be reasonably required to inform the other in ordinary course whether or not such other actually comes to know of it. A person "receives" a notice or notification when

(a) it comes to his attention; or

(b) it is duly delivered at the place of business through which the contract was made or at any other place held out by him as the place for receipt of such communications.

(27) Notice, knowledge or a notice or notification received by an organization is effective for a particular transaction from the time when it is brought to the attention of the individual conducting that transaction, and in any event from the time when it would have been

brought to his attention if the organization had exercised due diligence. An organization exercises due diligence if it maintains reasonable routines for communicating significant information to the person conducting the transaction and there is reasonable compliance with the routines. Due diligence does not require an individual acting for the organization to communicate information unless such communication is part of his regular duties or unless he has reason to know of the transaction and that the transaction would be materially affected by the information.

(28) "Organization" includes a corporation, government or governmental subdivision or agency, business trust, estate, trust, partnership or association, two or more persons having a joint or common interest, or any other legal or commercial entity.

(29) "Party", as distinct from "third party", means a person who has engaged in a transaction or made an agreement within this Act.

(30) "Person" includes an individual or an organization (See Section 1-102).

(31) "Presumption" or "presumed" means that the trier of fact must find the existence of the fact presumed unless and until evidence is introduced which would support a finding of its non-existence.

(32) "Purchase" includes taking by sale, discount, negotiation, mortgage, pledge, lien, issue or re-issue, gift or any other voluntary transaction creating an interest in property.

(33) "Purchaser" means a person who takes by purchase.

(34) "Remedy" means any remedial right to which an aggrieved party is entitled with or without resort to a tribunal.

(35) "Representative" includes an agent, an officer of a corporation or association, and a trustee, executor or administrator of an estate, or any other person empowered to act for another.

(36) "Rights" includes remedies.

(37) "Security interest" means an interest in personal property or fixtures which secures payment or performance of an obligation. The retention or reservation of title by a seller of goods notwithstanding shipment or delivery to the buyer (Section 2-401) is limited in effect to a reservation of a "security interest". The term also includes any interest of a buyer of accounts or chattel paper which is subject to Article 9. The special property interest of a buyer of goods on identification of such goods to a contract for sale under Section 2-401 is not a "security interest", but a buyer may also acquire a "security interest" by complying with Article 9. Unless a lease or consignment is intended as security, reservation of title thereunder is not a "security interest" but a consignment is in any event subject to the provisions on consignment sales (Section 2-326). Whether a lease is intended as security is to be determined by the facts of each case;

however, (a) the inclusion of an option to purchase does not of itself make the lease one intended for security, and (b) an agreement that upon compliance with the terms of the lease the lessee shall become or has the option to become the owner of the property for no additional consideration or for a nominal consideration does make the lease one intended for security.

(38) "Send" in connection with any writing or notice means to deposit in the mail or deliver for transmission by any other usual means of communication with postage or cost of transmission provided for and properly addressed and in the case of an instrument to an address specified thereon or otherwise agreed, or if there be none to any address reasonable under the circumstances. The receipt of any writing or notice within the time at which it would have arrived if properly sent has the effect of a proper sending.

(39) "Signed" includes any symbol executed or adopted by a party with present intention to authenticate a writing.

(40) "Surety" includes guarantor.

(41) "Telegram" includes a message transmitted by radio, teletype, cable, any mechanical method of transmission, or the like.

(42) "Term" means that portion of an agreement which relates to a particular matter.

(43) "Unauthorized" signature or indorsement means one made without actual, implied or apparent authority and includes a forgery.

(44) "Value". Except as otherwise provided with respect to negotiable instruments and bank collections (Sections 3-303, 4-208 and 4-209) a person gives "value" for rights if he acquires them

(a) in return for a binding commitment to extend credit or for the extension of immediately available credit whether or not drawn upon and whether or not a chargeback is provided for in the event of difficulties in collection; or

(b) as security for or in total or partial satisfaction of a pre-existing claim; or

(c) by accepting delivery pursuant to a pre-existing contract for purchase; or

(d) generally, in return for any consideration sufficient to support a simple contract.

(45) "Warehouse receipt" means a receipt issued by a person engaged in the business of storing goods for hire.

(46) "Written" or "writing" includes printing, typewriting or any other intentional reduction to tangible form.

§ 1–203. Obligation of Good Faith

Every contract or duty within this Act imposes an obligation of good faith in its performance or enforcement.

Official Comment

Purposes:

This section sets forth a basic principle running throughout this Act. The principle involved is that in commercial transactions good faith is required in the performance and enforcement of all agreements or duties. Particular applications of this general principle appear in specific provisions of the Act such as the option to accelerate at will (Section 1–208), the right to cure a defective delivery of goods (Section 2–508), the duty of a merchant buyer who has rejected goods to effect salvage operations (Section 2–603), substituted performance (Section 2–614), and failure of presupposed conditions (Section 2–615). The concept, however, is broader than any of these illustrations and applies generally, as stated in this section, to the performance or enforcement of every contract or duty within this Act. It is further implemented by Section 1–205 on course of dealing and usage of trade.

It is to be noted that under the Sales Article definition of good faith (Section 2–103), contracts made by a merchant have incorporated in them the explicit standard not only of honesty in fact (Section 1–201), but also of observance by the merchant of reasonable commercial standards of fair dealing in the trade.

§ 1–207. Performance or Acceptance Under Reservation of Rights

A party who with explicit reservation of rights performs or promises performance or assents to performance in a manner demanded or offered by the other party does not thereby prejudice the rights reserved. Such words as "without prejudice", "under protest" or the like are sufficient.

§ 1–208. Option to Accelerate at Will

A term providing that one party or his successor in interest may accelerate payment or performance or require collateral or additional collateral "at will" or "when he deems himself insecure" or in words of similar import shall be construed to mean that he shall have power to do so only if he in good faith believes that the prospect of payment or performance is impaired. The burden of establishing lack of good faith is on the party against whom the power has been exercised.

Official Comment

Purposes:

The increased use of acceleration clauses either in the case of sales on credit or in time paper or in security transactions has led to some confusion in the cases as to the effect to be given to a clause which seemingly grants the power of an acceleration at the whim and caprice of one party. This Section is intended to make clear that despite language which can be so construed and which further might be held to make the agreement void as against public policy or to make the contract illusory or too indefinite for enforcement, the clause means that the option is to be exercised only in the good faith belief that the prospect of payment or performance is impaired.

Obviously this section has no application to demand instruments or obligations whose very nature permits call at any time with or without reason. This section applies only to an agreement or to paper which in the first instance is payable at a future date.

ARTICLE 2. SALES

PART 1. SHORT TITLE, GENERAL CONSTRUCTION AND SUBJECT MATTER

§ 2–102. Scope; Certain Security and Other Transactions Excluded From This Article

Unless the context otherwise requires, this Article applies to transactions in goods; it does not apply to any transaction which although in the form of an unconditional contract to sell or present sale is intended to operate only as a security transaction nor does this Article impair or repeal any statute regulating sales to consumers, farmers or other specified classes of buyers.

§ 2–103. Definitions and Index of Definitions

(1) In this Article unless the context otherwise requires

(a) "Buyer" means a person who buys or contracts to buy goods.

(b) "Good faith" in the case of a merchant means honesty in fact and the observance of reasonable commercial standards of fair dealing in the trade.

(c) "Receipt" of goods means taking physical possession of them.

(d) "Seller" means a person who sells or contracts to sell goods.

. . .

(4) In addition Article 1 contains general definitions and principles of construction and interpretation applicable throughout this Article.

§ 2–104. Definitions: "Merchant"; "Between Merchants"; "Financing Agency"

(1) "Merchant" means a person who deals in goods of the kind or otherwise by his occupation holds himself out as having knowledge or skill peculiar to the practices or goods involved in the transaction or to whom such knowledge or skill may be attributed by his employment of an agent or broker or other intermediary who by his occupation holds himself out as having such knowledge or skill.

(2) "Financing agency" means a bank, finance company or other person who in the ordinary course of business makes advances against goods or documents of title or who by arrangement with either the seller or the buyer intervenes in ordinary course to make or collect payment due or claimed under the contract for sale, as by purchasing or paying the seller's draft or making advances against it or by merely taking it for collection whether or not documents of title accompany the draft. "Financing agency" includes also a bank or

other person who similarly intervenes between persons who are in the position of seller and buyer in respect to the goods (Section 2–707).

(3) "Between merchants" means in any transaction with respect to which both parties are chargeable with the knowledge or skill of merchants.

Official Comment

Purposes:

1. This Article assumes that transactions between professionals in a given field require special and clear rules which may not apply to a casual or inexperienced seller or buyer. It thus adopts a policy of expressly stating rules applicable "between merchants" and "as against a merchant", wherever they are needed instead of making them depend upon the circumstances of each . . . case. This section lays the foundation of this policy by defining those who are to be regarded as professionals or "merchants" and by stating when a transaction is deemed to be "between merchants".

2. The term "merchant" as defined here roots in the "law merchant" concept of a professional in business. The professional status under the definition may be based upon specialized knowledge as to the goods, specialized knowledge as to business practices, or specialized knowledge as to both and which kind of specialized knowledge may be sufficient to establish the merchant status is indicated by the nature of the provisions.

The special provisions as to merchants appear only in this Article and they are of three kinds. Sections 2–201(2), 2–205, 2–207 and 2–209 dealing with the statute of frauds, firm offers, confirmatory memoranda and modification rest on normal business practices which are or ought to be typical of and familiar to any person in business. For purposes of these sections almost every person in business would, therefore, be deemed to be a "merchant" under the language "who . . . by his occupation holds himself out as having knowledge or skill peculiar to the practices . . . involved in the transaction . . ." since the practices involved in the transaction are non-specialized business practices such as answering mail. In this type of provision, banks or even universities, for example, well may be "merchants." But even these sections only apply to a merchant in his mercantile capacity; a lawyer or bank president buying fishing tackle for his own use is not a merchant.

On the other hand, in Section 2–314 on the warranty of merchantability, such warranty is implied only "if the seller is a merchant with respect to goods of that kind." Obviously this qualification restricts the implied warranty to a much smaller group than everyone who is engaged in business and requires a professional status as to particular kinds of goods. . . .

A third group of sections includes 2–103(1)(b), which provides that in the case of a merchant "good faith" includes observance of reasonable commercial standards of fair dealing in the trade; . . . .

3. The "or to whom such knowledge or skill may be attributed by his employment of an agent or broker . . ." clause of the definition of

merchant means that even persons such as universities, for example, can come within the definition of merchant if they have regular purchasing departments or business personnel who are familiar with business practices and who are equipped to take any action required.

§ 2–106. Definitions: "Contract"; "Agreement"; "Contract for Sale"; "Sale"; "Present Sale"; "Conforming" to Contract; "Termination"; "Cancellation"

(1) In this Article unless the context otherwise requires "contract" and "agreement" are limited to those relating to the present or future sale of goods. "Contract for sale" includes both a present sale of goods and a contract to sell goods at a future time. A "sale" consists in the passing of title from the seller to the buyer for a price (Section 2–401). A "present sale" means a sale which is accomplished by the making of the contract.

(2) Goods or conduct including any part of a performance are "conforming" or conform to the contract when they are in accordance with the obligations under the contract.

(3) "Termination" occurs when either party pursuant to a power created by agreement or law puts an end to the contract otherwise than for its breach. On "termination" all obligations which are still executory on both sides are discharged but any right based on prior breach or performance survives.

(4) "Cancellation" occurs when either party puts an end to the contract for breach by the other and its effect is the same as that of "termination" except that the cancelling party also retains any remedy for breach of the whole contract or any unperformed balance.

PART 2. FORM, FORMATION AND READJUSTMENT OF CONTRACT

§ 2–202. Final Written Expression: Parol or Extrinsic Evidence

Terms with respect to which the confirmatory memoranda of the parties agree or which are otherwise set forth in a writing intended by the parties as a final expression of their agreement with respect to such terms as are included therein may not be contradicted by evidence of any prior agreement or of a contemporaneous oral agreement but may be explained or supplemented

(a) by course of dealing or usage of trade (Section 1–205) or by course of performance (Section 2–208); and

(b) by evidence of consistent additional terms unless the court finds the writing to have been intended also as a complete and exclusive statement of the terms of the agreement.

Official Comment

Purposes:

1. This section definitely rejects:

(a) Any assumption that because a writing has been worked out which is final on some matters, it is to be taken as including all the matters agreed upon;

(b) The premise that the language used has the meaning attributable to such language by rules of construction existing in the law rather than the meaning which arises out of the commercial context in which it was used; and

(c) The requirement that a condition precedent to the admissibility of the type of evidence specified in paragraph (a) is an original determination by the court that the language used is ambiguous.

2. Paragraph (a) makes admissible evidence of course of dealing, usage of trade and course of performance to explain or supplement the terms of any writing stating the agreement of the parties in order that the true understanding of the parties as to the agreement maybe reached. Such writings are to be read on the assumption that the course of prior dealings between the parties and the usages of trade were taken for granted when the document was phrased. Unless carefully negated they have become an element of the meaning of the words used. Similarly, the course of actual performance by the parties is considered the best indication of what they intended the writing to mean.

3. Under paragraph (b) consistent additional terms, not reduced to writing, may be proved unless the court finds that the writing was intended by both parties as a complete and exclusive statement of all the terms. If the additional terms are such that, if agreed upon, they would certainly have been included in the document in the view of the court, then evidence of their alleged making must be kept from the trier of fact.

§ 2-209. Modification, Rescission and Waiver

(1) An agreement modifying a contract within this Article needs no consideration to be binding.

(2) A signed agreement which excludes modification or rescission except by a signed writing cannot be otherwise modified or rescinded, but except as between merchants such a requirement on a form supplied by the merchant must be separately signed by the other party.

(3) The requirements of the statute of frauds section of this Article (Section 2-201) must be satisfied if the contract as modified is within its provisions.

(4) Although an attempt at modification or rescission does not satisfy the requirements of subsection (2) or (3) it can operate as a waiver.

(5) A party who has made a waiver affecting an executory portion of the contract may retract the waiver by reasonable notification re-

ceived by the other party that strict performance will be required of any term waived, unless the retraction would be unjust in view of a material change of position in reliance on the waiver.

§ 2-210. Delegation of Performance; Assignment of Rights

(1) A party may perform his duty through a delegate unless otherwise agreed or unless the other party has a substantial interest in having his original promisor perform or control the acts required by the contract. No delegation of performance relieves the party delegating of any duty to perform or any liability for breach.

(2) Unless otherwise agreed all rights of either seller or buyer can be assigned except where the assignment would materially change the duty of the other party, or increase materially the burden or risk imposed on him by his contract, or impair materially his chance of obtaining return performance. A right to damages for breach of the whole contract or a right arising out of the assignor's due performance of his entire obligation can be assigned despite agreement otherwise.

(3) Unless the circumstances indicate the contrary a prohibition of assignment of "the contract" is to be construed as barring only the delegation to the assignee of the assignor's performance.

(4) An assignment of "the contract" or of "all my rights under the contract" or an assignment in similar general terms is an assignment of rights and unless the language or the circumstances (as in an assignment for security) indicate the contrary, it is a delegation of performance of the duties of the assignor and its acceptance by the assignee constitutes a promise by him to perform those duties. This promise is enforceable by either the assignor or the other party to the original contract.

(5) The other party may treat any assignment which delegates performance as creating reasonable grounds for insecurity and may without prejudice to his rights against the assignor demand assurances from the assignee (Section 2-609).

PART 3. GENERAL OBLIGATION AND CONSTRUCTION OF CONTRACT

§ 2-301. General Obligations of Parties

The obligation of the seller is to transfer and deliver and that of the buyer is to accept and pay in accordance with the contract.

§ 2-302. Unconscionable Contract or Clause

(1) If the court as a matter of law finds the contract or any clause of the contract to have been unconscionable at the time it was made

the court may refuse to enforce the contract, or it may enforce the remainder of the contract without the unconscionable clause, or it may so limit the application of any unconscionable clause as to avoid any unconscionable result.

(2) When it is claimed or appears to the court that the contract or any clause thereof may be unconscionable the parties shall be afforded a reasonable opportunity to present evidence as to its commercial setting, purpose and effect to aid the court in making the determination.

Official Comment

Purposes:

1. This section is intended to make it possible for the courts to police explicitly against the contracts or clauses which they find to be unconscionable. In the past such policing has been accomplished by adverse construction of language, by manipulation of the rules of offer and acceptance or by determinations that the clause is contrary to public policy or to the dominant purpose of the contract. This section is intended to allow the court to pass directly on the unconscionability of the contract or particular clause therein and to make a conclusion of law as to its unconscionability. The basic test is whether, in the light of the general commercial background and the commercial needs of the particular trade or case, the clauses involved are so one-sided as to be unconscionable under the circumstances existing at the time of the making of the contract. Subsection (2) makes it clear that it is proper for the court to hear evidence upon these questions. The principle is one of the prevention of oppression and unfair surprise (Cf. Campbell Soup Co. v. Wentz, 172 F.2d 80, 3d Cir. 1948) and not of disturbance of allocation of risks because of superior bargaining power. The underlying basis of this section is illustrated by the results in cases such as the following:

Kansas City Wholesale Grocery Co. v. Weber Packing Corporation, 93 Utah 414, 73 P.2d 1272 (1937), where a clause limiting time for complaints was held inapplicable to latent defects in a shipment of catsup which could be discovered only by microscopic analysis; Hardy v. General Motors Acceptance Corporation, 38 Ga.App. 463, 144 S.E. 327 (1928), holding that a disclaimer of warranty clause applied only to express warranties, thus letting in a fair implied warranty; Andrews Bros. v. Singer & Co. (1934 CA) 1 K.B. 17, holding that where a car with substantial mileage was delivered instead of a "new" car, a disclaimer of warranties, including those "implied," left unaffected an "express obligation" on the description, even though the Sale of Goods Act called such an implied warranty; New Prague Flouring Mill Co. v. G. A. Spears, 194 Iowa 417, 189 N.W. 815 (1922), holding that a clause permitting the seller, upon the buyer's failure to supply shipping instructions, to cancel, ship, or allow delivery date to be indefinitely postponed 30 days at a time by the inaction, does not indefinitely postpone the date of measuring damages for the buyer's breach, to the seller's advantage; and Kansas Flour Mills Co. v. Dirks, 100 Kan. 376, 164 P. 273 (1917), where under a similar clause in a rising market the court permitted the buyer to measure his damages for non-delivery at the end of only one 30 day postponement; Green v.

Arcos, Ltd. (1931 CA) 47 T.L.R. 336, where a blanket clause prohibiting rejection of shipments by the buyer was restricted to apply to shipments where discrepancies represented merely mercantile variations; Meyer v. Packard Cleveland Motor Co., 106 Ohio St. 328, 140 N.E. 118 (1922), in which the court held that a "waiver" of all agreements not specified did not preclude implied warranty of fitness of a rebuilt dump truck for ordinary use as a dump truck; Austin Co. v. J. H. Tillman Co., 104 Or. 541, 209 P. 131 (1922), where a clause limiting the buyer's remedy to return was held to be applicable only if the seller had delivered a machine needed for a construction job which reasonably met the contract description; Bekkevold v. Potts, 173 Minn. 87, 216 N.W. 790, 59 A.L.R. 1164 (1927), refusing to allow warranty of fitness for purpose imposed by law to be negated by clause excluding all warranties "made" by the seller; Robert A. Munroe & Co. v. Meyer (1930) 2 K.B. 312, holding that the warranty of description overrides a clause reading "with all faults and defects" where adulterated meat not up to the contract description was delivered.

2. Under this section the court, in its discretion, may refuse to enforce the contract as a whole if it is permeated by the unconscionability, or it may strike any single clause or group of clauses which are so tainted or which are contrary to the essential purpose of the agreement, or it may simply limit unconscionable clauses so as to avoid unconscionable results.

3. The present section is addressed to the court, and the decision is to be made by it. The commercial evidence referred to in subsection (2) is for the court's consideration, not the jury's. Only the agreement which results from the court's action on these matters is to be submitted to the general triers of the facts.

§ 2-312. Warranty of Title and Against Infringement; Buyer's Obligation Against Infringement

(1) Subject to subsection (2) there is in a contract for sale a warranty by the seller that

(a) the title conveyed shall be good, and its transfer rightful; and

(b) the goods shall be delivered free from any security interest or other lien or encumbrance of which the buyer at the time of contracting has no knowledge.

(2) A warranty under subsection (1) will be excluded or modified only by specific language or by circumstances which give the buyer reason to know that the person selling does not claim title in himself or that he is purporting to sell only such right or title as he or a third person may have.

(3) Unless otherwise agreed a seller who is a merchant regularly dealing in goods of the kind warrants that the goods shall be delivered free of the rightful claim of any third person by way of infringement or the like but a buyer who furnishes specifications to the seller must hold the seller harmless against any such claim which arises out of compliance with the specifications.

§ 2–313. Express Warranties by Affirmation, Promise, Description, Sample

(1) Express warranties by the seller are created as follows:

(a) Any affirmation of fact or promise made by the seller to the buyer which relates to the goods and becomes part of the basis of the bargain creates an express warranty that the goods shall conform to the affirmation or promise.

(b) Any description of the goods which is made part of the basis of the bargain creates an express warranty that the goods shall conform to the description.

(c) Any sample or model which is made part of the basis of the bargain creates an express warranty that the whole of the goods shall conform to the sample or model.

(2) It is not necessary to the creation of an express warranty that the seller use formal words such as "warrant" or "guarantee" or that he have a specific intention to make a warranty, but an affirmation merely of the value of the goods or a statement purporting to be merely the seller's opinion or commendation of the goods does not create a warranty.

Official Comment

Purposes of Changes: To consolidate and systematize basic principles with the result that:

1. "Express" warranties rest on "dickered" aspects of the individual bargain, and go so clearly to the essence of that bargain that words of disclaimer in a form are repugnant to the basic dickered terms. "Implied" warranties rest so clearly on a common factual situation or set of conditions that no particular language or action is necessary to evidence them and they will arise in such a situation unless unmistakenly negated.

This section reverts to the older case law insofar as the warranties of description and sample are designated "express" rather than "implied".

2. Although this section is limited in its scope and direct purpose to warranties made by the seller to the buyer as part of a contract for sale, the warranty sections of this Article are not designed in any way to disturb those lines of case law growth which have recognized that warranties need not be confined either to sales contracts or to the direct parties to such a contract. They may arise in other appropriate circumstances such as in the case of bailments for hire, whether such bailment is itself the main contract or is merely a supplying of containers under a contract for the sale of their contents. The provisions of Section 2–318 on third party beneficiaries expressly recognize this case law development within one particular area. Beyond that, the matter is left to the case law with the intention that the policies of this Act may offer useful guidance in dealing with further cases as they arise.

3. The present section deals with affirmations of fact by the seller, descriptions of the goods or exhibitions of samples, exactly as any other part of a negotiation which ends in a contract is dealt with. No specific intention to make a warranty is necessary if any of these factors is made part of the basis of the bargain. In actual practice affirmations of fact made by the seller about the goods during a bargain are regarded as part of the description of those goods; hence no particular reliance on such statements need be shown in order to weave them into the fabric of the agreement. Rather, any fact which is to take such affirmations, once made, out of the agreement requires clear affirmative proof. The issue normally is one of fact.

4. In view of the principle that the whole purpose of the law of warranty is to determine what it is that the seller has in essence agreed to sell, the policy is adopted of those cases which refuse except in unusual circumstances to recognize a material deletion of the seller's obligation. Thus, a contract is normally a contract for a sale of something describable and described. A clause generally disclaiming "all warranties, express or implied" cannot reduce the seller's obligation with respect to such description and therefore cannot be given literal effect under Section 2–316.

This is not intended to mean that the parties, if they consciously desire, cannot make their own bargain as they wish. But in determining what they have agreed upon good faith is a factor and consideration should be given to the fact that the probability is small that a real price is intended to be exchanged for a pseudo-obligation.

5. Paragraph (1)(b) makes specific some of the principles set forth above when a description of the goods is given by the seller.

A description need not be by words. Technical specifications, blueprints and the like can afford more exact description than mere language and if made part of the basis of the bargain goods must conform with them. Past deliveries may set the description of quality, either expressly or impliedly by course of dealing. Of course, all descriptions by merchants must be read against the applicable trade usages with the general rules as to merchantability resolving any doubts.

6. The basic situation as to statements affecting the true essence of the bargain is no different when a sample or model is involved in the transaction. This section includes both a "sample" actually drawn from the bulk of goods which is the subject matter of the sale, and a "model" which is offered for inspection when the subject matter is not at hand and which has not been drawn from the bulk of the goods.

Although the underlying principles are unchanged, the facts are often ambiguous when something is shown as illustrative, rather than as a straight sample. In general, the presumption is that any sample or model just as any affirmation of fact is intended to become a basis of the bargain. But there is no escape from the question of fact. When the seller exhibits a sample purporting to be drawn from an existing bulk, good faith of course requires that the sample be fairly drawn. But in mercantile experience the mere exhibition of a "sample" does not of itself show whether it is merely intended to "suggest" or to "be" the character of the subject-matter of the contract. The question is whether the seller has so acted with reference to the sample as to make him responsible that the whole shall have at least the values shown by it. The circumstances aid in answering this question. If the sample has been drawn from an existing bulk, it must be regarded as describing values of the goods contracted for unless it is accompanied by an unmistakeable denial of such responsibility. If, on the other hand, a model of merchandise not on hand is offered, the mercantile presumption that it has become a literal description of the subject matter is not so strong, and particularly, so if modification on the buyer's initiative impairs any feature of the model.

7. The precise time when words of description or affirmation are made or samples are shown is not material. The sole question is whether the language or samples or models are fairly to be regarded as part of the contract. If language is used after the closing of the deal (as when the buyer when taking delivery asks and receives an additional assurance), the warranty becomes a modification, and need not be supported by consideration if it is otherwise reasonable and in order (Section 2–209).

8. Concerning affirmations of value or a seller's opinion or commendation under subsection (2), the basic question remains the same: What statements of the seller have in the circumstances and in objective judgment become part of the basis of the bargain? As indicated above, all of the statements of the seller do so unless good reason is shown to the contrary. The provisions of subsection (2) are included, however, since common experience discloses that some statements or predictions cannot fairly be viewed as entering into the bargain. Even as to false statements of value, however, the possibility is left open that a remedy may be provided by the law relating to fraud or misrepresentation.

§ 2–314. Implied Warranty: Merchantability; Usage of Trade

(1) Unless excluded or modified (Section 2–316), a warranty that the goods shall be merchantable is implied in a contract for their sale if the seller is a merchant with respect to goods of that kind. Under this section the serving for value of food or drink to be consumed either on the premises or elsewhere is a sale.

(2) Goods to be merchantable must be at least such as

(a) pass without objection in the trade under the contract description; and

(b) in the case of fungible goods, are of fair average quality within the description; and

(c) are fit for the ordinary purposes for which such goods are used; and

(d) run, within the variations permitted by the agreement, of even kind, quality and quantity within each unit and among all units involved; and

(e) are adequately contained, packaged, and labeled as the agreement may require; and

(f) conform to the promises or affirmations of fact made on the container or label if any.

(3) Unless excluded or modified (Section 2–316) other implied warranties may arise from course of dealing or usage of trade.

Official Comment

Purposes of Changes: This section, drawn in view of the steadily developing case law on the subject, is intended to make it clear that:

1. The seller's obligation applies to present sales as well as to contracts to sell subject to the effects of any examination of specific goods. (Subsection (2) of Section 2–316). Also, the warranty of merchantability applies to sales for use as well as to sales for resale.

2. The question when the warranty is imposed turns basically on the meaning of the terms of the agreement as recognized in the trade. Goods delivered under an agreement made by a merchant in a given line of trade must be of a quality comparable to that generally acceptable in that line of trade under the description or other designation of the goods used in the agreement. The responsibility imposed rests on any merchant-seller, and the absence of the words "grower or manufacturer or not" which appeared in Section 15(2) of the Uniform Sales Act does not restrict the applicability of this section.

3. A specific designation of goods by the buyer does not exclude the seller's obligation that they be fit for the general purposes appropriate to such goods. A contract for the sale of second-hand goods, however, involves only such obligation as is appropriate to such goods for that is their contract description. A person making an isolated sale of goods is not a "merchant" within the meaning of the full scope of this section and, thus, no warranty of merchantability would apply. His knowledge of any defects not apparent on inspection would, however, without need for express agreement and in keeping with the underlying reason of the present section and the provisions on good faith, impose an obligation that known material but hidden defects be fully disclosed.

4. Although a seller may not be a "merchant" as to the goods in question, if he states generally that they are "guaranteed" the provisions of this section may furnish a guide to the content of the resulting express warranty. This has particular significance in the case of second-hand sales, and has further significance in limiting the effect of fine-print disclaimer clauses where their effect would be inconsistent with large-print assertions of "guarantee".

. . .

6. Subsection (2) does not purport to exhaust the meaning of "merchantable" nor to negate any of its attributes not specifically mentioned in the text of the statute, but arising by usage of trade or through case law. The language used is "must be at least such as . . . ," and the intention is to leave open other possible attributes of merchantability.

7. Paragraphs (a) and (b) of subsection (2) are to be read together. Both refer, as indicated above, to the standards of that line of the trade which fits the transaction and the seller's business. "Fair average" is a term directly appropriate to agricultural bulk products and means goods centering around the middle belt of quality, not the least or the worst that can be understood in the particular trade by the designation, but such as can pass "without

objection." Of course a fair percentage of the least is permissible but the goods are not "fair average" if they are all of the least or worst quality possible under the description. In cases of doubt as to what quality is intended, the price at which a merchant closes a contract is an excellent index of the nature and scope of his obligation under the present section.

8. Fitness for the ordinary purposes for which goods of the type are used is a fundamental concept of the present section and is covered in paragraph (c). As stated above, merchantability is also a part of the obligation owing to the purchaser for use. Correspondingly, protection, under this aspect of the warranty, of the person buying for resale to the ultimate consumer is equally necessary, and merchantable goods must therefore be "honestly" resalable in the normal course of business because they are what they purport to be.

9. Paragraph (d) on evenness of kind, quality and quantity follows case law. But precautionary language has been added as a reminder of the frequent usages of trade which permit substantial variations both with and without an allowance or an obligation to replace the varying units.

10. Paragraph (e) applies only where the nature of the goods and of the transaction require a certain type of container, package or label. Paragraph (f) applies, on the other hand, wherever there is a label or container on which representations are made, even though the original contract, either by express terms or usage of trade, may not have required either the labelling or the representation. This follows from the general obligation of good faith which requires that a buyer should not be placed in the position of reselling or using goods delivered under false representations appearing on the package or container. No problem of extra consideration arises in this connection since, under this Article, an obligation is imposed by the original contract not to deliver mislabeled articles, and the obligation is imposed where mercantile good faith so requires and without reference to the doctrine of consideration.

11. Exclusion or modification of the warranty of merchantability, or of any part of it, is dealt with in the section to which the text of the present section makes explicit precautionary references. That section must be read with particular reference to its subsection (4) on limitation of remedies. The warranty of merchantability, wherever it is normal, is so commonly taken for granted that its exclusion from the contract is a matter threatening surprise and therefore requiring special precaution.

12. Subsection (3) is to make explicit that usage of trade and course of dealing can create warranties and that they are implied rather than express warranties and thus subject to exclusion or modification under Section 2-316. A typical instance would be the obligation to provide pedigree papers to evidence conformity of the animal to the contract in the case of a pedigreed dog or blooded bull.

13. In an action based on breach of warranty, it is of course necessary to show not only the existence of the warranty but the fact that the warranty was broken and that the breach of the warranty was the proximate cause of the loss sustained. In such an action an affirmative showing by the seller that the loss resulted from some action or event following his own delivery of the goods can operate as a defense. Equally, evidence indicating that the seller exercised care in the manufacture, processing or selection of the goods

is relevant to the issue of whether the warranty was in fact broken. Action by the buyer following an examination of the goods which ought to have indicated the defect complained of can be shown as matter bearing on whether the breach itself was the cause of the injury.

§ 2–315. Implied Warranty: Fitness for Particular Purpose

Where the seller at the time of contracting has reason to know any particular purpose for which the goods are required and that the buyer is relying on the seller's skill or judgment to select or furnish suitable goods, there is unless excluded or modified under the next section an implied warranty that the goods shall be fit for such purpose.

Official Comment

Purposes of Changes:

1. Whether or not this warranty arises in any individual case is basically a question of fact to be determined by the circumstances of the contracting. Under this section the buyer need not bring home to the seller actual knowledge of the particular purpose for which the goods are intended or of his reliance on the seller's skill and judgment, if the circumstances are such that the seller has reason to realize the purpose intended or that the reliance exists. The buyer, of course, must actually be relying on the seller.

2. A "particular purpose" differs from the ordinary purpose for which the goods are used in that it envisages a specific use by the buyer which is peculiar to the nature of his business whereas the ordinary purposes for which goods are used are those envisaged in the concept of merchantability and go to uses which are customarily made of the goods in question. For example, shoes are generally used for the purpose of walking upon ordinary ground, but a seller may know that a particular pair was selected to be used for climbing mountains.

A contract may of course include both a warranty of merchantability and one of fitness for a particular purpose.

The provisions of this Article on the cumulation and conflict of express and implied warranties must be considered on the question of inconsistency between or among warranties. In such a case any question of fact as to which warranty was intended by the parties to apply must be resolved in favor of the warranty of fitness for particular purpose as against all other warranties except where the buyer has taken upon himself the responsibility of furnishing the technical specifications.

3. In connection with the warranty of fitness for a particular purpose the provisions of this Article on the allocation or division of risks are particularly applicable in any transaction in which the purpose for which the goods are to be used combines requirements both as to the quality of the goods themselves and compliance with certain laws or regulations. How the risks are divided is a question of fact to be determined, where not expressly contained in the agreement, from the circumstances of contracting, usage of trade, course of performance and the like, matters which may constitute the

"otherwise agreement" of the parties by which they may divide the risk or burden.

4. . . . Although normally the warranty will arise only where the seller is a merchant with the appropriate "skill or judgment," it can arise as to nonmerchants where this is justified by the particular circumstances.

5. The elimination of the "patent or other trade name" exception constitutes the major extension of the warranty of fitness which has been made by the cases and continued in this Article. Under the present section the existence of a patent or other trade name and the designation of the article by that name, or indeed in any other definite manner, is only one of the facts to be considered on the question of whether the buyer actually relied on the seller, but it is not of itself decisive of the issue. If the buyer himself is insisting on a particular brand he is not relying on the seller's skill and judgment and so no warranty results. But the mere fact that the article purchased has a particular patent or trade name is not sufficient to indicate nonreliance if the article has been recommended by the seller as adequate for the buyer's purposes.

. . .

§ 2–316. Exclusion or Modification of Warranties

(1) Words or conduct relevant to the creation of an express warranty and words or conduct tending to negate or limit warranty shall be construed wherever reasonable as consistent with each other; but subject to the provisions of this Article on parol or extrinsic evidence (Section 2–202) negation or limitation is inoperative to the extent that such construction is unreasonable.

(2) Subject to subsection (3), to exclude or modify the implied warranty of merchantability or any part of it the language must mention merchantability and in case of a writing must be conspicuous, and to exclude or modify any implied warranty of fitness the exclusion must be by a writing and conspicuous. Language to exclude all implied warranties of fitness is sufficient if it states, for example, that "There are no warranties which extend beyond the description on the face hereof."

(3) Notwithstanding subsection (2)

(a) unless the circumstances indicate otherwise, all implied warranties are excluded by expressions like "as is", "with all faults" or other language which in common understanding calls the buyer's attention to the exclusion of warranties and makes plain that there is no implied warranty; and

(b) when the buyer before entering into the contract has examined the goods or the sample or model as fully as he desired or has refused to examine the goods there is no implied warranty with regard to defects which an examination ought in the circumstances to have revealed to him; and

(c) an implied warranty can also be excluded or modified by course of dealing or course of performance or usage of trade.

(4) Remedies for breach of warranty can be limited in accordance with the provisions of this Article on liquidation or limitation of damages and on contractual modification of remedy (Sections 2–718 and 2–719).

Official Comment

Purposes:

1. This section is designed principally to deal with those frequent clauses in sales contracts which seek to exclude "all warranties, express or implied." It seeks to protect a buyer from unexpected and unbargained language of disclaimer by denying effect to such language when inconsistent with language of express warranty and permitting the exclusion of implied warranties only by conspicuous language or other circumstances which protect the buyer from surprise.

2. The seller is protected under this Article against false allegations of oral warranties by its provisions on parol and extrinsic evidence and against unauthorized representations by the customary "lack of authority" clauses. This Article treats the limitation or avoidance of consequential damages as a matter of limiting remedies for breach, separate from the matter of creation of liability under a warranty. If no warranty exists, there is of course no problem of limiting remedies for breach of warranty. Under subsection (4) the question of limitation of remedy is governed by the sections referred to rather than by this section.

3. Disclaimer of the implied warranty of merchantability is permitted under subsection (2), but with the safeguard that such disclaimers must mention merchantability and in case of a writing must be conspicuous.

4. Unlike the implied warranty of merchantability, implied warranties of fitness for a particular purpose may be excluded by general language, but only if it is in writing and conspicuous.

5. Subsection (2) presupposes that the implied warranty in question exists unless excluded or modified. Whether or not language of disclaimer satisfies the requirements of this section, such language may be relevant under other sections to the question whether the warranty was ever in fact created. Thus, unless the provisions of this Article on parol and extrinsic evidence prevent, oral language of disclaimer may raise issues of fact as to whether reliance by the buyer occurred and whether the seller had "reason to know" under the section on implied warranty of fitness for a particular purpose.

6. The exceptions to the general rule set forth in paragraphs (a), (b) and (c) of subsection (3) are common factual situations in which the circumstances surrounding the transaction are in themselves sufficient to call the buyer's attention to the fact that no implied warranties are made or that a certain implied warranty is being excluded.

7. Paragraph (a) of subsection (3) deals with general terms such as "as is," "as they stand," "with all faults," and the like. Such terms in ordinary commercial usage are understood to mean that the buyer takes the entire

risk as to the quality of the goods involved. The terms covered by paragraph (a) are in fact merely a particularization of paragraph (c) which provides for exclusion or modification of implied warranties by usage of trade.

8. Under paragraph (b) of subsection (3) warranties may be excluded or modified by the circumstances where the buyer examines the goods or a sample or model of them before entering into the contract. "Examination" as used in this paragraph is not synonymous with inspection before acceptance or at any other time after the contract has been made. It goes rather to the nature of the responsibility assumed by the seller at the time of the making of the contract. Of course if the buyer discovers the defect and uses the goods anyway, or if he unreasonably fails to examine the goods before he uses them, resulting injuries may be found to result from his own action rather than proximately from a breach of warranty. See Sections 2–314 and 2–715 and comments thereto.

In order to bring the transaction within the scope of "refused to examine" in paragraph (b), it is not sufficient that the goods are available for inspection. There must in addition be a demand by the seller that the buyer examine the goods fully. The seller by the demand puts the buyer on notice that he is assuming the risk of defects which the examination ought to reveal. The language "refused to examine" in this paragraph is intended to make clear the necessity for such demand.

Application of the doctrine of "caveat emptor" in all cases where the buyer examines the goods regardless of statements made by the seller is, however, rejected by this Article. Thus, if the offer of examination is accompanied by words as to their merchantability or specific attributes and the buyer indicates clearly that he is relying on those words rather than on his examination, they give rise to an "express" warranty. In such cases the question is one of fact as to whether a warranty of merchantability has been expressly incorporated in the agreement. Disclaimer of such an express warranty is governed by subsection (1) of the present section.

The particular buyer's skill and the normal method of examining goods in the circumstances determine what defects are excluded by the examination. A failure to notice defects which are obvious cannot excuse the buyer. However, an examination under circumstances which do not permit chemical or other testing of the goods would not exclude defects which could be ascertained only by such testing. Nor can latent defects be excluded by a simple examination. A professional buyer examining a product in his field will be held to have assumed the risk as to all defects which a professional in the field ought to observe, while a nonprofessional buyer will be held to have assumed the risk only for such defects as a layman might be expected to observe.

. . .

§ 2–317. Cumulation and Conflict of Warranties Express or Implied

Warranties whether express or implied shall be construed as consistent with each other and as cumulative, but if such construction is unreasonable the intention of the parties shall determine which warranty is dominant. In ascertaining that intention the following rules apply:

(a) Exact or technical specifications displace an inconsistent sample or model or general language of description.

(b) A sample from an existing bulk displaces inconsistent general language of description.

(c) Express warranties displace inconsistent implied warranties other than an implied warranty of fitness for a particular purpose.

Official Comment

Purposes of Changes:

. . .

2. The rules of this section are designed to aid in determining the intention of the parties as to which of inconsistent warranties which have arisen from the circumstances of their transaction shall prevail. These rules of intention are to be applied only where factors making for an equitable estoppel of the seller do not exist and where he has in perfect good faith made warranties which later turn out to be inconsistent. To the extent that the seller has led the buyer to believe that all of the warranties can be performed, he is estopped from setting up any essential inconsistency as a defense.

. . .

§ 2-318. Third Party Beneficiaries of Warranties Express or Implied

Alternative A

A seller's warranty whether express or implied extends to any natural person who is in the family or household of his buyer or who is a guest in his home if it is reasonable to expect that such person may use, consume or be affected by the goods and who is injured in person by breach of the warranty. A seller may not exclude or limit the operation of this section.

Alternative B

A seller's warranty whether express or implied extends to any natural person who may reasonably be expected to use, consume or be affected by the goods and who is injured in person by breach of the warranty. A seller may not exclude or limit the operation of this section.

Alternative C

A seller's warranty whether express or implied extends to any person who may reasonably be expected to use, consume or be affected by the goods and who is injured by breach of the warranty. A seller may not exclude or limit the operation of this section with respect to injury to the person of an individual to whom the warranty extends.

Official Comment

Purposes:

1. The last sentence of this section does not mean that a seller is precluded from excluding or disclaiming a warranty which might otherwise arise in connection with the sale provided such exclusion or modification is permitted by Section 2–316. Nor does that sentence preclude the seller from limiting the remedies of his own buyer and of any beneficiaries, in any manner provided in Sections 2–718 or 2–719. To the extent that the contract of sale contains provisions under which warranties are excluded or modified, or remedies for breach are limited, such provisions are equally operative against beneficiaries of warranties under this section. What this last sentence forbids is exclusion of liability by the seller to the persons to whom the warranties which he has made to his buyer would extend under this section.

2. The purpose of this section is to give certain beneficiaries the benefit of the same warranty which the buyer received in the contract of sale, thereby freeing any such beneficiaries from any technical rules as to "privity." It seeks to accomplish this purpose without any derogation of any right or remedy resting on negligence. It rests primarily upon the merchant-seller's warranty under this Article that the goods sold are merchantable and fit for the ordinary purposes for which such goods are used rather than the warranty of fitness for a particular purpose. Implicit in the section is that any beneficiary of a warranty may bring a direct action for breach of warranty against the seller whose warranty extends to him [As amended in 1966].

3. The first alternative expressly includes as beneficiaries within its provisions the family, household and guests of the purchaser. Beyond this, the section in this form is neutral and is not intended to enlarge or restrict the developing case law on whether the seller's warranties, given to his buyer who resells, extend to other persons in the distributive chain. The second alternative is designed for states where the case law had already developed further and for those that desire to expand the class of beneficiaries. The third alternative goes further, following the trend of modern decisions as indicated by Restatement of Torts 2d § 402A . . . in extending the rule beyond injuries to the person.

PART 5. PERFORMANCE

§ 2–507. Effect of Seller's Tender; Delivery on Condition

(1) Tender of delivery is a condition to the buyer's duty to accept the goods and, unless otherwise agreed, to his duty to pay for them. Tender entitles the seller to acceptance of the goods and to payment according to the contract.

(2) Where payment is due and demanded on the delivery to the buyer of goods or documents of title, his right as against the seller to retain or dispose of them is conditional upon his making the payment due.

§ 2-508. Cure by Seller of Improper Tender or Delivery; Replacement

(1) Where any tender or delivery by the seller is rejected because non-conforming and the time for performance has not yet expired, the seller may seasonably notify the buyer of his intention to cure and may then within the contract time make a conforming delivery.

(2) Where the buyer rejects a non-conforming tender which the seller had reasonable grounds to believe would be acceptable with or without money allowance the seller may if he seasonably notifies the buyer have a further reasonable time to substitute a conforming tender.

Official Comment

Purposes:

1. Subsection (1) permits a seller who has made a non-conforming tender in any case to make a conforming delivery within the contract time upon seasonable notification to the buyer. It applies even where the seller has taken back the non-conforming goods and refunded the purchase price. He may still make a good tender within the contract period. The closer, however, it is to the contract date, the greater is the necessity for extreme promptness on the seller's part in notifying of his intention to cure, if such notification is to be "seasonable" under this subsection.

The rule of this subsection, moreover, is qualified by its underlying reasons. Thus if, after contracting for June delivery, a buyer later makes known to the seller his need for shipment early in the month and the seller ships accordingly, the "contract time" has been cut down by the supervening modification and the time for cure of tender must be referred to this modified time term.

2. Subsection (2) seeks to avoid injustice to the seller by reason of a surprise rejection by the buyer. However, the seller is not protected unless he had "reasonable grounds to believe" that the tender would be acceptable. Such reasonable grounds can lie in prior course of dealing, course of performance or usage of trade as well as in the particular circumstances surrounding the making of the contract. The seller is charged with commercial knowledge of any factors in a particular sales situation which require him to comply strictly with his obligations under the contract as, for example, strict conformity of documents in an overseas shipment or the sale of precision parts or chemicals for use in manufacture. Further, if the buyer gives notice either implicitly, as by a prior course of dealing involving rigorous inspections, or expressly, as by the deliberate inclusion of a "no replacement" clause in the contract, the seller is to be held to rigid compliance. If the clause appears in a "form" contract evidence that it is out of line with trade

usage or the prior course of dealing and was not called to the seller's attention may be sufficient to show that the seller had reasonable grounds to believe that the tender would be acceptable.

3. The words "a further reasonable time to substitute a conforming tender" are intended as words of limitation to protect the buyer. What is a "reasonable time" depends upon the attending circumstances. Compare Section 2–511 on the comparable case of a seller's surprise demand for legal tender.

. . .

PART 6. BREACH, REPUDIATION AND EXCUSE

§ 2–601. Buyer's Rights on Improper Delivery

Subject to the provisions of this Article on breach in installment contracts (Section 2–612) and unless otherwise agreed under the sections on contractual limitations of remedy (Sections 2–718 and 2–719), if the goods or the tender of delivery fail in any respect to conform to the contract, the buyer may

(a) reject the whole; or

(b) accept the whole; or

(c) accept any commercial unit or units and reject the rest.

§ 2–602. Manner and Effect of Rightful Rejection

(1) Rejection of goods must be within a reasonable time after their delivery or tender. It is ineffective unless the buyer seasonably notifies the seller.

(2) Subject to the provisions of the two following sections on rejected goods (Sections 2–603 and 2–604),

(a) after rejection any exercise of ownership by the buyer with respect to any commercial unit is wrongful as against the seller; and

(b) if the buyer has before rejection taken physical possession of goods in which he does not have a security interest under the provisions of this Article (subsection (3) of Section 2–711), he is under a duty after rejection to hold them with reasonable care at the seller's disposition for a time sufficient to permit the seller to remove them; but

(c) the buyer has no further obligations with regard to goods rightfully rejected.

(3) The seller's rights with respect to goods wrongfully rejected are governed by the provisions of this Article on Seller's remedies in general (Section 2–703).

Official Comment

Purposes of Changes: To make it clear that:

1. A tender or delivery of goods made pursuant to a contract of sale, even though wholly non-conforming, requires affirmative action by the buyer to avoid acceptance. Under subsection (1), therefore, the buyer is given a reasonable time to notify the seller of his rejection, but without such seasonable notification his rejection is ineffective. The sections of this Article dealing with inspection of goods must be read in connection with the buyer's reasonable time for action under this subsection. Contract provisions limiting the time for rejection fall within the rule of the section on "Time" and are effective if the time set gives the buyer a reasonable time for discovery of defects. What constitutes a due "notifying" of rejection by the buyer to the seller is defined in Section 1–201.

. . .

3. The present section applies only to rightful rejection by the buyer. If the seller has made a tender which in all respects conforms to the contract, the buyer has a positive duty to accept and his failure to do so constitutes a "wrongful rejection" which gives the seller immediate remedies for breach. Subsection (3) is included here to emphasize the sharp distinction between the rejection of an improper tender and the non-acceptance which is a breach by the buyer.

4. The provisions of this section are to be appropriately limited or modified when a negotiation is in process.

§ 2–605. Waiver of Buyer's Objections by Failure to Particularize

(1) The buyer's failure to state in connection with rejection a particular defect which is ascertainable by reasonable inspection precludes him from relying on the unstated defect to justify rejection or to establish breach

(a) where the seller could have cured it if stated seasonably; or

(b) between merchants when the seller has after rejection made a request in writing for a full and final written statement of all defects on which the buyer proposes to rely.

(2) Payment against documents made without reservation of rights precludes recovery of the payment for defects apparent on the face of the documents.

Official Comment

Purposes:

. . .

2. Where the defect in a tender is one which could have been cured by the seller, a buyer who merely rejects the delivery without stating his objections to it is probably acting in commercial bad faith and seeking to get out of a deal which has become unprofitable. Subsection (1)(a), following the

general policy of this Article which looks to preserving the deal wherever possible, therefore insists that the seller's right to correct his tender in such circumstances be protected.

. . .

§ 2–606. What Constitutes Acceptance of Goods

(1) Acceptance of goods occurs when the buyer

(a) after a reasonable opportunity to inspect the goods signifies to the seller that the goods are conforming or that he will take or retain them in spite of their nonconformity; or

(b) fails to make an effective rejection (subsection (1) of Section 2–602), but such acceptance does not occur until the buyer has had a reasonable opportunity to inspect them; or

(c) does any act inconsistent with the seller's ownership; but if such act is wrongful as against the seller it is an acceptance only if ratified by him.

(2) Acceptance of a part of any commercial unit is acceptance of that entire unit.

§ 2–607. Effect of Acceptance; Notice of Breach; Burden of Establishing Breach After Acceptance; Notice of Claim or Litigation to Person Answerable Over

(1) The buyer must pay at the contract rate for any goods accepted.

(2) Acceptance of goods by the buyer precludes rejection of the goods accepted and if made with knowledge of a non-conformity cannot be revoked because of it unless the acceptance was on the reasonable assumption that the non-conformity would be seasonably cured but acceptance does not of itself impair any other remedy provided by this Article for non-conformity.

(3) Where a tender has been accepted

(a) the buyer must within a reasonable time after he discovers or should have discovered any breach notify the seller of breach or be barred from any remedy; and

(b) if the claim is one for infringement or the like (subsection (3) of Section 2–312) and the buyer is sued as a result of such a breach he must so notify the seller within a reasonable time after he receives notice of the litigation or be barred from any remedy over for liability established by the litigation.

(4) The burden is on the buyer to establish any breach with respect to the goods accepted.

(5) Where the buyer is sued for breach of a warranty or other obligation for which his seller is answerable over

(a) he may give his seller written notice of the litigation. If the notice states that the seller may come in and defend and that if the seller does not do so he will be bound in any action against him by his buyer by any determination of fact common to the two litigations, then unless the seller after seasonable receipt of the notice does come in and defend he is so bound.

(b) if the claim is one for infringement or the like (subsection (3) of Section 2–312) the original seller may demand in writing that his buyer turn over to him control of the litigation including settlement or else be barred from any remedy over and if he also agrees to bear all expense and to satisfy any adverse judgment, then unless the buyer after seasonable receipt of the demand does turn over control the buyer is so barred.

(6) The provisions of subsections (3), (4) and (5) apply to any obligation of a buyer to hold the seller harmless against infringement or the like (subsection (3) of Section 2–312).

Official Comment

Purposes of Changes: To continue the prior basic policies with respect to acceptance of goods while making a number of minor though material changes in the interest of simplicity and commercial convenience so that:

. . .

4. The time of notification is to be determined by applying commercial standards to a merchant buyer. "A reasonable time" for notification from a retail consumer is to be judged by different standards so that in his case it will be extended, for the rule of requiring notification is designed to defeat commercial bad faith, not to deprive a good faith consumer of his remedy.

The content of the notification need merely be sufficient to let the seller know that the transaction is still troublesome and must be watched. There is no reason to require that the notification which saves the buyer's rights under this section must include a clear statement of all the objections that will be relied on by the buyer, as under the section covering statements of defects upon rejection (Section 2–605). Nor is there reason for requiring the notification to be a claim for damages or of any threatened litigation or other resort to a remedy. The notification which saves the buyer's right under this Article need only be such as informs the seller that the transaction is claimed to involve a breach, and thus opens the way for normal settlement through negotiation.

5. Under this Article various beneficiaries are given rights for injuries sustained by them because of the seller's breach of warranty. Such a beneficiary does not fall within the reason of the present section in regard to discovery of defects and the giving of notice within a reasonable time after acceptance, since he has nothing to do with acceptance. However, the reason of this section does extend to requiring the beneficiary to notify the seller that an injury has occurred. What is said above, with regard to the ex-

tended time for reasonable notification from the lay consumer after the injury is also applicable here; but even a beneficiary can be properly held to the use of good faith in notifying, once he has had time to become aware of the legal situation.

. . .

§ 2–608. Revocation of Acceptance in Whole or in Part

(1) The buyer may revoke his acceptance of a lot or commercial unit whose non-conformity substantially impairs its value to him if he has accepted it

(a) on the reasonable assumption that its non-conformity would be cured and it has not been seasonably cured; or

(b) without discovery of such non-conformity if his acceptance was reasonably induced either by the difficulty of discovery before acceptance or by the seller's assurances.

(2) Revocation of acceptance must occur within a reasonable time after the buyer discovers or should have discovered the ground for it and before any substantial change in condition of the goods which is not caused by their own defects. It is not effective until the buyer notifies the seller of it.

(3) A buyer who so revokes has the same rights and duties with regard to the goods involved as if he had rejected them.

Official Comment

Purposes of Changes: To make it clear that:

1. Although the prior basic policy is continued, the buyer is no longer required to elect between revocation of acceptance and recovery of damages for breach. Both are now available to him. The non-alternative character of the two remedies is stressed by the terms used in the present action. The section no longer speaks of "rescission," a term capable of ambiguous application either to transfer of title to the goods or to the contract of sale and susceptible also of confusion with cancellation for cause of an executed or executory portion of the contract. The remedy under this section is instead referred to simply as "revocation of acceptance" of goods tendered under a contract for sale and involves no suggestion of "election" of any sort.

2. Revocation of acceptance is possible only where the non-conformity substantially impairs the value of the goods to the buyer. For this purpose the test is not what the seller had reason to know at the time of contracting; the question is whether the non-conformity is such as will in fact cause a substantial impairment of value to the buyer though the seller had no advance knowledge as to the buyer's particular circumstances.

3. "Assurances" by the seller under paragraph (b) of subsection (1) can rest as well in the circumstances or in the contract as in explicit language used at the time of delivery. The reason for recognizing such assurances is that they induce the buyer to delay discovery. These are the only assurances involved in paragraph (b). Explicit assurances may be made either in

good faith or bad faith. In either case any remedy accorded by this Article is available to the buyer under the section on remedies for fraud.

4. Subsection (2) requires notification of revocation of acceptance within a reasonable time after discovery of the grounds for such revocation. Since this remedy will be generally resorted to only after attempts at adjustment have failed, the reasonable time period should extend in most cases beyond the time in which notification of breach must be given, beyond the time for discovery of non-conformity after acceptance and beyond the time for rejection after tender. The parties may by their agreement limit the time for notification under this section, but the same sanctions and considerations apply to such agreements as are discussed in the comment on manner and effect of rightful rejection.

5. The content of the notice under subsection (2) is to be determined in this case as in others by considerations of good faith, prevention of surprise, and reasonable adjustment. More will generally be necessary than the mere notification of breach required under the preceding section. On the other hand the requirements of the section on waiver of buyer's objections do not apply here. The fact that quick notification of trouble is desirable affords good ground for being slow to bind a buyer by his first statement. Following the general policy of this Article, the requirements of the content of notification are less stringent in the case of a non-merchant buyer.

6. Under subsection (2) the prior policy is continued of seeking substantial justice in regard to the condition of goods restored to the seller. Thus the buyer may not revoke his acceptance if the goods have materially deteriorated except by reason of their own defects. Worthless goods, however, need not be offered back and minor defects in the articles reoffered are to be disregarded.

7. The policy of the section allowing partial acceptance is carried over into the present section and the buyer may revoke his acceptance, in appropriate cases, as to the entire lot or any commercial unit thereof.

§ 2-609. Right to Adequate Assurance of Performance

(1) A contract for sale imposes an obligation on each party that the other's expectation of receiving due performance will not be impaired. When reasonable grounds for insecurity arise with respect to the performance of either party the other may in writing demand adequate assurance of due performance and until he receives such assurance may if commercially reasonable suspend any performance for which he has not already received the agreed return.

(2) Between merchants the reasonableness of grounds for insecurity and the adequacy of any assurance offered shall be determined according to commercial standards.

(3) Acceptance of any improper delivery or payment does not prejudice the aggrieved party's right to demand adequate assurance of future performance.

(4) After receipt of a justified demand failure to provide within a reasonable time not exceeding thirty days such assurance of due per-

formance as is adequate under the circumstances of the particular case is a repudiation of the contract.

Official Comment

Purposes:

1. The section rests on the recognition of the fact that the essential purpose of a contract between commercial men is actual performance and they do not bargain merely for a promise, or for a promise plus the right to win a lawsuit and that a continuing sense of reliance and security that the promised performance will be forthcoming when due, is an important feature of the bargain. If either the willingness or the ability of a party to perform declines materially between the time of contracting and the time for performance, the other party is threatened with the loss of a substantial part of what he has bargained for. A seller needs protection not merely against having to deliver on credit to a shaky buyer, but also against having to procure and manufacture the goods, perhaps turning down other customers. Once he has been given reason to believe that the buyer's performance has become uncertain, it is an undue hardship to force him to continue his own performance. Similarly, a buyer who believes that the seller's deliveries have become uncertain cannot safely wait for the due date of performance when he has been buying to assure himself of materials for his current manufacturing or to replenish his stock of merchandise.

2. Three measures have been adopted to meet the needs of commercial men in such situations. First, the aggrieved party is permitted to suspend his own performance and any preparation therefor, with excuse for any resulting necessary delay, until the situation has been clarified. "Suspend performance" under this section means to hold up performance pending the outcome of the demand, and includes also the holding up of any preparatory action. This is the same principle which governs the ancient law of stoppage and seller's lien, and also of excuse of a buyer from prepayment if the seller's actions manifest that he cannot or will not perform. (Original Act, Section 63(2).)

Secondly, the aggrieved party is given the right to require adequate assurance that the other party's performance will be duly forthcoming. This principle is reflected in the familiar clauses permitting the seller to curtail deliveries if the buyer's credit becomes impaired, which when held within the limits of reasonableness and good faith actually express no more than the fair business meaning of any commercial contract.

Third, and finally, this section provides the means by which the aggrieved party may treat the contract as broken if his reasonable grounds for insecurity are not cleared up within a reasonable time. This is the principle underlying the law of anticipatory breach, whether by way of defective part performance or by repudiation. The present section merges these three principles of law and commercial practice into a single theory of general application to all sales agreements looking to future performance.

3. Subsection (2) of the present section requires that "reasonable" grounds and "adequate" assurance as used in subsection (1) be defined by commercial rather than legal standards. The express reference to commer-

cial standards carries no connotation that the obligation of good faith is not equally applicable here.

Under commercial standards and in accord with commercial practice, a ground for insecurity need not arise from or be directly related to the contract in question. The law as to "dependence" or "independence" of promises within a single contract does not control the application of the present section.

. . .

4. What constitutes "adequate" assurance of due performance is subject to the same test of factual conditions. For example, where the buyer can make use of a defective delivery, a mere promise by a seller of good repute that he is giving the matter his attention and that the defect will not be repeated, is normally sufficient. Under the same circumstances, however, a similar statement by a known corner-cutter might well be considered insufficient without the posting of a guaranty or, if so demanded by the buyer, a speedy replacement of the delivery involved. By the same token where a delivery has defects, even though easily curable, which interfere with easy use by the buyer, no verbal assurance can be deemed adequate which is not accompanied by replacement, repair, money-allowance, or other commercially reasonable cure.

. . .

The adequacy of the assurance given is not measured as in the type of "satisfaction" situation affected with intangibles, such as in personal service cases, cases involving a third party's judgment as final, or cases in which the whole contract is dependent on one party's satisfaction, as in a sale on approval. Here, the seller must exercise good faith and observe commercial standards. . . .

The entire foregoing discussion as to adequacy of assurance by way of explanation is subject to qualification when repeated occasions for the application of this section arise. This Act recognizes that repeated delinquencies must be viewed as cumulative. On the other hand, commercial sense also requires that if repeated claims for assurance are made under this section, the basis for these claims must be increasingly obvious.

. . .

PART 7. REMEDIES

§ 2-703. Seller's Remedies in General

Where the buyer wrongfully rejects or revokes acceptance of goods or fails to make a payment due on or before delivery or repudiates with respect to a part or the whole, then with respect to any goods directly affected and, if the breach is of the whole contract (Section 2-612), then also with respect to the whole undelivered balance, the aggrieved seller may

(a) withhold delivery of such goods;

(b) stop delivery by any bailee as hereafter provided (Section 2-705);

(c) proceed under the next section respecting goods still unidentified to the contract;

(d) resell and recover damages as hereafter provided (Section 2–706);

(e) recover damages for non-acceptance (Section 2–708) or in a proper case the price (Section 2–709);

(f) cancel.

Official Comment

Purposes:

1. This section is an index section which gathers together in one convenient place all of the various remedies open to a seller for any breach by the buyer. This Article rejects any doctrine of election of remedy as a fundamental policy and thus the remedies are essentially cumulative in nature and include all of the available remedies for breach. Whether the pursuit of one remedy bars another depends entirely on the facts of the individual case.

. . .

§ 2–706. Seller's Resale Including Contract for Resale

(1) Under the conditions stated in Section 2–703 on seller's remedies, the seller may resell the goods concerned or the undelivered balance thereof. Where the resale is made in good faith and in a commercially reasonable manner the seller may recover the difference between the resale price and the contract price together with any incidental damages allowed under the provisions of this Article (Section 2–710), but less expenses saved in consequence of the buyer's breach.

(2) Except as otherwise provided in subsection (3) or unless otherwise agreed resale may be at public or private sale including sale by way of one or more contracts to sell or of identification to an existing contract of the seller. Sale may be as a unit or in parcels and at any time and place and on any terms but every aspect of the sale including the method, manner, time, place and terms must be commercially reasonable. The resale must be reasonably identified as referring to the broken contract, but it is not necessary that the goods be in existence or that any or all of them have been identified to the contract before the breach.

(3) Where the resale is at private sale the seller must give the buyer reasonable notification of his intention to resell.

(4) Where the resale is at public sale

(a) only identified goods can be sold except where there is a recognized market for a public sale of futures in goods of the kind; and

(b) it must be made at a usual place or market for public sale if one is reasonably available and except in the case of goods which are perishable or threaten to decline in value speedily the seller must give the buyer reasonable notice of the time and place of the resale; and

(c) if the goods are not to be within the view of those attending the sale the notification of sale must state the place where the goods are located and provide for their reasonable inspection by prospective bidders; and

(d) the seller may buy.

(5) A purchaser who buys in good faith at a resale takes the goods free of any rights of the original buyer even though the seller fails to comply with one or more of the requirements of this section.

(6) The seller is not accountable to the buyer for any profit made on any resale. A person in the position of a seller (Section 2–707) or a buyer who has rightfully rejected or justifiably revoked acceptance must account for any excess over the amount of his security interest, as hereinafter defined (subsection (3) of Section 2–711).

Official Comment

Purposes of Changes: To simplify the prior statutory provision and to make it clear that:

1. The only condition precedent to the seller's right of resale under subsection (1) is a breach by the buyer within the section on the seller's remedies in general or insolvency. . . .

2. In order to recover the damages prescribed in subsection (1) the seller must act "in good faith and in a commercially reasonable manner" in making the resale. This standard is intended to be more comprehensive than that of "reasonable care and judgment" established by the prior uniform statutory provision. Failure to act properly under this section deprives the seller of the measure of damages here provided and relegates him to that provided in Section 2–708.

. . .

§ 2–708. Seller's Damages for Non-acceptance or Repudiation

(1) Subject to subsection (2) and to the provisions of this Article with respect to proof of market price (Section 2–723), the measure of damages for non-acceptance or repudiation by the buyer is the difference between the market price at the time and place for tender and the unpaid contract price together with any incidental damages provided in this Article (Section 2–710), but less expenses saved in consequence of the buyer's breach.

(2) If the measure of damages provided in subsection (1) is inadequate to put the seller in as good a position as performance would have done then the measure of damages is the profit (including reasonable overhead) which the seller would have made from full performance by the buyer, together with any incidental damages provid-

ed in this Article (Section 2–710), due allowance for costs reasonably incurred and due credit for payments or proceeds of resale.

Official Comment

Purposes of Changes: To make it clear that:

. . .

2. The provision of this section permitting recovery of expected profit including reasonable overhead where the standard measure of damages is inadequate, together with the new requirement that price actions may be sustained only where resale is impractical, are designed to eliminate the unfair and economically wasteful results arising under the older law when fixed price articles were involved. This section permits the recovery of lost profits in all appropriate cases, which would include all standard priced goods. The normal measure there would be list price less cost to the dealer or list price less manufacturing cost to the manufacturer. It is not necessary to a recovery of "profit" to show a history of earnings, especially if a new venture is involved.

3. In all cases the seller may recover incidental damages.

§ 2–709. Action for the Price

(1) When the buyer fails to pay the price as it becomes due the seller may recover, together with any incidental damages under the next section, the price

(a) of goods accepted or of conforming goods lost or damaged within a commercially reasonable time after risk of their loss has passed to the buyer; and

(b) of goods identified to the contract if the seller is unable after reasonable effort to resell them at a reasonable price or the circumstances reasonably indicate that such effort will be unavailing.

(2) Where the seller sues for the price he must hold for the buyer any goods which have been identified to the contract and are still in his control except that if resale becomes possible he may resell them at any time prior to the collection of the judgment. The net proceeds of any such resale must be credited to the buyer and payment of the judgment entitles him to any goods not resold.

(3) After the buyer has wrongfully rejected or revoked acceptance of the goods or has failed to make a payment due or has repudiated (Section 2–610), a seller who is held not entitled to the price under this section shall nevertheless be awarded damages for non-acceptance under the preceding section.

§ 2–710. Seller's Incidental Damages

Incidental damages to an aggrieved seller include any commercially reasonable charges, expenses or commissions incurred in stopping delivery, in the transportation, care and custody of goods after the buyer's breach, in connection with return or resale of the goods or otherwise resulting from the breach.

§ 2-711. Buyer's Remedies in General; Buyer's Security Interest in Rejected Goods

(1) Where the seller fails to make delivery or repudiates or the buyer rightfully rejects or justifiably revokes acceptance then with respect to any goods involved, and with respect to the whole if the breach goes to the whole contract (Section 2-612), the buyer may cancel and whether or not he has done so may in addition to recovering so much of the price as has been paid

(a) "cover" and have damages under the next section as to all the goods affected whether or not they have been identified to the contract; or

(b) recover damages for non-delivery as provided in this Article (Section 2-713).

(2) Where the seller fails to deliver or repudiates the buyer may also

(a) if the goods have been identified recover them as provided in this Article (Section 2-502); or

(b) in a proper case obtain specific performance or replevy the goods as provided in this Article (Section 2-716).

(3) On rightful rejection or justifiable revocation of acceptance a buyer has a security interest in goods in his possession or control for any payments made on their price and any expenses reasonably incurred in their inspection, receipt, transportation, care and custody and may hold such goods and resell them in like manner as an aggrieved seller (Section 2-706).

§ 2-712. "Cover"; Buyer's Procurement of Substitute Goods

(1) After a breach within the preceding section the buyer may "cover" by making in good faith and without unreasonable delay any reasonable purchase of or contract to purchase goods in substitution for those due from the seller.

(2) The buyer may recover from the seller as damages the difference between the cost of cover and the contract price together with any incidental or consequential damages as hereinafter defined (Section 2-715), but less expenses saved in consequence of the seller's breach.

(3) Failure of the buyer to effect cover within this section does not bar him from any other remedy.

§ 2–713. Buyer's Damages for Non-Delivery or Repudiation

(1) Subject to the provisions of this Article with respect to proof of market price (Section 2–723), the measure of damages for non-delivery or repudiation by the seller is the difference between the market price at the time when the buyer learned of the breach and the contract price together with any incidental and consequential damages provided in this Article (Section 2–715), but less expenses saved in consequence of the seller's breach.

(2) Market price is to be determined as of the place for tender or, in cases of rejection after arrival or revocation of acceptance, as of the place of arrival.

§ 2–714. Buyer's Damages for Breach in Regard to Accepted Goods

(1) Where the buyer has accepted goods and given notification (subsection (3) of Section 2–607) he may recover as damages for any non-conformity of tender the loss resulting in the ordinary course of events from the seller's breach as determined in any manner which is reasonable.

(2) The measure of damages for breach of warranty is the difference at the time and place of acceptance between the value of the goods accepted and the value they would have had if they had been as warranted, unless special circumstances show proximate damages of a different amount.

(3) In a proper case any incidental and consequential damages under the next section may also be recovered.

§ 2–715. Buyer's Incidental and Consequential Damages

(1) Incidental damages resulting from the seller's breach include expenses reasonably incurred in inspection, receipt, transportation and care and custody of goods rightfully rejected, any commercially reasonable charges, expenses or commissions in connection with effecting cover and any other reasonable expense incident to the delay or other breach.

(2) Consequential damages resulting from the seller's breach include

(a) any loss resulting from general or particular requirements and needs of which the seller at the time of contracting had reason to know and which could not reasonably be prevented by cover or otherwise; and

(b) injury to person or property proximately resulting from any breach of warranty.

§ 2-716. Buyer's Right to Specific Performance or Replevin

(1) Specific performance may be decreed where the goods are unique or in other proper circumstances.

(2) The decree for specific performance may include such terms and conditions as to payment of the price, damages, or other relief as the court may deem just.

(3) The buyer has a right of replevin for goods identified to the contract if after reasonable effort he is unable to effect cover for such goods or the circumstances reasonably indicate that such effort will be unavailing or if the goods have been shipped under reservation and satisfaction of the security interest in them has been made or tendered.

§ 2-717. Deduction of Damages From the Price

The buyer on notifying the seller of his intention to do so may deduct all or any part of the damages resulting from any breach of the contract from any part of the price still due under the same contract.

§ 2-718. Liquidation or Limitation of Damages; Deposits

(1) Damages for breach by either party may be liquidated in the agreement but only at an amount which is reasonable in the light of the anticipated or actual harm caused by the breach, the difficulties of proof of loss, and the inconvenience or nonfeasibility of otherwise obtaining an adequate remedy. A term fixing unreasonably large liquidated damages is void as a penalty.

(2) Where the seller justifiably withholds delivery of goods because of the buyer's breach, the buyer is entitled to restitution of any amount by which the sum of his payments exceeds

(a) the amount to which the seller is entitled by virtue of terms liquidating the seller's damages in accordance with subsection (1), or

(b) in the absence of such terms, twenty per cent of the value of the total performance for which the buyer is obligated under the contract or $500, whichever is smaller.

(3) The buyer's right to restitution under subsection (2) is subject to offset to the extent that the seller establishes

(a) a right to recover damages under the provisions of this Article other than subsection (1), and

(b) the amount or value of any benefits received by the buyer directly or indirectly by reason of the contract.

(4) Where a seller has received payment in goods their reasonable value or the proceeds of their resale shall be treated as payments for the purposes of subsection (2); but if the seller has notice of the buy-

er's breach before reselling goods received in part performance, his resale is subject to the conditions laid down in this Article on resale by an aggrieved seller (Section 2–706).

§ 2–719. Contractual Modification or Limitation of Remedy

(1) Subject to the provisions of subsections (2) and (3) of this section and of the preceding section on liquidation and limitation of damages,

(a) the agreement may provide for remedies in addition to or in substitution for those provided in this Article and may limit or alter the measure of damages recoverable under this Article, as by limiting the buyer's remedies to return of the goods and repayment of the price or to repair and replacement of non-conforming goods or parts; and

(b) resort to a remedy as provided is optional unless the remedy is expressly agreed to be exclusive, in which case it is the sole remedy.

(2) Where circumstances cause an exclusive or limited remedy to fail of its essential purpose, remedy may be had as provided in this Act.

(3) Consequential damages may be limited or excluded unless the limitation or exclusion is unconscionable. Limitation of consequential damages for injury to the person in the case of consumer goods is prima facie unconscionable but limitation of damages where the loss is commercial is not.

Official Comment

Purposes:

1. Under this section parties are left free to shape their remedies to their particular requirements and reasonable agreements limiting or modifying remedies are to be given effect.

However, it is of the very essence of a sales contract that at least minimum adequate remedies be available. If the parties intend to conclude a contract for sale within this Article they must accept the legal consequence that there be at least a fair quantum of remedy for breach of the obligations or duties outlined in the contract. Thus any clause purporting to modify or limit the remedial provisions of this Article in an unconscionable manner is subject to deletion and in that event the remedies made available by this Article are applicable as if the stricken clause had never existed. Similarly, under subsection (2), where an apparently fair and reasonable clause because of circumstances fails in its purpose or operates to deprive either party of the substantial value of the bargain, it must give way to the general remedy provisions of this Article.

2. Subsection (1)(b) creates a presumption that clauses prescribing remedies are cumulative rather than exclusive. If the parties intend the term to describe the sole remedy under the contract, this must be clearly expressed.

3. Subsection (3) recognizes the validity of clauses limiting or excluding consequential damages but makes it clear that they may not operate in an unconscionable manner. Actually such terms are merely an allocation of unknown or undeterminable risks. The seller in all cases is free to disclaim warranties in the manner provided in Section 2-316.

§ 2-721. Remedies for Fraud

Remedies for material misrepresentation or fraud include all remedies available under this Article for non-fraudulent breach. Neither rescission or a claim for rescission of the contract for sale nor rejection or return of the goods shall bar or be deemed inconsistent with a claim for damages or other remedy.

Official Comment

Purposes: To correct the situation by which remedies for fraud have been more circumscribed than the more modern and mercantile remedies for breach of warranty. Thus the remedies for fraud are extended by this section to coincide in scope with those for non-fraudulent breach. This section thus makes it clear that neither rescission of the contract for fraud nor rejection of the goods bars other remedies unless the circumstances of the case make the remedies incompatible.

§ 2-725. Statute of Limitations in Contracts for Sale

(1) An action for breach of any contract for sale must be commenced within four years after the cause of action has accrued. By the original agreement the parties may reduce the period of limitation to not less than one year but may not extend it.

(2) A cause of action accrues when the breach occurs, regardless of the aggrieved party's lack of knowledge of the breach. A breach of warranty occurs when tender of delivery is made, except that where a warranty explicitly extends to future performance of the goods and discovery of the breach must await the time of such performance the cause of action accrues when the breach is or should have been discovered.

(3) Where an action commenced within the time limited by subsection (1) is so terminated as to leave available a remedy by another action for the same breach such other action may be commenced after the expiration of the time limited and within six months after the termination of the first action unless the termination resulted from voluntary discontinuance or from dismissal for failure or neglect to prosecute.

(4) This section does not alter the law on tolling of the statute of limitations nor does it apply to causes of action which have accrued before this Act becomes effective.

ARTICLE 3. COMMERCIAL PAPER

PART 1. SHORT TITLE, FORM AND INTERPRETATION

§ 3–104. Form of Negotiable Instruments; "Draft"; "Check"; "Certificate of Deposit"; "Note"

(1) Any writing to be a negotiable instrument within this Article must

(a) be signed by the maker or drawer; and

(b) contain an unconditional promise or order to pay a sum certain in money and no other promise, order, obligation or power given by the maker or drawer except as authorized by this Article; and

(c) be payable on demand or at a definite time; and

(d) be payable to order or to bearer.

(2) A writing which complies with the requirements of this section is

(a) a "draft" ("bill of exchange") if it is an order;

(b) a "check" if it is a draft drawn on a bank and payable on demand;

(c) a "certificate of deposit" if it is an acknowledgment by a bank of receipt of money with an engagement to repay it;

(d) a "note" if it is a promise other than a certificate of deposit.

. . .

§ 3–105. When Promise or Order Unconditional

(1) A promise or order otherwise unconditional is not made conditional by the fact that the instrument

(a) is subject to implied or constructive conditions; or

(b) states its consideration, whether performed or promised, or the transaction which gave rise to the instrument, or that the promise or order is made or the instrument matures in accordance with or "as per" such transaction; or

(c) refers to or states that it arises out of a separate agreement or refers to a separate agreement for rights as to prepayment or acceleration; or

(d) states that it is drawn under a letter of credit; or

(e) states that it is secured, whether by mortgage, reservation of title or otherwise; or

(f) indicates a particular account to be debited or any other fund or source from which reimbursement is expected; or

(g) is limited to payment out of a particular fund or the proceeds of a particular source, if the instrument is issued by a government or governmental agency or unit; or

(h) is limited to payment out of the entire assets of a partnership, unincorporated association, trust or estate by or on behalf of which the instrument is issued.

(2) A promise or order is not unconditional if the instrument

(a) states that it is subject to or governed by any other agreement; or

(b) states that it is to be paid only out of a particular fund or source except as provided in this section.

§ 3–106. Sum Certain

(1) The sum payable is a sum certain even though it is to be paid

(a) with stated interest or by stated installments; or

(b) with stated different rates of interest before and after default or a specified date; or

(c) with a stated discount or addition if paid before or after the date fixed for payment; or

(d) with exchange or less exchange, whether at a fixed rate or at the current rate; or

(e) with costs of collection or an attorney's fee or both upon default.

(2) Nothing in this section shall validate any term which is otherwise illegal.

§ 3–108. Payable on Demand

Instruments payable on demand include those payable at sight or on presentation and those in which no time for payment is stated.

§ 3–109. Definite Time

(1) An instrument is payable at a definite time if by its terms it is payable

(a) on or before a stated date or at a fixed period after a stated date; or

(b) at a fixed period after sight; or

(c) at a definite time subject to any acceleration; or

(d) at a definite time subject to extension at the option of the holder, or to extension to a further definite time at the option of the maker or acceptor or automatically upon or after a specified act or event.

(2) An instrument which by its terms is otherwise payable only upon an act or event uncertain as to time of occurrence is not payable at a definite time even though the act or event has occurred.

§ 3–110. Payable to Order

(1) An instrument is payable to order when by its terms it is payable to the order or assigns of any person therein specified with reasonable certainty, or to him or his order, or when it is conspicuously designated on its face as "exchange" or the like and names a payee. It may be payable to the order of

(a) the maker or drawer; or

(b) the drawee; or

(c) a payee who is not maker, drawer or drawee; or

(d) two or more payees together or in the alternative; or

(e) an estate, trust or fund, in which case it is payable to the order of the representative of such estate, trust or fund or his successors; or

(f) an office, or an officer by his title as such in which case it is payable to the principal but the incumbent of the office or his successors may act as if he or they were the holder; or

(g) a partnership or unincorporated association, in which case it is payable to the partnership or association and may be indorsed or transferred by any person thereto authorized.

. . .

§ 3–111. Payable to Bearer

An instrument is payable to bearer when by its terms it is payable to

(a) bearer or the order of bearer; or

(b) a specified person or bearer; or

(c) "cash" or the order of "cash", or any other indication which does not purport to designate a specific payee.

§ 3–112. Terms and Omissions Not Affecting Negotiability

(1) The negotiability of an instrument is not affected by

(a) the omission of a statement of any consideration or of the place where the instrument is drawn or payable; or

(b) a statement that collateral has been given to secure obligations either on the instrument or otherwise of an obligor on the instrument or that in case of default on those obligations the holder may realize on or dispose of the collateral; or

(c) a promise or power to maintain or protect collateral or to give additional collateral; or

(d) a term authorizing a confession of judgment on the instrument if it is not paid when due; or

(e) a term purporting to waive the benefit of any law intended for the advantage or protection of any obligor; or

(f) a term in a draft providing that the payee by indorsing or cashing it acknowledges full satisfaction of an obligation of the drawer; or

(g) a statement in a draft drawn in a set of parts (Section 3–801) to the effect that the order is effective only if no other part has been honored.

(2) Nothing in this section shall validate any term which is otherwise illegal.

§ 3–119. Other Writings Affecting Instrument

(1) As between the obligor and his immediate obligee or any transferee the terms of an instrument may be modified or affected by any other written agreement executed as a part of the same transaction, except that a holder in due course is not affected by any limitation of his rights arising out of the separate written agreement if he had no notice of the limitation when he took the instrument.

(2) A separate agreement does not affect the negotiability of an instrument.

Official Comment

Purposes: This section is new. It is intended to resolve conflicts as to the effect of a separate writing upon a negotiable instrument.

. . .

3. The section applies to negotiable instruments the ordinary rule that writings executed as a part of the same transaction are to be read together as a single agreement. As between the immediate parties a negotiable instrument is merely a contract, and is no exception to the principle that the courts will look to the entire contract in writing. Accordingly a note may be affected by an acceleration clause, a clause providing for discharge under certain conditions, or any other relevant term in the separate writing. "May be modified or affected" does not mean that the separate agreement must necessarily be given effect. There is still room for construction of the writing as not intended to affect the instrument at all, or as intended to affect it only for a limited purpose such as foreclosure or other realization of collateral. If there is outright contradiction between the two, as where the note is for $1,000 but the accompanying mortgage recites that it is for $2,000, the note may be held to stand on its own feet and not to be affected by the contradiction.

4. Under this Article a purchaser of the instrument may become a holder in due course although he takes it with knowledge that it was accompanied by a separate agreement, if he has no notice of any defense or claim arising from the terms of the agreement. If any limitation in the separate writing in itself amounts to a defense or claim, as in the case of an agreement that the note is a sham and cannot be enforced, a purchaser with notice of it cannot be a holder in due course. The section also covers limitations which do not in themselves give notice of any present defense or claim, such as conditions providing that under certain conditions the note shall be extended for one year. A purchaser with notice of such limitations may be a holder in due course, but he takes the instrument subject to the limitation. If he is without such notice, he is not affected by such a limiting clause in the separate writing.

. . .

PART 2. TRANSFER AND NEGOTIATION

§ 3-201. Transfer: Right to Indorsement

(1) Transfer of an instrument vests in the transferee such rights as the transferor has therein, except that a transferee who has himself been a party to any fraud or illegality affecting the instrument or who as a prior holder had notice of a defense or claim against it cannot improve his position by taking from a later holder in due course.

(2) A transfer of a security interest in an instrument vests the foregoing rights in the transferee to the extent of the interest transferred.

. . .

§ 3-202. Negotiation

(1) Negotiation is the transfer of an instrument in such form that the transferee becomes a holder. If the instrument is payable to order it is negotiated by delivery with any necessary indorsement; if payable to bearer it is negotiated by delivery.

(2) An indorsement must be written by or on behalf of the holder and on the instrument or on a paper so firmly affixed thereto as to become a part thereof.

. . .

PART 3. RIGHTS OF A HOLDER

§ 3-301. Rights of a Holder

The holder of an instrument whether or not he is the owner may transfer or negotiate it and, except as otherwise provided in Section 3-603 on payment or satisfaction, discharge it or enforce payment in his own name.

§ 3-302. Holder in Due Course

(1) A holder in due course is a holder who takes the instrument

(a) for value; and

(b) in good faith; and

(c) without notice that it is overdue or has been dishonored or of any defense against or claim to it on the part of any person.

(2) A payee may be a holder in due course.

(3) A holder does not become a holder in due course of an instrument:

(a) by purchase of it at judicial sale or by taking it under legal process; or

(b) by acquiring it in taking over an estate; or

(c) by purchasing it as part of a bulk transaction not in regular course of business of the transferor.

(4) A purchaser of a limited interest can be a holder in due course only to the extent of the interest purchased.

§ 3-303. Taking for Value

A holder takes the instrument for value

(a) to the extent that the agreed consideration has been performed or that he acquires a security interest in or a lien on the instrument otherwise than by legal process; or

(b) when he takes the instrument in payment of or as security for an antecedent claim against any person whether or not the claim is due; or

(c) when he gives a negotiable instrument for it or makes an irrevocable commitment to a third person.

§ 3-304. Notice to Purchaser

(1) The purchaser has notice of a claim or defense if

(a) the instrument is so incomplete, bears such visible evidence of forgery or alteration, or is otherwise so irregular as to call into question its validity, terms or ownership or to create an ambiguity as to the party to pay; or

(b) the purchaser has notice that the obligation of any party is voidable in whole or in part, or that all parties have been discharged.

(2) The purchaser has notice of a claim against the instrument when he has knowledge that a fiduciary has negotiated the instrument in payment of or as security for his own debt or in any transaction for his own benefit or otherwise in breach of duty.

(3) The purchaser has notice that an instrument is overdue if he has reason to know

(a) that any part of the principal amount is overdue or that there is an uncured default in payment of another instrument of the same series; or

(b) that acceleration of the instrument has been made; or

(c) that he is taking a demand instrument after demand has been made or more than a reasonable length of time after its issue. A reasonable time for a check drawn and payable within the states and territories of the United States and the District of Columbia is presumed to be thirty days.

(4) Knowledge of the following facts does not of itself give the purchaser notice of a defense or claim

(a) that the instrument is antedated or postdated;

(b) that it was issued or negotiated in return for an executory promise or accompanied by a separate agreement, unless the purchaser has notice that a defense or claim has arisen from the terms thereof;

(c) that any party has signed for accommodation;

(d) that an incomplete instrument has been completed, unless the purchaser has notice of any improper completion;

(e) that any person negotiating the instrument is or was a fiduciary;

(f) that there has been default in payment of interest on the instrument or in payment of any other instrument, except one of the same series.

(5) The filing or recording of a document does not of itself constitute notice within the provisions of this Article to a person who would otherwise be a holder in due course.

(6) To be effective notice must be received at such time and in such manner as to give a reasonable opportunity to act on it.

§ 3–305. Rights of a Holder in Due Course

To the extent that a holder is a holder in due course he takes the instrument free from

(1) all claims to it on the part of any person; and

(2) all defenses of any party to the instrument with whom the holder has not dealt except

(a) infancy, to the extent that it is a defense to a simple contract; and

(b) such other incapacity, or duress, or illegality of the transaction, as renders the obligation of the party a nullity; and

(c) such misrepresentation as has induced the party to sign the instrument with neither knowledge nor reasonable opportunity to obtain knowledge of its character or its essential terms; and

(d) discharge in insolvency proceedings; and

(e) any other discharge of which the holder has notice when he takes the instrument.

Official Comment

Purposes of Changes and New Matter:

. . .

4. Paragraph (a) of subsection (2) is new. It follows the decisions under the original Act in providing that the defense of infancy may be asserted against a holder in due course, even though its effect is to render the instrument voidable but not void. The policy is one of protection of the infant against those who take advantage of him, even at the expense of occasional loss to an innocent purchaser. No attempt is made to state when infancy is available as a defense or the conditions under which it may be asserted. In some jurisdictions it is held that an infant cannot rescind the transaction or set up the defense unless he restores the holder to his former position, which in the case of a holder in due course is normally impossible. In other states an infant who has misrepresented his age may be estopped to assert his infancy. Such questions are left to the local law, as an integral part of the policy of each state as to the protection of infants.

5. Paragraph (b) of subsection (2) is new. It covers mental incompetence, guardianship, ultra vires acts or lack of corporate capacity to do business, any remaining incapacity of married women, or any other incapacity apart from infancy. Such incapacity is largely statutory. Its existence and effect is left to the law of each state. If under the local law the effect is to render the obligation of the instrument entirely null and void, the defense may be asserted against a holder in due course. If the effect is merely to render the obligation voidable at the election of the obligor, the defense is cut off.

6. Duress is a matter of degree. An instrument signed at the point of a gun is void, even in the hands of a holder in due course. One signed under threat to prosecute the son of the maker for theft may be merely voidable, so that the defense is cut off. Illegality is most frequently a matter of gambling or usury, but may arise in many other forms under a great variety of statutes. The statutes differ greatly in their provisions and the interpretations given them. They are primarily a matter of local concern and local policy. All such matters are therefore left to the local law. If under that law the effect of the duress or the illegality is to make the obligation entirely null and void, the defense may be asserted against a holder in due course. Otherwise it is cut off.

7. Paragraph (c) of subsection (2) is new. It follows the great majority of the decisions under the original Act in recognizing the defense of "real" or "essential" fraud, sometimes called fraud in the essence or fraud in the factum, as effective against a holder in due course. The common illustration

is that of the maker who is tricked into signing a note in the belief that it is merely a receipt or some other document. The theory of the defense is that his signature on the instrument is ineffective because he did not intend to sign such an instrument at all. Under this provision the defense extends to an instrument signed with knowledge that it is a negotiable instrument, but without knowledge of its essential terms.

The test of the defense here stated is that of excusabie ignorance of the contents of the writing signed. The party must not only have been in ignorance, but must also have had no reasonable opportunity to obtain knowledge. In determining what is a reasonable opportunity all relevant factors are to be taken into account, including the age and sex of the party, his intelligence, education and business experience; his ability to read or to understand English, the representations made to him and his reason to rely on them or to have confidence in the person making them; the presence or absence of any third person who might read or explain the instrument to him, or any other possibility of obtaining independent information; and the apparent necessity, or lack of it, for acting without delay.

Unless the misrepresentation meets this test, the defense is cut off by a holder in due course.

8. Paragraph (d) is also new. It is inserted to make it clear that any discharge in bankruptcy or other insolvency proceedings, as defined in this Article, is not cut off when the instrument is purchased by a holder in due course.

. . .

§ 3–306. Rights of One Not Holder in Due Course

Unless he has the rights of a holder in due course any person takes the instrument subject to

(a) all valid claims to it on the part of any person; and

(b) all defenses of any party which would be available in an action on a simple contract; and

(c) the defenses of want or failure of consideration, non-performance of any condition precedent, non-delivery, or delivery for a special purpose (Section 3–408); and

(d) the defense that he or a person through whom he holds the instrument acquired it by theft, or that payment or satisfaction to such holder would be inconsistent with the terms of a restrictive indorsement. The claim of any third person to the instrument is not otherwise available as a defense to any party liable thereon unless the third person himself defends the action for such party.

ARTICLE 7. WAREHOUSE RECEIPTS, BILLS OF LADING AND OTHER DOCUMENTS OF TITLE

PART 2. WAREHOUSE RECEIPTS: SPECIAL PROVISIONS

§ 7–209. Lien of Warehouseman

(1) A warehouseman has a lien against the bailor on the goods covered by a warehouse receipt or on the proceeds thereof in his possession for charges for storage or transportation (including demurrage and terminal charges), insurance, labor, or charges present or future in relation to the goods, and for expenses necessary for preservation of the goods or reasonably incurred in their sale pursuant to law. If the person on whose account the goods are held is liable for like charges or expenses in relation to other goods whenever deposited and it is stated in the receipt that a lien is claimed for charges and expenses in relation to other goods, the warehouseman also has a lien against him for such charges and expenses whether or not the other goods have been delivered by the warehouseman. But against a person to whom a negotiable warehouse receipt is duly negotiated a warehouseman's lien is limited to charges in an amount or at a rate specified on the receipt or if no charges are so specified then to a reasonable charge for storage of the goods covered by the receipt subsequent to the date of the receipt.

. . .

(4) A warehouseman loses his lien on any goods which he voluntarily delivers or which he unjustifiably refuses to deliver.

§ 7–210. Enforcement of Warehouseman's Lien

(1) Except as provided in subsection (2), a warehouseman's lien may be enforced by public or private sale of the goods in block or in parcels, at any time or place and on any terms which are commercially reasonable, after notifying all persons known to claim an interest in the goods. Such notification must include a statement of the amount due, the nature of the proposed sale and the time and place of any public sale. The fact that a better price could have been obtained by a sale at a different time or in a different method from that selected by the warehouseman is not of itself sufficient to establish that the sale was not made in a commercially reasonable manner. If the warehouseman either sells the goods in the usual manner in any recognized market therefor, or if he sells at the price current in such market at the time of his sale, or if he has otherwise sold in conformity with commercially reasonable practices among dealers in the type of goods sold, he has sold in a commercially reasonable manner. A sale of more goods than apparently necessary to be offered to insure

satisfaction of the obligation is not commercially reasonable except in cases covered by the preceding sentence.

(2) A warehouseman's lien on goods other than goods stored by a merchant in the course of his business may be enforced only as follows:

(a) All persons known to claim an interest in the goods must be notified.

(b) The notification must be delivered in person or sent by registered or certified letter to the last known address of any person to be notified.

(c) The notification must include an itemized statement of the claim, a description of the goods subject to the lien, a demand for payment within a specified time not less than ten days after receipt of the notification, and a conspicuous statement that unless the claim is paid within that time the goods will be advertised for sale and sold by auction at a specified time and place.

(d) The sale must conform to the terms of the notification.

(e) The sale must be held at the nearest suitable place to that where the goods are held or stored.

(f) After the expiration of the time given in the notification, an advertisement of the sale must be published once a week for two weeks consecutively in a newspaper of general circulation where the sale is to be held. The advertisement must include a description of the goods, the name of the person on whose account they are being held, and the time and place of the sale. The sale must take place at least fifteen days after the first publication. If there is no newspaper of general circulation where the sale is to be held, the advertisement must be posted at least ten days before the sale in not less than six conspicuous places in the neighborhood of the proposed sale.

(3) Before any sale pursuant to this section any person claiming a right in the goods may pay the amount necessary to satisfy the lien and the reasonable expenses incurred under this section. In that event the goods must not be sold, but must be retained by the warehouseman subject to the terms of the receipt and this Article.

(4) The warehouseman may buy at any public sale pursuant to this section.

(5) A purchaser in good faith of goods sold to enforce a warehouseman's lien takes the goods free of any rights of persons against whom the lien was valid, despite noncompliance by the warehouseman with the requirements of this section.

(6) The warehouseman may satisfy his lien from the proceeds of any sale pursuant to this section but must hold the balance, if any, for delivery on demand to any person to whom he would have been bound to deliver the goods.

(7) The rights provided by this section shall be in addition to all other rights allowed by law to a creditor against his debtor.

(8) Where a lien is on goods stored by a merchant in the course of his business the lien may be enforced in accordance with either subsection (1) or (2).

(9) The warehouseman is liable for damages caused by failure to comply with the requirements for sale under this section and in case of willful violation is liable for conversion.

ARTICLE 9. SECURED TRANSACTIONS; SALES OF ACCOUNTS AND CHATTEL PAPER

PART 1. SHORT TITLE, APPLICABILITY AND DEFINITIONS

§ 9–101. Short Title

This Article shall be known and may be cited as Uniform Commercial Code—Secured Transactions.

Official Comment

This Article sets out a comprehensive scheme for the regulation of security interests in personal property and fixtures. It supersedes prior legislation dealing with such security devices as chattel mortgages, conditional sales, trust receipts, factor's liens and assignments of accounts receivable (see Note to Section 9–102).

Consumer installment sales and consumer loans present special problems of a nature which makes special regulation of them inappropriate in a general commercial codification. Many states now regulate such loans and sales under small loan acts, retail installment selling acts and the like. The National Conference of Commissioners on Uniform State Laws has proposed a Uniform Consumer Credit Code dealing with this subject. While this Article applies generally to security interests in consumer goods, it is not designed to supersede such regulatory legislation (see Notes to Sections 9–102 and 9–203). Nor is this Article designed as a substitute for small loan acts or retail installment selling acts in any state which does not presently have such legislation.

. . .

§ 9–105. Definitions and Index of Definitions

(1) In this Article unless the context otherwise requires:

. . .

(c) "Collateral" means the property subject to a security interest, and includes accounts and chattel paper which have been sold;

(d) "Debtor" means the person who owes payment or other performance of the obligation secured, whether or not he owns or has rights in the collateral, and includes the seller of accounts or chattel paper. Where the debtor and the owner of the collateral are not the same person, the term "debtor" means the owner of the collateral in any provision of the Article dealing with the collateral, the obligor in any provision dealing with the obligation, and may include both where the context so requires;

. . .

(*l*) "Security agreement" means an agreement which creates or provides for a security interest;

(m) "Secured party" means a lender, seller or other person in whose favor there is a security interest, including a person to whom accounts or chattel paper have been sold. When the holders of obligations issued under an indenture of trust, equipment trust agreement or the like are represented by a trustee or other person, the representative is the secured party;

. . .

§ 9-107. Definitions: "Purchase Money Security Interest"

A security interest is a "purchase money security interest" to the extent that it is

(a) taken or retained by the seller of the collateral to secure all or part of its price; or

(b) taken by a person who by making advances or incurring an obligation gives value to enable the debtor to acquire rights in or the use of collateral if such value is in fact so used.

PART 2. VALIDITY OF SECURITY AGREEMENT AND RIGHTS OF PARTIES THERETO

§ 9-201. General Validity of Security Agreement

Except as otherwise provided by this Act a security agreement is effective according to its terms between the parties, against purchasers of the collateral and against creditors. Nothing in this Article validates any charge or practice illegal under any statute or regulation thereunder governing usury, small loans, retail installment sales, or the like, or extends the application of any such statute or regulation to any transaction not otherwise subject thereto.

§ 9-206. Agreement Not to Assert Defenses Against Assignee; Modification of Sales Warranties Where Security Agreement Exists

(1) Subject to any statute or decision which establishes a different rule for buyers or lessees of consumer goods, an agreement by a buyer or lessee that he will not assert against an assignee any claim or defense which he may have against the seller or lessor is enforceable by an assignee who takes his assignment for value, in good faith and without notice of a claim or defense, except as to defenses of a type which may be asserted against a holder in due course of a negotiable instrument under the Article on Commercial Paper (Article 3). A buyer who as part of one transaction signs both a negotiable instrument and a security agreement makes such an agreement.

(2) When a seller retains a purchase money security interest in goods the Article on Sales (Article 2) governs the sale and any disclaimer, limitation or modification of the seller's warranties.

Official Comment

Purposes:

1. Clauses are frequently inserted in installment purchase contracts under which the conditional vendee agrees not to assert defenses against an assignee of the contract. These clauses have led to litigation and their present status under the case law is in confusion. In some jurisdictions they have been held void as attempts to create negotiable instruments outside the framework of Article 3 or on grounds of public policy; in others they have been allowed to operate to cut off at least defenses based on breach of warranty. Under subsection (1) such clauses in a security agreement are validated outside the consumer field, but only as to defenses which could be cut off if a negotiable instrument were used. This limitation is important since if the clauses were allowed to have full effect as typically drafted, they would operate to cut off real as well as personal defenses. The execution of a negotiable note in connection with a security agreement is given like effect as the execution of an agreement containing a waiver of defense clause. The same rules are made applicable to leases as to security agreements, whether or not the lease is intended as security.

2. This Article takes no position on the controversial question whether a buyer of consumer goods may effectively waive defenses by contractual clause or by execution of a negotiable note. In some states such waivers have been invalidated by statute. In other states the course of judicial decision has rendered them ineffective or unreliable—courts have found that the assignee is not protected against the buyer's defense by a clause in the contract or that the holder of a note, by reason of his too close connection with the underlying transaction, does not have the rights of a holder in due course. This Article neither adopts nor rejects the approach taken in such statutes and decisions, except that the validation of waivers in subsection (1) is expressly made "subject to any statute or decision" which may restrict the waiver's effectiveness in the case of a buyer of consumer goods.

. . .

§ 9–207. Rights and Duties When Collateral is in Secured Party's Possession

(1) A secured party must use reasonable care in the custody and preservation of collateral in his possession. In the case of an instrument or chattel paper reasonable care includes taking necessary steps to preserve rights against prior parties unless otherwise agreed.

(2) Unless otherwise agreed, when collateral is in the secured party's possession

(a) reasonable expenses (including the cost of any insurance and payment of taxes or other charges) incurred in the custody, preservation, use or operation of the collateral are chargeable to the debtor and are secured by the collateral;

(b) the risk of accidental loss or damage is on the debtor to the extent of any deficiency in any effective insurance coverage;

(c) the secured party may hold as additional security any increase or profits (except money) received from the collateral, but money so received, unless remitted to the debtor, shall be applied in reduction of the secured obligation;

(d) the secured party must keep the collateral identifiable but fungible collateral may be commingled;

(e) the secured party may repledge the collateral upon terms which do not impair the debtor's right to redeem it.

(3) A secured party is liable for any loss caused by his failure to meet any obligation imposed by the preceding subsections but does not lose his security interest.

(4) A secured party may use or operate the collateral for the purpose of preserving the collateral or its value or pursuant to the order of a court of appropriate jurisdiction or, except in the case of consumer goods, in the manner and to the extent provided in the security agreement.

PART 5. DEFAULT

§ 9-501. Default; Procedure When Security Agreement Covers Both Real and Personal Property

(1) When a debtor is in default under a security agreement, a secured party has the rights and remedies provided in this Part and except as limited by subsection (3) those provided in the security agreement. He may reduce his claim to judgment, foreclose or otherwise enforce the security interest by any available judicial procedure. If the collateral is documents the secured party may proceed either as to the documents or as to the goods covered thereby. A secured party in possession has the rights, remedies and duties provided in Section 9-207. The rights and remedies referred to in this subsection are cumulative.

(2) After default, the debtor has the rights and remedies provided in this Part, those provided in the security agreement and those provided in Section 9-207.

(3) To the extent that they give rights to the debtor and impose duties on the secured party, the rules stated in the subsections referred to below may not be waived or varied except as provided with respect to compulsory disposition of collateral (subsection (3) of Section 9-504 and Section 9-505) and with respect to redemption of collateral (Section 9-506) but the parties may by agreement determine

the standards by which the fulfillment of these rights and duties is to be measured if such standards are not manifestly unreasonable:

(a) subsection (2) of Section 9–502 and subsection (2) of Section 9–504 insofar as they require accounting for surplus proceeds of collateral;

(b) subsection (3) of Section 9–504 and subsection (1) of Section 9–505 which deal with disposition of collateral;

(c) subsection (2) of Section 9–505 which deals with acceptance of collateral as discharge of obligation;

(d) Section 9–506 which deals with redemption of collateral; and

(e) subsection (1) of Section 9–507 which deals with the secured party's liability for failure to comply with this Part.

(4) If the security agreement covers both real and personal property, the secured party may proceed under this Part as to the personal property or he may proceed as to both the real and the personal property in accordance with his rights and remedies in respect of the real property in which case the provisions of this Part do not apply.

(5) When a secured party has reduced his claim to judgment the lien of any levy which may be made upon his collateral by virtue of any execution based upon the judgment shall relate back to the date of the perfection of the security interest in such collateral. A judicial sale, pursuant to such execution, is a foreclosure of the security interest by judicial procedure within the meaning of this section, and the secured party may purchase at the sale and thereafter hold the collateral free of any other requirements of this Article.

Official Comment

Purposes:

1. The rights of the secured party in the collateral after the debtor's default are of the essence of a security transaction. These are the rights which distinguish the secured from the unsecured lender. This section and the following six sections state those rights as well as the limitations on their free exercise which legislative policy requires for the protection not only of the defaulting debtor but of other creditors. But subsections (1) and (2) make it clear that the statement of rights and remedies in this Part does not exclude other remedies provided by agreement.

. . .

3. Section 9–207 states rights, remedies and duties with respect to collateral in the secured party's possession. That section applies not only to the situation where he is in possession before default, as a pledgee, but also, by subsections (1) and (2) of this section, to the secured party in possession after default. Nevertheless the relations of the parties have been changed by default, and Section 9–207 as it applies after default must be read together with this Part. In particular, agreements permitted under Section 9–207 can-

not waive or modify the rights of the debtor contrary to subsection (3) of this section.

4. Section 1–102(3) states rules to determine which provisions of this Act are mandatory and which may be varied by agreement. In general, provisions which relate to matters which come up between immediate parties may be varied by agreement. In the area of rights after default our legal system has traditionally looked with suspicion on agreements designed to cut down the debtor's rights and free the secured party of his duties: no mortgage clause has ever been allowed to clog the equity of redemption. The default situation offers great scope for overreaching; the suspicious attitude of the courts has been grounded in common sense.

Subsection (3) of this section contains a codification of this long-standing and deeply rooted attitude: the specified rights of the debtor and duties of the secured party may not be waived or varied except as stated. Provisions not specified in subsection (3) are subject to the general rules stated in Section 1–102(3).

5. The collateral for many corporate security issues consists of both real and personal property. In the interest of simplicity and speed subsection (4) permits, although it does not require, the secured party to proceed as to both real and personal property in accordance with his rights and remedies in respect of the real property. Except for the permission so granted, this Act leaves to other state law all questions of procedure with respect to real property. For example, this Act does not determine whether the secured party can proceed against the real estate alone and later proceed in a separate action against the personal property in accordance with his rights and remedies against the real estate. By such separate actions the secured party "proceeds as to both," and this Part does not apply in either action. But subsection (4) does give him an option to proceed under this Part as to the personal property.

. . .

§ 9–503. Secured Party's Right to Take Possession After Default

Unless otherwise agreed a secured party has on default the right to take possession of the collateral. In taking possession a secured party may proceed without judicial process if this can be done without breach of the peace or may proceed by action. If the security agreement so provides the secured party may require the debtor to assemble the collateral and make it available to the secured party at a place to be designated by the secured party which is reasonably convenient to both parties. Without removal a secured party may render equipment unusable, and may dispose of collateral on the debtor's premises under Section 9–504.

Official Comment

Purposes:

Under this Article the secured party's right to possession of the collateral (if he is not already in possession as pledgee) accrues on default unless otherwise agreed in the security agreement. This Article follows the provisions of the earlier uniform legislation in allowing the secured party in most cases to take possession without the issuance of judicial process. In the case of collateral such as heavy equipment, the physical removal from the debtor's plant and the storage of the equipment pending resale may be exceedingly expensive and in some cases impractical. The section therefore provides that in lieu of removal the lender may render equipment unusable or dispose of collateral on the debtor's premises. The authorization to render equipment unusable or to dispose of collateral without removal would not justify unreasonable action by the secured party, since, under Section 9–504(3), all his actions in connection with disposition must be taken in a "commercially reasonable manner".

§ 9–504. Secured Party's Right to Dispose of Collateral After Default; Effect of Disposition

(1) A secured party after default may sell, lease or otherwise dispose of any or all of the collateral in its then condition or following any commercially reasonable preparation or processing. Any sale of goods is subject to the Article on Sales (Article 2). The proceeds of disposition shall be applied in the order following to

(a) the reasonable expenses of retaking, holding, preparing for sale or lease, selling, leasing and the like and, to the extent provided for in the agreement and not prohibited by law, the reasonable attorneys' fees and legal expenses incurred by the secured party;

(b) the satisfaction of indebtedness secured by the security interest under which the disposition is made;

(c) the satisfaction of indebtedness secured by any subordinate security interest in the collateral if written notification of demand therefor is received before distribution of the proceeds is completed. If requested by the secured party, the holder of a subordinate security interest must seasonably furnish reasonable proof of his interest, and unless he does so, the secured party need not comply with his demand.

(2) If the security interest secures an indebtedness, the secured party must account to the debtor for any surplus, and, unless otherwise agreed, the debtor is liable for any deficiency. But if the underlying transaction was a sale of accounts or chattel paper, the debtor is entitled to any surplus or is liable for any deficiency only if the security agreement so provides.

(3) Disposition of the collateral may be by public or private proceedings and may be made by way of one or more contracts. Sale or other disposition may be as a unit or in parcels and at any time and place and on any terms but every aspect of the disposition including the method, manner, time, place and terms must be commercially reasonable. Unless collateral is perishable or threatens to decline speedily in value or is of a type customarily sold on a recognized market,

reasonable notification of the time and place of any public sale or reasonable notification of the time after which any private sale or other intended disposition is to be made shall be sent by the secured party to the debtor, if he has not signed after default a statement renouncing or modifying his right to notification of sale. In the case of consumer goods no other notification need be sent. In other cases notification shall be sent to any other secured party from whom the secured party has received (before sending his notification to the debtor or before the debtor's renunciation of his rights) written notice of a claim of an interest in the collateral. The secured party may buy at any public sale and if the collateral is of a type customarily sold in a recognized market or is of a type which is the subject of widely distributed standard price quotations he may buy at private sale.

(4) When collateral is disposed of by a secured party after default, the disposition transfers to a purchaser for value all of the debtor's rights therein, discharges the security interest under which it is made and any security interest or lien subordinate thereto. The purchaser takes free of all such rights and interests even though the secured party fails to comply with the requirements of this Part or of any judicial proceedings

(a) in the case of a public sale, if the purchaser has no knowledge of any defects in the sale and if he does not buy in collusion with the secured party, other bidders or the person conducting the sale; or

(b) in any other case, if the purchaser acts in good faith.

(5) A person who is liable to a secured party under a guaranty, indorsement, repurchase agreement or the like and who receives a transfer of collateral from the secured party or is subrogated to his rights has thereafter the rights and duties of the secured party. Such a transfer of collateral is not a sale or disposition of the collateral under this Article.

Official Comment

Purposes:

1\. . . . The only restriction placed on the secured party's method of disposition is that it must be commercially reasonable. In this respect this section follows the provisions of the section on resale by a seller following a buyer's rejection of goods (Section 2–706). Subsection (1) does not restrict disposition to sale: the collateral may be sold, leased, or otherwise disposed of—subject of course to the general requirement of subsection (2) that all aspects of the disposition be "commercially reasonable". Section 9–507(2) states some tests as to what is "commercially reasonable".

. . .

5\. . . . Under subsection (3), the secured party in most cases is required to give reasonable notification of disposition to the debtor unless the debtor has after default signed a statement renouncing or modifying his right to notification of sale.

. . . Except for the requirement of notification there is no statutory period during which the collateral must be held before disposition. "Reasonable notification" is not defined in this Article; at a minimum it must be sent in such time that persons entitled to receive it will have sufficient time to take appropriate steps to protect their interests by taking part in the sale or other disposition if they so desire.

6. . . . [N]o period is set within which the disposition must be made, except in the case of consumer goods which under Section 9–505(1) must in certain instances be sold within ninety days after the secured party has taken possession. The failure to prescribe a statutory period during which disposition must be made is in line with the policy adopted in this Article to encourage disposition by private sale through regular commercial channels. It may, for example, be wise not to dispose of goods when the market has collapsed, or to sell a large inventory in parcels over a period of time instead of in bulk. Note, however, that under subsection (3) every aspect of the sale or other disposition of the collateral must be commercially reasonable; this specifically includes method, manner, time, place and terms. See Section 9–507(2). Under that provision a secured party who without proceeding under Section 9–505(2) held collateral a long time without disposing of it, thus running up large storage charges against the debtor, where no reason existed for not making a prompt sale, might well be found not to have acted in a "commercially reasonable" manner. See also Section 1–203 on the general obligation of good faith.

§ 9–505. Compulsory Disposition of Collateral; Acceptance of the Collateral as Discharge of Obligation

(1) If the debtor has paid sixty per cent of the cash price in the case of a purchase money security interest in consumer goods or sixty per cent of the loan in the case of another security interest in consumer goods, and has not signed after default a statement renouncing or modifying his rights under this Part a secured party who has taken possession of collateral must dispose of it under Section 9–504 and if he fails to do so within ninety days after he takes possession the debtor at his option may recover in conversion or under Section 9–507(1) on secured party's liability.

(2) In any other case involving consumer goods or any other collateral a secured party in possession may, after default, propose to retain the collateral in satisfaction of the obligation. Written notice of such proposal shall be sent to the debtor if he has not signed after default a statement renouncing or modifying his rights under this subsection. In the case of consumer goods no other notice need be given. In other cases notice shall be sent to any other secured party from whom the secured party has received (before sending his notice to the debtor or before the debtor's renunciation of his rights) written notice of a claim of an interest in the collateral. If the secured party receives objection in writing from a person entitled to receive notifica-

tion within twenty-one days after the notice was sent, the secured party must dispose of the collateral under Section 9–504. In the absence of such written objection the secured party may retain the collateral in satisfaction of the debtor's obligation.

Official Comment

Purposes:

1. Experience has shown that the parties are frequently better off without a resale of the collateral; hence this section sanctions an alternative arrangement. In lieu of resale or other disposition, the secured party may propose under subsection (2) that he keep the collateral as his own, thus discharging the obligation and abandoning any claim for a deficiency. This right may not be exercised in the case of consumer goods where the debtor has paid 60% of the price or obligation and thus has a substantial equity, and may be exercised in other cases only on notification to the debtor, unless the debtor has signed after default a statement renouncing or modifying his rights under this section, and (except in the case of consumer goods) to any other secured party who has given written notice of a claim of an interest in the collateral. In the latter case, notice must be given before the secured party receives the debtor's renunciation or before he sends his notice to the debtor. The secured party may keep the goods in lieu of sale on failure of anyone receiving notification to object within twenty-one days.

2. When an objection is received by the secured party he must then proceed to dispose of the collateral in accordance with Section 9–504, and on failure to do so would incur the liabilities set out in Section 9–507. In the case of consumer goods where 60% of the price or obligation has been paid the disposition must be made within 90 days after possession taken. For failure to make the sale within the 90-day period the secured party is liable in conversion or alternatively may incur the liabilities set out in Section 9–507.

In the absence of objection the secured party is bound by his notice.

3. After default (but not before) a consumer-debtor who has paid 60% of the cash price may sign a written renunciation of his rights to require resale of the collateral.

§ 9–506. Debtor's Right to Redeem Collateral

At any time before the secured party has disposed of collateral or entered into a contract for its disposition under Section 9–504 or before the obligation has been discharged under Section 9–505(2) the debtor or any other secured party may unless otherwise agreed in writing after default redeem the collateral by tendering fulfillment of all obligations secured by the collateral as well as the expenses reasonably incurred by the secured party in retaking, holding and preparing the collateral for disposition, in arranging for the sale, and to the extent provided in the agreement and not prohibited by law, his reasonable attorneys' fees and legal expenses.

Official Comment

Purposes:

Except in the case stated in Section 9–505(1) (consumer goods) the secured party is not required to dispose of collateral within any stated period of time. Under this section so long as the secured party has not disposed of collateral in his possession or contracted for its disposition, and so long as his right to retain it has not become fixed under Section 9–505(2), the debtor or another secured party may redeem. The debtor must tender fulfillment of all obligations secured, plus certain expenses: if the agreement contains a clause accelerating the entire balance due on default in one installment, the entire balance would have to be tendered. "Tendering fulfillment" obviously means more than a new promise to perform the existing promise; it requires payment in full of all monetary obligations then due and performance in full of all other obligations then matured. If unmatured obligations remain, the security interest continues to secure them as if there had been no default.

. . .

§ 9–507. Secured Party's Liability for Failure to Comply With This Part

(1) If it is established that the secured party is not proceeding in accordance with the provisions of this Part disposition may be ordered or restrained on appropriate terms and conditions. If the disposition has occurred the debtor or any person entitled to notification or whose security interest has been made known to the secured party prior to the disposition has a right to recover from the secured party any loss caused by a failure to comply with the provisions of this Part. If the collateral is consumer goods, the debtor has a right to recover in any event an amount not less than the credit service charge plus ten per cent of the principal amount of the debt or the time price differential plus 10 per cent of the cash price.

(2) The fact that a better price could have been obtained by a sale at a different time or in a different method from that selected by the secured party is not of itself sufficient to establish that the sale was not made in a commercially reasonable manner. If the secured party either sells the collateral in the usual manner in any recognized market therefor or if he sells at the price current in such market at the time of his sale or if he has otherwise sold in conformity with reasonable commercial practices among dealers in the type of property sold he has sold in a commercially reasonable manner. The principles stated in the two preceding sentences with respect to sales also apply as may be appropriate to other types of disposition. A disposition which has been approved in any judicial proceeding or by any bona fide creditors' committee or representative of creditors shall conclusively be deemed to be commercially reasonable, but this sentence does not indicate that any such approval must be obtained in any case

nor does it indicate that any disposition not so approved is not commercially reasonable.

Official Comment

Prior Uniform Statutory Provision: None.

Purposes:

1. The principal limitation on the secured party's right to dispose of collateral is the requirement that he proceed in good faith (Section 1–203) and in a commercially reasonable manner. See Section 9–504. In the case where he proceeds, or is about to proceed, in a contrary manner, it is vital both to the debtor and other creditors to provide a remedy for the failure to comply with the statutory duty. This remedy will be of particular importance when it is applied prospectively before the unreasonable disposition has been concluded. This section therefore provides that a secured party proposing to dispose of collateral in an unreasonable manner, may, by court order, be restrained from doing so, and such an order might appropriately provide either that he proceed with the sale or other disposition under specified terms and conditions, or that the sale be made by a representative of creditors where insolvency proceedings have been instituted. The section further provides for damages where the unreasonable disposition has been concluded, and, in the case of consumer goods, states a minimum recovery.

. . .

2. In view of the remedies provided the debtor and other creditors in subsection (1) when a secured party does not dispose of collateral in a commercially reasonable manner, it is of great importance to make clear what types of disposition are to be considered commercially reasonable, and in an appropriate case to give the secured party means of getting, by court order or negotiation with a creditors' committee or a representative of creditors, approval of a proposed method of disposition as a commercially reasonable one. Subsection (2) states rules to assist in the determination, and provides for such advance approval in appropriate situations. One recognized method of disposing of repossessed collateral is for the secured party to sell the collateral to or through a dealer—a method which in the long run may realize better average returns since the secured party does not usually maintain his own facilities for making such sales. Such a method of sale, fairly conducted, is recognized as commercially reasonable under the second sentence of subsection (2). However, none of the specific methods of disposition set forth in subsection (2) is to be regarded as either required or exclusive, provided only that the disposition made or about to be made by the secured party is commercially reasonable.

UNIFORM CONSUMER CREDIT CODE (1974 ACT)

Table of Sections

ARTICLE 1. GENERAL PROVISIONS AND DEFINITIONS

PART 1. SHORT TITLE, CONSTRUCTION, GENERAL PROVISIONS

PART 2. SCOPE AND JURISDICTION

PART 3. DEFINITIONS

PART 4. CONSUMER LOANS: MAXIMUM FINANCE CHARGES

PART 5. CONSUMER CREDIT TRANSACTIONS: OTHER CHARGES AND MODIFICATIONS

PART 6. OTHER CREDIT TRANSACTIONS

ARTICLE 3. REGULATION OF AGREEMENTS AND PRACTICES

PART 1. GENERAL PROVISIONS

PART 2. DISCLOSURE

PART 3. LIMITATIONS ON AGREEMENTS AND PRACTICES

PART 4. LIMITATIONS ON CONSUMERS' LIABILITIES

PART 5. HOME SOLICITATION SALES

ARTICLE 4. INSURANCE

PART 1. INSURANCE IN GENERAL

PART 2. CONSUMER CREDIT INSURANCE

PART 3. PROPERTY AND LIABILITY INSURANCE

ARTICLE 5. REMEDIES AND PENALTIES

PART 1. LIMITATIONS ON CREDITORS' REMEDIES

PART 2. CONSUMERS' REMEDIES

PART 3. CRIMINAL PENALTIES

ARTICLE 6. ADMINISTRATION

PART 1. POWERS AND FUNCTIONS OF ADMINISTRATOR

ARTICLE 1. GENERAL PROVISIONS AND DEFINITIONS

PART 1. SHORT TITLE, CONSTRUCTION, GENERAL PROVISIONS

§ 1.102 [Purposes; Rules of Construction]

(1) This Act shall be liberally construed and applied to promote its underlying purposes and policies.

(2) The underlying purposes and policies of this Act are:

(a) to simplify, clarify, and modernize the law governing consumer credit and usury;

(b) to provide rate ceilings to assure an adequate supply of credit to consumers;

(c) to further consumer understanding of the terms of credit transactions and to foster competition among suppliers of consumer credit so that consumers may obtain credit at reasonable cost;

(d) to protect consumers against unfair practices by some suppliers of consumer credit, having due regard for the interests of legitimate and scrupulous creditors;

(e) to permit and encourage the development of fair and economically sound consumer credit practices;

(f) to conform the regulation of disclosure in consumer credit transactions to the Federal Truth in Lending Act; and

(g) to make uniform the law, including administrative rules, among the various jurisdictions.

(3) A reference to a requirement imposed by this Act includes reference to a related rule of the Administrator adopted pursuant to this Act.

§ 1.103 [Supplementary General Principles of Law Applicable]

Unless displaced by the particular provisions of this Act, the Uniform Commercial Code and the principles of law and equity, including the law relative to capacity to contract, principal and agent, estoppel, fraud, misrepresentation, duress, coercion, mistake, bankruptcy, or other validating or invalidating cause supplement its provisions. In the event of inconsistency between the Uniform Commercial Code and this Act the provisions of this Act control.

§ 1.106 [Adjustment of Dollar Amounts]

(1) From time to time the dollar amounts in this Act designated as subject to change shall change, as provided in this section, according

to and to the extent of changes in the Consumer Price Index for Urban Wage Earners and Clerical Workers: U.S. City Average, All Items, 1967 = 100, compiled by the Bureau of Labor Statistics, United States Department of Labor, and hereafter referred to as the Index. . . .

§ 1.107 [Waiver; Agreement to Forego Rights; Settlement of Claims]

(1) Except as otherwise permitted in this Act, a consumer may waive or agree to forego rights or benefits under this Act only in settlement of a bona fide dispute.

(2) A claim by a consumer against a creditor for an excess charge, any other violation of this Act, a civil penalty, or a claim against a consumer for a default or breach of a duty imposed by this Act, if disputed in good faith, may be settled by agreement.

(3) A claim against a consumer, whether or not disputed, may be settled for less value than the amount claimed.

(4) A settlement in which the consumer waives or agrees to forego rights or benefits under this Act is invalid if the court as a matter of law finds the settlement to have been unconscionable at the time it was made. The competence of the consumer, any deception or coercion practiced upon him, the nature and extent of the legal advice received by him, and the value of the consideration are relevant to the issue of unconscionability.

Comment

Unlike UCC Section 1–102(3) which broadly permits variation by agreement, this Act starts from the premise that a consumer may not in general waive or agree to forego rights or benefits under this Act. Compare UCC Section 9–501(3). If not specifically provided for in the Act, waiver or agreement to forego must be part of a settlement, and settlements are subject to review as provided for in this section.

§ 1.110 [Obligation of Good Faith]

(1) Every contract or duty within this Act imposes an obligation of good faith in its performance or enforcement.

(2) "Good faith" means honesty in fact in the conduct or transaction concerned.

PART 2. SCOPE AND JURISDICTION

§ 1.201 [Territorial Application]

(1) Except as otherwise provided in this section, this Act applies to a consumer credit transaction entered into in this State. For the pur-

poses of this Act, a consumer credit transaction is entered into in this State if:

(a) pursuant to other than open-end credit, either a signed writing evidencing the obligation or offer of the consumer is received by the creditor in this State, or the creditor induces the consumer who is a resident of this State to enter into the transaction by face-to-face solicitation in this State; or

(b) pursuant to open-end credit, either the consumer's communication or his indication of intention to establish the open-end credit arrangement is received by the creditor in this State or, if no communication or indication of intention is given by the consumer before the first transaction, the creditor's communication notifying the consumer of the privilege of using the arrangement is mailed in this State.

(2) With respect to a consumer loan to which this Act does not otherwise apply, if a consumer who is a resident of this State, pursuant to solicitation in this State, sends a signed writing evidencing the obligation or offer of the consumer to a creditor in another state and receives the cash proceeds of the loan in this State:

(a) the creditor may not contract for or receive charges exceeding those permitted by the Article on Finance Charges and Related Provisions (Article 2); and

(b) the provisions on Powers and Functions of Administrator (Part 1) of the Article on Administration (Article 6) apply as though the loan were entered into in this State.

(3) The Part on Limitations on Creditors' Remedies (Part 1) of the Article on Remedies and Penalties (Article 5) applies to actions or other proceedings brought in this State to enforce rights arising from consumer credit transactions or extortionate extensions of credit, wherever entered into.

(4) Except as provided in subsection (2), a consumer credit transaction to which this Act does not apply entered into with a person who is a resident of this State at the time of the transaction is valid and enforceable in this State to the extent that it is valid and enforceable under the laws of another jurisdiction, but:

(a) a creditor may not collect through actions or other proceedings in this State an amount exceeding the total amount permitted if the Article on Finance Charges and Related Provisions (Article 2) were applicable; and

(b) a creditor may not enforce rights against the consumer in this State with respect to the provisions of agreements that violate the provisions on Limitations on Agreements and Practices (Part 3) and Limitations on Consumers' Liabilities (Part 4) of the Article on Regultion of Agreements and Practices (Article 3).

(5) Except as provided in subsections (2), (3), and (4), a consumer credit transaction entered into in another jurisdiction is valid and en-

forceable in this State according to its terms to the extent that it is valid and enforceable under the laws of the other jurisdiction.

(6) For the purposes of this Act, the residence of a consumer is the address given by him as his residence in a writing signed by him in connection with a consumer credit transaction until he notifies the creditor of a different address as his residence, and is then the different address.

(7) Notwithstanding other provisions of this section:

(a) except as provided in subsection (3), this Act does not apply if the consumer is not a resident of this State at the time of a consumer credit transaction and the parties have agreed that the law of his residence applies; and

(b) this Act applies if the consumer is a resident of this State at the time of a consumer credit transaction and the parties have agreed that the law of his residence applies.

(8) Each of the following agreements or provisions of an agreement by a consumer who is a resident of this State at the time of a consumer credit transaction is invalid with respect to the transaction:

(a) that the law of another jurisdiction apply;

(b) that the consumer consents to be subject to the process of another jurisdiction;

(c) that the consumer appoints an agent to receive service of process;

(d) that fixes venue; and

(e) that the consumer consents to the jurisdiction of the court that does not otherwise have jurisdiction.

(9) The following provisions of this Act specify the applicable law governing certain cases:

(a) applicability (Section 6.102) of the Part on Powers and Functions of Administrator (Part 1) of the Article on Administration (Article 6); and

(b) applicability (Section 6.201) of the Part on Notification and Fees (Part 2) of the Article on Administration (Article 6).

Comment

1. This section enables the enacting State to apply this Act for the protection of its own consumer residents in multi-state transactions to the extent consistent with the need for workable operating procedures on the part of creditors. The territorial applicability of the Act varies with the kind of protection safeguard involved. The major substantive protective provisions in this Act are those on rate ceilings (Parts 2 and 4 of Article 2), disclosure (Part 2 of Article 3), limitations on agreements and practices (Part 3 of Article 3), home solicitation sales (Part 5 of Article 3), limitations on consumers' liabilities (Part 4 of Article 3), and limitations on creditors' remedies (Part 1

of Article 5). Except for the disclosure provisions, this section allows the enacting State to apply all of these protective provisions to its own consumer residents when enforcement actions are brought against them in the enacting State.

. . .

2. Subsection (1) serves as a general residual provision governing those matters not specifically treated elsewhere in the section and controls the applicability of the disclosure provisions. Under this subsection the creditor has a measure of control over the applicability of the Act with respect to the disclosure requirements and can arrange his interstate operations in a manner which minimizes the operational difficulties arising from the variations in the disclosure requirements of the different state laws. This flexibility on the part of creditors with respect to the applicability of the disclosure provisions offers no threat to consumers because the Federal Consumer Credit Protection Act [15 U.S.C. § 1601 et seq.] assures consumers that disclosure requirements will be substantially similar in all states.

3. Creditors falling within the supervised lender category (Part 3 of Article 2) need be licensed only in the State where the loan is entered into, that is, where the debtor's writing is received [Subsection (1)]. However, in the case of a mail order loan to a consumer residing in an enacting State, even if the debtor's writing is received by the creditor in another State, the creditor may not exceed the rate ceilings of the enacting State and the Administrator may go into the creditor's State and investigate potential violations pursuant to Part 1 of Article 6 [Subsection (2)]. Of course, the general rule of subsection (1) that a transaction is entered into in the State where the consumer's writing is received yields whenever the creditor attempts to evade the Act by engaging in face-to-face solicitation in the State of the consumer's residence but contrives to have the consumer's writing sent the creditor in another State [Subsection (1)(a)].

. . .

§ 1.202 [Exclusions]

This Act does not apply to:

(1) extensions of credit to organizations;

(2) except as otherwise provided in the Article on Insurance (Article 4), the sale of insurance if the insured is not obligated to pay instalments of the premium and the insurance may terminate or be cancelled after non-payment of an instalment of the premium;

(3) transactions under public utility or common carrier tariffs if a subdivision or agency of this State or of the United States regulates the charges for the services involved, the charges for delayed payment, and any discount allowed for early payment;

(4) transactions in securities or commodities accounts with a broker-dealer registered with the Securities and Exchange Commission; [or]

(5) except with respect to the provisions on compliance with the Federal Truth in Lending Act (Section 3.201), [civil liability for viola-

tion of disclosure provisions (Section 5.203), criminal penalties for disclosure violations (Section 5.302)], and powers and functions of the Administrator with respect to disclosure violations (Part 1 of Article 6), pawnbrokers who are licensed and whose rates and charges are regulated under or pursuant to ordinances or other statutes [; or

(6) ceilings on rates or limits on loan maturities of credit extended by a credit union organized under the laws of this State or of the United States if these ceilings or limits are established by these laws or by applicable regulations].

PART 3. DEFINITIONS

§ 1.301 [General Definitions]

(1) "Actuarial method" means the method of allocating payments made on a debt between the amount financed and the finance charge pursuant to which a payment is applied first to the accumulated finance charge and any remainder is subtracted from, or any deficiency is added to, the unpaid balance of the amount financed. The Administrator may adopt rules not inconsistent with the Federal Truth in Lending Act further defining the term and prescribing its application.

(2) "Administrator" means the Administrator designated in the Article (Article 6) on Administration (Section 6.103).

(3) "Agreement" means the bargain of the parties in fact as found in their language or by implication from other circumstances including course of dealing, usage of trade, or course of performance.

(4) "Agricultural purpose" means a purpose relating to the production, harvest, exhibition, marketing, transportation, processing, or manufacture of agricultural products by a natural person who cultivates, plants, propagates, or nurtures the agricultural products. "Agricultural products" includes agricultural, horticultural, viticultural, and dairy products, livestock, wildlife, poultry, bees, forest products, fish and shellfish, and products thereof, including processed and manufactured products, and products raised or produced on farms and processed or manufactured products thereof.

(5) "Amount financed" means the total of the following items:

(a) in the case of a sale, the cash price of the goods, services, or interest in land, less the amount of any down payment made in cash or in property traded in, and the amount actually paid or to be paid by the seller pursuant to an agreement with the buyer to discharge a security interest in, a lien on, or a debt with respect to property traded in;

(b) in case of a loan, the net amount paid to, receivable by, or paid or payable for the account of the debtor, plus the amount of any discount excluded from the finance charge (paragraph (b)(iii) of subsection (20)); and

(c) in the case of a sale or loan, to the extent that payment is deferred and the amount is not otherwise included and is authorized and disclosed to the consumer as required by law:

(i) amounts actually paid or to be paid by the creditor for registration, certificate of title, or license fees, and

(ii) permitted additional charges (Section 2.501).

(6) "Billing cycle" means the time interval between periodic billing statement dates.

(7) "Card issuer" means a person who issues a credit card.

(8) "Cardholder" means a person to whom a credit card is issued or who has agreed with the card issuer to pay obligations arising from the issuance to or use of the card by another person.

(9) "Cash price" of goods, services, or an interest in land means the price at which they are offered for sale by the seller to cash buyers in the ordinary course of business and may include (1) the cash price of accessories or services related to the sale, such as delivery, installation, alterations, modifications, and improvements, and (b) taxes to the extent imposed on a cash sale of the goods, services, or interest in land. The cash price stated by the seller to the buyer in a disclosure statement required by law is presumed to be the cash price.

(10) "Conspicuous":

A term or clause is "conspicuous" when it is so written that a reasonable person against whom it is to operate ought to have noticed it. Whether or not a term or clause is conspicuous is for decision by the court.

(11) "Consumer" means the buyer, lessee, or debtor to whom credit is granted in a consumer credit transaction.

(12) "Consumer credit sale":

(a) Except as provided in paragraph (b), "consumer credit sale" means a sale of goods, services, or an interest in land in which:

(i) credit is granted either pursuant to a seller credit card or by a seller who regularly engages as a seller in credit transactions of the same kind;

(ii) the buyer is a person other than an organization;

(iii) the goods, services, or interest in land are purchased primarily for a personal, family, household, or agricultural purpose;

(iv) the debt is payable in instalments or a finance charge is made; and

(v) with respect to a sale of goods or services, the amount financed does not exceed $25,000.

(b) A "consumer credit sale" does not include:

(i) a sale in which the seller allows the buyer to purchase goods or services pursuant to a lender credit card, or

(ii) unless the sale is made subject to this Act by agreement (Section 1.109), a sale of an interest in land if the finance charge does not exceed 12 per cent per year calculated according to the actuarial method on the assumption that the debt will be paid according to the agreed terms and will not be paid before the end of the agreed term.

(c) The amount of $25,000 in paragraph (a)(v) is subject to change pursuant to the provisions on adjustment of dollar amounts (Section 1.106).

(13) "Consumer credit transaction" means a consumer credit sale or consumer loan or a refinancing or consolidation thereof, or a consumer lease.

(14) "Consumer lease":

(a) "Consumer lease" means a lease of goods:

(i) which a lessor regularly engaged in the business of leasing makes to a person, except an organization, who takes under the lease primarily for a personal, family, household, or agricultural purpose;

(ii) in which the amount payable under the lease does not exceed $25,000;

(iii) which is for a term exceeding four months; and

(iv) which is not made pursuant to a lender credit card.

(b) The amount of $25,000 in paragraph (a)(ii) is subject to change pursuant to the provisions on adjustment of dollar amounts (Section 1.106).

(15) "Consumer loan":

(a) Except as provided in paragraph (b), "consumer loan" means a loan made by a creditor regularly engaged in the business of making loans in which:

(i) the debtor is a person other than an organization;

(ii) the debt is incurred primarily for a personal, family, household, or agricultural purpose;

(iii) the debt is payable in instalments or a finance charge is made; and

(iv) the amount financed does not exceed $25,000 or the debt, other than one incurred primarily for an agricultural purpose, is secured by an interest in land.

(b) A "consumer loan" does not include:

(i) a sale or lease in which the seller or lessor allows the buyer or lessee to purchase or lease pursuant to a seller credit card, or

(ii) unless the loan is made subject to this Act by agreement (Section 1.109), a loan secured by an interest in land if the security interest is bona fide and not for the purpose of circumvention or evasion of this Act and the finance charge does not exceed 12 per cent per year calculated according to the actuarial method on the assumption that the debt will be paid according to the agreed terms and will not be paid before the end of the agreed term.

(c) A loan that would be a consumer loan if the lender were regularly engaged in the business of making loans is a consumer loan if the loan is arranged for a commission or other compensation by a person regularly engaged in the business of arranging those loans and the lender is not regularly engaged in the business of making loans. The arranger is deemed to be the creditor making the loan.

(d) The amount of $25,000 in paragraph (a)(iv) is subject to change pursuant to the provisions on adjustment of dollar amounts (Section 1.106).

(16) "Credit" means the right granted by a creditor to a consumer to defer payment of debt, to incur debt and defer its payment, or to purchase property or services and defer payment therefor.

(17) "Credit card" means a card or device issued under an arrangement pursuant to which a card issuer gives to a cardholder the privilege of obtaining credit from the card issuer or other person in purchasing or leasing property or services, obtaining loans, or otherwise. A transaction is "pursuant to a credit card" only if credit is obtained according to the terms of the arrangement by transmitting information contained on the card or device orally, in writing, by mechanical or electronic methods, or in any other manner. A transaction is not "pursuant to a credit card" if the card or device is used solely in that transaction to:

(a) identify the cardholder or evidence his credit-worthiness and credit is not obtained according to the terms of the arrangement;

(b) obtain a guarantee of payment from the cardholder's deposit account, whether or not the payment results in a credit extension to the cardholder by the card issuer; or

(c) effect an immediate transfer of funds from the cardholder's deposit account by electronic or other means, whether or not the transfer results in a credit extension to the cardholder by the card issuer.

(18) "Creditor" means the person who grants credit in a consumer credit transaction or, except as otherwise provided, an assignee of a creditor's right to payment, but use of the term does not in itself impose on an assignee any obligation of his assignor. In case of

credit granted pursuant to a credit card, "creditor" means the card issuer and not another person honoring the credit card.

(19) "Earnings" means compensation paid or payable by an employer to an employee or for his account for personal services rendered or to be rendered by him, whether denominated as wages, salary, commission, bonus, or otherwise, and includes periodic payments pursuant to a pension, retirement, or disability program.

(20) "Finance charge":

(a) Except as provided in paragraph (b), "finance charge" means the sum of all charges payable directly or indirectly by the consumer and imposed directly or indirectly by the creditor as an incident to or as a condition of the extension of credit, including any of the following types of charges which are applicable:

(i) interest or any amount payable under a point, discount, or other system of charges, however denominated;

(ii) time-price differential, credit service, service, carrying, or other charge, however denominated;

(iii) premium or other charge for any guarantee or insurance protecting the creditor against the consumer's default or other credit loss; and

(iv) charges incurred for investigating the collateral or creditworthiness of the consumer or for commissions or brokerage for obtaining the credit, irrespective of the person to whom the charges are paid or payable, unless the creditor had no notice of the charges when the credit was granted.

(b) The term does not include:

(i) charges as a result of default or delinquency if made for actual unanticipated late payment, delinquency, default, or other like occurrence, unless the parties agree that these charges are finance charges; a charge is not made for actual unanticipated late payment, delinquency, default or other like occurrence if imposed on an account that is or may be debited from time to time for purchases or other debts and, under its terms, payment in full or of a specified amount is required when billed, and in the ordinary course of business the consumer is permitted to continue to have purchases or other debts debited to the account after imposition of the charge;

(ii) additional charges (Section 2.501) or deferral charges (Section 2.503); or

(iii) a discount, if a creditor purchases or satisfies obligations of a cardholder pursuant to a credit card and the purchase or satisfaction is made at less then the face amount of the obligation.

(21) "Goods" includes goods not in existence at the time the transaction is entered into and merchandise certificates, but excludes money, chattel paper, documents of title, and instruments.

(22) "Insurance premium loan" means a consumer loan that (a) is made for the sole purpose of financing the payment by or on behalf of an insured of the premium on one or more policies or contracts issued by or on behalf of an insurer, (b) is secured by an assignment by the insured to the lender of the unearned premium on the policy or contract, and (c) contains an authorization to cancel the policy or contract financed.

(23) Except as otherwise provided, "lender" includes an assignee of a lender's right to payment, but use of the term does not in itself impose on an assignee any obligation of the lender.

(24) "Lender credit card" means a credit card issued by a supervised lender.

(25) "Loan":

(a) Except as provided in paragraph (b), "loan" includes:

(i) the creation of debt by the lender's payment of or agreement to pay money to the debtor or to a third person for the account of the debtor;

(ii) the creation of debt pursuant to a lender credit card in any manner, including a cash advance or the card issuer's honoring a draft or similar order for the payment of money drawn or accepted by the debtor, paying or agreeing to pay the debtor's obligation, or purchasing or otherwise acquiring the debtor's obligation from the obligee or his assignees;

(iii) the creation of debt by a cash advance to a debtor pursuant to a seller credit card;

(iv) the creation of debt by a credit to an account with the lender upon which the debtor is entitled to draw immediately; and

(v) the forbearance of debt arising from a loan.

(b) "Loan" does not include:

(i) a card issuer's payment or agreement to pay money to a third person for the account of a debtor if the debt of the debtor arises from a sale or lease and results from use of a seller credit card; or

(ii) the forbearance of debt arising from a sale or lease.

(26) "Merchandise certificate" means a writing not redeemable in cash and usable in its face amount in lieu of cash in exchange for goods or services.

(27) "Official fees" means:

(a) fees and charges prescribed by law which actually are or will be paid to public officials for determining the existence of or for perfecting, releasing, terminating, or satisfying a security interest related to a consumer credit transaction; or

(b) premiums payable for insurance in lieu of perfecting a security interest otherwise required by the creditor in connection with the transaction, if the premium does not exceed the fees and charges described in paragraph (a) which would otherwise be payable.

(28) "Open-end credit" means an arrangement pursuant to which:

(a) a creditor may permit a consumer, from time to time, to purchase or lease on credit from the creditor or pursuant to a credit card, or to obtain loans from the creditor or pursuant to a credit card;

(b) the amounts financed and the finance and other appropriate charges are debited to an account;

(c) the finance charge, if made, is computed on the account periodically; and

(d) either the consumer has the privilege of paying in full or in instalments or the creditor periodically imposes charges computed on the account for delaying payment and permits the consumer to continue to purchase or lease on credit.

(29) "Organization" means a corporation, government or governmental subdivision or agency, trust, estate, partnership, cooperative, or association.

(30) "Payable in instalments" means that payment is required or permitted by agreement to be made in more than four periodic payments, excluding a downpayment. If any periodic payment other than the downpayment under an agreement requiring or permitting two or more periodic payments is more than twice the amount of any other periodic payment, excluding a downpayment, a consumer credit transaction is "payable in instalments."

(31) "Person" includes a natural person or an individual, and an organization.

(32) "Person related to" with respect to an individual means (a) the spouse of the individual, (b) a brother, brother-in-law, sister, sister-in-law of the individual, (c) an ancestor or lineal descendant of the individual or his spouse, and (d) any other relative, by blood or marriage, of the individual or his spouse who shares the same home with the individual. "Person related to" with respect to an organization means (a) a person directly or indirectly controlling, controlled by, or under common control with the organization, (b) an officer or director of the organization or a person performing similar functions with respect to the organization or to a person related to the organization, (c) the spouse of a person related to the organization, and (d) a relative by blood or marriage of a person related to the organization who shares the same home with him.

(33) "Precomputed consumer credit transaction" means a consumer credit transaction, other than a consumer lease, in which the debt is a sum comprising the amount financed and the amount of the finance charge computed in advance. A disclosure required by the Federal Truth in Lending Act does not in itself make a finance charge or transaction precomputed.

(34) "Presumed" or "presumption" means that the trier of fact must find the existence of the fact presumed unless and until evidence is introduced which would support a finding of its non-existence.

(35) "Sale of goods" includes an agreement in the form of a bailment or lease of goods if the bailee or lessee pays or agrees to pay as compensation for use a sum substantially equivalent to or in excess of the aggregate value of the goods involved and it is agreed that the bailee or lessee will become, or for no other or a nominal consideration has the option to become, the owner of the goods upon full compliance with the terms of the agreement.

(36) "Sale of an interest in land" includes a lease in which the lessee has an option to purchase the interest and all or a substantial part of the rental or other payments previously made by him are applied to the purchase price.

(37) "Sale of services" means furnishing or agreeing to furnish services and includes making arrangements to have services furnished by another.

(38) "Seller" includes, except as otherwise provided, an assignee of the seller's right to payment, but use of the term does not in itself impose on an assignee any obligation of the seller.

(39) "Seller credit card" means either:

(a) a credit card issued primarily for the purpose of giving the cardholder the privilege of using the card to purchase or lease property or services from the card issuer, persons related to the card issuer, or persons licensed or franchised to do business under the card issuer's business or trade name or designation, or both from any of these persons and from other persons; or

(b) a credit card issued by a person except a supervised lender primarily for the purpose of giving the cardholder the privilege of using the credit card to purchase or lease property or services from at least 100 persons not related to the card issuer.

(40) "Services" includes (a) work, labor, and other personal services, (b) privileges with respect to transportation, hotel and restaurant accommodations, education, entertainment, recreation, physical culture, hospital accommodations, funerals, cemetery accommodations, and the like, and (c) insurance.

(41) "Supervised financial organization" means a person, except an insurance company or other organization primarily engaged in an insurance business:

(a) organized, chartered, or holding an authorization certificate under laws of this State or of the United States that authorizes the person to make loans and to receive deposits, including a savings, share, certificate or deposit account, and

(b) subject to supervision by an official or agency of this State or of the United States.

(42) "Supervised lender" means a person authorized to make or take assignments of supervised loans, under a license issued by the Administrator (Section 2.301) or as a supervised financial organization (subsection (41)).

(43) "Supervised loan" means a consumer loan, including a loan made pursuant to open-end credit, in which the rate of the finance charge, calculated according to the actuarial method, exceeds 18 per cent per year.

Comment

Subsection (1):

This subsection is derived from CCPA Section 107(a)(1)(A), 15 U.S.C. § 1606(a)(1)(A), and from Supplement I to Regulation Z(a). The intent is that with respect to the meaning and application of the defined term the Administrator will maintain by rule consistency between this Act and the Federal Truth in Lending Act.

The assumption underlying the actuarial method is that a periodic payment is applied first to the accumulated unpaid finance charge. If the payment exceeds the unpaid accumulated finance charge, the remainder of the payment is applied to reduce the unpaid balance of the amount financed.

To illustrate the application of this method assume that the amount financed on a four-month contract is $500, and that the finance charge is $12.56. Four monthly payments of $128.14 are contemplated. Thus the amount financed ($500) plus the finance charge ($12.56) equals the original unpaid balance ($512.56), which is divided into four equal monthly payments, the first payment being one month from date of contract. The application of the actuarial method is demonstrated below:

(A) Unpaid balance of amount financed		(B) Monthly rate		(C) Application of payment — Finance charge		(D) Amount financed		(E) Total monthly payment (C) + (D)
500.00	×	1%	=	5.00		123.14		128.14
376.86	×	1%	=	3.77		124.37		128.14
252.49	×	1%	=	2.52		125.62		128.14
126.87	×	1%	=	1.27		126.87		128.14
				12.56	+	500.00	=	512.56

Rate disclosure involves finding that rate which will generate the stated finance charge when applied to the unpaid balances of the amount financed according to the actuarial method. A monthly rate of 1% produces a finance charge of $12.56, the difference between the sum of the monthly payments and the amount financed. The annual percentage rate would be twelve times the monthly rate, or 12%. In mathematical literature this is generally referred to as the nominal annual rate.

Note the application of the actuarial method. In the first month the first $5 (1% × $500) of the monthly payment of $128.14 is applied to the finance charge, leaving a balance of $123.14. This remainder is then applied to reduce the unpaid balance of the amount financed from $500 to $376.86. The same process is repeated in subsequent months.

. . .

Subsection (5):

The term "amount financed" means the amount of credit extended to the consumer and includes not only the net price in sales and the net amount advanced in loans but also other amounts such as official fees, insurance charges, and other additional charges (Section 2.501) to the extent that payment is deferred. An advance payment of finance charge or a required compensating balance is deducted from the "net amount paid" under paragraph (b) of this subsection. The term is a key definition in Parts 2 (maximum finance charges, sales) and 4 (maximum finance charges, loans) of Article 2 for it determines the amount on which the finance charge is imposed. This definition is in harmony with Regulation Z Sections 226.2(d), 226.4(b), and 226.8(c)(7) and (d)(1).

The reference in paragraph (b) to Section 1.301(20)(b)(iii) relates to the practice of credit card issuers of paying sellers honoring credit cards less than the face amount of the cardholder's obligation. Paragraph (b) makes clear that this discount is a part of the amount financed even though the amount of the discount is not paid to the seller for the cardholder's account. Since the seller absorbs the discount in the price of his product, the amount of the discount redounds to the cardholder's benefit and is properly included in the amount financed. That is, the cardholder would pay the same price for the product purchased whether he pays cash or uses a credit card. However, if the goods are sold at one price pursuant to credit cards and at a lower price for cash, then the lower price would be the cash price pursuant to Section 1.301(9) and the differential would be a finance charge pursuant to Section 1.301(20) and not part of the amount financed. The discount problem need only be specially treated when use of the credit card results in a loan, as in the case of lender credit cards (Section 1.301(25)(a)(ii)), for in the case of sales pursuant to seller credit cards (Section 1.301(12)(a)(i)) the cash price of the property or services sold includes the discount, if any, which is thereby included in the amount financed.

. . .

Subsection (14):

Leasing has become a popular alternative to credit sales as a means of distributing goods to consumers and merits inclusion in a comprehensive consumer credit code. The four month term requirement in paragraph (a)(iii) excludes from the Act the innumerable hourly, daily, or weekly rental or hire agreements typically involving automobiles, trailers, home repair tools, sick room equipment, and the like. If the transaction, though in form a lease, is in substance a sale within the meaning of Section 1.301(35), it is treated as a sale for all purposes in this Act and the provisions on consumer leases are inapplicable. The Act requires disclosure of the elements of the consumer lease transaction (Section 3.202); places limits on advertising respecting consumer leases (Section 3.209); contains a number of limitations on agreements and practices applicable to consumer leases (Part 3 of Article 3) and on the lessee's liability (Part 4 of Article 3, notably Section 3.401); regulates insurance provided in relation to consumer lease transactions (Article 4); makes provisions for remedies and penalties in consumer lease transactions (Article 5); and gives the Administrator powers over consumer lease transactions (Article 6). Since a finance charge is not made in the usual consumer lease transaction, the rate ceiling provisions of the Act (Article 2) are inapplicable.

Subsection (15):

. . .

With respect to this Act's treatment of real property transactions, the 12% cut-off was chosen as a convenient line of demarcation between two dissimilar transactions—the home mortgage and the high rate, "small loan" type of real estate loan. The exclusion of the home mortgage was made because the problems of home financing are sufficiently different to justify separate statutory treatment. On the other hand, the high rate second mortgage transaction has been a major source of consumer complaint and merits full coverage by this Act. Since the Truth in Lending Act applies to real estate credit without regard to the rate of finance charge, the provision on compliance with Truth in Lending (Section 3.201) applies to all consumer real estate transactions without regard to the rate of the finance charge.

. . .

Subsection (17):

The meanings of "credit card" and "pursuant to a credit card" are broadly defined to allow for continuing technological developments in this area. The term "credit card" is defined to encompass the varied arrangements under which creditors equip consumers with some form of "card or device" that enables them to obtain credit from the issuing creditor or others. A "credit card" may be conceived of in its broadest sense as a repository of information, and a transaction is "pursuant to a credit card" when credit is obtained in accordance with the arrangement under which the card was issued by the transmission of some information on the card. Hence, a cardholder who telephones an airline and buys a ticket by giving the agent his credit card number or a cardholder who communicates the requisite information to a seller by using a device which gives off an electronic impulse is each engaging in a transaction "pursuant to a credit card" so long as they are acting within the terms of the arrangement. However, a creditor who himself extends credit to a consumer relying on the consumer's credit card issued by another creditor merely as an identification or verification of credit-worthiness of the consumer has not extended credit "pursuant to a credit card."

Moreover, use of a credit card to obtain a guarantee of payment or to effect an immediate transfer from the cardholder's deposit account is not "pursuant to a credit card" whether or not the payment or transfer results in a credit extension to the cardholder by the card issuer.

. . .

Subsection (20):

This definition, together with the provisions on "additional charges" (Section 2.501), is substantially similar to the concept of finance charge embodied in Regulation Z Section 226.4. In general, charges "incident to or as a condition of the extension of credit" are finance charges, whatever the parties call them, if imposed by the creditor on the consumer, unless the charge is excluded by paragraph (b) as a default or delinquency charge, an additional or deferral charge, or a credit card discount.

True default or delinquency charges are not finance charges and are separately regulated by Section 2.502. The test prescribed by Regulation Z Section 226.4(c) and Interpretation 226.401 is adopted in paragraph (b)(i) for determining when a charge is a true default or delinquency charge. In some instances this will leave the question of the applicability of the Act to depend on the factual determination whether a given charge is (1) a true late charge, which would make the Act inapplicable if there is no provision either for payment in instalments or a finance charge, or (2) a finance charge, which would make the Act applicable even though there is no provision for payment in instalments (Section 1.301(12)(a)(iv)). An example is the case in which an oil company extends 30-day credit with no right to defer payment further and imposes a charge for late payment but does not require surrender of the credit card if full payment is not made by the consumer when billed. . . .

Subsection (25):

The distinction between loans and sales is basic to the applicability of the rate ceiling provisions (Parts 2 and 4 of Article 2), the licensing provisions (Part 3 of Article 2), provisions relating to credit cards (Section 1.301(24) "lender credit card" and (39) "seller credit card"), and other provisions of the Act. The traditional concept of a loan as an advance of money or a commitment to advance money is continued in paragraph (a)(i) and (iv). The development of the credit card has blurred somewhat accepted boundaries between loans and sales and has necessitated a clarification of the rules in this regard. See the discussion of this matter in Comment to Section 1.301(39) "seller credit card." Use of a lender credit card, whether for purchases or cash advances, results in a loan.

The arrangement for the card issuer's payment to the person honoring the credit card may take different forms. It does not matter under paragraph (a)(ii) whether the arrangement calls for the third party to be the payee of a draft drawn by the cardholder on the card issuer, for the card issuer to take an assignment of the debt from the third party, or for the card issuer merely to pay to the third party the discounted amount of the cardholder's obligation. Each of these methods is sufficiently similar in function to be treated alike by this section.

Under this Act forbearance of debt is characterized on the basis of the nature of the original debt. Thus forbearance of debt arising from sales or leases is not a loan transaction within this Act (paragraph (b)(ii)). Sellers and lessors can enter into refinancings to meet the needs of consumers without having these transactions classified as loans resulting in the applicability of the licensing provisions and other provisions of the Act designed to regulate lenders.

Occasionally seller credit card issuers may allow their cardholders to obtain nominal cash advances pursuant to their credit card. An example is an automobile rental company which extends to its cardholders as a convenience the privilege of obtaining cash advances up to $40 in emergency situations. This is a loan transaction under paragraph (a)(iii), and if the finance charge exceeds 18% (Section 2.401(1)) the licensing provisions of Part 3 of Article 2 apply.

. . .

Subsection (28):

The problem arises how the Act applies to a transaction in which a seller credit card issuer allows a cardholder to make purchases and add them to an account payable at a fixed time after billing with no right to defer payment further and with a charge imposed for late payment. If the charge imposed is a "true" late payment under Section 1.301(20)(b)(i), the transaction is not a consumer credit sale because there is neither a finance charge nor the privilege of paying in instalments (Section 1.301(12)(a)(iv)). The Act's only coverage of such a case is a limit on the amount of the late charge (Section 2.601(2)). If the late charge is in fact a finance charge under the test set out in Section 1.301(20)(b)(i), the transaction is a consumer credit sale and the Act applies fully. The last "or" clause in paragraph (d) directs that such a transaction be treated as open-end credit. A similar result is reached by Regulation Z Section 226.2(r) and Interpretation 226.401.

Subsection (30):

Two guiding principles in determining the scope of the Act are: (1) The Act should not apply to the myriad credit transactions in which no finance charge is made and no substantial period of credit extension is involved. The old-fashioned 30-day department store charge account is an example. (2) The Act should apply to credit extended over a substantial period of time even though the creditor does not separately state a finance charge. The transactions of the credit jeweler who "buries" his finance charge and sells his merchandise for the same price on a 12-month instalment contract as for cash is an example. The drafting technique by which these ends are attained is the definition of consumer credit sales (Section 1.301(12)(a)(iv)) and consumer loans (Section 1.301(15)(a)(iii)) as transactions in which either a finance charge is made or which are payable in instalments. . . .

Subsection (33):

A credit transaction is precomputed whether the finance charge is "added-on" to the amount financed or, as is common in loan situations, the "discount" method is used and the finance charge is deducted from the face amount of the credit at the time of the credit extension. In both transactions the debt is expressed as a sum comprising the amount financed and the amount of the finance charge. If a loan transaction involves a principal of $2,000 repayable in 12 monthly instalments at an interest rate of 10% on the declining balance, the transaction is not precomputed even though the creditor must for purposes of the Federal Truth in Lending Act disclose a sum including both the $2,000 and the amount of the finance charge the debtor would pay if each instalment were paid on time.

. . .

Subsection (39):

Seller credit cards are issued primarily for the purpose of enabling cardholders to purchase property or services. Paragraph (a) applies to cards issued by card issuers who are themselves involved in the selling process either as retailers or as distributors who license or franchise retailers. So long as the card is issued for the purpose of purchasing from the issuer, a person related to the issuer, or a licensee or franchisee of the issuer, the card falls within paragraph (a) even though it may also be honored by sellers having no relation to the card issuer. For example, an oil distributor may issue a card for the purpose of allowing cardholders to buy petroleum products from independently owned franchisees of the issuer; the card falls within paragraph (a) even though it may also be honored by hotels, motels, and other service stations unrelated to the card issuer.

Paragraph (b) covers credit cards issued for the purpose of enabling cardholders to purchase from sellers unrelated to the card issuer. "Travel and entertainment" credit cards are the stereotype. The requirement that the card be honored by at least 100 unrelated retailers is designed to assure that this kind of card will be issued for bona fide sales purposes by entities large enough to be visible to the Administrator and will not be used as a subterfuge for masking unlicensed loans.

Although lender credit cards (Section 1.301(24)) are also used for purchasing property or services, they are increasingly utilized for cash loans. By classifying the use of credit cards issued by banks and licensed lenders as creating loans (Section 1.301(25)(a)(ii)), whether the card was used for purchases or cash advanced, the Act recognizes that credit card transactions are but one of many ways in which banks and other financial institutions extend credit and that it is not operationally desirable to introduce regulatory distinctions that would force these institutions to treat sales and loans pursuant to credit cards differently for purposes of maximum charges and other provisions of the Act.

Subsection (40):

The retail instalment sales acts often excluded from the definition of services those furnished by members of professions—physicians, dentists, and the like. This Act makes no such exclusion, but the definition of consumer credit sale in Section 1.301(12) excludes the usual arrangement that professional men use in selling their services in that they usually do not enter into instalment contracts with their patients or clients and do not impose finance charges. However, this Act does apply to the so-called "credit dentist" who sells his services on instalment contract with or without provision for a finance charge.

. . .

ARTICLE 2. FINANCE CHARGES AND RELATED PROVISIONS

PART 1. GENERAL PROVISIONS

§ 2.102 [Scope]

Part 2 of this Article applies to consumer credit sales. Parts 3 and 4 apply to consumer loans, including loans made by supervised lenders. Part 5 applies to other charges and modifications with respect to consumer credit transactions. Part 6 applies to other credit transactions.

PART 2. CONSUMER CREDIT SALES: MAXIMUM FINANCE CHARGES

§ 2.201 [Finance Charge for Consumer Credit Sales Not Pursuant to Open-End Credit]

(1) With respect to a consumer credit sale, except a sale pursuant to open-end credit, a creditor may contract for and receive a finance charge not exceeding that permitted in this section.

(2) The finance charge, calculated according to the actuarial method, may not exceed the equivalent of the greater of either of the following:

(a) the total of:

(i) 36 per cent per year on that part of the unpaid balances of the amount financed which is $300 or less;

(ii) 21 per cent per year on that part of the unpaid balances of the amount financed which exceeds $300 but does not exceed $1,000; and

(iii) 15 per cent per year on that part of the unpaid balances of the amount financed which exceeds $1,000; or

(b) 18 per cent per year on the unpaid balances of the amount financed.

(3) This section does not limit or restrict the manner of calculating the finance charge whether by way of add-on, discount, single annual percentage rate, or otherwise, so long as the rate of the finance charge does not exceed that permitted by this section. The finance charge may be contracted for and earned at the single annual percentage rate that would earn the same finance charge as the graduated rates when the debt is paid according to the agreed terms and the

calculations are made according to the actuarial method. If the sale is a precomputed consumer credit transaction:

(a) the finance charge may be calculated on the assumption that all scheduled payments will be made when due, and

(b) the effect of prepayment is governed by the provisions on rebate upon prepayment (Section 2.510).

(4) For purposes of this section, the term of a sale agreement commences with the date the credit is granted or, if goods are delivered or services performed ten days or more after that date, with the date of commencement of delivery or performance. Any month may be counted as $^{1}/_{12}$th of a year, but a day is counted as $^{1}/_{365}$th of a year. Subject to classifications and differentiations the seller may reasonably establish, a part of a month in excess of 15 days may be treated as a full month if periods of 15 days or less are disregarded and that procedure is not consistently used to obtain a greater yield than would otherwise be permitted. The Administrator may adopt rules not inconsistent with the Federal Truth in Lending Act with respect to treating as regular other minor irregularities in amount or time.

(5) Subject to classifications and differentiations the seller may reasonably establish, he may make the same finance charge on all amounts financed within a specified range. A finance charge so made does not violate subsection (2) if:

(a) when applied to the median amount within each range, it does not exceed the maximum permitted by subsection (2), and

(b) when applied to the lowest amount within each range, it does not produce a rate of finance charge exceeding the rate calculated according to paragraph (a) by more than eight per cent of the rate calculated according to paragraph (a).

(6) Notwithstanding subsection (2), the seller may contract for and receive a minimum finance charge of not more than $5 when the amount financed does not exceed $75, or $7.50 when the amount financed exceeds $75.

(7) The amounts of $300 and $1,000 in subsection (2) are subject to change pursuant to the provisions on adjustment of dollar amounts (Section 1.106).

Comment

1. **Purpose of rate ceilings provisions.** The purpose of this section and subsection (2) of Section 2.401 (Finance Charge for Consumer Loans) is to set ceilings and not to fix rates. Even under present statutes, considerable rate competition exists. The intent of this Act is to provide even more effective competition. Therefore, while this section sets rate ceilings, several sections are designed to generate sufficient competition to set rates. In addition, oth-

er provisions have been omitted by design, because they would have tended to restrict competition. Other provisions related to this section include:

(1) Disclosure of the finance charge both in dollar amounts and as annual percentages, as required by the Federal Truth in Lending Act and Section 3.201, is designed to facilitate comparative shopping. This is the most effective means of limiting prices. For most goods and services offered for sale in competitive markets, disclosure of the price generally has been deemed sufficient to regulate prices.

(2) The absence of special rate ceilings according to the type of credit grantors, type of item financed, or the form of credit extension is by design. Segmentation of the market for credit by differentiated rate ceilings tends to reduce competition and introduce rigidities into the market that benefit a few suppliers at the expense of others and work to the disadvantage of consumers.

(3) Greater freedom of entry to the credit field is fostered by several provisions, as well as by several deliberate omissions. Open-end credit may be offered both in connection with consumer credit sales, consumer loans, and supervised loans. No type of credit grantor is limited by this Act in the amount of credit that may be extended. By design the license required to make supervised loans is made readily accessible to those showing financial responsibility, character, and fitness. Provisions for minimum financial assets and for a showing of convenience and advantage have been deliberately omitted, since their inclusion would tend to restrict competition and require establishment of rates, rather than ceilings.

Because of the different cost structures that will be developed as a result of this Act, comparison of these rate ceilings cannot be made to existing rate ceilings. In this respect, the rate ceilings in this section are intimately related to other parts of the Act which provide for limitations on agreements and practices (Article 3, Part 3), limitations on creditors' remedies (Article 5, Part 1), limitations on consumers' liabilities (Article 3, Part 4), and consumers' remedies (Article 5, Part 2). These provisions will tend to raise operating costs of credit grantors above current levels. Other things being equal, these provisions would require higher rate ceilings than now exist to assure the same availability of credit to consumers. If they were not provided, the least credit-worthy consumers now in the market would be relegated to the illegal market.

The rate ceiling declines with the amount of credit granted by design. There are substantial fixed costs in granting consumer instalment credit. Up to a point the relative amount of fixed costs declines as the amount of credit granted increases. The present rate structure is designed not to restrict the amount of credit granted in any size category. Consequently, any changes in the rate ceilings provided would require a complete re-evaluation of the gradation in the rate structure, as well as of the other provisions of this Act which are closely related in an economic sense to rate ceilings.

2. **Explanation of operation of rate ceilings.** This explanation of maximum rates applies equally to finance charges made under Section 2.201 (finance charge for consumer credit sales not pursuant to open-end credit) and under subsection (2) of Section 2.401 (finance charge for consumer loans).

(1) **Other than precomputed transactions:** With respect to other than precomputed transactions the graduated rates permitted are calculated on unpaid principal balances. For example, Table A below illustrates the calculation of the monthly finance charge at the graduated rates on unpaid principal balances of various dollar amounts up to $1,500.

(2) **Precomputed transactions:** With respect to precomputed transactions, the graduated rates permitted are calculated on the periodic declining unpaid balances. The provisions for graduated rates should not be construed as requiring simultaneous liquidation of different portions of the original unpaid balance. Thus, the 21% annual rate permitted on unpaid balances exceeding $300, but not exceeding $1,000 does not apply to the initial unpaid balance in that range for the scheduled maturity of the transaction, but only to the extent that periodic declining unpaid balances fall within the range from $300.01 to $1,000.

The operation of this principle with respect to a precomputed transaction involving a $1,500 principal amount to be repaid in twelve months is illustrated in Table A below. The table shows the total dollar charge, the monthly payments and the charge earned each month when the rates stated in Sections 2.201 and 2.401(2) are computed on the unpaid balance as of each scheduled payment date and each payment is applied first to the earned charge and then to principal. It also shows the unpaid balances which result from applying the rates stated in Sections 2.201 and 2.401(2) and the parts of each unpaid balance to which each rate applies each month. The total dollar charge so computed is $211.71, but three cents is waived rather than increase the final payment.

3. **Explanation of subsection (5).** With respect to Sections 2.201(5) and 2.401(5), the variation permitted is limited to 8% of the rate of the finance charge and does not permit an eight percentage point variation. For example, if a credit grantor were to levy an annual add-on finance charge of $10 per $100 of initial unpaid balance, under the provisions of this section he could establish the following maximum range for one-year contracts:

Amount Financed	Finance Charge
$92.45–$107.55	$10.00

The median amount financed is $100; that is, this amount is $7.55 from both the upper and lower limits of the specified range. Alternatively, it is just halfway between $92.45 and $107.55.

The specified range is limited by the 8% requirement. On one-year contracts the add-on finance charge results in an actuarial rate of 17.972%. Sections 2.201(5)(b) and 2.401(5)(b) specify that the yield on the lowest amount within the range may not be more than 8% higher than the yield provided on the median amount. Thus the yield on the lowest amount may not exceed 19.40% [$17.972 + (.08 \times 17.972) = 19.4098$]. It follows that the lower amount must be such that the $10 credit service charge produces an annual rate not in excess of 19.40%. Interpolation from annuity tables shows that the lower amount must be about $92.45. Since the median is halfway between the upper and lower limits, the upper amount must be $107.55. These are close approximations; in actual practice precise limits can be determined.

To gain the convenience of using a single dollar amount of finance charge for a specified range of amounts financed the credit grantor must undercharge for amounts financed above the median. Thus the $10 finance charge is about $0.76 less than the $10.76 finance charge that could have been received by precise application of an add-on rate of $10 per $100 per annum on the initial unpaid balance. These results are summarized below for one-year monthly instalment contracts.

(A)	(B)	(C)	(D)	(E)
Amount financed	Actual finance charge	Accurate finance charge	Dollar difference (C) – (B)	Annual percentage rate
$107.55	$10.00	$10.755	–$0.755	16.74%
$100.00	$10.00	$10.00	0.00	17.97%
$ 92.45	$10.00	$ 9.245	+$0.755	19.40%

The 8% variation is derived from Regulation Z Section 226.5(c).

TABLE A

Amortization Schedule for $1,500 to be paid in 12 equal and consecutive monthly instalments of Principal Amount and Finance Charge combined with the charge computed at maximum graduated rates authorized by Sections 2.201 and 2.401(2)—36% per year on that part of the unpaid balances not exceeding $300, plus 21% per year on that part of the unpaid balances exceeding $300 but not exceeding $1,000, plus 15% per year on that part of the unpaid balances exceeding $1,000, yields $211.68.

	Unpaid Principal Balances Outstanding During Month				Application of $142.64 Monthly Payments	
Mo.	36%	21%	15%	Total	Charges	Principal
1	$300.00	$700.00	$500.00	$1500.00	$ 27.50	$ 115.14
2	300.00	700.00	384.86	1384.86	26.06	116.58
3	300.00	700.00	268.28	1268.28	24.60	118.04
4	300.00	700.00	150.24	1150.24	23.13	119.51
5	300.00	700.00	30.73	1030.73	21.63*	121.01
6	300.00	609.72	...	909.72	19.67	122.97
7	300.00	486.75	...	786.75	17.52	125.12
8	300.00	361.63	...	661.63	15.33	127.31
9	300.00	234.32	...	534.32	13.10	129.54
10	300.00	104.78	...	404.78	10.83	131.81
11	272.97	...	...	272.97	8.19	134.45
12	138.52	...	...	138.52	4.12**	138.52
	TOTALS				$211.68	$1500.00

* Finance Charge rates are applied to parts of Unpaid Principal Balances scheduled to be outstanding. For example, the Finance Charge on $1030.73 is computed as follows:

1/12 × 36% on	$ 300.00	=	$ 9.00
1/12 × 21% on	700.00	=	12.25
1/12 × 15% on	30.73	=	.38
	$1030.73		$21.63

** The charge earned the last month is $4.15, but three cents is waived and applied to principal to make the final payment equal to the others.

For purposes of disclosure under the Truth in Lending Act the credit grantor must determine the single annual percentage rate, which, when applied according to the actuarial method, earns the same dollar amount of finance charge that is produced by the graduated rates. Table B shows that an annual rate of 25.10% applied monthly to the periodic declining unpaid balances produces the same total dollar charge of $211.68 calculated by application of graduated rates in Table A.

TABLE B

Amortization Schedule for $1500 to be paid in 12 equal and consecutive monthly instalments of Principal Amount and Finance Charge combined showing that the Single Annual Percentage Rate of 25.10% computed by the Actuarial Method yields $211.68.

Mo.	Unpaid Principal Balances	Application of $142.64 Monthly Payments Charges	Principal
1	$1500.00	$ 31.38	$ 111.26
2	1388.74	29.05	113.59
3	1275.15	26.67	115.97
4	1159.18	24.25	118.39
5	1040.79	21.77	120.87
6	919.92	19.24	123.40
7	796.52	16.66	125.98
8	670.54	14.03	128.61
9	541.93	11.34	131.30
10	410.63	8.59	134.05
11	276.58	5.79	136.85
12	139.73	2.91*	139.73
	TOTALS	$211.68	$1500.00

* The charge earned the last month is $2.92 but 1 cent is waived and applied to principal to make the final payment equal to the others.

This Act is intended to give creditors the following choice in making their charges under Sections 2.201 and 2.401(2).

(1) The contract may be precomputed to include the dollar finance charge for payment according to schedule. In the example shown, the dollar finance charge of $211.68 would be added to the original unpaid principal, making a total of $1,711.68 to be repaid in twelve monthly instalments of $142.64.

A precomputed transaction is subject to delinquency charges pursuant to Section 2.502 or deferral charges pursuant to Section 2.503 in case of delinquency or deferral and to rebate for prepayment pursuant to Section 2.510 in case of prepayment in full.

(2) The contract need not be precomputed, but may provide for: (a) the addition of finance charges, computed on unpaid balances of the principal amount, at the rates specified in Sections 2.201 and 2.401(2); in this case there is no rebate for prepayment in full because charges are collected only as earned, and there are no separate charges for default or deferment; or (b) not more than the maximum single annual percentage rate computed on actual unpaid balances for the actual time outstanding. The single annual percentage is the rate which yields the charge for payment according to schedule when the rate is computed according to the actuarial method. In the example, the rate is 25.10%. In this case there is no rebate for prepayment in full because the charges are collected only as earned, and there are no separate charges for default or deferment.

4. **Explanation of Section 2.201(6).** Subsection (6) of this section permits minimum charges equal to finance charges for which the CCPA (15 U.S.C. § 1601 et seq.) requires no annual percentage rate disclosure. The CCPA does not set limits on the amounts of minimum charges, but does require annual percentage rate disclosure when the minimum charges exceed those permitted by subsection (6). Subsection (6) also sets limits on the amounts of minimum charges.

5. **Operation of 18% APR finance charge ceiling.** According to tables furnished by Financial Publishing Company, the 18% APR finance charge ceiling rate on unpaid balances of the amount financed permitted by subsection (2)(b) yields a greater finance charge than the sliding scale ceiling rates of 36%, 21% and 15% when applied to unpaid balances of the amount financed on amounts equal to or exceeding the following for the respective following number of equal monthly instalments (the corresponding Total of Payments, Finance Charge and amount of equal monthly instalments is set out below):

No. of Monthly Instalments	Unpaid Balance of Amount to be Financed	Total of Payments	Finance Charge	Amount of Monthly Instalments
3	$5,190.00	$5,346.51	$ 156.51	$1,782.17
6	5,853.00	6,164.16	311.16	1,027.36
9	5,953.00	6,408.45	455.45	712.15
12	6,016.00	6,618.72	602.72	551.56
15	6,011.00	6,757.50	746.50	450.50
18	5,985.00	6,874.02	889.02	381.89
24	5,906.00	7,076.64	1170.64	294.86
30	5,800.00	7,245.60	1445.60	241.52
36	5,695.00	7,412.40	1717.40	205.90
42	5,594.00	7,581.00	1987.00	180.50
48	5,491.00	7,742.88	2251.88	161.31
54	5,393.00	7,907.76	2514.76	146.44
60	5,301.00	8,077.20	2776.20	134.62
66	5,209.00	8,242.74	3033.74	124.89
72	5,121.00	8,410.32	3289.32	116.81
78	5,041.00	8,587.02	3546.02	110.09
84	4,958.00	8,754.48	3796.48	104.22
90	4,882.00	8,929.80	4047.80	99.22
96	4,810.00	9,108.48	4298.48	94.88
102	4,741.00	9,289.14	4548.14	91.07
108	4,676.00	9,473.76	4797.76	87.72
114	4,615.00	9,662.64	5047.64	84.76
120	4,554.00	9,848.40	5294.40	82.07

§ 2.202 [Finance Charge for Consumer Credit Sales Pursuant to Open-End Credit]

(1) With respect to a consumer credit sale pursuant to open-end credit, a creditor may contract for and receive a finance charge not exceeding that permitted in this section.

(2) For each billing cycle a finance charge may be made which is a percentage of an amount not exceeding the greatest of:

(a) the average daily balance of the open-end account in the billing cycle for which the charge is made, which is the sum of the amount unpaid each day during that cycle, divided by the number of days in that cycle; the amount unpaid on a day is determined by adding to any balance unpaid as of the beginning of that day all purchases and other debits and deducting all payments and other credits made or received as of that day;

(b) the balance of the open-end account at the beginning of the first day of the billing cycle [after deducting all payments and credits made in the cycle except credits attributable to purchases charged to the account during the cycle]; or

(c) the median amount within a specified range including the balance of the open-end account not exceeding that permitted by paragraph (a) or (b); a finance charge may be made pursuant to this paragraph only if the creditor, subject to classifications and differentiations he may reasonably establish, makes the same charge on all balances within the specified range and if the percentage when applied to the median amount within the range does not produce a charge exceeding the charge resulting from applying that percentage to the lowest amount within the range by more than eight per cent of the charge on the median amount.

(3) If the billing cycle is monthly, the finance charge may not exceed an amount equal to two per cent of that part of the maximum amount pursuant to subsection (2) which is $500 or less and one and one-half per cent of that part of the maximum amount which is more than $500. If the billing cycle is not monthly, the maximum charge for the billing cycle shall bear the same relation to the applicable monthly maximum charge as the number of days in the billing cycle bears to 365 divided by 12. A billing cycle is monthly if the closing date of the cycle is the same date each month or does not vary by more than four days from the regular date. Without regard to the length of the billing cycle, the finance charge may be computed at a daily rate that does not exceed $^{1}/_{365}$ths of 12 times the monthly charge permitted by this section for a billing cycle that is monthly.

(4) If the finance charge determined pursuant to subsection (3) is less than 50 cents, a finance charge may be made which does not exceed 50 cents if the billing cycle is monthly or longer, or the pro rata part of 50 cents which bears the same relation to 50 cents as the number of days in the billing cycle bears to 365 divided by 12 if the billing cycle is shorter than monthly.

(5) The amounts of $500 in subsection (3) are subject to change pursuant to the provisions on adjustment of dollar amounts (Section 1.106).

Comment

1. See Comment 1 to Section 2.201 for an explanation of the theory of rate regulation adopted by the Act.

2. Subsection (2) allows the creditor an option with respect to the balance on which the finance charge is imposed. The Federal Truth in Lending Act requires the creditor to disclose the method of determining the balance on which the finance charge is imposed (Regulation Z Section 226.7(a)(2) and (b)(8)). The average daily balance method authorized by paragraph (a) of subsection (2) is that commonly utilized by creditors employing electronic data processing equipment. Paragraph (b) of subsection (2), read with the bracketed material included, states the adjusted balance method under which the balance at the beginning of the cycle is reduced by all payments and credits during the cycle. Although under this method the balance is adjusted downward by payments and credits during the cycle, it is not adjusted upward by new purchases made within the cycle. The except clause is necessary to prevent the beginning balance from being reduced by returns of merchandise attributable to purchases made within the cycle the amounts of which had not been included in that balance. Paragraph (b) of subsection (2), read without the bracketed material, states the previous or beginning balance method under which the opening balance is neither decreased by payments or credits during the billing cycle nor increased by new purchases made during that period. Either the previous balance or the adjusted balance method is usable by a creditor with a manual system of entries. The brackets in paragraph (b) of subsection (2) acknowledge the as yet unresolved controversy in the Congress and the state legislatures about the comparative merit of the previous and adjusted balance methods.

. . .

PART 3. CONSUMER LOANS: SUPERVISED LENDERS

§ 2.301 [Authority to Make Supervised Loans]

Unless a person is a supervised financial organization or has obtained a license from the Administrator authorizing him so to do, he may not engage in the business of:

(1) making supervised loans, or

(2) taking assignments of and undertaking direct collection of payments from or enforcement of rights against consumers arising from supervised loans, but he may collect and enforce for three months without a license if he promptly applies for a license and his application has not been denied.

§ 2.302 [License to Make Supervised Loans]

(1) The Administrator shall receive and act on all applications for licenses to make supervised loans under this Act. Applications shall be in the form and filed in the manner prescribed by the Administra-

tor and contain or be accompanied by the information the Administrator requires by rule.

(2) The Administrator may not issue a license unless upon investigation he finds that the financial responsibility, character, and fitness of the applicant, and of the members thereof if the applicant is a partnership or association or of the officers and directors thereof if the applicant is a corporation, warrant belief that the business will be operated honestly and fairly within the purposes of this Act. In determining the financial responsibility of an applicant proposing to engage in making insurance premium loans, the Administrator shall consider the liabilities the lender may incur for erroneous cancellation of insurance.

(3) Upon written request, the applicant is entitled to a hearing on the question of his qualifications for a license if (a) the Administrator notifies the applicant in writing that his application has been denied, or (b) the Administrator does not issue a license within 60 days after the application for the license was filed. A request for a hearing may not be made more than 15 days after the Administrator mails a writing to the applicant notifying him that the application has been denied and stating in substance the Administrator's findings supporting denial of the application.

(4) The Administrator shall issue additional licenses to the same licensee upon compliance with all the provisions of this Act governing issuance of a single license. A separate license is required for each place of business. Each license remains in full force and effect until surrendered, suspended, or revoked.

(5) A licensee may not change the location of any place of business without giving the Administrator at least 15 days prior written notice.

(6) A licensee may conduct the business of making supervised loans only at or from a place of business for which he holds a license and only under the name in the license. Credit granted pursuant to a lender credit card does not violate this subsection.

Comment

1. This section is intimately related to the provisions on maximum finance charges (Parts 2 and 4 of Article 2) and disclosure (Part 2 of Article 3). A major objective of this Act is to facilitate entry into the cash loan field so that the resultant rate competition fostered by disclosure will generally force rates below the permitted maximum charges. To this end this section adopts a test of "financial responsibility, character and fitness" rather than the test of "convenience and advantage" often used in prior small loan laws. Competition is further encouraged by the absence of licensing requirements in consumer credit sales (Section 2.201) and in consumer loans not made by supervised lenders (subsection (1) of Section 2.401).

2. A secondary purpose is to reduce the likelihood of establishing localized monopolies in the granting of cash credit. Such monopolies tend to push rates charged to maximum permitted levels and to establish conditions under which some share of the anticipated monopoly profits are devoted to direct or indirect pressures to obtain the license.

. . .

§ 2.303 [Revocation or Suspension of License]

(1) The Administrator may issue to a person licensed to make supervised loans an order to show cause why his license with respect to one or more specific places of business should not be suspended for a period not in excess of six months or be revoked. The order shall set a place for a hearing and a time therefor that is no less than ten days from the date of the order. After the hearing the Administrator shall revoke or suspend the license or, if there are mitigating circumstances, may accept an assurance of discontinuance (Section 6.109) and allow retention of the license, if he finds that:

(a) the licensee has repeatedly and intentionally violated this Act or any rule or order lawfully made pursuant to this Act, or has violated an assurance of discontinuance; or

(b) facts or conditions exist which clearly would have justified the Administrator in refusing to grant a license for that place or those places of business were these facts or conditions known to exist at the time the application for the license was made.

(2) A revocation or suspension of a license is not lawful unless the Administrator, before instituting proceedings, gives notice to the licensee of the facts or conduct which warrant the intended action, and the licensee is afforded an opportunity to show compliance with all lawful requirements for retention of the license.

(3) If the Administrator finds that probable cause for revocation of a license exists and that enforcement of this Act requires immediate suspension of the license pending investigation, he, after a hearing upon five days' written notice, may enter an order suspending the license for not more than 30 days.

(4) Whenever the Administrator revokes or suspends a license, he shall enter an order to that effect and forthwith notify the licensee of the revocation or suspension. Within five days after entry of the order he shall deliver to the licensee a copy of the order and the findings supporting the order.

(5) A person holding a license to make supervised loans may relinquish the license by notifying the Administrator in writing of its relinquishment, but the relinquishment does not affect his liability for acts previously committed.

(6) Revocation, suspension, or relinquishment of a license does not impair or affect the obligation of any preexisting lawful contract between the licensee and any consumer.

(7) The administrator may reinstate a license, terminate a suspension, or grant a new license to a person whose license has been revoked or suspended if no fact or condition then exists which clearly would have justified the Administrator in refusing to grant a license.

§ 2.307 [Restrictions on Interest in Land as Security]

(1) A lender may contract for an interest in land as security, except to secure a supervised loan in which the amount financed is $1,000 or less. A security interest taken in violation of this section is unenforceable to the extent of that loan.

(2) The amount of $1,000 in subsection (1) is subject to change pursuant to the provisions on adjustment of dollar amounts (Section 1.106).

§ 2.308 [Regular Schedule of Payments; Maximum Loan Term]

(1) Supervised loans, not made pursuant to open-end credit and in which the amount financed is $1,000 or less, shall be scheduled to be payable in substantially equal instalments at substantially equal periodic intervals except to the extent that the schedule of payments is adjusted to the seasonal or irregular income of the debtor, and

(a) over a period not exceeding 37 months if the amount financed exceeds $300, or

(b) over a period not exceeding 25 months if the amount financed is $300 or less.

(2) The amounts of $300 and $1,000 in subsection (1) are subject to change pursuant to the provisions on adjustment of dollar amounts (Section 1.106).

§ 2.309 [No Other Business for Purpose of Evasion]

A supervised lender may not carry on other business for the purpose of evasion or violation of this Act at a location where he makes supervised loans.

PART 4. CONSUMER LOANS: MAXIMUM FINANCE CHARGES

§ 2.401 [Finance Charge for Consumer Loans]

(1) With respect to a consumer loan, including a loan pursuant to open-end credit, a lender who is not a supervised lender may contract for and receive a finance charge, calculated according to the actuarial method, not exceeding 18 per cent per year. With respect to a con-

sumer loan made pursuant to open-end credit, the finance charge shall be deemed not to exceed 18 per cent per year if the finance charge contracted for and received does not exceed a charge for each monthly billing cycle which is one and one-half per cent of the average daily balance of the open-end account in the billing cycle for which the charge is made. The average daily balance of the open-end account is the sum of the amount unpaid each day during that cycle divided by the number of days in the cycle. The amount unpaid on a day is determined by adding to any balance unpaid as of the beginning of that day all purchases, loans, and other debits and deducting all payments and other credits made or received as of that day. If the billing cycle is not monthly, the finance charge shall be deemed not to exceed 18 per cent per year if the finance charge contracted for and received does not exceed a percentage which bears the same relation to one and one-half per cent as the number of days in the billing cycle bears to 365 divided by 12. A billing cycle is monthly if the closing date of the cycle is the same date each month or does not vary by more than four days from the regular date.

(2) With respect to a consumer loan, including a loan pursuant to open-end credit, a supervised lender may contract for and receive a finance charge, calculated according to the actuarial method, not exceeding the equivalent of the greater of either of the following:

(a) the total of:

(i) 36 per cent per year on that part of the unpaid balances of the amount financed which is $300 or less;

(ii) 21 per cent per year on that part of the unpaid balances of the amount financed which exceeds $300 but does not exceed $1,000; and

(iii) 15 per cent per year on that part of the unpaid balances of the amount financed which exceeds $1,000; or

(b) 18 per cent per year on the unpaid balances of the amount financed.

(3) This section does not limit or restrict the manner of calculating the finance charge, whether by way of add-on, discount, single annual percentage rate, or otherwise, so long as the rate of the finance charge does not exceed that permitted by this section. The finance charge may be contracted for and earned at the single annual percentage rate that would earn the same finance charge as the graduated rates when the debt is paid according to the agreed terms and the calculations are made according to the actuarial method. If the loan is a precomputed consumer credit transaction:

(a) the finance charge may be calculated on the assumption that all scheduled payments will be made when due, and

(b) the effect of prepayment is governed by the provisions on rebate upon prepayment (Section 2.510).

(4) Except as provided in subsection (6), the term of a loan for purposes of this section commences on the day the loan is made. Any month may be counted as $^{1}/_{12}$th of a year, but a day is counted as $^{1}/_{365}$th of a year. Subject to classifications and differentiations the lender may reasonably establish, a part of a month in excess of 15 days may be treated as a full month if periods of 15 days or less are disregarded and that procedure is not consistently used to obtain a greater yield than would otherwise be permitted. The Administrator may adopt rules not inconsistent with the Federal Truth in Lending Act with respect to treating as regular other minor irregularities in amount or time.

(5) Subject to classifications and differentiations the lender may reasonably establish, he may make the same finance charge on all amounts financed within a specified range. A finance charge so made does not violate subsection (1) or (2) if:

(a) when applied to the median amount within each range, it does not exceed the maximum permitted by the applicable subsection, and

(b) when applied to the lowest amount within each range, it does not produce a rate of finance charge exceeding the rate calculated according to paragraph (a) by more than eight per cent of the rate calculated according to paragraph (a).

(6) With respect to an insurance premium loan, the term of the loan commences on the earliest inception date of a policy or contract of insurance payment of the premium on which is financed by the loan.

(7) The amounts of $300 and $1,000 in subsection (2) are subject to change pursuant to the provisions on adjustment of dollar amounts (Section 1.106).

Comment

1. For an extensive explanation of the purposes and operation of the rate ceilings provisions of this Act, see the Comment to Section 2.201. Subsection (1) sets the ceilings for all consumer loans not made by supervised lenders at 18% per annum, and this ceiling applies to open-end credit as well as to closed-end credit. The operation of open-end credit is such that a creditor cannot know whether he is exceeding a rate ceiling stated in terms of a rate calculated according to the actuarial method unless he calculates the rate on daily balances. In "deeming" that 1½% per month on the average daily balance is the equivalent of 18% per year, this subsection allows the creditor to use a somewhat simplified method of calculation.

2. The ceilings for loans by supervised lenders in subsection (2) also apply to open-end credit. This enables supervised lenders to serve the needs of higher risk consumers by the use of credit cards and other open-end credit plans.

Lenders are not required to use a graduated rate, but may find it more economical to use a single annual rate provided that it does not exceed the rate ceiling specified. Lenders may not levy delinquency charges (Section 2.502) and deferral charges (Section 2.503) on open-end credit accounts. By the same token a debtor is not entitled to rebates upon prepayment with respect to open-end accounts since at the time of his prepayment there will be no unearned prepaid finance charges on the open-end account.

. . .

PART 5. CONSUMER CREDIT TRANSACTIONS: OTHER CHARGES AND MODIFICATIONS

§ 2.501 [Additional Charges]

(1) In addition to the finance charge permitted by the parts of this Article on maximum finance charges for consumer credit sales and consumer loans (Parts 2 and 4), a creditor may contract for and receive the following additional charges:

(a) official fees and taxes;

(b) charges for insurance as described in subsection (2);

(c) annual charges, payable in advance, for the privilege of using a credit card which entitles the cardholder to purchase or lease goods or services from at least 100 persons not related to the card issuer, under an arrangement pursuant to which the debts resulting from the purchases or leases are payable to the card issuer;

(d) with respect to a debt secured by an interest in land, the following "closing costs," if they are bona fide, reasonable in amount, and not for the purpose of circumvention or evasion of this Act:

(i) fees or premiums for title examination, abstract of title, title insurance, surveys, or similar purposes,

(ii) fees for preparation of a deed, settlement statement, or other documents, if not paid to the creditor or a person related to the creditor,

(iii) escrows for future payments of taxes, including assessments for improvements, insurance, and water, sewer and land rents, and

(iv) fees for notarizing deeds and other documents, if not paid to the creditor or a person related to the creditor; and

(e) charges for other benefits, including insurance, conferred on the consumer, if the benefits are of value to him and if the charges are reasonable in relation to the benefits, are of a type that is not for credit, and are authorized as permissible additional charges by rule adopted by the Administrator.

(2) An additional charge may be made for insurance written in connection with the transaction:

(a) with respect to insurance against loss of or damage to property, or against liability arising out of the ownership or use of property, if the creditor furnishes a clear, conspicuous, and specific statement in writing to the consumer setting forth the cost of the insurance if obtained from or through the creditor and stating that the consumer may choose the person through whom the insurance is to be obtained;

(b) with respect to consumer credit insurance providing life, accident, or health coverage, if the insurance coverage is not required by the creditor and this fact is clearly and conspicuously disclosed in writing to the consumer, and if, in order to obtain the insurance in connection with the extension of credit, the consumer gives specific, dated, and separately signed affirmative written indication of his desire to do so after written disclosure to him of the cost thereof; and

(c) with respect to vendor's single interest insurance, but only (i) to the extent that the insurer has no right of subrogation against the consumer, and (ii) to the extent that the insurance does not duplicate the coverage of other insurance under which loss is payable to the creditor as his interest may appear, against loss of or damage to property for which a separate charge is made to the consumer pursuant to paragraph (a), and (iii) if a clear, conspicuous, and specific statement in writing is furnished by the creditor to the consumer setting forth the cost of the insurance if obtained from or through the creditor and stating that the consumer may choose the person through whom the insurance is to be obtained.

Comment

1. The two categories of charges a creditor is permitted to make at the inception of a credit extension are finance charges (Section 1.301(20)) and additional charges as enumerated in this section. In general, the charges designated as additional charges fall roughly into three classes: (1) those that would likely have been incurred had there been no credit extension (e.g., closing costs); (2) those closely related to the extension of credit but providing valuable subsidiary benefits to the consumer (e.g., the front-end credit card charge; life, accident, health, and property insurance); and (3) those ultimately payable to third parties with no portion of the charge returnable to the creditor by commission or otherwise (e.g., taxes; official fees for perfecting security interests). These classes are nonexclusive; for instance property insurance would sometimes fall within class (1) and closing costs fit into class (3) as well as in (1). Paragraph (e) of subsection (1) provides the Administrator with the flexibility needed to allow him to deal with new kinds of charges as new credit transactions evolve.

2. Though this section coincides with Regulation Z Section 226.4(a) in excluding premiums for insurance from the finance charge under certain stated conditions, it varies from Regulation Z Section 226.4(e) in that it does not include appraisal fees and credit report charges as additional charges. Section 1.301(20)(a)(iv) expressly designates these charges as part of the finance charge. Another variation from Truth in Lending is the treatment of vendor's single interest insurance (V.S.I.). Federal Reserve Interpretation 226.404 allows exclusion of the premium for V.S.I. insurance from the finance charge. Paragraph (c) of subsection (2) adopts a more sophisticated

test and allows the premium to be treated as an additional charge in limited situations in which the vendor's single interest coverage does not duplicate the coverage of other insurance under which loss is payable to the creditor as his interest may appear, against loss of or damage to property for which a separate charge is made to the consumer. In this case, the charge is sufficiently beneficial to the consumer to justify classifying the premium as an additional charge.

§ 2.502 [Delinquency Charges]

(1) With respect to a precomputed consumer credit transaction, the parties may contract for a delinquency charge on any instalment not paid in full within ten days after its due date, as originally scheduled or as deferred, in an amount, not exceeding $5, which is not more than five per cent of the unpaid amount of the instalment.

(2) A delinquency charge under subsection (1) may be collected only once on an instalment however long it remains in default. No delinquency charge may be collected with respect to a deferred instalment unless the instalment is not paid in full within ten days after its deferred due date. A delinquency charge may be collected at the time it accrues or at any time thereafter.

(3) A delinquency charge under subsection (1) may not be collected on an instalment paid in full within ten days after its scheduled or deferred instalment due date even though an earlier maturing instalment or a delinquency or deferral charge on an earlier instalment has not been paid in full. For purposes of this subsection a payment is deemed to have been applied first to any instalment due in the computational period (paragraph (a) of subsection (1) of Section 2.503) in which it is received and then to delinquent instalments and charges.

(4) If two instalments or parts thereof of a precomputed consumer loan are in default for ten days or more, the lender may elect to convert the loan from a precomputed loan to one in which the finance charge is based on unpaid balances. In this event he shall make a rebate pursuant to the provisions on rebate upon prepayment (Section 2.510) as if the date of prepayment were one day before the maturity date of a delinquent instalment, and thereafter may make a finance charge as authorized by the provisions on finance charge for consumer loans by lenders not supervised lenders (subsection (1) of Section 2.401) or finance charge for consumer loans by supervised lenders (subsection (2) of Section 2.401), whichever is appropriate. The amount of the rebate shall not be reduced by the amount of any permitted minimum charge (Section 2.510). If the creditor proceeds under this subsection, any delinquency or deferral charges made with respect to instalments due at or after the maturity date of the first delinquent instalment shall be rebated, and no further delinquency or deferral charges shall be made.

(5) The amount of $5 in subsection (1) is subject to change pursuant to the provisions on adjustment of dollar amounts (Section 1.106).

Comment

1. If a consumer is late in making a payment under a precomputed credit transaction, the creditor would receive no income for the period of delay unless a delinquency charge were permitted. The alternative of not permitting delinquency charges is rejected because the result would be to enforce a lower effective ceiling on finance charge rates for delinquent consumers than for consumers who pay promptly. Delinquency charges are inapplicable to open-end credit plans under which the finance charge continues to accumulate through any period of delay thus compensating the creditor for this period.

. . .

§ 2.503 [Deferral Charges]

(1) In this section and in the provisions on rebate upon prepayment (Section 2.510) the following defined terms apply with respect to a precomputed consumer credit transaction:

(a) "Computational period" means (i) the interval between scheduled due dates of instalments under the transaction if the intervals are substantially equal or, (ii) if the intervals are not substantially equal, one month if the smallest interval between the scheduled due dates of instalments under the transaction is one month or more, and, otherwise, one week.

(b) "Deferral" means a postponement of the scheduled due date of an instalment as originally scheduled or as previously deferred.

(c) "Deferral period" means a period in which no instalment is scheduled to be paid by reason of a deferral.

(d) The "interval" between specified dates means the interval between them including one or the other but not both of them; if the interval between the date of a transaction and the due date of the first scheduled instalment does not exceed one month by more than 15 days when the computational period is one month, or does not exceed 11 days when the computational period is one week, the interval may be considered by the creditor as one computational period.

(e) "Periodic balance" means the amount scheduled to be outstanding on the last day of a computational period before deducting the instalment, if any, scheduled to be paid on that day.

(f) "Standard deferral" means a deferral with respect to a transaction made as of the due date of an instalment as scheduled before the deferral by which the due dates of that instalment and all subsequent instalments as scheduled before the deferral are deferred for a period equal to the deferral period. A standard deferral may be for one or more full computational periods or a portion of one computational period or a combination of any of these.

(g) "Sum of the balances method," also known as the "Rule of 78," means a method employed with respect to a transaction to determine the portion of the finance charge attributable to a period of time before the scheduled due date of the final instalment of the transaction. The amount so attributable is determined by multiplying the finance charge by a fraction the numerator of which is the sum of the periodic balances included within the period and the denominator of which is the sum of all periodic balances under the transaction. According to the sum of the balances method the portion of the finance charge attributable to a specified computational period is the difference between the portions of the finance charge attributable to the periods of time including and excluding, respectively, the computational period, both determined according to the sum of the balances method.

(h) "Transaction" means a precomputed consumer credit transaction unless the context otherwise requires.

(2) Before or after default in payment of a scheduled instalment of a transaction, the parties to the transaction may agree in writing to a deferral of all or part of one or more unpaid instalments and the creditor may make at the time of deferral and receive at that time or at any time thereafter a deferral charge not exceeding that provided in this section.

(3) A standard deferral may be made with respect to a transaction as of the due date, as originally scheduled or as deferred pursuant to a standard deferral, of an instalment with respect to which no delinquency charge (Section 2.502) has been made or, if made, is deducted from the deferral charge computed according to this subsection. The deferral charge for a standard deferral may equal but not exceed the portion of the finance charge attributable to the computational period immediately preceding the due date of the earliest maturing instalment deferred as determined according to the sum of the balances method multiplied by the whole or fractional number of computational periods in the deferral period, counting each day as $^1/_{30}$th of a month without regard to differences in lengths of months when the computational period is one month or as $^1/_7$th of a week when the computation period is one week. A deferral charge computed according to this subsection is earned pro rata during the deferral period and is fully earned on the last day of the deferral period.

(4) With respect to a transaction as to which a creditor elects not to make and does not make a standard deferral or a deferral charge for a standard deferral, a deferral charge computed according to this subsection may be made as of the due date, as scheduled originally or as deferred pursuant to either subsection (3) or this subsection, of an instalment with respect to which no delinquency charge (Section

2.502) has been made or, if made, is deducted from the deferral charge computed according to this subsection. A deferral charge pursuant to this subsection may equal but not exceed the rate of finance charge required to be disclosed to the consumer pursuant to law applied to each amount deferred for the period for which it is deferred computed without regard to differences in lengths of months, but proportionately for a part of a month, counting each day as 1/30th of a month or as 1/7th of a week. A deferral charge computed according to this subsection is earned pro rata with respect to each amount deferred during the period for which it is deferred.

(5) In addition to the deferral charge permitted by this section, a creditor may make and receive appropriate additional charges (Section 2.501), and any amount of these charges which is not paid may be added to the deferral charge computed according to subsection (3) or to the amount deferred for the purpose of computing the deferral charge computed according to subsection (4).

(6) The parties may agree in writing at the time of a transaction that, if an instalment is not paid within ten days after its due date, the creditor may unilaterally grant a deferral and make charges as provided in this section. A deferral charge may not be made for a period after the date that the creditor elects to accelerate the maturity of the transaction.

Comment

1. The definitions in subsection (1) apply to Section 2.510 as well. See subsection (3) of Section 2.510.

2. These definitions and the other provisions of this section can be illustrated more readily than explained.

Assume the loan transaction specified in the example in Comment 2 to Section 2.201, and that the loan is made on July 1, 1974. It is then a "precomputed consumer credit transaction" (subsections (13) and (33) of Section 1.301), e.g., a "consumer loan" (subsection (15) of Section 1.301), of which the "amount financed" (subsection (5) of Section 1.301) is $1500, the "finance charge" (subsection (20) of Section 1.301) is $211.68, computed at an annual percentage rate of 25.10%, and the "total of payments" is $1711.68 and is payable in 12 equal monthly instalments of $142.64 each beginning on Aug. 1, 1974, and ending on July 1, 1975.

The "computational period" (paragraph (a) of subsection (1) of this section) is one month. The "periodic balances" (paragraph (e) of subsection (1) of this section) of, and other calculations applicable to, the transaction are:

Col. 1	Col. 2	Col. 3	Col. 4	Col. 5	Col. 6
Inst. No.	Inst. Due Date & Last Day of Each Comptnl. Period	Periodic Balances	Col. 3 ÷ by $11,125.92	Sum of Periodic Balances	Col. 5 ÷ by $11,125.92
1	Aug. 1, 1974	$ 1,711.68	12/78	$ 1,711.68	12/78
2	Sept. 1, 1974	1,569.04	11/78	3,280.72	23/78
3	Oct. 1, 1974	1,426.40	10/78	4,707.12	33/78
4	Nov. 1, 1974	1,283.76	9/78	5,990.88	42/78
5	Dec. 1, 1974	1,141.12	8/78	7,132.00	50/78
6	Jan. 1, 1975	998.48	7/78	8,130.48	57/78
7	Feb. 1, 1975	855.84	6/78	8,986.32	63/78
8	Mar. 1, 1975	713.20	5/78	9,699.52	68/78
9	Apr. 1, 1975	570.56	4/78	10,270.08	72/78
10	May 1, 1975	427.92	3/78	10,698.00	75/78
11	June 1, 1975	285.28	2/78	10,983.28	77/78
12	July 1, 1975	142.64	1/78	11,125.92	78/78
78		$11,125.92	78/78		

Col. 4 sets forth the fraction of the finance charge earned in each computational period as computed according to the "sum of the balances method" (paragraph (g) of subsection (1) of this section).

Col. 6 sets forth the fraction of the finance charge earned at the end of each computational period, also computed according to the sum of the balances method.

It will be noted that the fractions in Col. 4 and Col. 6, respectively, express more simply the fractions:

$$\frac{\text{Periodic balance}}{\text{Sum of all periodic balances under the transaction}}$$

and

$$\frac{\text{Sum of all periodic balances including computational period}}{\text{Sum of all periodic balances under the transaction}}$$

According to the "sum of the balances method" (paragraph (g) of subsection (1) of this section) the portion of the finance charge attributable to a period of time prior to the scheduled due date of the final instalment of the transaction is determined by multiplying the finance charge by a fraction the numerator of which is the sum of the periodic balances included within the period and the denominator is the total of all periodic balances under the transaction. Accordingly, in the assumed example, the portions of the total finance charge of $211.68 attributable to the periods ending, respectively, on Jan. 1, 1975, and Feb. 1, 1975, are $^{57}/_{78}$ths and $^{63}/_{78}$ths. Moreover, according to the "sum of the balances method" (the last sentence of paragraph (g) of subsection (1) of this section), the portion of the finance charge attributable to a specified computational period is the difference between the portions of the finance charge attributable to the periods of time including and excluding, respectively, that computational period; accordingly, in the assumed example the portion of the finance charge of $211.68 attributable to the computational period ending on Feb. 1, 1975, is $^{6}/_{78}$ths (i.e., $^{63}/_{78}$ths minus $^{57}/_{78}$ths) of $211.68, or $16.28.

3. Assume, further, that the consumer has paid the first 6 instalments, and that the parties have agreed to the deferral of the 7th instalment of $142.64 originally scheduled to be payable on Feb. 1, 1975, by 6 months until Aug. 1, 1975, or its equivalent, a deferral of the 7th and each of the five subsequent instalments of $142.64 each by one month each so that the 12th instalment originally scheduled for July, 1975 is payable on Aug. 1, 1975. The deferral is then a "standard deferral" (paragraph (f) of subsection (1) of this section) and the maximum deferral charge under subsection (3) of this section is $16.28, the finance charge so attributable to the computational period ending on Feb. 1, 1975, since the number of computational periods in the deferral period, the period in which no instalment is scheduled to be paid by reason of the deferral (paragraph (c) of subsection (1) of Section 2.503), is one.

The method of calculating deferral charges prescribed in subsection (3) of this section is that prescribed in the small loan laws of many States, e.g., New York Banking Law § 352(d)(4) computed by the application of the annual percentage rate of 25.10% (or 2.09 $^1/_6$% per month) to each amount deferred for the period of its deferral, as provided in U3C (1968 Draft) Sections 2.204(1) and 3.204(1) or subsection (4) of this section, the deferral charge would be $\$142.64 \times 6 \times .0209 \times {}^1/_6 = \$17.90$, or $1.62 more than the deferral charge of $16.28 as calculated according to subsection (3) of this section.

. . .

§ 2.504 [Finance Charge on Refinancing]

With respect to a consumer credit transaction except a consumer lease, the creditor by agreement with the consumer may refinance the unpaid balance and contract for and receive a finance charge based on the amount financed resulting from the refinancing at a rate not exceeding that permitted by the provisions on finance charge for consumer credit sales other than open-end credit (Section 2.201) if a consumer credit sale is refinanced, or for consumer loans (subsection (1) or (2) of Section 2.401, whichever is appropriate) if a consumer loan is refinanced. For the purpose of determining the finance charge permitted, the amount financed resulting from the refinancing comprises the following:

(1) if the transaction was not precomputed, the total of the unpaid balance and the accrued charges on the date of the refinancing, or, if the transaction was precomputed, the amount which the consumer would have been required to pay upon prepayment pursuant to the provisions on rebate upon prepayment (Section 2.510) on the date of refinancing, but for the purpose of computing this amount no minimum charge is permitted; and

(2) appropriate additional charges (Section 2.501), payment of which is deferred.

§ 2.505 [Finance Charge on Consolidation]

(1) In this section, "consumer credit transaction" does not include a consumer lease.

(2) If a consumer owes an unpaid balance to a creditor with respect to a consumer credit transaction and becomes obligated on another consumer credit transaction with the same creditor, the parties may agree to a consolidation resulting in a single schedule of payments. If the previous consumer credit transaction was not precomputed, the parties may agree to add the unpaid amount of the amount financed and accrued charges on the date of consolidation to the amount financed with respect to the subsequent consumer credit transaction. If the previous consumer credit transaction was precomputed, the parties may agree to refinance the unpaid balance pursuant to the provisions on refinancing (Section 2.504) and to consolidate the amount financed resulting from the refinancing by adding it to the amount financed with respect to the subsequent consumer credit transaction. In either case the creditor may contract for and receive a finance charge as provided in subsection (3) based on the aggregate amount financed resulting from the consolidation.

(3) If the debts consolidated arise exclusively from consumer credit sales, the transaction is a consolidation with respect to a consumer credit sale and the creditor may make a finance charge not exceeding that permitted by the provisions on finance charge for consumer credit sales other than one-end credit (Section 2.201). If the debts consolidated include a debt arising from a prior or contemporaneous consumer loan, the transaction is a consolidation with respect to a consumer loan and the creditor may make a finance charge not exceeding that permitted by the provisions on finance charge for consumer loans by lenders not supervised lenders (subsection (1) of Section 2.401) or consumer loans by supervised lenders (subsection (2) of Section 2.401), whichever is appropriate.

(4) If a consumer owes an unpaid balance to a creditor with respect to a consumer credit transaction arising out of a consumer credit sale, and becomes obligated on another consumer credit transaction arising out of another consumer credit sale by the same seller, the parties may agree to a consolidation resulting in a single schedule of payments either pursuant to subsection (2) or by adding together the unpaid balances with respect to the two sales.

§ 2.506 [Advances to Perform Covenants of Consumer]

(1) If the agreement with respect to a consumer credit transaction other than a consumer lease contains covenants by the consumer to perform certain duties pertaining to insuring or preserving collateral and the creditor pursuant to the agreement pays for performance of the duties on behalf of the consumer, he may add the amounts paid to

the debt. Within a reasonable time after advancing any sums, he shall state to the consumer in writing the amount of sums advanced, any charges with respect to this amount, and any revised payment schedule and, if the duties of the consumer performed by the creditor pertain to insurance, a brief description of the insurance paid for by the creditor including the type and amount of coverages. Further information need not be given.

(2) A finance charge may be made for sums advanced pursuant to subsection (1) at a rate not exceeding the rate of finance charge required to be stated to the consumer pursuant to law in a disclosure statement, but with respect to open-end credit the amount of the advance may be added to the unpaid balance of the debt and the creditor may make a finance charge not exceeding that permitted by the appropriate provisions on finance charge for consumer credit sales pursuant to open-end credit (Section 2.202) or for consumer loans (subsection (1) or (2) of Section 2.401), whichever is appropriate.

Alternative A:

§ 2.507 [Attorney's Fees]

With respect to a consumer credit transaction, the agreement may not provide for payment by the consumer of attorney's fees. A provision in violation of this section is unenforceable.

Comment

. . . In providing that no charge may be made for attorney's fees, this section reflects a policy decision to follow some small loan acts in treating this expense, like other collection costs, as part of the creditor's cost of doing business, rather than as a charge to be imposed on the defaulting consumer. The provisions made in this Act for rate ceilings and additional charges are generous enough to justify this treatment of attorney's fees and collection costs as part of general overhead.

Alternative B:

§ 2.507 [Attorney's Fees]

(1) With respect to a consumer loan in which the finance charge calculated according to the actuarial method is more than 18 per cent per year, the agreement may not provide for payment by the consumer of attorney's fees:

(a) if the loan is not pursuant to open-end credit and the amount financed is $1,000 or less; or

(b) if the loan is pursuant to open-end credit and the balance of the account at the time of default is $1,000 or less.

A provision in violation of this subsection is unenforceable.

(2) With respect to any other consumer credit transaction, the agreement may provide for payment by the consumer of reasonable attorney's fees not in excess of 15 per cent of the unpaid debt after default and referral to an attorney not a salaried employee of the creditor. A provision in violation of this subsection is unenforceable.

(3) The amounts of $1,000 in subsection (1) are subject to change pursuant to the provisions on adjustment of dollar amounts (Section 1.106).

Comment

. . . In providing in subsection (1) that no charge may be made for attorney's fees in supervised loans of $1,000 or less this section follows some small loan acts in treating this expense, like other collection costs, as part of the creditor's cost of doing business, rather than as a charge to be imposed on the defaulting consumer. Subsection (2) reflects a policy decision in other consumer transactions of treating attorney's fees not as part of the creditor's general overhead to be indirectly borne by all of his customers but as a charge to be imposed, at least in part, on the defaulting consumer who gives rise to the expense. This section allows the parties to agree that upon default and referral of the claim to an attorney a charge can be made. . . .

§ 2.509 [Right to Prepay]

Subject to the provisions on rebate upon prepayment (Section 2.510), the consumer may prepay in full the unpaid balance of a consumer credit transaction, except a consumer lease, at any time without penalty.

§ 2.510 [Rebate Upon Prepayment]

(1) Except as otherwise provided in this section, upon prepayment in full of a precomputed consumer credit transaction, the creditor shall rebate to the consumer an amount not less than the unearned portion of the finance charge computed according to this section. If the rebate otherwise required is less than $1, no rebate need be made.

(2) Upon prepayment of a consumer credit transaction, whether or not precomputed, except a consumer lease or one pursuant to open-end credit, the creditor may collect or retain a minimum charge not exceeding $5 in a transaction which had an amount financed of $75 or less, or not exceeding $7.50 in a transaction which had an amount financed of more than $75, if the minimum charge was contracted for and the finance charge earned at the time of prepayment is less than the minimum charge contracted for.

(3) In the following subsections these terms have the meanings ascribed to them in subsection (1) of Section 2.503: computational pe-

riod, deferral, deferral period, periodic balance, standard deferral, sum of the balances method, and transaction.

(4) If, with respect to a transaction payable according to its original terms in no more than [48] instalments, the creditor has made either:

(a) no deferral or deferral charge, the unearned portion of the finance charge is no less than the portion thereof attributable according to the sum of the balances method to the period from the first day of the computational period following that in which prepayment occurs to the scheduled due date of the final instalment of the transaction; or

(b) a standard deferral and a deferral charge pursuant to the provisions on a standard deferral, the unpaid balance of the transaction includes any unpaid portions of the deferral charge and any appropriate additional charges incident to the deferral, and the unearned portion of the finance charge is no less than the portion thereof attributable according to the sum of the balances method to the period from the first day of the computational period following that in which prepayment occurs except that the numerator of the fraction is the sum of the periodic balances, after rescheduling to give effect to any standard deferral, scheduled to follow the computational period in which prepayment occurs. A separate rebate of the deferral charge is not required unless the unpaid balance of the transaction is paid in full during the deferral period, in which event the creditor shall also rebate the unearned portion of the deferral charge.

(5) In lieu of computing a rebate of the unearned portion of the finance charge as provided in subsection (4) of this section, the creditor:

(a) shall, with respect to a transaction payable according to its original terms in more than [48] instalments, and a transaction payable according to its original terms in no more than [48] instalments as to which the creditor has made a deferral other than a standard deferral, and

(b) may, in other cases,

recompute or redetermine the earned finance charge by applying, according to the actuarial method, the annual percentage rate of finance charge required to be disclosed to the consumer pursuant to law to the actual unpaid balances of the amount financed for the actual time that the unpaid balances were outstanding as of the date of prepayment, giving effect to each payment, including payments of any deferral and delinquency charges, as of the date of the payment. The Administrator shall adopt rules to simplify the calculation of the unearned portion of the finance charge, including allowance of the use of tables or other methods derived by application of a percentage rate which deviates by not more than one-half of one per cent from the rate of the finance charge required to be disclosed to the consumer pursuant to law, and based on the assumption that all payments were made as originally scheduled or as deferred.

(6) Except as otherwise provided in subsection (5), this section does not preclude the collection or retention by the creditor of delinquency charges (Section 2.502).

(7) If the maturity is accelerated for any reason and judgment is entered, the consumer is entitled to the same rebate as if payment had been made on the date judgment is entered.

(8) Upon prepayment in full of a precomputed consumer credit transaction by the proceeds of consumer credit insurance (Section 4.103), the consumer or his estate is entitled to the same rebate as though the consumer had prepaid the agreement on the date the proceeds of insurance are paid to the creditor, but no later than 20 business days after satisfactory proof of loss is furnished to the creditor.

Comment

. . .

4. Subsection (4) of this section prescribes a method for computing the unearned portion of the finance charge and hence the rebate upon prepayment of a transaction payable according to its original terms in no more than [48] instalments as to which the creditor has made either no deferral or a "standard deferral" and a deferral charge according to the provisions applying to a standard deferral.

Assume the transactions described in Comment 2 to Section 2.201 and in Comments 2 and 3 to Section 2.503. Assume, further, that the consumer has paid not only $855.84, the total of the first six monthly instalments payable before the deferral, but also the deferral charge of $16.28, calculated according to subsection (3) of Section 2.503, $285.28, the total of the 7th and 8th instalments of $142.64 each payable as deferred on Mar. 1 and Apr. 1, 1975, and has prepaid on Apr. 15, 1975, $570.56, the then unpaid balance of his "total of payments." His total payments then aggregate $1,727.96. Then:

(1) According to subsection (4) of this section, the fraction of the finance charge of $211.68 to be used to determine the rebate is the fraction of which the numerator is the sum of periodic balances as rescheduled pursuant to the deferral, viz., $1,426.40 (the total of $570.56, $427.92, $285.28, and $142.64 payable as deferred on the 1st days of May, June, July, and August, 1975 respectively) divided by $11,125.92 (the sum of all the periodic balances under the original transaction). The fraction then is $1,426.40/11,125.92, or dividing both numerator and denominator by $142.64 (the amount of each instalment), $^{10}/_{78}$. The rebate, the unearned portion of the total finance charge of $211.68, is $211.68 × $^{10}/_{78}$ = $27.14.

(2) Deducting $27.14 from $1,727.96, the total paid on the transaction by the consumer, produces $1,700.82 as its net cost to the consumer.

Make the same assumptions as above, except that the deferral charge has been computed according to U3C (1968 Draft) Sections 2.204(1) and 3.204(1) or according to subsection (4) of Section 2.503 of this Act. His total payments then aggregate $1,729.58, the total of $1,711.68 (12 payments of $142.64 each) and the deferral charge of $17.90 calculated according to subsection (4) of Section 2.503. Then were the unearned portions of the finance charge and the deferral charge to be computed separately as formerly required by U3C (1968 Text) Sections 2.210(6) and 3.210(6):

(1) The unearned portion of the finance charge would have been computed without regard to the deferral, i.e., as the fraction of which the numerator is $855.84 (the total of the four prepaid periodic balances of $427.92, $285.28, and $142.64, and $00., as originally scheduled) and the denominator is $11,125.92 (the total of the 12 periodic balances as originally scheduled), or $855.84/$11,125.92, or, dividing both the numerator and the denominator by $142.64 (the amount of each instalment), $^6/_{78}$. The rebate, the unearned portion of the finance charge of $211.68, is $211.68 $\times$ $^6/_{78}$ = $16.28.

(2) As noted in Comment 3 to Section 2.503, the deferral charge, calculated as provided in U3C (1968 Draft) Sections 2.204(1) and 3.204(1), was $17.90. The unearned portion of that deferral charge is the fraction of which the numerator is four (the number of instalments remaining to earn the deferral charge) and the denominator is six (the number of instalments deferred). The unearned portion of the deferral charge of $17.90 is $17.90 $\times$ $^4/_6$ = $11.93.

(3) Deducting $28.21, the total of (a) $16.28, the unearned portion of the finance charge, and (b) $11.93, the unearned portion of the deferral charge, from $1,729.58, the total paid by the consumer, produces $1,701.37 as the net cost of the transaction to the consumer.

Consequently, the methods of calculating deferral charges according to subsection (3) of Section 2.503 of this Act and rebate of unearned finance charge according to subsection (4) of this Section not only permit more simple calculations, but also produce a lower cost to the consumer than under the corresponding provisions of the 1968 Draft of the U3C, viz. under the illustrations above, $1,700.82 as compared to $1,701.37.

. . .

PART 6. OTHER CREDIT TRANSACTIONS

§ 2.601 [Charges for Other Credit Transactions]

(1) Except as provided in subsection (2), with respect to a credit transaction other than a consumer credit transaction, the parties may contract for payment by the debtor of any finance or other charge.

(2) With respect to a credit transaction which would be a consumer credit transaction if a finance charge were made, a charge for delinquency may not exceed amounts allowed for finance charges for consumer credit sales pursuant to open-end credit (Section 2.202).

Comment

1. An economic fundamental of this Act is that too low a rate ceiling prevents both consumer and commercial debtors who need credit from getting credit at reasonable rates from legitimate creditors. Because basic usury laws had that effect, the legislatures in almost all the States have enacted

myriad exceptions to the usury statutes for consumer and commercial transactions such as small, industrial and instalment loan laws and prohibitions against a defense of usury by a corporation. The sale of goods, services, or interests in land on credit, whether in a consumer or commercial context, has been held by the courts of most of the States to be exempt from their usury laws under the time-price doctrine. That doctrine has been recognized and limited by the legislatures of most States which have enacted laws regulating consumer instalment sales.

This Act repeals the general usury statute as well as the exceptions to it, sets reasonable ceilings on all consumer credit rates, and in this section leaves the finance charge and other charges in transactions other than consumer credit transactions, such as:

(a) A transaction by a seller or lender not regularly engaged in similar credit transactions,

(b) A transaction over $25,000 in amount not involving real property,

(c) A transaction in which an organization is the debtor, and

(d) A transaction for a business purpose,

basically to the agreement of the parties. In all these types of transactions except the first, which is usually a family transaction or may be within subsection (15)(c) of Section 1.301, the debtors are usually sophisticated enough to take care of themselves in negotiating credit charges. It is difficult to impose an arbitrary rate ceiling for these transactions that will be high enough to allow for high risk business transactions without setting a limit that is so high as to be virtually meaningless. This Act contemplates the repeal of the general usury statute in any State which enacts it; hence the need for the time-price doctrine is eliminated in any such State. Given the basic philosophy of this Act, it should not be interpreted as rejecting the time-price doctrine in either its consumer or commercial context in any State which has not enacted the Act or which continues to have a general usury statute.

. . .

ARTICLE 3. REGULATION OF AGREEMENTS AND PRACTICES

PART 1. GENERAL PROVISIONS

§ 3.102 [Scope]

Part 2 of this Article applies to disclosure with respect to consumer credit transactions. The provision on compliance with the Federal Truth in Lending Act (Section 3.201) applies to a sale of an interest in land or a loan secured by an interest in land, without regard to the rate of finance charge, if the sale or loan is otherwise a consumer credit sale or consumer loan. Parts 3 and 4 of this Article apply, respectively, to limitations on agreements and practices, and limitations on consumers' liabilities with respect to certain consumer credit transactions. Part 5 applies to home solicitation sales.

PART 2. DISCLOSURE

§ 3.201 [Compliance with Federal Truth in Lending Act]

(1) A person upon whom the Federal Truth in Lending Act imposes duties or obligations shall make or give to the consumer the disclosures, information, and notices required of him by that Act and in all respects comply with that Act. To the extent the Federal Truth in Lending Act does not impose duties or obligations upon a person in a credit transaction, except a consumer lease, that is a consumer credit transaction under this Act, the person shall make or give to the consumer disclosures, information, and notices in accordance with the Federal Truth in Lending Act with respect to the credit transaction.

(2) The Federal Truth in Lending Act is deemed to apply to a credit transaction which is a consumer credit transaction under this Act, notwithstanding its inclusion in a class of transactions within this State which, by regulation of the Board of Governors of the Federal Reserve System, is exempt from the Federal Truth in Lending Act.

§ 3.202 [Consumer Leases]

(1) With respect to a consumer lease the lessor shall give to the lessee the following information:

(a) brief description or identification of the goods;

(b) amount of any payment required at the inception of the lease;

(c) amount paid or payable for official fees, registration, certificate of title, or license fees or taxes;

(d) amount of other charges not included in the periodic payments and a brief description of the charges;

(e) brief description of insurance to be provided or paid for by the lessor, including the types and amounts of the coverages;

(f) number of periodic payments, the amount of each payment, the due date of the first payment, the due dates of subsequent payments or interval between payments, and the total amount payable by the lessee;

(g) statement of the conditions under which the lessee may terminate the lease before the end of the term; and

(h) statement of the liabilities the lease imposes upon the lessee at the end of the term.

(2) The disclosures required by this section:

(a) shall be made clearly and conspicuously in writing, a copy of which shall be delivered to the lessee;

(b) may be supplemented by additional information or explanations supplied by the lessor, but none shall be stated, utilized, or placed so as to mislead or confuse the lessee or contradict, obscure, or detract attention from the information required to be disclosed by this section;

(c) need be made only to the extent applicable;

(d) shall be made on the assumption that all scheduled payments will be made when due and will comply with this section although rendered inaccurate by an act, occurrence, or agreement after the required disclosure; and

(e) shall be made before the lease transaction is consummated, but may be made in the lease to be signed by the lessee.

§ 3.203 [Notice to Consumer]

The creditor shall give to the consumer a copy of any writing evidencing a consumer credit transaction, except one pursuant to open-end credit, if the writing requires or provides for the signature of the consumer. The writing evidencing the consumer's obligation to pay the debt shall contain a clear and conspicuous notice informing the consumer that he should not sign it before reading it, that he is entitled to a copy of it, and, except in case of a consumer lease, that he is entitled to prepay the unpaid balance at any time without penalty and may be entitled to receive a refund of unearned charges in accordance with law. The following notice if clear and conspicuous complies with this section:

NOTICE TO CONSUMER:
1. Do not sign this paper before you read it.
2. You are entitled to a copy of this paper.
3. You may prepay the unpaid balance at any time without penalty and may be entitled to receive a refund of unearned charges in accordance with law.

§ 3.204 [Notice of Assignment]

A consumer may pay the original creditor until he receives notification of assignment of rights to payment pursuant to a consumer credit transaction and that payment is to be made to the assignee. A notification which does not reasonably identify the rights assigned is ineffective. If requested by the consumer, the assignee shall seasonably furnish reasonable proof that the assignment has been made and unless he does so the consumer may pay the original creditor.

§ 3.205 [Change in Terms of Open-End Credit Accounts]

(1) Whether or not a change is authorized by prior agreement, a creditor may change the terms of an open-end credit account applying to any balance incurred before or after the effective date of the change. If the change increases the rate of the finance charge or of additional charges, alters the method of determining the balance upon which charges are made so that increased charges may result, or imposes or increases minimum charges, the change is effective with respect to a balance incurred before the effective date of the change only if the consumer after receiving disclosure of the change agrees to it in writing or the creditor delivers or mails to the consumer two written disclosures of the change, the first at least three months before the effective date of the change and the second at a later time before the effective date of the change.

(2) A disclosure provided for in subsection (1) is mailed to the consumer when mailed to him at his address used by the creditor for mailing him periodic billing statements.

(3) If a creditor attempts to change the terms of an open-end credit account as provided in subsection (1) without complying with this section, any additional cost or charge to the consumer resulting from the change is an excess charge and is subject to the remedies available to the consumer (Section 5.201) and to the Administrator (Section 6.113).

§ 3.208 [Notice to Co-Signers and Similar Parties]

(1) A natural person, other than the spouse of the consumer, is not obligated as a co-signer, co-maker, guarantor, indorser, surety, or similar party with respect to a consumer credit transaction, unless before or contemporaneously with signing any separate agreement of obligation or any writing setting forth the terms of the debtor's agreement, the person receives a separate written notice that contains a completed identification of the debt he may have to pay and reasonably informs him of his obligation with respect to it.

(2) A clear and conspicuous notice in substantially the following form complies with this section:

NOTICE

You agree to pay the debt identified below although you may not personally receive any property, services, or money. You may be sued for payment although the person who receives the property, services, or money is able to pay. This notice is not the contract that obligates you to pay the debt. Read the contract for the exact terms of your obligation.

IDENTIFICATION OF DEBT YOU MAY HAVE TO PAY

____
(Name of Debtor)

____
(Name of Creditor)

____
(Date)

____
(Kind of Debt)

I have received a copy of this notice.

____
(Date)

____
(Signed)

(3) The notice required by this section need not be given to a seller, lessor, or lender who is obligated to an assignee of his rights.

(4) A person entitled to notice under this section shall also be given a copy of any writing setting forth the terms of the debtor's agreement and of any separate agreement of obligation signed by the person entitled to the notice.

§ 3.209 [Advertising]

(1) A seller, lessor, or lender may not advertise, print, display, publish, distribute, broadcast, or cause to be advertised, printed, dis-

played, published, distributed, or broadcast in any manner any statement or representation with regard to the rates, terms, or conditions of credit with respect to a consumer credit transaction that is false, misleading, or deceptive.

(2) Advertising that complies with the Federal Truth in Lending Act does not violate this section.

(3) This section does not apply to the owner or personnel, as such, of any medium in which an advertisement appears or through which it is disseminated.

PART 3. LIMITATIONS ON AGREEMENTS AND PRACTICES

§ 3.301 [Security in Sales and Leases]

(1) With respect to a consumer credit sale, a seller may take a security interest in the property sold. In addition, a seller may take a security interest in goods upon which services are performed or in which goods sold are installed or to which they are annexed, or in land to which the goods are affixed or which is maintained, repaired or improved as a result of the sale of the goods or services, if in the case of a security interest in land the debt secured is $1,000 or more, or, in the case of a security interest in goods the debt secured is $300 or more. The seller may also take a security interest in property to secure the debt arising from a consumer credit sale primarily for an agricultural purpose. Except as provided with respect to cross-collateral (Section 3.302) a seller my not otherwise take a security interest in property to secure the debt arising from a consumer credit sale.

(2) With respect to a consumer lease, except one primarily for an agricultural purpose, a lessor may not take a security interest in property to secure the debt arising from the lease. This subsection does not apply to a security deposit for a consumer lease.

(3) A security interest taken in violation of this section is void.

(4) The amounts of $1,000 and $300 in subsection (1) are subject to change pursuant to the provisions on adjustment of dollar amounts (Section 1.106).

§ 3.302 [Cross-Collateral]

(1) In addition to contracting for a security interest pursuant to the provisions on security in sales and leases (Section 3.301), a seller in a consumer credit sale may secure the debt arising from the sale by contracting for a security interest in other property if as a result of a prior sale the seller has an existing security interest in the other property. The seller may also contract for a security interest in the property sold in the subsequent sale as security for the previous debt.

(2) If the seller contracts for a security interest in other property pursuant to this section, the rate of finance charge thereafter on the

aggregate unpaid balances so secured may not exceed that permitted if the balances so secured were consolidated pursuant to the provisions on finance charge on consolidation (subsection (2) of Section 2.505). The seller has a reasonable time after so contracting in which to make any adjustments required by this section.

Comment

. . .

2. Subsection (1) allows cross-collateral to be taken either for separate debts or for consolidated debts, but subsection (2) . . . prevents the seller from taking the advantages of cross-collateral without also offering the buyer the lower rates that would have resulted had the debts been consolidated pursuant to Section 2.505(2).

§ 3.303 [Debt Secured by Cross-Collateral]

(1) If debts arising from two or more consumer credit sales, except sales primarily for an agricultural purpose or pursuant to open-end credit, are secured by cross-collateral (Section 3.302) or consolidated into one debt payable on a single schedule of payments, and the debt is secured by security interests taken with respect to one or more of the sales, payments received by the seller after the taking of cross-collateral or the consolidation are deemed, for the purpose of determining the amount of the debt secured by the various security interests, to have been applied first to the payment of the debts arising from the sales first made. To the extent debts are paid according to this section, security interests in items of property terminate as the debt originally incurred with respect to each item is paid.

(2) Payments received by the seller upon an open-end credit account are deemed, for the purpose of determining the amount of the debt secured by the various security interests, to have been applied first to the payment of finance charges in the order of their entry to the account and then to the payment of debts in the order in which the entries to the account showing the debts were made.

(3) If the debts consolidated arose from two or more sales made on the same day, payments received by the seller are deemed, for the purpose of determining the amount of the debt secured by the various security interests, to have been applied first to the payment of the smallest debt.

§ 3.304 [Use of Multiple Agreements]

(1) A creditor may not use multiple agreements with respect to a single consumer credit transaction with intent to obtain a higher finance charge than otherwise would be permitted by the provisions of the Article on Finance Charges and Related Provisions (Article 2).

(2) The excess amount of finance charge resulting from a violation of subsection (1) is an excess charge for the purposes of the provisions on rights of parties (Section 5.201) and the provisions on civil actions by Administrator (Section 6.113).

§ 3.305 [No Assignment of Earnings]

(1) A creditor may not take an assignment of earnings of the consumer for payment or as security for payment of a debt arising out of a consumer credit transaction. An assignment of earnings in violation of this section is unenforceable by the assignee of the earnings and revocable by the consumer. This section does not prohibit a consumer from authorizing deductions from his earnings in favor of his creditor if the authorization is revocable, the consumer is given a complete copy of the writing evidencing the authorization at the time he signs it, and the writing contains on its face a conspicuous notice of the consumer's right to revoke the authorization.

(2) A sale of unpaid earnings made in consideration of the payment of money to or for the account of the seller of the earnings is deemed to be a loan to him secured by an assignment of earnings.

§ 3.306 [Authorization to Confess Judgment Prohibited]

A consumer may not authorize any person to confess judgment on a claim arising out of a consumer credit transaction. An authorization in violation of this section is void.

§ 3.307 [Certain Negotiable Instruments Prohibited]

With respect to a consumer credit sale or consumer lease, [except a sale or lease primarily for an agricultural purpose,] the creditor may not take a negotiable instrument other than a check dated not later than ten days after its issuance as evidence of the obligation of the consumer.

Comment

This section, together with Sections 3.403, 3.404 and 3.405, states a major tenet of this Act: that the holder in due course doctrine should be abrogated in consumer cases. Whatever beneficial effects this doctrine may have in promoting the currency of paper is greatly outweighed by the harshness of its consequences in denying consumers the right to raise valid defenses arising out of credit transactions. The first step in abolition of the doctrine is the prohibition found in this section of the use of negotiable instruments in consumer credit sales and consumer leases. The presence of the bracketed language recognizes the strong tradition of the use of negotiable instruments in agricultural transactions in some States.

§ 3.308 [Balloon Payments]

(1) Except as provided in subsection (2), if any scheduled payment of a consumer credit transaction is more than twice as large as the average of earlier scheduled payments, the consumer has the right to refinance, without penalty, the amount of that payment at the time it is due. The terms of the refinancing shall be no less favorable to the consumer than the terms of the original transaction.

(2) This section does not apply to:

(a) a consumer lease;

(b) a transaction pursuant to open-end credit;

(c) a transaction primarily for an agricultural purpose;

(d) a transaction to the extent that the payment schedule is adjusted to the seasonal or irregular income or scheduled payments or obligations of the consumer; or

(e) a transaction of a class defined by rule of the Administrator as not requiring for the protection of the consumer his right to refinance as provided in this section.

§ 3.309 [Referral Sales and Leases]

With respect to a consumer credit sale or consumer lease, the seller or lessor may not give or offer to give a rebate or discount or otherwise pay or offer to pay value to the consumer as an inducement for a sale or lease for the consumer giving to the seller or lessor the names of prospective buyers or lessees, or otherwise aiding the seller or lessor in making a sale or lease to another person, if the earning of the rebate, discount or other value is contingent upon the occurrence of an event after the time the consumer agrees to buy or lease. If a consumer is induced by a violation of this section to enter into a consumer credit sale or consumer lease, the agreement is unenforceable by the seller or lessor and the consumer, at his option, may rescind the agreement or retain the property delivered and the benefit of any services performed, without any obligation to pay for them. A sale or lease that would be a referral sale or lease if credit were extended by the seller or lessor is nonetheless so because the property or services are paid for in whole or in part by use of a credit card or by a consumer loan with respect to which the lender is subject to claims and defenses arising from the sale or lease (Section 3.405), and the consumer has the same rights against the card issuer or lender that he has against the seller or lessor under this section.

Comment

. . .

2. The evil this section is aimed at is the raising of expectations in a buyer of benefits to accrue to him from events which are to occur in the

future. This provision has no effect on a seller's agreement to reduce at the time of the sale the price of an item in exchange for the buyer's giving the seller a list of prospective purchasers or assisting in other ways if the price reduction is not contingent on whether the purchasers do in fact buy or on whether other events occur in the future.

3. The misuse of the referral sale scheme has been so pervasive in some segments of vendor credit that this provision, in an effort to halt these practices, not only makes agreements in violation of this section unenforceable but also allows the buyer to retain the goods sold or the benefit of services rendered with no obligation to pay for them. Alternatively, the buyer may rescind the agreement, return the goods, and recover any payment. Use of a referral scheme subjects the offending seller or lessor to a penalty under Section 5.201. Creditors cannot evade this section by the use of credit cards or consumer loans.

PART 4. LIMITATIONS ON CONSUMERS' LIABILITIES

§ 3.401 [Restriction on Liability in Consumer Lease]

The obligation of a lessee upon expiration of a consumer lease [, except one primarily for an agricultural purpose,] may not exceed twice the average payment allocable to a monthly period under the lease. This limitation does not apply to charges for damages to the leased property or for other default.

Comment

This section is designed to protect consumer lessees against abuses associated with what are described in some areas of the country as "open-end" leases. Under such an agreement the parties contract that at the expiration of the lease the article leased, usually an automobile, will have a certain depreciated value and will be sold. If it brings less than the agreed depreciated value, the lessee is liable for the difference; if it brings more, the lessee is entitled to the surplus. Under such an agreement, the lessee will have no understanding of how much the lease might cost him unless he can accurately predict what the second hand market will be at the expiration of lease. Moreover, if the lessor sets an unrealistically high depreciated value the contingent liability of the lessee will increase accordingly, and the lessor can offer deceptively low rental payments to a gullible customer.

. . .

§ 3.402 [Limitation on Default Charges]

Except for reasonable expenses incurred in realizing on a security interest, the agreement with respect to a consumer credit transaction other than a consumer lease may not provide for any charges as a result of default by the consumer except those authorized by this Act. A provision in violation of this section is unenforceable.

§ 3.403 [Card Issuer Subject to Claims and Defenses]

(1) This section neither limits the liability of nor imposes liability on a card issuer as a manufacturer, supplier, seller, or lessor of property or services sold or leased pursuant to the credit card. This section may subject a card issuer to claims and defenses of a cardholder against a seller or lessor arising from sales or leases made pursuant to the credit card.

(2) A card issuer is subject to claims and defenses of a cardholder against the seller or lessor arising from the sale or lease of property or services by a seller or lessor licensed, franchised, or permitted by the card issuer or a person related to the card issuer to do business under the trade name or designation of the card issuer or a person related to the card issuer, to the extent of the original amount owing to the card issuer with respect to the sale or lease of the property or services as to which the claim or defense arose.

(3) Except as otherwise provided in this section, a card issuer, including a lender credit card issuer, is subject to all claims and defenses of a cardholder against the seller or lessor arising from the sale or lease of property or services pursuant to the credit card:

(a) if the original amount owing to the card issuer with respect to the sale or lease of the property or services as to which the claim or defense arose exceeds $50;

(b) if the residence of the cardholder and the place where the sale or lease occurred are [in the same state or] within 100 miles of each other;

(c) if the cardholder has made a good faith attempt to obtain satisfaction from the seller or lessor with respect to the claim or defense; and

(d) to the extent of the amount owing to the card issuer with respect to the sale or lease of the property or services as to which the claim or defense arose at the time the card issuer has notice of the claim or defense. Notice of the claim or defense may be given before the attempt specified in paragraph (c). Oral notice is effective unless the card issuer requests written confirmation when or promptly after oral notice is given and the cardholder fails to give the card issuer written confirmation within the period of time, not less than 14 days, stated to the cardholder when written confirmation is requested.

(4) For the purpose of determining the amount owing to the card issuer with respect to a sale or lease upon an open-end credit account, payments received for the account are deemed to have been applied first to the payment of finance charges in the order of their entry to the account and then to the payment of debts in the order in which the entries of the debts are made to the account.

(5) An agreement may not limit or waive the claims or defenses of a cardholder under this section.

§ 3.404 [Assignee Subject to Claims and Defenses]

(1) With respect to a consumer credit sale or consumer lease [, except one primarily for an agricultural purpose], an assignee of the rights of the seller or lessor is subject to all claims and defenses of the consumer against the seller or lessor arising from the sale or lease of property or services, notwithstanding that the assignee is a holder in due course of a negotiable instrument issued in violation of the provisions prohibiting certain negotiable instruments (Section 3.307).

(2) A claim or defense of a consumer specified in subsection (1) may be asserted against the assignee under this section only if the consumer has made a good faith attempt to obtain satisfaction from the seller or lessor with respect to the claim or defense and then only to the extent of the amount owing to the assignee with respect to the sale or lease of the property or services as to which the claim or defense arose at the time the assignee has notice of the claim or defense. Notice of the claim or defense may be given before the attempt specified in this subsection. Oral notice is effective unless the assignee requests written confirmation when or promptly after oral notice is given and the consumer fails to give the assignee written confirmation within the period of time, not less than 14 days, stated to the consumer when written confirmation is requested.

(3) For the purpose of determining the amount owing to the assignee with respect to the sale or lease:

(a) payments received by the assignee after the consolidation of two or more consumer credit sales, except pursuant to open-end credit, are deemed to have been applied first to the payment of the sales first made; if the sales consolidated arose from sales made on the same day, payments are deemed to have been applied first to the smallest sale; and

(b) payments received for an open-end credit account are deemed to have been applied first to the payment of finance charges in the order of their entry to the account and then to the payment of debts in the order in which the entries of the debts are made to the account.

(4) An agreement may not limit or waive the claims or defenses of a consumer under this section.

Comment

1. This section codifies a growing body of case law under UCC Section 9–206 to the effect that assignees take consumer paper subject to consumer claims and defenses. . . . The policy justifications for the section are to protect the consumer from the harshness of the holder in due course doctrine as well as to encourage financial institutions taking assignments of consumer paper to use discretion in dealing with sellers and lessors whose transactions give rise to an unusual percentage of consumer complaints. See Section 3.307.

2. The consumer, upon making a good faith attempt to obtain satisfaction from his seller or lessor, can assert his claim or defense against the assignee to the extent of the amount still owing to the assignee at the time the assignee learns of the claim or defense. If the assignee knows of the defense before any payments are made to him, the consumer can raise his claim or defense to the full amount of the assigned debt. Orderly procedures will necessitate some written record on the part of the assignee of the consumer's notification regarding his claim or defense, but the consumer ought to be able to rely on having given oral notification unless the assignee requests written confirmation. Hence, the assignee has the option of making his own written record upon receiving oral notice from the consumer or of requesting written notice from the consumer and allowing 14 days for the consumer to send his written confirmation. Subsection (3) uses the same tests for determining the amount owing on a debt as are used in Section 3.303.

§ 3.405 [Lender Subject to Claims and Defenses Arising from Sales and Leases]

(1) A lender, except the issuer of a lender credit card, who, with respect to a particular transaction, makes a consumer loan to enable a consumer to buy or lease from a particular seller or lessor property or services [, except primarily for an agricultural purpose,] is subject to all claims and defenses of the consumer against the seller or lessor arising from that sale or lease of the property or services if:

(a) the lender knows that the seller or lessor arranged for the extension of credit by the lender for a commission, brokerage, or referral fee;

(b) the lender is a person related to the seller or lessor, unless the relationship is remote or is not a factor in the transaction;

(c) the seller or lessor guarantees the loan or otherwise assumes the risk of loss by the lender upon the loan;

(d) the lender directly supplies the seller or lessor with the contract document used by the consumer to evidence the loan, and the seller or lessor has knowledge of the credit terms and participates in preparation of the document;

(e) the loan is conditioned upon the consumer's purchase or lease of the property or services from the particular seller or lessor, but the lender's payment of proceeds of the loan to the seller or lessor does not in itself establish that the loan was so conditioned; or

(f) the lender, before he makes the consumer loan, has knowledge or, from his course of dealing with the particular seller or lessor or his records, notice of substantial complaints by other buyers or lessees of the particular seller's or lessor's failure or refusal to perform his contracts with them and of the particular seller's or lessor's failure to remedy his defaults within a reasonable time after notice to him of the complaints.

(2) A claim or defense of a consumer specified in subsection (1) may be asserted against the lender under this section only if the consumer has made a good faith attempt to obtain satisfaction from the seller or lessor with respect to the claim or defense and then only to the extent of the amount owing to the lender with respect to the sale or lease of the property or services as to which the claim or defense arose at the time the lender has notice of the claim or defense. Notice of the claim or defense may be given before the attempt specified in this subsection. Oral notice is effective unless the lender requests written confirmation when or promptly after oral notice is given and the consumer fails to give the lender written confirmation within the period of time, not less than 14 days, stated to the consumer when written confirmation is requested.

(3) For the purpose of determining the amount owing to the lender with respect to the sale or lease:

(a) payments received by the lender after consolidation of two or more consumer loans, except pursuant to open-end credit, are deemed to have been applied first to the payment of the loans first made; if the loans consolidated arose from loans made on the same day, payments are deemed to have been applied first to the smallest loan; and

(b) payments received for an open-end credit account are deemed to have been applied first to the payment of finance charges in the order of their entry to the account and then to the payment of debts in the order in which the entries of the debts are made to the account.

(4) An agreement may not limit or waive the claims or defenses of a consumer under this section.

PART 5. HOME SOLICITATION SALES

§ 3.501 [Definition: "Home Solicitation Sale"]

"Home solicitation sale" means a consumer credit sale of goods or services, except primarily for an agricultural purpose, in which the seller or a person acting for him personally solicits the sale, and the buyer's agreement or offer to purchase is given to the seller or a person acting for him, at a residence. It does not include a sale made pursuant to a pre-existing open-end credit account with the seller or pursuant to prior negotiations between the parties at a business establishment at a fixed location where goods or services are offered or exhibited for sale, a transaction conducted and consummated entirely by mail or telephone, or a sale which is subject to the provisions of the Federal Truth in Lending Act on the consumer's right to rescind certain transactions. A sale that would be a home solicitation sale if credit were extended by the seller is nonetheless so because the goods or services are paid for in whole or in part by use of a credit card or by a consumer loan with respect to which the lender is subject to claims and defenses arising from the sale (Section 3.405), and the buyer has the same rights against the card issuer or lender that he has against the seller under this Part.

Comment

1. The Act singles out for special treatment consumer credit sales in which the buyer's order is given to the seller at a residence. An underlying consideration for Part 5 is the belief that in a significant proportion of such sales the consumer is induced to sign a sales contract by high pressure techniques. The Act recognizes that many buyers in such cases may be unwilling parties to the transaction and gives to them a limited right to cancel the sale. . . .

2. The definition of "home solicitation sales" differentiates between those types of transactions which have been the subject of particular abuse and those which have not. Although high pressure salesmanship can be practiced anywhere, the underlying theory of Section 3.501 is that the sale in the home is particularly susceptible to such methods. Two elements are required to bring a transaction within the definition. First, there must be personal solicitation at a residence. Second, the act of the buyer in binding himself by agreeing or offering to purchase, must also take place at a residence. The phrase "at a residence" rather than "in a residence" is used to prevent avoidance of the Act by the expedient of having the buyer sign the contract outside of, but in the immediate vicinity of, the home.

. . .

§ 3.502 [Buyer's Right to Cancel]

(1) Except as provided in subsection (5), in addition to any right otherwise to revoke an offer, the buyer may cancel a home solicitation sale until midnight of the third business day after the day on which the buyer signs an agreement or offer to purchase which complies with this Part.

(2) Cancellation occurs when the buyer gives written notice of cancellation to the seller at the address stated in the agreement or offer to purchase.

(3) Notice of cancellation, if given by mail, is given when it is properly addressed with postage prepaid and deposited in a mailbox.

(4) Notice of cancellation given by the buyer need not take a particular form and is sufficient if it indicates by any form of written expression the intention of the buyer not to be bound by the home solicitation sale.

(5) The buyer may not cancel a home solicitation sale if, by a separate dated and signed statement that is not as to its material provisions a printed form and describes an emergency requiring immediate remedy, the buyer requests the seller to provide goods or services without delay in order to safeguard the health, safety, or welfare of

natural persons or to prevent damage to property the buyer owns or for which he is responsible, and

(a) the seller in good faith makes a substantial beginning of performance of the contract before the buyer gives notice of cancellation, and

(b) in the case of goods, they cannot be returned to the seller in substantially as good condition as when received by the buyer.

§ 3.503 [Form of Agreement or Offer; Statement of Buyer's Rights]

(1) In a home solicitation sale, unless the buyer requests the seller to provide goods or services without delay in an emergency (subsection (5) of Section 3.502), the seller shall present to the buyer and obtain his signature to a written agreement or offer to purchase that designates as the date of the transaction the date on which the buyer actually signs and contains a statement of the buyer's rights that complies with subsection (2). A copy of any writing required by this subsection to be signed by the buyer, completed at least as to the date of the transaction and the name and mailing address of the seller, shall be given to the buyer at the time he signs the writing.

(2) The statement shall either:

(a) comply with any notice of cancellation or similar requirement of any trade regulation rule of the Federal Trade Commission which by its terms applies to the home solicitation sale; or

(b) appear under the conspicuous caption: "BUYER'S RIGHT TO CANCEL," and read as follows: "If you decide you do not want the goods or services, you may cancel this agreement by mailing a notice to the seller. The notice must say that you do not want the goods or services and must be mailed before midnight of the third business day after you sign this agreement. The notice must be mailed to:

____."

(insert name & mailing address of seller)

(3) Until the seller has complied with this section the buyer may cancel the home solicitation sale by notifying the seller in any manner and by any means of his intention to cancel.

§ 3.504 [Restoration of Down Payment]

(1) Within ten days after a notice of cancellation has been received by the seller or an offer to purchase has been otherwise revoked, the seller shall tender to the buyer any payments made by the buyer, any note or other evidence of indebtedness, and any goods traded in. A provision permitting the seller to keep all or any part of any goods traded in, payment, note, or evidence of indebtedness is in violation of this section and unenforceable.

(2) If the down payment includes goods traded in, the goods shall be tendered in substantially as good condition as when received by the seller. If the seller fails to tender the goods as provided by this section, the buyer may elect to recover an amount equal to the trade-in allowance stated in the agreement.

(3) Until the seller has complied with the obligations imposed by this section the buyer may retain possession of goods delivered to him by the seller and has a lien on the goods in his possession or control for any recovery to which he is entitled.

§ 3.505 [Duty of Buyer; No Compensation for Services Before Cancellation]

(1) Except as provided by the provisions on retention of goods by the buyer (subsection (3) of Section 3.504), and allowing for ordinary wear and tear or consumption of the goods contemplated by the transaction, within a reasonable time after a home solicitation sale has been cancelled or an offer to purchase revoked, the buyer upon demand shall tender to the seller any goods delivered by the seller pursuant to the sale, but he is not obligated to tender at any place other than his residence. If the seller fails to demand possession of goods within a reasonable time after cancellation or revocation, the goods become the property of the buyer without obligation to pay for them. For the purpose of this section, a reasonable time is presumed to be 40 days.

(2) The buyer shall take reasonable care of the goods in his possession before cancellation or revocation and for a reasonable time thereafter, during which time the goods are otherwise at the seller's risk.

(3) If a home solicitation sale is cancelled, the seller is not entitled to compensation for any services he performed pursuant to it.

ARTICLE 4. INSURANCE

PART 1. INSURANCE IN GENERAL

§ 4.102 [Scope [; Relation to Credit Insurance Act; Applicability to Parties]]

[(1)] This Article applies to insurance provided or to be provided in relation to a consumer credit transaction.

[(2) This Article supplements and does not repeal the Credit Insurance Act but to the extent of inconsistency between this Act and the Credit Insurance Act this Act controls. The provisions of this Act concerning administrative controls, liabilities, and penalties do not apply to persons acting as insurers, and the similar provisions of the Credit Insurance Act do not apply to creditors and debtors.]

Comment

. . .

The scope of this Article is broader than that of the NAIC Model Act.

. . .

§ 4.103 [Definition[s]: "Consumer Credit Insurance" [; "Credit Insurance Act"]]

In this Act:

[(1)] "Consumer credit insurance" means insurance, except insurance on property, by which the satisfaction of debt in whole or in part is a benefit provided, but does not include

(a) insurance provided in relation to a consumer credit transaction in which a payment is scheduled more than ten years after the extension of credit;

(b) insurance issued by an insurer as an isolated transaction not related to an agreement or plan for insuring consumers of or from the creditor; or

(c) insurance indemnifying the creditor against loss due to the consumer's default.

[(2) "Credit Insurance Act" means [NAIC Model Act, or any similar statute].]

§ 4.104 [Creditor's Provision of and Charge for Insurance; Excess Amount of Charge]

(1) Except as otherwise provided in this Article and subject to the provisions on additional charges (Section 2.501) and maximum finance charges (Parts 2 and 4 of Article 2), a creditor may agree to provide

insurance, and may contract for and receive a charge for insurance separate from and in addition to other charges. A creditor need not make a separate charge for insurance provided or required by him. This Act does not authorize the issuance of the insurance prohibited under any statute, or rule thereunder, governing the business of insurance.

(2) The excess amount of a charge for insurance provided for in agreements in violation of this Article is an excess charge for purposes of the provisions of the Article on Remedies and Penalties (Article 5) as to effect of violations on rights of parties (Section 5.201) and of the provisions of the Article on Administration (Article 6) as to civil actions by the Administrator (Section 6.113).

§ 4.105 [Conditions Applying to Insurance to Be Provided by Creditor]

If a creditor agrees with a consumer to provide insurance:

(1) the insurance shall be evidenced by an individual policy or certificate of insurance delivered to the consumer, or mailed to him at his address as stated by him, within 30 days after the term of the insurance commences under the agreement between the creditor and consumer, or the creditor shall promptly notify the consumer of any failure or delay in providing the insurance; and

(2) the creditor shall pay to the consumer or his estate all proceeds of consumer credit or property insurance received by the creditor in excess of the amount to which the creditor is entitled within ten days after receipt by the creditor of the proceeds.

§ 4.106 [Unconscionability]

(1) In applying the provisions of this Act on unconscionability (Sections 5.108 and 6.111) to a separate charge for insurance, consideration shall be given, among other factors, to:

(a) potential benefits to the consumer including the satisfaction of his obligations;

(b) the creditor's need for the protection provided by the insurance; and

(c) the relation between the amount and terms of credit granted and the insurance benefits provided.

(2) If consumer credit insurance otherwise complies with this Article and other applicable law, neither the amount nor the term of the insurance nor the amount of a charge therefor is in itself unconscionable.

Comment

It may be shown that an agreement about insurance, like other terms of a consumer credit contract, is unconscionable, and the effects are those specified in Sections 5.108 and 6.111. However, it is the intent of this section that the issue be judged in relation to the particular risks insured. The section lists only some of the factors to be considered, and indicates that a balancing of benefits, needs, and costs is required. In general, the creditor's need for insurance protection and the consumer's potential benefit are more patent in connection with extensions of credit that are substantial as to amounts and periods; the expense of providing exceptional coverage is suspect in relation to relatively small extensions of credit. The relation between the credit terms and the insurance terms must be taken into account in applying this section.

§ 4.107 [Maximum Charge by Creditor for Insurance]

(1) Except as provided in subsection (2), if a creditor contracts for or receives a separate charge for insurance, the amount charged to the consumer for the insurance may not exceed the premium to be charged by the insurer, as computed at the time the charge to the consumer is determined, conforming to any rate filings required by law and made by the insurer with the [Commissioner] of Insurance.

(2) A creditor who provides consumer credit insurance in relation to open-end credit may calculate the charge to the consumer in each billing cycle by applying the current premium rate to the balance in the manner permitted with respect to finance charges by the provisions on finance charge for consumer credit sales pursuant to open-end credit (Section 2.202).

§ 4.108 [Refund Required; Amount]

(1) Upon prepayment in full of a consumer credit transaction other than a consumer lease by the proceeds of consumer credit insurance, the consumer or his estate is entitled to a refund of any portion of a separate charge for insurance which by reason of prepayment is retained by the creditor or returned to him by the insurer, unless the charge was computed from time to time on the basis of the balances of the consumer's account.

(2) This Article does not require a creditor to grant a refund to the consumer if all refunds due to him under this Article amount to less than $1 and, except as provided in subsection (1), does not require the creditor to account to the consumer for any portion of a separate charge for insurance because:

(a) the insurance is terminated by performance of the insurer's obligation;

(b) the creditor pays or accounts for premiums to the insurer in amounts and at times determined by the agreement between them; or

(c) the creditor receives directly or indirectly under any policy of insurance a gain or advantage not prohibited by law.

(3) Except as provided in subsection (2), the creditor shall promptly make or cause to be made an appropriate refund to the consumer with respect to any separate charge made to him for insurance if:

(a) the insurance is not provided or is provided for a shorter term than that for which the charge to the consumer for insurance was computed; or

(b) the insurance terminates before the end of the term for which it was written because of prepayment in full or otherwise.

(4) A refund required by subsection (3) is appropriate as to amount if it is computed according to a method prescribed or approved by the [Commissioner] of Insurance or a formula filed by the insurer with the [Commissioner] of Insurance at least 30 days before the consumer's right to a refund becomes determinable, unless the method or formula is employed after the [Commissioner] of Insurance notifies the insurer that he disapproves it.

Comment

1. Subsection (1) concerns a premium for consumer credit insurance, or any part of it, that is not treated by the insurer as earned, even though the insurer has paid benefits for which the premium charge was made. If the premium was the subject of a separate charge to the consumer, a refund must be made. Making the refund is not practicable, however, and is not required, if the charge has been computed on the consumer's outstanding balances. Subsection (2)(a) recognizes that the insurer may, upon performance of its obligation, properly treat the premium as earned.

2. Subsection (2)(c) permits a creditor to derive from consumer credit insurance gains and advantages not prohibited by law such as dividends and refunds resulting from favorable mortality or morbidity experience with respect to insured consumers, and is predicated on the following conclusions: (1) although the gains and advantages may be large to the creditor, they are relatively insignificant to each insured consumer and the calculating, clerical, and mailing costs of returning them to insured consumers would be unreasonably disproportionate to the amounts involved, and (2) the requirement of Article 4 that premiums for consumer credit insurance be reasonable in relation to benefits (Section 4.203), if properly enforced by the State Insurance [Commissioner], will preclude the possibility of the use of consumer credit insurance as a device by creditors for concealing hidden charges from consumers.

. . .

4. A consumer is entitled to a refund rather than a credit in the event of a required rebate of any separate charge for insurance. This precludes a creditor from holding a rebate until the contract is sufficiently paid down to

have it constitute a prepayment in full which, particularly in long term contracts such as to finance a mobile home, gives the creditor free use of the consumer's money for a substantial period of time.

§ 4.109 [Existing Insurance; Choice of Insurer]

If a creditor requires insurance, upon notice to him the consumer has the option of providing the required insurance through an existing policy of insurance owned or controlled by the consumer, or through a policy to be obtained and paid for by the consumer, but the creditor for reasonable cause may decline the insurance provided by the consumer.

§ 4.110 [Charge for Insurance in Connection with a Deferral, Refinancing, or Consolidation; Duplicate Charges]

(1) A creditor may not contract for or receive a separate charge for insurance in connection with a deferral (Section 2.503), a refinancing (Section 2.504), or a consolidation (Section 2.505), unless:

(a) the consumer agrees at or before the time of the deferral, refinancing, or consolidation that the charge may be made;

(b) the consumer is or is to be provided with insurance for an amount or a term, or insurance of a kind, in addition to that to which he would have been entitled had there been no deferral, refinancing, or consolidation;

(c) the consumer receives a refund or credit on account of any unexpired term of existing insurance in the amount required if the insurance were terminated (Section 4.108); and

(d) the charge does not exceed the amount permitted by this Article (Section 4.107).

(2) A creditor may not contract for or receive a separate charge for insurance which duplicates insurance with respect to which the creditor has previously contracted for or received a separate charge.

PART 2. CONSUMER CREDIT INSURANCE

§ 4.201 [Term of Insurance]

(1) Consumer credit insurance provided by a creditor may be subject to the furnishing of evidence of insurability satisfactory to the insurer. Whether or not the evidence is required, the term of the insurance shall commence no later than when the consumer becomes obligated to the creditor or when the consumer applies for the insurance, whichever is later, except as follows:

(a) if any required evidence of insurability is not furnished until more than 30 days after the term otherwise would commence, the term may commence on the date the insurer determines the evidence to be satisfactory; or

(b) if the creditor provides insurance not previously provided covering debts previously created, the term may commence on the effective date of the policy.

(2) The originally scheduled term of consumer credit insurance shall extend at least until the due date of the last scheduled payment of the debt, except as follows:

(a) if the insurance relates to an open-end credit account, the term need extend only until payment of the debt under the account and may be sooner terminated after at least 30 days' notice to the consumer; or

(b) if the consumer is informed in writing that the insurance will be written for a specified shorter time, the term need extend only until the end of the specified time.

(3) The term of consumer credit insurance may not extend more than 15 days after the originally scheduled due date of the last scheduled payment of the debt, unless it is extended without additional cost to the consumer or as an incident to a deferral, refinancing, or consolidation.

§ 4.202 [Amount of Insurance]

(1) Except as provided in subsection (2):

(a) in the case of consumer credit insurance providing life coverage, the amount of insurance may not initially exceed the debt and, if the debt is payable in instalments, may not exceed at any time the greater of the scheduled or actual amount of the debt; or

(b) in the case of any other consumer credit insurance, the total amount of periodic benefits payable may not exceed the total of scheduled unpaid instalments of the debt, and the amount of any periodic benefit may not exceed the original amount of debt divided by the number of periodic instalments in which it is payable.

(2) If consumer credit insurance is provided in connection with an open-end credit account, the amounts payable as insurance benefits may be reasonably commensurate with the amount of debt as it exists from time to time. If consumer credit insurance is provided in connection with a commitment to grant credit in the future, the amounts payable as insurance benefits may be reasonably commensurate with the total from time to time of the amount of debt and the amount of the commitment. If the debt or the commitment is primarily for an agricultural purpose and there is no regular schedule of payments, the amounts payable as insurance benefits may equal the total of the initial amount of debt and the amount of the commitment.

Comment

. . .

3. Experience has demonstrated that limitations of these kinds are essential to the effectiveness of the requirement of Section 4.203(2) that premium rates be not unreasonable in relation to the benefits provided by consumer credit insurance.

§ 4.203 [Filing and Approval of Rates and Forms]

(1) A creditor may not use a form or a schedule of premium rates or charges, the filing of which is required by this section, if the [Commissioner] of Insurance has disapproved the form or schedule and has notified the insurer of his disapproval. A creditor may not use a form or schedule unless:

(a) the form or schedule has been on file with the [Commissioner] of Insurance for 30 days, or has earlier been approved by him; and

(b) the insurer has complied with this section with respect to the insurance.

(2) Except as provided in subsection (3), all policies, certificates of insurance, notices of proposed insurance, applications for insurance, endorsements, and riders relating to consumer credit insurance delivered or issued for delivery in this State, and the schedules of premium rates or charges pertaining thereto, shall be filed by the insurer with the [Commissioner] of Insurance. Within 30 days after the filing of any form or schedule, he shall disapprove it if the premium rates or charges are unreasonable in relation to the benefits provided under the form, or if the form contains provisions which are unjust, unfair, inequitable, or deceptive, encourage misrepresentation of the coverage, or are contrary to any provision of the [Insurance Code] or of any rule or regulation promulgated thereunder.

(3) If a group policy of consumer credit insurance has been delivered in another state, the forms to be filed by the insurer with the [Commissioner] of Insurance are the group certificates and notices of proposed insurance. He shall approve them if:

(a) they provide the information that would be required if the group policy were delivered in this State; and

(b) the applicable premium rates or charges do not exceed those established by his rules or regulations.

Comment

. . . Unlike the NAIC Model Act which is directed primarily to insurers, this section is directed to both creditors and insurers. Moreover, in its formulation as to the relationship of premium rates and charges to the benefits provided, subsection (2) follows New York Insurance Law Section 154.7. That provision, as construed by the New York Court of Appeals in Old Republic Life Insurance Company v. Wikler, 9 N.Y.2d 524, 215 N.Y.S.2d 481, 175 N.E.2d 147 (1961), gives the New York Superintendent of Insurance ample power as to premium rates for credit life and accident and health insurance. Doubt, whether reasonable or not, has been expressed whether equivalent power is conferred by the corresponding formulation of Section 7B of the NAIC Model Act.

. . .

PART 3. PROPERTY AND LIABILITY INSURANCE

§ 4.301 [Property Insurance]

(1) A creditor may not contract for or receive a separate charge for insurance against loss of or damage to property, unless:

(a) the insurance covers a substantial risk of loss of or damage to property related to the credit transaction;

(b) the amount, terms, and conditions of the insurance are reasonable in relation to the character and value of the property insured or to be insured; and

(c) the term of the insurance is reasonable in relation to the terms of credit.

(2) The term of the insurance is reasonable if it is customary and does not extend substantially beyond a scheduled maturity.

(3) With respect to a transaction, except pursuant to open-end credit, a creditor may not contract for or receive a separate charge for insurance against loss of or damage to property, unless the amount financed exclusive of charges for the insurance is $300 or more and the value of the property is $300 or more.

(4) With respect to a transaction pursuant to open-end credit, the Administrator may adopt rules consistent with the principles set out in subsections (1) and (2) prescribing whether, and the conditions under which, a creditor may contract for or receive a separate charge for insurance against loss of or damage to property.

(5) The amounts of $300 in subsection (3) are subject to change pursuant to the provisions on adjustment of dollar amounts (Section 1.106).

§ 4.302 [Insurance on Creditor's Interest Only]

If a creditor contracts for or receives a separate charge for insurance against loss of or damage to property, the risk of loss or damage not willfully caused by the consumer is on the consumer only to the extent of any deficiency in the effective coverage of the insurance, even though the insurance covers only the interest of the creditor.

§ 4.303 [Liability Insurance]

A creditor may not contract for or receive a separate charge for insurance against liability unless the insurance covers a substantial risk of liability arising out of the ownership or use of property related to the credit transaction.

ARTICLE 5. REMEDIES AND PENALTIES

PART 1. LIMITATIONS ON CREDITORS' REMEDIES

§ 5.102 [Scope]

This Part applies to actions or other proceedings to enforce rights arising from consumer credit transactions, to extortionate extensions of credit (Section 5.107), and to unconscionability (Section 5.108).

§ 5.103 [Restrictions on Deficiency Judgments]

(1) This section applies to a deficiency on a consumer credit sale of goods or services and on a consumer loan in which the lender is subject to claims and defenses arising from sales and leases (Section 3.405). A consumer is not liable for a deficiency unless the creditor had disposed of the goods in good faith and in a commercially reasonable manner.

(2) If the seller repossesses or voluntarily accepts surrender of goods that were the subject of the sale and in which he has a security interest, the consumer is not personally liable to the seller for the unpaid balance of the debt arising from the sale of a commercial unit of goods of which the cash sale price was $1,750 or less, and the seller is not obligated to resell the collateral unless the consumer has paid 60 per cent or more of the cash price and has not signed after default a statement renouncing his rights in the collateral.

(3) If the seller repossesses or voluntarily accepts surrender of goods that were not the subject of the sale but in which he has a security interest to secure a debt arising from a sale of goods or services or a combined sale of goods and services and the cash price of the sale was $1,750 or less, the consumer is not personally liable to the seller for the unpaid balance of the debt arising from the sale, and the seller's duty to dispose of the collateral is governed by the provisions on disposition of collateral (Part 5 of Article 9) of the Uniform Commercial Code.

(4) If the lender takes possession or voluntarily accepts surrender of goods in which he has a purchase money security interest to secure a debt arising from a consumer loan in which the lender is subject to claims and defenses arising from sales and leases (Section 3.405) and the net proceeds of the loan paid to or for the benefit of the consumer were $1,750 or less, the consumer is not personally liable to the lender for the unpaid balance of the debt arising from that loan and the lender's duty to dispose of the collateral is governed by the provisions on disposition of collateral (Part 5 of Article 9) of the Uniform Commercial Code.

(5) For the purpose of determining the unpaid balance of consolidated debts or debts pursuant to open-end credit, the allocation of payments to a debt shall be determined in the same manner as provided for determining the amount of debt secured by various security interests (Section 3.303).

(6) The consumer may be held liable in damages to the creditor if the consumer has wrongfully damaged the collateral or if, after default and demand, the consumer has wrongfully failed to make the collateral available to the creditor.

(7) If the creditor elects to bring an action against the consumer for a debt arising from a consumer credit sale of goods or services or from a consumer loan in which the lender is subject to claims and defenses arising from sales and leases (Section 3.405), when under this section he would not be entitled to a deficiency judgment if he took possession of the collateral, and obtains judgment:

(a) he may not take possession of the collateral, and

(b) the collateral is not subject to levy or sale on execution or similar proceedings pursuant to the judgment.

(8) The amounts of $1,750 in subsections (2), (3) and (4) are subject to change pursuant to the provisions on adjustment of dollar amounts (Section 1.106).

Comment

1. Where there has been a default with respect to a secured consumer credit transaction, the rights of the creditor and consumer are controlled by Part 5 (Default) of UCC Article 9 [U.C.C. § 9–501 et seq.], except to the extent that such rights are changed by this Act. . . .

2. The provisions of the UCC . . . are modified to some extent by this section with respect to proceedings to enforce rights arising from consumer credit sales and consumer loans in which the lender is subject to claims and defenses arising from sales and leases (Section 3.405). For both types of transactions, this section adopts the position of that line of cases under the UCC that directly or indirectly deny the creditor a deficiency if the creditor has not disposed of the collateral in good faith and in a commercially reasonable manner. See, e.g., Atlas Thrift Co. v. Horan, 27 Cal.App.3d 999, 104 Cal.Rptr. 315 (Cal.Ct.App.3d Dist.1972).

§ 5.104 [No Garnishment Before Judgment]

Before entry of judgment in an action against a consumer for debt arising from a consumer credit transaction, the creditor may not attach unpaid earnings of the consumer by garnishment or like proceedings.

§ 5.105 [Limitation on Garnishment]

(1) For purposes of this Part:

(a) "disposable earnings" means that part of the earnings of an individual remaining after the deduction from those earnings of amounts required by law to be withheld; and

(b) "garnishment" means any legal or equitable procedure through which earnings of an individual are required to be withheld for payment of a debt.

(2) The maximum part of the aggregate disposable earnings of an individual for any workweek which is subjected to garnishment to enforce payment of a judgment arising from a consumer credit transaction may not exceed the lesser of:

(a) 25 per cent of his disposable earnings for that week, or

(b) the amount by which his disposable earnings for that week exceed 40 times the Federal minimum hourly wage prescribed by Section 6(a)(1) of the Fair Labor Standards Act of 1938, U.S.C. tit. 29, § 206(a)(1), in effect at the time the earnings are payable.

In case of earnings for a pay period other than a week, the Administrator shall prescribe by rule a multiple of the Federal minimum hourly wage equivalent in effect to that set forth in paragraph (b).

(3) No court may make, execute, or enforce an order or process in violation of this section.

(4) At any time after entry of a judgment in favor of a creditor in an action against a consumer for debt arising from a consumer credit transaction, the consumer may file with the court his verified application for an order exempting from garnishment pursuant to that judgment, for an appropriate period of time, a greater portion or all of his aggregate disposable earnings for a workweek or other applicable pay period than is provided for in subsection (2). He shall designate in the application the portion of his earnings not exempt from garnishment under this section and other law, the period of time for which the additional exemption is sought, describe the judgment with respect to which the application is made, and state that the designated portion as well as his earnings that are exempt by law are necessary for the maintenance of him or a family supported wholly or partly by the earnings. Upon filing a sufficient application under this subsection, the court may issue any temporary order necessary under the circumstances to stay enforcement of the judgment by garnishment, shall set a hearing on the application not less than [five] nor more than [ten] days after the date of filing of the application, and shall cause notice of the application and the hearing date to be served on the judgment creditor or his attorney of record. At the hearing, if it appears to the court that all or any portion of the earnings sought to be additionally exempt are necessary for the maintenance of the consumer or a family supported wholly or partly by the earnings of the

consumer for all or any part of the time requested in the application, the court shall issue an order granting the application to that extent; otherwise it shall deny the application. The order is subject to modification or vacation upon further application of any party to it upon a showing of changed circumstances after a hearing upon notice to all interested parties.

§ 5.106 [No Discharge From Employment for Garnishment]

An employer may not discharge an employee for the reason that a creditor of the employee has subjected or attempted to subject unpaid earnings of the employee to garnishment or like proceedings directed to the employer for the purpose of paying a judgment arising from a consumer credit transaction.

§ 5.107 [Extortionate Extensions of Credit]

(1) If it is the understanding of the creditor and the consumer at the time an extension of credit is made that delay in making repayment or failure to make repayment could result in the use of violence or other criminal means to cause harm to the person, reputation, or property of any person, the repayment of the extension of credit is unenforceable through civil judicial processes against the consumer.

(2) If it is shown that an extension of credit was made at an annual rate exceeding 45 per cent calculated according to the actuarial method and that the creditor then had a reputation for the use or threat of use of violence or other criminal means to cause harm to the person, reputation, or property of any person to collect extensions of credit or to punish the non-repayment thereof, there is prima facie evidence that the extension of credit was unenforceable under subsection (1).

§ 5.108 [Unconscionability; Inducement by Unconscionable Conduct; Unconscionable Debt Collection]

(1) With respect to a transaction that is, gives rise to, or leads the debtor to believe will give rise to, a consumer credit transaction, if the court as a matter of law finds:

(a) the agreement or transaction to have been unconscionable at the time it was made, or to have been induced by unconscionable conduct, the court may refuse to enforce the agreement; or

(b) any term or part of the agreement or transaction to have been unconscionable at the time it was made, the court may refuse to enforce the agreement, enforce the remainder of the agreement without the unconscionable term or part, or so limit the application of any unconscionable term or part as to avoid any unconscionable result.

(2) With respect to a consumer credit transaction, if the court as a matter of law finds that a person has engaged in, is engaging in, or is likely to engage in unconscionable conduct in collecting a debt arising from that transaction, the court may grant an injunction and award the consumer any actual damages he has sustained.

(3) If it is claimed or appears to the court that the agreement or transaction or any term or part thereof may be unconscionable, or that a person has engaged in, is engaging in, or is likely to engage in unconscionable conduct in collecting a debt, the parties shall be afforded a reasonable opportunity to present evidence as to the setting, purpose, and effect of the agreement or transaction or term or part thereof, or of the conduct, to aid the court in making the determination.

(4) In applying subsection (1), consideration shall be given to each of the following factors, among others, as applicable:

(a) belief by the seller, lessor, or lender at the time a transaction is entered into that there is no reasonable probability of payment in full of the obligation by the consumer or debtor;

(b) in the case of a consumer credit sale or consumer lease, knowledge by the seller or lessor at the time of the sale or lease of the inability of the consumer to receive substantial benefits from the property or services sold or leased;

(c) in the case of a consumer credit sale or consumer lease, gross disparity between the price of the property or services sold or leased and the value of the property or services measured by the price at which similar property or services are readily obtainable in credit transactions by like consumers;

(d) the fact that the creditor contracted for or received separate charges for insurance with respect to a consumer credit sale or consumer loan with the effect of making the sale or loan, considered as a whole, unconscionable; and

(e) the fact that the seller, lessor, or lender has knowingly taken advantage of the inability of the consumer or debtor reasonably to protect his interests by reason of physical or mental infirmities, ignorance, illiteracy, inability to understand the language of the agreement, or similar factors.

(5) In applying subsection (2), consideration shall be given to each of the following factors, among others, as applicable:

(a) using or threatening to use force, violence, or criminal prosecution against the consumer or members of his family;

(b) communicating with the consumer or a member of his family at frequent intervals or at unusual hours or under other circumstances so that it is a reasonable inference that the primary purpose of the communication was to harass the consumer;

(c) using fraudulent, deceptive, or misleading representations such as a communication which simulates legal process or which gives the appearance of being authorized, issued, or approved by a government, governmental agency, or attorney at law when it is not, or threatening or attempting to enforce a right with knowledge or reason to know that the right does not exist;

(d) causing or threatening to cause injury to the consumer's reputation or economic status by disclosing information affecting the consumer's reputation for credit-worthiness with knowledge or reason to know that the information is false; communicating with the consumer's employer before obtaining a final judgment against the consumer, except as permitted by statute or to verify the consumer's employment; disclosing to a person, with knowledge or reason to know that the person does not have a legitimate business need for the information, or in any way prohibited by statute, information affecting the consumer's credit or other reputation; or disclosing information concerning the existence of a debt known to be disputed by the consumer without disclosing that fact; and

(e) engaging in conduct with knowledge that like conduct has been restrained or enjoined by a court in a civil action by the Administrator against any person pursuant to the provisions on injunctions against fraudulent or unconscionable agreements or conduct (Section 6.111).

(6) If in an action in which unconscionability is claimed the court finds unconscionability pursuant to subsection (1) or (2), the court shall award reasonable fees to the attorney for the consumer or debtor. If the court does not find unconscionability and the consumer or debtor claiming unconscionability has brought or maintained an action he knew to be groundless, the court shall award reasonable fees to the attorney for the party against whom the claim is made. In determining attorney's fees, the amount of the recovery on behalf of the consumer is not controlling.

(7) The remedies of this section are in addition to remedies otherwise available for the same conduct under law other than this Act, but double recovery of actual damages may not be had.

(8) For the purpose of this section, a charge or practice expressly permitted by this Act is not in itself unconscionable.

Comment

1. Subsections (1) and (3) are derived in significant part from UCC Section 2–302. Subsection (1), as does UCC Section 2–302, provides that a court can refuse to enforce or can adjust an agreement or part of an agreement that was unconscionable on its face at the time it was made. However, many agreements are not in and of themselves unconscionable according to their terms, but they would never have been entered into by a consumer if unconscionable means had not been employed to induce the consumer to

agree to the contract. It would be a frustration of the policy against unconscionable contracts for a creditor to be able to utilize unconscionable acts or practices to obtain an agreement. Consequently subsection (1) also gives to the court the power to refuse to enforce an agreement if it finds as a matter of law that it was induced by unconscionable conduct. Finally, subsection (1) includes provisions for court determination of unconscionability in a transaction that a consumer is led to believe will give rise to a consumer credit transaction so that, for example, a seller cannot bind the consumer to a short term sale contract payable in a lump sum on the assurance the seller will secure financing for the consumer, and then inform the consumer financing is unavailable and keep the downpayment or goods traded in as a penalty for non-payment.

In subsection (3) the omission of the adjective "commercial" found in UCC Section 2–302 from the provision concerning the presentation of evidence as to the conduct's or contract's "setting, purpose, and effect" is deliberate. Unlike the UCC, this section is concerned only with transactions involving consumers, and the relevant standard of conduct for purposes of this section is not that which might be acceptable as between knowledgeable merchants but rather that which measures acceptable conduct on the part of a businessman toward a consumer.

2. Subsection (2) provides a consumer remedy for unconscionable conduct in the collection of consumer credit debts. In recent years, there has been much legislative activity in this area. In subjecting this type of creditor conduct to the concept of unconscionability, this section provides a more flexible device for halting multifarious activities than the specific and somewhat rigid treatment contained in other legislation, and follows the lead of Section 6.111 of this Act which affords the Administrator the means to deal with this type of practice. Indeed this section considered as a whole confers on the consumer the ability to obtain relief in basically the same situations the Administrator is authorized to seek relief under Section 6.111, although not necessarily under the same conditions, e.g., no course of conduct is required. The section is not exclusive, however; subsection (7) stipulates that the remedies of this section are in addition to remedies otherwise available for the same conduct under law other than this Act so as to preserve, for example, the developing remedy for abusive debt collection in tort.

3. This section is intended to make it possible for the courts to police conduct which is, and contracts or clauses which are found to be unconscionable. The basic test is whether, in the light of the background and setting of the market, the needs of the particular trade or case, and the condition of the particular parties to the conduct or contract, the conduct involved is, or the contract or clauses involved are so one-sided as to be unconscionable under the circumstances existing at the time the conduct occurs or is threatened or at the time of the making of the contract. The principle is one of the prevention of oppression and unfair surprise and not the disturbance of reasonable allocation of risks or reasonable advantage because of superior bargaining power or position. The particular facts involved in each case are of utmost importance since certain conduct, contracts or contractual provisions may be unconscionable in some situations but not in others. . . .

4. Subsections (4) and (5) list a number of specific factors to be considered on the issue of unconscionability. It is impossible to anticipate all of

the factors and considerations which may support a conclusion of unconscionability in a given instance so the listing is not exclusive. The following are illustrative of individual transactions which would entitle a consumer to relief under this section:

Under subsection (4)(a), a sale of goods to a low income consumer without expectation of payment but with the expectation of repossessing the goods sold and reselling them at a profit;

Under subsection (4)(b), a sale to a Spanish speaking laborer-bachelor of an English language encyclopedia set, or the sale of two expensive vacuum cleaners to two poor families sharing the same apartment and one rug;

Under subsection (4)(c), a home solicitation sale of a set of cookware or flatware to a housewife for $375 in an area where a set of comparable quality is readily available on credit in stores for $125 or less;

Under subsection (4)(3), a sale of goods on terms known by the seller to be disadvantageous to the consumer where the written agreement is in English, the consumer is literate only in Spanish, the transaction was negotiated orally in Spanish by the seller's salesman, and the written agreement was neither translated nor explained to the consumer, but the mere fact a consumer has little education and cannot read or write and must sign with an "X" is not itself determinative of unconscionability;

Under subsection (5)(a) and (c), threatening that the creditor will have the consumer thrown in jail and her welfare checks stopped if the debt is not paid.

5. Since the remedies of this section are non-monetary in nature except for the ability to recover actual damages for unconscionable debt collection, subsection (6) authorizes an award of reasonable attorneys fees to the successful consumer or debtor. However, to discourage litigation seeking exculpation from merely bad bargains, provision is also made for recovery by a creditor if the court does not find unconscionability and the consumer's or debtor's action was known by the consumer or debtor to be groundless.

6. Subsection (8) prohibits a finding that a charge or practice expressly permitted by this Act is in itself unconscionable. However, even though a practice or charge is authorized by this Act, the totality of a particular creditor's conduct may show that the practice or charge is part of unconscionable conduct. Therefore, in determining unconscionability, the creditor's total conduct, including that part of his conduct which is in accordance with the provisions of this Act, may be considered.

§ 5.109 [Default]

An agreement of the parties to a consumer credit transaction with respect to default on the part of the consumer is enforceable only to the extent that:

(1) the consumer fails to make a payment as required by agreement; or

(2) the prospect of payment, performance, or realization of collateral is significantly impaired; the burden of establishing the prospect of significant impairment is on the creditor.

§ 5.110 [Notice of Consumer's Right to Cure]

(1) With respect to a consumer credit transaction, after a consumer has been in default for ten days for failure to make a required payment and has not voluntarily surrendered possession of goods that are collateral, a creditor may give the consumer the notice described in this section. A creditor gives notice to the consumer under this section when he delivers the notice to the consumer or mails the notice to him at his residence (subsection (6) of Section 1.201).

(2) Except as provided in subsection (3), the notice shall be in writing and conspicuously state: the name, address, and telephone number of the creditor to whom payment is to be made, a brief identification of the credit transaction, the consumer's right to cure the default, and the amount of payment and date by which payment must be made to cure the default. A notice in substantially the following form complies with this subsection:

(name, address, and telephone number of creditor)

(account number, if any)

(brief identification of credit transaction)

(date) is the LAST DAY FOR PAYMENT (amount) is the AMOUNT NOW DUE

You are late in making your payment(s). If you pay the AMOUNT NOW DUE (above) by the LAST DAY FOR PAYMENT (above), you may continue with the contract as though you were not late. If you do not pay by that date, we may exercise our rights under the law.

If you are late again in making your payments, we may exercise our rights without sending you another notice like this one. If you have questions, write or telephone the creditor promptly.

(3) If the consumer credit transaction is an insurance premium loan, the notice shall conform to the requirements of subsection (2) and a notice in substantially the form specified in that subsection complies with this subsection, except for the following:

(a) in lieu of a brief identification of the credit transaction, the notice shall identify the transaction as an insurance premium loan and each insurance policy or contract that may be cancelled;

(b) in lieu of the statement in the form of notice specified in subsection (2) that the creditor may exercise his rights under the law, the statement that each policy or contract identified in the notice may be cancelled; and

(c) the last paragraph of the form of notice specified in subsection (2) shall be omitted.

Comment

. . .

3. The forms of notice specified in this section are not mandatory. However, Section 5.111 provides that a default consisting of a failure to make a required payment may be cured by the consumer if he makes that payment before the expiration of the minimum period prescribed after written notice of his default and that prior to this time the creditor may not proceed against goods that are collateral or accelerate the maturity of the unpaid debt. This provision prevents the practice of some unscrupulous creditors who repossess collateral when a payment is only a day or two late. It also gives the average consumer the opportunity to rehabilitate his account, bring a billing error to the attention of or present a breach of warranty claim to the creditor, or negotiate a refinancing or deferral arrangement that may be required by a change in his financial circumstances.

. . .

§ 5.111 [Cure of Default]

(1) With respect to a consumer credit transaction, except as provided in subsection (2), after a default consisting only of the consumer's failure to make a required payment, a creditor, because of that default, may neither accelerate maturity of the unpaid balance of the obligation, nor take possession of or otherwise enforce a security interest in goods that are collateral until 20 days after a notice of the consumer's right to cure (Section 5.110) is given, nor, with respect to an insurance premium loan, give notice of cancellation as provided in subsection (4) until 13 days after a notice of the consumer's right to cure (Section 5.110) is given. Until expiration of the minimum applicable period after the notice is given, the consumer may cure all defaults consisting of a failure to make the required payment by tendering the amount of all unpaid sums due at the time of the tender, without acceleration, plus any unpaid delinquency or deferral charges. Cure restores the consumer to his rights under the agreement as though the defaults had not occurred.

(2) With respect to defaults on the same obligation other than an insurance premium loan and subject to subsection (1), after a creditor has once given a notice of consumer's right to cure (Section 5.110), this section gives the consumer no right to cure and imposes no limitation on the creditor's right to proceed against the consumer or goods that are collateral. For the purpose of this section, in open-end credit, the obligation is the unpaid balance of the account and there is no right to cure and no limitation on the creditor's rights with respect to a default that occurs within 12 months after an earlier default as to which a creditor has given a notice of consumer's right to cure (Section 5.110).

(3) This section and the provisions on waiver, agreements to forego rights, and settlement of claims (Section 1.107) do not prohibit a

consumer from voluntarily surrendering possession of goods which are collateral and the creditor from thereafter accelerating maturity of the obligation and enforcing the obligation and his security interest in the goods at any time after default.

(4) If a default on an insurance premium loan is not cured, the lender may give notice of cancellation of each insurance policy or contract to be cancelled. If given, the notice of cancellation shall be in writing and given to the insurer who issued the policy or contract and to the insured. The insurer, within two business days after receipt of the notice of cancellation together with a copy of the insurance premium loan agreement if not previously given to him, shall give any notice of cancellation required by the policy contract, or law and, within ten business days after the effective date of the cancellation, pay to the lender any premium unearned on the policy or contract as of that effective date. Within ten business days after receipt of the unearned premium, the lender shall pay to the consumer indebted upon the insurance premium loan any excess of the unearned premium received over the amount owing by the consumer upon the insurance premium loan.

§ 5.112 [Creditor's Right to Take Possession After Default]

Upon default by a consumer with respect to a consumer credit transaction, unless the consumer voluntarily surrenders possession of the collateral to the creditor, the creditor may take possession of the collateral without judicial process only if possession can be taken without entry into a dwelling and without the use of force or other breach of the peace.

Comment

1. Under Section 9–503 of the UCC a secured creditor has the right to take possession of collateral without resorting to legal process if he can do so without a breach of the peace. This raises delicate problems when it comes to repossessing furniture or other property that is within a home or apartment. The disputes that result from such a situation are rarely the type that get to the appellate courts for resolution. It is necessary, therefore, to make it clear that dwellings cannot be entered absent the consent of the occupants except under the supervision of the court. . . .

§ 5.113 [Venue]

An action by a creditor against a consumer arising from a consumer credit transaction shall be brought in the [county] of the consumer's residence (subsection (6) of Section 1.201), unless an action is brought to enforce an interest in land securing the consumer's obligation, in which case the action may be brought in the [county] in which the land or a part thereof is located. If the [county] of the consumer's residence has changed, the consumer upon motion may have the action removed to the [county] of his current residence. If the residence of the consumer is not within this State, the action may be brought in the [county] in which the sale, lease, or loan was made. If the initial papers offered for filing in the action on their face show noncompliance with this section, the [clerk] shall not accept them.

§ 5.114 [Complaint; Proof]

(1) In an action brought by a creditor against a consumer arising from a consumer credit transaction, the complaint shall allege the facts of the consumer's default, the amount to which the creditor is entitled, and an indication of how that amount was determined.

(2) A default judgment may not be entered in the action in favor of the creditor unless the complaint is verified by the creditor or sworn testimony, by affidavit or otherwise, is adduced showing that the creditor is entitled to the relief demanded.

Comment

Studies that have been performed of consumers who have legal action brought against them show a high rate of judgments taken by default, in excess of 90 per cent in some urban areas. Modern rules of procedure that require a complaint to contain only the barest of facts contemplate contested litigation. In the event judgment is taken by default there is not enough information in the pleadings to enable the court to enter an accurate award. This section provides that the minimum amount of information necessary to compute the award shall be brought to the attention of the court.

§ 5.115 [Stay of Enforcement of or Relief from Default Judgment]

At any time after entry of a default judgment in favor of a creditor and against a consumer in an action arising from a consumer credit transaction, the court which rendered the judgment, for cause including lack of jurisdiction to render the judgment, and upon motion of a party or its own motion, with notice as the court may direct, may stay enforcement of or relieve the consumer from the judgment by order upon just and equitable conditions.

Comment

The high rate of judgments by default arising out of consumer credit transactions suggests a need for broad judicial discretion to open or void such judgments and re-examine the claims upon which they were rendered in appropriate cases where cause exists. Particularly, the systematic practice by some process servers (usually private process servers) of filing an affidavit of service on the consumer when, in fact, the summons has never been served but stuffed in a "sewer" or elsewhere, cannot furnish the basis for a judgment. However, such discretion is generally associated with courts of general jurisdiction and most actions arising from consumer credit transactions fall within the purview of limited jurisdiction courts. This section is intended to confer that discretion upon any court with jurisdiction to entertain actions arising from consumer credit transactions.

§ 5.116 [Limitation on Enforcement of Security for Supervised Loan]

(1) Except as to a purchase money security interest, this section applies to a security interest in an item of goods other than a motor vehicle which (a) is possessed by a consumer, (b) is being used by him or a member of a family wholly or partly supported by him, (c) is or may be claimed to be exempt from execution on a money judgment under the laws of this State, and (d) is collateral for a supervised loan.

(2) Unless the consumer, after written notice to him of his rights under this section, voluntarily surrenders to the lender possession of any item of goods to which this section applies, the lender, without an order or process of the [ ] court, may not take possession of the item or otherwise enforce the security interest according to its terms. The notice to the consumer shall conform to any rule adopted by the Administrator.

(3) The court may order or authorize process respecting an item of goods to which this section applies only after a hearing upon notice to the consumer of the hearing and his rights at it. The notice shall be as directed by the court. The order or authorization may prescribe appropriate conditions as to payments upon the debt secured or otherwise. The court may not order or authorize process respecting the item if it finds upon the hearing both that the consumer lacks the means to pay all or part of the debt secured and that continued possession and use of the item is necessary to avoid undue hardship for the consumer or a member of a family wholly or partly supported by him.

(4) The court, upon application of the lender or the consumer and notice to the other, and after a hearing and a finding of changed circumstances, may vacate or modify an order or authorization pursuant to this section.

Comment

1. This section responds to the recommendation of the National Commission on Consumer Finance that security interests in household goods should not be allowed in any loan or consolidation transaction if the goods were not acquired by the use of that credit because in the event of default the right to repossess or threat to repossess these goods have far too disruptive an impact on the family life of the debtor to be in the public interest. However, since the section more appropriately directs itself to a limitation on the right to enforce a security interest rather than to the right to contract for one, the purview of it extends beyond household goods to goods that this State has

determined are entitled to exemption in accordance with the policy that a debtor should not be deprived of the necessities of life by his creditors if he is unable to pay his debts.

. . .

PART 2. CONSUMERS' REMEDIES

§ 5.201 [Effect of Violations on Rights of Parties]

(1) If a creditor has violated any provision of this Act applying to collection of an excess charge or amount or enforcement of rights (subsections (2) and (4) of Section 1.201), authority to make supervised loans (Section 2.301), restrictions on interests in land as security (Section 2.307), limitations on the schedule of payments on loan terms for supervised loans (Section 2.308), attorney's fees (Section 2.507), charges for other credit transactions (Section 2.601), disclosure with respect to consumer leases (Section 3.202), notice to consumers (Section 3.203), receipts, statements of account, and evidences of payment (Section 3.206), form of insurance premium loan agreement (Section 3.207), notice to co-signers and similar parties (Section 3.208), security in sales and leases (Section 3.301), no assignments of earnings (Section 3.305), authorizations to confess judgment (Section 3.306), certain negotiable instruments prohibited (Section 3.307), referral sales and leases (Section 3.309), limitations on default charges (Section 3.402), card issuer subject to claims and defenses (subsection (5) of Section 3.403), assignees subject to claims and defenses (subsection (4) of Section 3.404), lenders subject to claims and defenses arising from sales and leases (subsection (4) of Section 3.405), limitation on enforcement of security for supervised loan (Section 5.116), or assurance of discontinuance (Section 6.109), the consumer has a [claim for relief] [cause of action] to recover actual damages and also a right in an action other than a class action, to recover from the person violating this Act a penalty in an amount determined by the court not less than $100 nor more than $1,000. With respect to violations arising from sales or loans made pursuant to open-end credit, no action pursuant to this subsection may be brought more than two years after the violations occurred. With respect to violations arising from other consumer credit transactions, no action pursuant to this subsection may be brought more than one year after the scheduled or accelerated maturity of the debt.

(2) A consumer is not obligated to pay a charge in excess of that allowed by this Act and has a right of refund of any excess charge paid. A refund may not be made by reducing the consumer's obligation by the amount of the excess charge, unless the creditor has notified the consumer that the consumer may request a refund and the consumer has not so requested within 30 days thereafter. If the consumer has paid an amount in excess of the lawful obligation under the agreement, the consumer may recover the excess amount from

the person who made the excess charge or from an assignee of that person's rights who undertakes direct collection of payments from or enforcement of rights against consumers arising from the debt.

(3) If a creditor has contracted for or received a charge in excess of that allowed by this Act, or if a consumer is entitled to a refund and a person liable to the consumer refuses to make a refund within a reasonable time after demand, the consumer may recover from the creditor or the person liable in an action other than a class action a penalty in an amount determined by the court not less than $100 nor more than $1,000. With respect to excess charges arising from sales or loans made pursuant to open-end credit, no action pursuant to this subsection may be brought more than two years after the violation or passage of a reasonable time for refund occurs. With respect to excess charges arising from other consumer credit transactions no action pursuant to this subsection may be brought more than one year after the scheduled or accelerated maturity of the debt. For purposes of this subsection, a reasonable time is presumed to be 30 days.

(4) Except as otherwise provided, a violation of this Act does not impair rights on a debt.

(5) If an employer discharges an employee in violation of the provisions prohibiting discharge (Section 5.106), the employee within [ ] days may bring a civil action for recovery of wages lost as a result of the violation and for an order requiring reinstatement of the employee. Damages recoverable shall not exceed lost wages for six weeks.

(6) A creditor is not liable for a penalty under subsection (1) or (3) if he notifies the consumer of a violation before the creditor receives from the consumer written notice of the violation or the consumer has brought an action under this section, and the creditor corrects the violation within 45 days after notifying the consumer. If the violation consists of a prohibited agreement, giving the consumer a corrected copy of the writing containing the violation is sufficient notification and correction. If the violation consists of an excess charge, correction shall be made by an adjustment or refund. The Administrator and any official or agency of this State having supervisory authority over a supervised financial organization shall give prompt notice to a creditor of any violation discovered pursuant to an examination or investigation of the transactions, business, records, and acts of the creditor (Sections 2.305, 6.105 and 6.106).

(7) A creditor may not be held liable in an action brought under this section for a violation of this Act if the creditor shows by a preponderance of evidence that the violation was not intentional and resulted from a bona fide error notwithstanding the maintenance of procedures reasonably adapted to avoid the error.

(8) In an action in which it is found that a creditor has violated this Act, the court shall award to the consumer the costs of the action

and to his attorneys their reasonable fees. In determining attorney's fees, the amount of the recovery on behalf of the consumer is not controlling.

Comment

1. Rights that are accompanied by inadequate remedies or no remedy at all and limitations on agreements and practices that do not provide for sufficient penalties or for any penalty at all are generally ineffective to accomplish the desired result. They become little more than exhortatory, easily ignored, and meaningless proclamations. In order to protect rights created and to deter provisions of agreements and practices proscribed by legislation, suitable remedies and penalties must exist. Since an aggrieved party is one of the persons best able to enforce violations of rights and limitations, this section sets forth a right of action in the consumer in the event of violation by the creditor of each section of this Act that does not include its own provision for infraction and better to deter such practices, even of some that do, as in the case of referral sales and leases (Section 3.309).

2. Subsection (1) lists 22 provisions of this Act for the contravention of which actual damages and a penalty could be recovered. The formula used for the penalty is derived from the CCPA (15 U.S.C. § 1601 et seq.) with a minimum and a maximum recovery. Within this range a court may apportion penalties according to the seriousness of the offense and the overall circumstances of each violation. The penalty is designed not only to provide a deterrent to potential violators but also an incentive to a consumer to bring an action when a violation has occurred. Consequently, penalties may not be recovered in a class action, although actual damages may be if the enacting State's rules of civil procedure permits.

3. Subsections (2) and (3) set forth the rights of the consumer with respect to excess charges by the creditor. A refund rather than a credit of an excess charge must be made if requested by the consumer to prevent the creditor from holding a refund due until the contract is sufficiently paid down to have it credited as a prepayment in full. Subsection (3) imposes the same penalty on those who make excess charges or refuse to make refunds to which a consumer is entitled as that for violators of provisions listed in subsection (1). This provision is necessary because if the only rights the consumer had were those provided in subsection (2), it would be worth the creditor's gamble to make excess charges. The only thing that could be lost would be the illegal charge itself, and even that would be unlikely in view of the small percentage of consumers who would seek recovery.

. . .

5. Violations may occur for a variety of reasons, not all of them necessarily pernicious. Subsection (6) provides that if the creditor becomes aware of a violation, voluntarily notifies the consumer of the violation, and corrects the violation within 45 days after notification, he is not subject to a penalty. Such a provision encourages the autonomous correction of errors and violations. Voluntariness is considered to cease, however, either upon the commencement of an action against the creditor or upon his receipt of written notification from the consumer of the violation. Consistent with the idea that many errors and violations will be rectified upon knowledge without re-

sort to sanctions subsection (6) also provides that violations discovered pursuant to administrative examination or investigation shall promptly be brought to the attention of the creditor. Probably the most common type of creditor violation results from clerical mistake. No policy would be served in imposing liability for violations due to unintentional bona fide errors which occur notwithstanding the maintenance of procedures reasonably adapted to avoid them, and subsection (7) provides a creditor with an affirmative defense in such cases. Moreover, acts done or omitted in conformity with a rule, interpretation or declaratory ruling of the Administrator ought to result in no liability under this Act, except for refund of an excess charge. This Act so provides, as well as affording ample opportunity for creditor and consumer participation in the formulation and correction of rules. See Sections 6.104(4) and 6.107.

6. Subsection (8) directs the court to award to the consumer the costs of the action and to his attorney his reasonable fees in any action where it is found that a creditor has violated this Act. The direction to award attorney's fees should enable consumers to find attorneys to prosecute their cases, an essential element if the consumers' rights provided by this section are to be enforced, as an attorney is assured of adequate compensation. This is so whether or not the case goes to trial since any settlement offer will have to take the attorney's compensation into account.

PART 3. CRIMINAL PENALTIES

§ 5.301 [Willful and Knowing Violations]

(1) A supervised lender who willfully and knowingly makes charges in excess of those permitted by the Article on Finance Charges and Related Provisions (Article 2) applying to supervised loans (Part 4) is guilty of a misdemeanor and upon conviction may be [sentenced to pay a fine not exceeding $ [ ], or to imprisonment not exceeding one year, or both.

(2) A person who, in violation of the provisions of this Act applying to authority to make supervised loans (Section 2.301), willfully and knowingly engages without a license in the business of making supervised loans, or of taking assignments of and undertaking direct collection of payments from and enforcement of rights against consumers arising from supervised loans, is guilty of a misdemeanor and upon conviction may be [sentenced to pay a fine not exceeding $ [ ], or to imprisonment not exceeding one year, or both].

(3) A person who willfully and knowingly engages in the business of entering into consumer credit transactions, or of taking assignments of rights against consumers arising therefrom and undertaking direct collection of payments or enforcement of these rights, without complying with the provisions of this Act concerning notification (Section 6.202) or payment of fees (Section 6.203), is guilty of a misdemeanor and upon conviction may be [sentenced to pay a fine not exceeding $100].

ARTICLE 6. ADMINISTRATION

PART 1. POWERS AND FUNCTIONS OF ADMINISTRATOR

§ 6.104 [Powers of Administrator; Reliance on Rules; Duty to Report]

(1) In addition to other powers granted by this Act, the Administrator within the limitations provided by law may:

(a) receive and act on complaints, take action designed to obtain voluntary compliance with this Act, or commence proceedings on his own initiative;

(b) counsel persons and groups on their rights and duties under this Act;

(c) establish programs for the education of consumers with respect to credit practices and problems;

(d) make studies appropriate to effectuate the purposes and policies of this Act and make the results available to the public; [and]

(e) adopt, amend, and repeal rules to carry out the specific provisions of this Act, but not with respect to unconscionable agreements or fraudulent or unconscionable conduct [;

(f) maintain offices within this State; and]

[(g) appoint any necessary attorneys, hearing examiners, clerks, and other employees and agents and fix their compensation, and authorize attorneys appointed under this section to appear for and represent the Administrator in court].

(2) In addition to other powers granted by this Act, the Administrator shall enforce the Federal Truth in Lending Act, except to the extent otherwise provided by law.

(3) To keep the Administrator's rules in harmony with the rules of administrators in other jurisdictions that enact substantially the Uniform Consumer Credit Code, the Administrator, so far as is consistent with the purposes, policies, and provisions of this Act, shall:

(a) before adopting, amending, and repealing rules, advise and consult with administrators in other jurisdictions that enact substantially the Uniform Consumer Credit Code; and

(b) in adopting, amending, and repealing rules, take into consideration the rules of administrators in other jurisdictions that enact substantially the Uniform Consumer Credit Code.

(4) Except for refund of an excess charge, no liability is imposed under this Act for an act done or omitted in conformity with a rule, interpretation, or declaratory ruling of the Administrator, notwithstanding that after the act or omission the rule, interpretation, or rul-

ing is amended or repealed or is determined by judicial or other authority to be invalid for any reason.

(5) The Administrator shall report [annually on or before January 1] to the [Governor and Legislature] on the operation of his office, the use of consumer credit in this State, and the problems of persons of small means obtaining credit from persons regularly engaged in extending sales or loan credit. For the purpose of making the report, the Administrator may conduct research and make appropriate studies. The report shall include a description of the examination and investigation procedures and policies of his office, a statement of policies followed in deciding whether to investigate or examine the offices of credit suppliers subject to this Act, a statement of the number and percentages of offices which are periodically investigated or examined, a statement of the types of consumer credit problems of both creditors and consumers which have come to his attention through his examinations and investigations and the disposition of them under existing law, a statement of the extent to which rules of the Administrator pursuant to this Act are not in harmony with the rules of administrators in other jurisdictions that enact substantially the Uniform Consumer Credit Code and the reasons for these variations, and a general statement of the activities of his office and of others to promote the purposes of this Act. The report may not identify the creditors against whom action is taken by the Administrator.

§ 6.106 [Investigatory Powers]

(1) If the Administrator has cause to believe that a person has engaged in conduct or committed an act that is subject to action by the Administrator, he may make an investigation to determine whether the person has engaged in the conduct or committed the act. To the extent necessary for this purpose, he may administer oaths or affirmations, and, upon his own motion or upon request of any party, subpoena witnesses, compel their attendance, adduce evidence, and require the production of, or testimony as to, any matter relevant to the investigation, including the existence, description, nature, custody, condition, and location of any books, documents, or other tangible things and the identity and location of persons having knowledge of relevant facts, or any other matter reasonably calculated to lead to the discovery of admissible evidence.

(2) If the person's records are located outside this State, the person at his option shall make them available to the Administrator at a convenient location within this State or pay the reasonable and necessary expenses for the Administrator or his representative to examine them where they are located. The Administrator may designate representatives, including comparable officials of the State in which the records are located, to inspect them on his behalf.

(3) Upon application by the Administrator showing failure without lawful excuse to obey a subpoena or to give testimony, and upon reasonable notice to all persons affected thereby, the [ ] court shall grant an order compelling compliance.

(4) The Administrator may not make public the name or identity of a person whose acts or conduct he investigates under this section or the facts disclosed in the investigation, but this subsection does not apply to disclosures in actions or enforcement proceedings pursuant to this Act.

§ 6.107 [Application of [Administrative Procedure Act] [Part on Administrative Procedure and Judicial Review]]

Except as otherwise provided, the [State Administrative Procedure Act] [Part on Administrative Procedure and Judicial Review (Part 4) of this Article] applies to and governs all administrative action taken by the Administrator pursuant to this Article.

Comment

If the enacting State has an adequate State administrative procedure act reference should be made to it in this section. Otherwise Part 4 of Article 6 [Section 6.401 et seq.] should be enacted and referred to here. Brackets and bracketed language in this section and its caption should be retained or deleted dependent upon which course is followed. . . .

§ 6.108 [Administrative Enforcement Orders]

(1) After notice and hearing the Administrator may order a creditor or a person acting in his behalf to cease and desist from violating this Act. A respondent aggrieved by an order of the Administrator may obtain judicial review of the order and the Administrator may obtain an order of the court for enforcement of his order in the [ ] court. The proceeding for review or enforcement is initiated by filing a petition in the court. Copies of the petition shall be served upon all parties of record.

(2) Within 30 days after service of the petition for review upon the Administrator, or within any further time the court allows, the Administrator shall transmit to the court the original or a certified copy of the entire record upon which the order is based, including any transcript of testimony, which need not be printed. By stipulation of all parties to the review proceeding, the record may be shortened. After hearing, the court may (a) reverse or modify the order if the findings of fact of the Administrator are clearly erroneous in view of the reliable, probative, and substantial evidence on the whole record, (b) grant any temporary relief or restraining order it deems just, and (c) enter an order enforcing, modifying, and enforcing as modified, or

setting aside in whole or in part the order of the Administrator, or remanding the case to the Administrator for further proceedings.

(3) An objection not urged at the hearing shall not be considered by the court unless the failure to urge the objection is excused for good cause shown. A party may move the court to remand the case to the Administrator in the interest of justice for the purpose of adducing additional specified and material evidence and seeking findings thereon upon good cause shown for the failure to adduce this evidence before the Administrator.

(4) The jurisdiction of the court shall be exclusive and its final judgment or decree is subject to review by the [ ] court in the same manner and form and with the same effect as in appeals from a final judgment or decree in a [special proceeding]. The Administrator's copy of the testimony shall be available at reasonable times to all parties for examination without cost.

(5) A proceeding for review under this section shall be initiated within 30 days after a copy of the order of the Administrator is received. If no proceeding is so initiated, the Administrator may obtain an order of the court for enforcement of his order upon showing that his order was issued in compliance with this section, that no proceeding for review was initiated within 30 days after a copy of the order was received, and that the respondent is subject to the jurisdiction of the court.

(6) With respect to unconscionable agreements or fraudulent or unconscionable conduct by the respondent, the Administrator may not issue an order pursuant to this section but may bring a civil action for an injunction (Section 6.111).

§ 6.109 [Assurance of Discontinuance]

If it is claimed that a person has engaged in conduct which could be subject to an order by the Administrator (Sections 2.303 and 6.108) or by a court (Sections 6.110, 6.111, and 6.112), the Administrator may accept an assurance in writing that the person will not engage in the same or similar conduct in the future. The assurance may include any of the following: stipulations for the voluntary payment by the creditor of the costs of investigation or of an amount to be held in escrow as restitution to debtors aggrieved by past or future conduct of the creditor or to cover costs of future investigation, or admissions of past specific acts by the creditor or that those acts violated this Act or other statutes. A violation of an assurance of discontinuance is a violation of this Act.

§ 6.110 [Injunctions Against Violations of Act]

The Administrator may bring a civil action to restrain any person from violating this Act and for other appropriate relief including but not limited to the following: to prevent a person from using or employing practices prohibited by this Act, to reform contracts to conform to this Act and to rescind contracts into which a creditor has induced a consumer to enter by conduct violating this Act, even though a consumer is not a party to the action. An action under this section may be joined with an action under the provisions on civil actions by Administrator (Section 6.113).

§ 6.111 [Injunctions Against Unconscionable Agreements and Fraudulent or Unconscionable Conduct Including Debt Collection]

(1) The Administrator may bring a civil action to restrain a person to whom this Part applies from engaging in a course of:

(a) making or enforcing unconscionable terms or provisions of consumer credit transactions;

(b) fraudulent or unconscionable conduct in inducing consumers to enter into consumer credit transactions;

(c) conduct of any of the types specified in paragraph (a) or (b) with respect to transactions that give rise to or that lead persons to believe will give rise to consumer credit transactions; or

(d) fraudulent or unconscionable conduct in the collection of debts arising from consumer credit transactions.

(2) In an action brought pursuant to this section the court may grant relief only if it finds:

(a) that the respondent has made unconscionable agreements or has engaged or is likely to engage in a course of fraudulent or unconscionable conduct;

(b) that the respondent's agreements have caused or are likely to cause or the conduct of the respondent has caused or is likely to cause injury to consumers or debtors; and

(c) that the respondent has been able to cause or will be able to cause the injury primarily because the transactions involved are credit transactions.

(3) In applying subsection (1)(a), (b), and (c), consideration shall be given to each of the factors specified in the provisions on unconscionability with respect to a transaction that is, gives rise to, or that a person leads the debtor to believe will give rise to, a consumer credit transaction (subsection (4) of Section 5.108), among others.

(4) In applying subsection (1)(d), consideration shall be given to each of the factors specified in the provisions on unconscionability with respect to the collection of debts arising from consumer credit transactions (subsection (5) of Section 5.108), among others.

(5) In an action brought pursuant to this section, a charge or practice expressly permitted by this Act is not in itself unconscionable.

Comment

. . .

2. One purpose of this section is to afford the Administrator a means of dealing with new patterns of fraudulent or unconscionable conduct unforeseen and, perhaps, unforeseeable at the writing of this Act. Another is to give him a more flexible remedy for halting reprehensible creditor practices that have been specifically and somewhat rigidly treated in previous consumer credit legislation. For instance, this Act has no specific prohibition against the creditor's allowing the consumer to sign a credit agreement containing blanks. In some situations there may be legitimate reasons for a contract to contain blanks at the time of signing. However, if the creditor deliberately leaves blanks to be filled in after the consumer's signature and without his consent, the Administrator may seek to restrain the practice as fraudulent or unconscionable conduct under this section.

. . .

§ 6.112 [Temporary Relief]

With respect to an action brought to enjoin violations of the Act (Section 6.110) or unconscionable agreements or fraudulent or unconscionable conduct (Section 6.111), the Administrator may apply to the court for appropriate temporary relief against a defendant, pending final determination of the action. The court may grant appropriate temporary relief.

§ 6.113 [Civil Actions by Administrator]

(1) After demand, the Administrator may bring a civil action against a creditor to recover actual damages sustained and excess charges paid by one or more consumers who have a right to recover explicitly granted by this Act. In a civil action under this subsection, penalties may not be recovered by the Administrator. The court shall order amounts recovered under this subsection to be paid to each consumer or set off against his obligation. A consumer's action, except a class action, takes precedence over a prior or subsequent action by the Administrator with respect to the claim of that consumer. A consumer's class action takes precedence over a subsequent action by the Administrator with respect to claims common to both actions, but the Administrator may intervene. An Administrator's action on behalf of a class of consumers takes precedence over a consumer's subsequent class action with respect to claims common to both actions. Whenever an action takes precedence over another action under this subsection, the latter action may be stayed to the extent appropriate while the precedent action is pending and dismissed if the precedent action is dismissed with prejudice or results in a final judgment granting or denying the claim asserted in the precedent action. A defense available to a creditor in a civil action brought by a

consumer is available to him in a civil action brought under this subsection.

(2) The Administrator may bring a civil action against a creditor or a person acting in his behalf to recover a civil penalty of no more than $5,000 for repeatedly and intentionally violating this Act. A civil penalty pursuant to this subsection may not be imposed for a violation of this Act occurring more than two years before the action is brought or for making unconscionable agreements or engaging in a course of fraudulent or unconscionable conduct.

(3) The Administrator may bring a civil action against a creditor for failure to file notification in accordance with the provisions on notification (Section 6.202) or to pay fees in accordance with the provisions on fees (Section 6.203) to recover the fees the defendant has failed to pay and a civil penalty in an amount determined by the court not exceeding the greater of three times the amount of fees the defendant has failed to pay or $1,000.

§ 6.114 [Jury Trial]

The Administrator has no right to trial by jury in an action brought by him under this Act.

§ 6.115 [Consumer's Remedies Not Affected]

The grant of powers to the Administrator in this Article does not affect remedies available to consumers under this Act or under other principles of law or equity.

Comment

1. It is not the intention of the grant of powers to the Administrator or of any of the other provisions of this Act dealing with consumers' remedies to diminish in any way the availability of consumers' remedies under other principles of law or equity or to impede the development of judicially created law in this area. For example, the individual consumer has a cause of action under Section 5.201(2) and (3) to recover any charges in excess of those permitted in the Act and to recover a penalty in certain cases, and the Administrator may also bring an action under Section 6.113 to recover excess charges on behalf of consumers. Whether or not an action to recover excess charges by a class of private parties would lie depends upon the State law with respect to class actions. This Act does not specifically authorize such class actions nor does it preclude them. See also Section 5.105, Comment 7.

2. Various other consumers' remedies provided by other applicable law are not affected by this Act. Examples include the UCC provisions concerning the buyer's revocation of acceptance of goods delivered (UCC Section 2–608), the buyer's right to cancel the contract and to take a security interest in the goods delivered (UCC Section 2–711), the buyer's right to incidental and consequential damages (UCC Section 2–715), and the buyer's remedies for fraud (UCC Section 2–721). So, too, the limitations on contract provided

for in the UCC in regard to penalties, liquidated damages, and limitation of remedies (UCC Sections 2–718 and 2–719) continue to apply to transactions governed by this Act.

†